The Communist Party
of the Soviet Union

The Communist Party

of the

Soviet Union

by

LEONARD SCHAPIRO

Professor Emeritus of Political Science with
Special Reference to Russian Studies
in the University of London
(London School of Economics and Political Science)

SECOND EDITION, REVISED AND ENLARGED

He who seeks in Liberty anything
other than Liberty itself is destined
for servitude
ALEXIS DE TOCQUEVILLE

METHUEN & CO LTD
11 NEW FETTER LANE, LONDON EC4

First published as a University Paperback 1963
Reprinted 1964 and 1966
Second edition revised and enlarged 1970
Reprinted twice
Reprinted 1978

© 1960 and 1970 Leonard Schapiro

Printed in Great Britain at the
University Press, Cambridge

ISBN 0 416 18380 8

Contents

PART THREE: THE THIRD REVOLUTION

PART FOUR: SINCE STALIN DIED

EPILOGUE

APPENDICES

Preface to the First Edition

This book attempts to tell the story of a political party which for nearly forty-two years has wielded virtually all political power over what was formerly known as Russia. For some thirty years before, this party or, more accurately, a broad revolutionary movement composed of several warring factions had worked towards the overthrow of the monarchy. One faction, now known as the Communist Party of the Soviet Union, in the end achieved political power after the collapse of the Russian Empire in 1917. My story, therefore, which spans three-quarters of a century, falls into several distinct parts. It is necessary first to show the nature of the movement from which the bolsheviks, as the precursors of the present communists were known, emerged. If I have dwelt in some detail on this formative period, I would remind the reader of two reasons for this – though he will, I hope, discover them for himself if he is patient enough not to skip the earlier chapters: first, that without some knowledge of what happened in the formative years before the revolution of 1917 it is quite impossible to understand either the reason for the determination of the bolsheviks to overthrow what was on the face of it a democratic republican government, the Provisional Government of 1917, or much of their subsequent policy; and secondly, that existing histories are mostly silent on the all-important period between 1906 and 1917, and I thought it right to try to fill in this gap.

In the second instalment of the story the whole situation changes: what had hitherto been one party among several striving for power has become the sole party exercising power in the state. At this point it not only becomes something entirely different from what is usually called a 'party' in states in which several competing political parties exist side by side, but also raises a very difficult problem for the historian. For the history of the party can no longer be envisaged as something separate from the history of the country as a whole, but becomes increasingly identified with it. Yet I make no claim to have written anything in the nature of a history of the Soviet state. I have certainly tried to sketch in sufficient historical background as the story unfolds to make it intelligible. But my aim throughout has been to trace the development of the party – to show its ideas, its objectives, its successes and failures, its relations with the population, the effects which all these and other factors had upon the party machinery and upon the changes in the social and human composition of its membership. In a word, what I have tried to do is to write a kind of biography of the party, in which the story never wanders too far from the main subject whose life is being recounted – how far I have succeeded, others will have to judge. I can only hope that they will temper their judgement with some charitable reflection on the difficulty, and novelty, of the task.

It is however quite legitimate for the reader to ask why I should have attempted to separate off in this way the history of the party from the history of the country. I think there is a justification for this. The method of government which Lenin evolved after 1917 is, so far as I am aware, unique in the history of political systems – or was so until imitated in other countries. There have, of course, been autocracies, dictatorships, despotisms, autocratic democracies, or whatever one likes to call the Soviet system of government, throughout history. But Lenin's government had in addition the unique quality that it brought into being what were ostensibly independent political institutions – soviets, courts, trade unions and the like – but ensured from the first that each and every one of these institutions should function only under the control of a single political party, of which the members were linked by an ideology and by strict discipline. It seemed to me that a study of the key element of this novel system of government, its merits or defects, its difficulties and development, might in some small way contribute to the better understanding of political institutions.

With the third part of my story, which begins in 1928, a new factor enters – the personality of Stalin, and the dynamic imprint of his policy upon the life not only of the country – a story which has been told many times and which I have not tried to retell in any detail – but upon the nature and development of the party itself. Lenin certainly dominated the party, but he ruled through the party. After Stalin had emerged as the unchallengeable successor to Lenin it became apparent that he ruled over the party as often as he ruled through the party, that, in other words, there were times when his personal dictatorship was directed quite as much against the party itself as it was against the rest of the country. I was at first tempted to bring my story to a close with the death of Stalin, if only because events which have taken place in the six years which have elapsed since then are too near to us to enable us to form a balanced picture of them. But in the end I felt that to have done so would have been to risk leaving an essentially false impression. So much of what happened to, and in, the party during Stalin's lifetime was in such large measure due to the personal characteristics of this one powerful man that what I believe to be the essential features of this form of party government were at times eclipsed, or obscured. The events of the last six years have, at any rate, given us some indication of those features which seem to belong to the essential quality of the party and are part of its tradition – the fact that it is above the law, for example – and of those which are apparently more bound up with the idiosyncrasies of a particular man – for example, the use of mass terror. So I have added a fairly long Epilogue, in which, without giving a detailed history of the party between 1953 and 1958, I have at any rate tried to sift the ephemeral from the more permanent features.

It is an unfortunate fact that merely to write about the Soviet Union is to plunge oneself into current politics, if only because the present rulers of the Soviet Union make constant use of the picture which they seek to present of their past in order to influence the present. I had perhaps better state at the outset that I owe no allegiance to any political party – though I must confess that I have a certain predilection for a number of old-fashioned principles: respect for human life and dignity, freedom of thought and speech, justice, truth, and peace between man and man. It is not however only the rulers of the Soviet Union who bring politics to bear on the facts of Soviet history. Outside the USSR as well a 'committed' view of Marxism or Leninism, or of Soviet failures or achievements, leads to a number of historical approaches all of which seem to me to be erroneous. There are still some, I will not say historians, but publicists, whose *facts* (I say nothing of opinions) vary from time to time according to what is admitted or asserted by the government officials of the Soviet Union. The difficulty about this approach is its impermanence – works published a year or two ago are apt to look rather quaint if resurrected from charitable oblivion. Some, again, judge communist conduct by motive: thus, those who approve of the avowed aims and ultimate objectives of the bolsheviks or their successors, the communists, are prepared to condone actions which they might otherwise condemn; and conversely, those who are repelled by the price in human suffering which communist policy has at times exacted are apt to impute the lowest motives to those who put it into effect. I take the view that human motives are not only usually impossible to ascertain, but are in any case seldom unmixed, and it is therefore best to avoid making value judgements about them, and to leave the facts to speak for themselves.

Then there are those who have sought to look at Soviet history *sub specie aeternitatis* – this is an approach which is particularly frequent, perhaps predominant, in England. The historian projects himself, as it were, into the distant future and from his imaginary vantage point surveys the broad trend of developments in the Soviet Union since the revolution of 1917. The little difficulties and occasional roughness then fall into 'historical proportion'. What appeared to lesser minds at the time to have been due to such vulgar considerations as one man's personal ambition, or fear of popular revolt, is now seen to have unfolded as part of a continuous process of evolution which was moulded by ineluctable economic and historical forces. One fallacy of this approach seems to me to be the assumption which it necessarily makes that because things happened in a certain way therefore they had to happen in this way, irrespectively of the political actions of men. For example, it may well be the case that some form of industrial revolution had to take place in the Soviet Union for a whole variety of reasons in combination, which no party or government could have resisted. But I see no valid reason for assuming that it had to take place at the time and in the manner which Stalin determined, other than the reason that Stalin so determined it and was able to put his determination into effect. So we are back at politics again.

Anxious as I was to avoid what seemed to me to be these various pitfalls, I tried to confine myself to the unvarnished facts. The reader will, I hope, be able to judge for himself, with the aid of the footnote references (which were unhappily unavoidable) and with the aid of the Bibliographical Note, which will be found in an Appendix, how far my sources for the facts can be regarded as reliable. Included in the facts is of course an account of the theories upon which actions purported to be based. The reader will again judge if, and if so to what extent, theory and action were consistent. I have, of course, from time to time attempted to draw conclusions from the facts – a book which made no attempt to do this would be virtually unreadable. But I have always attempted to give a sufficient basis of facts to enable the reader to draw his own, different, conclusions if he should disagree with mine.

I should warn the reader at the outset that this book deals primarily with a political institution – a governing party. Now there are certain factors which operate in the case of every government, and I found that, whatever Marx or Lenin may have told us about the unique nature of government after a socialist revolution, in certain respects Soviet government continued to show remarkable similarity to other governments – not in its structure (which really was, I think, as I have already indicated, unique, though not perhaps in the way that Lenin meant it), but in the problems which faced it. For example, the administrative problem of devolution of responsibility arose even in so centralized a party as the Soviet Communist Party. Or again, all governments are concerned to retain power, though they may differ in the means which they adopt to this end, and the government of the communist party is no exception. All this would be too obvious to require stating, were it not for the fact that there are many to whom even the mention of 'power' in connection with a communist party is for some, presumably emotional, reason repellent. It is often said that such a view does not take sufficient account of Marxist, or Leninist, theory, upon which the actions of the party were based. But there are many, many actions of the party in the course of my story which would be quite unintelligible unless they were seen in the light of the fact that over long periods the party's hold over the country was precarious and a false move would have meant its downfall. To ignore this factor, which runs like a thread of scarlet through Soviet history, is to write about phantoms and not about what really happened, and so I make no apology for occasionally reminding the reader in the course of my narrative of the part played by considerations of power in events. I am strengthened in the belief that my judgement is the correct one by the fact that while I have discovered many instances in which it seemed to me that the theoretical considerations had to be sacrificed to the realities of the situation, I have as yet discovered no single instance in which the party was prepared to risk its own survival in power for considerations of doctrine. Nor, I confess, do I find this very surprising.

Finally, a word on value judgements. I have, as far as possible, avoided them, because I think the function of the specialist is that of analysing as honestly as he can, so that the reader, relying on the integrity of the analysis, can form his own judgement. With this in view I have tried to envisage as wide a range of readers' standards as I could, so as to furnish them all with a basis for judgement. Thus, one man may look to government solely as a means of ensuring the maximum economic development and the greatest material prosperity. Another may seek in it other qualities as well – its ability to develop the spiritual needs of the governed, their self-reliance, or their independence of thought. For some the aim of government is justice, for others territorial expansion – the list could easily be extended. Opinions may also differ as to the degree to which those who are subject to government ought to be allowed to decide for themselves what is best for them, or, on the contrary, ought to leave it to wiser, or more inspired, or more forceful, or more determined men than themselves to decide. If my own views on these issues seem occasionally to obtrude, I can only beg the reader's indulgence if he disagrees with them, and ask him to accept my assurance that I have done my best to put him in possession of sufficient facts, and I trust all the relevant facts, to enable him to form a judgement more in harmony with his own criteria of good government.

* * *

After some three years spent working on this book it is a great pleasure to have an opportunity at least to acknowledge some of the help and generosity of others which has made my work possible.

The writing of this work was undertaken at the invitation of the Research Program on the History of the CPSU. This Program, which is supported by a grant from the Ford Foundation, is administered by an inter-university Committee, of which Professors Merle Fainsod, Harold H. Fisher and Geroid T. Robinson are the members and Professor Philip E. Mosely is Chairman. The Program has helped me in many ways: it has enabled me to obtain printed or microfilm materials which I should otherwise not have been able to see, it has provided me with research assistance and with the means to travel in search of material (including a two months' stay in New York) and it has made available to me in MS. the results of research or memoirs which it has sponsored. I am deeply grateful for all this material help but even more for the kindly encouragement which I received throughout from the members of the Committee, and for their wise advice. I should particularly like to thank Professor Mosely, with whom as Chairman of the Committee I mostly had to deal, and who, in spite of the many calls on his time, was always willing to find the leisure to help when help was required. I should also like to thank Dr Alfred G. Meyer, formerly Director of the Research Program, and Mrs Josephine B. Bruno, the Executive Secretary of the Program, for much patient assistance on the administrative side.

It has been my good fortune to have enjoyed the collaboration for over a year of one of the most distinguished younger scholars in the field of Soviet Government, Dr T. H. Rigby, now of University College, Canberra. Dr Rigby's research, which was of the thoroughness and high quality which he brings to all his work, extended mainly to the structure, organization and composition of the party throughout the Soviet period, and to the top leadership of the party during the last twenty years. Chapters 13, 17 and 24 are very largely based on Dr Rigby's work, and the whole of Part Three and the Epilogue owes a great deal to his researches and ideas. For all this I wish to thank Dr Rigby, and not least for the care with which he read and commented on the manuscript at all its stages.

I should also like to thank Mr B. I. Nicolaevsky, who has so often, and with justice, in so many prefaces been referred to as the living encyclopaedia on the history of the Russian social democratic movement. Mr Nicolaevsky has most generously helped me with advice, and with the loan of books and documents. He has placed at my disposal the manuscript of a large collection of mostly unpublished documents relating to the pre-revolutionary years of the party which he is in the course of preparing, and which he is accompanying with the detailed and learned annotation which he alone is capable of producing. He has also read and commented on the whole of my manuscript and made innumerable valuable suggestions and criticisms.

Over and above the help of Messrs Nicolaevsky and Rigby, I have been singularly privileged in that a whole galaxy of other most eminent scholars in the field of Soviet studies has been willing to spare the time and effort to read and comment on all or on parts of the manuscript. I wish here to express my thanks to: Professor John A. Armstrong, Dr G. H. Bolsover, Mrs Xenia J. Eudin, Professor Merle Fainsod, Professor Harold H. Fisher, Mr David Footman, Dr O. H. Gankin, Dr Leopold H. Haimson, Professor John N. Hazard, Dr G. Katkov, Dr J. L. H. Keep, the late Professor V. Leontovitsch, Dr Alfred G. Meyer, Mr Alec Nove, Professor G. H. N. Seton-Watson, Mr Robert M. Slusser, Professor Donald W. Threadgold, Dr S. V. Utechin, Mr Bertram D. Wolfe, and Mr H. Willetts.

It is difficult to stress adequately the debt of gratitude which I owe to all these scholars. The variety of opinion in their comments, the depth of detailed scholarship, the penetration of judgement, were to me an education in themselves. They have saved me from innumerable errors of fact and judgement. But I alone am responsible for such errors of fact as still remain, which must be attributed to my obstinacy or ignorance. I should add in fairness to the scholars mentioned above, who did not all always agree with me, that such interpretation as I have put on the facts is entirely my own.

In addition, I wish to thank Dr S. V. Utechin for preparing the list of Congresses and Conferences of the party and the list of members and candidate members of the Politburo, which are printed as an Appendix.

I should also like to pay a tribute to the constant help which I have received from the librarians of those collections in which I have principally worked – the British Museum, the library of the London School of Economics and Political Science, the library of the Royal Institute of International Affairs, the Butler Library of Columbia University, and especially the Curator of its Archive of Russian and East European History and Culture, Mr L. F. Magerovsky, the New York Public Library, the Houghton Library, Harvard University, and the library of the Institute of Social History, Amsterdam.

I am particularly grateful to Mrs Lewinson (Dr Georgette Donchin), who has with great skill typed and retyped and completely edited the manuscript for the press, prepared the index, and has generally helped in many different ways to shorten the labour which the making of the book entailed.

I also wish to thank Professor Fainsod and the Harvard University Press for permission to reproduce from *How Russia is Ruled* the five charts which are printed as an appendix.

I am also grateful to the London School of Economics and Political Science for co-operation in various ways while I was writing the book.

My thanks are also due to my old friend Hywel Davies, who has read the manuscript with the eye of a poet, and has made the kind of suggestions for improvement which only a poet could perceive.

Lastly, I owe more than I can express to my wife. She has not only read and re-read the manuscript, and constantly helped by her judgement to improve it – that is, after all, perhaps the lot of wives who are unfortunate enough to have husbands who write. But she has also generously taken time off from her own work, which lies in another and more serene century than mine, to do indispensable and invaluable research for me.

LEONARD SCHAPIRO

The London School of Economics
and Political Science
June 1959

Preface to the Second Edition

Nearly ten years have elapsed since the manuscript of the first edition was completed. The most striking and unexpected event in the life of the party during this period was probably the fall of the First Secretary, Khrushchev. In my attempt to bring the book up to date, I have therefore tried to give a fairly full account of his period of office, and have used the information which has become available since his fall. For this period can now, in some ways, be regarded as closed: his many ideological and organizational innovations have proved ephemeral, and, in retrospect, somewhat naïve. Yet, there is one achievement to his credit which will probably prove as irreversible as the Revolution of February 1917 or the liberation of the serfs in 1861: his decision in 1956 to bring some of the horrifying facts of Stalin's era into the arena of public discussion. His successors have since tried to mute the discussion. But things can probably never be the same in Russia again, whatever the future may hold. I have dealt much more sketchily with the four years which have elapsed since Khrushchev's fall, the period of 'collective leadership'. I believe the present to be a period of transition, about which it is too early to make any confident pronouncements. However, I have yielded to the temptation to include some speculation on the present régime, and its future, in an Epilogue. I have been encouraged to do so by some criticisms which were levelled against the first edition; that it did not deal with the question of the role of the party in a totalitarian régime; and that it ended with a paragraph of speculation which should have been either expanded or omitted. I have tried to meet both of these just reproaches.

I have done my best to revise the text of the first edition up to the death of Stalin and to eliminate the many errors and inaccuracies which I have discovered since the book was published. (Some were already eliminated in the second printing.) In the work of revision I have had the greatest assistance from my former colleague, Paul Rosta. His meticulous checking of facts and searching of the text have not only made my task very much easier, but have, I am certain, uncovered many errors which I should have failed to spot. I am glad to be able to record my sincere gratitude to him. I have also had sage advice and help with suggestions and with the loan of materials from my colleague, Peter Reddaway. Dr Harold Shukman of St Antony's College, Oxford, gave me the benefit of his advice and great learning in the revision of the early part of the book. I wish to express my heart-felt thanks to both of them. But it is right to assure both them and Paul Rosta that any errors which still remain are the result of my own ignorance or obstinacy. I am also grateful to my College, The London School of Economics and Political Science, and to my colleagues in my department, for a period of sabbatical leave, which made it possible for me to complete this task of revision.

L.S.

Highgate,
February 1969

Introduction

The history of the revolutionary movement in Russia, of which social democracy was a part, begins with the Decembrists. The rising which these young noblemen attempted in 1825 was hastily improvised, and was easily crushed. But their political ideas foreshadowed the characteristic feature of the views of their successors. Only a minority of the Decembrists advocated constitutional aims – a limited monarchy, civil freedom and an elected supreme legislature. Most of them were Jacobin in politics, and more concerned with social reform than with liberty. They wanted the overthrow of the autocracy and a strong, centralized republican government as a necessary means for achieving social reforms.

It was to be expected that social reform should loom largest in the history of Russian revolutionary thought. The aspirations of the intellectual reformer were inevitably conditioned by the existence of a large peasant population. On the eve of the emancipation, in 1861, out of a total population of seventy-four millions, the peasants formed the overwhelming majority. Nearly half of them were privately owned serfs.[1] Ignorant, primitive, long suffering and patient, they were nevertheless capable of spontaneous outbursts of savage and pitiless revolt, and to the intellectual, dreaming of revolution, they were the one force which held out hope of the overthrow of the autocracy. But the peasants felt a veneration for the remote and almost legendary Tsar which was to remain unshaken throughout the century. Their enemies were the officials and the landlords whom they knew. Their desire was as much for land and relief from immediate hardships as for personal emancipation. Political liberty alone was therefore ill-adapted to solve the problem of the peasants.

The reign of Alexander II (1855–81) witnessed the rise of the populist movement (*narodnichestvo*). Its main inspiration came from

[1] No exact population figures are available for Russia before the first census of 1897. For sources upon which these estimates are based see Geroid Tanquary Robinson, *Rural Russia under the Old Régime. A History of the Landlord–Peasant World and a Prologue to the Peasant Revolution of 1917*, New York, 1949 (second printing), pp. 63, 284.

I

Alexander Herzen (1812–70). A passionate lover of liberty and justice, Herzen had been bitterly disillusioned not only by the collapse of the European revolutions, but also by his experience of mob rule in France. His long exile in England turned him against the dull inhumanity of Victorian capitalism. He resolved that Russia must never go the way of Western Europe, the way of capitalism and private enterprise. Russia must follow a separate path of her own. In Herzen's view the hope for this separate path to socialism and justice lay in the traditional Russian peasant commune, symbol of that socialism which was, he believed, instinctive to the Russian people. But the peasants were ignorant and backward. Let those, who like 'apostles' have 'the faith, the will, the conviction and the strength', speak to the people and train them for their destiny.

The doctrine that Russia could, by virtue of its traditional peasant commune, travel a separate path to socialism, and thus avoid the evils of capitalism, received more detailed exposition from N. G. Chernyshevsky (1828–89). A much colder and harder character than Herzen, Chernyshevsky was also the father of modern Russian radicalism, and influenced a generation of revolutionaries, including Lenin. Like Herzen (though without Herzen's love of freedom), like many if not most of the Russian *intelligentsia* of the period, he believed that socialism must come before freedom, since freedom is worthless where the economic means of enjoying it do not exist. A free and prosperous commune should, he believed, provide the basis for the society of the future.

The commune (*obshchina*) remained the lodestar of populist thinkers even after it had begun to disintegrate as an institution. This traditional form of land-tenure, which included a primitive form of self-government by peasant households, was shored up and strengthened by the Emancipation Act of 1861.[1] As it evolved in the course of practice during the century, the commune system tended to preserve the peasants as a separate social group. Three features distinguished the *obshchina*: first, that within it the peasant had no rights of property, but merely a right of user, within the commune and as determined by the commune; secondly, that he was restricted in his right to withdraw from the commune; thirdly, that he was subjected to a form of state paternalism, due partly to sentiment and partly to a desire to maintain an efficient system of tax collection. The peasant was subject to a separate system of laws based on what in theory was

[1] For a description of the various forms of this highly complex system see *ibidem*, pp. 66–80.

'customary' law, and in practice usually was arbitrary administration. Thus, the great majority of the population remained outside the influence of the habits of order, which only a universally applied system of civil law and civil rights could create.

This tendency to preserve the peasant in a world apart was supported, at any rate until 1905, both by the autocracy and by the populists, for different reasons. The autocracy believed that the foundations of support for the Tsar and the Church lay in these ancient peasant institutions. The populists, following Herzen and Chernyshevsky, saw in the commune the germ of the future socialist society. As against this, the richer and more enterprising peasants resented the commune, and wanted to attain full civil status, because the communal form of tenure restricted their ambition to expand their holdings. There were some thinkers who had the vision to see that this drag on the development of a normal legal society was also a drag on the development of free institutions. Thus the legal philosopher B. N. Chicherin, after the assassination of Alexander II in 1881, wrote to the new Emperor's minister and adviser, Pobedonostsev, urging the need to disband the commune. It was desirable, he wrote, that the peasant's sense of property should be strengthened, 'without which there can be no free civil society, and the absence of which always creates fertile ground for socialist disturbances'.[1] More than twenty years were to elapse before this advice was heeded, and it was then to prove too late.

As intellectual ferment grew during the 60's, under the impact of Alexander's reforms, populist thinkers turned increasingly to the problem of the individual's duty, and to the great gulf which lay between the intellectuals and the peasants. P. L. Lavrov (1823–1900), who was much occupied with the duty of the individual, believed, with Marx, that the road to socialism was being prepared by capitalism, of which the rise was beginning to be apparent in Russia. But Russian workers were not proletarians. They were close to the soil, and remained peasants at heart. The revolution would therefore come from the village, from the instinctive socialism of the *obshchina*. Lavrov believed that a conscious 'revolutionary minority' must devote itself for a long period to patient, preparatory and educative work among the people. For conspiracies and secret revolutionary societies planning to seize power he expressed withering contempt.

Until the 70's populism remained more a social philosophy than a

---

[1] *K. P. Pobedonostsev i ego korrespondenty*. Pis'ma i zapiski. S predisloviem M. N. Pokrovskogo. Volume I, Moscow, Petrograd, 1923, p. 111.

policy for revolution. But immediately after the emancipation of the serfs some signs of more violent activity began to appear. In 1861 leaflets and pamphlets calling for revolution were clandestinely circulated, and in the following year a short-lived conspiratorial society of revolutionaries was formed, called *Zemlia i Volia* (Land and Liberty). In 1866 an attempt was made on the life of the Emperor. All this activity had little following and less doctrine behind it. But an ideology for revolutionary activity was evolved by P. N. Tkachev (1844–85), the first Russian to teach that the revolution should be made by a small conspiratorial body of professionals, acting in the name of the people. According to Tkachev the revolutionary minority, or party, must first seize political power, and then transform society. It cannot, however, do so successfully without 'direct or indirect' support of the people. Therefore, before the revolution, every attempt should be made to organize a national uprising to coincide with the seizure of power by the revolutionary party. After the revolution, widespread propaganda will be required – indeed, propaganda can only become effective when once the revolutionary party has seized political power. Having consolidated its power, the revolutionary party, 'leaning on a national Duma', will carry out the social revolution – nationalization of land and of means of production, egalitarianism, gradual destruction of the family, and gradual 'weakening and abolition' of the central functions of government in favour of local self-governing communes.[1] There is no mention of liberty. The resemblance to bolshevism, such as it was eventually to become, is in some respects very striking, and it is with justice that Tkachev has often been described as the originator of many of Lenin's ideas. Lenin himself would later closely study Tkachev, and insist on Tkachev's articles as required reading for his own followers.[2] In contrast, Engels was very critical of his views, and engaged in open polemics with him.[3]

An important, and different, element in the development of more violent revolutionary activity was contributed to populism by M. A. Bakunin (1814–76). In contrast to Tkachev, Bakunin rejected not only the idea of a constitutional order, but of any order, even that of a revolutionary dictatorship. He saw salvation in the overthrow and

[1] See G. A. Kuklin, *Itogi revoliutsionnago dvizheniia v Rosii za sorok let (1862–1902 gg)*. Sbornik programm etc., Geneva, 1903, Part I, pp. 73–83, for some of Tkachev's articles from *Nabat* (The Tocsin), a paper published by him abroad, after his exile.

[2] See V. Bonch Bruevich in *Krasnaia Letopis'*, No. 3 (48), 1932, p. 113.

[3] *Fridrikh Engel's o Rossii. 1. Otvet P. N. Tkachevu, 1875 g. 2. Posleslovie k nemu, 1894.* (Translated by Vera Zasulich, with a preface by G. V. Plekhanov.) Geneva, 1894.

4

destruction of all existing society: from the resulting chaos, like a phoenix from the ashes, would arise a new brotherhood of men. His appeals were avowedly addressed to the darkest and most backward elements in Russian society – to the more primitive peasant, to the robbers and the outlaws. Like Lavrov, he called for missionary work among the people. But where Lavrov envisaged an educative mission to prepare peasant leaders for their task of making a better society, Bakunin's missionaries were to become apostles of revolt.

In the course of the 70's, the populists took the first steps towards creating an organization. They began to set up circles for discussion and for propaganda among the workers and peasants. In 1874 hundreds, probably thousands, of young men and women left their homes, assumed false names and provided themselves with false papers, and went to live among the peasants and workers – the latter were regarded as peasants in the factory. The naïve enthusiasm, faith and idealism behind this great missionary wave (the 'Going to the People', as it became known) is one of the most moving episodes in the whole of Russian history. Some of these young people, following Lavrov, aimed at creating by their propaganda future leaders of the revolution, others, more influenced by Bakunin, tried to stir up immediate revolt. They were all inexperienced in the ways of revolutionaries, and no match for the police, and very many of them were arrested. But more devastating than the arrests was the reaction of the peasants – their indifference, ignorance, suspicion, distrust and hostility. Those populist missionaries who escaped arrest came back to the cities bitterly disillusioned with the possibilities of bringing about a social revolution by propaganda among the peasants. They decided that organized action was needed. The result was the emergence in 1876 of the first Russian revolutionary party – *Zemlia i Volia* (Land and Liberty). The choice of name was influenced by the short-lived organization set up in 1862. *Zemlia i Volia* was founded by M. A. Natanson and A. D. Mikhailov, and G. V. Plekhanov, the future social democrat, was among its earliest adherents. The first programme adopted by *Zemlia i Volia* contained social rather than political demands: all land to the peasants, self-determination for all parts of the Russian empire, transfer of self-government functions to the peasant communes. But only a violent overthrow of the autocracy could achieve these aims. The programme accordingly called for agitation in order to arouse and stimulate revolutionary feeling. Of civil liberty there was not a word. But this essentially populist programme did not long satisfy the now more impatient and exasperated revolutionaries. Events helped to stimulate the trend towards more violent action. In the autumn of 1877 nearly two hundred young men and women, most of whom had already spent three years in prison awaiting trial, were sentenced for their part in 'going to the people'. In January 1878 a young girl, Vera Zasulich (another future social democrat), shot at and wounded the Governor of St Petersburg, General Trepov, as a reprisal for his orders to flog a young political prisoner. Her triumphant acquittal by a jury in defiance of the conclusive evidence against her, aroused a wave of sympathy in all progressive sections of society. Further terrorist acts soon followed. In 1878, under pressure from its more extreme members, a new programme and statute were adopted by *Zemlia i Volia* which called for a 'close and well-knit organization of formed revolutionaries' who would seek support among the *intelligentsia* and the workers as well as among the peasants. The programme demanded that the overthrow of the autocracy be carried out 'as speedily as possible', in view of the rapid development of capitalism (which it was feared would destroy the foundation of the ideal social order, the commune); and also called for the 'systematic destruction' of the most harmful or prominent persons in the government. But such acts of terror were still regarded as acts of vengeance, or self-defence, rather than as a means of political struggle. 'Only a class can arise against a class', proclaimed the first line of the illegal newspaper *Zemlia i Volia* in November 1878, echoing Marx.

In spite of the strong populist tradition against any kind of political objectives, pressure grew inside *Zemlia i Volia* for more concrete and immediate political action. This became evident at a Congress of the party which was held at Voronezh on 24 June 1879. A few days before the Congress, the more extreme members had met separately at Lipetsk and had decided that the aim of the party should now be the violent overthrow of the autocracy and the introduction of political liberties. But this political formulation was too far removed from traditional populism for the whole Congress to accept it, and the programme which was adopted tried to find a more socialist formulation. Political liberty, it stated, was not an aim, but only a means. The party would not pursue abstract socialist tenets, but aims of which the people is conscious, one of which is freedom. The immediate object was the overthrow of the régime in order to hand power over to the people: thereafter a freely elected Constituent Assembly would decide. The party must take the lead in overthrowing the autocracy, and must also prepare the people for the elections which would follow.

The task of organization was left to the conspiratorial party centre, the Executive Committee. (These two elements – the recognition of the priority of the political aim and the closely disciplined central conspiratorial organization – were later to win Lenin's praise.) But in the end the only activity of *Narodnaia Volia*, or People's Will (as the party called itself after the Voronezh Congress), proved to be the assassination of Alexander II. After unsuccessful attempts in 1879 and 1880, the Emperor was killed on 1 March 1881. It was a futile act of despair and political immaturity. The despair stemmed from the immense and apparently insuperable difficulty of ever organizing a people's rising. It was politically immature because these revolutionaries never considered in what manner the assassination of the Emperor would help to hand power over to the people, so long as the police, the army and the bureaucracy remained firmly under the control of the government machine. On the eve of his assassination (though this was not known at the time) the Emperor had agreed to the setting up of a consultative council, including representatives of the elected local government councils. This would have been, at any rate, a small step on the long road to constitutional government. But the murder led to the consolidation of the influence of those of the Emperor's advisers who favoured repressive measures to the exclusion of all else, and incidentally to the disintegration of the populist revolutionary movement. What had proclaimed itself as a political movement in the end proved to be a conspiracy, and nothing more.[1]

The Voronezh Congress of *Zemlia i Volia* was, however, significant for another reason. For it led to Plekhanov's break with *Zemlia i Volia*. Plekhanov had for some time been out of sympathy with the trend towards the primacy of political objectives which had been developing inside the party. Together with a few supporters – P. B. Aksel'rod, Vera Zasulich and Leo Deich – he soon after founded a separate organization, *Chernyi Peredel* ('Repartition of the Land'). In the first issue of *Chernyi Peredel* (the organ of the movement) Plekhanov argued that 'history has taught us' that political *coups d'état* have 'nowhere and at no time' been able to secure economic and political freedom to the people, and a long attack followed on Jacobinism. But, argued Plekhanov, 'an economic revolution on the land will inevitably bring with it the overturning of all other social relations'. In this, and in subsequent issues, Plekhanov and his supporters argued that it was

[1] For the best account in English of *Zemlia i Volia* and *Narodnaia Volia*, see David Footman, *Red Prelude*, The Life of the Russian Terrorist Zhelyabov, New Haven, 1945.

only through economic struggle that the people could gradually learn the meaning of and the need for political struggle. To preach general political aims to the people, which they could not understand, would only have the effect of turning them against all revolutionary activities. The future founders of Marxism were thus preaching for over a year the very heresy, which under the name of 'economism' they would later roundly condemn. *Chernyi Peredel* ceased publication with its fourth issue, in September 1881. By that date the founders of the movement were all living in emigration. Before long they had broken with populism, and had become converted to the doctrines of Marx and Engels. 'Almost half a social democrat' by the summer of 1880,[1] as he tells us, Plekhanov had certainly accepted some of the main principles of the Marxist theory of action by January 1881. In an open letter to *Chernyi Peredel* (with the aims of which he was no longer in sympathy) he asserted that socialism was the theoretical formulation of the 'antagonism and struggle of classes in existing society'. Revolutionaries' activity should consist in 'organizing the workers' estate' (he did not yet use the term 'class'), and 'in indicating to the worker the ways and means of his liberation'. But liberation could only be achieved with the co-operation of the people themselves, since the most heroic struggles by revolutionaries alone would only work out for the benefit of the higher classes of society.[2] Here were the clear tones of Marxism. On 25 September 1883, mainly on the initiative of Deich, Plekhanov and his supporters announced the publication in Geneva of a series of popular political pamphlets for workers to be called 'The Library of Contemporary Socialism', and thus founded the first Russian theoretical Marxist group. It became known as the Group for the Liberation of Labour.

For some ten years the theoretical development of Marxism as applied to Russian conditions was to be mainly the work of Plekhanov and Aksel'rod. The two men differed in origin, outlook and formation. Georgii Valentinovich Plekhanov was twenty-six in 1883. The son of a landowner, he had been trained for the career of an army officer, but soon abandoned it for the Petersburg Mining Institute. Essentially doctrinaire by temperament, he was attracted to Marxism by the systematic and scientific solution which it seemed to him to offer for the problem of revolution in Russia. His powerful and incisive intellect, his wide range of reading in political and social questions, and his ability to convince by the power of his analysis entitle him to a place

---

[1] See Plekhanov's reminiscences of this period in *Iskra*, No. 54, 1 December 1903.
[2] G. V. Plekhanov, *Sochineniia*, volume I, p. 134.

among outstanding Marxist theorists not only in Russia but in the movement generally. But his arrogance and intellectual pride made him impatient of those less educated than himself, and intolerant of opposition and criticism. He rightly regarded himself as the father of Russian Marxism, and he expected his leadership in theoretical questions to be acknowledged. But there were to be occasions when, spurred on by vanity, he came very near to sacrificing his principles.

Pavel Borisovich Aksel'rod was six years older. A Jew by birth, he became a revolutionary at the age of seventeen, burning with a mission to emancipate all the poor and oppressed of Russia. He had taken part in the 'going to the people', working as a carpenter, and had fled to Germany in 1874 to escape arrest. The deep impression made upon him at this time, and on subsequent visits, by the workers' movement then growing up in Germany was to last the whole of his life, and, more than any other leading Russian Marxist, Aksel'rod was to draw on German experience for his solution of Russian problems. The new working-class movement, the trade union, the proletariat educated for and conscious of its great historical mission – these were the elements of which Aksel'rod's thought would thereafter be formed. An intellectual, like Plekhanov, his road to Marxism had been both more practical and more emotional than scientific. Aksel'rod saw in Marxism a liberating force for living and suffering men, Plekhanov the scientific working out of the unalterable social law.[1]

There were indeed good reasons why Marxism should have attracted these former populists. It shared with traditional populism a belief in social change as the ultimate aim, regarding political liberty as but a means to that end. But, unlike populism, it offered a scientific basis for the belief in the future revolution: the evolution of capitalism on the model of Western Europe must lead Russia successively through the historical phases, first the 'bourgeois' phase of democracy, to be followed in time by the next phase, the social revolution. There were other reasons too. Marxism, at least in the interpretation put upon it by Plekhanov and Aksel'rod, rejected any form of Jacobin conspiracy, such as had repelled these two at Voronezh in 1879, and of which the assassination of 1 March 1881 had only proved the futility. Moreover, the foundation of Marx's teaching was that the ultimate socialist

[1] See Leopold H. Haimson, *The Russian Marxists and the Origins of Bolshevism* Cambridge, Mass., 1955, chapter ii, for an admirable account of the formation of these two men.

revolution would be brought about by the working class, which in the years of preparation that lay ahead would acquire the necessary consciousness for its task. To men who had lived through the disillusionment of trying to bring political consciousness to the Russian peasants this doctrine, with its reliance on a more educated class, more receptive to modern ideas, had an understandable attraction.

The application of Marxism to Russian conditions was not easy. Marx himself during his lifetime did not apparently envisage the possibility that capitalism on the Western scale and model could ever develop in Russia. Indeed, in 1877 Marx protested against the attempt to transpose his theory on the development of capitalism in Western Europe into a theory of general application to all countries.[1] In 1881, in reply to an enquiry by Vera Zasulich, Marx even committed himself to the cautious view that the peasant commune might in certain circumstances become 'a focal point for the social regeneration of Russia'.[2] A year before, when the news that Plekhanov had broken with the populists and had emigrated reached him, he had poured scorn in a private letter on 'these gentlemen who are opposed to any revolutionary activity, and are preparing for the leap all in one into the anarchist-communist-atheist millennium . . . by means of the dullest of dull doctrinaire views'.[3] But Marx died too soon to influence the first Russian steps in Marxism. In contrast, Engels to the end of his days maintained contact both in person and by correspondence with Plekhanov and Vera Zasulich, gave his encouragement and approval to the development of their ideas and, it may be supposed, influenced them.[4]

For over ten years the Group for the Liberation of Labour remained largely isolated from working-class political activity inside Russia.

[1] In a letter to the editor of *Otechestvennye Zapiski*, which was in fact never sent, and was only published after his death. For the text see *Lenin*, volume I, pp. 472–4. (There is an English version of the relevant parts in Karl Marx, *Selected Writings in Sociology and Social Philosophy,* edited by T. B. Bottomore and Maximilien Rubel, London, 1956, pp. 22–3.)

[2] Marx prepared several exhaustive drafts before sending his non-committal reply. See *Arkhiv K. Marksa i F. Engel'sa.* Pod redaktsiei D. Riazanova, part I, Moscow, 1924, pp. 265–86, for the above incident, and the documents. On the other hand, it may have been true, as Bernstein suggested, that Marx's support, even if hesitant, of the populists was due less to his conviction that they were right, than to a desire not to damp their revolutionary ardour too much – *ibidem*, p. 267.

[3] Letter to Sorge of 5 November 1880 quoted in *Gruppa 'Osvobozhdemie Truda'.* (Iz arkhivov G. V. Plekhanova, V. I. Zasulich i L. G. Deicha.) Pod redaktsiei L. G. Deicha. Sbornik I, Moscow, n.d., p. 134.

[4] The correspondence between the three of them is reprinted in *Perepiska K. Marksa i F. Engel'sa s russkimi politicheskimi deiateliami.* Second edition, Moscow, 1951, pp. 302–46. (The generous and warm-hearted Engels even insisted on helping Vera Zasulich financially when she was in need of medical treatment.) See pp. 825–97 *ibidem* for Engels' views on Russia in 1894.

In 1884 Deich, who was in charge of organizing contact with Russia, was arrested, and regular contact could not be resumed until 1895. During these years Plekhanov and Aksel'rod addressed themselves to the problem of translating Marxism into Russian terms. Two brilliant pamphlets by Plekhanov appeared in 1883 and 1884, and draft programmes were published, in 1884 and 1887.[1] There were three main difficulties in applying Marxist analysis to Russia. First, the fact that even when compared with the Western Europe of 1848, the development of capitalism in Russia was only in its infancy. The proletariat, though slowly growing, was in absolute figures small, and in comparison with the peasants, minute. The prospect of a proletarian majority was so remote that to wait for this majority (which Marx had foreseen as the prerequisite for the social revolution) meant waiting for a very long time. Secondly, the overwhelming majority of the population, the peasants, were interested not in socialism but in land. Yet the emergence, if the peasants' desire were satisfied, of a large class of smallholders, each endowed with that fierce love of his plot which is characteristic of the peasant, would be inconsistent with the fundamental aim of the social revolution – the national ownership of the means of production. And thirdly, in contrast, say, to the Germany or England of 1890, there was no political or civil freedom, and no middle-class parties in existence or in prospect in Russia. This meant that the modern workers' party, which Plekhanov and Aksel'rod were now hoping to create, must come into being without the advantage of political and civil liberties, such as parliamentary institutions or the right to associate in trade unions in which their German comrades were rapidly acquiring the maturity and political experience to fit them for their historic task. It meant, further, that in the event of liberal parties emerging in Russia in the future (which was not only likely, but, with the development of capitalism, in Marxist thinking axiomatic) the new workers' party would be faced with two equally undesirable alternatives: either to wait patiently until the liberals had made the bourgeois revolution, and thereafter to work for the social revolution in the remote future: or else to fight immediately on two fronts, both against the autocracy and against the liberals, and in so doing perhaps endanger the success of the bourgeois revolution.

Not all of these problems were ever raised, let alone solved, by the theorists in Geneva. Plekhanov argued with justice, and with foresight,

---

[1] *Sotsializm i politicheskaia bor'ba* and *Nashi raznoglasiia*. The programmes are reprinted in Plekhanov's *Sochineniia*, volume II, pp. 357–62 and 400–4.

that the peasant commune upon which the populists pinned their faith was fast disintegrating, and that with the development of capitalism a proletariat already existed, and was likely to grow. The task of socialism, therefore, was to lead this proletariat towards the accomplishment of its political task of liberation. This could only be achieved by the formation of a workers' party. Seizure of power by groups of conspirators, as envisaged by Tkachev, or terrorist conspiracies such as those of *Narodnaia Volia*, would at best accomplish nothing, and at worst, by bringing the bourgeoisie into power, present the workers with a better organized and more intelligent enemy. These early writings as yet scarcely tackled the problem of the peasant. The earlier draft programme of 1884 suggested the possibility of the workers' party co-operating with a peasant party, if such a party came into existence. The draft programme of 1887 envisaged certain economic demands for the benefit of the peasants, on the basis of which it was hoped to draw the workers and the peasants closer together, but evaded the main problem – the peasants' desire to become, and remain, smallholders. Nor did this programme deal with the question of the relation of the workers' party to liberal parties. On the contrary, it squarely laid the burden of achieving the basic political and civil freedoms upon the proletariat, whose first task must be the overthrow of the autocracy. Two years later, in 1889, Plekhanov did consider the probability that the workers' party would have to coexist for a substantial period of time side by side with liberal parties, and that the victory of the proletariat could only come after a fairly lengthy interval of preparation by the proletariat for its mission.[1] Yet this lengthy period of preparation was not likely to appeal to revolutionaries who are not, as a rule, endowed with a great deal of patience.

The answer was supplied by Plekhanov in 1892. The social democrats, he wrote, have no intention of 'becoming dissolved' in any other party. On the contrary, it will be very easy for the Russian social democrats (in contrast to their colleagues in Western Europe, where established liberal parties already exist) to gather around them all those members of the *intelligentsia* who stand hesitating 'between the bourgeoisie and the proletariat'. But this leadership will only be possible if the proletariat became the most determined and the boldest fighter for political liberty.[2] In other words, the proletariat should

[1] Plekhanov, *Sochineniia*, volume III, pp. 83–95 – 'Politicheskie zadachi russkikh sotsialistov'.
[2] Plekhanov, *Sochineniia*, volume III, pp. 409–10.

not wait passively for the bourgeoisie to seize political power, but should take the lead over the party of the bourgeoisie by attracting its intellectual champions to the side of the proletariat. This view was to become known as the doctrine of the 'hegemony' of the proletariat over the liberal parties. It was to fascinate Russian social democrats for a number of years to come, especially after Aksel'rod had developed it more fully in 1898 (the actual term, 'hegemony', was not, it seems, used by Plekhanov until 1901).[1]

In the conditions in which Russian social democracy was born, before the emergence of liberal parties, it was easy to see the attraction of 'hegemony': for it seemed to provide an alternative to the prospect of an interminably long wait. As the leader of the political struggle the proletariat would have an active task right from the start, and would point the way for the as yet unborn liberals. But what should be the relation of the workers' party to the liberals? Plekhanov, in 1892, regarded it as 'unthinkable' that the social democrats should, during their period of co-operation with the liberal spokesmen of the bourgeoisie, at the same time endeavour to explain to the proletariat the ultimate antagonism between their own interests and those of the bourgeoisie, as personified by the liberals. In later years, with the emergence of liberal parties on to the political scene, this issue would become the fertile source of disagreement inside the ranks of the social democrats. Another consequence of the idea of 'hegemony' was that it served to emphasize the importance of 'political' as compared with 'economic' struggle by the workers in their future party. For what chance had the workers to act as the leaders of, or as a magnet to, the liberal *intelligentsia* if they confined their demands to such matters as shorter hours and higher wages, but left untouched the civil liberties so dear to the liberal?

Meanwhile Marxist theory was being discussed inside Russia as well. The first volume of *Das Kapital* had appeared in Russian translation in 1872 (the censorship regarded it as too dull and academic to be in any way subversive). Its appearance immediately started discussion in intellectual circles on the significance of this novel analysis for Russia. The debate was 'legal' in the sense that it was carried on in strictly academic terms and within the narrow limits of the Russian censorship. One of the earliest converts to Marxism was N. I. Ziber, whose articles in the learned journals during 1876–8 did much to

---

[1] Plekhanov, *Sochineniia*, volume XII, p. 101. For Aksel'rod's views see his *K voprosu o sovremennykh zadachakh i taktike russkikh sotsial-demokratov*, Geneva, 1898.

spread sympathy with Marx's views long before Plekhanov and Aksel'rod had embraced Marxism. The main question in issue was: can Western capitalism, with its consequences both good and bad, develop in Russian conditions? The intellectuals who followed the populist tradition argued that it could not. The Marxist intellectuals who contested this populist view included P. B. Struve (1870–1944), S. N. Bulgakov, N. A. Berdyaev and M. I. Tugan-Baranovskii. They acquired the nickname of the 'Legal Marxists'. The description is inappropriate for two reasons: first, because even the leading 'Legal Marxist', Struve, engaged in underground political activity; secondly, because genuine conspirators like Lenin, Plekhanov and Martov joined in the debates in the pages of legally permitted publications. In 1893, the twenty-three-year-old Lenin made a great impression on a student meeting by the force of his attack on the populist V. P. Vorontsov at a lecture, and his early writings, particularly his *The Development of Capitalism in Russia*, completed in exile in 1899, were very influential in destroying much of the populist argument. Plekhanov's *Development of the Monist View of History*, legally published (under the name of Bel'tov) in 1895, likewise exercised great influence in arguing the case for Marxism. It remains to this day unexcelled as the best exposition of historical materialism.

But the temporary, and as events were to show, short-lived, co-operation against the populists of men like Struve on the one hand and Lenin and Plekhanov on the other did not mean a large area of identity of views. For Lenin and Plekhanov the acceptance of Marxist doctrine had been a conversion. For Struve Marxism was from the first not a faith but a promising hypothesis for political and historical enquiry. A passionate lover all his life of liberty and constitutionalism, he had embraced the theories of *Capital* precisely because he saw in the development of the capitalist system in Russia a promise of the legal order which in Western Europe was developing alongside of it. 'All contemporary material and spiritual culture,' he wrote in 1894, 'is closely bound up with capitalism.' The evolution of this culture was no easy matter, but a long and laborious business. But it was no use imagining, in the narrow nationalistic manner of the populists, that some kind of superior, indigenous Russian form of order could be built up without this laborious process. The most likely result in Russia of such a short-cut to utopia would be a return to serfdom. He ended with the much quoted words: 'No, let us confess our cultural backwardness, and let us go and learn from capitalism.'[1] But Struve was also attracted by the emphasis which Marxism laid on the mission of the workers' party to fight for civil and political freedom. In the absence of a middle class in Russia from which a strong, courageous liberal party could arise, Struve believed that the task of liberation from autocracy, and hence the achievement of civil and political liberty, could fall only on the shoulders of the proletariat. The subsequent political evolution of Struve shows how different his attraction to Marxism had been from the conversion of Lenin and Plekhanov. By 1901, if not before, Struve had come to the conclusion that the principles of liberalism need not depend either on the existence of a middle class or on an economic sub-structure of the kind that existed in Western Europe. His historical researches had convinced him, he wrote in 1901, that the doctrine currently accepted in Russia that liberalism had emerged 'as the political system of the bourgeoisie, and in the material interests of the bourgeoisie' was false. On the contrary, the origin of liberalism must be sought in the striving for freedom of conscience, and this was neither the prerogative of a class nor dependent on any particular system of economic relations. From this he drew the conclusion that liberal principles, founded on natural law, were of universal application.[2] It was consistently with this view that Struve in the following year became the ideological leader of a group which formed around the newspaper *Osvobozhdenie* (Liberation), which he edited abroad, and from which the future Russian liberal movement was to grow.

This evolution in Struve's thought from Marxism to liberalism was much influenced by the appearance in 1899 of the work of the German social democrat Eduard Bernstein – *Die Voraussetzungen des Sozialismus und die Aufgaben der Sozialdemokratie*.[3] Starting with a devastating attack on the economic foundations of Marxism in the light of actual developments, Bernstein argued that the path of reform and of steady pressure by democratic means had achieved much more for the workers than could ever be won by revolution. There was a fundamental fallacy in the Marxist doctrine of the ultimate seizure of power by the proletariat at a time when, after a long period of preparation, it has developed the necessary strength and maturity: so long as the working class is not strong enough to achieve power by parliamentary

---

[1] P. Struve, *Kriticheskiia zametki k voprosu ob ekonomicheskom razvitii Rossii*, St Petersburg, 1894, p. 288.
[2] See his 'V chem zhe istinnyi natsionalizm', reprinted in P. Struve, *Na raznyia temy (1893–1901 gg.)*, Sbornik statei, St Petersburg, 1902, pp. 526–55.
[3] It was published in Russian translation in the following year by the Russian Free Press Fund in London. The references which follow are to the Russian edition.

means, and without revolution, it is not fit to govern; but once it is strong enough to be fit to govern, it will achieve power without revolution.[1] True democracy, in Bernstein's view, does not lie, as visualized by the Jacobins and by Marx, in the oppression of the minority by the majority, but 'in a condition of society in which no single class enjoys special privileges in the light of the aims of society as a whole'.[2] A socialist party could never create democracy, because socialism can only develop where democracy exists, and democracy can only exist where the nation is ripe for it, and has reached understanding of what a legal order means.[3] The real purpose of socialism is best achieved where the socialist party 'works jointly with the radical bourgeoisie in order to achieve reform'.[4] But a so-called dictatorship of the proletariat, where the workers have not yet built up strong organizations of an economic nature of their own, and have not developed political maturity through the practice of self-government within their own organizations, can only mean 'the dictatorship of the club orators and the littérateurs'.[5]

The publication of this pamphlet was a bombshell for the European socialist parties. For years after, Lenin and Plekhanov joined in the chorus of Bernstein's critics in the German party, such as Kautsky and Rosa Luxemburg, in condemning this 'revisionism' and 'reformism' – the two words are still the strongest terms of abuse in the current communist vocabulary. At first sight the application of Bernstein's views to Russian conditions at the turn of the century might appear questionable – there was no parliamentary democracy in Russia, and therefore no path to power through a parliamentary victory was in prospect, as it was in Germany. But the explosive element of the doctrine was the fact that it attacked the very foundations of Marxism – the class struggle, and the peculiar historical mission of the proletariat as the only liberator class. One conclusion that could be drawn from it by Russians in 1899 was that the Russian workers should leave the fight for political freedom to the bourgeoisie, and concentrate on their own immediate economic needs. Another, that when once a liberal party did emerge in Russia, the workers' party should co-operate with it, and support it, rather than seek to exercise 'hegemony' over it. Each of these heresies in turn was to shake the foundations of Russian social democracy.

[1] *op. cit.*, pp. 42–3. Cf. Alfred G. Meyer, *Marxism. The Unity of Theory and Practice*, Cambridge, Mass., 1954, pp. 120–1, where a somewhat similar argument is adduced from Engels.
[2] *op. cit.*, p. 152.   [3] *op. cit.*, p. 208.   [4] *op. cit.*, p. 174.
[5] *op. cit.*, p. 229.

PART ONE

The Formative Years

I^1 The 'Economist' Controversy

When in 1889 Plekhanov told the First Congress of the Socialist International in Paris that the Russian revolution 'will succeed as a workers' revolution or it will not succeed at all' there seemed as yet little evidence to justify this view to his Western listeners. In the industrial countries of Western Europe the trade union movement was growing, mass workers' parties were in existence, and the civil liberties of constitutional systems provided the workers both with a means of exercising political pressure and with the opportunity for political self-education. In Russia at the end of the nineteenth century none of these circumstances existed. Trade unions were illegal, and strikes, even if unorganized, a criminal offence. Mutual aid societies, workers' clubs and similar organizations so familiar to the Western European worker were, if not strictly illegal, restricted and repressed under a system of criminal law in which the executive arm of the police was never at a loss, if required, to supplement the gaps left by legislation. Of political liberty there was, in 1889, no trace and little hope.

But the rapid development of industry, which had brought Plekhanov and the other Marxist theorists to the conclusion that Russia was now embarked on the road of Western capitalism, led to the growth of an industrial proletariat. In 1897 12·8% of the population of European Russia lived in towns (as against 33% in the United States, 54% in Germany and 77% in Britain). The workers numbered at least two and a half out of about 129 millions, and possibly more.[2] The populists persisted in their view that the Russian worker was really a peasant temporarily employed in the factory, who returned periodically to the farm, and argued that he should not be regarded as a proletarian in the usual sense. By the last decade of the century this traditional view was out of date. Nevertheless, the educational

---

[1] I am much indebted in this and in the next few chapters to Dr J. L. H. Keep's admirable doctoral dissertation *The Development of Social Democracy in Russia, 1898–1907* (quoted hereafter as *Keep*). This was published, with modifications, in 1963 in Oxford, under the title *The Rise of Social Democracy in Russia*.
[2] No exact figures are available. See *Keep*, p. 5, for various estimates.

standard of the Russian worker, though higher than that of the peasant, was well below that of the Western European worker.

The conditions of life and work of the Russian proletariat provided ample grounds for legitimate grievance. Wages were low – averaging 187·6 roubles annually for a man, half that amount for a woman, and a third for juveniles.[1] Hours were long, sanitary conditions in the factories were generally very bad, and living conditions a good deal worse. In spite of severe and often brutal police repression, the Russian workers, with little organization, succeeded in the last two decades of the century in wresting from the government a series of concessions. The law of 1 June 1882 prohibited the employment of children under 12, established an eight-hour day for juveniles under 15, and introduced a system of factory inspectors. A further law of 3 June 1886 required the regular payment of wages, prohibited payment in kind, increased the power of the inspectors, and imposed controls on the practice of employers of levying 'fines'. The law of 2 June 1897 established the eleven-and-a-half-hour day. Each of these modest milestones had been preceded by a wave of strikes, in which some of the future social democrats played the role of propagandists, if not organizers. Plekhanov (then still a populist) helped to organize the cotton spinners' strikes in Petersburg in 1878 and 1879 which led to the law of 1882. The legislation of 1886 was directly brought about by a strike of textile workers in the previous year. The modest ameliorations were often in practice nullified by evasion and corruption, but they taught the workers the important lesson that they could improve their lot by striking.[2] The mission which the Marxists set themselves was to persuade the workers that they could only improve their lot permanently and effectively by overthrowing the autocracy and by ultimately achieving political power.

The first workers' circles in Russia were organized by the populists. Several small circles were formed in Petersburg in the 60's and 70's. In 1877 fifty young populists, mainly girls and students, were tried for having conducted organized propaganda in the factories, and for distributing an illegal paper (*Rabotnik*, The Worker). In 1875 E. O. Zaslavkii founded the first large organization – it is said to have had

---

[1] A gold rouble was until 1897 equivalent to about two shillings and sixpence, or 50 U.S. cents.

[2] See *Obshchestvennoe dvizhenie v Rossii v nachale XX-go veka. Pod redaktsiei L. Martova, P. Maslova i A. Potresova.* Volume I, Petersburg, 1909 (quoted hereafter as *Obshchestvennoe dvizhenie*), pp. 224–9, where tables will be found, based on official data, analysing the incidence, nature and results of strikes for the period 1895–1904. In general, strikes led slightly more often to a success for the workers or to a compromise, than to a success for the employers.

two hundred members – called the South Russian Union of Workers. The second large organization, the Northern Union of Russian Workers was formed in December 1878 (or possibly earlier) by Stepan Khalturin and Victor Obnorskii. It also attained a membership of two hundred. These two groups, though short-lived, may rightly be considered the forerunners of the future social democratic organizations. Their programmes showed Marxist influence: they recognized that the liberation of the workers could only be achieved by the overthrow of the existing political order, and included demands for civil and political liberties.[1]

In the 80's working men's circles calling themselves Marxist or social democratic began to spring up in Petersburg and in some provincial cities. Their main activity was educational – the discussion of elementary economic and political questions from the Marxist point of view. The first of these circles, formed in the winter of 1883–4, and known as the Blagoev group, was directly influenced by Plekhanov's Group for the Liberation of Labour, and both he and Aksel'rod wrote for the two issues of an illegal paper published by Blagoev's group. But many of these circles owed little or nothing to the influence of Plekhanov's group abroad, and drew their inspiration from the study of Marxism inside Russia. The core of these indigenous circles was provided by former members of *Chernyi Peredel* and by workers trained by them. The number of these circles increased with great rapidity. The famine of 1891 acted as a stimulus to the *intelligentsia* to engage in revolutionary activity. At the same time the flow of starving peasants to the towns increased industrial unrest. In the last decade of the century social democratic groups could be numbered in dozens.

The primary aim of Plekhanov and his companions was the formation of a social democratic party in Russia. The first to attempt to put this idea into practice, however, were not the Russians, but the Polish and Jewish inhabitants of the Russian Empire. In 1882 a proletarian party, *Proletariat*, was founded in Warsaw. In the following year it held an illegal congress in Vilna with the avowed aim of uniting all circles of revolutionaries throughout the Russian Empire whose objective was the liberation of the working class. The attempt came to nothing, and *Proletariat* only survived for a short period. It was, how-

---

[1] The programme of the Northern Union is reprinted in *Lenin*, Volume II, pp. 609–11. For the Southern Union see Em. Iaroslavskii (editor), *Istoria VKP(b)*, volume I, part I, Moscow-Leningrad, 1926, p. 66; F. I. Dan, *Proiskhozhdenie Bol'shevizma. K istorii demokraticheskikh i sotsialisticheskikh idei v Rosii posle osvobozhdeniia krest'ian*. New York, 1946, p. 191.

ever, revived in 1888, when it united with other groups to form the Polish Socialist Party. In 1892–1893 the Polish Socialist Party split into two on the issue of national separatism. The internationalists broke away and formed the Social Democratic Party of the Kingdom of Poland. Its leaders, Rosa Luxemburg and Leo Iogiches (Tyshka) were to play an influential part in the history of Russian social democracy.

The Jewish social democratic movement, in the West and South-West of Russia, centred in Vilna and Minsk, was very different in development from the Russian movement. Like the Russian circles, the Jewish groups of the 80's were founded by intellectuals and worker intellectuals. But in contrast to the Russians, the Jewish social democrats were successful from the start in organizing mass action by Jewish workers in defence of their interests. In spite of repressions they succeeded in organizing underground mutual aid societies, strike funds, and even trade unions. In 1897 the various groups and organizations formed themselves into a national party, 'The General Jewish Workers' Union in Lithuania, Poland and Russia', known as the *Bund*. The *Bund* was by then already a mass party incorporating a wide network of workers' organizations, welded together over years of united struggle,[1] and it remained a mass party. Apart from the Georgian party, it was the only broadly based workers' party with anything like a democratic organization in Russia. In contrast, the Russian social democrats were seldom able to progress much beyond the stage of small, secret committees with little following among the workers. For example, in August 1904 the membership of the *Bund* was already 23,000, and two illegal social democratic trade unions were affiliated to it. The Russian party committees only contained 8,400 members by 1905.[2] The main reasons for this difference will become apparent later. But among subsidiary reasons two may be mentioned here. First, the higher educational level of the Jewish workers; and secondly, the fact that the majority of the Jewish workers were employed in small-scale workshops and factories, where close supervision presented greater difficulty for the police than in the large-scale industries of the Russian areas.

The relationship of the *Bund* to the Russian social democrats was to

---

[1] As A. Kremer, the early historian of the *Bund*, says, the 1897 Congress only set the seal on a union of organizations which had already worked in close co-operation for some years. Quoted in M. Rafes, *Ocherki po istorii 'Bunda'*, Moscow, 1923, pp. 41–2. See *ibidem*, pp. 315–26, for an example of the constitution of a Jewish workers' illegal strike fund organization, which skilfully combines solidarity, secrecy and democratic control.

[2] Rafes, *op. cit.* chap. XII, and p. 141; *BSE*, volume XI, col. 931.

be complicated by Jewish national aspirations. The first Jewish social democrats were anti-Zionist, assimilationist and mostly atheist, and accepted the Marxist doctrine that the struggle of the proletariat was one and indivisible. Anti-Semitism would disappear along with capitalism. But before long doctrine began to be modified in the light of experience. The occasional participation of Russian workers in anti-Jewish pogroms not unnaturally shook the *Bundist's* faith in the unity of the proletariat. The use of the Jewish language (Yiddish), originally avoided because it was not conducive to assimilation, was adopted for the practical purpose of more effective propaganda. As time went on, and relations between the *Bund* and the Russian party became more strained, the stress on the distinctiveness of the interests of the Jewish workers would become more marked. But as early as May 1895 the future menshevik leader, Julius Martov, then active in the Jewish organizations in Vilna, had formulated the need for a specifically Jewish party on the grounds that if at any time in the future the Russian proletariat were forced to sacrifice some of the party demands, it would be most likely to sacrifice 'demands which exclusively concern the Jews, such as freedom of religion or equality of civil rights for Jews'.[1] The demand for an autonomous Jewish party, though affiliated to the Russian party, put forward by the *Bund* soon led to conflict with the Russians. (Martov himself very shortly became a staunch opponent of *Bund* separatism.) Another factor also led to friction between the two. The *Bund* took considerable pride in the fact that it was a mass workers' party. It therefore became increasingly reluctant to put itself under the orders of what it regarded as a handful of squabbling intellectuals.

The success of the Jewish organizations in defending the interests of the workers gave considerable impetus to the development of the Russian movement. The Jewish solution of the problem of transforming a network of small circles, composed mainly of intellectuals, into a broader workers' organization was particularly influential. In technical terms, the problem was how to pass from 'propaganda' to 'agitation'. The difference between the two had been formulated by Plekhanov in 1891. 'The propagandist,' he wrote, 'presents many ideas to one individual, or to several individuals. The agitator presents one idea only, or a few ideas, but he presents them to a whole mass of persons. . . .' Thus, the intellectuals, and worker intellectuals, who

---

[1] L. (Iu.) Martov, *Povorotnyi punkt v istorii evreiskago rabochago dvizheniia*, Geneva, 1900, p. 9. Almost immediately afterwards Martov left the Jewish movement to devote himself to the Russian movement. See also Iu. Martov, *Zapiski sotsial-demokrata*, Berlin, 1922, pp. 245–7.

composed the circles, each went forth to create a mass movement.
The plan worked in the end, but there were some difficulties. The
worker intellectuals were often more concerned with their own self-
education, while the more backward workers felt estranged from their
more advanced comrades.[1] The successful experience among the
Jewish workers was set down in a pamphlet entitled *On Agitation (Ob
agitatsii)* by one of the leading *Bundists*, A. Kremer. It was edited
and supplied with a preface by Martov, reproduced on a hectograph,
and smuggled into Petersburg in 1894, at a time when social
democratic circles were rapidly multiplying. The main theme of this
influential pamphlet was that the proletariat must on no account
wait for the bourgeoisie to win freedom for it. 'The fight for the liberation of the proletariat must not be postponed until such time as the
bourgeoisie attains political freedom.' But the masses cannot be
induced to take up the cudgels for abstract ideas. The development
of proletarian consciousness is a gradual process, evolved in a
succession of battles for small, concrete demands. The aim of
the social democrats, therefore, should become 'continual agitation among factory workers based on existing minor demands and
needs'.[2]

Martov, whose presence in Vilna had been largely accidental, now
moved to Petersburg, to work in one of the Russian circles. Lenin was
already active in one of these circles, and late in 1895, on Martov's
suggestion, they joined forces to form the Petersburg Union of
Struggle for the Liberation of the Working Class (the name had been
suggested to Lenin by Aksel'rod in May). Martov recalls that the
intellectual social democrats showed a reluctance to adopt the new
idea – Lenin seemed to him 'cold, if not contemptuous' towards it. He
attributed Lenin's indifference to the habits of underground activity
which had led, as he wrote later, to an attitude of 'secretiveness not
only towards the police, but towards the working class as well'.[3] But
Lenin, if he did not sympathize with the theoretical basis of *On
Agitation*, that political consciousness should be allowed to grow
among the workers by guiding them through their economic struggle,
certainly recognized the practical value of the new formula for extending influence more widely. It was true, however, that his attention
was mainly engaged in putting his group through a period of intensive
theoretical training, so as to prepare them for their role as a nucleus of

[1] Iu. Martov, *Zapiski sotsial-demokrata*, Berlin, 1922, p. 277.
[2] *Ob agitatsii*. S poslesloviem P. Aksel'roda. Geneva, 1896, pp. 9, 11, 16, 21.
[3] Iu. Martov, *Zapiski sotsial-demokrata*, pp. 263–5.

the future political party.[1] The group, which consisted of seventeen
full members and five candidate members, included besides Martov,
Lenin's future wife, N. K. Krupskaia.[2] Martov himself soon became
converted to Lenin's views. There was some justification for this
insistence on the need for secrecy, at the expense of democracy. The
conditions of police surveillance were (until 1902, at any rate) considerably stricter in Petersburg than in Vilna, and the attempt
to form a mass party was consequently fraught with greater risk
of the arrest and loss of leaders. The joint political activity of
Lenin and Martov did not last long. They played an energetic part
in the great wave of strikes among the Petersburg textile and other
workers which began in December 1895, and were arrested together
with the other leaders of the Petersburg Union almost immediately.
They were to remain in prison and Siberian exile for over four
years.

There could have been no greater contrast, despite some outward
similarities, than that between these two men who were soon to become lifelong antagonists – Vladimir Il'ich Lenin (Ulianov) and Iulii
Osipovich Martov (Tsederbaum). Both were of comfortable middle-
class origin, each had witnessed early in life the insecurity of his own
position within that class. Lenin's family ranked as nobility by reason
of his father's service to the state. But the grim experience of the
execution of his brother in 1887 for a terrorist act had been followed
by a certain social ostracism meted out to the family of a revolutionary. Martov, a Jew, had from his earliest years been made aware of the
precarious nature of the sufferance extended to Jews by a society upon
which the veneer of law still lay very thin. Each from an early age
became convinced that salvation lay in revolution alone. But where
Lenin could subordinate everything to this one end, Martov could
never emancipate himself from his innate moral canon. Lenin could
veer, prevaricate, intrigue and sow confusion, seeking support from
the devil himself if it offered, without for a moment imagining that his
conduct might in itself be considered of any importance when judged
in relation to the ultimate end. He always attributed the worst motives
to his opponents; and there is a ring of sincerity about the surprise
which he occasionally revealed that his own conduct should have given
rise to genuine dismay among his fellow social democrats. But where
Lenin was supple as an athlete, Martov was rigid and angular, a

[1] *ibidem*, p. 265; N. K. Krupskaia, *Soiuz bor'by za osvobozhdenie rabochego klassa*,
1920, p. 4, quoted by M. A. Moskalev, in *Voprosy istorii*, No. 8, 1956, p. 100.
[2] See the definitive study of this organization, Richard Pipes, *Social Democracy
and The St Petersburg Labor Movement, 1885–1897*, Harvard, 1963, p. 84.

prisoner of standards of behaviour and of principles which he never thought of compromising. Brilliant as a pamphleteer, he was little adapted to Lenin's world of politics. He could neither plot behind the scenes nor dissemble his emotions on the grand stage where the party battles were fought out. On the first occasion when the two men clashed, Lenin proved easily the more dominating figure. Lenin enjoyed the advantage of complete conviction that his policy was the only right one, and that he alone knew how to put it into effect. He judged his political colleagues by the criterion of their willingness to do what he wanted them to do. Martov suffered from some of the indecision which is born of intellectual integrity. Though morally repelled by many of Lenin's actions, he was not for that reason prepared to condemn all his political judgements. Where Lenin successfully fought to annihilate Martov and his followers, Martov clung to the belief that the more rational, more logical, more sensible course of unity among all factions in the party must in the end prevail. For a counter-attack aimed at Lenin's political annihilation, for which at times the means seemed within his grasp, he had neither the aptitude, nor the character, nor, be it said in fairness, the necessary lack of moral scruples. Perhaps the course of personal relations between the two men after their rupture in 1903 best illustrates the contrast between them. Lenin, having classified Martov as 'soft', did his best thereafter to destroy him politically. Yet to the end of his days he retained a sincere affection for his one-time ally. For Martov, after the shock of what he regarded as Lenin's unprincipled conduct, personal relations were irrevocably at an end. But he retained his determination to try again and again to rebuild the broken political union.[1]

By the time of his arrest Lenin was already the author of several pamphlets and essays which had attracted attention, but he had not yet developed any of the ideas which were later to make so distinctive a mark upon the nature of the party. He had absorbed both Marx, and Plekhanov's interpretation of Marx. But he had also studied with care the Jacobin traditions of the Russian movement – Tkachev's writings and the conspiratorial organization of *Narodnaia Volia* – and Chernyshevsky's Slav radicalism had made a deep impression upon him. Together with Plekhanov and the 'Legal Marxists' he had joined in the great battle against the populists, arguing that capitalist development in Russia was inevitable and that the proletariat must wage a political

[1] Martov has at last found a biographer worthy of him. See Israel Getzler, *Martov, A Political Biography of a Russian Social Democrat*, Melbourne, 1967.

struggle, culminating in revolution. Yet in one respect Lenin's views already differed from those of the Geneva theoreticians. Whereas both Aksel'rod and Plekhanov visualized the need for a joint struggle by the proletariat and the democratic *intelligentsia* (from whom the future liberal parties were expected to emerge), Lenin had already emphasized 'the inevitable and urgent need for a full and final break with the ideas of the democrats'.[1] When in the spring of 1895 Lenin had gone on a pious pilgrimage to the masters in exile, he had listened dutifully while Plekhanov lectured him on his uncompromising attitude to the liberals. The gentler Aksel'rod was enthralled by this serious and modest young man, and fascinated by contact, after many years of isolation, with a real revolutionary for whom Marxism seemed 'not an abstract doctrine, but a weapon for the revolutionary battle'. But he also in his turn argued the need for joint action with the liberals.[2]

With the leading intellectuals safely under lock and key, the more practical younger social democrats in Petersburg threw themselves with energy into the development of a mass movement. The success of the strikes in December 1895 and the readiness with which the workers could be roused to action on the basis of concrete and intelligible demands, seemed to be proof of the sound sense of the policy of 'agitation'. As the base of the party became broader, so the pressure among workers grew for a more representative democratic organization in place of the existing self-appointed secret committees. When in February 1897 Martov, Lenin and a few others, enjoying a few days of freedom between prison and exile to Siberia, paid a visit to their Union, they discovered to their horror that the new leaders were inclined to yield to these demands. Lenin argued in vain (with Martov's support) that concentration on whole-time revolutionary activity was the surest way to bring down the autocracy.[3]

The attempt to widen the base of the party met with some success in Petersburg. The Union, which had already been active during Lenin's and Martov's short-lived leadership in late 1895, became much more active in mid-1896 when some thirty-five thousand textile workers struck for the ten-hour working day, and kept up the strike for four weeks. Another strike followed in early 1897, and the eleven-and-a-half-hour day was finally enacted in June of that year. The

---

[1] In 1894. *Lenin*, volume I, p. 171.

[2] See Aksel'rod's reminiscences reprinted in extract in *Lenin*, volume I, pp. 488–91.

[3] Martov, *Zapiski*, pp. 316–17; for Lenin's version see *Lenin*, volume IV, p. 387; and for criticism of Lenin's version see 'Peterburzhets' (ps. for Takhtarev), *Ocherk Peterburgskago rabochago dvizheniia 90-kh godov*. Po lichnym vospominaniiam. London, 1902, pp. 68–71.

strike movement of the last five years of the decade, in which nearly a quarter of a million workers in all participated, gave its shape to the young movement. It was inevitable, in Russian conditions, that the emphasis should have at the outset been on strikes for concrete economic demands rather than on political demonstrations. Sharp political slogans, particularly if directed against the Emperor, still frightened and repelled the Russian worker. Even Lenin had recognized this: in the numerous leaflets which he wrote in 1895 and 1896 (some from prison) for the Petersburg strikers, political questions are touched on very cautiously.[1] In October 1897 there appeared the first issue of an illegal workers' paper, *Rabochaia Mysl'* (The Workers' Thought), with a circulation of 500, which a year later became the organ of the Petersburg Union.

It had been the contention of *On Agitation* that starting with the assertion of practical, economic demands the workers would inevitably come to realize the necessity for making political demands. The blindness of the autocracy did much to ensure that this prediction came true. By brutal repression of peaceful strikes and demonstrations it inflamed hatred of the whole political régime. By making concessions only when faced with organized force, it nurtured the hope that the fortress could one day be stormed. The progress from economic to political demands is well illustrated in the pages of *Rabochaia Mysl'*. The intellectuals who ran this paper regarded it as their duty faithfully to reflect the opinions of the workers for whom it was written, and not to attempt to mould their views. The paper was therefore little concerned with theory. Its aim was to promote solidarity and unity, to stimulate the creation of strike funds, and to organize strikes and demonstrations, in the belief that capitalism and the autocracy would prove powerless against a united and organized working class. Yet, by 1900 *Rabochaia Mysl'*, still faithfully reflecting its worker readers, concluded that economic aims were not enough. In November 1900 it demanded responsible parliamentary government in place of the autocracy. In April 1901 it wrote of the need for 'new tactics, new forms of struggle', and called for a transition from 'individual strikes and small-scale clashes with the police' to mass strikes and political demonstrations 'against the entire government system'. The main fight now must be for freedom of assembly, of person, of press, and for the right to strike. The rights of the workers, it now argued, can never be achieved until the existing government, the ally of the bosses, had been overthrown. It was, of course, what Plekhanov had been

---

[1] For the text of these leaflets see *Lenin*, volume I, pp. 447–58 and 482.

urging for twenty years. But those for whom *Rabochaia Mysl'* wrote were impatient of advice from the émigré intellectuals, and indeed intolerant of intellectuals generally. Their conversion to revolutionary action was therefore more likely to be enthusiastic when the need for it had been discovered by bitter experience.

These beginnings of a mass party were not confined to Petersburg, but extended to several industrial areas. In Odessa, for example, the transition from the 'circles' to 'agitation' was immediately successful in 1900 and a widespread organization came into existence.[1] In Moscow, in contrast, the movement had been a complete failure.[2] It is impossible to estimate to what extent a mass workers' movement could have developed had it been left to its own initiative and to the guidance of the leaders of the Petersburg Union who after 1895 tended less to lead and dominate the movement than to allow it to follow its own impetus. For this development was not to be. The action of the émigré leaders was to transform the nature of the incipient movement in a way which they themselves did not all foresee. Meanwhile, at the turn of the century, Plekhanov and his friends watched the trend of social democracy inside Russia with increasing apprehension, suspicion and dismay.

While a practical movement was thus forming in the heat of the daily battle against the state and the employers, the All-Russian Social Democratic Labour Party was founded. The initiative for a foundation congress came from several quarters – many organizations were later to contend for the honour of being the sole originator of the idea. Plekhanov and Aksel'rod had urged the need for an all-Russian party since 1885. Lenin in his early writings also urged the need for such a party, but achieved nothing concrete towards it before his arrest. The question was certainly widely discussed inside Russia from the beginning of the 90's, but the main impulse came from the *Bund* after it was founded in 1897, and simultaneously from the Kiev social democrats, who had already discussed the question with other organizations. A. Kremer, of the *Bund*, made contact with all these organizations and, with the technical assistance of the *Bund*, a small illegal congress met in Minsk on 1 March 1898 – the First Congress of the All-Russian Social Democratic Labour Party.[3] The Congress

---

[1] P. A. Garvi, *Vospominaniia sotsial-demokrata*, Stat'i o zhizni i deiatel'nosti P. A. Garvi. New York, 1946, pp. 23–5.

[2] *Rabochee Delo*, No. 8, November 1900, p. 12.

[3] See especially A. Kremer, 'Osnovanie Bunda' in *Proletarskaia revoliutsiia*, No. 11, 1922, pp. 50–6; B. Eidel'man, 'K istorii vozniknoveniia rossiiskoi sots.-dem. rabochei partii', *ibidem*, No. I, 1921, pp. 20–81. Dates of events in Russia are given

was far from representative. There were only nine delegates representing the *Bund*, a Kiev group which edited a small illegal paper *Rabochaia Gazeta*, and the Petersburg, Kiev, Moscow and Ekaterinoslav Unions for the Liberation of Labour. The Congress elected a Central Committee of three – A. Kremer, B. L. Eidel'man of Kiev and S. I. Radchenko, who had been a member of Lenin's group of seventeen in 1895. *Rabochaia Gazeta* was declared the party newspaper, and Lenin, still in exile, was designated as editor of a series of pamphlets. The Congress also appointed as its representative abroad Plekhanov's organization in Geneva. The party statute adopted by the Congress was broadly democratic. The *Bund's* autonomy in matters 'especially concerning the Jewish proletariat' was recognized. The Central Committee, though given the right of co-opting new members (an essential provision where the risk of arrest was always present), was made responsible to periodic congresses. An extraordinary congress could be demanded by two-thirds of the local committees. Local committees were only obliged to carry out the directions of the Central Committee in 'the form which they consider most suited to local conditions', and could refuse to carry out directions 'in exceptional circumstances'. The Congress also issued a manifesto, the preparation of which had been entrusted to Struve, then still a Marxist – a slight which Plekhanov was not likely to forget. The main theme of the manifesto was that in its fight for socialism 'the Russian proletariat needs political freedom as much as it needs fresh air in order to breathe'. But, since in Eastern Europe, in contrast to Western Europe, the bourgeoisie is weak and cowardly, the workers alone must undertake the task of liberation.[1] The idea of the proletariat, as the only 'liberator class', which had originally drawn Struve to Marxism, is here plainly apparent.

It is difficult to see that this First Congress exercised very much practical influence. Most of the delegates, including two of the three Central Committee members, were arrested soon after the Congress, and the illegal press of the designated party newspaper was seized. Some of the local organizations began calling themselves 'Committees' of the 'R.S.-D.R.P.' (the initials in Russian of the name of the party),

[1] The decisions of the Congress, the party statute and the manifesto are reprinted in *KPSS v rez.*, volume I, pp. 11–15.

throughout in the calendar in use in Russia until February 1918 when Russia changed to the current calendar. The date in the nineteenth century was twelve days behind the date in the rest of Europe, and thirteen days behind in the twentieth century. Where dates prior to February 1918 are given in the current calendar, the Russian equivalent will be shown in parenthesis.

and continued to increase in number undisturbed by the absence of any central organization. In spite of the provision for co-opting new members, the Central Committee failed to re-form. This was due much less to police repressions than to the conflicts among the ideological leaders which were already raging at the end of 1898. These were for some years thereafter to centre around two questions: organization; and the heresy to which the name 'economism' was attached in party polemics.

So far as organization was concerned, a conflict was, broadly, already discernible between the older party intellectuals, who had emerged in the first 'circles' of the 80's; and the newer social democratic leaders who had come to the fore in the strike movement of the 90's. The former were much concerned with the professional side of revolution – security, unity of action, efficiency of organization. The latter more intent on practical action such as strikes, were indifferent to doctrine and impatient of advice. There was much to be said on both sides: if the older generation sinned on the side of over-emphasis on discipline and over-indulgence in theory, the younger (or, at any rate, newer) men were apt to endanger the progress of the movement through lack of experience in underground methods. Intolerant of the orders issuing from the more strictly conspiratorial centres (such as the Petersburg and other Unions of Struggle for the Liberation of Labour), they wanted the centre of political activity to be located in the much more open local factory and district circles, and in the mutual aid organizations. Part of the handicap from which the worker leaders suffered was that, being forced to earn their livings for long hours daily, they could not devote a great deal of time to the needs of security – often with disastrous results to themselves. Besides, as the movement grew, the police increased their vigilance. Leaders were not too numerous, and it was plain that loss of too many of them might result in a spontaneous movement outgrowing the control of any organization. Thus it came about that 'discipline' and 'organization' became increasingly the battle cry of the more theoretically inclined intellectuals, and 'democracy' that of the workers, and of those intellectuals who regarded it as their duty to express the views of the workers.

'Economism' was the label which was attached in party polemics to over-concentration on immediate concrete needs to the neglect of the main task – the winning of political freedom by the overthrow of the autocracy. The doctrine of *On Agitation* and of *Rabochaia Mysl'* amounted perhaps to little more than the common-sense view that a backward proletariat must learn to walk before it could run. Before long this view was blown up by its opponents into an ideological heresy denying the need for any political struggle, or the need for 'hegemony'. The Russian workers' first steps on the road to revolution were branded as an illegitimate offspring of Bernstein's 'reformism', and as a renunciation of the class struggle.

The battle developed among the émigrés in Switzerland. The comparative harmony which had subsisted among Plekhanov and his companions during the long years of isolation was rudely shaken by the arrival of new theorists from Russia. Plekhanov and Aksel'rod had long formulated their doctrines on the burning problems of the development of Russian social democracy. They were convinced of the need for it to be led by the intellectuals abroad – Aksel'rod had stressed this point to Lenin in 1895 – and convinced that they alone could provide the right leadership. The new men, with their more recent contacts with the young movement inside Russia, were not always inclined to defer to the authority of the masters. They soon formed a majority in the émigré organization in Geneva, now called the Union of Russian Social Democrats Abroad. At its first congress, in November 1898, Plekhanov and his followers came into conflict with the new men. Plekhanov and Aksel'rod, besides their understandable anxiety over the lack of strict organization in the Russian party, were passionate defenders of the need for 'political' as against 'economic' struggle. This was, in their minds, not only dictated by Marxist orthodoxy, but also closely linked with their theory of 'hegemony' of the proletariat, since the workers could never take the lead over the liberal intellectuals unless they concerned themselves with the fight for civil and political freedom. It was a theoretician's point: to the more practical revolutionaries it seemed obvious that the borderline between 'economic' and 'political' demands was not easy to define, and that a workman who began by demanding shorter working hours would, in Russian conditions, very soon be shouting 'down with the government'. Which you started with, therefore, seemed to Plekhanov's opponents more a matter of tactics than of doctrine.

Already in 1898 Aksel'rod had criticized the 'predominating' idea among Russian social democrats that their activity should be 'narrowed down' to organization of the workers for struggle against their employers and active participation in strikes.[1] In the same year Lenin

[1] P. Aksel'rod, *K voprosu o sovremennykh zadachakh i taktike russkikh sotsialdemokratov*, Geneva, 1898, p. 23.

joined in the battle, and Aksel'rod wrote the preface to Lenin's pamphlet (*The Tasks of the Russian Social Democrats*), in which Lenin attacked the policy of the Petersburg Union. 'Let no one be so simple minded as to think', wrote Aksel'rod in his preface, that the author is concerned 'to summon the workers to the barricades or to incite them to form conspiracies'.[1] What Aksel'rod believed was that in Russian conditions it was essential for the intellectuals actively to speed up the process by which the workers acquired their social democratic consciousness. But even some who were not 'simple minded' found difficulty in understanding what was meant by 'political' as distinct from 'economic' action, if it did not mean a summons to devote more attention to immediate revolution at the barricades, and less, or none, to organizing strikes.

Plekhanov, after the first clash with his younger opponents, had refused to continue to sponsor the publications of the Union of Russian Social Democrats Abroad. As a result of this, a new journal, *Rabochee Delo* (The Workers' Task), came into existence in April 1899. Grouped around it were the men who were now dubbed the 'Economists'. They included V. P. Akimov (Makhnovets), B. Krichevskii and A. Martynov (Piker). Yet achievement of political freedom as the main aim of the proletariat was clearly in the forefront of *Rabochee Delo*'s programme. The repeated allegations of Lenin, Plekhanov and even Aksel'rod that *Rabochee Delo* was 'economist', in the sense that it denied the need to fight for political objectives, were untrue. In its first issue *Rabochee Delo* announced that its ultimate aim was political, the overthrow of the autocracy. But it argued that in Russian conditions economic struggle was the 'fundamental condition for the growth of a mass workers' movement' which inevitably, since it led to conflicts with the police, led on to political struggle. In the same issue a review of Lenin's *The Task of the Russian Social Democrats* stated its complete agreement with the author's view. Bernstein's iconoclastic pamphlet (*Die Voraussetzungen des Sozialismus*), which appeared early in 1899, was attacked in *Rabochee Delo*, and so was *Rabochaia Mysl'* for its failure to deal in its pages with anything but the minor daily economic problems of the workers. The most that could with justice be said of the *Rabochee Delo* group is that its followers did not attach the same degree of dogmatic primacy to political over economic aims in Russian conditions; and that they tended to the view that the most important thing was that the workers should learn the need for political aims from their own experience. On the other hand, the

[1] See *Lenin*, volume II, pp. 167–90, 603–5.

younger social democrats grouped around *Rabochee Delo* were certainly unwilling to accept without question the ideological leadership of Plekhanov and Aksel'rod, whom they regarded as out of touch with Russian realities. There were also indications that *Rabochee Delo* was aiming at making itself the organizational centre of the entire Russian movement.[1]

The first to attack *Rabochee Delo* was Aksel'rod, and he was followed by Plekhanov.[2] Plekhanov's pamphlet was rather more virulent in character than had hitherto been usual, and it aroused considerable indignation, particularly as Plekhanov made use of what purported to be private letters written to him. These conflicts led to a split in April 1900, when Plekhanov's group broke away from the Union of the Russian Social Democrats Abroad and, together with a few supporters, founded the 'Social Democrat' Revolutionary Group. The main aim of this new group was declared to be to fight 'economism'.

But while the label of 'economism' was largely an invention, so far as *Rabochee Delo* was concerned, by its rivals for ideological leadership there were some inclinations towards 'economism' as a doctrine among isolated intellectuals, as the result of the influence of Bernstein. Bernstein himself did a great service to Plekhanov and his companions when he stated in his famous pamphlet that 'the greater, if not the greatest number' of Russian social democrats were very close to him in their views.[3] The statement was untrue – as the subsequent development of Russian social democracy was to show. But Bernstein's views influenced one party document, the so-called *Credo*, which was in the course of polemics given an influence out of all proportion to its importance. The author of the document was E. D. Kuskova, who with S. N. Prokopovich had maintained in debates against Plekhanov in Geneva the views which the latter attributed to *Rabochee Delo*. Neither Kuskova nor Prokopovich was a member of the *Rabochee Delo* group. Indeed these two individualists, with their lively originality, never fitted into the frame of any of the factions of Russian social democracy. Kuskova subsequently returned to Russia, and at a private gathering set down her views on a sheet of paper, which someone, probably Struve, took away and which she never saw again. The

[1] See for example No. 7, August 1900, p. 17, which stresses the need for 'serious organizational unification of our local committees, and the creation of a central party organ'.

[2] *Vademecum dlia redaktsii rabochago dela.* Sbornik materialov izdannyi gruppoi 'Osvobozhdenie Truda'. S predisloviem G. Plekhanova. Geneva, 1900, where Aksel'rod's original 'open letter' of 1899 is reprinted.

[3] Ed. Bernstein, *Usloviia vozmozhnosti sotsializma i zadachi sotsial-demokratii.* Translated from the German, London, 1900, p. 212, note.

ironical title *Credo* was not added by Kuskova.[1] The views expressed in the document may be summarized as follows. Nowhere in Western Europe has the working class won political freedom by its own efforts. But, where political freedom has been achieved by the efforts of the bourgeoisie, the workers, following the line of least resistance, utilize the opportunities presented by civil and political freedom for the advancement of their own aims. Hence the emphasis laid by Marx on political struggle. But in Russia, where political freedom does not exist, the line of least resistance, and the aim which should be followed by the workers, is precisely economic struggle. The fight for political freedom should be left to the bourgeoisie, and the task of Marxist intellectuals is to support the liberals in their battle for freedom, and to assist the workers in their economic struggle. Implicit in the *Credo*, though not expressly stated in it, was the abandonment of revolution in favour of reform, as preached by Bernstein. The bourgeoisie by themselves were not likely to drive on to the entire overthrow of the old order if they could achieve their comparatively modest aims by a compromise. The workers, so long as their demands remained strictly of an economic nature, could likewise hope to satisfy them in time with the aid of nothing more violent than strikes and trade union action. There was thus no room in the doctrine of Kuskova for one-class proletarian rule envisaged by Marx as the ultimate historical aim.

It was Lenin who realized how to exploit the *Credo*. Lenin had been drawn in early into the battle against the 'economists' – he maintained from his Siberian exile a regular correspondence with A. N. Potresov, and it was from him that he learnt in June 1899 that the heresies, which had already been discernible in Petersburg in 1896, were now also infecting the intellectuals in emigration.[2] Earlier in the year he had communicated his apprehensions over the new trend to Martov (also in Siberia), who for a while treated them with scepticism.[3] About the same time Lenin received from his sister, who had in turn received it from Struve, the short manuscript document with the heading *Credo*. He immediately gathered his comrades in Siberia and produced a Protest Resolution of Seventeen Social Democrats, attacking the *Credo*.[4] The protest was, incidentally, immediately published

[1] These facts are reconstructed from Kuskova's own story in *Byloe*, No. 10, pp. 324–6, note; cf. *Lenin*, volume II, p. 637.
[2] See Potresov's account in *Sotsial-demokraticheskoe dvizhenie v Rossii*. Materialy pod redaktsiei A. N. Potresova i B. I. Nikolaevskogo. Predislovie P. Lepeshinskogo. Vol. I, Moscow-Leningrad, 1928, pp. 346–8. (Quoted hereafter as *Materialy*.)
[3] Martov, *Zapiski sotsial-demokrata* pp. 398–402.
[4] *Lenin*, volume II, pp. 477–86, where the *Credo* is reprinted in full.

in Nos. 4–5 of *Rabochee Delo*. An editorial comment sincerely welcomed the protest, but pointed out that the *Credo* was only the 'muddled thinking' of individuals. It was certainly true that its main influence lay in the polemical value which Lenin's skill extracted from this, the first, if not the only, documentary evidence of the very existence of 'economism' as a doctrine. Before long the attack on 'economism' was to become Lenin's main weapon in building up a new organization.

II   The Birth of Iskra and the Second Congress

Lenin's exile in Siberia came to an end at the beginning of 1900, and he left Russia in July. He spent 1900 mainly in discussing and planning a scheme which had been maturing in his mind for some time. This was to create a newspaper which would not only serve to safeguard the ideological purity of party doctrine from the contamination of 'economism', but which at the same time would form an organizational centre for unifying the underground committees inside Russia. This idea was first formulated by Lenin in an article written in 1899, which remained unpublished.[1] The scheme was discussed at length with Plekhanov, Aksel'rod and Vera Zasulich in Switzerland. (Lenin's somewhat surprising insistence on bringing Struve in as a collaborator on the projected newspaper all but led to a break with Plekhanov. Plekhanov was finally pacified by Vera Zasulich, but Lenin's support of Struve was short-lived: by early 1901 it was Lenin who no longer wished to have anything to do with Struve, and Plekhanov who now insisted that Struve should be allowed to contribute. The quarrel became academic when Struve was arrested in March 1901.) By the end of 1900 agreement had been reached on policy, and on the composition of the editorial board – Plekhanov, Aksel'rod, Vera Zasulich, Potresov, Martov and Lenin, with two votes for Plekhanov. The bulk of the money was found by Potresov, who stood very close to Lenin at this period, and by a rich patroness of Lenin and his group, A. M. Kalmykova.[2] The announcement of the forthcoming publication contained the ominous phrase: 'Before uniting, and for the purpose of uniting, we must first decisively and definitely mark ourselves off from those who are not with us.'[3] It was as an engine of battle that *Iskra* (The Spark) came into being in Leipzig on 24 (11) December 1900.

---

[1] *Lenin*, volume II, pp. 500–4.
[2] See *Materialy*, pp. 356–7; B. Nikolaevskii, *A. N. Potresov. Opyt literaturno-politicheskoi biografii* in *A. N. Potresov. Posmertnyi sbornik proizvedenii*. Paris, 1937, p. 39.
[3] *Lenin*, volume IV, pp. 39–40.

It was quite clear from the start who the enemy was. Attacks on *Rabochaia Mysl'* began with the first issue, and *Rabochee Delo* was also an immediate target. The members of *Rabochee Delo* did not conceal their hostility to the suggestion that *Iskra* should now become both the oracle of truth and a self-appointed organizational centre, arguing that a party newspaper should be under the control of the party, and should not attempt to dictate over it by decrees, or to impose its authority through a network of agents.[1] Moreover, *Rabochee Delo* was the official organ of the only official party body abroad – the League of Russian Social Democrats Abroad, formed in 1888, and incorporating the Group for the Liberation of Labour. Since *Rabochee Delo* was obviously going to prove 'insubordinate', the best course from Lenin's point of view was a surgical operation. This was performed on Lenin's insistence, and with some reluctance on the part of Plekhanov, Martov and others.[2] A small independent group, *Bor'ba*, headed by D. B. Riazanov (Gol'dendakh), had in June 1901 mediated with some success between the two factions, and a congress was arranged for October. When the congress met, Lenin read an indictment charging *Rabochee Delo* with lapses from grace since June as shown in its articles published in September (these were the articles criticizing the role of *Iskra*), and led the *Iskra* group out of the congress.[3] Shortly afterwards the split was given formal recognition when *Iskra* set up a new Emigré League of Russian Revolutionary Democracy. The *Rabochee Delo* group was anxious to avoid a split, but was not ready to be told by the *Iskra* group what to say and what not to say. (*Rabochee Delo* supporters were incidentally about twice as numerous as *Iskra* supporters in the emigration at the end of 1900.[4]) Since, however, Lenin had decided six months before October 1901 that a new organization was necessary,[5] the split was perhaps a foregone conclusion.

During the two years 1901 and 1902, Lenin developed his ideas on organization which within a short time were to lead to a much more

---

[1] See the articles by Krichevskii and Martynov in No. 10, September 1901.

[2] *Pis'ma P. B. Aksel'roda i Iu. O. Martova.* Edited by F. Dan, B. Nikolaevskii and (Mrs) L. Tsederbaum-Dan. Berlin, 1924, p. 53. (Cited as *Pis'ma* hereafter.)

[3] For the document see *KPSS v rez*, volume I, pp. 22–7, and for further information and documents see A. S. Martynov, *Dva S''ezda. III-i ocherednoi s''ezd soiuza i 'ob''edinitel'nyi s''ezd.* Geneva, 1901; *Proletarskaia revoliutsiia*, No. 5 (76), 1928, pp. 166–83.

[4] At the Paris Congress of the Socialist International the *Rabochee Delo* candidate, Krichevskii, received twice as many votes as Plekhanov in elections to the International Committee – *Rabochee Delo*, No. 8, p. 52.

[5] In a letter to Aksel'rod dated 25 April 1901 – *Lenin*, volume IV, p. 582; volume XXVIII, pp. 223–4.

important split in the party. In an article published in the fourth issue of *Iskra* he argued that the newspaper must become not only the ideological but also the organizational centre of the party, through its network of agents. Lenin, and after his departure from Russia more particularly Martov, had in the course of 1900 taken practical steps to set up such a network. About a dozen agents, paid by *Iskra*, were living underground in Russia during 1901, and their work was directed by Lenin and Martov, with Krupskaia acting as secretary.[1] The basic principles of Lenin's system were set out in his pamphlet *What is to be done?* published in March 1902. In this powerful essay Lenin argued the case for a centralized, disciplined party, which would lead the workers' movement, and not follow in its wake. As its vanguard he envisaged a network of professional revolutionaries, united in doctrine and in aim and devoting themselves full time to the task of revolution. This, argued Lenin, was necessary, because 'political class consciousness can only be brought to the worker *from the outside*, that is to say from outside the economic struggle, outside the sphere of relations between workers and employers'. The accusation made by the opponents of *Iskra* that *Iskra* did not attach sufficient importance to the 'spontaneous' nature of the development of the workers' movement was, according to Lenin, misconceived: workers have no social democratic consciousness. 'The history of all countries bears witness that the working class by virtue of its own powers alone is capable solely of developing a trade union consciousness, i.e. the conviction of the necessity of uniting in trade unions, of urging struggle against their employers, bringing pressure on the government to pass this or that law which is necessary for the workers, and so forth.' But the vanguard of professional revolutionaries should not confine its activities to the workers: it should work among all sections of the population. It would necessarily take a long time before the proletariat could become the overwhelming majority in Russia, as Marx had envisaged they must be before they could take power in the capitalist systems of Western Europe. But Lenin now offered a short cut: revolution would never be brought about by the 'homespun' members of social democratic circles trying hard to keep abreast of the spontaneous workers' movement, but rather, 'give us an organization of revolutionaries – and we will overturn the whole of Russia'. The arguments of those who stressed the need for 'democracy' in the party were dismissed: in conditions of underground secrecy such democracy was

---

[1] *Lenin*, volume IV, pp. 107–13; *Pis'ma*, pp. 46–7; G. Zinoviev, *Sochineniia*, Leningrad, 1924–6, volume XV, p. 18.

inconceivable. For the value of free discussion as a method of arriving at the best course of action Lenin had no use: the whole conception of 'freedom of criticism', he argued, was false. 'People who were really convinced of the fact that they had advanced knowledge,' he said of his critics in *Rabochee Delo*, 'would be demanding not freedom for the new views alongside of the old views, but the replacement of the latter by the former.'[1] This was to become Lenin's guiding principle thereafter.

It is evident now, in retrospect, that these doctrines had little in common with the views developed by Plekhanov and Aksel'rod. It is a matter of controversy how far they can be reconciled with the views of Marx and Engels. Marx certainly believed in a centralized and disciplined party. But he had visualized the workers' party taking power within conditions of political freedom already achieved by the bourgeoisie. Lenin's conceptions had perhaps moved nearer to the conspiratorial ideas of *Narodnaia Volia*, and away from Marx's conception of the historic mission of an entire class.[2] But little disagreement was apparent at the time between Lenin and his colleagues. Potresov welcomed *What is to be done?* with enthusiasm, and with only one reservation: that the author had overstated the case against 'spontaneity' (*stikhiinost'*). Plekhanov and Aksel'rod merely made minor suggestions in the draft, which Lenin adopted. In private, however, Potresov, Aksel'rod and Plekhanov all had some misgivings, and later Plekhanov admitted publicly that his 'white-washing' of Lenin had been a mistake which he now greatly regretted.[3]

There is no doubt that Lenin's energy, strength of will and obvious superiority as an organizer all combined to mesmerize his colleagues into agreement. There were other reasons too for this public acceptance of Lenin's views. In the first place, the *Iskra* group, starting as a minority among the émigré theorists, was determined to assert its ascendancy over the rivals who, for a short time, had swept the field. 'Party democracy', 'spontaneity', 'freedom of discussion' were all slogans much canvassed by *Rabochee Delo*. A vigorous statement of the case against them was too valuable a weapon to be blunted by dissensions. Secondly, the opening of the century witnessed a rise of industrial unrest inside Russia. The annual number of workers involved in strikes doubled at the lowest estimate between 1900 and 1903.

[1] *Lenin*, volume IV, pp. 361–508. Emphasis as in the original, and translation my own throughout this book, unless otherwise indicated.
[2] As far back as 1895 Lavrov had foretold this evolution in Lenin's thought – see his article 'O programmnykh voprosakh', reprinted in *Lenin*, volume II, pp. 605–9.
[3] *Lenin*, volume IV, pp. 589–90; *Keep*, p. 136.

Revolution was in the air, and the men of *Iskra* would have been less than human if they had not welcomed a doctrine which put revolution so very much in the forefront.

The wave of industrial disturbances was in part a repercussion of the general European economic crisis, and in part a reaction to the policy of the autocracy: alarmed by the signs that the 'economic' demands of strikers were becoming tinged with a 'political' colour, the autocracy intensified its repressions. This in turn only served to drive the workers further along the road to 'politics'. Mass student demonstrations took place, and in some instances the workers came out in support of the students. Students expelled from the universities swelled the ranks of the professional revolutionaries, whom *Iskra* was fast enrolling. The professional classes and some of the landowners, industrialists and merchants were also aroused. Out of their indignation several progressive middle-class parties were eventually to emerge in 1905. For the time being they gave financial support to the revolutionary parties. The social democrats long derived their main income from the donations and subscriptions of the wealthy. Peasant disturbances, always endemic in Russian society, also became especially serious during 1902.

Iskra gained strength from this rising tide of unrest. Its agents worked hard, and successfully, to win over the existing committees inside Russia. Usually this was achieved by splitting a committee into an *Iskra* and an opposing group. In due course, on the crest of the revolutionary upsurge, the non-*Iskra* group died a natural death, unable to compete either with the greater financial and organizational resources of *Iskra's* professionals, or with the greater emotional appeal of *Iskra's* message. By July 1902, *Iskra* committees had already been successfully formed by such methods in Petersburg and in Moscow, and by the spring of 1903 the overwhelming majority of committees had followed.

Significantly, it was the industrial centres, where the beginnings of a mass workers' movement were observable (such as Ivanovo-Voznesensk) which resisted longest.[1] In some instances, even when there was a strong resistance to leadership by the intellectuals, and a demand for party democracy, *Iskra* was able to win by the argument that a

---

[1] *Pis'ma* pp. 70–1; materials on the nature of the campaign to win over committees to *Iskra* will be found in Lenin's letters of the period, *Lenin*, volume XXVIII, pp. 47–288; and in *Leninskii sbornik,* volume VIII; see also VI. Akimov, *Materialy dlia kharakteristiki razvitiia Rossiiskoi sotsial-demokraticheskoi partii,* Geneva, 1905, pp. 68–70; and A. N., 'Cherez tysiachi prepiatstvii' in *Osvoboditel'noe dvizhenie,* No. 1, Petersburg, March 1906, pp. 49–62.

conspiratorial organization was in existing conditions essential for success.[1] *Iskra* was unable to extend its influence in any way over the *Bund*, which maintained an attitude of somewhat contemptuous superiority in the face of *Iskra's* attacks. Most of the illegal newspapers which had retained some independence of *Iskra* disappeared. *Rabochaia Mysl'* ceased publication in December 1902, *Rabochee Delo* in February 1902, but published three issues under another name thereafter.

But although *Iskra* won over the majority of the committees, the workers' movement remained largely unorganized and outside their control. The new committees, which destroyed and replaced the old, often put an end to the attempts which some of these earlier organizations had made to link up with the workers' movement. The intellectuals in the *Iskra* committees, for all their theories, could only follow, and not lead, this spontaneous activity. Under its own impulse and in reaction against the methods of the autocracy, the workers' movement was turning towards 'political' and away from 'economic' demands – in plain language, was becoming more revolutionary. Before long loss of contact of the 'professionals' with the workers became apparent. It was not unusual for the 'professionals' to call a strike or a demonstration, only to meet with no response at all, and conversely for large-scale strikes to break out unknown to the 'professionals'.

There were a few among the Emperor's ministers who were far-sighted enough to see that the policy of meeting unrest by repression alone (and occasional enforced legislative concessions) was leading to disaster. Prince Sviatopolk-Mirskii (then head of the gendarmerie) warned after the 1901 strikes that the problem could only be tackled by removing some of the workers' legitimate causes for complaint. In the following year Count Witte urged that strikes should be legalized in Russia in line with the legislation of all civilized countries.[2] But the only serious attempt to tackle the problem came from the police, in the somewhat bizarre form of 'police socialism', which is usually associated with the name of S. V. Zubatov, who became head of the Moscow security police (*okhrana*) in 1901. It was first put into practice in 1901 in Moscow and in the areas where the *Bund* was most influential. Later it was extended to Petersburg. The pattern followed was the same: the workers were encouraged to set up elected organs (subject to police approval), through which strictly economic griev-

---

[1] For example, in Odessa – see P. A. Garvi, *Vospominaniia sotsial-demokrata. Stat'i o zhizni i deiatel'nosti P. A. Garvi.* New York, 1946, pp. 106–12.

[2] See M. Balabanov, *Ocherk istorii revoliutsionnogo dvizheniia v Rossii,* Leningrad, 129, pp. 490–1.

ances could be ventilated. In spite of the growing suspicion and resentment which the autocracy displayed towards these efforts, the more enterprising, even enlightened, police officers organized strikes. The numerous organizations, which the police, of course, endeavoured to keep under their own control, were an instantaneous success from the workers' point of view, and gathered in a vast mass membership. Where the membership of the underground party organizations could sometimes be numbered only in tens, the police-sponsored organizations could reckon their membership in thousands. In part these official organizations took the place of the somewhat broader based organizations which *Iskra* had largely succeeded in destroying; in part they were an attractive alternative to illegal working-class associations which at best could only be maintained in existence at considerable risk. The worker participants in the police-sponsored organizations indignantly denied that they were in any sense police agents, and claimed that, on the contrary, it was they who were exploiting the police. There was some justification for this view. Pleve (the Minister of Interior), at any rate, shared it when in 1903, after the strike wave of that year, he summarily dismissed Zubatov. Nevertheless, the movement was subsequently organized in Petersburg – thus directly contributing to the revolutionary outbreak of January 1905 which was led by a police agent.[1]

The 'economists' later claimed that the way in which the 'Zubatov' movement got rapidly out of control was clear proof of the ease with which the workers in Russian conditions passed from 'economic' to 'political' demands. But while the strange 'Zubatov' movement was not so much a police trick as a genuine attempt by the more far-sighted police officers to force a little enlightenment on a bigoted autocracy, it is easy to see what valuable ammunition it provided for *Iskra* in its fight against 'economism'. *Iskra* could argue that for the workers to confine themselves to economic demands was to play into the hands of the police. Nor is it difficult to imagine the triumph of the editors of *Iskra* when a police document recommending Bernstein's pamphlet as permitted reading fell into their hands.

[1] There is a good account of the Zubatov movement (on which a great deal of archive material has been published) in Balabanov, *Ocherk*, chapter xvi. All the published material has now been collected and analysed in an M.Phil Dissertation in the University of London by Dimitry Pospielovsky, entitled: *The Legal Trade Union Movement in Russia: the Police Socialism 1898–1903* (1967). For Witte's arguments against it, as liable to get out of control, see *ibidem*, pp. 523–4. For the police-sponsored 'Independent Jewish Workers' Party', designed to steal the *Bund*'s thunder, see Buchbinder in *Krasnaia Letopis'*, Nos. 2–3 and 4, and M. Rafes, *Ocherki po istorii 'Bunda'*, Moscow, 1923, pp. 76–80.

In view of the insignificance of the First Congress of 1898, and with so much dissension inside the party, there was considerable pressure for the summoning of a Second Congress. The *Iskra* group were naturally anxious that the Congress should not be held until they could be sure of a majority upon it. They were unable to prevent the summoning of a Congress at Belostok in April (March) 1902. But the representation at this gathering was so drastically depleted by mass arrests on the eve of the opening session that the *Iskra* emissary, F. I. Dan, had no difficulty in persuading the anti-*Iskra* majority of those present that the 'Congress' should be declared no more than a 'Conference'. The Belostok Conference nevertheless set up an Organizing Committee of three to prepare for the Second Congress, but this Committee was put out of action by arrests. Later Lenin succeeded in organizing another conference, at Pskov in November 1902, consisting almost entirely of *Iskra* supporters. The Pskov Conference appointed a fresh Organizing Committee, on which Iskrites predominated, and it was this Committee which made all the preparations for the Second Congress to be held in the summer of 1903.[1]

In preparation for the Second Congress the editorial board of *Iskra* spent 1902 discussing the party programme. Since it was a private discussion (the documents relating to it were not published until after 1917) it offers a revealing glimpse of the real views of a group which always sought to present an appearance of solidarity. Personal frictions also complicated the ideological debates. Lenin had now established his position as leader, and was no longer inclined to defer to the authority of Plekhanov. Plekhanov did not take to criticism easily, and his ruffled feelings had to be repeatedly soothed by Vera Zasulich. The collaboration in the pages of *Iskra* of the young and brilliant Trotsky, whom Plekhanov detested, did not contribute to harmonious relations. In formulating the programme three factors had to be taken into account which had arisen since the revised draft programme of Plekhanov's first Group for the Liberation of Labour was published in 1887. First, the emergence of a real movement of the working class, and the experience gained during its first ten years. Secondly, the awakening of the liberals. By 1902 the *zemstva* constitutionalists and liberals from among the *intelligentsia* had agreed upon a programme. In July Struve began to publish their organ, *Osvobozhdenie* (Liberation) in Stuttgart, and the emergence of a

---

[1] For the two conferences see *KPSS v rez.*, volume I, pp. 28–35, and *Pis'ma*, p. 80.

liberal party or parties appeared imminent. Thirdly, an illegal Group of Socialist Revolutionaries had been formed in 1901 by the older *Zemlia i Volia* populists, in conjunction with younger men. Its programme of distribution of all the land to the peasants for their use was more attractive than the jejune promises of minor concessions to the peasants contained in the draft of the social democratic programme which Plekhanov had published in 1887. Two serious competitors had thus appeared on the horizon.

During the discussion on the party programme agreement was reached to omit a number of points from the 1887 draft. One was the acceptance in principle in the early draft of terrorist acts as a method of struggle against absolutism. This point, inserted by Plekhanov (for what he thought were tactical reasons, and against his better judgement), was recognized in all sections of the party as inconsistent with social democracy. Another was the somewhat Utopian demand for 'direct legislation by the people'. Both points had been criticized by Lenin in his own draft programme in 1899.[1]

Much of the dispute in 1902 turned on questions of form. Plekhanov's first draft was severely criticized by Lenin, supported by Martov, as 'more suitable for a textbook of economics' than a fighting programme. Plekhanov, deeply affronted, withdrew his draft, and when Lenin presented his own, wrote ominously of 'a new split' if it were adopted. Through the peacemaking efforts of Vera Zasulich, and with the support of Aksel'rod, Plekhanov's second draft was adopted as a basis for discussion against Lenin's opposition. With some addenda it became the draft put forward to the Congress. Shortly afterwards another dispute arose over an article by Lenin discussing the policy towards the peasants to be put forward at the Congress. Again it was Vera Zasulich who narrowly averted a break between Lenin and Plekhanov.[2] The drafts under discussion in 1902 fell into two parts: the 'minimum' part, which contained those demands of the party which related to the first, bourgeois phase of the revolution, and consisted of the basic civil and political freedoms, and social reforms; and the 'maximum' part, which set out the objectives of the social or proletarian revolution. There was no disagreement on the 'minimum'

---

[1] See *Lenin*, volume II, pp. 505–28; the 1887 draft is reprinted *ibidem*, pp. 617–20.
[2] The draft programme as agreed by the editors of *Iskra* is printed in *Iskra*, No. 21 of 1 June 1902; the programme as adopted (with minor alterations) at the Congress is in *KPSS v rez.*, volume I, pp. 37–43. There is a good account of the dispute in *Pis'ma*, pp. 58–60, and many of the letters there reprinted relate to it. The documents on the dispute are in *Leninskii Sbornik*, volume II, pp. 15–170, and volume III, pp. 323–440. The best discussion of the theoretical divergences between the editors is in *Keep*, pp. 140–50, to which I am much indebted.

part of the programme. Significantly, it was over the 'maximum' part that disputes arose.

But not all these disputes were due to clashes of temperament, and it is likely that the deeper sources of the impending split in Russian social democracy lay in the theoretical differences on the aims of the social revolution which now emerged in discussion. According to Plekhanov, 'in Russia capitalism is becoming more and more the dominant means of production'. Lenin insisted that 'capitalism already has become dominant'.[1] The point of substance behind this fine distinction was that if capitalism had not yet become dominant, then, by Marxist theory, joint action by the proletariat and bourgeoisie against absolutism was still possible and desirable. Conversely, under Lenin's formula (which was the one adopted in the final draft) the time for a two-front struggle against both capitalism and absolutism simultaneously had already arrived. Logically the effect of adopting this formulation was to abandon the bourgeois stage of the revolution, despite the fact that civil and political freedom did not yet exist in Russia – in other words, to jettison the 'bourgeois' stage during which the proletariat would exercise hegemony over the liberal parties, and to work immediately for the social revolution.

That this was already in Lenin's mind (even if the other editors did not yet realize it) becomes evident when other points in dispute are examined, and in particular the discussions connected with the 'dictatorship of the proletariat'. This phrase was originally inserted by Plekhanov in his first draft, in the 'maximum' part of the programme. No other existing social democratic programme contained this phrase, but it was quite consistent with Marxist orthodoxy, and its omission from the Gotha programme of the German party had been criticized by Marx. In Marx's conception this dictatorship would precede the final historic stage, by which time the proletariat would already have become the overwhelming majority. In a peasant country this was a very remote contingency, and Plekhanov accordingly visualized the ultimate 'dictatorship of the proletariat' as taking place with the support of and jointly with the peasant smallholders. Lenin would have none of this. He was ready, indeed anxious, to include in the 'minimum' programme demands which would appeal to the peasants. But for Lenin the peasant remained a reactionary element, opposed to

---

[1] The view that capitalism already existed in Russia was reached by Lenin as far back as 1893 – see three letters to M. M. Maslov, of 1893 and 1894, *Lenin* (5), volume 46, pp. 1–6.

socialism. There would be no need, he explained, to say anything about dictatorship of the proletariat if there were any prospect of the proletariat being supported by the 'petty bourgeois' peasants. As it was, he wrote, while every kindness should be shown to the peasants in the practical (or 'minimum') part of the programme, 'we should not yield an inch' when it comes to the theoretical (or 'maximum') part. If the peasants did not accept the proletarian point of view, then 'when the dictatorship comes, we shall say about you (the peasants): "it's no use wasting words when you have got to use force"'. Vera Zasulich added a comment in the margin: 'Upon millions of people! Just you try!'[1] Meanwhile, Lenin urged that 'it is essential *first* to mark ourselves off from everyone, to single out the proletariat *exclusively* and alone, and *then* announce that the proletariat will liberate everyone, calls everyone to its side, invites everyone'. The pattern of the future dictatorship of the communist party was already inherent in these words, including proletarian dictatorship over the peasantry. Whether they realized it or not, Plekhanov, Potresov, and Aksel'rod (the position of Martov was less clearly discernible) were still thinking of a revolution in two stages – the bourgeois and the socialist stages. Lenin was, though perhaps not consciously, already looking towards an immediate socialist revolution.

The draft of the Programme presented to the Congress, and adopted without amendments of substance, began with an analysis of the growing contradiction in bourgeois societies between exploiting capitalism and the exploited masses. This contradiction could only be resolved by a social revolution carried out by the proletariat, which would 'destroy the division of society into classes'. Dictatorship of the proletariat was a 'necessary condition' for this revolution, in order to crush the resistance of the exploiters. In Russia, where capitalism had already become 'the dominant method of production', the immediate aim of the party was overthrow of the autocracy and its replacement by a democratic republic. There followed a series of demands for reforms which the democratic republic should ensure: political and civil freedoms, universal education, self-determination for all nationalities, election of judges, separation of church and state, and a militia in place of a standing army. There were also extensive demands for the improvement of conditions of industrial work, and for certain

[1] *Leninskii Sbornik*, volume II, p. 83, note. Cf. Lenin's views on the dictatorship of the proletariat in *Lenin*, volume XII, pp. 183–9, in an article 'Marksizm i revizionizm' written in 1908, in which he argues that complete 'proletarianization' is unnecessary as a condition for the proletarian revolution, but that its absence will necessitate 'decisive blows against the enemy'.

concessions to be made to the peasants 'in the interests of the free development of class war in the villages'.[1]

When the Second Congress met in Brussels on 30 (17) July 1903 serious theoretical differences divided Lenin from his colleagues on *Iskra*. But Lenin always attached much more importance to the question of organization than to doctrine. And so far as organization was concerned there was certainly general unanimity that *Iskra* should dominate the party. As events were to show, where Lenin miscalculated was in assuming that there would be the same agreement on the necessity for Lenin to dominate *Iskra*. As he had already written in September 1902, it was essential that both the Central Committee and the editorial board of the Central Organ (*Iskra*) should, in the interests of unity, contain individuals 'who are in complete agreement'.[2] But the Central Organ would be in emigration, the Central Committee would be inside Russia. Which was to be the controlling body? There was never any doubt about this in Lenin's mind. The Congress provided him with an opportunity for putting his intentions into practice – at the cost of splitting the party.

The Congress delegates, though handpicked, nevertheless included a few who could not be relied on to support *Iskra* at every step. The basis of representation had been laid down by the Organizing Committee set up at Pskov in November. There were 57 delegates in all, but of these only 43 were voting delegates. Aksel'rod, Vera Zasulich and Potresov, as representatives of a newspaper and not of an organization, had no vote. Since eight of the 43 delegates had two votes each, the total number of votes was 51. Of this total, five votes went to the *Bund* – an inadequate number, out of all proportion to the size of the *Bund* in relation to the very small Russian party. The *Bund*'s relations with *Iskra* were far from cordial. It had no intention of accepting control by *Iskra* over its organization and its excommunication at the Congress was a virtual certainty,[3] since the 46 'Russian' votes would certainly oppose the *Bund*'s claim to retain the autonomy conceded to it by the First Congress.[4] So far as other questions were

---

[1] See *KPSS v rez.*, volume I, pp. 37–43; for the text of the draft submitted to the Congress see *Iskra*, No. 21, 1 June 1902. The only differences between the two are the addition to the programme as voted of the demand for elected judges; and a few modifications of detail in the demands relating to legislation for the improvement of working conditions.

[2] *Lenin*, volume V, p. 180.

[3] See for example Lenin's letter to one of the members of the Organization Commission, E. M. Aleksandrova, in May 1903, *Leninskii Sbornik*, volume VIII, pp. 355–6. Cf. *Protokoly II*, p. 48.

[4] 'Russian' in this context means regional – national identity, not ethnic composition.

concerned, two of the 46 votes represented the émigré *Rabochee Delo* group (the League of Russian Social Democrats Abroad, from which Lenin and his followers had split off in October 1901), and one the small surviving anti-*Iskra* organization in Petersburg. Two more votes represented a group known as *Iuzhnyi Rabochii*, which, though in general agreement with *Iskra*, had in the past shown a tendency towards an independent view in matters of organization. Nevertheless, there was in prospect an *Iskra* majority of at least 41 votes to 10 – provided the *Iskrites* all voted on the same side. Although there were rumours at the outset of disagreements on organization, the early stages of the Congress (the first three sessions were entirely devoted to trivial disputes on procedure) appeared to give no cause for alarm. The early debates on the programme showed no sign of disunity, and successive paragraphs went through with solid majorities. Martynov, one of the 'economist' *Rabochee Delo* delegates, delivered a devastating attack on Lenin's theory that, left to themselves without guidance from the intellectuals, workers can achieve nothing beyond trade unionism. He argued that this was contrary to Marx's and Engels's fundamental thesis that all class struggle is a political struggle. But he made no converts. The whole programme was in the end voted unanimously with one delegate (Akimov) abstaining.

Nevertheless, by the time of the sixteenth and seventeenth meetings it was becoming apparent that the *Iskra* majority was no longer solid. Several very close votes revealed that a number of Iskrites were voting with the *Bund*, the 'economists' and the *Iuzhnyi Rabochii* group against Lenin. Even allowing for some division on issues of principle, the main reason for the breach must probably be sought elsewhere. The most likely explanation is that Lenin in action had already succeeded in antagonizing all but his most steadfast supporters. Feverish activity had been going on behind the scenes in a series of private meetings convened by Lenin, rumours of which were no doubt buzzing among all the delegates. At these meetings Lenin had discussed with his immediate supporters the action to be taken against two delegates who had failed to show sufficient 'hardness' at the outset of the Congress. In defiance of Lenin, they had urged the admission to the Congress as a participant without vote of D. B. Riazanov (Gol'dendakh), who represented the small literary group, *Bor'ba*. *Bor'ba* had certainly not endeared itself to Lenin. It had attempted to mediate between the dissident groups of émigrés in 1901; and Riazanov had in a pamphlet sternly criticized the draft party programme – incidentally blaming Lenin for the defects which he saw in it. But

Riazanov was an educated Marxist scholar, and had been elected as a delegate by the Odessa Committee, until *Iskra's* agents had succeeded in getting the election set aside. The proposal to admit him, supported by the Organizing Committee, was a reasonable one. Lenin now discovered, to his consternation, a clear division into 'hard' and 'soft' *Iskrites* on this issue ('hard' and 'soft' were to become the main criteria thereafter in Lenin's characterization of party members). Among the 'hards' at these private discussions were now ranged Lenin, his brother, his wife, Plekhanov and stalwart underground agents like Zemliachka, N. E. Bauman, P. A. Krasikov and two others; among the 'softs' were Martov, Deich, Trotsky, Aksel'rod, Zasulich, Krokhmal', and Potresov.[1]

The full effect of this division among the *Iskrites* only became apparent at the twenty-second session when the draft of the party Rules (including the machinery for party control) came up for discussion. Martov had hitherto voted with Lenin at all the divisions which had taken place on the programme: he now changed sides. The occasion was the discussion of the first paragraph of the draft statute, which defined membership. Lenin's draft proposed to define a party member as one 'who accepts the programme, and supports the party both materially and by personal participation in one of the party organizations'. Martov's draft also required acceptance of the programme and material support as a condition of membership, but extended membership to anyone 'who gives the party his regular personal co-operation, under the direction of one of the party organizations'. There had hitherto been no discussion of the draft Rules among the party leaders. A month or two before the Congress Martov had sent his draft of the Rules to Lenin for comment, and Lenin had expressed no substantial disagreement with it.[2] The difference between the two wordings was in Russian conditions at most of academic importance. It would be many years before the party could boast of a regular party membership in the ordinary sense of the term,

---

[1] For these private meetings of the *Iskra* group, of which there were four, see *Protokoly II*, p. 532, a note by the Marx-Engels-Lenin Institute editors of the verbatim report of the Congress. See also Lenin's account of the Congress written shortly after it in *Leninskii Sbornik*, volume VI, pp. 220–49. Both Lenin and the editors, whose account is much more detailed, but who do not disclose the source of their information, stress that the split over Paragraph One of the party Rules was directly connected with the dissensions over Riazanov. For Riazanov's criticism of the programme see *Materialy dlia vyrabotki partiinoi programmy* (vypusk II i III), Geneva, 1903.

[2] *Protokoly 2-go ocherednogo s"ezda Zagranichnoi Ligi russkoi revoliutsionnoi sotsial-demokratii.* Edited by I. Lesenko and F. Dan. Geneva, 1904, pp. 58–9; *Lenin*, volume VI, pp. 190–1.

as distinct from a network of underground agents. It was, of course, the case, and this was argued at very great length, that Lenin's formula envisaged much stricter discipline over members and consequent repression of individual opinions. But the real importance of the dispute over a difference in the wording lay in the division which it caused. Lenin's version was outvoted by 28 votes to 23. Plekhanov supported Lenin; Martov's majority included the *Bund* delegates and the two 'economists'. These seven votes would have given Martov and his supporters a majority against Lenin sufficient to dominate the Congress thereafter, had he had the intention to do so. A number of contests now followed over various relatively unimportant clauses of the draft Rules in each of which Martov – now always ranged against Lenin – successfully carried the day by a narrow majority.

The situation changed at the twenty-seventh session, when the report of a commission appointed by the Congress on the status of the *Bund* came up for debate. It was the old issue: the *Bund* wished to preserve its autonomy in all matters concerning the Jewish proletariat, the commission reflected the unanimous view of all the Russian members (among whom there were many Jews) that the *Bund* should be brought under central, in other words, *Iskra's* control. By 41 votes to 5 (with 5 abstentions) the Congress rejected the *Bund's* claim to autonomy and soon afterwards the five *Bund* delegates walked out of the Congress. In the course of the debate on the *Bund* there were two further departures. The 'economist' delegates argued that because the Congress had voted that the *Iskrite* Emigré League of Russian Revolutionary Social Democracy was to be the sole representative abroad of the party, their presence was no longer justified, since the organization which they represented no longer existed. Thus Martov lost seven votes at a blow. He had voted against both the *Bund* and the 'economists' – eloquent proof of the fact that no conspiracy of any kind had existed between him and these dissident delegates. The departure of the seven delegates left a total of 44 votes. Of these Lenin now controlled a majority, 24.

Lenin was quick to exploit this advantage. His aim was to secure effective control over the party organs, and hence over the party. The Congress had already agreed on the machinery of party control. The party Rules had designated a Central Committee of three to operate inside Russia and had appointed *Iskra* as Central Organ of the party for ideological leadership. Supreme over both of these there was to be a Party Council, consisting of five members – two appointed by the

Central Committee, two by the Central Organ and the fifth elected by the Congress. It was quite certain that the Congress would elect Plekhanov to the Party Council, and he still supported Lenin. But unless Lenin could ensure his own majority both on the Central Committee and on the editorial board of the Party Central Organ, *Iskra,* he could not be sure of the appointment of his own nominees to the Party Council. A series of private discussions by Lenin's 'bloc' of twenty-four now took place, from which Martov's group were excluded. In an endeavour to heal the breach, Martov put forward a compromise list of candidates for the Central Committee. One of Lenin's supporters, S. I. Gusev, apparently used this opportunity to circulate a false list, allegedly emanating from Martov's group, and containing names of notoriously weak and vacillating candidates, with the aim of discrediting Martov.[1]

With his firm majority of twenty-four votes against twenty Lenin could be sure of putting through his own list of candidates to the Central Committee of three. The editorial board presented more difficulty, since it was generally assumed that the original six (who formed the intellectual aristocracy of the party) would be re-elected. Four of these, Martov, Potresov, Aksel'rod and Zasulich, were now unlikely to support Lenin. By eliminating three of the hostile members – Potresov, Aksel'rod and Zasulich – Lenin could ensure that the two representatives of *Iskra* on the Party Council would necessarily be himself and Martov. Of the five members of the Party Council he could be sure of the support of Plekhanov, and of the two members appointed from the Central Committee. Martov would thus find himself outvoted by the four remaining members of the Council.

Lenin's proposal that the editorial board of *Iskra* should be limited to Plekhanov, Martov, and himself was not in itself unreasonable, since these three had in the past been the most active editors. But Lenin's tactics with regard to the elections to party organs were now clear to everyone, and they aroused angry hostility. In order to strengthen his argument that the editorial board of *Iskra* would work more smoothly if it were composed of Plekhanov, Martov, and himself, Lenin alleged that Martov had in private already agreed to this proposal. This suggestion, which implicated Martov in Lenin's intrigue against Aksel'rod, Zasulich and Potresov, incensed Martov,

---

[1] For the evidence on this see L. (Iu.) Martov, *Ob odnom nedostoinom postupke* (Otvet Leninu, Liadovu i Ko), Geneva, 1904, where the decision of the arbitrators appointed to investigate the incident will be found; and *Lenin,* volume VI, p. 56, and pp. 223-4.

who denied it with almost hysterical vehemence.[1] The incident subsequently almost led to an open break between Lenin and Martov,
which was patched up by an exchange of letters in which each admitted that he had 'misunderstood' the other. But Martov never forgave
what he regarded as a breach of faith. When eventually Plekhanov,
Lenin and Martov were elected to the editorial board, it was a foregone conclusion that Martov would refuse to serve upon it. In this
election, as in the elections to the Central Committee, Martov and his
supporters (who disposed of twenty votes) abstained. The elections
were carried through by Lenin's bloc of twenty-four votes against the
abstention of the remainder. Eight of the fourteen non-voting delegates expressed their solidarity with Martov's group.[2] G. M. Krzhizhanovskii, F. V. Lengnik and V. A. Noskov (Glebov) were elected to
the Central Committee – all were close supporters of Lenin and had
played an active part in the preparation of the Second Congress. After
these stirring events the Congress ended in a calmer atmosphere.
Martov announced that in spite of what had taken place 'the decisions
of the Congress are lawful',[3] and a number of policy resolutions were
voted in quieter mood.

Such then was the majority upon the strength of which Lenin and
his followers would henceforth call themselves the 'bolsheviks' (or
majoritarians) and dub their opponents the 'mensheviks' (or minori-
tarians). Used at first in inverted commas, the terms passed into
current use in the party, at any rate within a year. It was a measure of
the tactical ineptitude of Martov and his followers that they accepted
this damaging nickname, even at times when their supporters were in
the majority on the party committees.

Lenin, who devoted considerable polemical energy to analysis of the
Second Congress, subsequently gave a variety of explanations for the
split: it had all been due to an intrigue by the 'opportunists', headed
by Martov, to gain a majority with the support of the *Bund* and the
'economists'; it had been merely a vulgar struggle by Martov and his

[1] In order to bolster his argument, Lenin flourished a piece of paper which
allegedly contained the agreement with Martov – but when years later this paper
was printed, it suggested that what Martov had agreed to was only a method of
election, but leaving the possibility open that the editorial board of *Iskra* would
be reduced to three: three members, unnamed, to be elected by the Congress to the
Central Committee, and to the editorial board, and these six to co-opt the remaining
members 'if required'; *Leninskii Sbornik*, volume VI, pp. 60, 65. But though the
paper did not contain what Lenin alleged at the time, it is possible that Lenin
believed that he had secured Martov's agreement verbally – see *Lenin*, volume VI,
p. 42.
[2] *Protokoly II*, pp. 359–84. The names of the Central Committee members were
not published in the stenogram for security reasons.
[3] *ibidem*, p. 386.

supporters for seats on the party organs; it had been a profound disagreement on principle, going to the very roots of party philosophy, as evidenced by the difference of views over paragraph one of the party statute. Martov attributed the split to Lenin's insatiable lust for personal power. It was true that important theoretical differences already existed between Lenin and his fellow editors on *Iskra*. The discussions in 1902 had revealed them. But very little question of principle is discernible in the incident which actually led to the split. All *Iskrites*, including the future mensheviks, were fully compromised by their endorsement of Lenin's dictatorial principles of party organization. At this date, at all events, Martov had no more than Lenin the remotest intention of allowing party organization to develop on democratic lines. In harrying the *Bund* and the other dissidents at the Congress, Martov and his followers had shown themselves as enthusiastic as Lenin. Moreover, once dictatorship from the top downwards was accepted as the principle of organization, it was logical enough that Lenin should be that dictator. Who else was it to be? Lenin asked one of his confidants a few months later: Plekhanov? – who for all his learning was incapable of organizing anything? Martov? – an excellent journalist, but an 'hysterical intellectual, who needs watching all the time'? Aksel'rod? Zasulich? Potresov? Dan? Trotsky? The very idea was enough 'to make a chicken laugh'.[1] The future of Russian social democracy was to show that Lenin's assessment of the practical talents of his colleagues was not very far off the mark.

[1] N. Valentinov, *Vstrechi s Leninym*, New York, 1953, pp. 167–8.

III Lenin against Iskra:
the 1905 Revolution

Efforts to break the deadlock between the party leaders on the composition of the editorial board of *Iskra* began immediately after the Congress. Lenin, Plekhanov and Noskov (the only member of the newly created Central Committee then outside Russia) offered to restore the original editorial board of six, provided Lenin were one of the two representatives of the editorial board on the Party Council of Five. This proposal, which would have given Lenin a majority of four to one on the Council with Plekhanov and the two Central Committee representatives, was declined. Further negotiations between the two factions early in October (the bolsheviks had now been joined by Lengnik from Russia) proved equally abortive: this time Lenin and Plekhanov refused to co-opt more than two of the old board.[1] In a letter to another Central Committee member, Krzhizhanovskii, Lenin had made preparations for war. The task, he wrote, was to keep the Martovites out of the local committees, and above all to find money, since Martov's opposition disposed over the party's two main sources of revenue.[2] Meanwhile, the oppositionists, at a meeting in Geneva, elaborated the lines of their future policy. They would work inside the local party organizations, in order to influence the centre through them; they would boycott the Central Organ, *Iskra*, until the old editorial board was restored; and, with, or if need be without, the permission of the Central Committee would continue activity as a literary group.[3]

The majority of the émigrés supported Martov. This became evident at the end of October 1903 when the *Iskrite* Emigré League of Russian Revolutionary Social Democracy met for its Second

---

[1] For these negotiations see *Pis'ma*, pp. 89–90; further materials on the negotiations are printed in *Leninskii Sbornik*, volumes VI and VII.

[2] See *Lenin*, volume XXVIII, p. 296, written in the second week of September 1903.

[3] Printed from the MS., partly in Martov's and partly in Trotsky's writing, in *Pis'ma*, pp. 94–6.

Congress. The Central Committee opened the attack by attempting to impose on the League new Rules designed to subject the League to its own orders. Emotional and acrimonious debate followed, which showed how deeply Lenin's tactics had wounded his former colleagues, and in particular Martov. When the meeting passed a vote of censure on Lenin and voted its own Rules, the Central Committee, in the person of Lengnik, declared the Congress illegal, and the bolsheviks stamped out in a body.[1]

This proved too much for Plekhanov. That same evening he announced to Lenin his intention of exercising his power of co-option in order to restore the old board of *Iskra*, threatening to resign if Lenin did not agree. Somewhat unwisely, perhaps, Lenin chose to resign himself – though there was truth in what Martov wrote later that Lenin's authority would have been irreparably damaged had he found himself in sole charge of *Iskra* without Plekhanov. Plekhanov now made an unsuccessful attempt to reach some agreement with the Central Committee (one member, at any rate, Krzhizhanovskii, was less intransigent than Lenin). A last-minute effort by the Central Committee to compromise, made on Lenin's initiative on 25 November 1903, was rejected by the opposition, who suspected that the offer was a trick. On 26 November Plekhanov co-opted the entire old board. Plekhanov's subsequent explanation for his change of front was that he acted in the interests of party peace. It is possible that personal considerations also played a part in his decision. Although he had staunchly supported Lenin in public, even at the Emigré League Congress in October, he had for some time past felt misgivings over Lenin's extreme views and tactics, and he may have feared the prospect of being left in isolated alliance with such a partner.

With all inhibitions now gone, the flood-gates of recrimination were opened, and Lenin's one-time allies now poured into print what hitherto they had suffered in silence. In a circular letter to the local committees the editors of *Iskra* explained their view of the split in the party. While both sides had agreed on the need 'to create a strong centralized party organization', Lenin had wanted to grant 'enormous powers' to certain persons in order to ensure the domination of certain 'hard' *Iskrites*. The majority of the board had opposed this, since it would have subjected the committees inside Russia to the émigrés, and would, by creating a system of orders from above and subordination from below, have prevented the emergence of real leaders in

---

[1] The proceedings of this Congress are reported in *Protokoly 2-go ocherednogo s"ezda Zagr.anichnoi Ligi russkoy revolutsionnoi sotsial-demokratii*. Geneva, 1904.

Russia.[1] Plekhanov wrote bitter articles on Lenin's 'Bonapartism', and on 'What is not to be done', Martov produced a pamphlet on the 'State of siege' in the party.[2] But recrimination was not enough. The entire board of *Iskra*, as its members now admitted, had compromised itself by accepting Lenin's line both in the campaign against the 'economists' and in the battle before the Second Congress for the capture of the local committees. The early beginnings of a mass party had been sacrificed to centralized control. If the *Iskra* group was now breaking with Lenin, it was also necessary for them to re-examine the whole question of the relations of the central party organization both to the local committees and to the mass workers' movement.

This task was attempted by Aksel'rod at the end of 1903 and the beginning of 1904. He argued that *Iskra* had been wrong in its worship of centralism, and, in attempting to combat the 'economists' demand for autonomy, had gone to the other extreme. The intellectual professionals, idealized by Lenin, were in reality nothing more than a radical bourgeoisie, like the Jacobins. There was no proletarian party in Russia, and the task of social democracy was now to create one. This however could not be achieved by the mechanical method of ousting intellectuals and replacing them by workers. The task before the social democrats was to encourage the worker members to develop to the full their independence and political consciousness, since, in the more broadly based party which would thus evolve, the need for leadership by the intellectuals would disappear.[3] *Iskra* was less successful with its concrete proposals for making the party more democratic. Aksel'rod admitted that centralized discipline was essential so long as the Russian autocracy remained unshaken. One writer argued that 'centralism' and 'democracy' were by no means irreconcilable, thus introducing into Russia a formula which in Lenin's hands would later become notorious. But he did not explain how these apparent incompatibles were to be harmonized.[4] In practice, it does not seem that there was much difference in the degree of democracy between a

[1] N. Shakhov, *Bor'ba za s"ezd* (Sobranie dokumentov), Geneva, 1904, pp. 14–19; *Leninskii Sbornik*, volume VII, pp. 257, 267.

[2] *Iskra*, No. 52, 20 (7) November 1905; No. 65, 14 (1) May 1904; L. Martov, *Bor'ba s 'osadnym polozheniem' v Rossiiskoi sotsial-demokraticheskoi rabochei partii* S prilozheniem pisem N. Lenina, G. Plekhanova i F. Dana. (Otvet na pis'mo Lenina), Geneva, 1904.

[3] 'Ob"edinenie rossiiskoi sotsial-demokratii i eia zadachi' – *Iskra*, No. 55, 28 (15) December 1903, and No. 57, 28 (15) January 1904. See also his preface to 'Rabochii', *Rabochie i intelligenty v nashikh organizatsiiakh*. S predisloviem P. Aksel'roda. Geneva, 1904.

[4] *Rabochie i intelligenty*, p. 6; Cherevanin (n.i.), *Organizatsionnyi vopros*, s predisloviem L. Martova, Geneva, 1904, pp. 28–9.

bolshevik and a menshevik controlled committee at this date, in spite of these opinions. But in line with the new, more liberal ideas of party discipline which *Iskra* now advocated, Plekhanov invited Martynov and others hitherto regarded as heretics to contribute to *Iskra*, and both Plekhanov and Martov repudiated some of their former attacks on *Rabochee Delo*.

Iskra did not however confine itself to soul-searching. War between Russia and Japan had broken out on 9 February (27 January) 1904. It was an unpopular war among all classes, and *Iskra* conducted a considerable propaganda campaign, printing and distributing many thousands of leaflets through the underground organizations inside Russia.[1] As Lenin had feared, his opponents remained in the stronger financial position, and held the whip hand over the bolshevik-dominated Central Committee because they could (and did) refuse to part with the party funds for the Central Committee's use.[2] Since Plekhanov together with Martov and Aksel'rod, who had been appointed to it as the representatives of *Iskra*, now commanded a majority on the highest party organ, the Council, *Iskra* was technically within its rights.

Plekhanov's action had thus undermined Lenin's position, and nullified his victory at the Second Party Congress. Lenin at once went over to the counter-attack. His immediate impulse was to seize the Central Organ and printing press 'by revolutionary means', but the Central Committee would not support him in his step.[3] He accordingly adopted more constitutional tactics. He had been co-opted to the Central Committee after his break with Plekhanov. His plan now was to win over a sufficient number of the local committees inside Russia to make possible the summoning of a new party Congress, which would give him control over all the organs of the party. This plan was seriously hampered by the reluctance of the Central Committee, in spite of its all-bolshevik composition, to support it. (The Central Committee's composition was at this date somewhat different from that at the end of 1903.[4]) The Committee members, appalled by the expense and difficulties involved in summoning another party

---

[1] *Sotsial-demokraticheskie listovki, 1894–1917 gg.* Bibliograficheskii ukazatel'. Tom I. Listovki tsentral'nykh uchrezhdenii i zagranichnykh organizatsii. Pod redaktsiei B. P. Birmana, G. I. Kramol'nikova i P. G. Sennikovskogo. Sostavleno bibliotekoi instituta Lenina, Leningrad, 1931, pp. 129–96.

[2] See *Leninskii Sbornik,* volume VIII, pp. 119, 124–6, 129; *Pis'ma,* pp. 101, 109–11.

[3] *Leninskii Sbornik,* volume VII, pp. 277–8.

[4] By the end of 1903 the Central Committee, in addition to Lenin and the original three, consisted of R. S. Zemliachka, L. B. Krasin, L. E. Gal'perin, M. Essen and G. Gusarov. But Krzhizhanovskii left the Central Committee in the spring of 1904, and Zemliachka and Gusarov in the summer.

Congress, preferred to seek a solution in some kind of accommodation with the mensheviks. During 1904 Lenin's relations with the Central Committee, after months of acrimonious correspondence, became increasingly strained, and by the summer, though still technically a member, Lenin had virtually been ousted from the Committee. By July 1904 the Central Committee made a move towards a compromise with *Iskra*: in an announcement, published in *Iskra*, it recognized the full authority and legality of the editorial board, deplored dissensions in the party, asserted its opposition to the calling of a Congress, condemned agitation to that end, and called on Lenin to return to the editorial board. A conference in Geneva, representing both factions in the party, welcomed this announcement by an overwhelming majority, in spite of a demonstrative protest and walk out by one of the bolsheviks present. The following month the Central Committee put precept into practice by co-opting three mensheviks.[1] By October 1904 a joint commission of *Iskra*, the Central Committee and the Emigré League had been created for all technical party activities, though the *Iskra* editors were still reluctant to part with control over the funds which remained in their possession.[2]

Lenin, however, had foreseen that the Central Committee would 'capitulate' and had not been idle while these developments were taking place. In the space of one year, 1904, with the aid of the indefatigable Krupskaia in Geneva, and of a group of new lieutenants operating inside Russia, he virtually rebuilt his disciplined network of followers which the split had impaired. The Central Committee, of which he still formally remained a member, could not be relied on to support him. The Rules of the party adopted at the Second Congress provided that the Party Council must summon a Congress if it were demanded by a number of local committees representing half the total possible votes at a Congress. Throughout the best part of 1904 Lenin's new agents worked feverishly to win over by fair means or foul the necessary majority. Before long Lenin's one-man party was issuing pamphlets, without the authority of the Central Committee. His right hand in this new publication venture, condemned by the Party Council on 1 September 1904, was V. Bonch-Bruevich – one of the few members of the new group of lieutenants who was to remain closely associated with Lenin thereafter. Lenin himself produced a pamphlet, *One Step Forward, Two Steps Backward*: Aksel'rod's apprehension of

[1] E. Aleksandrova, V. Krokhmal' and V. Rozanov.
[2] *Iskra*, No. 72, 25 (12) August 1904, p. 9; *Kratkii otchet o sobranii chlenov Rossiiskoi Sots.-dem, rabochei partii 2-go sentiabria 1904 goda: v Zheneve*. Geneva, 1904 p. 1; *Pis'ma*, pp. 109–11.

excessive domination by intellectuals was dismissed out of hand. To the charge that he was a Jacobin, Lenin retorted: 'A Jacobin who is indissolubly linked to the *organization* of a proletariat which has *realized* its class interest is precisely what a *revolutionary social democrat* is.' To be afraid of the dictatorship of the proletariat or of conspiratorial organization and to sigh for democratic liberties was opportunism.[1] By the end of 1904 Lenin was able to launch a rival newspaper, *Vperëd* (Forward).[2]

All this activity required money. The amount of money which Lenin could divert from those committees which supported him, out of the contributions which they were obliged to forward to the Central Committee, was at best infinitesimal, and private benefactors had to be found.[3] In August 1904 Lenin called a conference of his supporters and agents in Geneva, which in effect became a rival 'Central Committee' and issued a declaration demanding a Third Congress. It was largely a propaganda move, because as late as March 1905 Lenin in a private letter expressed doubt whether the statutory half of the committees had expressed themselves in favour of a Congress.[4] After November Lenin's rival 'Central Committee' called itself the 'Bureau of the Committees of the Party Majority'. But the Party Council still refused to call a Congress, on the grounds that the demand for it, alleged to exist by this Bureau, was artificial, and shortly afterwards expelled Lenin from the Central Committee. In February 1905 the Russian police played into Lenin's hands by a wholesale arrest of nine of the eleven members of the Central Committee. The two members who remained at liberty, L. B. Krasin and A. I. Liubimov, were now more inclined to support Lenin's plan to call a Congress, if only to re-create a representative party organ inside Russia. This now seemed particularly urgent as Russia was in the throes of revolution.[5] With these two Lenin now concluded an agreement to call a Congress, if

[1] *Lenin*, volume VI, p. 303.

[2] The first number appeared on 4 January 1905 (22 December 1904). The paper was edited by Lenin, A. A. Bogdanov, M. S. Ol'minskii, V. V. Vorovskii and A. V. Lunacharskii.

[3] There is no evidence where the funds came from.

[4] For the resolution see *KPSS v rez.*, volume I, pp. 60–6; the letter is in *Lenin*, volume XXVIII, pp. 463–4. Some of the agents who made the illegal journey from Russia to attend this conference should be noted, since they were to figure for some years to come as Lenin's close supporters: they included A. A. Bogdanov, A. V. Lunacharskii, M. Liadov, S. I. Gusev, P. A. Krasikov, V. A. Desnitskii (Stroev) and R. S. Zemliachka (she had by this date left the Central Committee, in protest against its conciliatory policy). Others, not present in Geneva, were M. M. Litvinov and E. D. Stasova. The latter's activities as secretary in the Petersburg Committee were of particular assistance to Lenin.

[5] *Leninskii Sbornik*, volume XVI, pp. 81, 90–3.

necessary against the decision of the Party Council. As a concession to the conscience of the rump of the Central Committee, Lenin's Bureau agreed that the presence of delegates from three-quarters of the committees should be necessary before the Congress could open. Ten days, an obviously inadequate period in underground conditions, were fixed for the completion of the elections.[1] An attempt to obtain the agreement of the Council, on the eve of the Congress, failed owing to the insistence of Martov and Plekhanov that sufficient time must be allowed for elections to take place if they were to be real, and not rigged elections.[2]

Thus, when the Congress known in bolshevik nomenclature as the Third (the mensheviks repudiated its legality) opened in London on 25 (12) April 1905 it lacked authority from the highest party instance, the Council. The bolsheviks argued that the Council had forfeited its rights by its refusal to recognize the demand from the local committees for a Congress. In view of the hurried elections and of the way in which Lenin's agents had been creating splinter committees for the purpose of passing resolutions in favour of a Congress, it is impossible to say to what extent the bolshevik claim that half of the local party committees supported the calling of the Congress was true. In one instance, at any rate, the 'committee' which the delegate claimed to represent appears to have been a 'committee' of one; while in other instances the bolshevik committee was rivalled by a parallel menshevik organization, which would claim to be the larger of the two. The votes of one delegation were doubled by a claim, clearly unfounded, that it represented four committees, when in fact at most it represented two. These and other irregularities were revealed either at the Congress or shortly afterwards. The support of three-quarters of the committees, required by the agreement with Krasin and Liubimov, was certainly not obtained (only twenty of the thirty-four committees entitled to send delegates were represented), and Lenin admitted that the Congress was formally illegal.[3] But the tide of revolution in Russia was rising fast, while these quarrels were going on, and the demand for a Congress to put an end to party disunity was genuine enough in many committees. It was a time when energetic action was bound to win support among many of the underground professionals who craved for action and knew little and cared less for the rights and wrongs as between Lenin and Martov. Lenin's forcible methods counted for

[1] *Tretii S"ezd RSDRP*. Sbornik dokumentov i materialov. Moscow, 1955, pp. 70–2. The agreement was published in *Iskra*, No. 95.
[2] *Protokoly III*, pp. 32–3.
[3] *Lenin*, volume VII, p. 251.

more with them than theoretical niceties. His success in calling this Congress emphasized the lines on which the Bolshevik party was developing – a disciplined order of professional committee men, grouped round a band of conspirators who were all linked by personal allegiance to their chieftain, Lenin, and ready to follow him in any adventure, so long as his leadership appeared sufficiently radical and extreme. The views of a group of committees from the Urals illustrated this new trend in the party: these committees wrote (in a letter to *Iskra*) of the need to combine 'the highest degree of (political) consciousness with absolute obedience' to an all powerful central organization – and dismissed the suggestion that the one might be excluded by the other.[1]

The Congress did not prove as well disciplined as Lenin had hoped, consisting as it did entirely of bolsheviks. The names of those who were for the next few years to form the core of bolshevik leadership figured prominently – Bogdanov, Kamenev, Rykov, and the two Central Committee members now siding with Lenin, Liubimov and Krasin. All the delegates were professional committee men, with the exception of three, who were pamphleteers. There was no disagreement on the need for energetic steps to forward an armed uprising. Nevertheless, some of the Congress delegates showed uneasiness over the irregular nature of the proceedings, and not all of them had yet learnt to be as disciplined as their comrades from the Urals. There was in fact a divergence between Lenin and many of the delegates on the purpose of the Congress. Lenin intended it to bring about the final break with those who had opposed him: the delegates, for the most part, looked to the Congress to reunite the party. A number of them pointed out that the émigré mensheviks (with whom Lenin was principally familiar) should not be confused with the mensheviks of the underground in Russia.[2] Lenin was therefore unable to put through either a harsh condemnation of Plekhanov, or a resolution requiring all mensheviks to submit to discipline on pain of exclusion. Certain resolutions adopted, which were not for publication, instructed a newly elected Central Committee to bring about reunification of the party, but stressed that the conditions for reunification must be approved at a further Congress. However, committees refusing to submit to the Congress were to be dissolved. A published resolution invited mensheviks to participate in organizations upon terms of

[1] *Tretii S"ezd*, p. 146.
[2] *Lenin*, volume XXVIII, p. 452 (Letter to S. I. Gusev, 29 January 1905: 'For God's sake . . . put through an unconditional split, a split, a split!'). Cf. volume VII. p. 58; pp. 100–1; and for Krasin's views at the Congress see *Protokoly III*, p. 388.

submission to party discipline.[1] The remaining decisions of the Congress reaffirmed what were now becoming the main tenets of bolshevism. Lenin's formulation of the first paragraph of the party Rules on membership was adopted, and the Party Council was abolished. Otherwise the new Rules followed the pattern of strict centralization adopted at the Second Congress. The preparation and organization of an armed uprising was declared to be one of the main tasks of the party. All revolutionary activity by the peasants was to be supported, including confiscation of the landlords' land and of state domains; the counter-revolutionary nature of all shades of liberals, including the most radical, must be explained to the workers: this was in line with the activity of *Vperëd*, which since its inception had been devoting much space to attacking the liberals. Finally, a resolution was passed which ran counter to orthodox principles of social democracy – that participation of members of the party in a provisional revolutionary government might in certain circumstances be desirable.

The mensheviks, outmanoeuvred by Lenin, improvised a simultaneous meeting in Geneva. It was attended by the delegates of fourteen committees who on arrival at the bolshevik Congress had immediately walked out on the grounds that it was neither legally convened nor representative. These delegates were joined by a number of menshevik émigrés. The resolutions adopted by this conference showed signs of the deep division which was beginning to form in the menshevik ranks. On the one hand were those who, following Aksel'rod, pinned their faith on a mass workers' party into which the underground organizations with all their regrettable conspiratorial features would eventually be absorbed. On the other there were those who clung to the underground party and to the disciplined organization created by *Iskra*, while deploring the shape which it was taking under Lenin's impact. At the time of the conference, when a revolution was sweeping over Russia, with complete disregard for the social democratic committees, it was natural enough that the latter view should have predominated. Hence, in spite of very sharp and detailed criticism of the irregularities of the bolshevik Congress and of the methods used by Lenin's agents in preparing it, the main stress of the menshevik conference was on reunification. In an effort to bring about reconciliation, the assembled mensheviks disclaimed any pretension to represent the whole party, and declared their meeting a party conference and not a Congress. In place of a Central Committee they

[1] *Lenin*, volume VII, pp. 130–2, 454; *KPSS v rez.*, volume I, pp. 81, 90.

elected an 'Organization Committee' – thus leaving Lenin and the all-bolshevik Central Committee as elected at the Third Congress in possession of the 'firm name'. They also urged the immediate reunification of the disrupted local organizations as a first step towards ultimate party unity at the centre. The 'mass party' view found some expression in resolutions calling for a struggle for the eight-hour day and for freedom to strike and to form trade unions, and for encouragement to the workers' efforts to start forming trade unions and other clubs and associations. Its influence was perhaps also to be seen in a further resolution on organization, which proposed a greater degree of democracy in the local committees, but left untouched the powers of the centre. But in the main, revolutionary resolutions predominated. The masses must be prepared for the 'inevitable' armed uprising, and social democrats must be ready to take control of the spontaneous movement; class warfare among the peasants must be exacerbated; and liberals must only be supported if they in turn are truly on the side of revolution. While rejecting participation in any provisional government, the mensheviks nevertheless envisaged the possibility of immediate seizure of power by the proletariat if the revolution in Russia should spread to other countries.[1]

Thus, there was much truth in the view held by many mensheviks that nothing divided the two factions except Lenin's intransigence and determination to create a party subordinate to his own commands. But Plekhanov blamed both factions for the split and broke with the mensheviks.[2] For some time he remained in an ivory tower, criticizing both factions in the pages of a small periodical, *The Diary of a Social Democrat*.

Meanwhile, in Russia, the revolution movement had started which was to culminate in the first major defeat of the autocracy. On 28 (15) July 1904 discontent exacerbated by the war with Japan found expression in the assassination of Pleve, the Minister of the Interior, by a young socialist revolutionary. The autocracy, with little prospect of support in any section of society, hesitated between repression and concession, and choose concession. Under the comparatively mild ministry of Prince Sviatopolk-Mirskii a short period of 'confidence' was inaugurated. Events soon proved how dangerous a situation can arise when an unpopular and repressive government is forced to adopt

---

[1] *Pervaia obshcherusskaia konferentsiia partiinykh rabotnikov.* Otdel'noe prilozhenie k. No. 100 'Iskry', Geneva, 1905, *passim*.
[2] Plekhanov, *Sochineniia*, volume XIII, p. 286; *Perepiska G. V. Plekhanova i P. B. Aksel'roda*, redaktsiia i primechaniia P. A. Berlina, V. S. Voitinskogo i B. I. Nikolaevskogo, volume II, Moscow, 1925, p. 234. (Hereinafter cited as *Perepiska*.)

a policy of even slight relaxation. One result was the new impetus which was given to the political aspirations of the progressive middle class. Another was the development of the so-called Petersburg Society of Russian Factory and Workshop Workers. This legally tolerated organization had existed since 1903, and was encouraged by the police in Petersburg even after the original efforts in the direction of police socialism associated with Zubatov had been suppressed. Now, under the leadership of its president, the priest George Gapon, it grew with great rapidity. By the end of 1904 its branches covered the city, and its membership rose to 8,000. Outwardly harmless enough in its mainly social and educational and quite unpolitical activities, it responded to a need of the workers for a mass organization which the social democratic underground could not satisfy. Gapon himself, although in touch with the police, played a double role, and maintained within the approved non-political organization something like a secret revolutionary committee. At the beginning of January 1905, the dismissal of four men by one of the large Petersburg factories led to a strike which became general within a few days, with Gapon as its accepted leader. The workers' demands were at first limited to immediate economic needs, and they were not at the outset prepared to accept the revolutionary slogans of the social democrats, and socialist revolutionaries, who were active in the mass meetings. But before many days the crowds became more revolutionary, and Gapon, who was as much led by the mob as its leader, was forced to echo them. On 20 (7) January at a crowded and enthusiastic meeting Gapon proposed a dramatic plan: to march to the palace in a body and petition the Emperor. What Gapon proposed was something between the peaceful march which has subsequently become enshrined as a legend, and open revolution. We will say to the Emperor, he told the crowd, 'Your Majesty, we cannot go on like this, it is time to give the people their freedom.' If he agrees, he must swear an oath. If we are kept out, 'we shall force our way through'. If the troops fire on us, we will defend ourselves. 'Part of the troops will then come over to us – and we will then make a revolution, we will build barricades, sack the stores of arms and ammunition, storm the prison, capture the telephone and telegraph. . . . The socialist revolutionaries have promised us bombs . . . and we will win through.'[1] There were police agents present in the crowd. Gapon warned the Minister of the Interior of

[1] Reprinted, from an account of this meeting contributed to *Iskra*, No. 86, by a social democrat who was present at it, by Nevskii, in *Krasnaia Letopis'*, No. 1, pp. 36–8. (Nevskii was himself in Petersburg at the time.) Cf. Father George Gapon, *The Story of my Life*, London, 1905, p. 170.

the intended procession, and stressed that it would be peaceful, and that the Emperor had nothing to fear. Enclosed with the warning was a programme of demands for a Constituent Assembly and for full civil and political freedom for all.[1] On the following day, 22 (9) January, a vast crowd with Gapon in his priest's robes at its head converged on the palace. The government was prepared for a revolutionary storm, and, ill accustomed to demonstrations of this magnitude, lost its head. The crowd was in fact unarmed, and the socialist revolutionaries had failed to provide any bombs. But when the crowd surged towards the palace (the Emperor was out of town) the troops fired, and there were serious casualties. That some attempt was made to put Gapon's plan of two days before into action seems probable. For barricades went up, at least two stores of arms were in fact stormed, and an attempt was made to break open the town prison and to seize the telegraph office.[2] The truth seems to be that the demonstration only failed to develop into a revolution for lack of organization, and because the troops did not side with the crowd. But it was widely believed that the Emperor had fired on a peaceful unarmed crowd in cold blood, and the incident caused consternation and horror all over Russia, and outside. It is no exaggeration to say that from this day on, known thereafter as Bloody Sunday, faith in the Emperor's love and care for his people was shattered. The same night Gapon issued an open call to revolt which was answered throughout Russia.[3]

But 22 (9) January 1905, if the most dramatic moment of the year, was not the real beginning of the revolution. The impetus to this vast national protest against the autocratic régime had already been given by the middle classes. Beginning in the autumn of 1904, the two groups which were united under the aegis of the Union for Liberation, the *Zemstva* and the progressive members of the professional class, were organizing conferences, banquets, and unions which put forward constitutional demands. This movement, which continued throughout 1905, was now reinforced by industrial and peasant unrest. Following Bloody Sunday, industrial strikes and disturbances of all kinds continued for most of the year throughout the length and breadth of the country, in a mounting wave. In some instances the workers' demands were of an economic nature, in others revolution-

---

[1] *Revoliutsiia 1905–1907 gg. v Rossii.* Dokumenty i materialy. Nachalo pervoi russkoi revoliutsii. Ianvar'-mart 1905 goda, Moscow, 1955, pp. 28–31.
[2] Details in Nevskii, *loc. cit.*, pp. 14–72; *Revoliutsiia 1905–1907 gg., Nachalo*, pp. 31 ff.
[3] *Sviashchennika Georgiia Gapona* . . ., p. 15 (a pamphlet printed illegally at the time, and distributed in large quantities).

ary. The workers, though unwilling to accept the organizational leadership of the social democrats, who seemed to them remote and out of touch with their needs, nevertheless often accepted the revolutionary formulations which poured out in thousands of leaflets. In some cases the social democrats did lead the movement. The *Bund*, for example, within its area of activity, called an organized strike with concrete political demands. In the heart of Russia the railway workers formed their own strike organization and maintained a railway strike for over a month. But these were exceptional cases. For the most part the disorders were unorganized, and lacked leadership and definite aim. The peasant disturbances continued throughout the year and into 1906.

With the situation completely out of control, the government alternated between repressions and organized *pogroms* on the one hand, and panic concessions on the other. Courts-martial were set up, death sentences became usual, and troops were used without restraint both in the towns and in the villages. The repressions served to alienate the sympathy of even the most moderate sections of society, while the concessions helped to whet the appetite for more. On 19 (6) August, a fortnight before peace was concluded with Japan, an imperial rescript had promised that a State Duma with consultative powers would be convened. But by October the country was in the throes of a general strike. Now, in the midst of a complete stoppage of normal life, the Emperor was persuaded against his judgement to sign a manifesto on 30 (17) October. This promised full civil freedom – of person, of speech, of conscience, and of association; and a State Duma with full legislative powers, elected on a wide suffrage. It was a momentous promise because, if fulfilled, it would transform the autocracy into a constitutional monarchy. But in those excited and troubled days few believed that it would be fulfilled, or that freedom could be attained in Russia except by the methods of self-help. There was little welcome for the manifesto. Even the progressive members of the middle class for the most part rejected it out of hand, while the peasants were aroused by the news of it to fresh outbreaks of violence. A strange situation prevailed in Russia in 1905. A panic-stricken government was confronted by almost an entire nation, conscious of its power and yet unable to effect its aims – if indeed it was clearly conscious of them. But, in the midst of the chaos and the carnage, the masses of the Russian people gained their first experience of self-organization. Entire districts were at times under the control of self-appointed 'governments'. Trade unions were formed in open defiance of the legal ban on their existence. Armed bands were formed for defence, mainly against the anti-Jewish or other racial *pogroms* let loose with government connivance. The irony of the situation reached its height in Tiflis, where the local social democrats were for a time entrusted with arms by the local military commander, since they alone were capable of keeping order and preventing a massacre of the Armenian population.[1]

For the most part the social democratic committees could encourage, but could not lead or organize this movement. Both factions of the party noted with dismay the negligible influence which social democrats were exercising on the workers. But whereas Lenin's *Vperëd* drew the moral that what was needed was better organization, more fighting detachments, more discipline, more obedient conspiratorial committees, *Iskra* drew the conclusion that what was required was not a closed band of conspirators, but 'a wide organization based on the working masses, acting independently'. At their conference in 1905 the menshevik leaders had discussed the idea of setting up some form of workers' congress which would voice the interests of the whole working class. The idea came from Aksel'rod. He developed it at length later in the year, after the publication of the Emperor's first promise of an advisory Duma, in a series of letters and in a pamphlet. In his view this workers' congress should embrace the entire working class, independently of party allegiance. It would be able to speak in the name of all the workers, and would put forward the demand for the election of a People's Duma, as the first step towards the summoning of a Constituent Assembly.[2] It was under the influence of this view that the mensheviks tried to take an active part in and to encourage the trade unions and other forms of worker organizations which were springing up in 1905, without seeking to control them. The bolsheviks, in contrast, powerless to control these organizations, either stood aloof from them or actively opposed them. For Lenin, in particular, non-party mass organizations were anathema if they meant that the social democrats were to be lost in a 'neutral' mass which they could not control. The idea of a workers' congress was also opposed by the bolsheviks, who took the view that insurrection must precede the formation of such a congress, which could only be set up after the revolution had been successful.

---

[1] The weapons were issued on the word of I. Ramishvili, the (menshevik) social democrat leader, that they would be returned. Ramishvili kept his word – though he had some difficulty with his followers. (From the unpublished memoirs of P. A. Garvi, who was at that date in Tiflis.)

[2] See P. B. Aksel'rod, *Narodnaia duma i rabochii s''ezd*, Geneva, 1905.

Towards the end of the year the Petersburg Menshevik Group, which was five times the size of the bolshevik Committee, took the initiative in organizing the Petersburg Soviet of Workers' Deputies. The Petersburg Soviet was far from Aksel'rod's ideal. Half strike-committee, half an improvised organ of self-government, the Soviet, although formed in response to an appeal to the workers by the mensheviks, was non-party in composition though largely proletarian. But its organizers were mostly mensheviks. During the short period of its existence, from 26 (13) October until 16 (3) December, the Soviet led the strikes then in progress in the capital, but at the same time worked with success for such measures as the defiance of the censorship. Under its leadership, the printers were able to control publications, and a whole number of social democratic and other newspapers sprang up during these 'days of freedom', as the period later became known. But an attempt by the Soviet to introduce the eight-hour day failed and provoked the final reaction of the autocracy. Within the limits of its small budget (it was only 34,315 roubles, or less than £3,500 for the two months of its existence) the Soviet also endeavoured to provide the workers with subsistence when strikes were followed by lockouts.

Inspired by the revolution, the émigré leaders, with the exception of Aksel'rod and Plekhanov, returned to Petersburg in order to take a more active part. *Iskra* was on 13 November replaced by a paper published in Russia named *Nachalo* (The Beginning), on which Martov, Dan, Aksel'rod and Trotsky collaborated. Lenin's activity was mainly confined to the Petersburg Committee and to editing the bolshevik newspapers. For the Soviet he had little sympathy and a good deal of suspicion. The outstanding social democratic figure in the public eye during these days was undoubtedly L. D. Trotsky, then twenty-six years old. This young Jewish revolutionary, of arresting appearance, and endowed with pyrotechnical brilliance of speech and pen which few in the party could rival, had joined *Iskra* from the start. He had enjoyed Lenin's protection, but Plekhanov had been seized by instant dislike of the newcomer, and frequent friction on the editorial board caused by Trotsky's articles had had to be smoothed out, as usual, by Vera Zasulich. After 1903 Trotsky had broken with Lenin, and had been the author of some of the most biting (and prophetic) attacks on Lenin's ideas on organization. He had left the menshevik faction in October 1904. But his views on the perspective of the revolution, though quite unacceptable to the more orthodox like Plekhanov or Aksel'rod, enjoyed some support in the menshevik ranks. In the Petersburg Soviet Trotsky, a natural tribune of the people, and a mob orator of rare talent, found new outlets for his energies. Even his enemies were forced to concede his oratory, his courage and his striking defiance of the autocracy during the short life of the Soviet, and especially during the last days of its existence when Trotsky presided over it.

The end came so easily and rapidly that general decline of revolutionary fervour among the Petersburg proletariat must be regarded as one of the contributory causes. As menshevik writers were subsequently to point out, this demoralization was only to be expected where the proletariat was not only unarmed but isolated, without support from the garrison troops, and without the aid of a middle-class party sufficiently organized to be ready to take over the reins of government from the crumbling autocracy. On 16 (3) December the Soviet was surrounded by troops and all its members arrested. A few days later an appeal by the workers' and social democratic organizations to rise for 'the last and final battle' met with scarcely any response.

Soviets also sprang up during 1905 in many provincial cities. The usual pattern was the non-party assembly of workers, with the socialist parties losing their political identity in a coalition. In the Moscow Soviet, for example, coalition was the only possible pattern, since, if anything, socialist revolutionary influence predominated there, and bolshevik attempts to subordinate this Soviet to their own exclusive leadership proved unsuccessful. In contrast to Petersburg, Moscow was not heavily garrisoned. Moreover, there existed in Moscow a number of fighting detachments, organized mainly by the socialist revolutionaries, but also by the social democrats. Lenin, in particular, had repeatedly urged the need to form such detachments both as organs of attack and defence, and for subsidiary tasks such as hold-ups in order to raise funds for the rising, or for the killing of police spies. The Moscow Soviet grew out of the strike committee formed during October to direct the railway strike which was then in progress. It had a much larger proportion of intellectuals than the Petersburg Soviet, and was correspondingly more inclined to follow revolutionary slogans. A strike in December in Moscow led to the immediate intervention of troops, and there were casualties among the civilian population. On 20 (7) December the Moscow Soviet issued a call for a general strike, and urged that 'all efforts should be made to transform the strike into an armed uprising'. The initiative for the rising came from the bolsheviks, but the appeal was signed jointly by the Soviet, the Bolshevik Social Democratic Committee, the Menshevik Group and the Committee of the Socialist Revolutionary Party. Barricades were put up in the streets by the fighting detachments, with the assistance of the crowds which were enraged by the action of the troops. For about a week sporadic guerrilla fighting was kept up by these detachments in Moscow, and for a little longer in one of Moscow's suburbs. It was a hopeless fight from the start. The detachments were heavily outnumbered by the troops, who were rapidly reinforced, and received little if any support from the population once fighting had actually started. By the beginning of 1906 all attempts at armed rising all over Russia had been put down, and military reprisals by the armed forces and by field courts-martial began.[1]

This marked the end of the revolution of 1905. Sporadic violence and strikes would continue for some years, indeed were never wholly absent from the Russian scene, but the back of the movement had been broken. It failed for two reasons. First, because in the last resort the troops proved loyal to the autocracy. There had, it is true, been mutinies in the Black Sea fleet in Odessa and in the naval base at Kronstadt, and unrest in certain units, but the bulk of the troops obeyed their orders and did not come out in sympathy with the strikers. The second reason was that the middle-class parties which had only been founded in October, were neither sufficiently prepared nor united to take over power. However, the Duma, in accordance with the Emperor's promise, was to meet in the spring of 1906. The electoral law of 24 (11) December 1905 provided for a franchise which on paper was a good deal wider than that to be found at the same period in many countries of Western Europe. The disenfranchised were workers in factories which employed less than fifty persons, small craftsmen, casual labourers, and peasants without property. In March 1906 the Fundamental Laws (promulgated by decree, before the Duma had assembled) guaranteed civil freedoms and legalized the trade unions. There were, however, certain reservations, of which the overriding one was the degree of discretionary power left in the hands of the executive. An entirely new situation, therefore, faced the social democratic party in 1906.

[1] The 1905 revolution has been treated in English in two monographs, Sidney Harcave, *First Blood: The Russian Revolution of 1905*, London, 1964; and Solomon M. Schwarz, *The Russian Revolution of 1905, The Workers' Movement and the Formation of Bolshevism and Menshevism*, Chicago, 1967. See also Alexander Fischer, *Russiche Sozialdemokratie und Bewaffneter Ausstand im Jahr 1905*, Wiesbaden, 1967. A vast literature exists in Russian consisting of documents and memoirs, much of it published in the half-century year 1955. In general, the later publications are a good deal less reliable in quality than the earlier.

IV   Attempts at Reunion

Under the impact of the revolution a largely spontaneous movement for reunification developed among the sundered bolshevik and menshevik party organizations. During 1905 these small committees were beginning to extend their influence more widely and to attract more followers. By mid-1905 the number of enrolled members of the organizations of both factions could be reckoned in thousands, if not tens of thousands, and some organizations were several hundred strong.[1] With this extension of their activity grew distaste for interfactional struggles. Both factions fully supported every form of revolutionary action, both were actively trying to fan revolt throughout the country, and to urge the striking workers to overthrow the autocracy. Absorbed in the immediate importance of this task, bolsheviks and mensheviks alike in the underground committees began to feel that the issues which divided them were much less important than the aims which united them. By the summer of 1905 many parallel bolshevik and menshevik committees merged on the spot. In September 1905 a southern regional conference of some fifteen bolshevik and menshevik organizations decided that the time had come for their organizations to merge. In November the Petersburg Bolshevik Committee and Menshevik Group decided to unite, without reference to the Central Committee.[2] Bolshevik agents inside Russia were urging upon the Central Committee the need for reunion. For a short time there even appeared a joint bolshevik-menshevik newspaper, *Severnyi Golos*.

Lenin, whatever his personal views on the matter, was unable to resist this pressure from below. The all-bolshevik Central Committee inside Russia was for a time inclined to encourage unification by the

[1] For details of membership of organizations at this time see Martov in *Obshchestvennoe dvizhenie*, volume III, pp. 568–9, 572–4.
[2] *Resheniia iuzhno-russkoi uchreditel'noi konferentsii rossiskoi R.S.-D.R.P.*, avgust 1905 goda, Geneva, 1905, p. 3; *Revoliutsiia 1905–1907 gg. v Rossii ... Vysshii pod"em revoliutsii 1905–1907 gg.* Vooruzhennoe vosstanie. Noiabr'-dekabr' 1905 goda, Moscow, 1955, volume I, p. 416.

obvious and simple method of fusing the sundered committees and groups. But Lenin was opposed to this. He had insisted at the Third Congress that unification should only take place at a Congress, and an (unpublished) resolution to this effect had been adopted. Under pressure from Lenin the Central Committee was forced to break off its negotiations with the mensheviks and to insist on the summoning of a further Congress.[1] In December 1905, at their conference at Tammerfors in Finland, the bolsheviks resolved to call another party Congress at which unification should take place. This Congress was to be called by a joint committee, consisting of the Central Committee and of the Menshevik Organization Committee which they had set up in May 1905. Elections to the Congress were to take place by 'platforms'.[2] This meant that delegates elected to the Congress would be committed in advance to the policy of one or other faction, and the Congress thus divided into bolsheviks and mensheviks from the start. No doubt Lenin hoped that the bolsheviks would be in a majority. The mensheviks, who met in separate conference about the same time, opposed this method of election to the Congress, and urged election of delegates by both menshevik and bolshevik organizations voting jointly. As a symbolical concession, in the interests of party unity, they solemnly adopted Lenin's formulation of paragraph one of the party Rules.[3]

In the end, Lenin's insistence on election of delegates by 'platforms' prevailed, and a system of representation was agreed. But the chances of unity were destroyed in advance. At the Congress, which met in Stockholm from 23 April to 8 May (10–25 April) 1906, and which is known as the Fourth (Unification) Congress, the 112 voting delegates represented the separate bolshevik and menshevik organizations. Although no exact figures of the size of the party can be given in view of the prevalently loose nature of membership,[4] it had most probably doubled since mid-1905. The delegates were young – the average age was thirty – and mainly drawn from the liberal professions, though one-quarter were workers in origin. Less than half were Russian by nationality. Jews formed nearly a quarter, and there was a

[1] The documents relating to these negotiations are reprinted in *Protokoly IV*, pp. 563–601. For Lenin's views at different stages see *Lenin*, volume VIII, pp. 7–8, 21–3, 202–5; 241–7; volume XXVIII, p. 492.

[2] *KPSS v rez.*, volume I, pp. 98–9; *Lenin*, volume VIII, pp. 515–17.

[3] *Lenin*, volume VIII, pp. 466–7.

[4] According to the left-wing independent newspaper *Tovarishch*, the total number of members enrolled in Russian (bolshevik and menshevik) organizations was about 70,000 in October 1906. At the same date the *Bund* numbered 33,000, the Polish social democrats 28,000, and the Lettish S.-D.'s 13,000. See *Lenin*, volume X, p. 483.

large Georgian contingent. Most had worked in the social democratic movement since the First Congress of 1898, or before, and had experienced both prison and exile.[1] Each delegate represented 300 party members. Minority views were safeguarded, as well as the representation of organizations which did not rise to 300 members. It was possibly as fair a method of representing both factions in the party as could be devised. Lenin's hopes that bolsheviks would be in a majority were disappointed, since of the 112, sixty-two were mensheviks as against forty-four or forty-six bolsheviks. Plekhanov was easily the most respected figure in the party, as the voting in the elections to the Bureau or Steering Committee of the Congress showed; Lenin failed to secure the absolute majority required. (Martov was not present.)

In spite of the serious theoretical issues which, as will be seen below, divided the two sections of the party, and on which the menshevik majority could have enforced its view, an atmosphere of conciliation prevailed. There was more banter, fewer charges of 'treason' or 'opportunism'. Lenin displayed a greater spirit of conciliation than ever before, or after. When the 'economist' Akimov, who was then in Stockholm, asked for leave to be present at the Congress it was Lenin who immediately proposed that he should be invited to attend as a non-voting delegate. It was a striking contrast to Lenin's attitude on the question of Riazanov's attendance at the Second Congress three years before. In the course of debate Lenin went out of his way to emphasize that he was 'far from holding the opinion' that bolsheviks and mensheviks could not work together in one party.[2] At the conclusion of the Congress Lenin and a number of other bolsheviks, describing themselves as members of the 'former' bolshevik faction, issued a declaration enumerating those decisions of the Congress which they regarded as mistaken. They declared their determination not to permit another split in the party, but claimed the democratic right, while loyally accepting all decisions of the majority, to propagate their views in 'comradely' debate with the aim of winning the majority over to their side.[3] Time would show how much sincerity there was in these gestures.

[1] *Protokoly IV*, pp. 480–2.
[2] *Protokoly IV*, p. 476. According to M. Liadov, *Iz zhizni partii. Vospominaniia*, Moscow, 1956, pp. 164–5, the object of supporting the admission of Akimov was to discredit the mensheviks by their association with such an obvious 'opportunist'; according to what Lenin told Lunacharskii, he had no intention of letting the mensheviks 'lead us along after them on a chain' – see A. Lunacharskii, 'Iz vospominanii o Lenine v 1905 godu', *Proletarskaia revoliutsiia*, volume 97–8, pp. 89–90.
[3] *Protokoly IV*, pp. 604, 254, 341, 573–7, 9, 51; *KPSS v rez.*, volume I, pp. 120–4.

On the important question of organization, the menshevik majority proved devoid of any constructive ideas. The symbolic paragraph one of the party Rules, in Lenin's formulation, was duly adopted. The phrase, 'democratic centralism' was incorporated in the new party constitution – it had already been adopted by the bolsheviks at Tammerfors a few months before – but there was little to suggest that it could have any great meaning in practice.[1] The mensheviks were divided on the issue of centralized control over the party. The majority, which included the leaders Martov and Dan, stood very close to the bolsheviks in their belief that only a strictly centralized organization could successfully lead the revolutionary movement to its victorious end. Only a minority, influenced by their experience of the Soviets, and by work in the new trade union organizations, believed that the most urgent task of social democracy was to create a mass party.[2] Hence, the Rules as voted, retained all the essential features of a centralized underground organization.[3]

The Congress also resolved to readmit the *Bund* on the basis of autonomy, and to admit the Polish and Lettish social democratic parties on the same basis, though their admission into the party before long gave Lenin once again a majority on the party organs. The concession to the *Bund* of autonomy in questions of organization and propaganda aroused opposition not only from some bolsheviks but also among the Caucasian mensheviks. The Georgian majority of the Caucasian social democrats feared the possible repercussions of the special privileges of the Jews upon the smaller national organizations in the Caucasus. One of the eleven delegates from Tiflis was a bolshevik – the young Dzhugashvili, later to become famous as Stalin. He voted with Lenin for the readmission of the *Bund*, but many other bolsheviks voted against it. In the *Bund* the mensheviks were to gain an ally against the bolsheviks. The editors of the proposed new party newspaper, *Sotsial-Demokrat*, elected by the Congress were all mensheviks. There was, however, nothing either in the party Rules or in the resolutions of the Congress to prevent Lenin and the bolsheviks from continuing to publish a newspaper of their own. The new Central Committee, as elected at the Congress, consisted of seven

[1] It will be recalled that, in the Russian context, the phrase was of menshevik origin. Historically, the phrase originated in the German Social Democratic Movement, and was first used in 1865 by J. B. Schweitzer, one of the principal followers of Lasselle. See Leo Valiani, 'La Storia della socialdemocrazia ledesca (1863–1914)' in *Rivista Storica Italiana*, Anno LXXX, fascicolo 1, 1968, p. 38.
[2] See on this Martov in *Obshchestvennoe dvizhenie*, volume III, pp. 585–6.
[3] *KPSS v rez.*, volume I, pp. 135–6.

mensheviks and three bolsheviks. Later it was increased by the addition of two Polish social democrats, one Lettish, and two members of the *Bund*.[1]

The Congress merely papered over the theoretical differences on policy which had revealed themselves in the course of 1905. The first disagreement related to the revolution itself. Although no bolsheviks, and few mensheviks, were as yet prepared to admit this, it was apparent by 1906 that it had failed, or had at any rate received a serious set-back. In the heat of battle each faction had bent its energies towards inviting the masses to greater revolutionary activity. In the Moscow rising bolsheviks and mensheviks had fought side by side. Yet, in retrospect it became clear that the revolution of 1905 had been largely spontaneous, and that social democrats had not been able to exercise real leadership. Some, like Plekhanov, who shortly after Bloody Sunday was sufficiently carried away to call upon the workers to 'arm themselves', now asserted that the Moscow rising had been a mistake. This view was unpopular with bolsheviks and mensheviks alike. The bolsheviks attributed the Moscow failure to lack of determination and organization. The mensheviks attributed it primarily to the fact that the troops had remained loyal to the autocracy. Both were agreed that armed struggle as such was desirable, and that the task of the social democrats was to organize an armed uprising in the immediate future. But to the bolsheviks this meant creating a general staff of insurrection and a network of armed detachments which would go into action at a signal from above. To the mensheviks preparation for insurrection meant intensified political activity among the masses so as to spur them on to revolt. Then, when the revolution came, social democrats would lead it to victory. These conflicting views are reflected in the menshevik resolution adopted at the Fourth Congress, and in the draft resolution proposed by the bolsheviks, which failed to secure a majority. Aksel'rod put forward a third view, which won very little support at the Congress. The tactics of the mensheviks and of the bolsheviks, he said, differed little in practice. The real task of social democrats, that of 'raising our proletariat to the status of a conscious and organized, that is to say, independent political force' is divided by an 'impassable gulf' from armed actions, and 'is quite inconsistent with the aim of preparing the masses for a decisive battle against

---

[1] The editors included Martov, Dan and Potresov. The menshevik Central Committee members included none of the prominent leaders. The bolsheviks were V. A. Desnitshy, L. B. Krasin and A. I. Rykov. (Rykov was later replaced by A. A. Bogdanov.) The Poles were A. S. Varskii and F. E. Dzerzhinskii. For full list see *Lenin*, volume IX, p. 515.

reaction with weapons in their hands.'[1] He foresaw the need for a period of political preparation before the proletariat was ripe to fulfil its mission of becoming the dominant power in the state. As a concrete step in this direction he advocated at the Fourth Congress, as before it, that the social democrats should take the lead in convening a national workers' congress. This, he argued, would achieve a good deal more than strikes and demonstrations, since it could become a unifying focal point for the whole social democratic and workers' movement. His doctrine fell on deaf ears within his own faction, who feared that the authority of the social democratic committee men would soon become engulfed in a spontaneous self-organized workers' movement. A few months after the Fourth Congress the mensheviks joined with the bolsheviks in condemning any attempt to organize a workers' congress as 'a breach of party discipline'.[2]

The majority of the party was still intoxicated with the heat of battle, and refused to believe that the wave of revolution had receded. Much debate therefore centred in the course of 1905 and 1906 on the question of what the policy of the social democrats should be in the event of a successful revolution leading to the formation of a provisional government. Most mensheviks on this question followed the accepted interpretation of the views of Marx prevalent in the social democratic parties in Western Europe. According to this view, the revolution in Russia could only lead to the replacement of 'feudalism' by a 'bourgeois capitalist' form of society. The provisional government could therefore only be a bourgeois government formed by the liberal parties. For social democrats to participate in such a government would be wrong, since not only would it mean the anticipation of the next historic phase, the proletarian revolution, but it would also dull the class-consciousness of a proletarian party, compromise its integrity in the eyes of the masses and distract it from its next main task, the overthrow of the bourgeois government. The social democrats must therefore remain a party of extreme opposition to the provisional government – driving it towards more radical measures. Some mensheviks, however, were not content to accept this counsel of doctrinal perfection. As the revolution of 1905 developed, some of them began to incline towards the extreme views of Trotsky and his

[1] *Protokoly IV*, pp. 284-5; for the two resolutions see *KPSS v rez.*, volume I, pp. 128–9, 108–9.
[2] At the Tammerfors Conference, in November 1906, at which mensheviks were in the majority, see *KPSS v rez.*, volume I, p. 143. For Aksel'rod's views in 1906 see *Protokoly IV*, pp. 283–4; *Perepiska* (letter of 1 September 1906); and 'Po povodu odnoi zametki' in *Sotsial-Demokrat*, No. 1, of 17 September 1906.

ally Helphand (Parvus). These two argued that the impetus of the revolution might be such that the proletariat could be led on to press immediately for the maximum programme of full socialist transformation of society, the moment the bourgeois phase of the revolution had been accomplished. The bourgeois phase, Trotsky argued, was only a stage: in the interests of its own self-preservation the proletariat should aim at 'uninterrupted revolution', without giving the bourgeois state any time to establish itself, and this in turn would lead on to the dictatorship of the proletariat. This doctrine of 'uninterrupted revolution' had a respectable ancestry in the views of Marx during a short period after the German revolution of 1848, when he had urged the Communist League not to be misled by 'democratic talk of freedom', but to take as its battle-cry 'The Revolution in Permanence', and to press its demands for immediate transition to the social revolution. But these views were a temporary aberration from Marx's scientific analysis, formed under the impetus of what he believed was the rising tide of revolution. Before long Marx's more fundamental belief in the development of the historical process by necessary stages had reasserted itself, and he was criticizing those who 'make sheer will instead of real conditions the driving-wheel of revolution. While we say to the workers: you have fifteen or twenty or fifty years of bourgeois and national wars to go through, not just to alter conditions, but to alter yourselves and qualify for political power – you on the contrary say: we must obtain the power at once or we might as well lay ourselves down to sleep.' Martov also had inclinations towards 'uninterrupted revolution', but viewed the probability as an unavoidable evil, and not, like Trotsky, as a desirable aim.[1]

Lenin, on one sole occasion, in September 1905, also used this traditional phrase. 'From the democratic revolution,' he wrote, 'we shall begin straightaway within the measure of our strength . . . to pass to the socialist revolution. We stand for uninterrupted revolution. We will not stop halfway.' But this was an isolated statement. His considered opinion was stated in the course of 1905 with more regard for traditional Marxist doctrine. The view that the achievement of the maximum programme of the socialist revolution could be attempted immediately after the democratic revolution had succeeded, he

[1] For Trotsky's views see his *Itogi i perspektivy*, Moscow, 1919 (a reprint of a pamphlet published in 1906); for Martov's views see *Iskra*, No. 93, 17 (4) March 1905, p. 4, and *Pis'ma*, p. 146; on Marx see *Selected Works*, volume I, pp. 98–108, and Boris Nicolaevsky and Otto Maenchen-Helfen, *Karl Marx: Man and Fighter*, translated by Gwenda David and Eric Mosbacher, London, 1936, pp. 204–20.

argued, was 'inept' and 'semi-anarchist'. 'Without the consciousness and the organization of the masses, without preparing and educating them in the course of open class struggle against the entire bourgeoisie, there can be no thought of a socialist revolution.' The only way to this lies through the democratic republic. 'Anyone who wants to reach socialism by any road other than political democracy will inevitably be led on to inept and reactionary results, both in the economic and the political sense.' Having thus enunciated his view of revolution in orthodox Marxist fashion, Lenin proceeded to explain what he meant by 'political democracy' in Russian conditions. This would necessarily be a dictatorship, since 'the achievement of the transformations which are immediately and inevitably necessary to the proletariat and the peasantry will evoke violent opposition from the bourgeoisie and the landlords', which must be broken. This dictatorship, however, could not be a dictatorship of the proletariat, but a 'revolutionary demo-cratic dictatorship of the proletariat and the peasantry'. Since it would not be a proletarian dictatorship, it could not as yet, or at any rate at first, attack the foundations of capitalism. But it could radically alter land tenure in the peasants' favour, introduce complete 'demo-cratization', improve the conditions of the workers, and, 'last but not least' (the words are in English in the original) carry the flames of revolution across to the rest of Europe.[1] After 1905 Lenin's conception of the first phase of the next revolution therefore excluded the liberal parties from the provisional government. In theory, it differed from Trotsky's conception in conceding that the dictatorship would be exercised jointly with peasant, and therefore 'bourgeois', parties. Both at the Third and at the Fourth Congresses, he urged participa-tion of social democrats in what he called the 'provisional revolution-ary government'. But it was a measure of the extent to which his ideas were misunderstood outside his own party (and inside it too) that the Kadet leader, Miliukov, interpreted this to mean that the bolsheviks were willing to participate in a *bourgeois* provisional government.[2]

Lenin now assigned a vital part to the peasants in the future revolu-tion. Although he had already realized in 1902, in the course of the disputes over the party programme with his colleagues on *Iskra*, the importance of attracting the peasants, it required the revolution of 1905 to open his eyes to their importance as a revolutionary force. The peasants were playing an important part in Russia in 1905 in

[1] *Lenin*, volume VIII, pp. 186, 41, 62–3.
[2] *KPSS v rez.*, volume I, pp. 78, 110; Donald W. Treadgold, *Lenin and his Rivals: The Struggle for Russia's Future, 1898–1906*, London, 1955, p. 175.

adding to the general upheaval, but, in so far as there was any socialist leadership among them, this was mainly provided by the socialist revolutionaries, and not by the social democrats. Gapon's programme too had been a rousing call to the peasants, and Lenin had for a while seen Gapon frequently when he arrived in Switzerland after Bloody Sunday.[1] Both Gapon and the socialist revolutionaries offered the peasants the one thing in which they were interested – land. The austere offers of the social democrats, who up to 1905 had expected the peasants to follow their leaders, the proletariat, in return for minor concessions,[2] could not compete with such promises. By March 1905 at any rate, Lenin had realized the 'true democratic and revolutionary content' behind the peasants' hunger for land, and the advisability for social democrats to support it. The all-bolshevik Third Congress in April 1905 promised support for all peasant revolutionary activity, including expropriation of the landlords' land.[3] But this view, though good practical politics for making a revolution, came into conflict with the view of most Marxists, that to encourage the peasant in his natural desire to become a smallholder would create an entrenched petty bourgeoisie whose love of property would prove an obstacle to the future development of socialism.

In an endeavour to make a more attractive offer to the peasants, and at the same time to meet this theoretical objection, the mensheviks at the Fourth Congress in 1906 proposed the 'municipalization' of land. This envisaged the confiscation of all land and its administration for the peasants' benefit by democratically elected local organs. To this policy, which in view of the menshevik majority was adopted by the Congress, Lenin opposed a programme of 'nationalization' by the state of all land. In his analysis of Lenin's proposal Plekhanov pointed out that to anyone who envisaged (as an orthodox Marxist must) the first phase of the revolution as a bourgeois democratic one, nationalization of all land could only add to the strength of an hostile state. Hence, Lenin's demand for nationalization, Plekhanov contended, was only consistent with the views of one who had in his mind already jettisoned the first or bourgeois phase, and was thinking of immediate transition to the second, socialist phase. Plekhanov's main argument

---

[1] N. Krupskaia, *Vospominaniia o Lenine*, Moscow, 1932, pp. 85–90.

[2] For details of these concessions, see the programme adopted in 1903, *KPSS v rez.*, volume I, pp. 42–3. The principal concessions had been worked out by Lenin as a means of attracting the peasants as early as 1895 – see Iu. Martov, *Zapiski Sotsial-Demokrata*, Berlin, 1922, pp. 331–2. This was the return to the peasants, of the *otrezki* – a portion of their land which had been 'cut away' by the Emancipation Act of 1861.

[3] *Lenin*, volume VII, p. 161; *KPSS v rez.*, volume I, p. 80.

was that it was necessary to destroy the despotic and semi-Asiatic system of land ownership in Russia, if only as a guarantee against a counter-revolutionary restoration. Lenin replied that the peasants would never accept municipalization; that the only guarantee against a counter-revolutionary restoration was in any case the outbreak of revolution in other Western countries; and that nationalization, coupled with seizure of the land by peasant committees, was the only way to teach the peasants the need for completing the socialist revolution. As Lenin made clear shortly after the Congress, 'we must call upon the peasants to seize the land'; the juridical recognition of this seizure, in the form of a confiscation decree, would come later.[1] One consequence of Lenin's views on land policy was to render him more prepared to co-operate with the socialist revolutionaries. But for the time being the more immediate question was that of relations with the liberals.

The revolution of 1905 had led to the formation of several progressive but comparatively moderate political parties which, for want of a better term, must be designated as 'liberal'. The largest of these parties, the Constitutional Democrats, known for short as *Kadety*, emerged out of the fusion of two movements – the Union for Liberation, and the *zemstva* constitutionalists, among whom there was a large proportion of liberal-minded landowners active in the local government organizations. These two elements were different in outlook. Whereas the 'Liberationists' were by temperament radical reformers, the *zemstva* men were usually moderate constitutionalists, with a strong strain of cautious conservatism, who, in spite of dislike of the arbitrary autocracy, were equally repelled by violent or over-hasty opposition to it. The more radical Liberationists, though emotionally always more in sympathy with revolutionary activity by the proletariat, were driven into union with the constitutionalists because of the apprehension they felt when they saw the violent and anarchical nature of the revolutionary movement. After a year of energetic public campaigning, which played a major part in forcing the autocracy into making its concessions, the future *Kadety* met in a Congress in Moscow in the middle of October 1905, and emerged as an organized party, ready to take its share in the political life of the

---

[1] *KPSS v rez.*, volume I, pp. 124, 116–18; *Protokoly IV*, pp. 59–63, 81–3, 143–9; *Lenin*, volume IX, pp. 149–56, 184–200. For an original analysis of the importance of this debate, as revealing Plekhanov's fears of the possibility that an Asiatic, bureacratic form of dictatorship would be the result of Lenin's proposals see Karl A. Wittfogel, *Oriental Despotism. A Comparative Study of Total Power*, Oxford, 1957, chapter ix. See also Samuel H. Baron *Plekhanov: The Father of Russian Marxism*, London, 1963, pp. 295–307.

country. The programme adopted at this foundation Congress left open the question whether the future state was to be monarchical or republican. Its provisions included a demand for full civil and political freedom, universal franchise, the eight-hour day and other progressive labour legislation, and the expropriation of land for the benefit of the peasants on the basis of fair compensation. The leader of the new party, P. N. Miliukov, explained that what divided the *Kadety* from parties further to the right was their refusal to sacrifice the interests of the workers to those of the landowners and industrialists. As for what he called 'our allies on the left', the *Kadety* were unable to accept either their demands for a democratic republic or their policy of the nationalization of all means of production. But solidarity with, and indeed admiration of, the proletariat for the part which it had played in bringing the autocracy to its knees were the keynotes of most speeches at the Congress. As for the Emperor's manifesto of 17 October, which was issued while the Congress was in session, the new party showed little confidence that its promises would be implemented. The *Kadety* set themselves the task of fighting the forthcoming elections to the State Duma with the object of forcing the autocracy to accept this body as a fully sovereign legislature, and to set up a government responsible to it. They were prepared to accept nothing less. The Congress did not satisfy all the heterogeneous elements of which it was composed, and there was fission both to the left and to the right. A small group of 'critical socialists', as they called themselves, remained outside the *Kadet* organization: this group now included E. D. Kuskova and S. Prokopovich, the former 'economists'. On the right a number of other groups emerged, of which the most important was the 'Union of 17 October' (known as the 'Octobrists') most of whom believed that the only safe road for Russia was cautious progress towards freedom, and that the progressive political parties should accept the October manifesto, moderate their demands, and work with what had now in effect become a constitutional monarchy in an effort to build up legal order as a secure foundation for reform.

Thus, many of the members of the liberal parties which emerged in Russia in 1905 were a good deal more radical than their liberal counterparts in Western Europe. To the bolsheviks this made no difference, and Lenin in particular was always careful to emphasize that no distinction should or could be drawn between more or less radical liberals. All of them would inevitably ally themselves with the autocracy against the workers, and all would inevitably betray. The workers must therefore neither support liberals nor ally themselves with them. Although the Third (all-bolshevik) Congress had paid lip service to the traditional social democratic doctrine of support for liberals until such time as the bourgeois democratic phase of the revolution was accomplished,[1] in practice, in the pages of Lenin's newspaper *Vperëd*, the liberals were constantly attacked. 'Support' was in its columns interpreted as meaning at most assistance to fugitives from the police, or passing clandestine literature. Lenin's intransigent hostility to the liberals was indeed consistent with his view, already formulated in 1902, that capitalism was already dominant in Russia, and that the time for co-operation with the liberals was therefore over, and with his conception of the 'revolutionary democratic dictatorship of the proletariat and the peasantry'. The mensheviks, in theory at any rate, were prepared to accept the need for a more or less prolonged bourgeois democratic phase of revolution in which the social democrats would act as an extreme opposition to a liberal democratic government. Some of them, therefore, began to favour joint action with the liberals in all efforts directed against the autocracy. At the same time they still believed that social democrats should constantly expose the cowardice or reactionary hesitation of liberals, and thereby endeavour to drive them leftwards, on a more revolutionary course. Though they continued to believe that in the second phase, the social revolution, the liberals would be eliminated, this was apparently regarded as still sufficiently remote not to preclude co-operative action at present.

One of the casualties of 1905 was the menshevik belief in the 'hegemony' of the proletariat which, with the emergence of the liberals as an active and independent force, ceased to have much relation to facts. So far as Lenin was concerned, unlike the mensheviks, he had never envisaged leadership by the party of the proletariat over independent liberal parties, but had rather contemplated the eventual emergence of the social democrats as the sole organized party, although drawing its members and support from all classes.[2] But the mensheviks, faced with the evident fact that the *Kadety* were going to think and act for themselves, in spite of their admiration for the role played by the proletariat in the revolution, quietly abandoned their once cherished doctrine. Trotsky described 'hegemony' as 'hypocrisy', and Plekhanov as 'absurd'.[3]

Indeed, there could have been no more eloquent proof of the

[1] *KPSS v rez.*, volume I, pp. 82–3.
[2] See A. N. Potresov in *Iskra*, No. 78, 20 (7) November 1904, p. 5.
[3] See *Keep*, pp. 211–12.

absurdity of 'hegemony' than that provided by the elections to the First Duma in the spring of 1906. The wide franchise enacted after the October Manifesto offered considerable opportunities to social democratic candidates. Since the method of election was indirect, and by a system of *curiae* of voters under which factory workers voted separately, the chances were particularly good for social democratic candidates in the workers' *curiae*. But the sympathies of many of the radically minded bourgeoisie and intelligentsia for the workers' movement promised successes in other *curiae* as well. However, in the atmosphere of distrust for the promises of the autocracy, the first inclination among all social democrats was to boycott the elections. The franchise, though wide, was unjust, because it was weighted in favour of the property owners. Political parties still had a precarious standing, and there was therefore no guarantee that electoral canvassing and agitation would be free from police interference.

In the bolshevik view the Duma would necessarily be a reactionary body, whatever its composition, and could only aim at compromise with the autocracy. By participating in the elections the social democrats would merely encourage false illusions among the workers that they might after all achieve their object without revolution, by parliamentary means. The proper course for social democrats was to take no part in the elections, and if and when the Duma assembled, to exploit the conflicts which would arise between the Duma and the people, when the people realized that it had been betrayed. These views were widespread not only among the bolshevik leaders but among party members generally. The mensheviks were divided in their views, but in the main tended to believe that the elections should be exploited as a means of focusing the attention of the masses on the problems which faced them in their struggle. The Duma itself could (such at any rate was Plekhanov's view) serve as a valuable source of experience for the workers, and would teach them that only a really democratic Constituent Assembly could fully satisfy their demands. In the event, the bolsheviks in December 1905 decided in favour of a complete boycott of the Duma elections. Lenin himself, though at one time apparently hesitant upon the issue, and anxious to exploit the elections in some form for the opportunities for agitation which they offered, acceded to the general opinion inside his faction in favour of complete boycott.[1] The menshevik leaders failed to agree on

---

[1] See *Pis'ma*, p. 148, and the reference *ibidem* to the memoirs of a participant in this conference, of which no protocols exist. For the resolution see *KPSS v rez.*, volume I, pp. 100–1.

a common policy, and left the question of participation in the elections or boycott to the decision of their local committees. The socialist revolutionaries, like the bolsheviks, decided to boycott the elections. The result of this policy was complete disorganization so far as the workers were concerned. In most districts where social democratic influence, whether bolshevik or menshevik, was strong, the elections were boycotted by the worker voters. Left to themselves, the workers tended to take part in the elections, and in some cases returned candidates of social democratic sympathies. In the Caucasus, where the strong menshevik organizations were opposed to the boycott from the start, the social democrats organized the elections in an orderly manner and received more than twice as many votes as all the other parties together.[1] The peasants remained impervious to all propaganda in favour of boycott (which emanated from the socialist revolutionaries), and in the absence of socialist candidates, voted for the *Kadety*. The result of the political ineptitude of the socialists was to rally popular support to independent candidates or to *Kadety*, who in the end proved to be the strongest single party in the Duma, with 179 out of 478 seats. Eighteen social democrats were elected.[2]

When the Fourth Party Congress assembled in Stockholm on 23 April 1906, the elections were nearly complete, and the *Kadet* victory and the failure of the policy of boycott were evident. The mensheviks now rejected boycott out of hand. Their resolution, which was passed by the Congress, not only sanctioned participation in those elections which still remained to be held (this referred to the Caucasus), but also deemed it desirable that social democrats in the Duma should form a special group. This group, under the control of the central party organization, should aim to drive the bourgeois parties on towards more resolute opposition to the autocracy, and to do all in its power to exacerbate the conflicts between it and the Duma. Lenin and some sixteen bolsheviks voted for this resolution, but many bolsheviks abstained, including Stalin. Lenin, and those who voted with him, explained their change of front by asserting that the forthcoming elections were of no practical importance. This was a transparent 'face-saver', since the Caucasian elections could clearly not be so

[1] See B-ov (M. Balabanov) and F. Dan, *Rabochie deputaty v pervoi gosudarstvennoi Dume*, St Petersburg, n.d., pp. 31–59.

[2] 38 were 'moderates' and 50 'centre' deputies; there were also 94 left-wing so-called 'Labourites', or *Trudoviki*. The remainder were mainly non-party peasants. No right-wing members were elected. See J. L. H. Keep, 'Russian Social Democracy and the First Duma' in *The Slavonic and East European Review*, volume XXXIV, December 1955, p. 186, note 27. And see *ibidem*, pp. 182–5, for much information on the election and on the policy of the parties towards it.

dismissed. The truth was that the highly organized Caucasian mensheviks were very unlikely to take much notice of any resolution barring them from participation in elections which they were already fully determined to carry through. Lenin continued thereafter stoutly to maintain that the tactics of boycotting the First Duma elections had been correct, and it was only in 1920 that he first publicly stated that the boycott had been a mistake.[1]

Thus the Fourth Congress ended with the two factions nominally reunited, in very changed conditions from 1903. Revolution was at the ebb, the constitutional era had dawned, and a strong middle-class party had emerged upon the scene, determined to create conditions of political and civil liberty. New opportunities seemed to be opening up for social democrats, of a kind which in some of the countries of Western Europe were already leading to the emergence of the working class as a conscious political force. The Russian party was not destined to profit from these opportunities.

[1] See *Lenin*, volume XXV, p. 204. For the resolution see *KPSS v rez.*, volume I pp. 127–8; for the Congress voting see *Protokoly IV*, p. 374.

V The First and Second Dumas

Lenin and the bolsheviks viewed their defeat at the Fourth Congress as only a temporary set-back, and they set out to overcome it. According to Martov, the Central Committee elected at this Congress (on which mensheviks were in the majority) came up from the very first against 'the existence within the party . . . of efforts to create some special, centralized organization designed to prepare and lead an armed uprising'.[1] He was referring to the secret bolshevik 'Centre', the official existence of which is usually only acknowledged by Soviet historians after 1907, but which was in fact set up at Stockholm during the Fourth Congress in the spring of 1906. Its exact composition is unknown, but it certainly included Lenin, A. A. Bogdanov and Krasin – the two last named were members of the Central Committee.[2] The nature of this Centre can only be reconstructed from scraps of information found in memoirs. 'At the very Congress,' wrote one of Lenin's closest supporters, 'the bolsheviks set up their own inner and, so far as the party was concerned, illegal Central Committee.'[3] Another bolshevik refers in his memoirs to secret bolshevik funds which, unbeknown to the Central Committee, were administered by Krasin. The ostensible unification, he adds, 'had practically no influence on our bolshevik affairs. We certainly did not disarm as a strong, independent revolutionary faction'. This secret activity was directed by Lenin.[4]

Lenin still believed at this period that the tide of revolution was rising, that the lull was only temporary, and that the social democrats should be prepared to seize the next opportunity when it arose. His

[1] *Protokoly V*, p. 86.
[2] The six-volume history of the C.P.S.U. now (1969) in course of publication in the Soviet Union has a passing reference to the Centre which it identifies as the editorial board of *Proletarii*, in August 1906: see P. N. Pospelov and others (ed.) *Istoriia Kommunisticheskoi Partii Sovetskogo Soiuza*, volume II, Moscow, 1966, p. 193.
[3] G. Zinoviev, *Istoriia Rossiiskoi kommunisticheskoi partii (bol'shevikov).* Populiarnyi ocherk. Moscow, Petrograd, 1923, p. 124. Cf. M. Liadov, *Iz zhizni partii. Vospominaniia.* Moscow, 1956, pp. 166, 190.
[4] Vlad. Bonch-Bruevich, *Bol'shevistskie izdatel'skie dela v 1905–1907 gg. Moi vospominaniia.* Leningrad, 1933, pp. 17–18.

sense of the urgent need to bring about a victorious national uprising was strengthened by the publication during 1906 of the projected land reforms of the new Prime Minister, P. A. Stolypin. These reforms contemplated the break-up of the traditional peasant commune so as to make possible the emergence of a strong class of individual land-owning peasants. Stolypin had recognized that the peasant communes, far from being strongholds of support for the autocracy (as most of the Emperor's advisers had hitherto believed), were, on the contrary, a breeding ground for revolutionaries. The new peasant landowners, whom Stolypin envisaged, would become a bulwark for the defence of order against the tide of revolution. For Lenin, the prospects of a successful revolution were bound up with a mass rising of a land-hungry peasantry. He foresaw, and later explained in print, that Stolypin's reforms, if allowed to proceed to completion, might jeopardize the very prospect of revolution.[1] An immediate revolution, more powerful than that of 1905, was therefore the answer. But this could only be achieved with a network of fighting detachments, controlled by a close-knit organization of revolutionaries, who would accept Lenin's leadership. There was no room in such an organization for 'soft' mensheviks. Therefore it was necessary, in Lenin's view, to prevent the formal unification of the party from becoming a reality, and to work for the summoning of another congress at which the bolsheviks could once again secure control over the party organs.

The tactics which the bolsheviks adopted in 1906 and 1907 consisted of making every effort to discredit the officially elected party leadership among party members. When they thought they detected signs of the menshevik leaders falling victims to 'constitutional illusions', they blamed them for violating the resolutions of the party Congress. But when, as occasionally happened, the Central Committee issued extreme revolutionary appeals, they blamed its menshevik majority for 'adventurousness'. Inside the Central Committee Bogdanov and Krasin bombarded the majority with protests, circulating them among party members when they were rejected.[2] The bolsheviks were supported inside the Petersburg Committee by G. E. Zinoviev, whose co-option Lenin had arranged. Zinoviev, a young firebrand who had few scruples and a rare gift for intrigue, soon proved a valuable assistant for work behind the scenes. With his aid Lenin achieved before long a bolshevik majority in the Petersburg

---

[1] *Lenin*, volume XII, p. 193.
[2] See pamphlet published for the Fifth Congress reprinted in *Lenin*, volume X, pp. 421–34, and the debates at the Fifth Congress, *passim*.

Committee, which was scarcely less important than the Central Committee. The new bolshevik mouthpiece, *Proletarii*, was published under its auspices.

All this activity required separate funds, since Lenin could not rely for his own secret operations on official party funds administered by the Central Committee. A large sum (sixty thousand roubles) was handed over to Lenin, Bogdanov and Krasin during this period, 1906–7, by Gorky's wife, as trustee for a life insurance policy of the bolsheviks' benefactor, the industrialist Morozov, who had died in 1905.[1] The total official budget of the Central Committee for the whole period between the Fourth Congress and the Fifth Congress (in May 1907) was only twenty thousand more.[2] But a much greater source of income for the bolsheviks was provided by the proceeds of armed hold-ups, or, as they were called, 'expropriations'. This method of obtaining funds for the party had been generally accepted during the anarchy prevailing in the country in 1905. It had been practised by the party's fighting detachments as an integral part of the process of insurrection. But there was also a good deal of 'unofficial' plain robbery, thinly veiled as revolutionary activity, which tended to discredit the party among its would-be supporters, and to demoralize it within. All mensheviks, the *Bund* and many bolsheviks viewed the practice of 'expropriations' with distaste. Lenin, and some of his immediate supporters, however, recognized the importance of this source of funds. At the Fourth Congress the great majority of delegates had voted against 'expropriations' as a means of struggle, except in cases where a local revolutionary government was already established, when seizure of state-owned funds was to be permitted.[3] Lenin and a number of bolsheviks abstained in the voting and ignored the resolution after the Congress. During 1906 and 1907 an epidemic of armed 'expropriations' both of government and of private property spread all over the country, bringing in substantial funds to the private bolshevik exchequer.

Bolshevik sources are naturally reticent about this activity, which was unlawful not only in terms of the law of the land but of party discipline. Even the mensheviks were at the time reluctant to discuss the subject, for fear of discrediting the party, especially in the eyes of the German social democrats. But memoirs of the period throw some

---

[1] For a brilliant sketch of this strange figure by Maxim Gorky see *M. Gor'kii v epokhu revoliutsii 1905–1097 godov. Materialy, vospominaniia, issledovaniia.* Moscow 1957, pp. 12–35. According to Gorky, Morozov shot himself.
[2] *Protokoly V*, pp. 94–7, 188.
[3] *KPSS v rez.*, volume I, pp. 130–1.

light on this question. The general control over operations was in Lenin's hands. The technical direction was largely in the hands of Krasin, an engineer of distinction with outstanding organizing ability. This conspiratorial activity brought the bolsheviks into co-operation with the socialist revolutionary terrorists. The socialist revolutionary bomb which was intended, but failed, to kill Stolypin in August 1906, was manufactured in one of Krasin's underground laboratories. The main centres of activity were the Urals and the Caucasus.[1] Some funds also reached the bolshevik exchequer as the result of a tour in 1906 of workers' organizations in the United States. The money was ostensibly collected for the party as a whole, but in fact reached the bolsheviks alone.[2] Since no accounts were published by the bolsheviks for any period before September 1908, an exact calculation of the total amount of these funds is impossible. But they are not likely to have been far short in the period 1906–8 of several hundred thousand roubles.[3]

The mensheviks did not exploit their majority at the Fourth Congress and made little attempt to assert their predominance over the bolsheviks. After the Congress their aims remained conciliation and unity. They took no steps to counter the disorganizing activity of the bolsheviks, and none to assert ideological leadership. *Sotsial-Demokrat*, the central organ of the party, with its all-menshevik editorial board (which included Martov and Dan), never sought to speak in the name of the whole party for fear of exacerbating factionalism. The openly factional *Proletarii*, which Lenin controlled through the Petersburg committee, was tolerated without protest, and apparently without suspicion. Confident that unity had been achieved, the mensheviks maintained no separate organization. For the most part, they failed to discern, or at any rate to attach importance to, bolshevik tactics. 'The bolsheviks behave as if the split were already achieved,'

---

[1] See, for example, *Proletarskaia revoliutsiia*, No. 58, 1926, pp. 11–12; B. Bibineishvili, *Kamo*, Moscow, 1934; N. Krupskaia, *Vospominaniia o Lenine*, Moscow, 1932, pp. 116, 161–2; S. M. Pozner (ed.), *Protokoly pervoi konferentsii voennykh i boevykh organizatsii R.S.-D.R.P.*, Moscow, 1932, pp. 341–3. And see L. Martov, *Spasiteli ili uprazdniteli* (Kto i kak razrushal R.S.-D.R.P.), Paris, 1911, pp. 17–19.

[2] Based largely on unpublished sources collected in several MS. studies prepared by Mr B. I. Nicolaevsky. These MS. studies, which I was enabled to use by the courtesy of the late Mr Nicolaevsky and of the Research Program on the History of the CPSU, contain not only a fund of information on published materials relating to the period, but also a large number of documents reprinted from various public and private archives which have never been published. I have drawn freely on these studies in this and following chapters, and take this opportunity to acknowledge my debt of gratitude to Mr Nicolaevsky and to the Research Program.

[3] This is the figure given by Bogdanov in his polemical leaflets and pamphlets, issued after his break with Lenin in 1909.

Plekhanov commented to Aksel'rod in January 1907, 'while the mensheviks behave as if it will never take place.'[1] Probably the majority of mensheviks, like the bolsheviks, still believed that a new uprising was imminent, and that the task of all social democrats was to prepare for it. For this, unity was the first aim.

The difference of outlook between Lenin and the menshevik leaders became evident as soon as the question arose of the policy to be adopted towards the First Duma. Lenin's view was not in doubt. The Duma, with its strong *Kadet* leadership, was counter-revolutionary: it was only a matter of time before the *Kadety* would reveal the true meaning of their fine phrases about freedom and reform, and would make a deal with the autocracy at the expense of the workers. Participation in the elections had been a mistake anyway, in his opinion. Instead of encouraging 'constitutional illusions', social democrats should be spending their time organizing fighting detachments and training for insurrection. But now that there was in fact a social democrat contingent inside the Duma, its task should be to devote its energies to exposing the hypocrisy of the *Kadety*.[2] The behaviour of the *Kadety* during the three months of the First Duma's existence bore little relationship to Lenin's prognosis. The *Kadety* did not make a deal with the autocracy, but on the contrary rejected such overtures as were made towards compromise. Before the Duma opened on 10 May (27 April) 1906 its legislative powers, as outlined in the manifesto of 17 October, had been curtailed. The *Kadety*, flushed with the confidence which the electorate had shown in them, were determined to demand full constitutional government, with a ministry responsible to the Duma, and would be satisfied with nothing less. Their intransigent attitude soon led to a deadlock, which was solved by the Emperor dissolving the Duma on 8 July. Historians will long debate the question whether this fatal set-back to the development of constitutional government in Russia was due more to the hostility of the monarchy to a limitation of its powers which it accepted against its will, or to the failure of the *Kadety* to accept progress towards liberty by stages.[3]

After the arrival of the Caucasian delegates, the mensheviks inside

---

[1] *Perepiska*, volume II, pp. 228–9.

[2] See the draft resolution on the Duma, proposed by Lenin at the Fourth Party Congress in 1906, but rejected by its menshevik majority, *KPSS v rez.*, volume I, pp. 114–16.

[3] For the latter view see, for example V. Leontovitsch, *Geschichte des Liberalismus in Rusiland*, Frankfurt, 1957, and V. A. Maklakov, *Vlast i obshchestvennost' na zakate staroi Rossii.* (Vospominaniia sovremennika). Three volumes, Paris, 1936. For the former view see P. N. Miliukov, *Vospominaniia* (1895–1917). Two volumes New York, 1955.

the Duma organized a 'fraction', totalling eighteen, including the Georgian leaders I. Ramishvili and N. Zhordania. The 'fraction' voluntarily put itself under the direction and discipline of the Central Committee.[1] But the social democrats played little part in the First Duma. Consistently with their theory they should have supported the *Kadety*, up to the point of establishing a full 'bourgeois democratic' government and thus accomplishing the first phase of the revolution. Plekhanov logically summed up his view of what the policy should be in the phrase: 'Join for the kill, then go your separate ways.' But few of the mensheviks in the Duma were disciplined or consistent enough to see tactics in this light. To them the Duma was merely a forum from which mass revolt could be fomented. They took for granted that the Emperor was waiting for a chance to destroy the Duma. They believed that the Duma would prove a rallying point for mass action since the workers would rise in its defence. Instead of co-operating with the *Kadety*, as often as not they devoted themselves to empty rhetoric, blaming the *Kadety* for not being what they never pretended to be – uncompromising revolutionaries. They therefore spent their time trying to drive the *Kadety* even further to the left than this quite radical, and incidentally, like the social democrats, still unlegalized, party was prepared to go. This was not very different from Lenin's point of view, and indeed Lenin agreed that the social democratic deputies 'had adopted a correct attitude' on the whole.[2]

Since there were no bolsheviks in the Duma, the tactics of the social democratic 'fraction' can properly be regarded as those of the mensheviks. The menshevik deputies in the Duma were in fact carrying out the resolution supported by the menshevik majority at the Fourth Congress, which enjoined them to 'drive the bourgeois parties further to the left' by their criticism inside the Duma, and thereby to fan the flames of revolution.[3] But the mensheviks also believed it was their duty to support the *Kadety* in all activity designed to consolidate the 'bourgeois revolution'. Few of them appear to have reflected in those turbulent days that the two aims were in practice incompatible. In June 1906 the Central Committee declared its support for the Duma in all activity aimed at forcing the autocracy to grant a government of ministers responsible to the Duma. When, after the dissolution of the Duma, some two hundred deputies, mostly *Kadety*,[4] travelled to Vyborg in Finland and issued an appeal calling for a nation-wide

---

[1] Balabanov i Dan, *op. cit.*, pp. 96–8.
[2] *Lenin*, volume IX, p. 392.
[3] *KPSS v rez.*, volume I, pp. 127–8.
[4] But social democrats also signed the manifesto.

campaign of passive resistance, the mensheviks capped this by calling for a general strike. The response to these appeals was eloquent proof of the illusions shared by bolsheviks and most mensheviks alike that the revolutionary wave was still rising. There were two sporadic revolts in the fleet, which were quickly suppressed, and which were probably unconnected with the appeal; and some 80,000 stopped work for a day in Petersburg.

The June 1906 resolution of the Central Committee declaring support for the Duma in its conflict with the autocracy was used by Lenin to drive a further wedge between the two factions in the party. Lenin argued that the policy of the Fourth Congress was directed at the overthrow of the Duma, and not at making it work. (He omitted to mention that the resolution of the Congress on the Duma had also enjoined the social democratic deputies to 'exacerbate the conflict between the Duma and the government'. Nothing was more calculated to do this than a demand for a responsible ministry.) Talk of discipline, Lenin continued, was mere 'sophistry'. He now induced the bolshevik-dominated Petersburg Committee to pass a resolution of protest against the tactics of the Central Committee, thus bringing the Petersburg Committee and the Central Committee into head-on collision. Furthermore, at a subsequent local party conference he put through another resolution demanding that a new congress should meet as soon as possible 'in view of the difference of opinion which has arisen between the party leadership and the majority of the party'.[1] The views of the Petersburg Committee were stated to enjoy the support of the Polish social democrats, and of certain other party organizations.

The divergence between the two party factions widened as the time for the campaign for elections to the Second Duma approached. Lenin, who in spite of his own hesitations in 1905, had hitherto defended the boycott of the elections, now suddenly changed his mind. The tactics of boycott, he wrote in September 1906, must be 'reconsidered': 'history had demonstrated' that the Duma is a valuable forum for agitation.[2] But Lenin, then almost alone among his close supporters to hold this view, was still far from agreement with the mensheviks. The latter, although not prepared to go as far as Plekhanov, who advocated a common platform with the liberals until the attainment of a Duma with full powers, were prepared to work jointly with the *Kadety* in order to keep out reactionary right-wing

[1] *Lenin*, volume IX, pp. 326–7, 473–9.
[2] *Lenin*, volume X, pp. 26–32.

candidates. They viewed such tactical agreements as part of their general mission to make the *Kadety* 'more revolutionary'.[1] The bolsheviks, in their passionate hatred of the liberals, would probably have preferred a reactionary to a liberal Duma, and occasionally got very near to saying so.[2] But in any case Lenin's views on the role of the peasants in the revolution (and possibly the common interest in 'expropriations') were drawing him very much closer to the socialist revolutionaries than to the *Kadety*. At the end of 1906 a party conference held at Tammerfors worked out a compromise solution which permitted 'local agreement with revolutionary and opposition democratic parties' at the discretion of the local organizations, provided that danger existed of a right-wing candidate's victory. But this conference, on which the mensheviks had a majority, was not prepared to pander to the vanity of the bolsheviks by passing a resolution asserting that the tactics of boycott of the First Duma had been proved correct.[3]

The electoral compromise worked well enough in most of the country, and bolsheviks and mensheviks co-operated fairly harmoniously in the electoral campaign. The local social democrats continued to display the same trend towards unity which remained natural to them so long as they were not goaded into splits and dissensions by their leaders. The campaign in Petersburg was a notable exception. Here the acrimonious disputes over electoral policies led to an open split between the bolshevik majority and the menshevik minority on the Committee.[4] The real victors in this incident were possibly the socialist revolutionaries, who carried off many of the Petersburg workers' votes.[5]

Shortly afterwards Lenin followed up this split with a vitriolic pamphlet in which he accused the mensheviks of 'treason'. He suggested that they had plotted and conspired with the *Kadety* to split the Petersburg social democrats in return for concessions to their own candidates. At this point the long-suffering Central Committee lost patience, and arraigned Lenin before a party court of honour. At the first sitting of the court Lenin boldly justified his action. 'You say to

[1] See e.g. *Sotsial-demokrat*, No. 6, 16 (3) October 1906, pp. 2–5.
[2] See *Keep*, p. 339.
[3] See *KPSS v rez.*, volume I, pp. 139–44.
[4] The whole complicated story of this electoral campaign is admirably treated in *Keep*, pp. 329–53.
[5] Martov however disagreed with Aksel'rod's view that the large S-R vote had been due to factional disputes, and attributed it to the dictatorial, and hence unpopular, methods of the social democrats inside the workers' organizations – *Pis'ma*, pp. 156–7.

me,' he told the court, '"you have sown confusion among the proletariat". I reply: I deliberately and calculatingly sowed confusion in the ranks of that part of the Petersburg proletariat which was under the leadership of the mensheviks who split off on the eve of the elections. What is more, I am determined always to act in the same way in the case of a split. It was my duty ... to break the ranks of the mensheviks who were leading the workers in the footsteps of the *Kadety*. .... Against such political opponents I waged then ... and shall *always* wage a war of *destruction*.' The hearing was adjourned, pending the then imminent meeting of the Fifth Congress, and was never resumed.[1]

The composition of the Second Duma in 1907 reflected the conflicts of the past year: while the moderates had lost, the extremists at either end had gained. The number of *Kadety* was halved, but social democrats now numbered sixty-five as compared with eighteen. Nearly one-third of the deputies were workers and peasants.[2] The Second Duma was, if possible, more hostile to the monarchy than the First, and even less willing to co-operate. But the *Kadety*, chastened by their experience, were anxious to avoid endangering the survival of the Duma by provoking further conflicts. The social democrats constituted themselves into a 'fraction', which adopted rules similar to those which had been adopted by the 'fraction' of the First Duma: the 'fraction' was to act as a party organ, under the constant leadership and control of its central institutions. Mensheviks were in the majority: thirty-six of them as against eighteen bolsheviks. The remaining eleven, without declaring for any one side, generally voted with the mensheviks. Apart from its activities in the Chamber, the 'fraction' maintained constant contact with the proletariat. It was flooded with petitions, delegations, and directives of every nature; it organized meetings and investigations. In fact, by its activities outside the Chamber the 'fraction' in the four months of its existence came near to laying the foundations of a broadly based workers' party and to providing a political organization which the workers could look upon as their own.

Inside the Chamber there was less scope for social democratic activity. Stolypin, though anxious to secure the co-operation of the Duma, was not prepared to enlarge the limits of the constitution, and

---

[1] *Lenin*, volume X, pp. 307–15; volume XI, pp. 216–28, 567. (Emphasis in the original.)
[2] For details see Alfred Levin. *The Second Duma. A Study of the Social-Democratic Party and the Russian Constitutional Experiment.* New Haven, 1940, pp. 67–9.

was moreover inhibited by the Emperor's hostility to constitution-alism. He was ready to embark on a vast programme of reforms, but at the same time made it plain that he would not shrink from stern measures to restore public order. On the other hand, there was little reason to believe that the violent and extremist left-wing parties would be restrained by anything except police action. In this atmos-phere compromise and normal parliamentary procedure had little chance of success. The *Kadety* tried to some extent to swallow their principles and to pretend that the Duma was really a parliament, in the hope that some day in the distant future the present make-believe might turn into reality. Their 'betrayal' infuriated the social demo-crats, bolshevik and menshevik alike, who denounced both the *Kadety* and the government with equal vehemence. There was usually little difference in tactics between bolshevik and menshevik deputies. The bolsheviks outside the Duma showered the 'fraction' with criticism, but no serious issues of principle were discernible in their attacks. In truth, the social democrats in the Second Duma were all faithfully following the injunctions of the Fourth Congress to make the Duma 'more revolutionary' and to expose its 'counter-revolutionary' nature in the eyes of the masses. But they failed of their purpose. They did not succeed in making either the Duma or the masses more revolu-tionary. By torpedoing the efforts of the *Kadety* and the Octobrists to save some semblance of a parliamentary régime from the wreckage of the First Duma period, they helped to precipitate a second crisis. By the end of April, if not before, the Emperor and Stolypin had decided that a pretext must be found for dissolving the Duma and for amend-ing the electoral law in such a manner as to ensure a more co-operative Third Duma.[1] A pretext would soon be found. Meanwhile, with the Duma in its death throes, the social democratic leaders were meeting in distant London for another of their interminable congresses – the Fifth in the series in bolshevik nomenclature.

The bolsheviks had begun their agitation for a Fifth Congress shortly after the end of the Fourth. The Central Committee at first opposed the suggestion. Plekhanov also argued with some force that a congress would waste both time (since a Russian congress lasted two or three times as long as that of a Western European party) and con-siderable funds; its only purpose could be to give Lenin a chance to try his luck again. But most mensheviks were hypnotized by the pros-pect of unity, and they believed that full and frank discussion of

---

[1] V. N. Kokovtsov, *Iz moego proshlago. Vospominaniia 1903–1919 g.g.*, Volume One, Paris, 1933, pp. 259 ff.

differences with the bolsheviks must bring it about. At the Tammerfors Conference at the end of 1906 they agreed that a congress should be called for the spring of 1907.

The Congress met in London on 15 May 1907. Lenin had not wasted his time, his organizing ability, or the advantage of superior financial resources which the bolshevik centre enjoyed over the mensheviks. Of the Russian delegates entitled to vote, bolsheviks now formed a slight majority: some ninety, as against some eighty-five mensheviks. Exact figures cannot be stated, since the number of delegates whose mandates were accepted by the mandates commission of the Congress kept changing throughout the Congress.[1] But the bolsheviks were more often than not sure of a majority owing to the support of the forty-five Polish and twenty-six Lettish delegates. The mensheviks could usually rely on the fifty-five votes of the *Bund* delegates. Trotsky and a few of his supporters voted independently of the factions.

The Russian delegates were said to represent about 100,000 and the representatives of the *Bund*, the Poles and the Letts another 50,000 between them. These figures were more a paper estimate than a reality, except in the case of the *Bund* and of a few well-established organizations, like that of Tiflis with its 3,300 members. Few registered members attended party meetings, and even fewer paid their dues. Analysis of the social composition of the delegates does not disclose any notable difference between bolsheviks and mensheviks, except that the menshevik delegates had mostly served longer in the party than the bolshevik. There was, however, a noticeable difference in racial composition: nearly a third of the menshevik delegates were Georgians, and many, about a fifth, were Jews – in contrast to the bolshevik delegates, of whom only one-tenth were Jews.[2] As Plekhanov had foreseen, the Congress was costly both in time and in money. Session after session was devoted to wrangles about procedural points and about the validity of delegates' mandates. The total cost of the Congress was 100,000 roubles, and at the end of it the delegates were short of £2,000 for their return journey to Russia. They were rescued by Plekhanov, who succeeded in borrowing this sum

[1] For an analysis of the strength of the two factions at different stages of the Congress see A. S. Bubnov, *VKP(b)*, Moscow, Leningrad, 1931, p. 404. The number of bolshevik voting delegates varied from 81 to 90, and of mensheviks from 80 to 85. The most recent edition of the proceedings of the Congress, published in Moscow in 1963, gives the number of bolsheviks as 89 and mensheviks as 88 – see *Piatyi (Londonstii) S"ezd RSDRP*. Aprel'–mai 1907 goda. Protokoly. Moscow, 1963, pp. xii, 621–31.

[2] This latter fact gave rise to an anti-Semitic joke, carefully recorded and republished by Stalin (who was present at the Congress as a non-voting delegate) forty years later. See *Stalin*, volume II, pp. 50–1.

from an industrialist, Joseph Fels, against a promise to repay by the end of the year signed by all the delegates. The money was repaid, after repeated demands, but not until after the 1917 revolution.

The Congress made no momentous contributions to doctrine, but it did show the deep division which now existed between the bolsheviks and the mensheviks. The bolsheviks proposed a resolution censuring the Central Committee during the past year for failing to express the will of the party; however, the Poles voted with the mensheviks or abstained, and the Letts voted with the mensheviks – with the result that the resolution was rejected. But the bolsheviks were able to assert their policy on relations with the non-proletarian parties in a resolution which reflected the bolsheviks' uncompromising hostility to the *Kadety* and more sympathetic attitude towards the socialist revolutionary and populist parties. The resolution on the Duma adopted by the Congress reiterated the views which had prevailed at the Fourth Congress: the Duma was to be treated as a forum for propaganda, and in no case as a legislature. But the slogan of 'a government responsible to the Duma' was roundly condemned. The Duma 'fraction' was to remain under the direction of the Central Committee. *Sotsial-Demokrat*, which had ceased publication in December 1906, was reinstituted as the party organ, but the mensheviks lost control of it.[1]

On one question, that of 'expropriations', Lenin suffered serious defeat. Although the subject had not been openly discussed in the party hitherto, the demoralizing effects of this practice were well known, and aroused disquiet in some bolsheviks as well as in the mensheviks, the Poles, and the *Bund*. The mensheviks had the additional incentive of wishing to deprive Lenin of his most important source of funds for the bolshevik private exchequer. Their resolution on this subject was voted by the Congress by 170 votes to 35, with 52 abstentions. The resolution recited the prevalence of 'partisan attacks' on both 'government agents and representatives of the bourgeoisie' as a result of which 'expropriations of both state and private property' were increasing; it went on to condemn the demoralizing effects of this activity on party members, and the general disrepute caused to the party; and prohibited any member of the party from taking 'any part whatever' in either 'partisan' activities or in 'expropriations', or from assisting them in any way. This high majority for the resolution was

---

[1] *KPSS v rez.*, volume I, pp. 155–68; on *Sotsial-Demokrat*, which did not resume publication until February 1908, and which remained thereafter under bolshevik domination, see *Lenin*, volume XIV, p. 471.

due to the support or abstention of some Poles and some bolsheviks. Tyshka, the leader of the Polish social democrats, for example, voted for the resolution, and Zinoviev abstained. (Krasin was under arrest and was not at the Congress, Bogdanov had no vote.[1]) The Congress finally elected a Central Committee of fifteen members and twenty-two candidates. Of the members, five were bolsheviks, four were mensheviks, and the *Bund*, the Poles and the Letts contributed two each. Thus the Central Committee reflected the uneasy compromise which the newly joined national parties were at this date trying to effect.[2] The Congress had not ended in complete victory for Lenin, in spite of its bolshevik majority. Above all, he had failed to secure control of the Central Committee, since the five bolshevik members could only out-vote the four mensheviks and the two *Bund* members with the support of the Poles and the Letts. The Congress concluded on 1 June 1907, within a few weeks of a crisis inside Russia which was to create very different conditions for the social democrats from those envisaged in London.

On 3 June 1907 the Emperor issued a manifesto dissolving the Second Duma and promulgating a new electoral law under which the suffrage was considerably restricted. The immediate occasion for the dissolution was the refusal of the Duma (including the *Kadet* deputies) to waive the immunity of the members of the social democratic 'fraction', and to surrender them for trial on a charge of fomenting an uprising among the armed forces. The alteration of the suffrage was avowedly in violation of the fundamental law establishing the Duma, according to which no change in the electoral laws could be made without the assent of the Duma. The dissolution was accompanied by the arrest of most of the social democratic deputies, and by widespread arrests of social democrats and socialist revolutionaries throughout the country. It was an openly avowed *coup d'état*.

The trial of the social democratic deputies was held in secret, the evidence adduced included that of a police informer and was in part manufactured, and the sentences were severe. Moreover, in indicting the entire 'fraction' the government was largely visiting the sins of the more revolutionary bolsheviks upon the heads of the somewhat more constitutional mensheviks. On the other hand no government can be blamed for taking steps to restrain even members of the legislature from inciting to disaffection in the armed forces, and there is little doubt but that the social democratic party as a whole was engaged in

---

[1] *KPSS v rez.*, volume I, pp. 168–9; *Protokoly V*, pp. 609–10.
[2] For names see *Protokoly V*, p. 786.

just this. The Duma 'fraction' was a party organ, under the direction of the Central Committee and subject to party discipline. It was now saddled with responsibility for the policy of the party as a whole. The accused deputies maintained in their defence that an armed uprising was foreign to Marxist doctrine, which looked to the future revolution as an historical process which would inevitably, but without any conspiracy or preparation, lead to a clash with the state. This may have been true of Western European Marxism: it was certainly not true of Russian social democracy as a whole. At the Fourth Congress both bolsheviks and mensheviks had voted a resolution that an armed uprising was 'inevitable' and that the main task of the party was agitation among all sections of the population, including in particular the army, in order to ensure the success of the rising. The party maintained a wide network of organizations among the soldiers, and published some twenty illegal soldiers' periodicals and newspapers. The sole aim of this propaganda effort was to cause disaffection. This military organization was by 1907 in fact almost entirely under bolshevik control.[1] Agitation in the armed forces went side by side with the technical task of organizing the fighting detachments, on which Lenin placed considerable reliance not only for the eventual armed rising, but for the immediate task of 'expropriations'. At the end of 1906 a conference of 'Military and Fighting Organizations' had met in Tammerfors. It was all-bolshevik in composition, and met in defiance of the Central Committee. It adopted a series of revolutionary resolutions, any one of which was sufficient to establish complicity in a conspiracy to overthrow the government.[2] It was true that some mensheviks were beginning to think in terms of a social democratic party which, in conjunction with the liberals, would by political pressure force the monarchy to yield on the issue of a government responsible to the Duma. But in June 1907 they were still organizationally, and often temperamentally, linked with the bolsheviks, whose sole concern was to promote another armed uprising. For this they paid the penalty in the trial of the social democratic 'fraction' of the Duma.

The government expected the dissolution of the Duma to be followed by a general strike and an armed rising.[3] But, as it turned out,

[1] According to one estimate, there were some fifty organizations of revolutionaries active among the armed forces in 1905–6, and the majority were bolshevik. See S. E. Rabinovich, *Vserossiiskaia voennaia konferentsiia bol'shevikov 1917 goda*, Moscow, 1931, p. 8.
[2] *KPSS v rez.*, volume I, pp. 145–54.
[3] See a circular of the police department of the Ministry of the Interior, No. 7643 of 19 April 1907, in the Library of Congress.

Stolypin's move was received by the public with apathy and indiffer-ence. In the course of the next few months the social democratic achievements of 1905 were systematically swept away. Numerous arrests and even more frequent resignations decimated the party committees. The legal newspapers which had survived since 1905 were closed down. Once again the party leaders went into emigration. The policy of revolution at all costs had proved completely bankrupt.

VI   Towards the Final Split

Immediately after the dissolution of the Second Duma in June 1907, the question arose of the policy to be adopted in the elections to the Third Duma. At a party conference held at the beginning of August 1907, Lenin, now convinced of the error of boycott, found himself in a minority of one among the bolsheviks. In contrast to his colleagues, who still clung to the hope that a new uprising was imminent, and regarded participation in the Duma as a brake on revolutionary ardour, Lenin now foresaw a period of preparation in which the Duma could play a useful part as a platform for propaganda. His views were contested by Bogdanov, who had hitherto supported him. It was the beginning of the end of the partnership. Lenin found himself voting for participation in the elections with mensheviks and the Polish, Lettish and *Bund* delegates.[1]

The new Duma met on 1 November 1907. The effects of the revised electoral law were clearly evident in its composition. The majority of the deputies were right-wing, or liberal-conservative Octobrists. Of the radicals, the *Kadety* now numbered only fifty-four, the social democrats eighteen. The great majority of the latter were mensheviks. Of the five bolsheviks, one, V. E. Shurkhanov, was an agent of the police. During the years which followed the *coup d'état* of June 1907 the social democratic 'fraction' could at most use the Duma as the one permitted forum from which it could criticize the government without restraint and voice socialist doctrines. The fleeting opportunity which the Second Duma had presented for making the 'fraction' the focal point of a new, legal mass movement was gone and also whatever hope there may have been of forcing the monarchy to accept the principle of a government responsible to the Duma. For almost five years the 'fraction' fought to voice its views, under constant fire from two sides. Inside the Chamber the social democrats suffered abuse from the now much more numerous right-wing reactionaries;

---

[1] There are no verbatim reports of this conference or of the one which preceded it in Petersburg, but accounts based on police agents' reports are reprinted in *Lenin* volume XII, pp. 452–4. For the resolution – see *KPSS v rez.*, volume I, pp. 173–8.

outside it, from the bolsheviks, who for the most part had not been reconciled to the abandonment of the boycott forced upon them by Lenin.

The 'fraction' clashed from the outset with the new Central Committee, which attempted to assert its control. But the deputies, remembering the fate which had befallen their predecessors in the Second Duma, felt safer without any formal link with the controlling organs of the party. They adopted a resolution that the 'fraction' was an 'autonomous group', which, while listening attentively to the voice of the party, took its decisions independently.[1] The Central Committee returned to the attack at a plenary meeting in August 1908, and again at a party conference at the end of the year. On both occasions resolutions were passed placing the 'fraction' under the control of the Central Committee. At the conference the small menshevik contingent fought valiantly in defence of the 'fraction' and succeeded in toning down some of the harsher condemnations emanating from the bolsheviks.[2] But the question had already become academic. For the Central Committee and the bulk of the party organization was by 1908 in process of disintegration, and the 'fraction' was thereafter left largely to its own devices.

For some four or five years the plight of the party organization was to be pitiable. Before long the membership of Russian underground committees, nominally a hundred thousand strong in 1907, declined drastically. The decline was less severe in the Caucasus. In the course of one year after the Fifth Congress, in many committees where membership had been reckoned in hundreds it was now reckoned in 1910 at ten thousand, and this was probably an over-estimate.[3] In the summer of 1909 only five or six bolshevik committees in all were functioning regularly in Russia.[4] The principal reason for this decline was a combination of apathy and intensified government repression, and both bolshevik and menshevik committees, where they remained separate, were affected. But in general the bolsheviks tended to leave party work for a long time (many returned in 1917). In contrast, mensheviks usually tried to throw themselves into work in such of the trade unions or other worker organizations as were still tolerated. Since trade unions, although technically legal, led a precarious life

---

[1] *Pis'ma*, p. 189.

[2] See *KPSS v rez.*, volume I, pp. 188–9; *Otchet kavkazskoi delegatsii ob obshchepartiinoi konferentsii . . .*, Paris, 1909, pp. 13–27; *KPSS v rez.*, volume I, pp. 198–201.

[3] *Proletarii*, No. 30, 23, (10) May 1908; *Pravda*, No. 2, 16 (3) April, 1910 p. 3.

[4] *Protokoly soveshchaniia razshirennoi redaktsii 'Proletariia' 1909 g.*, Moscow, 1934, p. 139. (Cited hereafter as *Protokoly soveshchaniia*.)

and were invariably closed down if their connexion with any under-ground social democratic committee became known to the police,[1] the mensheviks had an additional incentive for severing their contacts with moribund underground committees.

June 1907 proved more of a watershed to the mensheviks than it did to the bolsheviks. Lenin's confident expectation of revolution had betrayed him: but he had laid the foundations of his organization. Even if he did not say so in terms, his idea of the next phase of the revolution was much closer to a proletarian and peasant uprising than to the more orthodox 'bourgeois democratic' phase. Since this could not in his view be allowed to follow its own spontaneous course, it required the leadership of a disciplined and devoted band of pro-fessional revolutionaries who would do the right thing at the right moment. Lenin had when necessary not hesitated to be disloyal and destructive – but he had been consistent. The mensheviks, on the other hand, had fallen between two stools. They believed that the principles of scientific Marxism could be applied in Russia, but they hankered after an immediate revolution, and in the end they lost both. As Marxists they dreamt of a mass proletarian party on the Western European model. Yet they were only human, and goaded to exaspera-tion by their hatred and distrust of the government. Hence, as ultra-revolutionaries, they worked to destroy and discredit the first steps towards that constitutional government in Russia which in the countries of Western Europe had made possible the emergence of mass social democratic parties. During the five years 1908 to 1912 Lenin could, for all his disappointment, continue where he had left off. The mensheviks were now forced to reconsider the object of their existence.

Broadly four groups of mensheviks can be distinguished during this period. There were the influential Georgians, notably N. Zhordania and N. Ramishvili, in the underground Caucasian committee (apart from E. P. Gegechkori and N. S. Chkheidze in the Duma). The con-ditions in which the Caucasians worked were different from those which the Russians had to face, and their outlook was not always identical with that of their colleagues. Next, there was a group of intellectuals inside Russia, of whom the leading figure was A. N. Potresov, one of the most balanced, educated and intelligent of Russian social democrats. They used the limited opportunities for legally tolerated publication inside Russia to develop the theory of

---

[1] See Instructions Nos. 72182, 73614 and 73615, dated 10 May and 27 July 1907, of the Police Department of the Ministry of Interior, in the Library of Congress.

social democracy as applied to the new conditions of police repression. Thirdly there were the 'practicals', as they were called, the men whose work lay mainly in the surviving trade unions, or in other lawful workers' activities. Finally, there were the leaders in emigration – Martov, Dan, Aksel'rod, and for a short time Plekhanov. By January 1908 the menshevik leaders abroad had succeeded in obtaining some financial backing from wealthy sympathizers, and at a conference at the end of the month decided to found a paper, *Golos Sotsial-Demokrata* (The Voice of the Social Democrat). Plekhanov, unable to attend through illness, was fully in sympathy with this first step towards ensuring 'the triumph of social democratic principles over bolshevik Bakuninism'.[1] The founding of this newspaper was an important step for the mensheviks, who had lost their control over the party paper, *Sotsial-Demokrat*.

Although there were to be differences of opinion between leading mensheviks on many matters in the years to come, they evolved a basic doctrine on the tasks of social democracy which won fairly general acceptance among their followers. Since this doctrine has so far in histories of the party mostly received recognition in the distorted form in which bolshevik polemics have treated it – as a policy of 'liquidating' the underground party and of restricting themselves to legally permitted activity – it is worth examining what it really was. Fundamental to the new view was the recognition that the revolution which began in 1905, but which was never completed, was in essence a bourgeois democratic revolution. It had failed, because a bourgeois democratic régime had not evolved from it. The main reason for the failure had been the fact that the bourgeois liberal parties had not proved strong enough to press the revolution to its logical end by assuming power. By implication this was a belated recognition that Plekhanov had been right when during the period of the first two Dumas he had urged in vain the need to give full support to the liberals in their efforts to achieve a responsible government.

In the light of this reassessment, the mensheviks now began to reconsider the role which the social democratic party should play. Most of them were agreed that the function of the old, secret underground committees, geared towards organizing insurrection, and with but slender contacts with the day-to-day activities and interests of the workers, was now spent. As Potresov repeatedly emphasized, there was in reality no party in existence, and never had been in the sense in

---

[1] *Perepiska*, volume II, p. 250; *Pis'ma*, pp. 252–5.

which Marx conceived it – only the embryo of a party. The task was to build it. This could not be achieved by attempting to restore the old, rapidly disintegrating underground committees, but only by creating a mass party, by utilizing such legal opportunities for workers' activities as still remained in order to build up a party of workers, not of professional conspirators. There were isolated individuals, or so at any rate Martov believed, who were opposed to the continued existence of any underground, illegal party. But their views did not find their way into print, and were never at any time influential, if only for the reason that those who held them broke with the party. The great majority of mensheviks recognized that in Russian conditions illegal party committees would for a long time have to continue to exist in order to support and develop lawful activity in the workers' organizations. But in order to overcome the isolation from the workers which had hitherto characterized the underground committees, they advocated joint conferences (which would have to be secret) of all party members, both those engaged in lawful activity, and those working underground.[1] Another motive behind the advocacy of such conferences was the belief that much of the dissension between bolsheviks and mensheviks could be overcome if once the bolshevik members could be freed from the conspiratorial atmosphere in which their leaders endeavoured to preserve them.

Aside from questions of doctrine, many mensheviks were by 1908 heartily sick of bolshevik tactics, and particularly of 'expropriations', which were now beginning seriously to discredit the party. For the secrecy hitherto shrouding this subject had been rudely shattered. In defiance of the ban imposed by the Fifth Congress, the bolsheviks had not disbanded Krasin's organization for 'expropriations', and on 13 June 1907 a particularly daring bank robbery had taken place in Tiflis. Organized by Krasin, it had been carried out by the Caucasian bolshevik bandit Kamo, whose courage and personal devotion to the cause he believed in almost made him a legendary figure. The Tiflis robbery yielded 341,000 roubles, most of them in 500-rouble notes, of which the numbers were known to the police. Subsequent attempts to change these notes abroad led to arrests and publicity in which for the first time the Russian social democrats were openly implicated in a robbery.[2] The effect on the mensheviks was electric. Plekhanov urged

[1] For the most complete statement of the menshevik view on organizational questions at this period see *Otchet kavkazskoi delegatsii*, pp. 28–45.
[2] For the story of Kamo and the Tiflis robbery see Bertram D. Wolfe, *Three Who Made a Revolution. A Biographical History*. London, 1956, chapter xxii, which is based on the available evidence in memoirs, etc.

the need for a complete break with the bolsheviks, and the first issue of *Golos Sotsial-Demokrata* in February 1908 stated in its editorial that either the party must destroy 'this camarilla', or 'the camarilla' will end by destroying the party.[1] Many bolsheviks, too, were shocked by the incident, and Lenin himself, possibly with the reaction of German social democratic opinion in mind, began to reconsider the advisability of remaining associated with the two men most closely concerned in the policy of 'expropriations', Krasin and Bogdanov.

At the conclusion of the Fifth Congress a new enlarged Bolshevik Centre had been set up, in anticipation, as Zinoviev later described it, that the 'shot-gun marriage' with the mensheviks would not last.[2] The fifteen members who composed it were far from united. Bogdanov and another member, Marat (V. L. Shantser), were opposed to Lenin on the issue of participation in the Duma. Of the remaining twelve, only two, I. F. Dubrovinskii (Innokentii) and L. B. Kamenev, had sided with Lenin on the issue of 'expropriations' at the Fifth Congress. Before long it was to become apparent that several members of the Centre, notably Dubrovinskii, V. P. Nogin and A. I. Rykov, did not support Lenin in his efforts to bring about a final break with the mensheviks, but were anxious for reunification. For the next few years this Centre, thinly disguised as the enlarged editorial board of the bolshevik newspaper, *Proletarii*, functioned abroad as the directing leadership of the bolsheviks.

The Central Committee representation in Russia virtually disintegrated in the course of 1908. The party had designated a small sub-committee of Central Committee members to work inside Russia. But of the sub-committee of five, set up in August 1908, there was before long only one left at liberty, and he only escaped arrest for a few months thereafter. The full meeting of the Central Committee or Plenum, consisting of all members who were either living abroad or who could make the illegal journey from Russia, with the candidate members replacing the members who could not attend, could only meet abroad. But the Plenum, with its compromise composition of bolsheviks, mensheviks and representatives of the national parties, was paralysed by dissensions.

The scandal raised by the Tiflis robbery contributed to these dissensions in the Central Committee. Nor were relations rendered more

---

[1] See *Materialy*, p. 175; *Perepiska*, volume II, pp. 250–1; for Plekhanov's views as early as March 1907 see *ibidem*, p. 170.
[2] *Protokoly V*, p. 264; G. Zinoviev, *Istoriia R.K.P.(b)*, p. 129.

harmonious by the split in the hitherto united Baku party organization which Dzhugashvili (Stalin) successfully engineered at the end of 1907. At the beginning of 1908 Lenin and the bolsheviks were unable to control the Central Committee, because of the uncertain support of the Lettish and Polish representatives. Hence, in a series of meetings abroad during the next few months of 1908 the Central Committee condemned 'expropriations', denied its responsibility for the Tiflis scandal, and ordered both an investigation on the spot into the Tiflis and Baku scandals and a general investigation into 'expropriations' by the executive of the émigré party groups, the so-called Central Bureau of Emigré Organizations, on which the mensheviks were in a majority.[1] The investigation, which was conducted by G. V. Chicherin (the future People's Commissar for Foreign Affairs, then a menshevik), was obstructed by the two bolshevik members of the Central Bureau of Emigré Organizations, mainly on the pretext that the enquiry endangered the security of the party. This was somewhat ironical, because one of the two bolshevik members, Zhitomirskii, was later discovered to be an agent of the police. By August 1908, however, Lenin had won the support of both the Polish and Lettish members of the Central Committee, and with their help was able to put an end to the unwelcome investigation. At a meeting of the Central Committee, after various condemnatory resolutions attacking the mensheviks had been passed, the investigation was transferred to a new sub-committee headed by Zinoviev, which effectively stifled further action.[2]

The support of the Lettish members on an issue of this kind was not surprising, since the Lettish party was not only implicated in 'expropriations', but was also in receipt of a subsidy from the private funds of the Bolshevik Centre. But the change of view of the Polish social democrats was more dramatic. As recently as April 1908 their leader, Tyshka, who had taken an active part in the investigation, had been whole-heartedly in favour of a full and free enquiry. Although the other leading Polish social democrat, Rosa Luxemburg, had supported Lenin at the Fifth Congress on the issue of armed uprising, the Poles in general, since the Congress, had adopted an attitude of neutrality as between the Russian factions. That they should now have thrown in their lot with Lenin was due to several reasons. One was the

---

[1] The decisions of the Central Committee of early 1908 are in unpublished minutes which were made available to me by the late Mr Nicolaevsky.

[2] See *KPSS v rez.*, volume I, p. 190; see *ibidem*, p. 208, for a reference to a protest at the end of the year by the Caucasian organization against the stifling of the investigation.

financial support which they too were getting from the well-stocked exchequer of the Bolshevik Centre. The other was their need for an ally against their rival faction in Poland, the Polish socialist party (PPS), with whom the mensheviks were in fairly close relations. In spite of their 'tartar-mongolian savagery' – so Rosa Luxemburg wrote privately to Tyshka a little later – the bolsheviks were the more valuable side to back from the Polish point of view.[1] For the next three years the services of Tyshka (*'la miniature Ausgabe de Net-schaeff'*, as Plekhanov, who detested him, had described him to Engels) were to prove of the greatest importance to Lenin.

Although Lenin had thus successfully suppressed the unwelcome investigation into bolshevik finances, he nevertheless decided to break with the policy of 'expropriations', and with Bogdanov and Krasin who had been the main instruments in carrying it out. But these two, as technical managers of the robberies and as the financial officers of the Bolshevik Centre, retained control of the proceeds which formed the bulk of the bolsheviks' capital resources. A fortuitous circumstance enabled Lenin to look elsewhere for the building up of a new exchequer, which would not be controlled by Bogdanov and Krasin. In the course of 1906 a wealthy student, one N. P. Shmidt, of social democratic leanings, then in prison, bequeathed a large fortune to the social democratic party, and shortly afterwards committed suicide. Since the party was at that date nominally united, the bolsheviks were not solely entitled to this inheritance. However, since the executrices of Shmidt were two young sisters it proved comparatively easy to exert pressure upon them. Each was in due course wooed by a bolshevik, the elder in marriage, the younger outside wedlock. When the husband of the elder sister broke with the bolsheviks, and proved obstinate over handing over more than a portion of the estate, the lover of the younger eventually succeeded, by methods which (according to Martov, confirmed from bolshevik memoirs) included threats of violence, in diverting the whole of the estate to the bolshevik exchequer. The man who played the useful part of the lover was a newcomer in the Bolshevik Centre since the Fifth Congress, Victor Taratuta.[2] He had also been since that date, 1907, a candidate member of the Central Committee. All these operations took some time. But in the course of 1908 part of this money became available to Lenin, and

---

[1] *Protokoly soveshchaniia*, pp. 126, 260–3; Tyshka's views appear from a letter dated 11 April 1908, in the archives of G. Aleksinskii in Columbia University Library.

[2] See Wolfe, *op. cit.*, chapter xxii; Martov, *Spasiteli ili uprazdniteli*, pp. 20–1, 22–7.

since his correspondence shows that by mid-1909 the bolsheviks were once again in possession of ample funds[1] it would appear that the whole of the Shmidt inheritance had by that time been realized. The total sum received by the bolsheviks is stated by a communist historian to have amounted to 'about 280,000 roubles'.[2]

This substantial capital was to be the subject of acrimonious dispute for years to come. Together with his other assets, such as the proceeds of former 'expropriations' still unspent, it gave Lenin a great advantage over the impoverished mensheviks in providing him with wages for his professional agents, for the subsidy of allies like the Poles, for the expenses of more intensive propaganda and for more effective control over elections. Lenin was successful in keeping these new funds out of the control of Krasin and Bogdanov. In August 1908 the Bolshevik Centre replaced Bogdanov and Krasin by a new financial commission headed by Zinoviev. Its other members were Krupskaia, Taratuta and the police agent Zhitomirskii.[3]

This important move was only part of a surgical operation performed by Lenin in the course of 1908 and 1909 for the elimination of inconvenient allies. An ultra-left wing had been forming within the bolshevik faction for some time. In the political sphere this left wing, when its efforts to put through a boycott of the elections had failed, had taken up an attitude of extreme hostility to the Duma 'fraction'. It included Bogdanov, Lunacharskii, the future People's Commissar for Education, and G. Aleksinskii, who had been a deputy in the Second Duma – one of the few to escape Stolypin's round-up in June 1907. In May 1908 these left-wing trends had found expression in a resolution adopted at a conference of bolsheviks in Moscow criticizing the conduct of the 'fraction' in the sharpest terms. A substantial number of those present at the conference, nearly half, went so far as to demand the recall of the social democratic delegates from the Duma. Bogdanov, Aleksinskii and Marat, the ideological leaders of these hotheads, did not go so far as to demand recall, but urged the need for serving an 'ultimatum' on the 'fraction' calling upon it to mend its ways.[4] These extreme views in the party acquired the party

---

[1] *Lenin*, volume XXVIII, p. 546; cf. *Protokoly soveshchaniia*, p. 135, from which it appears that in June 1909 the realization of the balance of the inheritance, 125,000 roubles, was imminent. In the spring of 1908 the bolsheviks were short of money (see *Lenin*, volume XXVIII, pp. 539, 542), hence the inference is that funds became available during the interval.

[2] Em. Iaroslavskii, *Ocherki po istorii V.K.P.(b)*, volume I, Moscow, 1937, p. 204.

[3] *Protokoly soveshchaniia*, p. 284, note 127 (the fifth member, Kotliarenko, was responsible for illegal transport.)

[4] See *Lenin*, volume XII, pp. 507–9, 511–12.

nicknames, respectively, of 'otzovism' ('recallism') and 'ultimatism'. But the views of the left-wing ideologists were not confined to ultra-revolutionary fears of allowing the proletariat to be lulled by 'constitutional illusions'. For Bogdanov, a physician and a philosopher of distinction, was also the leader of an intellectual group, which included Maxim Gorky and Lunacharskii. The members of this group, although in no way agreed on all points, shared a readiness to modernize Marxism by the infusion of new, contemporary ideas into it. Lunacharskii and the literary members of the group evolved a pseudo-religious proletarian mystique of the 'collectivity' as the religion of the future, which acquired the name of 'God-construction'. Bogdanov expounded philosophical views on the nature of sense-perceptions which a number of Marxists, Plekhanov and Martov included, had already attacked as contrary to historical materialism since he first made them public early in the century. Krasin, although essentially a practical man, must also be included in Bogdanov's group because of close friendship with him, and with Gorky and Lunacharskii.[1]

Lenin had always disagreed with Bogdanov's philosophical views and may well, as he later asserted[2] have already before 1909 refuted them in writing, but failed to publish his writings for lack of time. By common consent philosophy had hitherto been regarded as irrelevant, neutral ground. As one of the prime movers of the Third Congress and as one of the editors of the bolshevik paper, *Vperëd*, and later as the organizer of 'expropriations', Bogdanov had worked closely with Lenin without a thought for philosophical disagreements. Lenin had even ridiculed Plekhanov's attempts to discredit Bogdanov for philosophical views which, according to Lenin, were 'completely irrelevant to the question of the social revolution'.[3]

Early in 1908 the first issue of *Proletarii* to appear abroad after the closing down of the socialist papers in Russia carried an announcement that questions of philosophy were a matter of individual opinion.[4] But by that date relations between Lenin on the one hand, and Krasin and Bogdanov on the other, were already very strained. The fact that Krasin was equally involved suggests that the quarrel

[1] For Lunacharskii's views see his *Religiia i sotsializm*, the first part of which was published in 1908. For a summary of Bogdanov's philosophical views see Gustav A. Wetter, *Der Dialektische Materialismus*, seine Geschichte und sein System in der Sowjetunion, Freiburg, 1952, pp. 102–5. (An English translation of this standard work was published in New York and in London in 1959.)
[2] *Lenin*, volume XXVIII, p. 528.
[3] *Protokoly III*, p. 217.
[4] *Lenin*, volume XXVIII, p. 531–2.

had little connexion with the nature of sense-perceptions. It is more probable that one of the main subjects of dispute was the question of the further disposal of the proceeds of the Tiflis robbery, which Bogdanov and Krasin wanted to use for an attempt to rescue Kamo from prison. But none of this aspect of the quarrel was made public. The dispute was throughout presented as one on issues of ideology. Lenin, anxious not to quarrel with Gorky, took pains to explain why it was now necessary to break with the heretical opinions of Gorky's friend Bogdanov in a lengthy correspondence. Gorky was unconvinced, and the two remained slightly estranged for over a year. But Gorky understood little of politics, had a great admiration for Lenin, and seems to have borne him no ill will for the attacks on his friends.

By the middle of 1908 Lenin had ousted Bogdanov from the editorial board of *Proletarii*. On 23 February 1909 Bogdanov and Krasin were in effect expelled from the bolshevik faction when the Bolshevik Centre voted to condemn them for misappropriating party funds.[1] This accusation, which was made in secret, was immediately followed by a public attack on Bogdanov's philosophical views in *Proletarii*, in violation of the truce on philosophical questions. Thus the public quarrel on philosophy was not unconnected, so far as *Proletarii* was concerned, with the private quarrel on money. In the course of 1908 Lenin had gone to London to work in the library of the British Museum on his main attack on the views of Bogdanov and Lunacharskii which appeared in the spring of 1909 under the title *Materialism and Empiriocriticism*. The public break came in June 1909 at a meeting of the Bolshevik Centre, or, as it called itself, the enlarged editorial board of *Proletarii*. This conference denounced 'otzovism' and 'ultimatism', condemned Bogdanov and Lunacharskii for their opinions, and formally expelled Bogdanov. No mention was made either of Krasin or of money. In the event, considerable sums of money did remain in Bogdanov's hands. The Bolshevik Centre renounced all claim to that part of the money which consisted of the Tiflis 500-rouble notes, known to the police, and which were eventually burnt.[2] But Bogdanov also apparently retained certain other funds of the Bolshevik Centre, which for years afterwards formed the subject of an acrimonious dispute between him and other members of the left group.

[1] *KPSS v rez.*, volume I, pp. 219–23; *Protokoly soveshchaniia*, pp. 159–64.
[2] Based on a letter from Bogdanov to Jan Straujan, dated 3 January 1912, in the Aleksinskii archives. See also a police report in M. A. Tsiavlovskii (editor), *Bol'sheviki. Dokumenty po istorii bol'shevizma s 1902 po 1916 god byvshago moskovskago okhrannago otdeleniia ...*, Moscow, 1918, p. 39.

Bogdanov and his group now withdrew from the bolshevik faction and formed an opposition group which chose the name of *Vperëd* – the name of the first bolshevik newspaper. In a series of spirited leaflets circulated inside the party, Bogdanov attacked the Bolshevik Centre and revealed much of the real history of the dispute which Lenin had sought to conceal behind a smokescreen of philosophy. As had once the editors of *Iskra*, Bogdanov now proceeded to accuse Lenin of doing to him what he, Bogdanov, had for years helped Lenin to do to others. *Vperëd* continued as a separate extreme left-wing group for some years to come. For a short time the group published a little periodical, but it never achieved any considerable influence. Its views were curious rather than remarkable. But it won the distinction of being the first faction in the Russian social democratic party to found a party school. The idea of founding a school originated early in 1909 with Gorky, who provided the money, and with Bogdanov. An approach was made to *Proletarii* for support, but in the state of relations which prevailed this was not likely to meet with any response. The school eventually opened in August 1909, in Capri, where Gorky was then living. In a further endeavour to keep the peace it invited the Bolshevik Centre to assume the ideological direction of the school's activities, but received no reply. The few months of the Capri school's existence were far from untroubled. Under a constant attack from *Proletarii*, it suffered from the further disadvantage that five of its thirteen pupils and one member of its Council proved to be acting in Lenin's interests, and before long organized a split in an endeavour to break up the school. However, the remaining eight pupils completed the course and were sent into Russia early in 1910. There they were promptly arrested. One of the turbulent Leninists also happened to be an agent of the police.[1]

While thus engaged in disposing of the left extremists within the bolshevik faction, Lenin had not lost sight of the main enemy, the mensheviks. The break with Bogdanov, whatever other motives may have contributed to it, also had the mensheviks in mind. For association with so eccentric a Marxist as Bogdanov left Lenin's faction open to telling attacks on the grounds of breaches of orthodoxy. In one of his letters to Gorky Lenin stresses this aspect of his dispute with Bogdanov: so far from weakening the bolsheviks, he writes in rejoinder to Gorky, a break with Bogdanov will strengthen their position. The

---

[1] *Lenin*, volume XIV, pp. 485–7; *Otchet pervoi vysshei s.-d. shkoly dlia rabochikh* (avgust-dekabr' 1909 goda), Paris, 1910, *passim*, where the documents are reprinted.

mensheviks will no longer be able to attack them on theoretical grounds, and will be reduced to politics – 'which means death to them.'[1]

From 1908 onwards Lenin's attack on the mensheviks always took the same form: they were the 'liquidators' who were striving, openly and secretly, for the disbanding of the underground party, they wanted to confine social democratic politics solely to legally permitted activity, and were thus playing into the hands of Stolypin. Since the allegation in this bald form was untrue (indeed mensheviks inside Russia were being imprisoned and exiled at least as often as bolsheviks) and there was no evidence in menshevik speeches or articles to support it, bolshevik party polemics had to be bolstered by distorting trivialities. There was some remark that Potresov was supposed to have made to Plekhanov in the *couloirs* of the Mannheim Congress of the German social democratic party in 1906. Then, there was the remark supposedly made by B. I. Gol'dman (Gorev), a menshevik member of the Central Committee, in Moscow in the spring of 1908 (he denied it) to the effect that 'it is time to disband all this'. Another favourite was a letter in which a member of the *Bund* Central Committee was supposed to have revealed to Zinoviev a menshevik 'plot' to destroy the party: the letter itself was never published, and its bolshevik interpretation was subsequently disputed both by the *Bundist* concerned, and by the mensheviks.[2] Had there existed in Russia a mature, educated workers' party this kind of chicanery would not have been worth the effort devoted to it. But the Russian committee men were for the most part ill-versed in the elements of politics: the better educated and politically mature workers left the party in disgust at the antics of their leaders, and polemics of this kind were not ill-adapted to the educational level of many of those who remained.

The allegation that the mensheviks wanted to 'liquidate' the underground party was thus an invention for the purposes of factional polemics. But it was true that they were for the most part disillusioned with the Central Committee which Lenin now controlled with the help of the Letts and Poles, and reluctant to have anything to do with it,

[1] *Lenin*, volume XXVIII, p. 536, letter of 24 March 1908. (Gorky's letters to Lenin for this period have not been published.) Several attacks on Bogdanov's views did appear in the early issues of *Golos Sotsial-Demokrata*, before the break between him and Lenin became known.

[2] See e.g. Iu. Kamenev, *Dve partii*. S. predisloviem N. Lenina, i prilozheniem pisem i zaiavlenii tt. B. Vil'iamova, Al. Vlasova, Innokentieva, E., i gruppy rabochikh. Paris 1911, pp. 202–3; *Leninskii sbornik*, volume XXV, p. 26, note 12; and cf. *Lenin*, volume XII, pp. 505–6.

and their attitude stiffened after the Central Committee had become discredited in their eyes by its action in first obstructing and then stifling the enquiry into the Tiflis robbery. One menshevik member, M. I. Broido, resigned on this issue as a protest. The other menshevik members, B. I. Gol'dman (Gorev) and A. S. Martynov, stressed in July 1908 in a circular addressed to all menshevik organizations that the Central Committee had not only brought the party into disrepute by its conduct, but that its representation inside Russia had virtually disintegrated together with the rest of the party organization there. They further argued that the reconstruction of the underground party organization was at present impossible; that a party conference was also not in present conditions possible; and that for the time being the Central Committee should, in so far as it still survived, confine its activities to the collection of information.[1] Implicit in this argument, however, was the intention to work within the limits possible in Russia for the creation of a mass, educated workers' movement, out of which in the fullness of time a new, responsible social democratic party could be formed – underground or open, or both, as the circumstances might require. The disintegration of the party was a fact and no 'liquidation' on the part of the menshevik leaders was needed to complete the process. But, since in the future reformed party which they visualized there could be no room for Lenin's conspirators and 'expropriators', it was understandable that Lenin should have devoted so much energy to attacking the mensheviks as 'liquidators'. Besides, the new organization envisaged by the mensheviks was less an organization for revolution than a mechanism for servicing lawful, social democratic activity. Revolution for them remained only the ultimate aim: for the bolsheviks it was the immediate objective. The views of Gorev and Martynov were broadly the views of Potresov and of the other leading party workers inside Russia. But some of the Caucasian leaders were not always prepared to go quite so far in jettisoning the remnants of even a discredited party organization, and of the leaders abroad Martov in particular, whose fundamental aim always remained party unity, viewed the policy of his colleagues with some suspicion.[2]

[1] This little-known document, which is important as a corrective to the usual version of 'liquidation', was published on 20 April 1910 under the title 'Neobkhodimoe dopolnenie k "dnevnikam" G. V. Plekhanova'.

[2] Cf. Martov's views at a private meeting of menshevik leaders in Paris on 6 October 1909: 'We are in the dark whether there really is a "liquidation" movement, or whether there are only words which go contrary to the old menshevik tradition'. (From a MS. minute of the meeting made by G. V. Chicherin, in the archives of I. S. Bisk, and made available to me by the late Mr Nicolaevsky.)

In the face of such waverings among his opponents, Lenin saw a chance of reconstructing his own bolshevik organization by sacrificing his left wing, and by seeking to attract to his side the 'healthy', 'party minded' and 'anti-liquidation' elements among the mensheviks – that is to say, those who still clung to the hope of rebuilding the existing underground organization. In this aim, to which he devoted the next four years, Lenin received help from a possibly unexpected quarter. At the end of 1908 Plekhanov, who had collaborated throughout the year on the menshevik *Golos Sotsial-Demokrata*, quarrelled with his colleagues. The cause of the quarrel was unrelated to the policy of the newspaper. It arose out of Plekhanov's disapproval of an article by Potresov on the origins of Russian social thought. This article was written for a collective work on the Russian social movement of which Plekhanov and Potresov were joint editors, together with Martov and the economist Maslov. The four volumes eventually published contain the most moderate and objective analysis of Russian social and political development, from the Marxist point of view, produced in Russia before or since. Plekhanov criticized Potresov's failure in his article to appreciate the importance of 'hegemony'. The real reason for the quarrel seems to have been a failure by Potresov to stress sufficiently Plekhanov's personal role in the early movement. Neither the co-editors nor Aksel'rod, who was brought into the dispute, agreed with Plekhanov's strictures. To their complete consternation, Plekhanov, when his demands for the suppression of the article were rejected, threatened to join Lenin, and to denounce them all as 'opportunists'.[1] He did not, for the time being, join Lenin, but in 1909 he restarted his *Diary of a Social Democrat* which had been suspended, and proceeded to attack his former colleagues as 'liquidators' in a manner which differed little from Lenin's. He also formed a group which he called the 'Party Mensheviks'. He remained sufficiently independent to criticize the bolsheviks on occasion, when he disapproved of their policy, but his main effort was directed against the mensheviks. His group abroad attracted few mensheviks of note. But the weight of his authority gave to the charge that the mensheviks were 'liquidators' a new and quite unwarranted reality. His support of the charge helped to discredit the mensheviks in the eyes of the German social democrats, and to sow a great deal of confusion among menshevik worker followers who understood little of

[1] There is correspondence on this quarrel in *Materialy*, pp. 186–94, and in *Perepiska*, volume II, pp. 250–1, 284–7. See also Nicolaevsky, *Potresov*, pp. 56–61. (See note 2 on p. 37 for reference.) I have also used some of Martov's unpublished letters made available to me by the late Mr Nicolaevsky.

what was happening in the party, but respected the great name of Plekhanov.

Plekhanov's conduct still remains an enigma. He may possibly, like Martov, have had genuine hesitations about jettisoning the fragments of the old organization, however discredited. But he could not have failed to be aware of the nature of the campaign which he was now supporting. His differences with Lenin were too deep to be healed by Lenin's break with Bogdanov, of whose philosophical views Plekhanov disapproved – though no doubt this was one factor which made the reconciliation with Lenin easier. Moreover, until the quarrel with Potresov, Plekhanov had worked closely with his 'liquidator' colleagues without a word of protest. According to Aksel'rod, Plekhanov had been one of the very first among the mensheviks to urge, in 1906, the need to break with the old underground party, and to create a new party subordinated to a mass workers' party.[1] But Plekhanov's character was complex and not always consistent. He was perhaps on this occasion swayed by ruffled vanity to actions which he subsequently regretted.

Trotsky also remained uncommitted to either faction. But, unlike Plekhanov, Trotsky, instead of exacerbating interfactional disputes, devoted his efforts to trying to bring about the union of all factions. From October 1908 he published in Lemberg (Lvov) and then in Vienna a newspaper, *Pravda* (The Truth), designed for illegal circulation inside Russia. The financial support came from two devoted wealthy sympathizers, A. Ioffe, who was to remain a lifelong friend of Trotsky's, and M. I. Skobelev, the son of a Baku oil magnate. Trotsky had the gift of inspiring such personal loyalties. In marked contrast to the factional newspapers, *Pravda* avoided all sharp polemics. In its endeavour to bring about party unity it devoted itself to the general problems of the workers and of social democracy, and tried to find common ground between the bolsheviks and the mensheviks. *Pravda* achieved a certain popularity among its worker readers, to whom unity among their leaders at all times seemed an obviously desirable aim. But it was the object of constant attack by the newspapers which Lenin controlled, since Lenin's aims excluded all compromise with the mensheviks as a faction.

Meanwhile Lenin was facing a more serious difficulty. He was

---

[1] According to P. A. Garvi, in his unpublished memoirs in the Archive of Russian and East European History and Culture of the Butler Library of Columbia University.

beginning to lose support within the bolshevik faction itself. For many leading bolsheviks were anxious to see a united party. These 'conciliators', as they were called, viewed with more favour the policy urged by the mensheviks since 1908 that unification should take place on the basis of joint conferences of underground and legal party workers. They included several who had been elected as members or candidates of the Central Committee at the Fifth Congress, notably Dubrovinskii, Rykov and Nogin. Modern Soviet histories, written after Stalin's conflict with the opposition in the twenties, include Zinoviev and Kamenev as 'secret' conciliators, but available evidence suggests that they were more often the most reliable supporters of Lenin's point of view, even if on occasions they intervened in an attempt to moderate his tactics.

In these circumstances the menshevik leaders were successful in calling together a Plenum of the Central Committee in Paris at the beginning of January 1910. In view of the disagreements among the bolshevik leaders, the mensheviks were confident that they would at last succeed in bringing about unity in the party. Lenin, who was opposed to this meeting, was on this occasion in a minority not only in the party as a whole, but within his own faction. The Plenum reached a compromise which can be summarized as follows:

1. The Plenum recognized that a mass party could now at last be created. To this end and to promote unity a party conference should be summoned as soon as possible. But as a preliminary, local joint conferences should be summoned of both underground and legal party workers. In a passage which carefully avoided the word 'liquidators' the resolution condemned both the extremists on the left wing of the party, and those who 'underestimate' and 'deny' the role of the underground party. This part of the Plenum's decisions was resisted by Lenin.

2. The party organs were to be reconstructed on the basis of the Central Committee as elected at the Fifth Congress. Of these members, seven (known as the 'Sem'ërka') were to operate inside Russia – two each from the two factions, and one each from the three national parties. Three mensheviks inside Russia, P. A. Garvi, K. M. Ermolaev and I. A. Isuv (all 'practicals'), were designated to nominate the two mensheviks on the 'Sem'ërka'. Abroad, the regular party organ was to be a small executive committee of the émigré organizations, known as the Foreign Bureau of the Central

Committee (*Z.B.Ts.K.*). This consisted of five members – one from each faction and one from each of the three national parties. There were also complex provisions for calling a meeting abroad of a full Plenum of the Central Committee of fifteen in certain specified circumstances.

3. The editorial board of the party newspaper, *Sotsial-Demokrat*, which Lenin had controlled since it reappeared in 1908, was re-organized with the avowed intention of making it the common mouthpiece of both factions. The bolsheviks agreed to stop *Proletarii*. The mensheviks, on the other hand, were successful in making their decision to stop *Golos Sotsial-Demokrata* dependent on *Sotsial-Demokrat* first proving itself to be a really joint organ. *Vperëd* was recognized as a 'literary group', and a subsidy was promised to *Pravda*.

4. The question of the Shmidt inheritance and the 'expropriations' gave rise to heated discussions. But eventually the spirit of compromise prevailed. The resolution adopted condemned violations of party discipline by 'certain comrades', which had, however, been due only to an 'incorrect appreciation' of the interests of the party. As for the money which remained in their hands, the bolsheviks promised to restore part of it immediately to the Central Committee. The remainder was to be handed over to three German social democrats, Franz Mehring, Klara Zetkin and Karl Kautsky, as trustees. The bolsheviks reserved the right to demand the return of the money from the trustees if the mensheviks refused to co-operate with the party organs inside Russia, or if they continued to publish their factional organ. Otherwise this portion of the money too was to be paid over to the Central Committee.[1]

This compromise depended for its success on Lenin's good faith, the impartiality of the German trustees, and the co-operation of the menshevik 'practicals'. For all their majority at the Plenum meeting, the mensheviks had not ensured either a condemnation of the anti-'liquidator' campaign in terms sufficiently strong to make it impossible for Lenin in future to use it for his object of splitting the party or succeeded in removing the ill-gotten bolshevik monies from

[1] No records of this Plenum meeting have been published. There is an incomplete and unpublished minute in the Aleksinskii archives, and an account of it in Martov's *Spasiteli ili uprazdniteli* (Paris, 1911). Further information can be culled from party polemics in *Sotsial-Demokrat* and *Golos Sotsial-Demokrata* in 1910 and 1911, and from correspondence. The account of the decisions which appeared in *Sotsial-Demokrat* is reprinted in *KPSS v rez.*, volume 1, pp. 234–43.

Lenin's actual control. Hence, the arrangements made on paper very soon proved to be worthless. For this failure at a decisive moment the menshevik leaders were not entirely responsible, because their majority depended on the support of the *Bund*, of Trotsky's group and of their Caucasian colleagues, all of whom urged compromise and conciliation. But Martov admitted in private that the bolder policy of making it impossible for Lenin to split the party would have meant 'taking the responsibility for the final wrecking of the old party institutions', and this the mensheviks felt unable to do.[1]

Events soon showed that Martov had miscalculated in supposing that the 'practicals' inside Russia could be persuaded to co-operate with bolsheviks in rebuilding the old central party organ. They did not trust Lenin, and thought that the proposed 'Sem'ërka' was doomed to be ineffective because Lenin would use it for the sole purpose of inter-factional warfare. There was another reason why the 'practicals' were not likely to be enthusiastic about the compromise. There were signs of revival of working-class activity inside Russia, after the long period of apathy, and Garvi and his colleagues were now hoping to create the kind of mass party which they did not believe could ever be created in partnership with Lenin. The first step towards implementing this policy was taken at the beginning of 1911, when a conference of 'legal party workers' decided that the time had come for the mensheviks to set up a revived underground party organization of their own in preparation for the forthcoming elections to the Fourth Duma, and for support of and for co-operation with the legal movement.[2] Such new menshevik organizations were set up in Petersburg, and in several other centres in the course of 1911, and formed the basis of the menshevik party in its revived form after 1912. The efforts to set up the 'Sem'ërka' inside Russia accordingly foundered immediately. The bolshevik members were both 'conciliators'. One of them, Nogin, whose duty it was to approach the three menshevik 'practicals' selected by the Plenum, was frank enough to tell them that in his view Lenin had no intention of allowing a joint Central Committee of bol-sheviks and mensheviks to become a reality. The three mensheviks then decided not to nominate members to the committee of seven. Their refusal was fully exploited by Lenin thereafter in order to attack the 'liquidators' for wrecking the agreement arrived at by the Plenum.

---

[1] In a letter to Potresov, of 23 February 1910, unpublished, made available to me by the late Mr Nicolaevsky.
[2] The resolutions of this conference are reprinted in *Listok Golosa Sotsial-Demokrata*, No. 1, 25 June 1911.

Martov also blamed the 'unexpected' refusal of the three for the break down of the agreement, and Aksel'rod in later years reproached Garvi, one of the three, for their decision.[1] But it is doubtful if, having regard to Lenin's scarcely disguised hostility to the compromise, the results would have been very different in the end had two mensheviks joined the 'Sem'ërka'.

The agreement on the party press remained a dead letter. Having been forced to close down *Proletarii*, Lenin was anxious to ensure that the pages of *Sotsial-Demokrat* should be available to him to continue his campaign against the 'liquidators'. His two supporters on the editorial board, Zinoviev and a Pole, gave him a majority against the two mensheviks, Martov and Dan. He immediately exploited it in order to transform what had been intended as an inter-factional organ into the mouthpiece of the bolsheviks – or more accurately, of Lenin and his immediate supporters, like Zinoviev and Kamenev. For the bolshevik faction was by 1910 already split wide open by the prevalence of 'conciliators' among it. Martov and Dan fought a losing battle on *Sotsial-Demokrat*, but were almost immediately once again restricted to *Golos Sotsial-Demokrata* for the expression of their views, and remained powerless against Lenin in influencing the contents of *Sotsial-Demokrat*. *Pravda* did not fare any better under the agreement. The subsidy was paid for a time, but before long Kamenev, designated as the Central Committee delegate on the editorial board of *Pravda*, had quarrelled with Trotsky. Since Lenin, as will be seen shortly, retained control over virtually all the funds at the disposal of the whole party, the subsidy to *Pravda* was promptly withdrawn. In the course of 1910 Lenin had renewed personal contacts with Plekhanov, which had remained severed since 1903. By exploiting Plekhanov's dislike of Trotsky, he persuaded him to join in the publication of a newspaper inside Russia to compete with *Pravda*.

The resolution on party funds was not worth the paper it was written on, and money remained a bone of contention for years. The only organ of the Central Committee in existence (since the 'Sem'ërka' had not yet been set up) was the *Z.B.Ts.K.*, and Lenin was not prepared to hand any of the money over to this body which he could not be sure of controlling. Lenin's majority on the *Z.B.Ts.K.* depended on the support of its Polish and Lettish members (since the *Bundist*

---

[1] Unpublished letter of Martov to Potresov, made available to me by the late Mr Nicolaevsky dated 17 April 1910 – cf. his article in *Golos Sotsial-Demokrata* for November 1910, 'Kuda prishli', see also *Materialy*, p. 384.

and the menshevik were unlikely to support him). How precarious this support was became evident quite early in 1910 when a newly appointed Lettish member proved to be anti-bolshevik.[1] The money which should have gone to the Central Committee therefore remained in Lenin's hands. The balance, which he had undertaken to transfer to the trustees, also remained in Lenin's name in a bank in Paris until June 1911. When soon after the Plenum the *Z.B.Ts.K.* drew the attention of the trustees to the fact that the agreement had not been fulfilled, and called upon them to take steps to have the money transferred to them, they replied somewhat tartly, through Klara Zetkin, that since Lenin had agreed to hand the money over if and when requested there was no need to insist on the transfer. It does not appear that the trustees were at any time told the precise sum which was to be handed over to them, or that they took any steps to find out.[2] Thus, until June 1911 the position remained that half the capital of over 200,000 roubles was at Lenin's unrestricted disposal, and half deposited in his name under a promise to transfer it to the three trustees if required.

At the end of 1910 Lenin precipitated a crisis by requesting the 'return' to him of the money (with which he had not so far parted) on the grounds that the mensheviks had broken the agreement arrived at in January at the Plenum. He demanded that a new Plenum of the Central Committee should meet abroad to decide the question.[3] After a good deal of conflict, it was agreed that the question whether a Plenum should be called would be decided by the Central Committee members inside Russia (the 'Sem'ërka'). But the attempt to assemble the 'Sem'ërka' (which in any case lacked menshevik members) was frustrated by the arrest of its two bolshevik members inside Russia. The arrest of these two was not entirely a coincidence, since it was Malinovskii, a bolshevik agent of the police, who had denounced them.[4] The interests of the police, to create as much division in the social democratic party as possible, coincided with those of Lenin, who can scarcely have regretted seeing two such staunch 'conciliators' as Nogin and Lindov removed from the scene.

Lenin, with the support of the Poles, and of Zinoviev and Kamenev, now urged that the foreign Plenum should be called. Presumably he hoped that he could secure a majority on this Plenum, just as

[1] See *Lenin*, volume XIV, p. 516.
[2] *Listok Golosa Sotsial-Demokrata*, No. 3, February 1912.
[3] *Lenin*, volume XV, pp. 581 ff.
[4] *Lenin*, volume XV, p. 729; D. Sverchkov, *Na zare revoliutsii*, Leningrad, 1924, p. 308.

the *Z.B.Ts.K.* had placed its hopes on the 'conciliators' in the Russian 'Sem'ërka'. The usual legalistic argument ensued, but Lenin decided to act without regard for formalities. At a private meeting of his own adherents (Kamenev, Zinoviev, Tyshka, Rykov and the bolshevik member of the *Z.B.Ts.K., Dr Semashko) a plot was worked out to summon a meeting, ostensibly supposed to be a Central Committee Plenum, for 5 June 1911. Invitations were issued on 27 May 1911 to representatives of the *Bund*, the Letts and the mensheviks to attend. On the same day, 27 May, Dr Semashko walked out of the *Z.B.Ts.K.*, taking with him the records, and the cash-box. On 10 June 1911, Lenin's pseudo-Plenum met. The menshevik and *Bund* delegates now walked out on the grounds that the meeting had no party constitutional authority behind it. It was indeed a hand-picked assembly. Not all the delegates to the 1910 Plenum were invited, and not all who were invited had attended the 1910 Plenum. Several Central Committee members and candidates (elected by the Fifth Congress in 1907) had been passed over. Unperturbed by these irregularities, the meeting pronounced the *Z.B.Ts.K.* dissolved, and set up an Organizing Commission, charged with preparing a party conference, and a Technical Commission to deal with funds, printing and transport.

This, however, was only halfway to victory, since two problems remained. One was the likely effect on the German trustees of this bold move. Lenin's high-handed action and Dr Semashko's rape of the cash-box immediately became the subject of numerous protests in the party papers and at meetings – by the *Bund*, the Caucasians, the Letts, *Vperëd, Pravda,* Plekhanov, the *Z.B.Ts.K.* and the great majority of social democratic groups in exile. The other difficulty was the fact that in carrying out this *coup* Lenin had had to rely on the support of 'conciliators' – the only bolshevik member of the Central Committee still at liberty was Rykov, a staunch 'conciliator'. The 'conciliators' were prepared to solve the deadlock created by the conflict with the *Z.B.Ts.K.* in this unorthodox manner. They could not be relied on to act on the lines desired by Lenin when the time came for the final party conference. Both the new bodies set up were 'conciliator' in their majority. This had largely been the result of pressure from an unexpected quarter – Tyshka.[1]

The importance of Tyshka lay in the influence which he could exercise over the German trustees, not only by himself but possibly

[1] *Lenin*, volume XV, pp. 631–4.

also through Rosa Luxemburg,[1] who was a close friend of two of them, Klara Zetkin and Kautsky. Lenin had paid a secret visit to Kautsky a short time before, and had achieved nothing.[2] Meanwhile the mensheviks were also making every effort to put their case to the trustees. A pamphlet by Martov exposing the bolsheviks' financial dealings, which had been published in May 1911, was translated into German for the trustees' benefit. The mensheviks' efforts were successful at any rate to the extent that in June the trustees at long last demanded the transfer of the agreed portion of the capital to their name and Lenin in fact transferred a certain sum to Berlin. It seems that at this point Tyshka, hitherto a faithful tool of Lenin, began to see himself in the role of arbiter of the affairs of the Russian party. Tyshka successfully persuaded the trustees – in the face of repeated protests from the *Z.B.Ts.K.* – to transfer sums totalling 30,000 francs to the 'Technical Commission'. The fact that this Technical Commission was no more than a private agency set up by Lenin without any party authority did not apparently deter the trustees.[3] Lenin was quick to make use of this 'proof' that the trustees had adjudicated in favour of the bolsheviks.

The German social democrat leaders who acted as trustees seem to have been very ill-informed about what was happening in the Russian party. They regarded the conflicts which were taking place within it with understandable distaste. But their efforts to preserve a position of neutrality were, to say the least, singularly ill-judged. To have left the disputed fund in Lenin's hands until June 1911, and furthermore to pay out thereafter sums to the flagrantly illegal 'Technical Commission', was in effect to back Lenin against his opponents. Of the three trustees, Franz Mehring throughout was a sick man, and Kautsky seems to have left matters largely to Klara Zetkin. Two circumstances at first inclined Kautsky to support Lenin. First, the fact that his information was largely derived from Rosa Luxemburg and Tyshka, whose views were not likely to have been unbiased; and secondly the support which Plekhanov was showing for Lenin. The whole story of bolshevik finances had been kept very quiet, and

---

[1] For the relationship between Tyshka (Leo Jogiches) and Rosa Luxemburg see J. P. Nettl, *Rosa Luxemburg*, Volume I, London, 1966, pp. 378–84.
[2] Unpublished letter, Martov to Potresov, 28 April 1911, made available to me by the late Mr Nicolaevsky.
[3] *Listok Golosa Sotsial-Demokrata*, No. 3, February 1912; *Informatsionnyi biulleten' TK*, Nos. 1 and 2; Martynov in *Golos Sotsial-Demokrata*, No. 26, December 1911; *Listok Z.B.Ts.K.*, No. 1, 8 September 1911. There is also much detail in a copy of a letter written to the trustees in July 1911 by Dan and Martov, preserved in the *Bund* archives in New York.

Martov's pamphlet in the spring of 1911 provoked Kautsky to an outburst of indignation against Martov for washing dirty linen in public.[1]

The first conflict between Lenin and Tyshka had ended in a compromise, which left Tyshka dominating the new 'party' organs. It was not to be expected that Lenin would content himself for long with a situation in which these organs, which he had created, remained in the hands of 'conciliators'. In the spring and summer of 1911 Lenin organized a party school at Longjumeau near Paris, with the assistance of Zinoviev. Several pupils who had shown the right qualities when acting as agents of the bolsheviks inside Russia were trained at this school – notably G. K. Ordzhonikidze, a Georgian. The Organizing Commission had been set up by Lenin's 'Plenum' in June to send representatives illegally into Russia, and there prepare a new party conference. But Rykov and its other 'conciliator' members visualized this forthcoming conference as a genuine attempt to unite all party members. An appeal which they issued was couched in conciliatory terms, calculated to attract the widest possible response from both factions.[2] In August 1911 the 'conciliator' member of the Organizing Commission, Rykov, returned to Russia to make preparations for a party conference. He was promptly arrested – on the denunciation of another police agent working for the bolsheviks in Paris, Briandinskii. The arrest was not fortuitous. The detailed report by Briandinskii to the police has since been published and shows that this skilful agent was well informed on the state of affairs inside the party, and on the views of Rykov, as well as on the value of arresting both Rykov and his sympathizers on the committees inside Russia (of whom Rykov had prepared detailed lists with Briandinskii's aid) in the interests of party disunity.[3] The two other 'conciliators', Nogin and Lindov, had been under arrest since April 1911. The field in Russia therefore lay open to Ordzhonikidze, who was sent into Russia with two others about the same time as Rykov, but alone escaped arrest. After a few months of feverish activity, Ordzhonikidze had gathered sufficient appearance of support to set up in Russia a so-called Russian Organizing Commission (*R.O.K.*). This body now claimed to speak in the name of the

---

[1] *Dnevnik Sotsial-Demokrata* No. 15, October 1911, p. 16. The allegations contained in this pamphlet (*Spasiteli ili uprazdniteli*), though violent in tone, appear to be confirmed by bolshevik and police sources, and by documents in Aleksinskii's archives relating to the period.

[2] This appeal was printed as a leaflet, but has not been re-published. It is listed as item 565 in *Sotsial-Demokraticheskie listovki 1894–1917 gg.* (See note 1, p. 58 for full reference.)

[3] M. A. Tsiavlovskii, *op. cit.*, pp. 48–57.

whole party, and called for immediate elections to a party conference by all 'genuine' supporters of the party. At the same time it assumed the right of authority over the Organizing Commission and the Technical Commission abroad.

Relations between Lenin and Zinoviev on the one hand and Tyshka, the leading figure in these latter two bodies, had already reached breaking point in October, when Tyshka's Technical Commission had refused to provide funds for the publication of the November issue of *Sotsial-Demokrat*. Lenin and Zinoviev, whose funds had apparently by this date been depleted by the expenses of organizing the *R.O.K.*, were reduced to borrowing money to enable them to publish their paper. The days of the Organizing and Technical Commissions, which had in any case been temporary improvisations, were numbered. In November 1911 they were denounced by the *R.O.K.* The Leninist members walked out – and Zinoviev seized the cash and the printing press in the manner now become familiar. Tyshka, outwitted by Lenin, and frustrated in his own plans, broke with Lenin. In a series of bitter pamphlets and articles he now poured abuse on Lenin, accusing him of the conduct in which he, Tyshka, had for the past three years usually been an enthusiastic partner.

Meanwhile, the *R.O.K.* proceeded undisturbed to prepare the conference, which was summoned to meet in Prague on 18 January 1912.

VII   Lenin Overplays his Hand

Lenin had stolen a march on his rivals. Party support for the *R.O.K.* was small – at most one-fifth of the party, according to Trotsky's estimate, endorsed Lenin's action. No member or candidate of the last Central Committee to be elected played any part in its formation. Nor could the *R.O.K.* claim the support of the only party organ still lawfully in existence under the decisions of the 1910 Plenum – the *Z.B.Ts.K.* – which opposed Lenin throughout. The *R.O.K.* thus had little claim to represent the bolshevik faction – and none to represent the Russian social democratic party. But all this counted for little in a party as politically inexperienced as the Russian. The average party member was anxious for unity and impatient of inter-factional quarrels. To anyone who spoke with apparent authority, and in the name of the party, he was generally prepared to give his support. Lenin had therefore won the first round. The menshevik leaders, from their dominant position in January 1910, were now forced back on the defensive.

The *R.O.K.* issued invitations to attend a conference at Prague to the national parties and to a number of groups within the Russian party. The 'liquidators' were pointedly omitted. The national parties, *Vperëd*, Trotsky and Plekhanov all refused. The conference met on 18 January 1912; the fourteen voting delegates (of whom two were police agents) claimed to represent ten party committees. The actual existence of most of these 'committees' was later disputed, and some party organizations which did exist had been left unrepresented. Trotsky claimed that only one organization among those allegedly represented actually existed. In spite of Plekhanov's refusal to attend, two of his followers were among the delegates as so-called 'party mensheviks'. One of the two disturbed the harmony of the proceedings by protesting repeatedly against the irregularity of the conference. Unperturbed, this little gathering of rebels (for that is all it was) constituted itself as a conference representing virtually all existing party organizations, passed a number of resolutions, and elected a Central Committee. The 'liquidators' were pronounced to be outside the party, and the funds still held by the German social democrat trustees were declared to be the property of the bolsheviks. Resolutions on policy towards the Duma were also adopted, to which reference is made below.[1]

This new Central Committee consisted of Lenin's closest and 'hardest' followers. Its seven members included Lenin, Zinoviev, Ordzhonikidze, the Armenian bolshevik Spandarian and Roman Malinovskii, the police agent. Among the five alternate members were A. S. Bubnov, M. I. Kalinin and E. D. Stasova. Shortly afterwards the Committee co-opted two further members, I. V. Dzhugashvili (Stalin) and I. S. Belostotskii. Belostotskii had been trained at Lenin's party school at Longjumeau during the summer of 1911. A number of members were designated for work inside Russia, including three Caucasians – Ordzhonikidze, Spandarian and Stalin.

The blow struck by the bolsheviks at the Prague Conference stimulated Lenin's opponents to fresh efforts to restore unity in the party. Attempts had been going on for some time past. The main advocacy for unification came from Trotsky's group. Trotsky's attitude was that there were faults on both sides – if the bolsheviks sinned by usurping rights which belonged to the party as a whole, the mensheviks were wrong in treating the underground party with disdain. Throughout the year Trotsky urged the need to call a conference at which all who had the true interests of the party at heart could and should be reunited. His activity was much abused by Lenin, but also treated with some suspicion by the mensheviks, who, possibly unjustly, saw in Trotsky's criticism of themselves a continuation of what they considered to be the dishonest campaign against 'liquidationism'. The *Golos Sotsial-Demokrata* group had some time previously formulated its demands for unification in a letter circulated to the party early in 1911.[2] Both Trotsky and the mensheviks contemplated that those working in the legal organizations as well as underground workers should be represented at a conference. Since this conference would have to be illegal, those social democrats who were really opposed to the reconstitution of an underground party were not likely to attend it, and real 'liquidators', if they existed, would automatically be excluded. Various other efforts to reach a compromise were made throughout the year.

---

[1] *KPSS v rez.*, volume I, pp. 265–87; *Lenin*, volume XV, pp. 651–4; *Vserossiiskaia konferentsiia Ros. Sots.-dem. Rab. partii 1912 goda. Izdanie Tsentral'nago Komiteta*, Paris, 1912, *passim*.

[2] This undated letter was reprinted by Martov in his *Spasiteli ili uprazdniteli* pp. 42–7, but the approximate date can be fixed by internal evidence.

None of these efforts bore any fruit in 1911. One reason was the practical difficulty and the expense of organizing a conference – a task which presented even greater problems for the mensheviks, who were contemplating a genuinely representative conference, than for the bolsheviks, who were not. Moreover, many mensheviks did not believe that reunion with Lenin and his supporters was either practicable or desirable. The Lettish and Polish social democrats, the *Bund* and the Caucasians, all had interests of their own which often outweighed their desire for party unity. Plekhanov maintained an attitude of aloof disapproval of both sides, criticizing the bolsheviks for their excesses, but supporting their campaign against the 'liquidators'. But at the end of the year, after the *R.O.K.* had been set up, the *Bund* called a meeting of representatives of the three largest minority organizations working inside Russia – the *Bund*, the Lettish social democrats and the Caucasians. The aim of this meeting was to summon a general unification party conference. The following year, under the impact of the Prague Conference, a meeting of protest was held in Paris on 12 March, at which the *Bund*, *Pravda* and *Golos Sotsial-Demokrata* were represented. It was also attended by a delegate from the *Vperëd* group, and by two delegates from a group of 'conciliator' bolsheviks who had since the summer of 1911 broken with Lenin and set themselves up as the 'Party Bolsheviks'.[1] These groups decided to hold a genuinely all-party conference. Invitations were issued to all groups and factions, but neither the Polish social democrats nor Plekhanov accepted. The Prague Central Committee, of course, ignored the invitation, but one bolshevik (to the delight of Trotsky) attended as a delegate from Moscow.

The conference met in Vienna from 25 August to 2 September 1912. The delegates had little more in common than their frustration at having been outwitted by Lenin, and blamed each other for the disintegration of the party. The bolshevik delegate was a police agent, with instructions from the police to break up the conference if possible. He was assisted in his efforts by Aleksinskii, representing *Vperëd*. Trotsky, as chairman, was anxious to preserve harmony, and Martov's reference to Lenin and his followers as 'charlatans' produced a head-on conflict with him. But in spite of this heated atmosphere, a spirit of conciliation prevailed in the end. The conference decided to forego calling itself an all-Russian Conference, and contented itself with the title 'Conference of R.S.-D.R.P. Organizations'. Instead of a

[1] *Lenin*, volume XV, p. 659. For the resolution see *Pravda*, No. 25, 6 May (23 April) 1912.

Central Committee, it set up an 'Organization Committee' to work inside Russia, consisting of seven members, including *Bund* and Lettish representatives. The general policy approved by the Vienna Conference was in line with that of the Petersburg menshevik organization: to create a mass party, to which the illegal organizations should become subordinate. The resolution adopted on the state of the party was couched in conciliatory terms, calculated not to exacerbate existing discords.[1]

Once again therefore two rival organizational centres – the bolshevik Central Committee and the Organization Committee – existed side by side. The next few years, during which Lenin redoubled his campaign against the 'liquidators', were soon to show that the advantages lay on Lenin's side. He had once again secured the 'firm name' – Central Committee – a fact which counted for a great deal. He had the help of Plekhanov's followers, who, while calling themselves 'party mensheviks', sowed confusion in the rank and file.

Meanwhile the question of money arose once again. Lenin had retained at least half of the Shmidt inheritance. The Longjumeau school, the *R.O.K.* and the Prague Conference must all have cost him considerable sums, and by the time of the Prague Conference bolshevik funds were low.[2] The mensheviks, dependent on contributions from wealthy sympathizers, were always in low financial water. Both sides had made unsuccessful attempts throughout the summer of 1911 to obtain the money remaining in the hands of the German trustees. The trustees had, perhaps unwittingly, been 'neutral' on Lenin's side. But towards the latter half of 1911 a change in their attitude became perceptible. Visits and letters to the Germans by mensheviks, *Bundists* and Trotsky may have had some effect. Moreover, the influence of Rosa Luxemburg, with whose ultra-revolutionary views on German social democratic policy Kautsky was by now in open disagreement, may have been waning. By November 1911 the trustees, bewildered by a situation which they could not resolve, had made the illness of Mehring the excuse for laying down their functions. They had expressed their willingness to pay over the money if

[1] See *Lenin*, volume XVI, pp. 708–11; *Izveshchenie o konferentsii organizatsii R.S.-D.R.P., Izdanie Organizatsionnago Komiteta*, Vienna, September 1912, *passim*; M. A. Tsiavlovskii, *op. cit.*, pp. 111–19.

[2] *Lenin*, volume XXIX, p. 19; *Tsiavlovskii*, pp. 101–2 – from agents' reports it would appear that the total funds available at this date were only 30,000 francs, but police agents would not necessarily be well informed on finance, which Lenin kept very much under his own control. Illegal literature alone, which was sent into Russia by the bolsheviks in preparation for the *R.O.K.*, was seven times larger in quantity for the one month, August, than the average monthly quantity over the previous six months – *Sotsial-Demokrat*, No. 24, October 1911.

agreement could be reached between Lenin and his opponents as to who should be the recipients. Until then the money was to remain in their name in a bank in Berlin.[1]

It was this money which, in the changed circumstances of 1912, each side now set out to claim. Immediately after the Prague Conference Lenin sent one of the bolshevik Duma deputies, Poletaev, to try to persuade Kautsky to part with the money. Lenin himself also went to Berlin, and threatened Kautsky with legal proceedings if he did not hand over the trust funds. But all these efforts were unavailing. Lenin may by this date have somewhat overplayed his hand. Having quarrelled with Tyshka in the autumn of 1911, he had shortly afterwards engineered a break-away in the Polish social democratic party. This split was designed to leave the two leaders, Tyshka and Rosa Luxemburg, isolated in their party. Lenin's main advocates with Kautsky (Poletaev in fact obtained his introduction to Kautsky from Rosa Luxemburg) was therefore no longer by the date of this attempt likely to plead his cause. But the mensheviks were no more successful in persuading Kautsky when a member of their Organization Committee visited him after the Vienna Conference. Further attempts by them proved equally abortive. The money, so far as is known, was never returned to the Russian social democratic party, and was certainly in the hands of the trustees as late as 1915.[2]

Immediately after Prague Lenin made one of those rapid changes of policy which characterized him – he decided to compete with the mensheviks in their policy of 'legality'. Some time before, in the summer of 1911, when the idea of launching a legal daily paper for workers had been raised in discussion by a group of mensheviks inside Russia, the bolsheviks had derided the suggestion. It would only serve, they argued, to create illusions among the workers that a legal press was possible inside Russia without the overthrow of the monarchy. The proposal was, however, very popular among the workers, and the reaction of the authorities was immediately to arrest those who had originated it. Trotsky's *Pravda* had remained the most

---

[1] See their letter of 18 November 1911 reprinted in *Listok Golosa Sotsial-Demokrata*, No. 3, February 1912.

[2] Much of the story of the relations between the party and the trustees over the question of this money between 1910 and the war has to be sought in unpublished documents, and the whole subject awaits exhaustive treatment. I have used materials assembled by Mr Nicolaevsky in his studies referred to in note 2, page 90, and documents deposited in the Institute for Social History at Amsterdam. See also: N. Poletaev in *Proletarskaia revoliutsiia*, No. 4 (16) 1923, pp. 3–6; *Vospominaniia o Vladimire Ilyiche Lenine*, volume I, Moscow, 1956, p. 272; O. Piatnitskii, *Zapiski bol'shevika*, Fifth edition, Moscow, 1956, pp. 153, 164.

popular of the newspapers imported illegally from abroad. When therefore Lenin in February 1912 decided to launch his own legal daily paper, he did not scruple to use the title *Pravda* – to the indignation of Trotsky. The first issue of the bolshevik *Pravda* appeared on 5 May (22 April) 1912. It was published until the outbreak of war, and played a big part, as *Iskra* had once done, in enabling Lenin to rebuild his organization inside Russia. For, in spite of the bold claims made on behalf of the *R.O.K.*, this organization was in 1912 still virtually non-existent. *Pravda* also became the main vehicle for bolshevik attacks on 'liquidators', which were now stepped up. Plekhanov was a regular contributor to its pages. Bogdanov and the rest of the *Vperëd* group were also for a time invited to contribute (the issues of empiriomonism, 'otzovism' and 'ultimatism' were now as dead as the Dodo) but, with the exception of the adaptable Aleksinskii, did not continue their connexion for very long. Bolshevik sources are reticent about the financing of *Pravda*, seeking to show that it relied solely on the workers' contributions which figured prominently in its pages. There is no doubt, however, that in addition private benefactors also helped to finance it. Zinoviev recalls that 'a few thousands' were raised from such well-wishers. One substantial benefactor was V. A. Tikhomirnov, a wealthy student, who was active in the students' bolshevik circle in Kazan' which included the young V. M. Molotov.[1]

The mensheviks also succeeded in launching a legal daily in Petersburg, *Luch* (The Ray), which appeared from September 1912 onwards, and to which all leading mensheviks contributed. *Luch* never succeeded in equalling the circulation of *Pravda*. But, like *Pravda*, it soon became a legal cover for an underground organization. That the underground party was a necessary evil in Russian conditions for the time being, so as to provide assistance to all possible forms of permitted activity, became the keynote of *Luch*. This was essentially the view of the 'practicals' inside Russia, rather than of the intellectuals outside. Conflicts on this issue arose with Trotsky, who was at the outset a supporter of *Luch*.[2]

The bolsheviks also entered into competition with the mensheviks in the trade unions, which they had hitherto neglected. The attitude of the two factions to the trade unions which existed precariously in

[1] Tikhomirnov's opportune benefaction to the bolsheviks, though quite widely known at the time, is never mentioned in Soviet literature, with one exception – the authorized biography of Molotov in volume 41 of *Entsiklopedicheskii slovar'* 'Granat', Part II, p. 63 (by A. Arosev).

[2] See e.g. *Luch*, No. 109 (195), 14 May 1913, p. 2; *Pis'ma*, pp. 284–6. On *Luch* generally there is much valuable information in Garvi's unpublished memoirs.

Russia on the eve of the First World War was very different. The mensheviks argued (citing Marx in support) that trade unions should not be tied to any party. The aim of social democrats inside the unions should be to encourage and help the workers in their activity, to lead them and guide them, but not to dominate them or to endanger their existence by insisting on a formal link between the unions and the party. The mensheviks thus viewed the unions as an end in themselves, as an essential part of the conscious, organized political life of the proletariat. To the bolsheviks the unions were only a means to one end – armed insurrection. The object therefore, in their view, was to weld the unions into mass instruments which in the hour of need would be ready to support the rising. With this in mind, the Prague Conference had resolved that bolsheviks should aim to create illegal party cells within the unions, closely linked to the appropriate party committees. These disciplined cells inside the unions should try to achieve control over all strike activity.[1]

Thus the bolsheviks after 1912 became active participators in the permitted workers' organizations, and the mensheviks were making all efforts to reconstruct an illegal party machine. This raises the question how far any real differences of theory now survived between the two factions. There were certainly differences of doctrine on the land question and on the future of the national components of Russia. But these problems related to the, as yet remote, day when the monarchy would be overthrown. The charge of 'liquidation' in the form levelled by Lenin at the mensheviks was plainly false. Mensheviks were suffering arrest and exile as often, if not more often, than the bolsheviks. By early 1913 already quite an extensive network of illegal, underground menshevik committees was in existence. All mensheviks, including the 'practicals', fully realized that in Russian conditions an underground, illegal party organization was essential if any political work was to continue. But coupled with the bolshevik charge of 'liquidationism' went another, that of 'reformism' – the accusation that the mensheviks had now abandoned the ultimate revolution, and were, like the followers of Bernstein in Germany, restricting their aims to demand piecemeal reforms. Now, although in contrast to their attitude in 1906 the mensheviks no longer thought that a revolution was imminent (no one in his senses could have

---

[1] See *KPSS v rez.*, volume I, p. 277. The difference of attitude of the two factions towards the trade unions already became evident in 1907 at a party conference in July in Kotka in Finland, at which no agreement could be reached on this question. See *ibidem*, pp. 178–9 and p. 180, for the menshevik and Lenin's draft resolutions respectively on the question of trade unions.

thought this in 1912 or 1913), it was not true that they had abandoned ultimate revolution as at any rate theoretically necessary and inevitable. Indeed, the menshevik leaders, always doctrinaire in the extreme, were very sensitive to the charge of 'reformism', and always anxious to repudiate the suggestion that the acceptance of a necessary, temporary lull meant any change in doctrine. Fear of 'reformism' was one of the main reasons why Martov, in particular, was always inclined to suspect that his followers inside Russia might after all turn out to be guilty of something like the 'liquidationism' of which they were constantly accused. So long as legal activity is regarded only as preparation for the ultimate revolution, all is well, Martov wrote in 1911. But if it should become a policy of legality at all costs, based on the doctrine that the workers by winning piecemeal reforms will gradually evolve or 'grow into' a constitutional system which will make a revolution unnecessary, then this is reformism, and must be fought tooth and nail.[1] It was precisely because they accepted ultimate revolution as part of doctrine, and regarded legal activity as merely the best method of preparation for it, that the mensheviks made reunion with the bolsheviks the keystone of their policy. After all, since, as they saw it, no fundamental issue of doctrine divided the two factions, and since both bolsheviks and mensheviks were the intellectual vanguard of the same class, the proletariat, it followed that their battle was one and the same. For the moment the excesses of some individuals were disturbing this natural unity. But this could not last, since in the end according to Marxism it is not individuals who make history, but classes. There is no need to over-emphasize 'fighting' the bolsheviks, another menshevik wrote in 1913. In practice the social democratic movement has for the time being become a movement of struggle for partial reforms and individual rights, and bolshevism will have to adapt itself to this, or it will disappear.[2]

Many mensheviks also believed that the worst inter-factional conflicts were merely the growing pains of a young party struggling for existence. When once social democray emerged on to the broad 'German' path as a legal, recognized party, all these distasteful intrigues would become a thing of the past. All these reasons kept the mensheviks from any attempt during these years at taking a leaf out of Lenin's book – from trying to seize control of the party and excluding Lenin and his followers. In the final analysis the real division in

[1] See his 'Zametki publitsista, "likvidatorstvo" i perspektivy', in *Delo Zhizni*, No. 1, pp. 2–12.
[2] K. Oranskii, 'Kak osushchestvit' edinstvo', in *Nasha Zaria*, No. 1, 1913, pp. 40–4.

the party was much more one of temperament and tactics than of doctrine.

The climax of Lenin's offensive against the mensheviks was reached in the precincts of the Duma, inside the social democratic 'fraction'. Bolshevik and menshevik deputies in the Third Duma had worked inside one 'fraction' and, for Russian conditions, in comparative harmony. This exceptional state of affairs had been due to the isolation from its party leaders which the 'fraction' enjoyed, if only because for much of the period of its existence there had been no Central Committee functioning inside Russia. The 'fraction' was thus able to maintain the relative independence from party control which it had asserted at the outset. In the summer of 1912 the Third Duma's term expired, and elections for the Fourth were fixed for September. In preparation for these elections bolsheviks and mensheviks enunciated their policy in advance. The bolsheviks, among whom all ideas of boycott were now quite forgotten, had decided at the Prague Conference that participation in the forthcoming elections was 'absolutely necessary'. The social democratic 'fraction' when elected should be subordinated to 'our party' as a whole. The resolution skated lightly over the fact that the great majority of the party did not at that date acknowledge the leadership of the Prague group. There was one significant point in the resolution: in the workers' *curiae* (it will be recalled that Russian elections were indirect, and by social *curiae*, or colleges of electors) only 'our own' candidates must be put forward, and in no circumstances must there be any electoral agreements here 'with other parties or groups'. An explanatory parenthesis revealed that by 'groups' was meant 'liquidators'. The Vienna Conference had also dealt at length with the then imminent elections. The resolution emphasized above all the need for party unity. In particular, no competing social democratic candidatures were to be tolerated and candidatures should be agreed with the bolshevik Central Committee. The election when it came was fought in an atmosphere of co-operation. Candidatures were discussed, with the bolsheviks proving the tougher bargainers, especially where the workers' *curiae* were concerned. Thus, according to Martov,[1] in three instances out of six the bolshevik candidates owed their election to the support of the 'liquidators'. It was notable that the worker voters were emphatic on the need for unity in the Duma 'fraction'. Thousands of instructions to deputies from worker electors testified to this desire for social democratic unity in the Duma, and all the social democratic deputies were

[1] In *Nasha Zaria*, No. 10–11, 1913, pp. 72, 90.

returned upon their express promise that they would endeavour to preserve a united 'fraction'. In the end six bolsheviks and seven mensheviks were elected. Among the bolshevik deputies was the police agent Roman Malinovskii, a member of the bolshevik Central Committee.

The traditions of the social democrats in the Third Duma carried on for a time into the Fourth. Declarations in favour of unity were made by all the deputies. One bolshevik deputy, Petrovskii, went so far as to publish a conciliatory interview in the menshevik paper *Luch*, dissociating himself from past attacks on the 'liquidators', and expressing doubt whether 'liquidationism' really existed. At the end of December 1912 all except two of the deputies (one of the two was Malinovskii) voted for a resolution in the 'fraction' that there should be only one daily party newspaper and that meanwhile all social democratic deputies should, as a step towards party union, contribute to both *Pravda* and *Luch*. This was too much for Lenin. He hastily summoned a meeting in Cracow, where he was living at the time. It took place in the second week of January 1913, and was attended by the six bolshevik Duma deputies. Shortly afterwards, on the instructions of the Central Committee, the agreement of December 1912 was repudiated by the bolshevik deputies, and this led to a period of strained relations in the 'fraction'. The bolsheviks had in fact already decided to effect a split. But in view of the strong temper in favour of unity among the workers they thought that a preliminary period of propaganda was essential, during which sufficiently convincing pretexts to befuddle worker opinion could be found. By October 1913, at a further meeting summoned by Lenin, the time was considered ripe. In preparation for the final split, a suitable resolution was now adopted, declaring that unity in the 'fraction' was 'possible and necessary', but that this unity was being threatened by the seven mensheviks. Shortly afterwards an ultimatum was presented to the seven mensheviks, demanding equal rights for the six bolsheviks with the seven mensheviks. As evidence of victimization the ultimatum instanced the persuasion to which the six had been subjected to write for *Luch*; the refusal by the 'fraction' to establish the post of a second secretary for a bolshevik; and the fact that a menshevik and not a bolshevik had been appointed as member of the Duma budget commission. The bolsheviks now declared themselves a separate 'fraction'.[1]

---

[1] A. Badaev, *Bol'sheviki v gosudarstvennoi dume. Vospominaniia.* Eighth edition, Moscow, 1954, pp. 168, 170, 182, 326 ff.

The leading part in effecting the split had been played by Roman Malinovskii, one of the most enigmatic characters in the bolshevik ranks. He had for years been an agent of the police, and it was on the instructions of the police that in 1911 he went over to the bolsheviks. He was then a prominent member of the Metal Workers' Union. He signalized his 'conversion' by arranging for the arrest of a large group of 'liquidators' engaged in legal work. Subsequently he helped the bolsheviks to win control of his union from the mensheviks. Whatever services he rendered to the police, his services to Lenin's cause were undeniable. He had organized the arrest at the right moment of people whom Lenin wanted out of the way. He had planned and organized the split in the Duma 'fraction' about a year before it took place – on Lenin's instructions, and against the views of the rest of the bolshevik deputies. Inside the Duma he was the most violent and the most uncompromising bolshevik – earning Lenin's admiration for speeches, to the drafts of which both Lenin and the police authorities had made amendments. As a member of the Central Committee he could keep the police informed of the secret deliberations of the bolshevik leaders. That he was able to serve two masters in this manner was, of course, due to the fact that the immediate aims of Lenin and of the police were identical – to cause the maximum of disruption and disunity in the social democratic movement. Had Malinovskii been playing his double role with Lenin's complicity (and this question must, in the absence of evidence, remain an open one) he could scarcely have helped Lenin more.

Malinovskii's activity became openly suspect early in 1914, when after a scene in the Duma he resigned his seat on police instructions and went straight to Lenin in Cracow. Rumours that Malinovskii was a police agent were now buzzing everywhere, and were given wide circulation in the menshevik press, which demanded an enquiry. Lenin immediately rallied to Malinovskii's defence. Indeed his reaction could have been consistent with complicity in Malinovskii's police activities. As against this, it was natural enough for Lenin to fight with all his might against an accusation which had emanated from his political opponents. The end of the drama came after the revolution, when Malinovskii, who had spent the war conducting propaganda for the bolsheviks among Russian prisoners in Germany (by arrangement with the German authorities), returned voluntarily to Russia. As Malinovskii well knew, the imperial police records were now available, and his role as agent plainly revealed. He was put on trial, and shot. His repeated requests that Lenin should be called to give evidence were refused, and his plea that Lenin must have known of his connexions with the police was rejected. Malinovskii had done his work, and the temper of the workers was now, in November 1918, violently against him. It was not now in Lenin's interests to soil bolshevik reputation with the defence of Malinovskii.[1]

The prevalence of police agents among the bolsheviks, often in high places, has repeatedly been noted. Among the mensheviks important agents were rare – the one known case was that of V. Abrosimov, a menshevik delegate to the Vienna Conference and a leading 'practical' in Petersburg, who entered the service of the police in 1912 or 1913. There were three main reasons for this striking difference. In the first place, the main object of the police – to keep the two factions disunited – could be better achieved from the bolshevik than from the menshevik side, and would-be agents were accordingly assigned to the bolsheviks. Secondly, the conspiratorial and unscrupulous bolshevik was more akin in temperament to the kind of adventurer to whom the double life of a police agent appealed than the more doctrinaire and idealistic menshevik. And thirdly, the bolshevik was as often as not a professional revolutionary, living on the salary which the Central Committee paid him. In contrast the menshevik, who was very rarely supported by the party, had to earn his living as best he could. It was not only easier for the professional conspirator to add a further, different kind of conspiracy to his daily round, but also tempting to draw the extra emoluments. For the bolsheviks paid little – but the police were not ungenerous.

The splitting of the Duma 'fraction' was the logical consequence of Lenin's policy since 1910, if not since 1903. Nevertheless, it caused a profound shock when once it happened, and many of the workers were bewildered and outraged. Trotsky, the *Bund* and the Caucasians rallied behind the menshevik deputies. The Polish social democrats, apart from Lenin's splinter group of oppositionists, also supported them.[2] Even Plekhanov, who had continued to lash the 'liquidators' in the pages of *Pravda* (to the dismay of his closest friends, Aksel'rod and Vera Zasulich), was beginning to have doubts. At a meeting with a group of his émigré followers in August 1913 Plekhanov had decided to found a new paper which would seek to unite the best elements of both factions. In a letter of 9 December 1913 after the split in the 'fraction', he resigned from the International Socialist

---

[1] For a detailed account of the case of Malinovskii, in which all the available evidence is studied, see Wolfe, *op. cit.*, chapter xxxi. Mr Wolfe rejects the suggestion of Lenin's complicity in Malinovskii's connexions with the police.

[2] *Lenin*, volume XVII, pp. 694–5.

Bureau in protest against this 'last blow struck at our unity', and urged the Socialist International to make an effort to bring about that control in Russian social democracy which all healthy elements in both factions desired. Nevertheless, he still blamed the split on certain 'regrettable decisions' adopted by the 'liquidators'. But a little later, in May, 1914, he succeeded in starting a new paper, *Edinstvo* (Unity), in the pages of which his criticism of Lenin now became sharper, and his hostility to the 'liquidators' somewhat less intransigent.[1] Meanwhile, it was evident that the aim of the bolsheviks was to perpetuate the division inside the party. The split in the 'fraction' was soon followed by intensive preparations for a party congress, which was to set the seal on the bolsheviks' claim to speak in the name of the whole party. For greater effect it was planned to coincide with the forthcoming congress of the Socialist International.[2]

Outmanœuvred, outwitted and bewildered, the menshevik leaders had also turned to the Socialist International as their last hope. The experience of the international socialist movement with its wayward Russian brothers had not hitherto been very happy. As far back as 1905 an offer by the German social democratic leader, A. Bebel, to mediate on the differences which had arisen between the two Russian factions was snubbed by the bolsheviks at their Third Congress. From the beginning there had been disputes on the question of the representation of the Russian social democrats on the Social International. More recently, there had been the unfortunate experiences of Kautsky, Mehring and Klara Zetkin in their role as trustees of party monies. It was Rosa Luxemburg who now urged the International Socialist Bureau to return to the charge, in a speech in which she blamed Lenin for the Duma split and attacked his policy over the past years. For many years a supporter of Lenin's tactics, the leader of the Polish social democrats had now herself been the victim of Lenin's methods, and was thus able to speak with personal feeling.[3] The Bureau adopted a resolution, offering its services as mediator, but emphasizing that it was not prepared to rake up past differences. The Duma mensheviks, the menshevik Organization Committee, the *Bund* and the Lettish social democrats accepted the offer immediately.[4]

---

[1] See G. Plekhanov, *Sochineniia*, volume XIX, pp. 560–1, 493 ff. The text of the letter to the I.S.B. reprinted in this volume omits the paragraph in which Plekhanov blamed the seven 'liquidators' for the split. For the full original text see *Bulletin of the International Socialist Bureau*, Supplement No. 11, p. 6.

[2] Badaev, *op. cit.*, pp. 325 ff.; *Istoricheskii arkhiv*, No. 1, 1957, pp. 30–2.

[3] For her speech see '1. Beilage des Vorwärts', No. 306, 21 November 1913, p. 2

[4] O. H. Gankin and H. H. Fisher, *The Bolsheviks and the World War. The Origin of the Third International*, Stanford, 1940, pp. 93–4, 96–8.

The bolsheviks soon after 'warmly welcomed' the International's proposal, and went on to point out that all that was required for unity was for the 'liquidators', who had broken away from the original organization formed in 1898, to submit to the bolsheviks in every respect. A little later, in reply to a request from Huysmans of the Executive Committee of the International Socialist Bureau, Lenin wrote that the difference between bolsheviks and mensheviks was the same as that which divided social democratic revolutionaries from reformists everywhere else.[1] Early in 1914 the chairman of the International Socialist Bureau, Emile Vandervelde, visited Russia and had conversations with representatives of both factions. He behaved with correct impartiality, though he did privately admit to Martov that his sympathies lay with the mensheviks.[2]

The International Socialist Bureau followed up its offer by convening a conference of all groups and factions of the Russian social democratic party and of the national parties federated with it. This unification conference met in Brussels on 16 and 17 July 1914. No report of its proceedings was ever published, but in view of the Russian police interest in this unwelcome step towards social democratic unity, several agents attended, and their reports have been preserved.[3] The following groups were represented: the bolshevik Central Committee; the menshevik Organization Committee (which also spoke for the Caucasian organization); the menshevik 'fraction' of the Duma; Plekhanov, representing the *Edinstvo* group; the *Vperëd* group; the *Bund*; the Lettish social democrats; the two portions of the sundered Polish social democrats; and the Polish socialist party. Lenin did not attend, but was represented by a Central Committee delegation of three, led by Inessa Armand – an active bolshevik, to whom Lenin at the time stood very close. She was armed with an enormous memorandum, to which a number of private instructions were appended. The memorandum, drafted with the skill and force which Lenin so well commanded, reiterated the familiar bolshevik case, and especially blamed the 'liquidators' for their 'slanderous' allegations both about the bolsheviks' money dealings, and about Malinovskii. It ended by asserting that bolshevik policy had been correct throughout, '*and we shall not retreat from it*' – the words were underlined in Lenin's text. The private instructions explained what tactics were to be adopted in different contingencies

[1] *Lenin*, volume XVII, pp. 681–2.
[2] *Pis'ma*, pp. 290–1; E. Vandervelde, *Three Aspects of the Russian Revolution*, 7 May–25 June 1917. Translated by Jean E. H. Findlay, London, 1918, p. 19.
[3] Tsiavlovskii, *op. cit.*, pp. 146–8.

which might arise, and added that 'so long as the group of liquidators does not satisfy the conditions which we put forward . . . any moves towards a rapprochement are out of the question'.[1]

This time Lenin found almost no supporters. His memorandum, which was read out at the conference by Inessa Armand, was severely criticized. Even Plekhanov went so far in his criticism that he was stopped and not allowed to continue by the chairman: Plekhanov asserted that the real reason why Lenin was so unwilling to reach agreement with the rest of the party was because he did not wish to be forced to disgorge the large sums of party money which he had misappropriated by 'thieving'. Lenin's only ally was the Lettish delegate.[2]

At the end of the Brussels Conference a resolution was voted by all except the bolshevik and Lettish delegates. Even the pro-Lenin group of the Polish social democratic party voted for the resolution. This recorded that there were no tactical disagreements sufficiently important to justify a split between the various Russian groups, and called for unity upon five conditions: acceptance of the party programme; recognition of the principles that the minority should always accept the decisions of the majority; that the organization of the party 'must be secret at present'; that all groups renounce blocs with the bourgeois parties; and that all agree to participate in a general unification congress.[3] It was intended that the Executive Committee of the International Socialist Bureau should report to the forthcoming Congress of the Socialist International, which was due to meet in August 1914 in Vienna.

The Brussels Conference had not achieved very much, but it was nonetheless the most important step towards unity which had yet been made. The bolsheviks, or those of them who supported Lenin, could now no longer persist in their policy of maintaining the split at all costs, except in open defiance of the Socialist International. One of its leaders, Huysmans, privately warned the bolshevik delegates at Brussels that failure to support the resolution meant disruption of the efforts of the International to promote unity, and that he would so report at the forthcoming Congress of the Socialist International.[4] Plekhanov's authority was at long last no longer at Lenin's service.

[1] *Lenin*, volume XVII, pp. 543–71.
[2] At the Fourth Congress of the Lettish party, at the end of the previous January, the pro-bolsheviks had secured a majority of one among the delegates, and had thus captured the Central Committee. Lenin took an active part in the Congress – *Lenin*, volume XVII, pp. 696–7.
[3] Gankin and Fisher, *op. cit.*, pp. 131–2.
[4] *Lenin*, volume XVII, p. 738.

There was also more unity now on the non-bolshevik side than ever before. With the weight of the International behind them there was more likelihood than there had been in 1910 that the menshevik leaders would find the necessary courage to break with Lenin for good if he persisted in his policy of disunity at all costs. If Lenin were isolated in his intransigence, there was every chance that many of his 'conciliator' followers, who had rejoined him in 1912, would break away again. The bolshevik organization was, moreover, in a poor state in 1914, as compared with 1912. The underground committees were disrupted. There were no funds, and the circulation of *Pravda* had fallen drastically under the impact of the split in the Duma 'fraction'.[1]

Intensive propaganda for unity now began inside Russia. The mensheviks and the organizations supporting them drew up an appeal to the Russian workers, blaming the bolsheviks for the split and urging support for the efforts of the International to reunite the whole party.[2] But it was too late. War broke out, the Vienna Congress of the Socialist International never met, and before long the Russian social democrats were rent asunder by new and even less reconcilable dissensions.

[1] On the general state of the bolsheviks in the spring of 1914 see a letter from Krupskaia to Stasova, dated 6 March 1914, recently printed in *Istoricheskii arkhiv*, No. 1, 1957, pp. 26–7. The circulation of *Pravda* had fallen from its maximum figure of 40,000 daily to 20,000 or 25,000, according to Potresov in November 1913 – see *Materialy*, p. 249. According to the information of the police, the circulation averaged 25,000 in the first three months of 1914 – *Krasnyi arkhiv*, volume 64, p. 140.

[2] See *Sotsial-demokraticheskoe dvizhenie v Rossii*. Materialy pod redaktsiei A. N. Protresova i B. I. Nikolaevskogo. Predislovie P. Lepeshinskogo. Moscow-Leningrad, 1928, pp. 397–400. The war prevented its publication, and it was eventually first printed in 1915 in No. 7 of *Informatsionnyi listok zagranichnoi organizatsii Bunda*.

VIII   War and Revolution

The first reaction of the Russian proletariat to the war was a patriotic upsurge. Political appeals denouncing the war found little response, and there were no strikes. The situation changed by the summer of 1915. Rising costs, shortage of commodities, economic depression, defeat and disorganization had had their effect. There were major strikes in the capital and in Moscow. The mayor of Petrograd recorded that the workers were now putting forward demands for immediate peace and for the overthrow of the autocracy. By 1916 the situation was even more unsettled, though no one as yet foresaw that a revolution was imminent.[1]

Of the radical parties, the *Kadety* supported the war effort; their conflicts with the government were mainly caused by the inefficiency with which the war was conducted and their demand for a representative ministry. The socialist revolutionaries were far from united in their attitude to the war; some supported and some opposed it. The troubled history of the Russian social democrats during the war became closely interwoven with international socialism. The solidarity of the Socialist International had failed when put to the test. In 1907, at Stuttgart, its Congress had resolved to 'exert every effort to prevent the outbreak of war'. But, 'should war break out nonetheless', the duty of socialists would be to utilize the resulting political and economic crisis in order to 'rouse the peoples and thereby to hasten the abolition of capitalist class rule'. This part of the resolution had been proposed by Lenin, Martov and Rosa Luxemburg. It had been adopted with more enthusiasm than circumspection, and masked the profound divisions which in reality existed between the several parties,[2] but it was never repudiated at subsequent congresses, and

---

[1] M. Balabanov, *Ocherk istorii revoliutsionnogo dvizheniia v Rossii*. Leningrad, 1929, p. 296; *Golos*, No. 81, 16 December 1914; Iv. Menitskii, *Rabochee dvizhenie i sotsial-demokraticheskoe podpol'e Moskvy v voennye gody* (1914–17 g.g.) Moscow, 1923, pp. 10, 201–2.

[2] Text in Gankin and Fisher, *op. cit.*, p. 59; for the circumstances in which it came to be voted, and for the real feelings of the parties which voted it, see Milorad M. Drachkovitch, *Les Socialismes Francais et Allemand et le Problème de la Guerre, 1870–1914*, Geneva, 1953, pp. 223–30.

remained the accepted policy of the International. When war broke out the socialist parties of all the belligerents, except Russia and Serbia, voted in support of credits for the conduct of the war. The leaders of the International, headed by Kautsky, supported the action of these socialists, arguing in various forms that the demands of socialism must be postponed until the peril to one's country had been averted. Socialists of the belligerent countries now found themselves fighting on opposite sides, and only a few small dissident groups endeavoured to keep alive the ideals of internationalism. The Second International thus suffered a severe blow from which it was never to recover.

The Russian social democrats in the Duma refused to vote for the war budget, and issued a declaration in August (July) 1914 repudiating the war, and calling on the international proletariat to work for its termination. In spite of the split in the 'fraction', both bolsheviks and mensheviks signed the declaration, which, incidentally, was drafted by a group of mensheviks headed by P. A. Garvi.[1] The effect inside Russia was to stimulate the government to new repressive measures against the social democratic organizations. They were to remain disorganized and decimated for the rest of the war. Outside Russia the prestige of Russian socialism was enhanced, at any rate among the small minority of social democrats who remained true to the principles of internationalism.

The Duma 'fraction' escaped arrest for the time being. But the five bolsheviks were arrested at the end of 1914 (in disregard of their immunity as Duma deputies), when taking part in a conference near Petrograd, summoned to discuss Lenin's theses on the war. These theses, as will be seen, envisaged the defeat of Russia as the 'lesser evil', and thus went much further than the Duma declaration. The government was accordingly able to accuse the bolshevik deputies of disloyalty. They were tried, sentenced and exiled to Siberia, together with Kamenev and others present at the conference. The seven mensheviks continued on in the Duma, under the leadership of Chkheidze. Although they were not always consistent, they continued to oppose the war, and one of their number who in 1915 defied the 'fraction' and voted for war credits was expelled.

Outside the Duma, the social democrats of both factions who remained inside Russia for the most part opposed the war. The disciplined bolsheviks succeeded in presenting the appearance of deter-

---

[1] Nicolaevsky in P. A. Garvi, *Vospominaniia Sotsial-demokrata. Stat'i o zhizni i deiatel'nosti P. A. Garvi*, New York, 1946, p. xxxii; text in Badaev, *op. cit.*, pp. 346–7.

mined opposition to the war, though many of them wavered, and some, like Krasin, openly put patriotism first. There was even less unanimity among the mensheviks. Virtually all were agreed that the first essential was the re-establishment of the shattered Socialist International so that by its efforts the war could be brought to an end on just terms, without territorial annexations, or payment of indemnities. Again, nearly all were agreed that it was their duty to press for democratic reforms. But beyond this there was less unanimity. An influential group, headed by Potresov and embracing most of the leading 'liquidators', believed that the defeat of Germany would be a progressive factor, which would advance the development of socialism. They therefore argued that their duty lay in not actively opposing Russian efforts to win the war. The only path was 'through patriotism to the international reign of brotherhood and equality'. But Potresov and his group were all opposed to supporting the monarchy to the extent of voting for the war budget, and endorsed the stand taken by the Duma 'fraction'. The majority of mensheviks took up a more internationalist standpoint, refused to regard the victory of either side as preferable, and believed that all efforts should be directed towards bringing the war to an end.[1] Only a small minority supported the war unconditionally.

Among the leaders abroad, the war created new divisions and enmities which often cut across the political alignments which had formed after 1905. Plekhanov, for example, now found himself isolated both from the majority of the mensheviks and from Lenin. Reconciled once again with his former allies, Deich and (after 1917) Vera Zasulich, he argued the need for unconditional support of the war until victory of the Western democracies. But his following inside Russia was small. His break with Lenin, which had been building up since the split in the Duma fraction, was now final. For Lenin the attitude of the leading socialists of the belligerent countries to the war was conclusive proof that they were hopelessly sunk in the quagmire of reformism and opportunism. His views on the war and on socialist tasks arising out of it were formulated immediately on his arrival in September 1914 in Switzerland from Austria, where he had been living. Lenin argued that the socialists of the Second International, by betraying their duty to turn the war into a civil war, had proved both

[1] See the report of the menshevik Organization Committee to the Copenhagen Conference of the International in January 1915, Gankin and Fisher, *op. cit.*, pp. 267–71. For the views of the Potresov group see a collection of essays called *Samozashchita*, published in 1916. (Potresov's article 'Patriotizm i mezhdunarodnost" is reprinted in Nicolaevsky, *Potresov*, pp. 212–24.)

their ideological bankruptcy and their repudiation of class warfare. The war was a bourgeois, imperialist struggle for markets and plunder. The proletariat has no fatherland: since the workers are merely used as cannon fodder for the profit of the bourgeoisie, their only course is revolution. Propagation of and preparation for revolution was therefore the immediate task of social democrats in all the belligerent countries. Although Lenin repudiated the argument that a victory of relatively advanced Germany over reactionary Russia would be preferable to a Russian victory, he nonetheless regarded the defeat of Russia as the 'lesser evil', since this would lead to the break away from the Russian Empire of the oppressed national groups which composed it, and hence to a weakening of the monarchy.[1]

Lenin from the outset of the war staked everything on revolution both in Russia and in the other countries of Europe, and the whole of his policy was geared to this one end. He did not necessarily regard such revolutions as imminent, nor did he believe that they could happen simultaneously in all countries. On the contrary, he wrote in August 1915, the unequal economic and political development of different capitalist systems inevitably means that socialism will at first be victorious in a few countries, or even in one isolated country. But the victorious proletariat of that one country 'will then stand up *against* the rest of the capitalist world, attract to itself the oppressed classes of other countries, arousing them to insurrection against the capitalists, and if necessary even using its military forces against the exploiting classes and their states'.[2] If Lenin hoped that this pioneer of world revolution would be Russia, he did not say so. Nor did he at any time predict revolution in Russia or elsewhere as about to take place – as late as 22 January 1917 he was not prepared to say more than that popular risings, ending with the ultimate victory of socialism would come about 'in the next few years'.[3]

Lenin's formulation of the 'law of unequal development' of different capitalist systems was later to be used to explain how it came about that an ostensibly 'proletarian' revolution, such as the bolsheviks would one day claim to have effected, happened first in a country in which the proletariat was most backward and least numerous, and not, as Marx had foreseen, in circumstances where the proletariat formed the overwhelming majority. But during the war Lenin did not as yet have to face this theoretical problem. He argued that the Russian

[1] *Lenin*, volume XVIII, pp. 44–6.
[2] *ibidem*, pp. 232–3.
[3] *Lenin*, volume XIX, p. 357.

revolution would in the first place take the form of 'completing' the bourgeois revolution of 1905 – the proletariat would for this purpose ally itself with the petty bourgeois peasants. Only thereafter would the second phase become possible, 'the kindling of the flames of socialist revolutions' in all Europe, in alliance with the proletariat of other countries.[1] Thus, as in 1905, when he first developed his doctrine of the 'revolutionary democratic dictatorship of the proletariat and the peasantry', Lenin was still, in theory at all events, accepting the orthodox two phases of revolution, and, moreover, was envisaging the socialist revolution in one country, Russia, as possible only with the support of the proletariat of other countries. But Lenin repeatedly made it plain that there would be no place in the 'revolutionary democratic dictatorship' for anyone but those whom he considered real revolutionaries. There was to be no reunion with the mensheviks,[2] and no sharing of power with them in the future revolutionary dictatorship.

The main lines of bolshevik policy, as he envisaged it after the revolution had taken place, were sketched by him in a series of Theses published in October 1915. It would not be enough merely to demand the summoning of a Constituent Assembly; the important question would be who was in power when the elections to it took place. Should Soviets arise, as they had arisen in 1905, they should be treated as organs of insurrection against the bourgeoisie. On no account must social democrats participate in a Provisional Government side by side with 'social chauvinists' – i.e. mensheviks, or socialist revolutionaries. If the 'social chauvinists' should be victorious in Russia, 'we should be against the defence of *their* fatherland in the present war'. The bolsheviks will be against the 'chauvinists', even if they are revolutionaries and republicans, and stand 'for the union of the international proletariat for the socialist revolution'.[3] Here, in a few bold strokes, was the pattern of action which was put into effect in Russia less than two years later.

In the international sphere Lenin from the first envisaged a break with the Socialist International. As so often before, it was not unity that he sought for, but a final rupture with those who were not prepared to accept his policy. As he wrote to Alexandra Kollontay – then still a menshevik, but soon to become one of his followers – as

---

[1] *ibidem*, pp. 311–13; cf. pp. 314–18.

[2] 'The fundamental thing is a split with the Organization Committee and with Chkheidze and Co' he wrote to A. M. Shliapnikov in March 1916. See *Lenin*, volume XXIX, p. 229.

[3] *Lenin*, volume XVIII, pp. 311–13.

early as December 1914: 'You emphasize that "we must put forward a slogan that will *unite* all". Frankly, I am more afraid at the present time of such indiscriminate unification than of anything else.'[1] The following year he wrote of the need to create a third, truly Marxist International, cleansed of opportunism and chauvinism. The break with the Second International was for the bolsheviks now 'irrevocable'.[2] It was this irrevocable decision which precluded any reunion of the bolsheviks even with those mensheviks who were the most internationalist in outlook, such as Martov. The menshevik Organization Committee was represented in Switzerland by a 'Secretariat in Exile' which included Aksel'rod, Martov and Martynov. Like Lenin, these menshevik leaders repudiated the war as a bourgeois, imperialist war of plunder, and like Lenin they saw the only ultimate solution in revolution. Where they differed from Lenin was in their belief that the only hope for socialist revolutions in the belligerent countries lay in restoring the unity of international socialism, which had been so rudely shattered. Nor were they prepared, like Lenin, to advocate the defeat of Russia as the 'lesser evil'. They regarded the victory of any of the imperialist belligerents, with its consequent annexations of territory and subjection of foreign nationals, as a disaster. To prevent this it was essential, in their view, to maintain and encourage in every way the solidarity of socialists of all countries, so that they could together mobilize the proletariat to bring pressure upon the governments to conclude a speedy and just peace, without annexation of territory, or war indemnities. This was the first step. Thereafter, the only hope for the prevention of future wars lay in the universal victory of socialism, which would put an end to further imperialist plunder.[3]

Trotsky, who spent the early years of the war in Paris, was close in his views to the menshevik 'Secretariat in Exile'. In the pages of a daily paper, *Nashe Slovo* (Our Word), he developed his argument for a republican United States of Europe. The organization of the dictatorship of the proletariat on an all-European scale (the United States of America was excluded from his scheme for the time being) was for him the only counter-balance to the retrograde forces of nationalism and patriotism.[4] Trotsky also constantly emphasized the need for unity among all social democrats and rejected the final break with the

---

[1] *Lenin*, volume XXIX, p. 162.

[2] *Lenin*, volume XVIII, p. 217.

[3] Their views were voiced in a news-sheet, *Izvestiia zagranichnago sekretariata organizatsionnago komiteta R.S.-D.R.P.*, of which ten issues appeared between February 1915 and January 1917.

[4] *Nashe slovo*, Nos. 22 and 23 and 24, February 1915, and Nos. 24 (411), 25 (412), 28 (415) and 29 (416), 1916.

Second International urged by Lenin. But the fact that in the interests of union with the bolsheviks he was prepared to break with those mensheviks who supported the war, notably Plekhanov, prevented any lasting union between Trotsky and the 'Secretariat in Exile' and especially Aksel'rod. For the leading mensheviks abroad were divided not only on the question of their future relations with 'defensists' like Plekhanov, but also on the advisibility of attempting any kind of reconciliation with Lenin. Martov, who was prepared to go much further than his colleagues, not only in repudiating the 'defensists', but in attempting to make peace with Lenin, for a time collaborated with Trotsky on *Nashe Slovo*. The venture was short lived, since it led to friction both between Martov and Trotsky, and between Martov and his colleagues of the 'Secretariat in Exile'.

In the end, attempts at reunification of the Russian social democrats abroad proved abortive. A conference of all groups planned early in 1915 came to nothing,[1] and the attempt was not renewed. In spite of the apparent identity of the main aim – revolution (even Lenin grudgingly conceded that Martov was the 'most decent' among the mensheviks[2]) – there was a deep gulf between the bolsheviks and the mensheviks on the nature of this revolution. Lenin was thinking of revolution in one country, at the weakest point of the imperialist chain, and only thereafter of its spread to other countries. The mensheviks, and Trotsky, were thinking of co-ordinated, simultaneous risings of a united, organized, world or European proletariat.

The bolsheviks abroad were little more united than the mensheviks, and Lenin, with the aid of Zinoviev, engaged in spirited polemics throughout the war with his fellow exiles. New figures had appeared on the scene in Switzerland, mainly intellectual bolsheviks, and very different from the underground committee-men of whom Lenin had before the war built up his main following inside Russia. Among the new arrivals were N. I. Bukharin, N. V. Krylenko and G. L. Piatakov, all of whom were to play leading parts in Russia after the revolution. They had as yet no experience of Lenin's methods at close quarters, and suffered the shock of his uncompromising assault on their views with considerable dismay. For Bukharin however, a man of brilliant if erratic intellect but of little practical sense, Lenin in spite of all their disagreements retained respect and even affection. Much of this war-time squabbling was tedious and of little consequence.[3] But two of the

---

[1] *Pis'ma*, p. 336; Gankin and Fisher, *op. cit.*, pp. 162–73.
[2] In October 1914 – *Lenin*, volume XVIII, p. 54.
[3] It is dealt with in detail in Gankin and Fisher, *op. cit.*, pp. 213 ff.

questions in dispute – national self-determination and the theory of the state – were of importance both as a foretaste of future dissensions inside the bolshevik party and as an instance of Lenin's practical adaptation of theoretical Marxism to the needs of revolution when contrasted with the doctrinal scruples of more orthodox or traditional Marxists, who would later be dubbed 'left-wing'.

Marx and Engels left little precise guidance on the problem of nationalism. But in so far as they dealt with it, they treated nationalism as a transient force, characteristic of the capitalist phase of society. It could hamper the class struggle for a time; but it would eventually yield to proletarian class consciousness, which was essentially international. The orthodox followers of Marx, or those who regarded themselves as such, were faced in Eastern Europe with nationalism as a much more acute problem than it had been for Marx in the countries of Western Europe. Rosa Luxemburg, the most influential opponent of Polish nationalism, argued that Polish social democrats should not strive for Polish independence, but for revolution in Russia, which would, when accomplished, allow Poland her autonomy within a free Russia. The issue of national self-determination had been the most hotly debated question among Polish social democrats. It was over this that in 1893 Rosa Luxemburg and Tyshka had split off from the Polish socialist party to form the Polish social democratic party, which had played so large a part in Lenin's conflicts with the mensheviks before the war. The Russian social democrats adopted as part of their programme in 1903 the right of each nation within the Russian Empire to self-determination, without at the time either fully debating, or realizing, all the implications of this decision. After 1912 dissensions on the question of nationalism arose between the two factions. The mensheviks at their Vienna Conference in 1912, now dependent on their alliance with the *Bund*, the Caucasians and other national parties, accepted in principle national cultural autonomy within a unified future democratic state. This was the policy of the *Bund*, among others, which in turn derived from the views of two prominent Austrian socialists, Karl Renner and Otto Bauer. Lenin supported full national self-determination. He devoted several articles to the subject, and Stalin also produced a somewhat uneducated work on nationalism at Lenin's request.[1]

It was Lenin's defence of the unrestricted right of each Russian nation to self-determination which was the object of attack in war-time

---

[1] On the history of this question see Richard Pipes, *The Formation of the Soviet Union. Communism and Nationalism, 1917–1923*. Cambridge, Mass., 1954, pp. 21 ff.

exile, especially from Rosa Luxemburg and from Bukharin. Bukharin, who was supported by Piatakov, argued that to preach self-determination endangered the world solidarity of the proletariat, and would deflect the proletariat of the individual countries from their main task, the overthrow of capitalism, by encouraging the workers to nurture illusions that they could achieve their liberation under capitalism.[1] But for Lenin, who was thinking in the more practical terms of fostering the best conditions for a revolution in Russia, national self-determination was too powerful a weapon for hastening the disintegration of the Russian Empire to be readily jettisoned. Moreover, on analysis it becomes clear that Lenin only envisaged the break away of the national groups of the Empire as a 'transition stage' on the road to reintegration under socialism. He insisted that the social democratic party should remain one and centralized, and should never be allowed to become a loose federation of national parties.[2] Thus, even after the various nationalities had severed their connexion with the Empire, they would continue to be linked through a united party which could work within each nation for the reintegration of the former multinational unity after the victory of socialism. And, as Lenin was never tired of emphasizing, to defend the right to self-determination did not mean to advocate separatism. On the contrary, it was to be hoped that when once the oppressive Russian monarchy had fallen, those nations which had exercised the right to secede would return to the fold voluntarily.[3]

Lenin also clashed with Bukharin on the question of what happens to the state after the victory of socialism. Bukharin had argued that since the state was merely an organization of the ruling class which existed for the sole purpose of exploiting the proletariat, it must disappear with the social revolution which abolishes class relationships. This view was no more than a restatement of the argument frequently advanced by Engels that the state was destined to 'wither away' when once class exploitation had been abolished. But neither Marx nor Engels had applied himself to defining the concrete process by which a revolution would be completed, beyond occasional references to the 'dictatorship of the proletariat' which would intervene between the outbreak of revolution and the establishing of socialism. Lenin now supplied some of the omissions in polemics with Bukharin. It was true, he wrote, that the state would gradually wither away after

[1] Gankin and Fisher, *op. cit.*, pp. 219–21.
[2] *Lenin*, volume XVI, p. 512; volume XIX, p. 40.
[3] See e.g. his letter to Shaumian of 6 December 1913, *Lenin*, volume XVII, pp. 89–91; and cf. volume XIX, p. 245.

the bourgeoisie had been expropriated. But socialists stand for the utilization of the contemporary state and its institutions in order to liberate the working class during the transition from capitalism to socialism. This period of transition, which is itself also a form of the state, will be the dictatorship of the proletariat.[1] Bukharin's 'left' views were also shared by *Vperëd*, which (bereft of Aleksinskii, who had become a war patriot) continued throughout the war as a separate group.

Apart from engaging in argument with his fellow bolsheviks, Lenin also devoted his energies to building up a following in international socialism. He did not make much progress in this direction, nor did he succeed in achieving unity among those who at first followed his lead. Two international conferences of dissident socialists who disagreed with their leaders in the Second International were held during the war – at Zimmerwald and at Kienthal. At the former, in September 1915, thirty-eight participants from eleven countries, including Germany and France, adopted a manifesto which called upon the working class to struggle for peace. At this conference Lenin and Zinoviev headed a left group, to which Karl Radek, two Swedish, one Dutch one German and one Lettish delegates gave their support. The 'Zimmerwald Left', as it became known, proposed as an alternative to the manifesto a call to civil war as the only means of ending the imperialist war. At the second and somewhat larger conference at Kienthal in April 1916, a resolution of a more concrete nature was adopted by the majority. The proletariat was now enjoined to 'raise the call for an immediate truce'. The 'Zimmerwald Left', with some Swiss, Polish, Serbian and Italian, but no longer with Swedish, support (the Swedes were now in prison), proposed an even more radical call to the proletariat of the belligerent powers: 'Lay down your weapons. You should turn them only against the common foe – the capitalist governments.'[2]

The call 'lay down your weapons' raised the question of what would happen if the proletariat of one belligerent obeyed it but the proletariat of another did not. Was the pacifist belligerent to submit to conquest and annexation? Before long this problem was to become a very actual one in Russia. But as yet it was little discussed. Lenin, however, had in part supplied the answer in an article published in

[1] For Bukharin's views see an article by him written in December 1916, reprinted in Gankin and Fisher, *op. cit.*, pp. 236–9. For Lenin's reply see *Lenin*, volume XIX, pp. 294–7. Lenin's reply to Bukharin was later expanded in *State and Revolution*.

[2] These conferences are dealt with in full detail in Gankin and Fisher, *op. cit.*, chapters iv, v and vi, where the texts of the documents quoted are reprinted.

October 1915. If, he then wrote, the party of the proletariat were to achieve power in Russia during the war, it would immediately offer peace to all belligerents, upon condition that all colonial and dependent peoples were liberated. This offer would certainly be refused. 'Then we should have to prepare and lead a revolutionary war,' with the object of rousing to insurrection all the colonies and the dependent countries of Asia, such as India, China and Persia, as well as the socialist proletariat of Europe.[1] It should be noted that this proved to be the only part of Lenin's detailed programme of action adumbrated during the war which was never implemented: when the time came the bolshevik call for peace was not made in this form, nor did revolutionary war follow rejection of the bolshevik peace offer.

Inside Russia during the war social democratic activity was disorganized, intermittent and not very effective. The bolsheviks were somewhat better organized, and the more united. In spite of the setback caused by the arrest of the bolshevik Duma deputies, a number of organizations were reconstituted which were run by the Russian Bureau of the Central Committee in Petrograd. In the later stages of the war when home morale began to collapse, the bolsheviks' direct call to oppose the war, to come out on strike and to raise an insurrection was beginning to find a slight response. The Russian Bureau, which after the autumn of 1916 consisted of A. M. Shliapnikov, Molotov and P. Zalutskii, was under Lenin's direction. For Lenin maintained regular correspondence with Shliapnikov, who stood very close to him, and had spent a part of the war in Sweden and Denmark. The Russian Bureau was in contact with a number of underground committees whose total membership has been (somewhat optimistically) estimated at ten thousand.[2] It was handicapped by lack of money. Although offers of German money, made through such agents of the Germans as Trotsky's former ally Parvus, reached the Russian Bureau, they were rejected, according to Shliapnikov. There is no evidence to suggest that at this date the bolsheviks inside Russia were in possession of ample means.[3]

[1] *Lenin*, volume XVIII, p. 313.
[2] V. Volosevich, *Bol'shevizm v gody mirovoi voiny*, Leningrad, n.d. (1929). A rather less optimistic picture emerges from the contemporary reports sent in to the party organ, *Sotsial-Demokrat*, which are reprinted in *Bol'sheviki v gody imperialisticheskoi voiny. 1914 – fevral' 1917*. Sbornik dokumentov mestnykh bol'shevistskikh organizatsii. GAU NKVD Tsentral'nyi Arkhiv Revoliutsii. Moscow, 1939, pp. 62–4, 80–8, 95–6, 100–1, 132, 172, 174–5, 186–7, 201–4.
[3] See A. Shliapnikov, *Kanun semnadtsatogo goda*. Vospominaniia i dokumenty o rabochem dvizhenii v revoliutsionnom podpol'e za 1914–1916 gg. Part I, Second edition, Part II, Third edition, Moscow, Petrograd, 1923, Part I, pp. 65, 209; Part II, pp. 100–3.

The menshevik organization was at first even less effective than the bolshevik. Unlike the more disciplined bolsheviks, the mensheviks were disinclined to accept such leadership as emanated from the 'Secretariat in Exile'. Moreover, their attitude to the war placed them at a disadvantage so far as practical work was concerned. The minority who were 'defensist', in Potresov's limited sense, found in practice that it was difficult to demand democratic reforms and at the same time to urge that the war effort should not be opposed. Some, like Cherevanin, attempted to draw a fine distinction between 'not actively opposing the war' and 'helping the success of the war'. The internationalist majority, among whom all shades of opinion prevailed, tried to steer an uneasy course between limited approval of the war and all out disapproval of the government. The Petersburg menshevik group urged (in January 1915) that while the war, as a matter of national self-defence, should not be opposed, no trust should be placed in the government, and of course no credits voted.[1] Lenin's simple formula that Russian defeat was the lesser evil was both more direct and, as time went on, more popular, and Dan, who was an internationalist, noted with dismay at the end of 1915 that the bolsheviks were attracting the most vigorous elements among the workers.[2]

In the course of 1915 a new opportunity presented itself to the mensheviks which some of them were quick to exploit. By August 1915 the leader of the Octobrists, Guchkov, had been successful in putting through a scheme for setting up all over Russia a network of so-called War Industry Committees. These committees were intended to bring more closely together the industrialists, the workers and the government, and thus to encourage greater effort in production for war needs. The new organization covered every branch of military supply, and – to the dismay of the Emperor and Empress – made provision for delegates from the workers in the relevant industries. The workers' delegates held separate meetings as a Workers' Group, and had their own office. The new scheme raised a storm among social democrats which helped to accentuate the divisions which already existed. The bolsheviks opposed all participation in an organization designed to help the war, and were supported by the more extreme internationalists. The menshevik 'Secretariat in Exile' also ruled that no mensheviks should seek election to the committees. Inside Russia the internationalists, headed by Dan, now in exile in Siberia, advocated

[1] *Nashe delo*, No. 5–6; *Izvestiia zagr. sekr. O.K. R.S.-D.R.P.*, No. 1, p. 2.
[2] *Pis'ma*, p. 355.

limited participation. Social democratic delegates, in their view, should enter the committees both in order to propagate the need for peace and in order to protect the workers from exploitation.[1] The 'liquidator' practicals, like P. A. Garvi, immediately welcomed the new opportunity for concrete social democratic activity, and ignored the views of the 'Secretariat in Exile'. In the election of delegates to the Central War Industry Committee, held in November 1915 (after an unsuccessful attempt by the bolsheviks to frustrate it), a strong Workers' Group of 'liquidators', headed by K. A. Gvozdev and B. O. Bogdanov, was returned.

Left thus alone in the field, the 'liquidators' were soon dominant in the workers' groups inside this new organization, which was attracting like a magnet the support of workers from all over the country. These mensheviks in the workers' groups, unlike the social democrats in the First Duma in 1906, were prepared to support the left-wing members of the Duma, including the *Kadety*, in their struggle to wrest a more democratic form of government out of the monarchy. By the end of 1916 the new Minister of the Interior, Protopopov, reported that the workers' groups were engaging in revolutionary activity. In conjunction with the progressive members of the Duma they were demanding a 'Save the Country' government, and were organizing meetings in support of the more radical demands of the Duma. At the end of December 1916 the Central Workers' Group in Petrograd organized a conference of workers' delegates to the War Industry Committees, composed of the Duma social democratic 'fraction', and of representatives from twelve cities, from the factories and from the trade unions. This conference declared that the present régime had brought the country to the edge of disaster. The only solution lay in complete democratization of the system of government. The task of the workers was to strive towards this end by mass political action which would give the 'necessary impetus and decisiveness' to the struggle which was already being waged by the Duma. The greatest possible numbers should be gathered around the workers' groups, the idea of a workers' congress should be put forward, and steps taken for its practical realization.[2] This last proposal, first put forward by Aksel'rod eleven years before, was to lead to momentous results.

By 1917 popular discontent was assuming alarming proportions,

[1] *ibidem*, p. 356. For the views of various bolshevik committees opposing participation see *Bol'shevizm v gody* . . . pp. 66–9, 55, 87.

[2] A. Shliapnikov. *op. cit.*, Part II, pp. 173–7 and 143–7. For full details of the activity of the Workers' Group in Petrograd see the numerous documents printed in *Krasnyi arkhiv*, No. 57, 1933, pp. 43–84; and No. 6 (67), 1934, pp. 28–92.

and strikes were rapidly increasing in extent and frequency. The Central Workers' Group had by its agitation contributed to this unrest sufficiently to cause the arrest of all its members on 27 January on the charge of fomenting an insurrection. Their last act had been to call a demonstration for the day of the re-opening of the Duma, 14 February 1917. The bolsheviks, alarmed by the ascendancy which the Workers' Group appeared to be gaining over the masses, countered this by calling a strike for 13 February, the anniversary of the trial and condemnation of the five bolshevik deputies of the Fourth Duma. It was a measure of the spontaneous character of the Russian revolution that the workers did not respond to either appeal; but their reaction showed, if anything, the influence of the Workers' Group. They ignored the bolshevik call – there was no unrest or strike activity whatever on the 13th. But the following day, in place of a demonstration before the Duma, there was a mass strike of nearly a hundred thousand workers in sixty enterprises in Petrograd, which continued the following day.[1] A lull then followed until 19 February. Demonstrations by women queueing for bread now started off a further chain of strikes in the capital. By 25 February the strike was general, and two days later the monarchy was on the verge of collapse. Power was precariously in the hands of a Provisional Committee of the Duma, and the troops in the capital were siding with the crowds. Some of the mutinous soldiers went to the prisons and, among other political prisoners, freed the arrested members of the Workers' Group. The Group members went straight from prison to the Tauride Palace, where the Duma met. The tide of revolution was rising fast. The memories of these seasoned menshevik revolutionaries (for this, for all Lenin's vilification, is what they were) now went back to another Soviet, twelve years before, which had failed because it had been convened too late, and because the bourgeoisie had not supported it. This time the revolution must not be allowed to fail. The members of the Workers' Group acted with feverish haste. Together with representatives of the trade unions and of the co-operatives, and also the left-wing Duma parties, they set up a Provisional Executive Committee of the Soviet of Workers' Deputies. This Committee proceeded immediately to call for elections to a Soviet, and summonses to send their delegates to the Palace went out to the factory workers. The same evening the Petrograd Soviet held its first meeting, and

---

[1] N. Avdeev, *Revoliutsiia 1917 goda. (Khronika sobytii.)*, volume I, Moscow. 1923, pp. 14–36; I. Iurenev in *Proletarskaia revoliutsiia*, No. 2 (25), 1924, pp. 131–3.

began straightaway to take administrative steps for the assurance of food supplies.[1]

Three days later the Emperor had abdicated and a Provisional Government had been formed by the moderate progressives in the Duma. The monarchy had crashed in ruins. By the irony of history it had fallen to the 'liquidators' to play a greater part in its overthrow than any other group in the social democratic party. True to the menshevik tradition, they had taken immediate steps to create a Soviet which would provide, as they believed, a focal point to rally the worker masses. For the time being the mensheviks held the ascendancy within this strange assembly which now arose side by side with the newly born Provisional Government. They were not destined to enjoy it for long.

[1] Avdeev, *loc. cit.*; P. A. Garvi in *Sotsialisticheskii vestnik*, No. 2–3, 1957, pp. 47–8.

PART TWO

From Lenin to Stalin

IX The Road to Power

The general disintegration, which caused the precipitous collapse of the monarchy left the problem of authority unresolved. The Provisional Government, formed at first of the moderate progressive members of the Duma who had done most to bring the monarchy to its knees, found itself from the outset in competition with a rival authority, that of the soviets of workers' and soldiers' delegates which sprang up throughout the land. Beneath the mood of exaltation which the revolution engendered, the reality of impending chaos soon threatened. To the Provisional Government the revolution stood for democratic freedoms, for liberation from oppression, and for a chance at long last to prosecute effectively a war which a reactionary and inefficient monarchy had hampered. They saw little hope for the new democracy in Russia if the older democracies of Britain and France fell before the onslaught of Imperial Germany. They realized the need for order. But they had neither the inclination, nor perhaps the means, to take the kind of measures which alone could have restored it. The soviets, in which mensheviks and socialist revolutionaries predominated until September 1917, viewed the imperialist war with disgust and the bourgeois Provisional Government with suspicion. For the most part (there were exceptions among them, but their voices were of little effect) the socialists made their support of the war conditional upon the Provisional Government making immediate efforts to conclude peace on just, democratic terms. Their propaganda to the soldiers, even if they did not intend it, was little less disruptive than that of the frankly defeatist bolsheviks. The socialist leaders at first refused to enter the government, but in domestic matters they supported it, though only to the extent to which it was ready to put into immediate effect extreme socialist and democratic measures. Their strength lay in the popular support which they enjoyed both in the towns and in the army. In the villages a peasant war, symptomatic of the chronic land hunger, fast gathered momentum.

The socialist parties, even if by their conduct they contributed to the growing disorder, were in the last resort prepared to co-operate with the Provisional Government, provided they could impose their own policy upon it. It was with such intentions that some of their leaders eventually entered the government, and thereafter progressively drove it farther to the left – acting under pressure from the soldiers and workers whose spokesmen they were. The bolsheviks were determined to destroy the Provisional Government. They were prepared neither to join it, nor to support it. They made uninhibited promises of immediate peace and distribution of land to the peasants and encouraged the growing chaos on the land, in industry and in the army, from which they hoped to reap the reward of power. After April, at any rate, they were convinced that nothing but the passing of power to the soviets, in which they hoped they would be in a majority, could ensure the survival of a revolutionary régime. As time went on their bid for power, by fair means or foul, became increasingly apparent. The Provisional Government (with a majority composed of comparatively moderate socialists, after July) wrestled in vain with growing disorder. What was widely believed to be an attempted *coup d'état* by the bolsheviks in July for a short time united all the socialists behind the government and against the bolsheviks. But, soon after, an attempt by General Kornilov (himself a left-wing supporter of the revolution, though backed by right-wing industrialists) to restore order by imposing a military dictatorship turned the tables. The Provisional Government, forced to choose between what it rightly or wrongly regarded as 'counter-revolution' and the bolsheviks, jettisoned Kornilov, and thereby alienated those remnants of the army which might have been prepared to support it. Bolsheviks and socialists now co-operated in the defence of the revolution, but the bolsheviks alone were the winners. Their popularity in many parts of the country, and in the capital, grew rapidly. On 25 October 1917 they voted themselves into office in the name of the Second All-Russian Congress of Soviets, on which they had a small majority, having previously seized effective power in the capital by force of arms.

* * *

Thus, in the course of eight months the bolsheviks, who in numbers and influence could have been dismissed as negligible at the beginning of 1917, had placed themselves in sole, if precarious, control over the former Russian Empire. We are concerned with the development of policy and organization within the party during these crucial months. Few bolshevik organizations had survived the war unscathed. When the monarchy fell, there was a fair-sized organization in the capital, the

Petersburg Committee,[1] as well as the Russian Bureau of the Central Committee, which consisted of Molotov and two others – Shliapnikov and Zalutskii, a figure of little influence. Several other committees were able to start their legal existence immediately after the revolution of February 1917, including the Moscow city and provincial organizations. Some seventy further organizations emerged into the open in the course of March or early April, many of which had presumably retained some remnants of an underground organization during the war. But over half of these organizations were still joint bolshevik-menshevik organizations, and many of them remained joint for some time. By October the Central Committee was in touch with a total of 163 all-bolshevik organizations.[2] When the monarchy fell, Molotov was in charge of the secretarial duties of the Russian Bureau of the Central Committee. But almost immediately, on her return from exile, Stasova, who had had many years of experience in the past as party secretary, took over from Molotov, and thereafter maintained the general conduct of the small secretariat, of which the staff in 1917 only totalled some half-dozen. Sverdlov exercised general supervision.[3]

Lenin did not arrive in Petrograd until 3 April. During the month which elapsed before his arrival the policy pursued by the party on the two burning issues – the attitude to the war and the policy towards the Provisional Government – was very different from what Lenin had in mind. For a short time Shliapnikov endeavoured to put Lenin's views, as he knew them, into practice, and on 23 March, for example, the Russian Bureau under his guidance issued a declaration demanding fraternization at the front, immediate negotiations for an end to the war and the turning of the war into civil war against the imperialists.[4] But shortly afterwards the arrival in Petrograd of Stalin and Kamenev from exile changed the picture. By virtue of their seniority they took over the Russian Bureau and the direction of policy. The slogan 'down with the war' was useless, Stalin now wrote in *Pravda*

[1] This Committee (which had continued to call itself Petersburg, not Petrograd Committee) claimed a membership of 16,000 by May 1917 – see *Perepiska sekretariata Ts. K. RSDRP(b) s mestnymi partiinymi organizatsiiami (mart-oktiabr' 1917 g.). Sbornik dokumentov.* Volume I, Moscow, 1957, p. 481. (Cited hereafter as *Perepiska sekretariata.*)

[2] *ibidem*, pp. 481–506. The membership of the Moscow committees totalled 30,000 by May 1917. The remaining committees varied in size of membership from a few dozen to several thousand.

[3] E. D. Stasova, *Stranitsy zhizni i bor'by*, Moscow, 1957, pp. 83–96; K. T, Sverdlova, 'Deiatel'nost'la. M. Sverdlova v 1917 godu' in *Voprosy istorii* (Moscow). No. 6, 1956, pp. 5–15.

[4] Quoted in *Proletarskaia revoliutsiia*, No. 4 (63'), 1927, pp. 50–2, from *Pravda*.

on 29 March. The proper course was 'pressure on the Provisional Government' to induce it to open peace negotiations. Kamenev wrote in similar terms.[1] The divisions inside the party became apparent at an All-Russian Party Conference, held between 1 and 3 April, at which 58 organizations were represented. Three main groups could be discerned: the centre group, which included Stalin and Kamenev, and was supported by the Moscow City Organization, now reinforced by the return from exile of Nogin and Rykov; a more radical left-wing group, headed by Shliapnikov and Molotov, which included Alexandra Kollontai, and was supported by the Moscow Provincial Organization, which embraced 13 provinces; and a small right-wing group. Stalin succeeded in winning unanimous approval for a resolution on relations with the Provisional Government: this was based on the assumption, which no one questioned, that a long period of bourgeois middle-class democratic government had now begun, and that dictatorship of the proletariat only related to the very distant future. It called for 'vigilant control' over the activities of the Provisional Government and support for the Petrograd soviet as the 'beginning of a revolutionary power'. The moderate views of Stalin and Kamenev on the attitude to the war were also accepted, in spite of considerable opposition, by a majority vote. It was a position which did not much differ from that of the mensheviks and it was therefore not surprising that the conference should have agreed, though with some reluctance, to embark on exploratory discussions on unification with the mensheviks.[2]

Meanwhile Lenin, chafing in Switzerland for some means to get him back to Russia, had, with Zinoviev's support, been formulating a very different policy. His views were clearly summarized in a telegram sent to Alexandra Kollontai and others towards the end of March: 'Our tactics: absolutely distrust, no support of new government. Kerensky particularly suspect; to arm proletariat only guarantee; *no rapprochement with other parties*. The last is *conditio sine qua non*. We do not trust Chkheidze.' The full development of his views was contained in a set of Theses on policy prepared jointly with

[1] *Stalin*, volume III, pp. 4–8; *Pravda*, 28 March 1917.

[2] The complete transcript of the proceedings of this conference is said to have been lost during the July disturbances, though an abridged form of it has survived in the archives of the Institute of Marxism-Leninism – see F. I. Drabkina, 'Vserossiiskoe soveshchanie bol'shevikov v marte 1917 goda', in *Voprosy istorii* (Moscow), No. 9, 1956, pp. 4–16. The complete record was however published by Trotsky from a copy in his possession in L. Trotsky, *Stalinskaia shkola fal'sifikatsii*, Berlin, 1932, pp. 225–90. Drabkina's and Trotsky's versions are obviously very similar. See also E. N. Burdzhalov, 'O taktike bol'shevikov v marte-aprele 1917 goda' in *Voprosy istorii*, No. 4, 1956, pp. 38–56.

Zinoviev on 17 March and a number of 'Letters from Afar' written between 20 and 26 March.[1] Lenin clearly visualized seizure of power by the armed proletariat, 'fusing the police, the army and the bureaucracy with the people armed to a man', but not by the existing soviets. What he had written of the soviets in 1905 as 'organs of revolutionary power', he now wrote, required reconsideration.[2]

On 3 April 1917, while the All-Russian Party Conference was still in session, Lenin arrived in Petrograd. He had travelled through Germany by arrangement with the German government, a fact which immediately gave rise to rumours that the bolsheviks were acting as agents of the Germans in trying to knock Russia out of the war.[3] The impact of Lenin's arrival on the party was electric; but he too was apparently influenced by the evidence of the popularity of the soviets. The policy which he now urged, both at the conference, and in *Pravda* a few days later, was indeed very different from what the conference had accepted just before his arrival and differed somewhat from what he had himself written in Switzerland. There should be no question of unification with the mensheviks. Nor should the bolsheviks support the Provisional Government in any way: they should work not for a parliamentary republic, 'but a republic of soviets of workers', soldiers' and peasants' deputies in the whole country . . . confiscation of all landlords' estates, nationalization of all land . . . a single national bank . . . elimination of the army and police.' As for the war, there could be no genuinely democratic peace without the overthrow of capitalism, and Lenin now urged 'the widest propaganda of this view in the army in the field' and 'fraternization'.[4]

There was little, if anything, in these views which differed fundamentally from Lenin's policy for years past. But the demand for an immediate socialist revolution, even in the form of the passing of all power to the soviets, though implicit in Lenin's views as far back as 1905 if not earlier, had never before been formulated so baldly, and the party leaders were startled. *Pravda* immediately disowned Lenin's view as 'unacceptable in that it starts from the assumption that the bourgeois democratic revolution is ended. . . .'.[5] Both Kamenev and

[1] *Lenin*, volume XXIX, p. 343 (Chkheidze was the menshevik chairman of the Petrograd soviet); volume XX, pp. 9–47.
[2] *Lenin*, volume XX, pp. 34–5.
[3] The documents from the archives of the German Foreign Ministry relating to this transaction, which were captured by the Allied Forces during the Second World War, have now been published – see *Lenins Rückkehr nach Russland 1917. Die deutschen Akten.* Edited by Werner Hahlweg, Leiden, 1957.
[4] *Lenin*, volume XX, pp. 79, 88.
[5] On 21 (8) April 1917.

Zinoviev, and a number of others such as Rykov and Nogin, who, unlike Zinoviev and Kamenev, had already had serious differences with Lenin before 1917, continued to oppose this part of Lenin's policy thereafter. Stalin, in contrast, very soon accepted Lenin's views. In spite of Lenin, a joint bolshevik-menshevik bureau was set up to prepare a conference on union, which a number of right-wing bolsheviks entered.[1] Nor were Lenin's views on relations with the mensheviks immediately accepted by the party rank and file. As late as September and October there were still 28 local party organizations which, despite all efforts of the Central Committee, remained joint bolshevik-menshevik.[2]

In spite of this unpromising beginning, Lenin before long succeeded in winning over most of the party to his views. This success was in part due to his intellectual superiority over his opponents; in part to the appearance of compromise with which he exercised his leadership; and in part to the growing revolutionary mood of the rank and file of the party which was straining for power and had little regard for theoretical niceties. A series of party resolutions in the last week of April stressed that there was no question of seizure of power by the soviets until the bolsheviks had won a majority in them.[3] This possibility was still sufficiently remote to comfort the more hesitant leaders – at the First All-Russian Congress of Soviets which met on 3 June, the bolsheviks were still a small minority of the mainly socialist revolutionary and menshevik delegates.[4] At the Seventh All-Russian Party Conference, which met from 24 to 29 April, a resolution which similarly linked passage of power to the soviets with the winning of a bolshevik majority was adopted with only three dissenting votes and eight abstentions. There was a good deal more opposition at this conference to a resolution calling for nationalization of land and for various forms of state control over industrial undertakings, which was only passed by 71 votes to 39, with 8 abstentions; and Lenin's proposal to break finally with the Second International did not receive a single vote in support.[5]

---

[1] N. Avdeev, *Revoliutsiia 1917 goda (khronika sobytii)*, volume II, Moscow, 1923, pp. 10–11. Its efforts were abortive.
[2] *Perepiska Sekretariata*, Volume I pp. 481–506. The total number of organizations listed is 163.
[3] *VII Konf.* (Moscow, 1934). pp. 29, 242–3, 256–8.
[4] 105 out of 777 voting delegates whose party allegiance was disclosed. There were 285 SR's and 248 mensheviks – W. H. Chamberlin, *The Russian Revolution 1917–1921*, volume I New York, 1935, p. 159.
[5] For the resolutions of this conference, which also dealt with the attitude to the war, with the national question (reiterating the demand for full autonomy for minorities, while stressing that the right to autonomy must not be confused with the

In spite of these concessions to the 'constitutional illusions' prevalent in his party, it is unlikely that this emphasis on the winning over of a majority in the soviets as a condition for seizing power represented, so far as Lenin was concerned, anything more than a tactical recognition of the popular support which the soviets enjoyed. The proletariat cannot conquer, he wrote some years later, 'without winning over to its side the majority of the population. But to limit this winning over of the population to, or to make it conditional on, "acquiring" a majority of votes in an election, *while the bourgeoisie is in power* is impracticable imbecility, or simply cheating the workers.'[1] But in addition to overcoming the hesitations in the top leadership of his own party Lenin had further to temper his tactics to developing circumstances. So long as the soviets, with their largely menshevik and socialist revolutionary composition, enjoyed greater popular support than the bolshevik party organizations, it was necessary for Lenin to restrain the ardour of the rank and file for immediate impetuous action, for two reasons. One was the fear that the Executive Committee of the Petrograd Soviet might take alarm at bolshevik intentions and decide to support the Provisional Government in measures aimed at curbing the bolsheviks. The other was the realization that revolutionary temper in the capital would not guarantee victory unless a seizure of power by the bolsheviks at the centre could be relied on to find a ready response all over the country.

The rapidly changing balance of forces can be illustrated by the salient moments of the history of the rise of the bolsheviks in the capital. In April a note on Russian war aims dispatched to the Allied Powers by the Kadet foreign minister, Miliukov, provoked angry demonstrations in the capital, under the slogan 'Down with the government'. Yet there was no doubt where authority lay, so far as the crowd was concerned, since it obediently yielded to the request of the Petrograd Soviet to disperse.[2] By June the position was very different. After some hesitation the bolshevik party leaders, yielding to the insistent demand of the rank and file, called a demonstration for 10 June. On 9 June the First All-Russian Congress of Soviets, which was then in session, forbade the demonstration, and the bolshevik Central Committee decided to call it off. Party emissaries, with

---

[1] *Lenin*, volume XXIV, p. 641.
[2] N. Sukhanov, *Zapiski o revoliutsii*, Berlin, St Petersburg, Moscow, 1923, volume III, pp. 293–5.

---

expediency of autonomy in any particular case, which could only be decided by the party in the interests of the class struggle of the proletariat) and with revision of the party programme, see *KPSS v rez.*, volume I, pp. 332–53.

some difficulty, persuaded the demonstrations to disperse. But Lenin had the satisfaction of noting that this time it was the party, not the soviet, which had stopped the crowds. There is little doubt that at that date a rising would have been premature, and *Pravda* on 10 June warned against premature demonstrations, promising that the party would call the workers and soldiers out into the streets 'in case of necessity'. In spite of the moral victory of the soviet, and despite the scarcely disguised intention of the bolsheviks to seize power by force, the socialists in the soviets were not yet prepared to take any steps towards disarming the bolsheviks and their supporters in the capital.[1]

The position was very different a few weeks later. On 3 and 4 July crowds of workers and soldiers broke out in an angry and disorderly armed demonstration in the streets of Petrograd, determined to force the Petrograd Soviet to take power. There were several hundred casualties. The Provisional Government at last decided to take steps to repress the bolsheviks. In this move they had the support of the great majority of the members of the socialist parties in the Petrograd Soviet, whose representatives were by now sitting in the government. The Provisional Government not only accused the bolsheviks of planning a *coup d'état*, but revived the charge, allegedly on new evidence, that the bolshevik leaders were in the pay of the Germans. These charges had their effect. Lenin and Zinoviev went into hiding in order to avoid arrest and trial, and other leaders were arrested. No attempt seems to have been made to disarm the bolshevik force, the Red Guard (to which reference is made below), nor was the charge of complicity with the Germans ever pursued to a trial. The extent to which it rested on fact is also examined below. Although the measures which the Provisional Government took were in themselves ineffective, there is no doubt that the whole incident of the July disturbances, caused a serious ebb in the fortunes of the bolsheviks. The charge that they had planned a rising was probably untrue – in the sense that they were aiming at a direct seizure of power. At any rate, the report of an official enquiry held soon after suggests that, while the armed demonstration was undoubtedly organized by a number of leading bolsheviks in Petrograd and Kronstadt, no concrete plans were made for the seizure of any vital points in the capital, or for deposition of the Provisional Government.[2]

---

[1] On the attitude of the socialists in the soviet see I. Tsereteli, 'Nakanune iiul'skogo vosstaniia', *Novyi zhurnal* (New York), No. 52, 1958, pp. 162–98.

[2] *Baltiiskie moriaki v podgotovke i provedenii velikoi oktiabr'skoi sotsialisticheskoi revoliutsii*, edited by R. N. Mordvinov, Moscow, 1957, pp. 162–74. For two versions of a short speech by Lenin on the occasion, as reported to the enquiry and as subsequently summarized by Lenin, contrast pp. 169 and 349 *ibidem*.

But though the July demonstration may thus have been no more than a reconnaissance in force, it seriously altered the whole situation of the bolsheviks. Their popularity waned almost as rapidly as it had waxed,[1] their leader was now in hiding, and the socialist parties had at long last turned against them – had turned counter-revolutionary, as the bolsheviks put it. By the middle of July Lenin jettisoned the soviets as organs of power, since they had become organs of reaction. Only the 'revolutionary masses of the people' can take power, he now wrote, turning away from the socialist parties who have betrayed the revolution and who have supported a government 'which must now be overthrown'.[2] Lenin did not, however, indicate what organs were to take power, if it was not to be the soviets. When on 26 July the Sixth Bolshevik Party Congress met in Petrograd, Lenin and Zinoviev were absent, and the task of explaining the new policy fell to Stalin, who proposed a resolution embodying the new tactics. The familiar slogan 'All power to the soviets' was now out of date. The bolsheviks were to take on the role of 'front rank fighters against counter-revolution', and without being tempted into a 'premature battle' were to prepare for the ultimate seizure of power by the 'revolutionary classes'. There was no indication in the resolution of the organs which would take the place of the soviets, and many members were disturbed by this difficulty. If the intention was that the party should take over government in the name of the 'revolutionary masses', which was certainly in Lenin's mind, no one at the Congress was prepared to utter this unorthodox view for which Marx at any rate provided no authority. Many delegates were unwilling to throw over the soviets, some were not reconciled to the view that the time was ripe to pass from the bourgeois to the socialist revolution. Yet the resolution was adopted unanimously, with only four abstentions.[3] Once again those who hesitated could comfort themselves with the reflection that the fatal day was still far off. One speaker probably expressed a fairly general view when he said at a meeting of the Petersburg Committee in the middle of October: 'We must realize that when we take power we shall have to lower wages ... we shall have to introduce terror. ... We have no right to refuse to

[1] Chamberlin, *op. cit.*, pp. 178–9; Em. Iaroslavskii, *Istoriia VKP(b)*, volume IV, Moscow, Leningrad, 1929, p. 151. And see also the replies to questionnaires addressed to the delegates to the Sixth Party Congress in *Shestoi S''ezd RSDRP (bol'shevikov), avgust 1917 goda.* Protokoly. Moscow, 1958, pp. 321–66.

[2] *Lenin*, volume XXI, pp. 33–8.

[3] *KPSS v rez.*, volume I, pp. 374–6.

adopt these means, but neither is there any need to rush towards them.'[1]

Less than a month after the Congress, as a result of the abortive Kornilov attempt, and of the Provisional Government's denunciations of Kornilov, the tide turned in favour of the bolsheviks as rapidly as it had ebbed in July. In the capital and elsewhere the socialists, who had moved half-heartedly against the bolsheviks after the July riots, were now co-operating with the bolsheviks in organizing committees for struggle against counter-revolution. The hitherto semi-illegal, but tolerated, Red Guard was now being openly armed. In many soviets throughout the country elections held in September and October were returning bolshevik majorities for the first time. Moreover, in many provincial centres, owing to the weakness of the authority of the local organs of the Provincial Government, all virtual power was in fact passing to the local bolshevik-dominated soviet.[2] Early in September Lenin seems to have believed that the bolsheviks could once again hope to seize power through winning a majority in the soviets, but soon abandoned this view. On 5 September the Central Committee was faced with a demand by Lenin for immediate insurrection by means of revolutionary detachments which would arrest the government and seize power. His demand found no supporters in the Central Committee.[3] The view prevalent in the party at the time was that the bolsheviks should pave the way for the assumption of power by the soviets by participating in the forthcoming Council of the Republic – a constitutional improvisation designed by the Provisional Government to solve the growing deadlock of power.

The Second All-Russian Congress of Soviets was due to meet on 20 October. In a series of articles published in the party press between 10 and 21 October Lenin now outlined, with increased urgency and passion, his plan of insurrection. Power, he argued, must be seized independently of the soviets. It was necessary to fight 'the constitutional illusions and hopes based on the forthcoming Congress of Soviets'. True, the new proletarian government must be responsible

[1] *Pervyi legal'nyi peterburgskii komitet bol'shevikov v 1917 godu.* Sbornik materialov i protokolov zasedanii peterburgskogo komiteta RSDRP(b) ... za 1917 god. Moscow, Leningrad, 1927, p. 296 (Volodarskii).

[2] This is revealed by the replies to questionnaires furnished by the bolshevik delegates to the Second All-Russian Congress of Soviets. See *Vtoroi vserossiiskii s'ezd sovetov rabochikh i soldatskikh deputatov.* Sbornik dokumentov. Moscow, 1957, pp. 227–386.

[3] *Protokoly tsentral'nogo komiteta RSDRP(b).* Avgust 1917-fevral' 1918. Moscow, 1958, pp. 55-62.

to the soviets – after new elections had been held. But mere assumption of power by the soviets without insurrection could not create a proletarian government.[1] On 10 October the majority of the Central Committee was won over to his views. At a stormy meeting, which Lenin and Zinoviev still in hiding attended secretly, Lenin's resolution that 'an armed rising is inevitable and the time perfectly ripe' was adopted against the dissenting votes of Kamenev and Zinoviev.[2] Nine full members of the Central Committee of 22 were, however, not present, and of those at least three, Nogin, Rykov and Miliutin, would certainly have opposed the resolution. A full meeting would thus have revealed an opposition approximating to a quarter of the members.

Lenin returned to hiding after this historic meeting, and preparations for the insurrection went ahead in the capital mainly under the direction of Trotsky. Trotsky, who had been arrested after the July disturbances, had been released on bail in the changed atmosphere after the Kornilov affair. After his return to Petrograd in May 1917 he had revived a small group known as the *Mezhraiontsy*, which had been formed in 1913, and which occupied a half-way position between the bolsheviks and the mensheviks. By mid-July at any rate Trotsky had expressed his open solidarity with Lenin,[3] though the fusion of the *Mezhraiontsy* with the bolsheviks did not take place until August, at the Sixth Congress. Indeed, the divisions between Lenin and Trotsky had long been overtaken by events, and the bond between them, now that Lenin was openly committed to the design of passing immediately from the bourgeois to the socialist revolution (which Trotsky had advocated in 1905), was much stronger than anything which kept them apart.

Trotsky, no less than Lenin, realized the importance of the seizure of actual power by the party. The organization of the practical moves for the insurrection – the seizure of important points in the capital on the night of 24–25 October, on the eve of the meeting of the Second Congress of Soviets (the date of its meeting had been postponed from 20 to 25 October), and the arrest of the Provisional Government on the night of 25 October – was his work. But Trotsky realized more than Lenin the importance of making the actual seizure of power

---

[1] *Lenin*, volume XXI, pp. 221–8, 235–41; cf. also pp. 287–9.

[2] *Protokoly tsentral'nogo komiteta*, pp. 83–6. For the subsequent attempts by Zinoviev and Kamenev to make their protest in wider party circles and the reactions of Lenin to these attempts see my *The Origin of the Communist Autocracy*. Political Opposition in the Soviet State. First Phase 1917–1922. London, 1955, pp. 59–62.

[3] L. Trotsky, *Sochineniia*, volume III, Part I, Moscow, Leningrad, n.d., pp. 149, 165–6, 201–2.

coincide with the symbolic assumption of power by a vote of the Congress of Soviets. Lenin had never been entirely won over to this view.[1] There was much force in Trotsky's judgement. The soviets rather than the party attracted the mass allegiance, which the bolsheviks exploited. In the provinces it was through their majorities in the Soviets that the bolsheviks were extending their influence. A report to the Petersburg Bolshevik Committee on the mood of the workers ten days before the insurrection of 24–25 October revealed that loyalty was in general to the Petrograd Soviet rather than to the party.[2] Even within the party itself, as the Sixth Congress and the opposition to insurrection inside the Central Committee had revealed, many members identified the victory of the party with a victory of the soviets. When the bolshevik delegates to the Second Congress of Soviets were questioned on their views as to what the future form of government should be, the overwhelming majority of them replied 'All power to the soviets', and some of them more specifically that power must be vested in a coalition of all 'democratic parties' – meaning thereby all parties of the left, excluding, of course, the *Kadety*.[3] What was to become known as the bolshevik revolution was to them a victory of the soviets over the Provisional Government.

The Second All-Russian Congress of Soviets of Worker and Soldier Delegates probably gave a fair picture of the strength of the bolsheviks in the country. It did not represent the peasants in the villages, but only the workers, and the peasants in uniform. About 300 delegates out of some 650 were bolsheviks, and in addition about half of the socialist revolutionaries supported the bolsheviks. The remaining socialist revolutionaries and the mensheviks each numbered seventy or eighty. The total bolshevik and pro-bolshevik strength was therefore about 380 out of 650, or rather over half.[4]

Reliable information is lacking on the size and composition of the party, and only rough estimates of its development in this respect during these vital eight months is possible. The official estimate of the strength of the party in January 1917, before the emergence of the conspiratorial organizations into the open and the return of party members from exile, is 23,600.[5] but this is at best a guess. At the

[1] L. Trotsky, *Lenin*. Authorized translation, London, 1925, p. 117.

[2] *Pervyi legal'nyi peterburgskii komitet*, pp. 312–15.

[3] *Vtoroi vserossiiskii s"ezd* (Moscow, 1957), pp. 386–98.

[4] *Vtoroi vserossiiskii s"ezd sovetov rabochikh i soldatskikh deputatov*. With an introduction by Ia. A. Iakovlev. Moscow, Leningrad, 1928. Figures were not reliable. For an estimate of 390 bolsheviks and pro-bolsheviks see Chamberlin, *op. cit.*, p. 320.

[5] *BSE*, volume XI, p. 533.

time of the Seventh All-Russian Conference, in the last week of April, 79,204 party members were represented by 149 delegates. The largest concentrations were in the Petrograd province and in the Urals (over 14,000 each), with Moscow province (7,000) and the Donets Basin (5,000) next in importance.[1] The strength of the party increased rapidly in the next few months. Sverdlov told the Sixth Congress in August that the number of organizations had grown from 78 to 162, and he estimated the total strength of the party at 200,000.[2] No information is available on party membership by October, but it may be presumed that a further increase took place, since the very incomplete data on the membership of individual organizations available to the Central Committee Secretariat show an increase after August in the case of a number of organizations.[3]

Virtually no details are available on the social composition of the party at this period. But it is fairly certain that the party drew its supporters mainly from the factories and the army – its support among the peasants working on the soil, as distinct from peasants in uniform, was negligible. A very rough estimate of the extent to which the factory workers actually enrolled in the party can be obtained from the answers to questionnaires supplied by the delegates to the Sixth Congress. A sample of replies from the organizations in twenty-five towns shows that the percentage of organized bolsheviks among the factory workers in the towns at this date varied from 1 per cent to 12 per cent – the average for the twenty-five towns being 5.4 per cent.[4] A little more information is available on the composition of the party élite in August 1917, since 171 of the 267 delegates to the Congress completed questionnaires about themselves, the results of which have been published. Russians (92) and Jews (29) predominated among these 171 delegates, whose age averaged 29. Almost all had worked in the social democratic movement for years, the great majority as bolsheviks, mostly as organizers and propagandists, or secretaries or members of party committees. Since 94 of those who replied had received higher or secondary education, and only 72 were listed as workers or soldiers by occupation, it may fairly be estimated that over half the delegates, as revealed by this sample, were intellectuals.[5]

[1] *Sed'maia (aprel'skaia) vserossiiskaia konferentsiia RSDRP (bol'shevikov)* ... Protokoly. Moscow, 1958, p. 149.
[2] *Shestoi s"ezd RSDRP (bol'shevikov). Avgust 1917 goda.* Protokoly. Moscow, 1958, p. 36.
[3] *Perepiska sekretariata*, Volume I pp. 481–506.
[4] *Shestoi s"ezd* (1958 edition), pp. 317–90.
[5] *ibidem*, pp. 294–300.

The composition of the Central Committee elected by the Sixth Congress should be noted. Its 22 full members[1] no longer represented anything like the hard core of well-tried lieutenants which Lenin had laboured to build up as the party leadership in the years before the revolution, culminating with the Prague Conference in 1912. Some indeed still belonged to the category of hard-core Leninists – Stalin, Bubnov, Sverdlov, Stasova and Dzerzhinskii, for example. Kamenev and Zinoviev, who had belonged to this category for years, were now opponents of Lenin's views on insurrection. Other bolsheviks of long standing were far from accepting Lenin's lead without question. Such were Bukharin, who had clashed with Lenin on theoretical questions during the war, and Nogin and Rykov, who had for years refused to support Lenin in his uncompromising war on the mensheviks. Finally, the adhesion of Trotsky at the head of his group of *Mezhraiontsy* introduced into the top councils of the party a group of men who had not been through the discipline of work in Lenin's party machine under Lenin's vigorous leadership. Trotsky himself became a member of the Central Committee, as well as Uritskii, and Ioffe, another member of the group, a candidate member.

The organization of the party was necessarily somewhat loose and fluid during these dramatic months, and information on it is incomplete. We can draw, it is true, on the information contained in the correspondence of the Secretariat with local party organizations, but since only 129 out of a total of some 1,700 letters sent out by the Secretariat during this period have been published, the picture is very approximate.[2] The general impression gleaned from the selection of letters available is that the Secretariat was quite unable to exercise anything like complete control over local organizations. From time to time emissaries were sent out to stimulate or co-ordinate their activities, but in the main the local party committees were left to work out their policy and tactics as best they could, using the central press of the party for guidance. This was not always to the liking of all the local organizations, and complaints that they were not being visited frequently enough by emissaries from the centre recur constantly in their correspondence with the Secretariat. Nevertheless, within its

[1] Its exact composition was not revealed at the Sixth Congress for publication, but its composition can be reconstituted from the Central Committee meeting reports which were subsequently published. See also *Shestoi syezd* (1958 edition) pp. 439 and 252, which gives some names: Lenin, Zinoviev, Kamenev and Trotsky headed the list with the majority of votes.

[2] *Perepiska sekretariata*, Volume I p. vi. The remaining letters are stated by the editors to be 'as yet undiscovered'.

limitations the Secretariat worked to maintain the kind of detailed control over local activities which would in later years become so characteristic of the organization of the party. There were constant demands for detailed information on the work and progress of the party in the provinces in order to compile the central records. It is not unreasonable to assume that Sverdlov's reports to Lenin played an important part in deciding his tactics. There is also in one case, at any rate, a list of candidates recommended by the Central Committee to a local organization for election.

The Sixth Congress adopted a new set of party Rules (these had not been completely revised since the Fifth Congress in 1907). Several new provisions reflected the greater emphasis on party discipline which had developed since 1907. A new condition of membership was adopted – submission to all party directives – and provisions were laid down for expulsion, and appeals against expulsion. The Congress was to meet annually, the Central Committee plenary sessions at least once in two months. An amendment designed to give greater autonomy to party organizations of national minorities was rejected.[1] In between plenary sessions the Central Committee in practice acted through a smaller sub-committee, which dealt with the current work of the party, and when necessary set up further sub-commissions for special tasks. The importance of the Secretariat after the Sixth Congress was enhanced by the appointment to it of five members of the Central Committee – three, in addition to Stasova (a candidate member) and Sverdlov.[2]

The meeting of the Central Committee of 10 October also set up a Political Bureau, intended as a temporary measure until the rising. Lenin, Zinoviev, Kamenev (the last two in spite of, or because of, their adverse vote), Trotsky, Stalin, Sokol'nikov and Bubnov were elected.[3] But there is no evidence that this precursor of the Politburo ever functioned. The organization of the rising was in the hands of the Military Revolutionary Committee of the Petrograd Soviet, which was formed on 12 October, and of which Trotsky was chairman. This improvised general staff of the revolution maintained control over the military units in the capital which were prepared to support the bolsheviks, and also controlled the Red Guard. This force, which had been organized by the bolsheviks after June, and which the Provisional Government had been unable, or unwilling, to disarm, was the

[1] *KPSS v rez.*, volume I, pp. 384–5; *Shestoi s''ezd* (1958 ed.), p. 175.
[2] *Protokoly Ts. K.*, pp. 12–13.
[3] *ibidem*, p. 86.

real armed might behind the bolshevik *coup d'état*. Organized through the factory and shop committees, which in turn were under Central Committee control, the Red Guard numbered some 20,000 on the eve of the Second Congress of Soviets.[1] The Military Revolutionary Committee acted through commissars, of whom there were several hundred by the date of the rising. These commissars were mainly appointed to the military units in the capital, and to those factories where, owing to the prevalence of menshevik or socialist revolutionary influence, the bolsheviks could not rely on their own factory committees to mobilize worker support. The work of the Military Revolutionary Committee and its commissars was under the general supervision of individual members of the Central Committee, each responsible for a particular sector of activity, such as the railways or posts and telegraphs, and one member was entrusted with the supervision of the rising in Moscow. The evidence does not disclose any organizational links before the rising with any other provincial centre, though it is probable that they existed.[2] The Military Revolutionary Committee remained the main centre of government for the first few weeks, until its dissolution on 5 December 1917.

Much effort was devoted by the party during these crucial months to developing its press. At the time of the Sixth Congress 41 newspapers and journals were being produced, 27 in Russian and the remainder in the languages of various minorities. A large proportion of this propaganda effort was directed at the army. The total number of copies printed was almost a million and a half a week, or 320,000 a day, at the time of the Sixth Congress.[3] This activity was costly, because of the rising prices of paper and printing-presses, and because the outlay could not be recouped by sales, since much of the

[1] On the Red Guard see Chamberlin, *op. cit.*, pp. 307–8. There were also Red Guards in a few provincial centres, but none of the contingents seems to have exceeded a few dozen or hundreds, except in Kiev, and Odessa – see *Vtoroi s''ezd* (1957 edition), pp. 227–386. There is no evidence for the assertion in the new *Short History* of the party, published in 1959, that the Red Guard numbered 200,000 in October 1917 – see *Istoriia Kommunisticheskoi partii Sovetskogo Soinza,* Moscow, 1959, p. 234.

[2] *Protokoly Ts. K.,* pp. 119–21; *Doneseniia komissarov petrogradskogo voenno-revoliutsionnogo komiteta,* Moscow, 1957, pp. 5–16. There is no evidence of what part, if any, was played by a Military Revolutionary 'Centre', consisting of five, including Stalin, which was set up on 16 October, and which modern Soviet historians describe as the real organizing force of the revolution, presumably because it did not include Trotsky – see *Protokoly Ts. K.,* p. 104. For a detailed study of the organization of the rising the work of S. P. Mel'gunov, *Kak bol'sheviki zakhvatili vlast'. Oktiabr'skii perevorot 1917 goda,* Paris, 1953, is quite indispensable. The minutes of the Military Revolutionary Committee have been published. See D. A. Chugaev and others (ed.), *Petrogradskii Voenno-revoliutsionnyi komitet,* Dokumenty i materialy, three volumes, Moscow, 1966–7.

[3] *Shestoi s''ezd* (1958 edition), pp. 147–50.

party periodical literature was in fact distributed free.[1] But propaganda of this nature was an important weapon, and the party rightly attached the greatest importance to it.

The lavish expenditure of funds on propaganda, and presumably also on weapons for the Red Guard, which the party was able to afford helped to swell the rumours that the source of bolshevik funds was Germany. When the accusation was officially launched by the Provisional Government in July, the evidence which it allowed to be published was inconclusive, and the enquiry was never pursued to a finish. The accusation was vehemently denied by Lenin personally and by the party as a whole, both at the time and subsequently. The capture by the Allied forces in the Second World War of the archives of the German Foreign Ministry has thrown some new light on the whole much-debated question of whether Lenin and the bolsheviks were German 'agents'. The Provisional Government's allegation was that money from official German sources had reached the bolsheviks through the principal agency of Parvus (Helphand), who was in Stockholm. Parvus, a former social democrat, and at the time of the 1905 revolution a close associate of Trotsky, had become during the war a financial adventurer of somewhat unsavoury reputation. Parvus's contacts with Lenin were stated to have been through Haniecki, who was in Parvus's employment, and Kozlovskii, an otherwise undistinguished social democrat in Petrograd. Haniecki certainly stood very close to Lenin, and had been used by him in 1911 with other Polish social democrats to effect or at all events encourage, a split in the Polish party. After October 1917 Haniecki worked as a bolshevik in government service, at any rate until 1932. While the evidence of the Provisional Government as published is in itself inconclusive, the sincerity of Lenin's denials is open to some doubt. For on two occasions he specifically denied that he or the party had ever had any financial or commercial dealings with either Haniecki or Kozlovskii.[2] Yet two private letters written by Lenin in April 1917 to Haniecki (one of them also addressed to Radek) which were seized by the police and subsequently published appear to refer to money transactions with Haniecki and Kozlovskii: one letter complains that 'we have so far received . . . no money from you' and ends 'Be extremely careful

[1] See for example a report of the Don Provincial Committee, which shows that a daily newspaper issue of 4,500–4,800 copies entailed a daily loss of about 200–250 roubles. Paper alone cost 360 roubles – *Perepiska Sekretariata*, Volume I p. 339.
[2] In *Novaia zhizn'* of 24 (11) July 1917, reprinted in V. Vladimirova, *Revoliutsiia 1917 goda (Khronika sobytii)*, Moscow, Leningrad, 1923–24, volume III, p. 329; and on 8 August (26 July), *ibidem*, p. 360.

and meticulous in your relations'; the other contains the phrase, 'We have received the money (2,000) from Kozlovskii'.[1] It is also known that the Central Committee discussed the 'controversial affairs' of Haniecki and Kozlovskii on no less than eight occasions in August and September 1917, though the account of these discussions was omitted from the verbatim reports of the meetings of the Central Committee for the period concerned when they were published.[2]

The documents from the archives of the German Foreign Ministry leave no doubt that from 1915 onwards the Germans were seeking means to subsidize not only the bolsheviks but all revolutionaries who were opposed to the war. There is also no doubt that large sums were paid over to Parvus, who was one of their two principal agents for seeking contacts with the bolsheviks, though the documents are inconclusive on the question whether any of the funds intended for them in fact reached them before the revolution of February 1917. But the documents do raise a strong probability that substantial sums reached the bolsheviks after March 1917. In a report of 3 December 1917 to the Emperor, the German Foreign Minister Kühlmann claimed that it was not until the bolsheviks had 'received from us a steady flow of funds through various channels and under different labels' that they were able to build up their propaganda effort.[3] It is extremely improbable that the Foreign Minister could have reported in these terms on a matter for which he was directly responsible unless his claim was founded in fact.

The probability that funds for propaganda purposes at any rate came from the Germans is further strengthened by the fact that no other source for what must have been substantial sums has come to light. The funds certainly could not have come from the official source of party revenue – the ten per cent of their income which local organizations were bound to forward to the Central Committee – since revenue from this source was admittedly negligible.[4] It also appears that 'special funds' were placed at the disposal of the Press

---

[1] *Proletarskaia revoliutsiia* (Moscow), No. 9 (21), 1923, pp. 227–32.
[2] *Protokoly Ts. K.*, p. 250 – a note by the Institute of Marxism-Leninism. The materials omitted are said to be insufficient to 'ascertain the subject matter of the questions discussed'. For discussion of the evidence on this whole question, before the publication of the German documents, see S. P. Mel'gunov, *Zolotoi nemetskii kliuch bol'shevikov*, Paris, 1940.
[3] *Germany and the Revolution in Russia 1915–1918*. Documents from the Archives of the German Foreign Ministry. Edited by Z. A. B. Zeman. London, Oxford, New York, 1958, *passim*. The document quoted is No. 94. A similar report was made by Kühlmann to the Army High Command on 29 September 1917 – see Document No. 71.
[4] *Perepiska sekretariata*, Volume I pp. 50–1.

Bureau of the Central Committee, which Molotov headed, in order among other things to help the financing of local papers.[1] Whether, assuming that bolshevik funds came from the Germans, the bolsheviks could properly be described as 'German agents' is another matter, and depends on the meaning attached to the word 'agent'. There is no evidence that the bolsheviks at any time received instructions from the Germans on their policy or tactics. If the Germans did indeed pay them, as seems very probable, it was because bolshevik aims coincided with their own – to knock Russia out of the war. On the other hand, from the point of view of the Provisional Government, the receipt of money from an enemy in order to help to subvert the lawful government of the country could fairly be regarded as treason.

The germs of the dissensions which were to shake the party for many years after November 1917 were already inherent in the circumstances of its development which have been described. There was first of all the lack of homogeneity in the Central Committee after August 1917. There was next the deep division between those who visualized the bolshevik revolution as a soviet victory, and those like Lenin or Stalin for whom it was primarily a party victory. Thirdly, there were many in the party for whom the acceptance of money from any imperialist power for the purposes of making a revolution was contrary to bolshevik ethics,[2] and the suspicion that Lenin might have done so may perhaps explain their subsequent readiness to jettison him as leader. Above all, the loose discipline which the Central Committee had perforce to tolerate in local organizations in revolutionary conditions led to self-reliance, anarchy and independence of mind which the Central Committee was to take years to eradicate.

[1] I. S. Sazonov, 'Biuro pechati pri Ts. K. RSDRP (b) v 1917 godu', *Istoricheskii arkhiv* (Moscow), No. 5, 1955, pp. 200–1. See also *Perepiska sekretariata*, Volume I p. 339, for a reference to the 'special funds' and *passim* for instances of quite substantial subsidies, when necessary, by the Central Committee to local organizations for their propaganda purposes.

[2] See, for example, Bukharin's explanation of the ethics of revolutionaries taking money from the imperialists at the Fourth Congress of the Communist International in 1922.

X The Party in the Civil War

The Second All-Russian Congress of Soviets created a new organ of government: the Council of People's Commissars. Headed by Lenin, it was all bolshevik in composition. The left socialist revolutionaries, now become a separate party, had been offered some seats on the Council of People's Commissars, but had refused. At this date they still hoped that the bolsheviks would come to an agreement for a broader coalition with the mensheviks and (right) socialist revolutionaries. Since both these socialist parties had denounced the bolshevik *coup*, and many, probably most, of their delegates had walked out of the Congress in protest, the prospects for such a settlement were not bright. The Congress also set up a new All-Russian Central Executive Committee – in place of the one elected by the First All-Russian Congress on which the bolsheviks were in a minority. On the new All-Russian Central Executive Committee the bolsheviks were allotted 62 seats, and the left socialist revolutionaries 29. Various small left-wing political groups of no influence shared the remaining 10 seats.

For about a week after the *coup d'état* the fate of the bolsheviks hung in the balance. On 26 October Kerenskii, who had escaped from Petrograd on 25 October with the object of mobilizing some military action against the bolsheviks, began his march on the capital, together with General Krasnov, who had hastily assembled a force of a few hundred cossacks. But on 29 October a rising in Petrograd of the military cadets against the bolsheviks was defeated, with heavy casualties. By 1 November Kerenskii was in flight and Krasnov captured. The 'neutrality' of the garrison troops had determined the issue. In Moscow the bolshevik uprising, timed to coincide with the rising in the capital, had met with resistance, and its outcome was in doubt until 2 November, when the bolsheviks achieved their victory. For the moment no military opposition was imminent, but preparations for forming an anti-bolshevik volunteer army among the Don cossacks started at once.

The political events of the first days must be viewed against this background. To many of Lenin's followers it seemed evident that if the bolsheviks persisted in their refusal to share power with the two major socialist parties, behind whom stood large sections, the majority indeed of the population, the prospect of a civil war was inevitable. Several bolshevik leaders were in favour of a broader based government which would include the socialists. Negotiations for such a coalition were precipitated on 29 October, when the All-Russian Executive Committee of the Union of Railway Workers (on which bolsheviks were in a minority) threatened a railway strike if a coalition were not formed. In the discussions which ensued, Lenin, as he frankly admitted,[1] merely played for time. But many of his colleagues took the attempt seriously, and were even prepared to negotiate on the basis that Lenin and Trotsky would be omitted from the future government. These 'waverers' included Zinoviev and Kamenev, as well as the former 'conciliators' Rykov and Nogin.

The question of the press was closely bound up with the question of coalition, and indeed with the whole problem of the treatment to be meted out to the socialists, who had rejected the bolshevik *coup*. Bolshevik practice within a few days of 25 October was already at variance with Lenin's repeated promises that when once they were in power the bolsheviks would guarantee to each political party which could muster a sufficient number of supporters facilities for publishing its newspaper.[2] Some socialist and liberal papers, as well as the conservative papers, were closed down in these first few days. To many of Lenin's followers such action seemed a violation of the promises contained in the party programme, especially in view of the impending elections to the Constituent Assembly. When therefore on 4 November the All-Russian Central Executive Committee passed a decree giving the bolsheviks control over all newsprint and wide powers of closing down newspapers critical of the régime, the 'waverers' resigned in protest from the Central Committee and from their government appointments. They were supported by a number of other People's Commissars. The revolt did not last long, and the critics soon relented. They were eventually readmitted to the Central Committee and to their former offices.

The negotiations for coalition with the mensheviks and the right socialist revolutionaries broke down, and the question was quietly

---

[1] In the Central Committee on 1 November 1917 – see the official minute in *Proletarskaia revoliutsiia*, No. 10 (1922), pp. 465–70.

[2] See e.g. an article published by Lenin on 15 September 1917, *Lenin* (4), volume XXV, p. 352.

shelved.[1] But another problem loomed ahead as the elections to the Constituent Assembly approached. These elections had been fixed to begin on 12 November by the Provisional Government, and reiterated promises that only the bolsheviks could ensure that they would be duly held had formed part of bolshevik attacks on the Provisional Government. It was quite certain that the peasants would, in any free election, return a majority of socialist revolutionary deputies. Lenin had even found it necessary on 26 October at the Second Soviet Congress to pander to popular faith in the Constituent Assembly by announcing that the bolsheviks would yield to the 'popular masses' if their party were outvoted in the elections.[2]

As the unwelcome elections approached, Lenin was at first inclined to postpone them, but was dissuaded on the grounds that the bolsheviks were still too weak to flout popular demand. Lenin had already in 1915 stated that the important question so far as the Constituent Assembly was concerned would be: who is in power when the elections take place?[3] But the bolsheviks' hold on the country in November 1917 was still far too precarious and their organizations too weak for them to hope to be able to rig the elections in their own favour. Their supporters, the left socialist revolutionaries, were in a similar predicament: as a new party, only recently formed, they could not hope to compete in a free election with the candidates of the main socialist revolutionary party. Thus, like the bolsheviks, they were faced with the alternatives of either accepting political eclipse or establishing their rule by further violence, and like the bolsheviks they chose the latter. Their fate was in any case linked to that of the bolsheviks after 9 December, when several of their members agreed to enter the Council of People's Commissars in coalition with the bolshevik members.

As the results of the elections became known, clear hints were being dropped in bolshevik and left socialist revolutionary circles that force would be required as a corrective to the ballot box.[4] The result of the balloting, in which, according to a detailed survey, 'the vast majority' of the electorate voted freely, was an assembly in which out

---

[1] For details on the negotiations for coalition and for the treatment of the press see Leonard Schapiro, *The Origin of the Communist Autocracy*, Political Opposition in the Soviet State, First Phase 1917–1922, London, 1955, pp. 70–80.

[2] *Vtoroi vserossiiskii s"ezd sovetov rabochikh i soldatskikh deputatov*, edited with an introduction by Ia. A. Iakovlev, Moscow, Leningrad, 1928, p. 57.

[3] 'The whole question *now* is who will summon it' (the Constituent Assembly), *Lenin*, volume XVIII, p. 311.

[4] For Lenin's views on the subject in private conversation early in December 1917 see G. A. Solomon, *Sredi krasnykh vozhdei. Lichno perezhitoe i vidennoe na sovetskoi sluzhbe.* Two volumes, Paris, 1930. Vol. I, p. 17.

of the 707 deputies, 370 were socialist revolutionaries, 175 bolsheviks, 40 left socialist revolutionaries, 17 *Kadety* and 16 mensheviks. The bolsheviks secured just under one-quarter of the total of all votes cast. Half the country voted for socialism but against bolshevism. The bolsheviks had a majority in the industrial centres, and polled about half the votes in the army.[1] More important, they had a majority in the sections of the army closest to the capital and to Moscow.[2] On the day of its opening, 5 January 1918, the Constituent Assembly rejected a bolshevik declaration by 237 votes to 136 (the declaration endorsed the decrees passed by the Second Soviet Congress and thus pre-judged the form which Russian society was to take). The bolsheviks and left socialist revolutionaries then withdrew. On the following day the Red Guards refused to admit the remaining delegates to the adjourned session, and the Constituent Assembly was at an end. Lenin's instincts had not failed him. The dispersal of the Assembly caused little stir either inside the party or in the country at large. Only two bolsheviks in the All-Russian Central Executive Committee (one was a recent recruit, Riazanov) had voted against the decision to disperse it. A demonstration in the capital (unarmed, on the insistence of the socialist revolutionary leader, Chernov)[3] was scattered by the rifles of the Red Guard, with a number of casualties. Shortly after-wards, in the middle of January, a Third All-Russian Congress of Soviets, after carefully rigged elections, approved by an overwhelm-ing majority the policy adopted towards the Constituent Assembly by the bolsheviks and left socialist revolutionaries.

The refusal to come to terms with the socialists and the dispersal of the Constituent Assembly led to the logical result that revolution-ary terror would now be directed not only against traditional enemies, such as the bourgeoisie or right-wing opponents, but against anyone, be he socialist, worker or peasant, who opposed bolshevik rule. The bolsheviks had from the start provided themselves with effective instruments of action. The Military Revolutionary Committee of the Petrograd Soviet contained a section for combating counter-revolu-tion, headed by Dzerzhinskii, and this section acted as the punitive arm of the party until the establishment of the *Vecheka* on 6 or 7

---

[1] I. S. Mal'chevskii (editor), *Vserossiiskoe uchreditel'noe sobranie*, Moscow, Leningrad, 1930, p. 115; Oliver Henry Radkey, *The Election of the Russian Con-stituent Assembly of 1917*, Cambridge, Mass., 1950, pp. 57–8, 80 and chapter v *passim*.

[2] As Lenin noted when the analysis of the voting was published some years later – see *Lenin*, volume XXIV, p. 638.

[3] See B. Sokolov, 'Zashchita uchreditel'nogo sobraniia' in *Arkhiv russkoi revo-liutsii*, volume XIII, pp. 5–70.

December 1917. The Second Congress of Soviets abolished capital punishment on 26 October 1917. But the decree of the Congress did not in practice hamper the *Vecheka*, and was quietly ignored until its official repeal in June 1918. Terror, however, remained sporadic for the first months and did not acquire an organized character until the summer of 1918, after the outbreak of the civil war, the assassination of several bolshevik leaders and an attempt on Lenin's life. The murder of the former Emperor together with all the members of his family, his personal physician and three servants, on 16–17 July 1918, was but one incident in this new régime of terror. But if terror was thus now intensified in part as a weapon of self-defence, systematic lawlessness by bolsheviks against their political opponents had been everywhere tolerated, and indeed encouraged, from the first.

The first acts of the new government concerned the two burning problems upon the solution of which the bolsheviks' hope to win over the peasants depended – peace and land. The question of peace, however, also raised the wider issue of relations between the bolsheviks and their allies, the left socialist revolutionaries, and affected relations among the bolshevik leaders themselves. In October 1915 Lenin had linked his peace policy, in the event of a bolshevik victory, with 'revolutionary war' when he declared that the bolsheviks on coming to power would propose as a preliminary to a revolutionary uprising an all-round peace, on terms which the imperialist powers were certain to refuse. This would be designed to kindle revolutions in the capitalist countries and revolt in the colonial and semi-colonial territories.[1] This policy was repeatedly reaffirmed after the revolution of February 1917, and the bolsheviks thereafter continued at one and the same time to demoralize the army by preaching fraternization and promising peace; to deny indignantly that they intended to conclude a separate peace with the Germans; and to promise 'revolutionary war'.[2]

The Germans had not been deceived by this demagogy, and no doubt realized the obvious fact that if the army were thoroughly demoralized, all hopes of 'revolutionary' war would be unrealistic. They were confident that, once the bolsheviks were in power, they could force them to conclude peace on German terms. But, unlike the Germans, many of Lenin's followers were deceived by his tactics, and so were the left socialist revolutionaries. They did not however demur when, after the seizure of power, the Second Soviet Congress adopted a decree on peace which differed fundamentally from the call to world

---

[1] *Lenin*, volume XVIII, p. 313; and see pp. 150–1 above.
[2] For details see my *The Origin of the Communist Autocracy*, pp. 89–95.

revolution envisaged by Lenin in 1915. In place of a defiant summons to revolt, the bolsheviks now offered negotiation: they demanded an immediate armistice and immediate discussions by all belligerents of 'just and democratic peace terms', which must exclude all forcible annexation of territory; but at the same time they were careful to emphasize that the decree was 'in no sense' an ultimatum, and that any counter-suggestions would be considered.

The bolshevik appeal to all belligerents remained unanswered, and the proposal for a general armistice was ignored. On 7 November 1917 the Commander-in-Chief was ordered to offer an immediate armistice to the enemy, and on his refusal was dismissed, and subsequently lynched. Direct appeals to the soldiers were now broadcast by the bolsheviks, calling upon them to take into their own hands the question of peace. On 20 November armistice negotiations were opened with the Central Powers, and an armistice was signed on 2 December. Thus, by the time the bolsheviks opened negotiations for a peace treaty with the Central Powers at Brest-Litovsk on 9 December, they had made further inroads into the morale of an already demoralized army.

Protracted negotiations for a peace treaty, in which Trotsky as People's Commissar for Foreign Affairs played the leading part on the Russian side, began on 9 December 1917. From 7 January, when Lenin came out squarely in favour of the acceptance of the German peace terms, the bolshevik Central Committee was in a fever of debate, unable to decide what its proper course should be. The divided counsels in the party leadership reflected the dissension in the rank and file of the party. In a referendum of the views of local soviets held during February (of which the results were not published at the time) a small majority of the city soviets voted for war, while a small majority of the village soviets voted for peace. A majority of the Petrograd Committee and the entire Moscow Regional Bureau were in favour of revolutionary war. On 28 January 1918 Trotsky forestalled a German ultimatum with a statement in which, while refusing to sign an annexationist peace, Russia at the same time declared the state of war with the Central Powers at an end. But on 18 February[1] the Germans resumed their advance into Russia, and the decision could no longer be postponed. The final vote in the Central Committee took place on 23 February, after the receipt of the severe terms of peace offered by the Germans. Lenin now threatened to resign if the terms

[1] On 31 January 1918 the calendar in Soviet Russia was advanced to 14 February in order to bring it into line with the calendar in force in the rest of Europe.

were not accepted, and secured a majority of those who voted. Of the fifteen members of the Central Committee present, seven voted for peace, four voted against it, and four abstained. Stalin and Zinoviev voted with Lenin, Trotsky abstained. Bukharin voted against the peace.

The decision to submit to terms of peace which condoned annexation of territory by the Central Powers shook the party to its foundations. More was at issue than a mere question of expediency – the question, as Lenin put it, of buying time by sacrificing space. For the advocates of revolutionary war the acceptance of the terms forced upon them by the imperialist Central Powers seemed a betrayal of their duty as revolutionaries. In an endeavour to show that revolutionary war was not an impossibility, they stressed that though the army was demoralized, the population was not, and that a partisan war in depth was not a hopeless dream. But Lenin and his supporters like Stalin, Zinoviev and even Trotsky, dismissed the alternative of revolutionary war out of hand. Whatever other considerations swayed them, it is clear that they realized that this course would mean the end of their precarious hold on the country. The only units of the army where morale was still good were anti-bolshevik, and in the patriotic upsurge created by the resumption of hostilities the defeatist bolsheviks would soon be swept away. (The Germans had foreseen that this factor would be the decisive one, as the German Foreign Office appreciation at the time reveals.) Peace was signed on 3 March 1918.[1]

The decision to accept the German peace terms marked the end of the coalition with the left socialist revolutionaries, who now stormed out of the government to rouse the country to revolutionary war. Within the party it produced an open opposition movement, led by

[1] For further details and sources see my *The Origin of The Communist Autocracy*, chapter vi. The question whether German financial support of the bolsheviks after the seizure of power played any part in influencing Lenin's decision to conclude the peace on German terms cannot be answered conclusively one way or the other on available evidence. According to the documents of the German Foreign Ministry, 15 million marks were assigned 'for use on political propaganda in Russia' on 10 November 1917. According to German information the new government was destitute, and after the peace had been signed, on 13 May 1918, the German ambassador in Moscow Mirbach sought authority 'to continue to provide the bolsheviks with a minimum of essential goods and to maintain them in power'. Shortly afterwards he was authorized to use 'larger sums', and 40 million marks was authorized, though in view of the assassination of Mirbach on 6 July 1918 it is possible that none of this money ever reached Russia. The German Foreign Ministry also asserted that 'considerable sums' had been spent by Mirbach 'to persuade' the Soviet Congress to ratify the Peace of Brest-Litovsk – see *Germany and the Revolution in Russia 1915–1918*, Documents from the Archives of the German Foreign Ministry, edited by Z. A. B. Zeman, Oxford, 1958, Documents Nos. 75, 92, 124, 128, 129, 131, 132, 133, 135.

Bukharin, which became known as 'Left Communism'. The defection of the left socialist revolutionaries was of little importance. Impatient for results, they were more often than not reluctant to stomach the means which were necessary if they were to be achieved. Their union with the bolsheviks had been due to two main factors: a desire to ensure peace and to give land to the peasants. When they saw the failure in practice of the immediate Utopia which they had pictured to themselves, the alliance was at an end. The bolsheviks, to whom the alliance had never been more than a temporary expedient, welcomed the break when it came. Indeed, the alliance was already at breaking point before the issue of peace arose. It had served its purpose in the critical first phase of bolshevik rule by enabling the bolsheviks to claim that they enjoyed peasant support, and by going some way towards allaying the demand for a coalition government.

The left socialist revolutionaries' agitation against peace with Germany grew in intensity after the treaty had been signed and ratified, and culminated on 6 July 1918 in a small-scale revolt in the streets of Moscow and Petrograd and the assassination by one of their members of the German ambassador, von Mirbach. The revolt was unorganized, and was easily suppressed, even with the very scanty armed forces at the disposal of the government. But it served as a useful reminder to the bolsheviks that unless they remained united they were liable to be swept away; it reinforced the bolshevik argument that from political opposition to armed revolt in the streets was only a step; and helped to provide justification for systematic terrorism against all political opponents.

The revolt of the left communists inside the party was led by Bukharin. The left communists did not include any of that group of 'waverer' bolsheviks who had opposed Lenin on the issue of coalition. The two opposition movements were in fact very different in origin and temperament – the one founded mainly on hesitation or fear, the other inspired by extreme revolutionary zeal. Furthermore, the left communists did not, for the most part, draw their support from those bolsheviks who had disagreed with Lenin before the revolution. Dissenters such as Rykov or Nogin, once over the shock of November 1917, were to remain loyal to Lenin to the end. The left communists included a good many prominent bolsheviks, several members of the Central Committee, including Alexandra Kollontai, and Inessa Armand. Their outlook was emotional rather than rational. The left communists attacked the proposed peace as a betrayal of the international idea of socialism, as a capitulation to imperialism, and as a contamination of the purity of bolshevism in the name of expediency. Although at first they enjoyed considerable support in the rank and file, among whom ultra-revolutionary appeals were always certain of an immediate response, a short period of intense and quite free debate inside the party, between the acceptance of the German terms on 23 February 1918 and the ratification of the peace treaty on 15 March 1918, reduced their following drastically. At the Seventh Party Congress, which met between 6 and 8 March 1918, Bukharin's resolution against the treaty of peace was easily outvoted. At the Fourth Extraordinary All-Russian Congress of Soviets a week later, which voted overwhelmingly in favour of ratification of the treaty, the group of left communists contented themselves with abstaining.[1]

Like the 'waverers', the left communists had gone too far to draw back. The treaty of Brest-Litovsk was the logical culmination of Lenin's tactics for seizure of power, which the left communists had fully endorsed. For all its harsh terms, the treaty gave the bolsheviks (or communists, as they now called themselves after the Seventh Congress) the breathing space which they sought. But the price paid for it was high. By its terms Russia renounced all rights over Riga and some territory in Livonia behind it, over the whole of Courland and Lithuania and a part of Belo-Russia, agreed to evacuate the Ukraine, Estonia, Livonia and Finland, ceded Kars, Ardahan and Batum in the Caucasus to Turkey, and recognized the German-protected government of the Ukraine. There was, however, a mutual waiver of indemnities. In economic terms the loss represented 27 per cent of the sown area, 26 per cent of the population, 26 per cent of the railways, and three-quarters of the iron and steel.[2]

The breathing space did not last long. By the early summer of 1918 the new Soviet régime was in the throes of a civil war. The victory of the Red Army in the civil war was one of the major successes of the communist party. Both the organization and the supply of the Red Army were largely its work. The organization was mainly Trotsky's achievement, who after the peace of Brest-Litovsk was appointed People's Commissar for War. His disregard for the susceptibilities of some of his colleagues, when the interests of efficiency demanded it, was to make him enemies who were not disposed to forget or forgive. Stalin's first conflict with Trotsky took place during the civil war.

[1] See my *The Origin of the Communist Autocracy*, chapter viii.
[2] Based on official calculations made some time later, quoted in A. L. P. Dennis, *The Foreign Policies of Soviet Russia*, London, 1924, p. 40.

Trotsky's achievements as political organizer of the army were scarcely less important than his success as a military organizer. The ruthless discipline and fanaticism of the communist elements were an essential ingredient of victory in a largely peasant army where desertion, indifference and poor morale were often more serious obstacles to military success than lack of military training or equipment. As Trotsky recognized, in the last resort victory was due to the fact that of the two evils, the White forces and the communist forces, the peasants in the end preferred the communists.[1]

The civil war left a lasting imprint on the communist party. For three years a small band of men, convinced that they alone were on the side of history, grappled with enemies on all sides and faced incredible hardships. It was true that they had themselves helped to create their enemies by defying the vote of the majority of the country and by challenging the whole world. And their own doctrinaire intransigence was responsible for many of the hardships. But they emerged from the civil war with the sense that they had battled alone against considerable odds and won, and with enhanced conviction that their cause was just.

The supply of the Red Army was directly linked with the policy of the communists towards the peasants and towards industry during the civil war. In the army Trotsky was successful in subordinating considerations of Marxist theory to the prime need for efficiency. His colleagues were less successful in this respect in grappling with the problems of industry and the land. It will be recalled that bolshevik policy towards the land was 'nationalization', and that since 1906 the bolsheviks had defended this policy of nationalization against the mensheviks' plan for municipalization. As late as their Sixth Congress in August 1917 the bolsheviks reaffirmed their policy of nationalization of the land. There was, however, little possibility of putting theory into practice, nor in any case would the prospect of a centralized state control of exploitation of the land have appealed very much to the peasants. In practice, therefore, bolshevik agitators before October 1917 sought to win over the peasants both by promising to satisfy their hunger for more land and by encouraging them to seize their landlords' land. No sooner had they captured power than the bolsheviks without hesitation jettisoned their programme of nationalization in favour of that of the socialist revolutionaries. The socialist revolutionary scheme, while abolishing property in, and sale

---

[1] L. Trotsky, *Kak vooruzhalas' revoliutsiia*, three volumes, Moscow, 1923–5, volume I, pp. 14–21, volume III (2), p. 7.

and lease of, land, provided for the distribution of all land for the use of the labouring peasantry. The land was to be divided up according to the size of the family, the productivity of the soil and other similar factors. The effect in practice, if not in law, was to leave untouched the existing system of smallholdings. The adoption by the bolsheviks of the policy of their rivals was only a tactical move designed to win over the peasants, as Lenin subsequently admitted.[1] The bolsheviks, in any case, had no administrative machinery available in the villages to put through any policy. The seizure and division of land took place very much on the peasants' own initiative. The results incidentally showed how little foundation there had been in the repeated promises of the socialist revolutionaries that all-round redivision of the land could solve the problem of land hunger. In the majority of provinces the increase in individual peasant holdings did not exceed half a *desiatina*, and in many it was less.[2] This was partly due to the fact that some 8,000,000 left the towns in order to claim a share of the land, thus reducing the share of the villagers. The main achievement, from the point of view of the peasants, was the elimination of the landlords.[3]

Further development of bolshevik policy in the villages was dictated even more by expediency than by doctrine. Having destroyed the existing food distribution apparatus and prohibited private trade, the new government discovered that the peasants were unwilling to deliver food to the towns for nothing in return. By the summer of 1918 supplies of food had dropped catastrophically. The communists now sought the solution in force. Their freedom of action had hitherto been somewhat inhibited by their alliance with the left socialist revolutionaries. But after the break between the two parties this factor no longer mattered. The ruthless war unleashed against the peasants after May 1918, thinly disguised as 'class war', substantially contributed to the open revolt of the left socialist revolutionaries in July. The policy adopted was a combination of three measures: the institution of a system of barter of manufactured goods for grain; the setting up in the villages of so-called 'committees of the poor' which were organizations of the poorest peasants of which the purpose was to expropriate produce from the better-off peasants; and the arming of

---

[1] *Lenin*, volume XXVI, p. 446.
[2] A *desiatina* = 2·7 acres.
[3] For detailed figures of the extent to which the peasant holdings of land increased as the result of this seizure, based on the official publications of the People's Commissariat of Agriculture, see S. N. Prokopovich, *Narodnoe khoziaistvo SSSR*, New York, 1952, volume I, pp. 132–4.

'food detachments' of townsmen for what Lenin called a 'crusade' for bread. In practice only the last yielded any results. The small supply of goods for barter went mainly to the 'committees of the poor'. These, in turn, served to unleash class warfare in the villages. The proceeds of the expropriations they kept for themselves. By the end of 1918 they had succeeded in provoking a wave of risings in several districts, and they were disbanded.

But Lenin's 'crusade' gave positive results. Some 20,000 to 45,000 strong during the period up to 1920, the food detachments succeeded by 1920 in forcing out of the peasants supplies of which the total quantity approximated to nearly half the average supplies for the years 1914–17. Yet the basic failure of the attempt to devise a system of food supply independently of any market was most graphically illustrated by the fact that, in spite of severe police repression of private trading, the illegal 'black' market accounted for more food supplied to the towns than the official system.[1] Another positive result of the 'crusade', from the communist point of view, was to extend a form of proletarian dictatorship over the villages which in time of civil war was a valuable instrument of control over the politically unreliable peasantry.

An extreme doctrinaire like Bukharin was prepared to justify the methods of compulsion used against the peasants by the argument that since the peasants needed a strong worker state to defend them against the landlords, the exaction of food from them was really in their own interests. The peasants, however, did not see it in this light, and from the economic point of view the results were disastrous. Forced to deliver produce at machine-gun point, and unable to obtain the manufactured goods which they needed, the peasants ceased to produce. By 1921–2 production on the land had fallen to about half of the total for 1913, and the land under cultivation to three-quarters. Meanwhile, as the civil war drew to a close at the end of 1920, deserters and returning soldiers swelled the forces of rebellion in the village. By the end of 1920 the extent of peasant risings, involving bands totalling tens of thousands, amounted almost to a guerrilla war, directed primarily against the food detachments, and following the simple slogan 'Down with the communists!'[2] The peasants in the ranks of the Red Army, where they formed the majority, had played their part in winning the civil war. But with the end of the civil war, as Lenin

[1] *ibidem*, pp. 148 ff.
[2] See *Revoliutsionnaia Rossiia*, Tallinn, No. 6, April 1921, pp. 23–8 (Tambov); No. 11, August 1921, pp. 22–5 (Ukraine); No. 14/5, Nov./Dec. 1921, pp. 33–6 (Tobol'sk); cf. the speech of Skvortsov-Stepanov, *X S''ezd*, pp. 69–72.

conceded, the 'overwhelming majority' of them turned against communist rule.

Thus, in regard to the land, the party was guided largely by expediency and did not during the period of the civil war attempt to put into practice any of its doctrines. Even the unleashing of class war in the villages, though consistent with doctrine, was mainly a by-product of compulsory exaction of food. The situation was different as regards industry. Here measures of expediency were intermingled with measures dictated by doctrine – the desire to introduce 'communism' right from the start. Inseparable from doctrine, was the urgent desire to smash the existing social and economic system in order to prepare the vacuum which the new power would eventually fill. But this could not be achieved during the civil war. The substantial loss of resources inflicted by the treaty of Brest-Litovsk, the exigencies of the civil war, the drop in supplies of food from the villages, the ravages of disease and class war – all combined to defeat any possibility of socialist planning. Furthermore, the party itself, torn by dissensions, did not succeed for several years after the revolution in establishing effective control over the loose, unco-ordinated machinery of government and industry. The whole disjointed complex of industry eventually ground to a standstill, and, as on the land, threatening signs of revolt appeared. But there was one solid achievement to the credit of 'war communism' (as the period from mid-1918 to the spring of 1921 became known), and Lenin would repeatedly emphasize it: state capitalism was consolidated, and this, he claimed, was an essential step towards socialism.

One of the early steps of the new government was to decree on 14 November 1917 workers' control of industry. This primitive, but popular, syndicalist measure had been advocated by the bolsheviks after the February revolution both in order to win support and as part of their campaign to cause general disintegration. Within a few months it was evident that its results were disastrous. The inexperienced workers welcomed the new system as a method of settling scores with the owners and management, and as an opportunity of providing for their own interests, in complete disregard of the repercussions of their actions on the enterprise as a whole. From mid-1918 onwards the communists struggled to counteract some of the anarchy which workers' control had unleashed, and to restore such features of capitalist management as works discipline, one-man management and modern efficiency systems.

The evident failure of workers' control served to weaken the influence of the left communists, who were its enthusiastic advocates. This group, after the ratification of the peace treaty, no longer advocated 'revolutionary war', but continued for a short time to press for extreme left-wing measures, including wide-scale nationalization, fearing that the moral betrayal of socialism implicit, in their view, in the peace with Germany would lead to a similar betrayal of principles on the home front. The left communists ceased to exist as a separate group by the summer of 1918. But the heritage of their doctrinaire and emotional passion for pure revolutionary socialism would be seen before long in internal party opposition. Worker communists, too, would long remember with regret the sweet but short-lived anarchy of the days of 'workers' control'.

Extensive nationalization of industrial undertakings was decreed in the course of the civil war. But this was dictated less by doctrine than by other factors, such as the 'punitive' use of confiscation, during the short period of workers' control, as the only method of resolving the conflicts which this system invariably provoked. A decree of 28 June 1918, nationalizing all large-scale industrial undertakings, was hurriedly passed, apparently as a means of preventing them from falling under German control under the economic provisions of a supplementary agreement to the treaty of Brest-Litovsk, then under negotiation. The process of nationalization continued thereafter unabated. But the central machinery, the Supreme Council of National Economy (VSNKh) set up at the end of 1917 for the purpose of controlling the nationalized enterprises, was quite unequal to its task. In August 1920 of over 37,000 nominally 'nationalized' industrial undertakings, more than 30,000 were not even listed in the central records. Yet, in comparison with 1913, the bureaucratic machine was estimated to contain double the number of employees in relation to workers employed in productive tasks. Working without plan or system between its forty or more directorates, the Supreme Council of National Economy failed to achieve co-ordination in the supply of raw materials necessary to keep production going. That industry was not entirely paralysed was largely due to the existence of a semi-legal 'underground' organization of private enterprise, on which the state machinery was at times entirely dependent for the raw materials which it was incapable of supplying itself.[1]

'War communism' embodied all the extremes of 'left' theory. Lenin, after it had been abandoned, would variously describe it as forced

[1] The facts and figures are taken mainly from L. Kritsman, *Geroicheskii period velikoi russkoi revoliutsii*, Second edition, Moscow, Leningrad, 1926.

upon the bolsheviks by the civil war, as a mistaken attempt at an immediate transition to socialism without a preliminary period of adapting the old economic system to a socialist economy, and as a commendable attempt.[1] Its main elements were: highly centralized control; the rejection of commercial market or monetary forms of distribution in favour of production for direct use, and distribution by rationing of basic goods and services free, or at nominal prices; and an egalitarian wages policy in industry. The combined effects of all these factors on industry were catastrophic. The food shortage produced near starvation in the towns among the industrial proletariat. The drain of industrial workers to the villages in search of food halved the industrial proletariat by 1920 as compared with 1917. By 1921 overall production had fallen to between a quarter and a third of the figure for 1913, and production per individual worker to about the same. Hunger, lack of incentives, and the government policy of trying to put down as 'speculation' the attempts by workers to obtain food in the villages, while at the same time failing to provide it by official means, had by the end of the civil war brought the temper of the proletariat to breaking point. Strikes and disorders were becoming frequent, and, more ominously, as had happened in the days of the tsars, 'economic' protest was rapidly developing into 'political' protest against communist rule.

The evident failure of 'war communism' did not shake the faith of the majority of the communist leaders that all problems could be solved by more centralization, more control and more decrees. At the end of 1918 a former menshevik, Larin, had advocated the need to return to a modified form of free trading with the villages, but found little support. Lenin's argument that anything short of a forcible campaign against the peasants would enable them to starve the régime into submission won the day. Trotsky's proposals in the Central Committee at the beginning of 1920 for a form of limited free trade, very much on the lines of the New Economic Policy adopted a year later, were rejected by eleven votes to four. As late as the end of 1920, the Supreme Council of National Economy was taking steps to extend the net of nationalization even more widely.[2]

Meanwhile, the communist party itself was becoming divided by internal dissensions. The party organs were as yet powerless to enforce strict discipline, nor were attempts to maintain unanimity by

[1] *Lenin*, volume XXVI, p. 388; volume XXVII, p. 29; pp. 38–9; pp. 58–9.
[2] See my *The Origin of the Communist Autocracy*, pp. 215–17, where sources will be found.

force as yet regarded as consistent with party practice. The party Rules, adopted at the Eighth Party Conference in December 1919, permitted free discussion inside the party of all questions until such time as a decision had been reached, and this rule was respected until 1921. There was a good deal less respect for another rule entitling party organizations to elect their own committees,[1] and appointment of committees from the top downwards was rapidly becoming the usual practice. By the end of 1920 the policy and methods of Lenin and his supporters among the leaders of the party had been causing criticism and dissatisfaction for some time both among the trade union communists and among a left-wing group of the party leadership, on whom the mantle of the former left communists had fallen. But neither of these critical trends was of sufficient importance to shake the unity of the party while the civil war was in progress. Critics contained themselves in the confident hope that once victory had been achieved all would be put right.

The two socialist parties, in spite of all repressions, managed to survive the civil war. They were a thorn in the side of the communists, a permanent reminder to them in the midst of their difficulties of the many warnings which these political opponents had given in the past. Yet, though severely harassed, they were not extinguished. They had a chequered career during the civil war, and their part in it has been much distorted by both communist and non-communist historians. Neither the socialist revolutionaries (apart from their ill-fated left-wing) nor the mensheviks had supported the seizure of power by the bolsheviks in October 1917. They were accordingly branded as 'counter-revolutionaries'. If by 'counter-revolutionaries' was meant that these socialists preferred a capitalist restoration to communist rule, the reverse was the case: for each of these parties in turn threw away the opportunities which it had to rally effective opposition to the communist régime for fear that this would play into the hands of the reactionary side in the civil war.

This was probably why so long as the civil war raged the communists, while constantly harassing the two socialist parties by arrests and administrative repression, nevertheless suffered their continued existence. The position changed when the end of the civil war came in sight. Although the socialist revolutionaries did not in fact usually lead the peasant revolts which were taking place, it was natural enough for the communists to anticipate that they might yet do so. The mensheviks, who had drastically lost support among the workers in 1917,

[1] *KPSS v rez.*, volume I, pp. 462, 467.

were rapidly recovering ground in spite of all obstacles which were put in their way. As late as 1920 the mensheviks secured the election of 45 delegates in the Moscow soviet, over 225 in Kharkov and substantial delegations in some two dozen other soviets. In many, if not all, of the trade unions, mensheviks and their supporters far outnumbered the handful of unpopular communists, who dominated the trade union organs, and in three unions at least mensheviks predominated until 1921 in spite of all communist efforts to dislodge them. Zinoviev, always prone to exaggerate, estimated in 1921 the total anti-communist following in the trade unions variously at 90 and 99 per cent. Even Trotsky admitted that anti-communists were 'very numerous'. More alarming from the communist point of view, even communists were beginning by 1920 to listen to mensheviks in the unions with respect. The days were over when, as in 1918 or 1919, the very word 'freedom' in the mouth of a menshevik would be greeted by the communists with whistles, catcalls and cries of 'shame'. The time was fast approaching when the socialist parties would either have to be given legal recognition or destroyed.[1]

* * *

Isolated from the outside world and immersed in the immediate problems of the civil war, the new Soviet state nonetheless laid the foundations of its foreign policy during these years. Almost from the first it was the party which decided all questions of foreign policy, not the People's Commissariat for Foreign Affairs. For a short time the post of Foreign Commissar was held by Trotsky. A dynamic personality with views of his own, Trotsky was not always inclined to consult the views of his colleagues, let alone yield to their objections. For two weeks between the signing of the peace on 3 March 1918 and its ratification, Trotsky conducted informal negotiations with the Allied Powers in an endeavour to enlist their military support against the Germans on the bolshevik side. Lenin and the other supporters of the peace, like Stalin, only reluctantly gave their consent to these negotiations, and there were subsequent recriminations between Trotsky and his colleagues. After Trotsky's appointment as Commissar for War, the experiment of allowing such latitude in the conduct of foreign relations was never repeated. The new Commissar, G. V. Chicherin (a former menshevik), was not even a member of the Central Committee. The responsibility for foreign affairs was vested

[1] I have dealt in detail with the policies and fates of the mensheviks and socialist revolutionaries in my *The Origin of the Communist Autocracy*, chapters ix and xi.

increasingly in the Central Committee and later in the Politburo when it was set up in 1919. Lenin towards the end of his life approved this 'fusion', as he called it, of party and government in the case of foreign affairs.[1] It was a fusion in which 'the government' played a very subordinate, executive role.

Until the question of the peace shook the party to its foundations, the problem of foreign relations had hardly been considered. All accepted as incontrovertible that the Russian example would quickly be followed by other European peoples, or at all events persuaded themselves that this was incontrovertible, fearing that without such further revolutions the new Russian régime was doomed. Brest-Litovsk introduced a new factor into the doctrine of world revolution: henceforward, as Lenin emphasized in his argument in favour of the peace, since a socialist government had come to power in Russia, all questions of foreign policy must be decided 'exclusively' with the developing and strengthening of the socialist revolution in Russia in mind.[2] This was not an abandonment of world revolution, but a practical recognition of the fact that world revolution was not one and indivisible, and of the fact that the continued existence and strength of one revolutionary state were the best guarantee for spreading revolution to other states. The left communists with some bitterness dotted the i's of this new policy on 20 April 1918 in their political programme: 'In foreign policy,' they foretold, 'aggressive tactics of exposure of the imperialist powers will be replaced by a policy of diplomatic manœuvre by the Russian state amidst the imperialistic powers.' The Soviet republic will not only conclude trade agreements with them, but will also develop organic economic and political bonds with them, use their military and political support, 'and take loans from them'.[3] The left communists did not foresee that all this need not preclude the new state from furthering the cause of world revolution at the same time.

That diplomatic manœuvre could be combined with the furthering of revolutions became evident in 1919 – the most critical year of the civil war. Allied intervention in the civil war had taken place mainly in the second half of 1918. British forces had landed in Archangel on 2 August and in Baku on 14 August. On 3 August Japanese and British troops had landed in Vladivostok, to be followed shortly by American and French troops. But these Allied forces were small and of

[1] *Lenin*, volume XXVII, p. 413.
[2] *Lenin*, volume XXII, p. 194.
[3] Quoted from the political Programme or Theses of the left communists, which are reprinted in *Lenin*, volume XXII, pp. 561–71, from the first issue of *Kommunist*, a factional periodical published by the left communists for a time in Moscow.

little military significance, and the divided opinions on the question of intervention among the several powers were widely known. For a time, in January 1919, it seemed that a Soviet appeal to President Wilson for peace, issued on 24 December 1918, was going to lead to a settlement. But the prospect of Soviet defeat in the civil war seemed imminent to the Allied Powers, and by March 1919 it was evident that all hopes of the Allies agreeing to negotiate were dashed. It was about this time that Lenin told the Eighth Party Congress that the existence of the Soviet state side by side with the imperialist states was inconceivable. 'In the end, one or the other must conquer', but until then a number of terrible clashes was 'inevitable'. It was an idea to which he frequently returned, in order to draw the moral that until the Soviet state was strong enough to defeat its sworn enemies, its proper course was to exploit whatever divisions there were between the capitalist states.[1]

The appeal for peace and the tentative negotiations which accompanied it were only one facet of the dual Soviet foreign policy, combining diplomacy with the simultaneous furthering of world revolution. Thus, it was during the negotiations with the Allied Powers, indeed at the most hopeful moment in the negotiations, on 24 January 1919, that invitations were issued to a founding congress of a new, Third Communist International. Those invited included the left-wing groups in England, Ireland, France and the United States. The foundation of the Third International (the Comintern), which Lenin had decided on as far back as September 1914, took place in Moscow on 4 March 1919. Unrepresentative, in fact if not on paper, its first Congress was a propaganda gesture more than an organizational move. But the propaganda was not unsuccessful, and its results were at first sufficient to keep the hope of imminent revolutions alive. The appeal of the First Comintern Congress to workers everywhere to rally to the support of the Soviet régime in Russia appeared to be acting as a stimulus to the industrial unrest which was widespread in the countries of Europe ravaged and disorganized by the war. For the time being, the Soviet leaders, fighting for their survival, and anxious to encourage support wherever they could, showed a marked tolerance to the ideological diversities of the nascent communist movements in Europe.

The first clear indication that foreign communist parties were expected to conform to instructions issued by their Russian brothers

[1] See *Lenin*, volume XXIII, pp. 292–3 – November 1918; volume XXIV, p. 122; and Volume XXV, pp. 498–513, for a speech in November 1920.

was the publication in June 1920 of Lenin's *The Children's Disease of 'leftism' in Communism*. This vigorous pamphlet provided detailed directions on the tactics which the individual new-born communist parties should pursue in their countries. It interpreted the experience of the Russian party for universal application in advanced industrial countries with developed trade union and parliamentary institutions. The main theme of the pamphlet is condemnation of ultra-revolutionary romanticism which disdains to exploit the opportunities provided by democratic institutions. For the first time Lenin now admitted that the bolshevik boycott of the elections to the First Duma in 1906 had been a mistake. This mistake should not be repeated. British communists, for example, should 'if necessary, use every kind of trick, cunning, illegal means, concealment of the truth or prevarication' in order to get into and stay in the trade unions. They should learn to support the Labour Party leaders by their votes 'as the rope supports the hanged man'. There were similar injunctions for the communists of other countries. Lenin's motives in condemning 'leftism' were not, however, limited to devising correct tactics for the foreign parties. The 'children's disease' had erupted by this date with some violence within the Russian party and it was therefore a matter of some importance for Lenin to discredit the left-wing elements which existed among the foreign parties from whom the Russian left-wing oppositionists might in future seek support.

At the Second Congress of the Comintern, in July and August 1920, Zinoviev, Lenin's 'maid of all work', who had become President of the Executive Committee of the International at its foundation, strove to transform the International from a loose federation into a 'single world communist party' of which the national parties would be sections. Conditions for membership and for the internal discipline of individual parties were voted. These 21 conditions were designed both to model all parties on the Russian pattern and to exclude the troublesome left wings which were likely to be critical of the Russian party. The Congress also adopted resolutions on policy in the colonial and 'semi-colonial' territories, to which the Russians, particularly Lenin, attached supreme importance, regarding them as the weakest point in the armour of the imperialist powers. Lenin's Theses on colonialism, although not acceptable to all delegates without some compromise, became the policy of the International. Communists were to aim at bringing about 'a close alliance of all national and colonial liberation movements with Soviet Russia'; and at supporting what Lenin called the 'bourgeois democratic' national movements.

But because of the susceptibilities of some of Lenin's critics, 'bourgeois democratic' became 'national revolutionary' movements in the resolution as amended. The effect was the same: the communists must support a nationalist and bourgeois movement so long as such support would strengthen the Soviet Union and weaken the imperialists.[1]

The first steps in what was soon to become the complete subordination of communist parties to the Russian party were thus taken in the summer of 1920. Although dissident voices were raised at the Second Comintern Congress, the great majority accepted Soviet leadership without demurring. The prestige of the first country in which a communist party had won power was at its highest, and while the Congress held its deliberations the Red Army was sweeping on victoriously to the gates of Warsaw. Hopes that revolution would break out all over Europe ran high.

[1] See *The Communist International 1919–1943*. Documents. Selected and edited by Jane Degras. Volume I 1919–1922, Oxford, 1956, pp. 127 ff., 138–44. 166–72,

XI The Communist Rule under Threat

Victory in the civil war at the end of 1920 raised anew the whole question of the survival of communist party rule. The peasants were now in open revolt, and among the proletariat discontent began to assume threatening proportions. Party rule was accepted during the civil war, in spite of its unpopularity. The majority of the nation tolerated the party, though less for love of the communists than for fear of the return of the landlords. But now that the civil war was over, and any prospect of a restoration of the old order so remote as to be discounted, the basis of communist rule was to be challenged.

Within the party itself, trends of opposition to the leadership, which had played only a subordinate role while the overriding needs of the civil war commanded all allegiance, now acquired new importance. Two centres of discontent had been building up for some time before the end of 1920. One such centre was among the communists in the trade unions, whose spokesmen acquired the nickname of the 'Workers' Opposition'; their leader was Shliapnikov, himself a former worker. The trade union communists had ensured themselves by 1920 a dominant position in the leading organs of nearly all trade unions. They had achieved this position very largely by force and electoral fraud. The dissident communist trade unionists also regarded their own privileged position in the unions as justified, and did not oppose the methods which were used to oust their political opponents, such as mensheviks. But there were three matters on which many of the trade union communists found themselves in conflict with the policy of the party leaders.

The first cause of friction was the practice, much encouraged by Lenin after the breakdown of workers' control in the factories, of employing non-communist experts and specialists. This concession to the practical needs of industry outraged many radical worker communists to whom it appeared as an unwarranted concession to the class enemy, and as lack of faith in the working class. The second source of discontent was the growing habit of the central party organs of disregarding party democracy in such matters as the election of local union committees, and their readiness to substitute nomination for the methods of election prescribed in the party Rules. From the point of view of the centre, these authoritarian practices were often dictated by the requirements of maintaining an unpopular minority in power in the face of opposition inside the union from the non-communist workers. But the members of the Workers' Opposition, while they accepted their monopolistic position in the unions, often disagreed with the methods which were necessary to maintain it, and jibbed at party discipline. They demanded for themselves the freedom which they were actively engaged in denying to the majority of their fellow-workers.

Thirdly, there was dissension between many of the rank and file communist trade unionists and the party leaders on the question of the function of the trade unions. Until 1922 the party leaders regarded the trade unions' role in a socialist state, where by definition no conflict could arise between the workers and their 'own' government, as limited to maintaining work discipline and to increasing production. The voice of organized labour, according to this view, was sufficiently represented by the participation of trade union leaders in the counsels of the central party and government organs. The rank and file trade unionists were far from satisfied that the voice of the leaders (who were in any case usually appointed, not elected) was the voice of the communist workers. By the end of 1920 the opposition trade unionists were demanding that control over industry should be exercised by a central organ directly elected by 'the unions' – by which they meant elected by those who almost alone now enjoyed any voice inside the unions, the communists in the trade union committees. Their demand was reinforced by reliance on a passage in the party programme, adopted in 1919, and, though disregarded in practice, never modified, that the trade unions 'must achieve the actual concentration in their hands of all management of the entire national economy'.

The second centre of dissent was among the so-called Democratic Centralists. The leading Democratic Centralists were in the majority of cases former left communists, though Bukharin was no longer of their number. They objected to the increasingly authoritarian practices of the party centre. Their interpretation of the party principle of democratic centralism differed from Lenin's. As a prominent Democratic Centralist said at the Ninth Party Congress, in March 1920: 'Comrade Lenin says that the essence of democratic centralism is contained in the fact that the [party] Congress elects the Central Committee, while the Central Committee manages [the party]. We cannot agree with this somewhat fanciful view.' Fanciful or not, it was rather late to take issue with Lenin over a view which he had held since 1902, if not before. The Democratic Centralists also advocated reforms which were designed to allow more real powers to the executive committees of the local soviets. In much the same way as the members of the Workers' Opposition, the Democratic Centralists accepted the rigged elections by means of which communists won their majorities in the local soviets, but resented the growing centralization by which Lenin and his colleagues kept the party as a whole in power.[1] Analysis of these two party opposition movements shows that though many of the leaders were intellectuals, the largest number of their prominent adherents were industrial workers, or former industrial workers. These workers were mostly comparatively young men, about a third of whom had joined the party before 1904, and another third between 1908 and 1913.[2]

Neither of these critical trends caused very serious difficulty while the war was in progress. By the end of 1920, the party rank and file began to hope for relaxation of the discipline which they had for so long endured in the interests of the national emergency. The unrest in the party as a whole precipitated a crisis at the top. Its immediate cause was Trotsky. Trotsky had by 1920, while still retaining control over the army, turned his energies to the critical situation in industry. In contrast to Lenin, whose skill in leadership consisted in saying a little less than he intended to do, Trotsky's method was a blunt frankness, designed to stimulate revolutionary ardour. He made no secret of his view that the basis of the proletarian dictatorship was iron discipline, and that the trade unions would be subjected to this discipline in the interests of production.

Appointed People's Commissar of Transport and later Chairman of the openly dictatorial so-called Central Transport Committee (*Tsektran*) he lost no time in putting his theories into practice. The catastrophic condition of transport called for stern measures, which were fully backed by the Central Committee. But Trotsky's methods caused an uproar among the trade union communists. Coming on top of the already existing pressure for more democratic practices inside the party, Trotsky's policy led to widespread discontent in the rank and

---

[1] Further details on these two opposition trends in the party will be found in my *The Origin*, chapter xii.

[2] I have drawn for this information on the analysis of these opposition movements made by Dr S. V. Utechin in a dissertation for the degree of B.Litt. in the University of Oxford, 'The Origin of the Ruling Class in Soviet Society'.

file, not only with him, but with the general direction of the party as practised by its central organs. By the end of 1920 the dissensions in the party at large spread to the Central Committee. No one in the Central Committee of nineteen championed the views of either the Workers' Opposition or the Democratic Centralists, which indeed all the top leaders strongly opposed, if only as a challenge to their own authority. But the Central Committee was broadly divided on the issue of less or more stern party dictatorship and discipline.[1]

Plainly, in the event of an open debate and vote, the more 'liberal' faction was likely to prove the more popular. This faction of ten in all headed by Lenin, included Zinoviev, Kamenev and Stalin, and the two trade union leaders, Tomskii and Rudzutak. Trotsky's supporters included Bukharin, the head of the *Vecheka*, Dzerzhinskii, and the three men at the head of the party secretarial organization – Krestinskii, Preobrazhenskii and Serebriakov. A proposal, supported by Lenin, for the immediate abolition of the unpopular *Tsektran* led to a division of opinion among the members of the Central Committee; all efforts to reach a compromise failed. The only solution lay in appealing to the party as a whole to decide between the conflicting views of their leaders. The issue between the leaders was presented in January 1921 to the party at large as a division between a more moderate conciliatory wing, and a more extreme, harsh, dictatorial wing.[2] Lenin's lieutenant, Zinoviev, the party boss of Petrograd who was renowned for his ruthlessness, now took the lead in attacking Trotsky as a 'dictator'. His personal antagonism to Trotsky had been a marked feature in the relations of the party leaders since 1918, if not before. Zinoviev now painted the rosy future of party democracy if once the menace of Trotsky's iron grip over the party were defeated. In his enthusiasm to disparage Trotsky, he allowed himself to be so far carried away as to undermine Trotsky's authority in the Baltic Fleet stationed in the naval base of Kronstadt, thus helping to precipitate a sailors' revolt a few months later.[3]

In view of this open split among the party leaders, a party debate on the basis of rival policies, or 'platforms', was inaugurated largely at the instigation of Zinoviev, in preparation for the Tenth Party Congress which was due to meet in March 1921. Lenin later claimed that he had not wanted such a public party debate, but he never disowned

[1] This conflict is fully treated in my *The Origin*, chapter xiv, where references will be found to the sources.
[2] See the announcement in *Izv. Ts.K.*, No. 27 of 27 January 1921.
[3] For details of Zinoviev's activities in the Baltic Fleet see A. S. Pukhov, 'Kronshtadt i baltiiskii flot pered miatezhem 1921 goda' in *Krasnaia letopis'*, No. 6 (39), 1930, pp. 174–97.

any of Zinoviev's moves. The Workers' Opposition and the Democratic Centralists, and several minor groups, took advantage of the invitation issued by the Central Committee to publish their 'platforms'. The adherence to the Workers' Opposition in 1921 of Alexandra Kollontai, a colourful if somewhat unstable figure, transformed this rather drab movement into a clarion call for freedom in the party. To the charge that freedom of discussion was being curtailed the Workers' Opposition added the complaint, of which much would be heard so long as criticism was allowed, that the party was losing its true proletarian composition and was fast becoming a caste of self-seeking officials.

Trotsky's programme in contrast bluntly advocated the fusion of trade union organs with the state machinery and military discipline and compulsion as the normal methods of maintaining industrial efficiency. Lenin's Theses, which became the so-called 'Platform of the Ten', were a masterpiece of diplomatic understatement, and certainly held out hope, at all events to the more credulous, that greater freedom would now be tolerated: the state functions of the unions 'will gradually increase', but the tempo of fusion must not be speeded up; the principal method for ensuring discipline in industry is persuasion, though 'proletarian compulsion' is 'in no way' excluded; all trade union organs should be elected – but 'of course', under the 'overall control of the party'.[1]

But six days before the Tenth Party Congress, due to open on 8 March 1921, the party was shaken to its very foundations by the news that the sailors of the Baltic Fleet and the garrison of the naval base at Kronstadt had revolted and had set up a Provisional Revolutionary Committee.[2]

[1] Lenin's original Theses have not been preserved, but they formed the basis of the Platform of the Ten, as it was called when presented to the Tenth Party Congress. Both this Platform and Trotsky's Theses are reprinted in G. Zinoviev (editor), *Partiia i soiuzy (K diskussii o roli i zadachakh profsoiuzov)*, Leningrad, 1921, pp. 9–32 and 354–60, and 249–50. Bukharin's Theses, also signed by Larin, Preobrazhenskii, Serebriakov and Sokol'nikov, are *ibidem*, pp. 371–7, and those of the Workers' Opposition at pp. 361–70. For the Theses of the Democratic Centralists see *Lenin*, volume XXVI, pp. 573–6, and for those of Ignatov see *ibidem*, pp. 576–8. A separate view was also expressed by Nogin, and will be found in an article reprinted in Zinoviev, *op. cit.*, pp. 304–16.

[2] The best accounts of the Kronstadt revolt will be found in Chapter v of D. Fedotoff-White, *The Growth of the Red Army*, Princeton, 1944 and in George Katkov, 'The Kronstadt Rising', in *St Antony's Papers* No. 6, Soviet Affairs No. 2, edited by David Footman, London, 1959. See also Robert V. Daniels. 'The Kronstadt Revolt of 1921: Study in the Tyrannies of Revolution', in *American Slavic and East European Review*, 1951, p. 241. The best Soviet account is A. S. Pukhov, *Kronshtadtskii miatezh v 1921 g.*, Leningrad, 1931. And see my *The Origin*, Chapter xvi for further discussion of the immense literature of this subject.

In the last week of February 1921 a particularly big wave of strikes and demonstrations swept Petrograd. Its origin was only in part directly political, since many of the resolutions passed at meetings were aimed at the armed detachments which were being used by the government to foil the attempts of the starving workers to obtain food in the neighbouring countryside. There was, however, also a more clearly political undercurrent in some of the resolutions which reflected the activity of menshevik agitators. The strikes were quickly and effectively suppressed by a combination of force and concessions. Private foraging expeditions were sanctioned, and food supplies were rushed to Petrograd. At the same time the communist party organization in Petrograd, led by Zinoviev, maintained its discipline in face of the threat, and succeeded in restoring order by wholesale arrests.

But the unrest in Petrograd sparked off more serious events in the naval base of Kronstadt, which is situated on an island in the Finnish Gulf some seventeen miles to the west of the city. The sailors, long renowned for their savage revolutionary ardour, had been in a state of ferment for some time past – Zinoviev's private feud with Trotsky had been a contributory factor. The sailors had made some contacts with the strikers and confidently expected that if they now raised the standard of revolt against the rule of the communist party, their demands would be spontaneously supported in Petrograd and throughout the country. On 28 February the crew of the battleship *Petropavlovsk* voted the resolution which embodied the insurgents' programme. Its main demands were: immediate re-election of the soviets by free and secret ballot 'in view of the fact that the existing soviets do not express the will of the workers and peasants'; freedom of speech and press for all workers' and peasants' political parties; freedom of meeting and association in unions for both workers and peasants; liberation of all political prisoners; the abolition of the specially privileged position of the communist party and abolition of all armed communist detachments, 'since no one party can enjoy privileges for the propaganda of its ideas and receive money from the state for this purpose'; full rights for the peasants to do what they like with their land, and the right of individual, small-scale manufacture – but, in each case, provided no hired labour was employed; and equal rations for all. Next day a mass meeting was held in the main square of Kronstadt, which some 12,000 attended. Among those who addressed the meeting were Kalinin, who had been hurriedly dispatched to Kronstadt to investigate the situation, and the military commissar who accompanied him. They were loudly heckled, and the *Petropavlovsk* resolution was enthusiastically voted by the crowd in defiance of their protests.

On 2 March a Provisional Revolutionary Committee, headed by a naval clerk, Petrichenko, and consisting entirely of ratings of proletarian or peasant origin, was set up. The communist leaders in Moscow immediately demanded that the Committee should surrender: the demand was rejected out of hand. The Provisional Revolutionary Committee lasted for fifteen days, during which it published a daily newspaper.[1] It refused to resort to arms, except in self-defence, confidently expecting that the justice of its cause would be evident enough to ensure that the revolt spread to the mainland. During the fifteen days of the rule of the Provisional Committee about a quarter of the communists in Kronstadt, both civilian and naval, resigned from the party: thirty per cent of all the communists in the fleet and in the garrison, at the lowest estimate, supported the insurgents, and forty per cent were 'neutral'.[2] But there was no popular outbreak against the communists inside Kronstadt. A few were put under arrest, but there were no executions and no lynchings.

On 7 March military operations, directed from Moscow by Trotsky and led by Tukhachevskii, the outstanding commander of the civil war, were begun, and on 18 March the fortress was finally stormed by the Red Army. The soldiers' reluctance to fire on sailors and workers was overcome by a combination of promises, threats, cajoling and lies. After the fall of Kronstadt hundreds, if not thousands, were massacred, but no public trial was ever held.

The revolt of the proletariat against the dictatorship of the proletariat was something for which Marxist doctrine had made no provision. The Tenth Party Congress when it met on 8 March was dominated by the plain evidence of the growing unpopularity of communist rule over those whom it claimed to represent, of which the Kronstadt revolt was only the culminating proof. As Lenin admitted to the Congress, 'we have failed to convince the broad masses'.[3] The mood of the Congress was one of resentment, disappointment, anger, bewilderment and fear. The Kronstadt revolt was immediately branded as 'counter-revolution'. In the sense that the revolt was directly or indirectly aimed at the restoration of a capitalist, let alone a

---

[1] Reprinted in full as an appendix to *Pravda o Kronshtadte*, Prague, 1921.
[2] According to Trotsky, as quoted by Smilga, *X S"ezd*, p. 225. And see N. Kornatovskii (editor), *Kronshtadtskii miatezh. Sbornik statei, vospominanii i dokumentov.* Leningrad, 1931, pp. 13–15.
[3] *X S"ezd*, p. 382.

monarchist, society the charge was not remotely true. Not a shred of evidence has ever been adduced to show that the rising in Kronstadt was financed by foreign capital, or led or inspired by monarchists, socialist revolutionaries or mensheviks. It was from start to finish a spontaneous, popular uprising. Lenin once admitted as much, in one of those flashes of honesty which still distinguished him from many of his followers, when he said that in Kronstadt 'they do not want the White Guards, and they do not want our power either'.[1] But more usually he associated himself with the party line, of which Trotsky was the main initiator – to the dismay of the insurgents, who had at first exempted Lenin from the general contempt which they felt for all the communist leaders.[2] Yet, if once it was accepted that communist party rule and socialism were identical – and both Lenin and his followers were fully committed to this view – 'counter-revolution' it had to be.

Lenin now applied himself to consolidating party rule on a new and more secure basis. It is necessary at this point to look at the theory of revolutionary government which underlay the communist party's policy in the first few years of power. At the centre of the doctrine lay the idea of the 'dictatorship of the proletariat', which Marx on one sole occasion had asserted would intervene between the conquest of power by the proletariat and the establishment of socialism.[3] How far Marx had meant by this the exercise of arbitrary power by one party against everyone who disagreed with it has been questioned by leading Marxists.[4] There is indeed nothing in the writings of Marx which suggests that he ever contemplated the communist party as an instrument of rule after the revolution. But Lenin certainly interpreted Marx's phrase as justifying the use of what he had called 'unlimited power based on violence, and bound by no laws'[5] in order to ensure the survival of Soviet government against its opponents. Lenin, with the prospect in mind that the final 'proletarian' revolution would take place in Russia at a time when the proletariat was still very small, had

---

[1] *Lenin*, volume XXVI, p. 248.

[2] See the insurgents' newspaper quoted in *Pravda o Kronshtadte*, pp. 150-1.

[3] In his 'Critique of the Gotha Programme', in May 1875.

[4] In particular by Karl Kautsky. See his *Demokratie oder Diktatur*, Berlin, 1918; and *The Dictatorship of the Proletariat*, translated by H. J. Stenning, Second Edition, London, 1920. For Lenin's replies to him see *Lenin*, volume XXIII, pp. 331–412, and volume XXV, pp. 429–47. Whatever be the correct interpretation of Marx's phrase 'revolutionary dictatorship of the proletariat', it was nonetheless the case that the idea that the individual's liberty would require protection from the state after the revolution is absent from Marx's thought: he believed that with the ending of exploitation such a necessity could not arise.

[5] In 1906, *Lenin*, volume IX, pp. 94–5 – but frequently reiterated after the 1917 revolution – e.g. in 1920 – volume XXV, p. 436.

already envisaged in 1902 that when once the proletariat seized power it would have to exercise forcible dictatorship over the peasant majority.[1] Certainly, in common with all bolsheviks, Lenin had foreseen revolutionary terror on the Jacobin model as a necessary means for dealing with counter-revolutionaries. Terror against those elements who were regarded as by nature opposed to the revolution – the bourgeoisie, and the 'petty bourgeosie' among the peasants – had therefore a long history in bolshevik theory. Lenin's peculiar contribution was the use of terroristic means against socialist opponents, and the recognition of the need to use terror even against the proletariat in the case of those waverers who were unwilling immediately to accept bolshevik leadership – the 'semi-proletariat', as Lenin sometimes called it.

But while Lenin was ready enough to admit, and indeed to justify, the use of 'revolutionary violence' against the bourgeoisie, when exercised by 'the toiling masses' of the workers and the poor peasants, it was some time before he was prepared to concede what had in practice become equally evident – the use of violence against the 'toiling masses' in the name of the 'toiling masses'. The keynote of Lenin's *State and Revolution*, written in August–September 1917 (though not published until after the October *coup d'état*), is that the new order to be set up by the worker masses will need little or no force to back it, because its edge will be directed against the small minority of exploiters by the great majority of toilers. The revolutionary state, he wrote, 'will begin to die away' immediately after the proletariat has seized power and destroyed the bourgeois state, since no state machinery is necessary where no class divisions exist any longer. Although in the transition from capitalism to communism some form of state machinery will still be needed, nevertheless, since democratic rights will be enjoyed by a vast majority, 'no special machinery for repression' will be required. The armed people will be able to deal with the small minority of exploiters 'without any special apparatus'. As for the normal business of 'proletarian' government, since the mass of the population will participate in 'day-to-day administration', it would follow, according to Lenin, that 'all will administer in turn and will quickly become accustomed to no one administering'.[2]

It is unlikely that the more utopian parts of this represented Lenin's convictions. Only six months after writing *State and Revolution* he

[1] See pp. 46–7 above.
[2] *Lenin*, volume XXI, pp. 369–455.

angrily brushed aside talk of the state withering away as a premature 'violation of historical perspective'.[1] As the first years of bolshevik rule rolled on, Lenin's utterances on the subject of government began to approximate more to reality. By 1919 he was prepared to admit that the dictatorship of the proletariat really meant the dictatorship of its vanguard, the party, and he argued that the dictatorship of a class and that of the party were indistinguishable.[2] Practical people know, he said in 1921, that the suggestion that every worker can administer the state is a 'fairy tale'.[3] A year before he had frankly admitted that 'revolutionary violence' was also essential 'against the faltering and unrestrained elements of the toiling masses themselves'. A 'desperate class struggle', he added, was the motive power of all progress.[4] It would indeed have been difficult to deny that the workers and the peasants were in fact bearing the burden of the dictatorship quite as much as the bourgeoisie.

It was also early in 1920 that Lenin wrote various drafts of a pamphlet on the dictatorship of the proletariat which he never completed. Nothing now remained in his thought of the utopianism of *State and Revolution*. The domination of one class, he notes, 'excludes freedom and equality'. The dictatorship of the proletariat is 'the continuation of the class struggle by other means'. Its four stages are the repression of the exploiters, the 'neutralization' of the petty bourgeoisie by persuasion or by force, the subordination to the needs of dictatorship of the necessary expert talent, and the training of all in a 'new discipline'. The overriding 'will of the majority' means the decision of all citizens -- but without the bourgeoisie, and without the 'waverers'.[5] That the 'majority' might in fact be the 'waverers', and that the decision of 'all citizens' would therefore be in fact that of the party, was by 1920 becoming obvious. Yet, while insisting to the end of his life on the need for dictatorship, Lenin continued to maintain at the same time that the Soviet system was the most democratic and the most free in the world. Soviet freedom differed from so-called freedom in the bourgeois world because it gave rights only to the workers and to the toiling peasantry, and properly deprived of all right to freedom and

[1] At the Seventh Party Congress, in polemics with Bukharin – *Lenin*, volume XXII, p. 365.
[2] *Lenin*, volume XXIV, p. 436; volume XXV, p. 188.
[3] *Lenin*, volume XXVI, p. 103.
[4] See *Kommunist*, No. 5, 1957, p. 21.
[5] *Lenin*, volume XXV, pp. 1–12. For an argument that Lenin's theory of the state showed no inconsistency over the years, since it was always dependent on the rate at which classes were in practice eliminated, see Edward Hallett Carr, *The Bolshevik Revolution 1917–1923*, volume I, London, 1950, pp. 233–49.

equality both the capitalists and those, such as the socialists, who were supporters of the bourgeoisie.

Faced with a simultaneous revolt of both the proletariat and the peasants, the Tenth Congress was prepared for drastic measures aimed at preserving party rule. The peasants, on whom ultimately the régime depended for its survival, had at all costs to be appeased. The question of the reversal of the economic policy of the country and the replacement of 'war communism' by a policy based on a free market had already been raised in the Political Bureau a month before the Tenth Congress met. But the proposal had then run into serious opposition inside the party leadership and had been referred to a commission for further discussion. The Congress now voted the abolition of the forcible exaction of produce from the peasants and its replacement by a graduated tax in kind, and also sanctioned a limited form of local trade. These were the first steps of what became known as the New Economic Policy (NEP), of which the development will be examined later. Lenin's proposals on the eve of the Tenth Congress had run into immediate opposition from his colleagues, which was only overcome when he threatened to resign.[1] The precipitous decision to make concessions to the peasants, agreed almost without debate by the Congress, was undoubtedly influenced by the Kronstadt revolt, though Lenin had been contemplating the need for such concessions some time before the revolt broke out. No sooner was it adopted than over two hundred delegates from the Congress were sent off to harangue the hesitant Red Army soldiers who were being driven across the ice at pistol point into beleaguered Kronstadt. An experienced political commissar noted that the news that the hated forcible collection of grain had been abolished, and that the peasants would once again be allowed to trade, brought about a 'radical change in the mood' of the peasant soldiers.[2]

The radical break with doctrine which was implicit in NEP created a deep division in the ranks of the communist party which was to prove of great importance for its future history. The need for Lenin's steadying hand in a time of crisis was never felt more than in March 1921. Bukharin, for example, hitherto the main theorist of the policy of 'war communism', changed his views almost on the spot, and became

[1] No official account of these dissensions has been published, but they were widely known in the higher party circles at the time. I have used an account contained in the unpublished memoirs of N. Valentinov (N. V. Vol'skii), who was at the time close to the leading economic circles.

[2] S. E. Rabinovich, 'Delegaty 10-go s"ezda RKP(b) pod Kronshtadtom v 1921 godu' in *Krasnaia letopis'*, No. 2 (41), 1931, p. 32.

thereafter the advocate of what he believed to be Lenin's views. But other economic theorists among the communist leaders, such as Piatakov and Preobrazhenskii, retained their doubts. To the orthodox Marxist there were two theoretical objections to NEP. One was the apparent sacrifice of a planned economy, based on heavy industry, to the prosperity of persons who were regarded as the natural enemies of socialism – the peasant smallholders. The other, and more important, theoretical objection went to the very roots of Marx's doctrine that the political 'superstructure' of every society is determined by its economic base. If the economic base was now to become the free market, a prosperous peasantry and light industry, it seemed inevitable that sooner or later the political superstructure would have to change in conformity with the base, and alongside of revived capitalism the political features of the bourgeois state would replace the socialism believed to have been won in the revolution. Lower down the intellectual scale, the followers of the Workers' Opposition regarded NEP as a betrayal of the workers in the interests of the inferior peasants.

Lenin's argument was that the only way of saving the revolution was by agreement with the peasants. The attempt at direct transition to communism had been a grave mistake. The proper road was from small-scale production to state capitalism, and thence to socialism, and only thereafter to communism. The 'petty bourgeois' peasant would not be converted overnight. But with the development of co-operation, of mechanization and electrification on a national scale, the mentality and habits of the peasant could be refashioned, so that from an enemy of socialism he would turn into its supporter. This process would take generations, but not centuries. However, the condition for the 'decisive success' of this policy was timely support of the Russian revolution by revolutions in one or several advanced countries. Meanwhile, so long as the state retained control over the 'commanding heights' of heavy industry and foreign trade, there was no danger of losing the achievements of the revolution to a capitalist restoration.[1]

The crisis which faced the Tenth Congress could not, however, be solved by economic means alone. Indeed, so far as Lenin was concerned, the economic reform was only subsidiary to the political reform if the supremacy of the communist party and its monopoly of

---

[1] Lenin's short argument at the Tenth Congress was subsequently elaborated by him in one of the last things he wrote – 'O kooperatsii', *Lenin*, volume XXVII, pp. 391–7, written in January 1923.

power was to be preserved. His immediate reforms in the political sphere were to prove of more lasting effect than his economic policy. Lenin may have believed that the peasants would eventually be converted to socialism by example and peaceful precept. But what was more important, and more in tune with his whole outlook, was his faith in the absolute primacy of the political machinery, if properly organized, over economic and social forces. His attention at the Tenth Party Congress, while the rifles of the Red Army were mowing down the worker and peasant insurgents in Kronstadt to the accompaniment of exhortations from all the leading communists, was accordingly devoted to perfecting the political machine. To maintain the monopoly of all power in communist hands during a civil war, and in the conditions of violent hatred of man for man was one thing. To maintain it under the conditions of the truce with the peasants now envisaged was another, and required quite a different party machine.

Lenin and his supporters in the Central Committee won their victory over Trotsky on the popular issue of more democracy in the party and less dictatorial interference from the top in the trade unions. The victory of the Platform of the Ten headed by Lenin was a foregone conclusion at the Congress, and their resolution on the trade unions was adopted by an overwhelming majority at the Congress. The fruits of the victory of the faction of moderation were duly embodied in resolutions. In the trade unions, ran one resolution, 'it is above all necessary to put into practice . . . on a wide scale the principle of election to all organs . . ., and to do away with the method of appointment from the top'. A further long resolution on party democracy, adopted on Bukharin's proposal, seemed to meet many of the criticisms of the Workers' Opposition. The military form of centralization in the party, it stressed, had been dictated by civil war conditions and was no longer applicable. All party members must be ensured 'an active part in the life of the party, in the discussion of all questions arising in the party'. Moreover, 'the nature of workers' democracy excludes every form of appointment in place of election as a system'.[1] This resolution also went a long way to meet the criticisms of the intellectual Democratic Centralists, who appear to have been, unlike the Workers' Opposition, more amenable to persuasion by resolutions and withdrew their 'platform' at the Congress. To symbolize the new, more moderate policy now promised in inner party affairs, the three secretaries of the party, Krestinskii, Preobrazhenskii and Serebriakov, were

---

[1] The resolutions are printed in *KPSS v rez.*, volume I, pp. 516–27 and 534–49.

replaced, and also removed from the Central Committee. They had been deluged with attacks, mainly by Zinoviev, who had endeavoured to blame them for the dictatorial system prevalent in the party. They had also sided with Trotsky on the trade union issue; moreover, one of them, Preobrazhenskii, was soon to become the principal theoretical opponent of NEP, and may be presumed to have opposed its introduction on the eve of the Congress. These were more important reasons than their 'dictatorial' practices (they appear, in fact, to have been comparatively mild and conciliatory during their term of office in the Secretariat) to explain their removal from the party leadership.[1]

Meanwhile, very different plans were in preparation for dealing with discipline inside the party. Lenin had hinted at them on the second day of the Congress, when he asserted that the time had come 'to put an end to opposition, to put the lid on it', but the resolutions tabled to date did not suggest that the threat would be implemented. On the last day of the Congress Lenin suddenly produced two new resolutions, on 'Party Unity', and on 'The Syndicalist and Anarchist Deviation in our Party'. 'I do not think it will be necessary for me to say much on this subject', was his characteristic introduction to what was to prove a milestone in the history of the party.

The first resolution on Party Unity drew attention to the fact that there had been signs in the party, even before the eve of Congress debate on the trade unions, of the formation of 'groups with separate platforms and with the determination to a certain extent to become self-contained and to create their own group discipline'. It went on to suggest that the existence of opposition inside the party had given encouragement to the enemies of the revolution, as the Kronstadt rising had shown, and went on to lay down new limits for criticism of party policy by members of the party: 'Everyone who criticizes in public must keep in mind the situation of the party in the midst of the enemies by which it is surrounded. . . .' The resolution called for the immediate dissolution of all groups with a separate platform, on pain of immediate expulsion from the party. The last clause of the resolution, which remained secret until January 1924, conferred on the Central Committee full disciplinary powers, including the power of expulsion from the party, with the proviso that where the offender was a member of the Central Committee a two-thirds vote of full members, candidate members and members of the Control Commission was

[1] On the whole conflict with the secretaries and their removal see my *The Origin*, pp. 267–71, 320–1.

required to decide on his expulsion. (This proviso was of practical interest to the leader of the Workers' Opposition, Shliapnikov, who, on Lenin's particular insistence, was elected to the Central Committee at the Tenth Congress.)

The second resolution condemned the views of the Workers' Opposition on the role of the trade unions in exercising control over industry as 'inconsistent with membership' of the party, since they offended against Marxism. It further went on to incorporate Lenin's distinctive views on the role of the party into the canons of orthodox Marxism: 'Marxism teaches us that only the political party of the working class, i.e. the communist party, is capable of uniting, educating and organizing such a vanguard of the proletariat and of the working masses as is capable of resisting the inevitable petty-bourgeois waverings of these masses . . . [and] their trade union prejudices.' Here was the central doctrine of *What is to be Done?*[1]

The charges against those who were nicknamed the Workers' Opposition were flagrantly unjust. This group of critics had never had any press, or separate organization or discipline of its own. Its emergence at the Tenth Congress with its own 'platform' had been solely due to the insistence by the Central Committee, on the initiative of Zinoviev, that elections to this Congress should take place by 'platforms'. So far from supporting the demands of the Kronstadt insurgents some members of the Workers' Opposition were, at the very moment when the resolution was passed, actively and enthusiastically engaged in shooting the insurgents down. As for their views on the role of the trade unions in the control of industry, whether or no they offended against Marxism, they differed little from the assertion contained in the party programme that the trade unions 'must achieve the concentration in their hands of all management of the entire national economy'. But the traditions of the party were not those of justice, but of expediency, and expediency dictated to the frightened men at that Congress the need for unity in the face of the enraged proletariat and peasants. The resolutions were passed by overwhelming majorities, and were little criticized – even by followers of the Workers' Opposition. The mood of the Congress was well voiced by Radek in prophetic words: 'In voting for this resolution I feel that it can well be turned against us, and nevertheless I support it. . . . Let the Central Committee in a moment of danger take the severest measures against the best party comrades, if it finds this

[1] *X S"ezd*, pp. 523–36; *KPSS v rez.*, volume I, pp. 527–33.

necessary. . . . Let the Central Committee even be mistaken! That is less dangerous than the wavering which is now observable.'[1] Few indeed of those present at the Congress, including many elected to the Central Committee, and Radek himself, were to survive unscathed through the subsequent years.

[1] *X S"ezd*, p. 540.

XII Lenin's Conflict with his Colleagues

Having assured victory over the party at the Tenth Congress, Lenin soon showed that little remained of the resolutions on trade union and party democracy with which he had sought to pacify his critics. The hated *Tsektran* was immediately restored, in spite of the fact that the Central Committee had split over the very issue of its abolition, urged by Lenin and his faction. The ink was scarcely dry on the trade union resolution which deprecated 'reconstruction of the trade union organizations from the top' when a conflict arose between the Central Committee and the communists in the Metal Workers' Union – incidentally the oldest pro-bolshevik union. In May 1921 the communist 'fraction' in this union rejected the Central Committee's list of candidates for its own controlling committee by 120 votes to 40, whereupon the Central Committee ignored the vote and appointed a committee consisting of its own nominees. Shliapnikov's demand to be allowed to resign from the Central Committee in protest was rejected.

The resolution on 'party democracy' was equally ignored. Throughout 1921 and 1922 the ferment of protest grew in the rank and file of the party, directed against the dictatorship of the party bureaucracy, its entrenched immunity from control, its indifference to criticism and its readiness to ride rough-shod over the views of local committees. Much of this criticism was no doubt inspired by the resentment against NEP, which now favoured the peasants at the expense of the proletarian communists who had hitherto enjoyed a monopoly of privilege. The Central Committee and its organs (much strengthened, as will be seen later), the Control Commission and even the *Vecheka* attempted to stifle this criticism. Critics were dealt with by victimization, transfer and even expulsion from the party. Discussion groups, which had been expressly authorized by the Tenth Party Congress, were closed down for their 'demagogic, non-party character', and a number of elected organizations were disbanded and restocked with Central Committee nominees.[1]

[1] I have dealt fully with these developments after the Tenth Congress in Chapter xvii of my *The Origin*.

In February 1922, a group of twenty-two supporters of the former Workers' Opposition decided in despair to appeal for a hearing to the Communist International. They were treated with scant sympathy by the Executive Committee of the International. A commission (headed by the Bulgarian Kolarov, and including among its members Klara Zetkin) was appointed, which duly condemned their complaints as unfounded. There was little risk at that date that the International would side against the Russian party, but the raising of this issue in the forum of world communism was none the less a serious blow to Russian prestige. The twenty-two were duly condemned by the Eleventh Party Congress in March 1922 – not, ostensibly, for appealing to the International, but for maintaining a separate 'faction' inside the party. But although the party leaders at this Congress were for the most part solidly behind the drive to stifle criticism, the rank and file of the delegates were not. It was a turbulent assembly, which in the end defied the Central Committee by refusing to vote the expulsion of Shliapnikov and Alexandra Kollontai from the party.[1]

The absence of Lenin, whose health was beginning to fail, from all the meetings except the opening and the closing sessions, was never more clearly felt. The new leaders who were to step into his shoes – Zinoviev, Stalin, Kamenev, Trotsky, Bukharin – carefully noted that much remained to be done if discipline in the party was to be raised to the necessary pitch. On this, if on nothing else, they were all agreed. One solitary voice – that of the scholar Riazanov, against whom Lenin's venom had been directed in the far-off days of the Second Congress – warned that if the leaders governed by issuing orders which they were afraid to submit to preliminary discussion, chaos, corruption and bureaucracy would be the inevitable results. 'They say,' he commented, with the bitter wit which characterized him, 'that the English Parliament can do everything except change a man into a woman. Our Central Committee is far more powerful than that. It has already changed more than one not very revolutionary man into an old woman, and the number of these old women is increasing daily.'[2]

The introduction of NEP affected not only the communist party: it spelt the end of the vestiges of overt political activity by the two socialist parties – the mensheviks, and the socialist revolutionaries.[3]

---

[1] *ibidem*, pp. 334–6.
[2] *XI S″ezd*, p. 83.
[3] Both parties continued clandestine activities for some time thereafter, with increasing risk of attracting severe police repressions. A group of socialist revolutionary leaders was sentenced after a show trial in 1922. There were a number of minor trials of mensheviks in 1920, but the main show trial did not take place until

The mensheviks had long advocated the policy which Lenin inaugurated under the name of NEP. The socialist revolutionaries were the traditional champions of the peasant's freedom to till his own land. To have left these parties at large would inevitably have invited the question why those who had been proved wrong should not yield power to those who had been proved right. Moreover, once it was admitted, as the transition to NEP necessarily admitted, that the bourgeois revolution had not yet been completed, it followed for anyone familiar with the rudiments of Marxism that the main theoretical justification for the dictatorship of the proletariat, in its guise of the dictatorship of the communist party, ceased to exist. But Lenin and his followers were less interested in doctrine than in preserving their own rule. No communist was prepared to quarrel with Lenin's repeated assertions that prison was the only place for mensheviks and socialist revolutionaries. At the Tenth Party Conference, in May 1921, Radek, with rather more frankness than Lenin, dotted the i's by explaining that if the mensheviks were left at liberty, now that the communists had adopted their policy, they would demand political power; while to concede freedom to the socialist revolutionaries when the 'enormous mass' of the peasants was opposed to the communists would be suicide.[1]

* * *

The resolution on NEP adopted by the Congress merely referred to replacement of requisitioning by a tax in kind, and to exchange by the peasants of their surplus products 'on a local scale'. As the full policy unfolded in the course of 1921 and after, it became apparent that a much more fundamental change was taking place.[2] The first intention had been to permit only cautiously and with severe limitations the return of the private enterprise so much feared by the doctrinaires. But the 'demon' of capitalism, as Bukharin called it, once released was not so easily tamed. Indeed, throughout the period of war communism, it had maintained a vigorous enough underground existence, in the face of all repressions, and may even have been the main factor which had prevented total economic breakdown.

A decree which followed shortly after the Tenth Congress aban-

[1] *X Konf.*, pp. 66–7.
[2] There is a good account of NEP in Edward Hallett Carr, *The Bolshevik Revolution 1917–1923*, volume II, London, 1952, chapter xix.

1931. It is one of the curiosities of Soviet constitutional law that there is no legal enactment rendering political activity by parties other than the communist illegal. But the wide interpretation of 'counter-revolution' has in practice always proved adequate to cover such activity.

doned any limitations on the peasant's right to trade in his surplus products, and in May 1921 the Tenth Party Conference recognized that the New Economic Policy had been established for a 'long period, measured in years', and that its 'fundamental lever' was exchange of goods.[1] The concession, however, came too late in the year to affect the spring sowing, and the new policy was in any case frustrated in 1921 by a failure of the harvest, followed by a disastrous famine. By the following spring further concessions were made to the peasants. In March 1922 the tax in kind was limited to ten per cent of production, and seizure of livestock as a penalty for non-payment was prohibited. In May 1922 a further decree in effect recognized the right of the peasant to treat his holding as his own, to lease his land and to hire labour to work it. Thus, though public ownership was in theory preserved, the peasant was offered security to develop his holding with the prospect that industry would be rewarded in a free market. The new agrarian code enacted at the end of 1922 embodied these provisions.

The success of the new policy became plainly evident by the end of 1922. Lenin claimed that any 'serious discontent' among the peasants with the régime was now 'completely out of the question',[2] and by 1923 overall agricultural production had risen to nearly three-quarters of the 1913 level. The pacification of the revolt in the countryside had not, however, been due entirely to NEP. In the course of 1922 the whole might of the Red Army had been employed to put down peasant rebellion.

NEP was mainly intended as a means of appeasing the peasants, and had not primarily been designed to extend to industry. Before long the new wind began to blow in industry too. This was inevitable, since, if the peasant was to be encouraged to produce by the prospects of profits earned on a free market, goods had to be manufactured in order to provide him with something in exchange for his money. In the course of 1921 the harm done during the civil war by the policy of headlong nationalization was progressively undone. Several decrees in the summer of 1921 ensured for the small industries in the countryside the same security and opportunity to trade as was offered to the peasant smallholders. A further step taken about the same time permitted the return to private management, through leasing, of enterprises which were nominally nationalized. This permission applied in practice only to small concerns, and only half of the enterprises so leased were restored to their former owners, the remainder being

---

[1] *KPSS v rez.*, volume I, p. 574.
[2] *Lenin*, volume XXVII, p. 347.

leased to co-operatives and state institutions. Large-scale industry, as Lenin repeatedly claimed remained in the hands of the state.

The application of commercial principles was, however, soon extended to the nationalized industries as well. In August 1921 the operation of these industries was removed from direct state control and management and placed on the basis of independent commercial management. The principle of the market was thereby extended to the state sector too, since the state-owned industries were now forced to sink or swim in accordance with their ability to compete. This process of transition to commercial principles was completed by the end of 1922.

It was unavoidable that transition to the market as the basis of agriculture and industry should lead to a revival of internal trade and to orthodox finance. As Lenin pointed out, the intention had been to exchange the products of industry 'more or less' in a socialist manner, but 'the private market turned out stronger than we'.[1] The same was true of finance, where the return to orthodoxy was imposed by the restoration of the free market, rather than by deliberate design. During the years of 'war communism', the absence of a market and rampant inflation had virtually reduced financial policy to the printing of ever-increasing quantities of worthless paper currency. Now (with the advice and assistance of a former *Kadet* minister, Kutler) the currency was stabilized and related to its gold backing, public borrowing was restored and private savings encouraged, and a certain freedom in banking policy was allowed – under the general supervision of a state-owned bank.

NEP told more unevenly on the revival of industry than on that of agriculture. Light industry benefited from the peasants' newly acquired purchasing power, but heavy industry stagnated – with consequent hardship to the great majority of the workers who were employed in it. Over half a million were unemployed by the end of 1922, and real earnings of workers in 1922–3 were still less than half of their earnings in 1913.[2] By the end of 1922, if not before, it was openly admitted that heavy industry could not be restored without state subsidies. The problem was to find the capital for these subsidies. Imperial Russia had developed her industry to a large extent by means of substantial loans from foreign capitalists. But these debts had been repudiated by the communists immediately after the

[1] *ibidem*, p. 68.
[2] S. N. Prokopovich, *Narodnoe khoziaistvo SSSR*, volume II, New York, 1952, pp. 97–8.

revolution, and their refusal thereafter to agree to any terms of settlement of the debts of the overthrown régime was to preclude any likelihood of foreign loans, on the hope of which for some time reliance was placed. The other source of potential capital was foreign trade, the pursuit of which after 1921 became an increasing preoccupation of foreign policy. It was not coincidental that an Anglo-Soviet trade agreement was signed in London by Krasin on behalf of Soviet Russia the day after Lenin had announced NEP to the Tenth Party Congress.

*   *   *

Indeed, the effects of NEP upon the foreign policy of the RSFSR were soon to become apparent. The prospect of further revolutions had by 1921 receded. Attempts to foment them in Poland, in the Baltic States and in Germany had failed. Besides, although in Lenin's view the ultimate success of NEP was linked with the victory of communism in one or more important industrial countries, the immediate need of the Soviet state was for normal trade relations with, and, if possible, financial backing from, the capitalist powers. The new wind was soon blowing up storms in the Comintern. At the Third Congress of the Comintern, in June and July 1921, the Russian delegation, firmly led by Lenin, though not unanimous behind the scenes, sounded the retreat from world revolution. It was plain that Russia now needed trade relations with the capitalist states, and fomenting of revolutions was not the best way of achieving them. But it was no longer quite so easy as in 1920 to assert the primacy of Russian interests over all else. Voices were heard from dissident groups, who were still grudgingly allowed a hearing at this Congress, that the retreat was more in the immediate interests of the RSFSR than of ultimate world revolution. It was the last occasion on which even this tolerance would be allowed to left-wing critics. There was sympathy for, and even informal links with, the Russian left opposition among the dissident foreign groups, especially the German KAPD and the Dutch Left, which were too dangerous for the Russians to suffer for long. The disciplinary powers of the Executive, still centred in Moscow, and completely under Russian domination, were increased, and the KAPD was shortly afterwards expelled. A resolution was voted on the structure of communist parties, which assimilated them even more in organization to the Russian party than had the twenty-one points adopted by the Second Congress.[1] Henceforward the

[1] For the text see *Thesen und Resolutionen des III Weltkongresses der Kommunistischen Internationale*, Hamburg, 1921, pp. 105 ff.

progressive subordination of the Comintern to Moscow, and the era-
dication of dissent by discipline, were only a matter of time.

At the Fourth Comintern Congress, which met in November–
December 1922, the keynote of a more obedient gathering was the
need to direct all action in such manner as to help the Soviet state.
Lenin, now a very sick man, addressed the Congress in what was to
prove his last public appearance but one. Most of his speech was
devoted to the justification of Soviet internal policy. At the very end,
somewhat incoherently, and almost as an afterthought, he made a few
remarks on the resolution on party organization passed by the previous Congress. It was too 'Russian', he said, it was related to Russian
experience and unintelligible to non-Russian comrades, who had
signed it 'without understanding or reading it'. 'I have formed the
impression that we made a great mistake over this resolution, and
namely that we have ourselves cut off our path to further progress.'
In itself the resolution is 'excellent', but 'we have not understood how
to make our Russian experience acceptable to foreigners'.[1] His
Russian colleagues, who included Zinoviev, Trotsky and Bukharin,
may well have listened to these remarks with consternation. But
Lenin's words had no practical effect upon the Congress, which
shortly afterwards proceeded to pass a further resolution which,
so far from modifying the 'Russian' nature of the resolution of
the Third Congress, now wrote into the constitution of the International an almost exact replica of the institutional devices for strict
centralized discipline which were at that date being perfected inside
Russia.[2] The Congress delegates were not to blame for implementing Leninism according to their lights, even if Lenin was somewhat unaccountably throwing doubts on the system which he had
created.

As revolution in Europe receded into the background the RSFSR
made some progress in more conventional diplomatic relations. A
number of trade agreements had been concluded and imports and
exports were rising. Negotiations for more ambitious commercial
relations with the capitalist powers had ended in failure. At a conference at Genoa in April and May 1922 an all-round agreement was
attempted between the RSFSR and the Allied Powers, from which
Russia hoped to secure *de jure* recognition and foreign loans for the
development of her industry. But this attempt foundered on the

[1] *Lenin*, volume XXVII, pp. 354–5.
[2] *The Communist International 1919–1943*. Documents. Selected and edited by
Jane Degras, volume I, 1919–1922, Oxford, 1956, pp. 436–42.

thorny question of Allied claims arising from the repudiation by Russia of the public debts of the former government and from the nationalization of foreign-owned enterprises. However, this failure at Genoa was more than counterbalanced by the diplomatic success scored by the RSFSR against the Allied Powers at the neighbouring Rapallo, on 16 April 1922, on Easter Sunday, while the Genoa Conference was resting from its labours. A political and commercial alliance with Germany was clandestinely concluded. The two outcasts, the vanquished Germany penalized by the Treaty of Versailles and revolutionary Russia, cemented the beginning of an alliance from which each was to gain in strength in its relations with the Allied Powers. The alliance was further bolstered by secret agreements between Russia and Germany, for which tentative negotiations had been going on throughout 1921, providing for the manufacture by Germany in Russia of the military equipment prohibited to her under the terms of the Treaty of Versailles.

* * *

By the end of 1921 Lenin had been compelled to abandon full-time work, and in May 1922 he suffered his first stroke. Thereafter, except for a few months in the second half of 1922, he was a total invalid until his death on 21 January 1924. He continued at intervals to dictate articles and memoranda whenever his health permitted, but his writings and views during these last years have not all been published by his successors, and it is not yet possible to make a complete assessment of the attitude of the dying man to the machine which he had created and which he no longer had the strength to control. There is no doubt, however, that on a number of important issues he was by 1922 in sharp disagreement with his colleagues, and that his views were circumvented or ignored. The disagreement over the treatment of foreign communist parties has already been noted. Rather more important was Lenin's decided view, towards the end of his life, that steps should be taken to limit the vast powers which Stalin was building up behind the scenes. Stalin's successful handling of this explosive threat to his ambitions must be postponed till a later chapter. But another serious cause of disagreement between the dying Lenin and his followers was the question of the treatment of the national minorities.

It will be recalled that Lenin had insisted on making self-determination for all the national components of the Empire part of bolshevik doctrine, in spite of opposition from some of his colleagues. This policy was an important element in bolshevik propaganda before October 1917, and was reaffirmed after the seizure of power. On 2 November 1917 a decree proclaimed the sovereign equality of all the peoples of Russia, recognized their right to self-determination, including the right of secession, and promised the abolition of all national privileges and restrictions. This promise was progressively modified as soon as the national minorities began to take advantage of it to assert their claims to independence. Even immediately after October 1917 the policy was not implemented without hesitation or qualification. Thus, though Finland's independence was recognized, with some reluctance, on 18 December 1917, this did not prevent the Soviet government from intervening to support a revolutionary *coup* in Finland a few weeks later. (The issue was decided by the treaty of Brest-Litovsk.)

During the next few years the Moslem borderlands, the Caucasus and Siberia enjoyed at times various degrees of freedom from Russian control. But this was due much less to doctrine than to the dislocation caused by the civil war. Indeed, the policy of insisting on the unfettered right to self-determination proclaimed for purposes of vote catching proved singularly ill-adapted to the realities of the Russian situation. Economic factors alone would have driven any Russian government towards attempting to reintegrate as much of the former empire as possible into some form of unity. Moreover, as the control of the communist party was progressively extended in the wake of the Red Army over the territories of the national minorities, it was inevitable that the obsession with centralized control which characterized the Russian party should influence the course of its relations with the non-Russian peoples.[1]

It was, therefore, hardly surprising that the slogan of self-determination should barely have survived the attempt by the national minorities to put the offer of separatism into practice. The bolshevik organizations established in the borderlands during the period of the Provisional Government were used, with the support of troops prepared to follow the bolsheviks, to overthrow, or more often to attempt to overthrow, the newly established national governments. Theory soon began to show signs of changing to something more in accordance with practice. In January 1918 Stalin asserted that independence in any particular case would only be recognized upon the demand of

[1] Soviet doctrine and practice on the policy towards the non-Russian elements of the former Empire are admirably studied and fully documented by Richard Pipes in his *The Formation of the Soviet Union. Communism and Nationalism. 1917–1923.* Cambridge, Mass., 1954.

the working population of that area, and that self-determination must be viewed as a method of struggling for socialism.[1]

However, this frank formulation of intentions was modified in July 1918 when the first Soviet constitution of the All-Russian Socialist Federal Soviet Republic (RSFSR) was adopted. Article Two of the constitution described the RSFSR as a 'federation of national Soviet republics'. But federation, in the normally accepted sense, means a free union of states which retain a considerable autonomy of action. When the party programme was voted in March 1919 by the Eighth Party Congress it became evident that the communist conception was far from this. The programme, adopted at a time when the civil war was still in progress and much of the borderlands still outside bolshevik control, made the best of both worlds. It began by reaffirming the principle of self-determination and the right of secession, but immediately after proceeded to qualify it in two respects: first, by 'proposing' a federal union of states organized on the Soviet pattern 'as one of the transitional forms on the path to complete unity'; and secondly, by declaring that the question of who in any particular case must be regarded as the bearer of the will of a nation on the issue of separatism must be decided 'according to the historical stage of development of that nation'.[2] Evidently the decision was to be left to the party leaders in Moscow. This formulation was in practice to provide a basis upon which the decision of small Moscow-dominated parties, mainly Russian in nationality, operating among minorities, could be treated, when expediency required it, as the 'bearers of the will' of the whole nation. This convenient formula enabled the communists during the civil war not only to agitate for national self-determination in territories in which they were not yet in control; but also, in the case of territories where they were in control, to resist nationalist movements aimed at separatism. The programme also echoed Lenin's exhortations to the Congress against the attempt of any one nation to assert itself over others – a fault to which, as he said, the Russians were particularly prone; and against offending national susceptibilities in the case of formerly subject nations.

As far back as 1903 *Iskra* had broken with the *Bund* over the issue of autonomy, and the principle that the social democratic party must remain one and indivisible, even in respect of the party organizations in areas of the Russian Empire which should decide to secede, was

---

[1] *Stalin*, volume IV, pp. 30–7.
[2] *KPSS v rez.*, volume I, pp. 416–17.

reaffirmed by Lenin in 1915.[1] This principle was enforced after the seizure of power. The *Bund*, for example, fought a losing battle to retain some measure of autonomy, but by 1921 was forced to submit. (A 'right' wing, led by R. Abramovich, which refused to capitulate, shared the fate of the mensheviks.) But the *Bund* was never in control of any separate geographical area. The position was different in such territories as the Ukraine, the Moslem borderlands or Georgia, where parties could evolve with a territorial area of their own, with strong local interests, and with at any rate some indigenous membership. In the course of the civil war Moscow successfully enforced the principle that communist parties operating in the national territories were no more than regional committees of the Russian party, subordinate to the Central Committee in the same way as any other local committee, and without any right to autonomy or separate identity. The principle was embodied in the party Rules in December 1919.[2] But the opposition which this policy aroused in the national parties left deep scars, of which the traces were to be visible for many years.

The natural result of this policy was the emergence of nationalist sentiments in cases where the local party consisted of native communists. Lenin, who by 1920 was already becoming increasingly apprehensive of the working out in practice of communist policy among the national minorities, blamed friction on the chauvinism of the Russian communists or of those communists of other nationalities who identified themselves with the Russians. Yet the Russian communists were only doing to the minorities, including the national communist parties, what they were doing in Russia itself: it was not so much chauvinism but over-centralization and insistence on exclusive communist rule which were the causes of the trouble.

Lenin was, of course, fully behind the policy of allowing only one centralized party – indeed, he had been the main author of this principle. But the conduct of policy towards the national minorities was in practice very largely in the hands of Stalin. Stalin had been put in charge by Lenin in October 1917 of a People's Commissariat of Nationality Affairs (*Narkomnats*), which in time became the main instrument first for suppressing all competing national councils or organizations which grew up in the RSFSR during the civil war; and thereafter for reinforcing central direction over the parties in the reconquered national territories. For the latter purpose Stalin relied

---

[1] See pp. 150–1 above.

[2] *KPSS v rez.*, volume I, p. 464: 'Party organizations which serve the territories of the federal components of the RSFSR are . . . wholly subordinate to the Central Committee of the Russian Communist Party (bolsheviks)'.

principally on a close band of faithful agents, whom he could place at the head of the main national parties. Thus at different times L. M. Kaganovich headed the Turkestan Bureau, Molotov the Ukraine Central Committee, Ordzhonikidze the Caucasian Bureau (which was set up in February 1920 for the purpose of establishing communist rule all over the Caucasus), and S. M. Kirov the Azerbaijani Central Committee. The prevalence of such Russians and assimilated non-Russians at the head of national organizations was in keeping with the general predominance of Russians in the party as a whole. As late as 1922 Great Russians still formed 72 per cent of the party membership; and if allowance is made for the assimilation of many of those listed as Ukrainians (5·88 per cent) or Jews (5·20 per cent), the Russian-speaking element in the party was probably nearer 80 per cent.[1] This predominance of Great Russians, and assimilated non-Russians, over all others was due less to chauvinism than to two other factors: first, that in a centralized party, such as the leaders were anxious to create, it was often easier to get Moscow's orders carried out through Russian or Russified agents than to deal, say, with non-Russian-speaking Tatars; and secondly, that the urban population, from which the communists drew their main support, was predominantly of Russian stock.

From 1919 onwards Lenin became increasingly critical of the way in which policy towards the national minorities was being implemented by his party. But he failed to make his criticism effective. This was in part due to the fact that Stalin, who was already building up his own power complex inside the party with the aid of his close supporters, was able to ignore Lenin's views. But serious conflict began over the reconquest of Georgia. Georgia had profited by the civil war to proclaim its independence, and the Georgian Republic was recognized by the Allied Powers. There was a long social democratic tradition in Georgia, and the mensheviks had won 105 out of 130 seats in elections to the Georgian National Assembly in February 1919 (the remaining seats went to nationalists, federalists and socialist revolutionaries). The bolsheviks in Georgia remained what they had been before the revolution – a small knot of conspirators, without mass support.

For two and a half years the Georgian mensheviks, at the helm of government, attempted with some success to put into practice socialist policies. On 7 May 1920 the RSFSR signed a treaty with Georgia, represented by its menshevik government, 'unreservedly' recognizing its

[1] Pipes, *op. cit.*, pp. 269–70, based on the figures of the 1922 census.

independence, renouncing all Russian claims to Georgia, and undertaking to refrain from 'any kind of interference' in Georgian internal affairs. Almost immediately afterwards, the communists inside Georgia (whom the mensheviks had by a secret clause in the treaty unwisely agreed to legalize) began to prepare for the reconquest. In February 1921 they engineered a rebellion and the Red Army entered soon after. The RSFSR had already adopted this pattern of reconquest in several cases during the civil war without, apparently, any objection from Lenin. But the case of Georgia was different: the reconquest could no longer be regarded as a part of civil war operations, Georgia was governed by social democrats, freely elected, and its independence had been recognized by the Allied Council – to say nothing of the RSFSR. There is no doubt that this flagrant breach of faith aroused opposition from some leaders. According to Trotsky, Lenin also at first opposed the betrayal of Georgia, advocated mainly by the Georgians, Stalin and Ordzhonikidze. But his opposition was perhaps more due to fear of the consequences than to any principle. For he withdrew his objection when it became apparent that the Allied Council would not intervene in favour of Georgia, and when Lloyd George had so assured Krasin, the Soviet representative in London. Nevertheless, after the conquest, Lenin continued to bombard Ordzhonikidze, who now became the real ruler of Georgia, with directives urging moderation in the relations between the Caucasian Bureau (the Moscow-appointed communist body set up in February 1920 to carry out the reconquest of the Caucasus) and the central committees of the individual Caucasian communist parties, and advising concessions to the Georgian mensheviks. Ordzhonikidze ignored all these exhortations.[1]

The reconquest of Georgia virtually completed the reintegration of the former Empire, so far as it lay in the power of the communists to accomplish it at that stage: the attempt to carry communism to Poland by force of arms had met with defeat, while communist revolutions fomented in the three Baltic States had been crushed. Meanwhile the pattern of centralized administration, which the communist party had successfully grafted on to the machinery of the RSFSR Soviet system, was also extended to the borderlands, as they were progressively reincorporated. The seventeen autonomous regions and republics formed between 1920 and 1923 were in practice as little autonomous as any part of the RSFSR, inasmuch as even their official sphere of competence – such as public health or

---

[1] *ibidem*, pp. 235 ff.

education – was under the overall surveillance of the communist party and of the RSFSR Commissariats. At the centre the People's Commissariat for Nationalities, headed by Stalin since 1917, progressively extended its bureaucratic control over all matters affecting national minorities.

By the end of 1922 the time was considered ripe to give formal recognition to a reincorporation which was already a fact. It was about this time that several trends of nationalist opposition, which had been smouldering for some time inside the native communist parties, came into prominence. In general, these trends expressed the disillusionment of natives who had loyally supported the communist cause during the civil war but had lost faith in communist promises to eliminate national inequalities when once the war was won. One of the most active centres of this form of native communist nationalism was Georgia, where resistance by the Georgian communist party to the ever-encroaching dictatorship of Ordzhonikidze's Caucasian Bureau led to serious friction. The culminating grievance of the Georgian communists was the failure of Ordzhonikidze to take the Georgian party into his confidence over the plan for creating a formal Soviet Union, which was first discussed in September 1922. The plan was intended both to legalize existing practice and to create a formal international unit which could speak in one voice in the long-drawn diplomatic battle with the outside world which was foreseen now that the prospect of revolution in Europe had receded.

The plan for union was completed by early December 1922. On 26 December the Tenth Congress of Soviets of the RSFSR approved it, and on 29 December the articles of Union were signed by representatives of the communist parties of the four republics concerned – the RSFSR, the Ukraine, Belorussia and Transcaucasus. Stalin's control over the selection of delegates and the improved party discipline by this date ensured that the opposition was outvoted. Work was now begun on the draft of the constitution of the Union of Soviet Socialist Republics (USSR). The final version of the Constitution which emerged from the drafting commission was the work of the Politburo and was opposed both by those who pressed for even more centralization and by those who pressed for real republican autonomy. The Constitution of the USSR was finally approved and put into effect by the Central Executive Committee on 6 July 1923 and ratified by the Second All-Union Congress of Soviets on 31 January 1924. It followed (so far as the federal question was concerned) the articles of union, and left to the republics sole competence only in the sphere of the republican Commissariats of Agriculture, Interior, Justice, Education, Health and Social Security. Moreover, as everyone knew, in practice their competence even in these spheres would be severely limited by the party machine, controlled in Moscow, of which the Constitution made no mention. The right of secession, 'guaranteed' in the Constitution, was no more than a mockery. The Council of Nationalities, which under the new Constitution was to be set up in the Soviet Congress, was certain to be handpicked by Stalin, since the Central Committee apparatus would control the elections to it.

Lenin, disabled by illness, took no part in any of the final debates. He had commented adversely on constitutional proposals put forward by Stalin in September 1922, but his criticism was ignored.[1] In his public actions, however, Lenin at first supported the Caucasian Regional (*Krai*) Committee against the Georgian Central Committee. A telegram from Lenin to the Georgian communists on 21 October 1922, at the height of the conflict between them and Ordzhonikidze, roundly reprimanded the Georgians for the 'ill-bred' and 'impertinent' tone of their attacks on Ordzhonikidze.[2] But at the end of October the entire Georgian Central Committee resigned. A commission of three, headed by Dzerzhinskii, was then sent out to investigate. The commission was set up on Lenin's initiative, and Dzerzhinskii was selected for his 'impartiality'. The commission duly reported, exonerating the Caucasian Committee and blaming the Georgians, whose leaders were now recalled to Moscow.

In the next few weeks something happened to make Lenin change his mind and decide that the fault in this conflict did not lie with the Georgians. For in the last days of December Lenin dictated three notes on the national question which gave a very different picture and of which the existence only became known some months later. 'I am much to blame before the workers', Lenin began his first note, for not interfering 'sufficiently energetically' in the national question before now. Lenin then analysed the Georgian situation, roundly blaming Stalin and Ordzhonikidze for their 'Great Russian chauvinism' –

---

[1] Copies of Lenin's letter and Stalin's reply are among Trotsky's papers now deposited in the Library of Harvard University.

[2] This telegram is quoted in full in L. Beria, *K voprosu ob istorii bol'shevistskikh organizatsii v Zakavkaze*. Ninth edition, Moscow, 1952, pp. 245–6, allegedly from the archives of the Georgian branch of the Marx-Engels-Lenin Institute. But the source is suspect, since Beria's lecture was written for the purpose of falsifying party history in the Caucasus and of glorifying Stalin's role (see pp. 404–5 below). The telegram was not reprinted in 1957, when an additional volume of the fourth edition of Lenin's works was published, volume 37, containing hitherto unpublished materials. However, the text of the telegram was printed in 1965 in volume 54 of the Fifth (complete) edition of Lenin's works, at pp. 299–300.

assimilated Russians were always, he pointed out, worse in this respect than Russians themselves. The argument that 'we needed a single apparatus' was quite unjustified: the apparatus that was called 'ours' was in truth no more than the old imperial apparatus 'annointed with a little Soviet holy oil'. In such conditions the right of free secession from the union would be 'nothing but a scrap of paper, incapable of defending the minorities' from the inroads of the Russian chauvinist bureaucrats. After a further diatribe against chauvinism, Lenin in his last letter passed to practical proposals. There could be no doubt that the Union 'must be retained and strengthened'. But the possibility should be considered of retaining the union 'only in the military and diplomatic spheres, and in all other respects restoring the full independence of the separate commissariats'. The harm which such autonomy could cause would be 'infinitely smaller' than that which would result 'if, on the eve of the emergence of the East and at the beginning of its awakening we should undermine our prestige there with even the slightest rudeness or injustice to our own minorities', or adopt 'something like imperialistic relations' towards them.[1]

An extraordinary blindness to facts pervades these documents. The national policy was not the result of any particular chauvinism on the part of former imperial bureaucrats, but, as Lenin himself emphasized, the work of Stalin and Ordzhonikidze, his own pupils, and of other leaders of the party. Increasing the number of commissariats left to republican jurisdiction would have made little difference so long as the system of all-pervading centralized party control, which Lenin had created and of which he never so far as is known spoke a word in criticism, was allowed to continue. For Lenin the fault still lay in the failure of individuals to live up to high standards – standards which, in so far as they ever existed among those whom Lenin had himself chosen as his followers, had long been corrupted by a power which recognized no legal restraints.

Indeed, the evidence which exists on Lenin's last thoughts suggests irresistibly that though he was obsessed with the obvious defects of the party apparatus, the remedy which he proposed for them took little account of the realities. The constant refrain recurring through his last writings is the corruption of the party apparatus, its failure to win the confidence of the rank and file, its bureaucratic indifference to the

[1] *Lenin*, fourth edition, volume XXXVII, pp. 553–9. These three notes were first published in the USSR in 1956. They were known to scholars outside from a text which was published in the émigré press, but the authenticity of this text was only established after Trotsky's death, when his papers were deposited in Harvard University Library.

needs of the governed and its preoccupation with its own interests, its inefficiency – all the charges, in fact, which were made by the Workers' Opposition until these critics were silenced. As Lenin nears his death, we catch glimpses of his thought which suggest that he was attempting to console himself for his disappointment over the failure of communist party rule to live up to his expectations. The new apparatus, he argues, is after all only the same bureaucratic apparatus as the apparatus of the old régime – 'only slightly repainted on the surface', and one which 'we took over in its entirety from the preceding epoch'.[1] It was true that the bolsheviks had taken over very large numbers of the staff of the civil service inherited from the imperial régime, altering the old system only to the extent of superimposing a thin crust of all-powerful and irresponsible communists upon it. But the comparison between the communist bureaucracy and that of imperial Russia was unfair to the old régime, in which some elements of legal order and of restraint over the executive had already begun to take root. The communists had destroyed all vestiges of this incipient legal order.

Like the Workers' Opposition, Lenin saw, and deplored, the symptoms, but failed to diagnose the disease. It is, however, only fair to remember that any line of Lenin's suggesting that the time had come to question the unlimited power of the communist party would certainly have been sedulously suppressed by his successors had it been found after his death. Good-will, exhortation, conscientious application to their duties by leading communists – these were all the remedies which Lenin was able to propose. For years Lenin had laboured to build up an obedient following of men who would stop at nothing in the party interest. Now that these men were in power – the Stalins, the Zinovievs, the Ordzhonikidzes and the Dzerzhinskiis – it was too late to expect a regeneration in their moral character. Lenin, who yielded to no one in the methods which he was prepared to use to achieve his ends, himself always retained some sparks of idealism in the process. He had a natural asceticism of character which power did not corrupt, and could do evil without losing sight of the ultimate good in which he believed. Like most idealists, he expected the same of his followers.

In the end, the obsession with power which dominated Lenin's outlook since the days of *What is to be Done?* had proved the only

---

[1] cf. the same idea expressed in his speech at the Fourth Congress of the Comintern, in November 1922, in which he criticized excessive 'Russification' of the foreign communist parties – volume XXVII, pp. 354–5.

durable element in his thought. As so many of his critics had foretold in the party debates before the revolution, he had merely effected a seizure of power by his party: he had failed to create a free workers' state. When faced with a revolt of the peasants, Lenin had the wisdom to see that the solution lay not in further strife and violence, but in a long period of harmony between classes with different interests. But fear is a good master – and fear of a conflagration was real in 1921. Once over the panic, Lenin's rigid inability to see facts except within the framework of his own dogma reasserted itself. He knew of only one rule in politics: no compromise with opponents, and no adoption of their policy or views until you have first destroyed them. He made no difference in this respect between Stolypin and Shliapnikov. A great revolutionary but not a statesman, Lenin failed to see in time, if he ever did, that harmony, and not further strife, was the only political solution in 1921, even though such political harmony could only have been achieved at the cost of sacrificing the monopoly of power which the communists had built up for themselves. 'They say Martov is dying too,' was one of the last things Lenin said to his wife. Did the thought cross his mind that the quarrel in 1903 with his old friend, now hounded into exile, and all the consequences that flowed from that quarrel, had not in the end been worth while?

XIII Party Composition and Machinery
1917 – 1922

In the five years between the seizure of power in October 1917 and Lenin's retirement from active politics towards the end of 1922 the party went through two phases of rapid growth, and two of sharp contraction. The first phase of growth reflected the attractions held out by the party after it became the governing power. But by the Eighth Congress, in March 1919, it was recognized that an open-door policy on recruitment threatened the party with an influx of careerists. It was accordingly decided to undertake a registration of party members, numbering about 250,000, with the aim of sifting out those who were 'unworthy'.[1]

The party was reduced to about 150,000, or a little over half, by the autumn of 1919, and immediately launched out upon a second period of headlong growth. Because of the civil war the bolshevik régime now had its back to the wall, membership of the party involved personal risk, and the view taken was that mass recruitment presented little danger of attracting the wrong type. During the 'Party Week' held in October–December 1919, approximately 200,000 new recruits entered the party, and by the time of the Ninth Congress in March 1920, its size was given as 611,978.[2] Recruitment continued at a reduced rate throughout the next year, and there were almost three-quarters of a million in the party by March 1921, when the Tenth Congress met.

The Tenth Congress, which was in so many ways a watershed in the party's development, also inaugurated a new stiffening in recruitment policy. On the one hand, with the end of the civil war, membership of the party no longer called for self-sacrifice, and the green light was given to careerists. On the other hand, the Kronstadt insurrection

---

[1] According to A. Bubnov, *BSE*, volume XI, p. 531, the membership grew from 115,000 on 1 January 1918 to 251,000 on 1 January 1919, but other sources differ. For the Congress resolution see *KPSS v rez.*, volume I, pp. 441–2, and for the Central Committee instruction on who should be purged see Merle Fainsod, *Smolensk under Soviet Rule*, Cambridge, Mass., 1958, p. 210. (For list of Abbreviations see p. 642 below.)

[2] *Izv. Ts.K.*, No. 15, 24 March 1920; Bubnov, *loc. cit.*

and the signals of revolt inside the party placed a premium on 'proletarian' orthodoxy and discipline. The Congress intimated that the party would be purged, and on 30 June 1921 *Pravda* announced that the purge was to begin on 1 August. Manual workers and peasants were to be subjected to the minimum of formalities. The edge of the purge was to be directed against officials who had served under the old régime, former members of other political parties, and party members occupying responsible posts or employed in the state administration. Recruitment was to stop forthwith, except for a limited acceptance of manual workers and peasants under special conditions. It was later explained that, while poor peasants should be kept in the party at all costs, 'kulak elements' must be weeded out, as these had the conscious or unconscious aim of disrupting the party.[1] The purge was entrusted to a central checking commission of five, appointed by the Central Committee and functioning through local subordinate checking commissions.[2]

Despite warnings that the purge was not to be used to victimize such 'other thinkers' as 'former' members of the Workers' Opposition, it was not surprising, under the prevailing conditions, that the announcement of the purge was widely interpreted in the party as a further attempt to bludgeon the rank and file into unquestioning obedience to their leaders.[3] How many communists were in fact expelled in this purge for their opinions or for outspoken criticism it is impossible to say. Up to the beginning of 1922 some 136,386 members, or one-fifth of the party, were expelled. Eleven per cent of those expelled were said to have been excluded 'for refusing to carry out party directions', and many of these were no doubt actual or potential oppositionists. The commonest reasons for expulsion were 'passivity' (34 per cent), careerism, drunkenness, bourgeois mode of life, etc. (25 per cent), and bribe-taking, extortion, etc. (9 per cent).[4]

The contraction of the party during the years 1921–2 was not due solely to expulsions. Many people were leaving the party of their own free will. The end of the civil war naturally led to a cooling of revolutionary ardour, and this accounted for many of the withdrawals. Disappointment, confusion, and the disgust which the more orthodox or left-wing party members felt after the adoption of the New

[1] *SPR*, No. 2, pp. 74–7.
[2] *ibidem*, pp. 77–8.
[3] See e.g. *Izv.Ts.K.*, No. 33, October 1921.
[4] *Izv.Ts.K.*, No. 40, March 1922. Former members of other parties formed nearly five per cent of those expelled, or some 6,000. A third of them were former mensheviks.

Economic Policy and because of the suppression of independent thought within the party, accounted for many more. As early as March 1921 the Central Committee had made public mention of the 'widespread individual and group withdrawals' and ordered a thorough study of the type of person involved.[1] The Workers' Opposition alleged that defections had acquired the character of a mass exodus, involving mainly the worker element in the party. Large-scale withdrawal continued throughout 1921 and 1922, and in the latter year, according to official figures, totalled 14,100.[2]

What with the purge and defections, between March 1921 and January 1922 the number of members and candidate members in the party fell from 730,000 to 515,000. Thereafter, decline in membership became less precipitous, and by 1 January 1923 total membership, including candidate members, stood at 485,500.[3] In this period of relative stability of membership, the communist party took shape, having purged itself of both its extremes – of most of its revolutionary romantics as well as of its more blatant careerists. Many of the features which characterized it for years thereafter were already recognizable.

What kind of people made up the communist party in these first years of its rule? It was first of all a party of youth. At the end of 1919 over half the members were under 30, and only 10 per cent of the party were aged over 40. Party members were, in their overwhelming majority, young men of little political experience, and with little formal education. Even in October 1919 only 20 per cent of the party had been members before the seizure of power two years earlier, and only 8 per cent had joined before the February revolution. A further 4·5 per cent were former members of other left-wing parties. At the same period only 5 per cent of the party had had a higher education and 8 per cent a secondary education.[4] It was, further, an overwhelmingly masculine party, despite the tradition of female participation in the Russian revolutionary movements. Only 7·5 per cent of the party members in 1922 were women, but the recruitment of women was slightly on the increase.[5]

The thorny question of determining the social composition of the party is beset by two main difficulties. The first, and more obvious, is that there was a premium on concealing non-proletarian origin and

[1] *SPR*, No. 2, p. 79.
[2] *Izv.Ts.K.*, No. 4 (52), April 1923.
[3] *ibidem*.
[4] *Izv.Ts.K.*, No. 15, 24 March 1920. These percentages are based on samples of up to 20,000 members.
[5] *Izv.Ts.K.*, No. 1 (49), January 1923.

that this was often made easy by the confusion of public records. Concealment of bourgeois origin was a frequent reason for expulsions from the early 20's on. How many went undetected no one will ever know. The second difficulty is one of definition. In the party records of these early years a man's social class was registered not according to the social position of his parents, or his current employment, but according to the social position in which he found himself at the time of the revolution. In October 1919, when the party was on the eve of its second phase of post-revolutionary expansion, 52 per cent of party members were workers in the sense that they had originally been employed as such, 15 per cent were peasants, 18 per cent were white-collar workers and 14 per cent were 'intellectuals'. Yet at the same time only 11 per cent were actually employed in industry, and, since even many of these were employed in managerial and administrative positions, the proportion who actually were manual workers was quite insignificant. No less than 53 per cent of party members at that time were working in government offices, and 8 per cent were party or trade union officials. Twenty-seven per cent were in the Red Army.[1]

Little data is available on the social composition of the second wave of recruits brought into the party in the last quarter of 1919 and during 1920. It is clear, however, that this influx led to a much stronger peasant representation at the expense of the 'worker element'. By September 1920 there were over 180,000 full and candidate members in the rural cells, almost a five-fold increase as compared with October 1919.[2] Many of these recruits were 'rural proletarians' or 'rural intelligentsia', but a substantial proportion were classified as peasants. The official class analysis shows a reduction of the proportion of 'workers' from 57 per cent in 1918 to 41 per cent in 1921, and an increase in the 'peasant' representation over the same period from 14·5 per cent to 28 per cent. The white-collar workers and intelligentsia rose slightly to 31 per cent.[3]

The 1921 purge appears to have hit the peasant and white-collar elements in the party hardest of all. There was thus a slight redressing of the balance in favour of the workers, which continued throughout 1922.[4] However, by 1922 the party was once again showing signs of concern at the extent to which it had lost ground among the peasantry,

[1] *Izv.Ts.K.*, No. 15, 24 March 1920. Based on samples of from 17,000 to 30,000 members.
[2] *Izv.Ts.K.*, No. 8, 2 December 1919, and No. 22, 18 September 1920.
[3] Bubnov, *loc. cit.*
[4] *Izv.Ts.K.*, No. 40, March 1922, and No. 10 (46), October 1922.

though the encouragement given to the recruitment of peasant members in 1922 went further than Lenin wished, and was given against his advice.[1]

When one looks beyond the official 'class' analyses, the party's achievements at this stage in increasing its worker element are not impressive. Only 12 per cent of 1922 recruits were actually employed as workers at the time of joining the party. About 30 per cent were in the Red Army, but only a seventh of these were actually serving in the ranks.[2] Thus the existing restrictions on recruitment, ostensibly aimed at keeping it to *bona fide* proletarians, were obviously being applied in such a way as to let in mainly those workers who had earned promotion and were thus moving out of their class.

An attempt may now be made to take stock of the social composition of the party at the end of the first five years of its rule. An official class analysis of the party published early in 1923 put the proportion of workers at 45 per cent, of peasants at 26 per cent, and of 'others' at 29 per cent. In an effort to counter the impression that over half the party was non-proletarian, another analysis added to the workers those white-collar employees and others who had no more than a primary education, and thus arrived at the conclusion that 'proletarian elements' made up about two-thirds of the party.[3]

However, these figures take no account of changes in the social position of members occurring since the revolution. A large proportion of 'worker' and 'peasant' communists were already in positions of relative privilege and authority at the time of joining the party, quite apart from those who were promoted after joining. A more realistic social analysis could have been made in terms of current employment in 1923. Although the raw material for such an analysis was available to the Central Committee in the data compiled in a party census held in 1922, none appears to have been made, and indeed it is very probable that any such analysis, if published, would have provided ammunition for the opposition.

The nearest available approximation to an analysis by actual occupation is a breakdown according to different types of party cell. This shows 18 per cent of the party as members of industrial or transport cells, 24 per cent of military cells, 19 per cent of cells in the Soviet administration, and 30 per cent in peasant cells.[4] (The remaining 9 per

---

[1] For details of this further instance of the way in which Lenin's views were disregarded by this date see my *The Origin*, pp. 340–2.
[2] *Izv.Ts.K.*, No. 10 (46), October 1922.
[3] *Izv.Ts.K.*, No. 1 (49), January 1923, and No. 4 (52), April 1923.
[4] *Izv.Ts.K.*, No. 11–12 (47–8), November–December 1922.

cent of party members were presumably central and local party officials, students, or non-employed.) What proportion of those in industry were managerial and office staff, party and trade union officials, and what proportion were manual workers, one can only guess. Nor is there any way of knowing how many in military cells were in the administrative, commanding and party staffs, and how many were Red Army men, though the ratio of 6 to 1 for 1922 recruits gives some clue to this. A breakdown does exist, however, of the members of peasant cells, although this covers only one province said to be representative. Only a quarter of the members of these cells were engaged in farming, while two-thirds of them were employed as government, party or co-operative officials.[1] It can be calculated from these figures that, even if half of the members of industrial and military cells were ordinary workers and Red Army men respectively – a very generous estimate – something like two-thirds of all party members in 1922 were employed in positions of greater or lesser authority and privilege.

An examination of the ruling élite of the party during these formative years reveals several striking features. At the policy-making level at the summit, a high proportion of newcomers had emerged on the eve of the seizure of power side by side with Lenin and his close collaborators. Thus, the twenty-two full members of the Central Committee elected at the Sixth Congress in August 1917 included a number who had only recently joined the party, of whom Trotsky was the most outstanding, and several, like Bukharin, who though bolsheviks of longer standing, had never worked closely under Lenin's orders. Much of the friction of the early years of communist rule owes its explanation to this factor. The position is quite different when one comes to examine the actual party apparatus, the men in the key jobs. Here Lenin's pre-revolutionary collaborators predominated. Thus, an analysis of some four hundred of the main executants of policy in key positions in national life after the bolsheviks had seized power shows that the overwhelming majority of them had been loyal executants of Lenin's policies for many years before the revolution, working in the underground committees, in the fighting organizations, in trade unions and in the bolshevik press. The organizational structure after the revolution was therefore in this respect very close to the pre-revolutionary underground structure.[2] The degeneration in the

---

[1] *Izv.Ts.K.*, No. 1 (49), January 1923.
[2] This analysis was made by Dr S. V. Utechin in his dissertation 'The Origin of the Ruling Class in Soviet Society' (Oxford).

character of higher party officialdom which both Lenin and the oppositionists inside the party were alleging after 1921 was not therefore due to any change in the social origin of the higher élite of the party, but to the corruption brought about by the exercise of unbridled power.

A similar picture emerges when one analyses the place occupied in the party after 1917 by those rank and file party members who had joined before October 1917 – the 'underground men', as they were known. In general, the successive waves of post-revolutionary recruits had had the effect of swamping them. Even in so privileged a group as the delegates to party congresses, 'underground men' formed little over a third in 1921 and less than half in 1922. But it was significant first, that the closer one came to the centre of power, the stronger became the representation of the older bolsheviks in the party apparatus; and, secondly, that the tendency to use old bolsheviks in the party apparatus in the local organizations was showing a natural increase by 1922.[1] The majority of the rapidly expanding army of party officials were, however, already of the post-revolutionary generation – the fact alone that the average age of delegates to party congresses between 1917 and 1921 remained constant at almost 30 illustrates the extent to which this élite was being rejuvenated.

It was frequently asserted by the critics within the party that party officialdom was becoming less proletarian in its composition. Yet the reason for the growing prevalence of intellectual and white-collar communists in the party apparatus was easily explained. The machinery of party bureaucracy was growing both larger and more complicated, the range of tasks with which it was called upon to deal was constantly increasing, and higher educational standards than those normally found in a manual worker were required in order to man it. An analysis of nearly 15,000 leading party officials made in 1921 showed that scarcely more than a third were of proletarian origin.[2] Nor were the proletarian elements necessarily to be found among the pre-revolutionary 'men of the underground'. On the contrary, a very large proportion of the committee men in pre-revolutionary times were of intellectual or white-collar origin; and, conversely, a high proportion of the older revolutionaries of proletarian origin were by 1921 in revolt against the party leadership, and fast being winkled

[2] *Izv.Ts.K.*, No. 9, 20 December 1919, No. 39, March 1922, and No. 42, June 1922. The information on the Congress delegates is based on reports made at the successive congresses.

[3] *Izv.Ts.K.*, No. 39, March 1922.

out. Thus, by 1921, at all events, the dictatorship was proletarian in name rather than by social origin.

*   *   *

By 1922 Lenin's leadership of the bolsheviks, virtually undisputed since 1903, was coming to an end. His authority was still great, but his advice could be, and was, disregarded. Although it was not yet obvious at the time, far and away the greatest amount of direct power had been amassed by Stalin. It is, of course, plain that Lenin's rise to power and ability to maintain his party in the saddle was in large measure due to his control over the apparatus. But the apparatus until 1921 was comparatively simple to handle. The great machine which was beginning to grow up after 1920–21 required a full-time specialist in administration at the head of it. It was a task beyond the conciliatory and mild Krestinskii, the first formally designated secretary of the party. But Molotov, appointed (among others) in 1921, also proved quite unequal to the new task, and Stalin, whose gifts lay in this field, was perhaps the obvious choice to succeed him in 1922. From 1919 and 1922 Stalin was People's Commissar of State Control, later the Workers' and Peasants' Inspection, or *Rabkrin*. This appointment (made, apparently, with Lenin's approval, though by 1921, at any rate, Lenin was very critical of Stalin's performance of his office[1]) put into Stalin's hands a great engine of control over the entire machinery of the state. It soon became a commissariat above all commissariats, the eye of the party inside the whole administrative machine.

The rules relating to party structure were set out in the party Rules, which were periodically revised. At this time the Rules in force were those adopted in August 1922 at the Twelfth Party Conference. These laid down that party congresses should be held annually, and that smaller and less formal party conferences should also be held annually, in the intervals between congresses. The hierarchy of organizations for the RSFSR (i.e. the hierarchy of committees which functioned between the meetings of the congresses or conferences) was: Central Committee, regional (*oblast'*) committees or committees of national parties, provincial (*guberniia*) committees, district (*uezd*) committees, rural (*volost'*) committees, and industrial and Red Army cells, or party cells in individual institutions. Relations between the regional committees and the committees of the national parties were not defined and these

---

[1] See a letter from Lenin to Stalin, dated 29 September 1921, while Stalin still headed this Commissariat in *Lenin*, volume XXVII, pp. 14–20. Stalin's reply is on pp. 490–1.

outstations of the Central Committee (which is what they were) could be used to exercise control over a recalcitrant national committee. Apart from this, all the organizations enumerated stood in a hierarchical relation of subordination – the lower organization was subordinated in all matters to the next higher. In particular, every lower committee when elected required the confirmation of the next higher committee. All provincial secretaries – the key men in the network of secretariat control – were required to be party members of pre-October 1917 standing, and their election in each case required confirmation by the next higher instance, which in practice meant the central organs of the party.[1] In 1922 these latter provisions were interpreted to mean that the central party organs not only had the right to say who was to be 'elected' as secretary of each committee, but also to remove and replace the members of a committee, where its composition as elected did not meet with their approval.

Lenin had always sought to exercise complete control over the bolshevik movement from a single centre consisting of himself and a few close collaborators. Although the Political Bureau (Politburo) set up on the eve of the seizure of power was abolished soon after, and no similar organ was set up at the Seventh Congress in March 1918, the refusal of the left communists to enter the new Central Committee, and the frequent absence of its members meant that in practice decisions were taken by a small inner group of Central Committee members. It may well have been the case that during 1918 Lenin got used to running things alone with Sverdlov, who acted as secretary of the Central Committee, and that his experience of attempting to govern through the full Central Committee at the beginning of 1919 convinced him that a smaller body was essential. Moreover, during the civil war, all policy and direction relating to the organization of resources for purposes of the war rested with the Council of Workers' and Peasants' Defence, set up on 30 November 1918, of which Lenin was chairman and whose five members included Trotsky and Stalin. At all events, it was at the Eighth Congress, in March 1919, that the Politburo was reconstituted.

The vesting of policy-making authority in an inner group like the Politburo was thus scarcely a departure from traditional procedure. Indeed, the attempt to make the Central Committee, a body of nineteen full members and eight candidate members, the real decision-making body in the party between Congresses and conferences would have been more of a departure from practice. Nevertheless, the leaders

[1] *KPSS v rez.*, volume I, pp. 654–64.

were fully aware that any change threatening to supplant the Central Committee elected by and responsible to the Party Congress by some smaller group would meet with suspicion and resistance at the Congress. Their diffidence is clearly shown in the fact that the suggestion to establish the Politburo was put forward by Zinoviev as a 'personal proposal'. Their expectations of resistance were not disappointed, and the suspicions aroused were clearly voiced by Osinskii, a former left communist and at the time a democratic centralist.

The leaders sugared the pill by providing that the Central Committee as a whole was still to meet at least fortnightly and that members of the Central Committee who were not in the Politburo might nevertheless attend its meetings, without the right of voting. The Politburo was to deal only with matters requiring urgent decision and was to report on all its activity to the full Central Committee. The proposal was accepted by the Congress on these terms. From 1919 to 1921 the Politburo consisted of Lenin, Trotsky, Stalin, Kamenev and Krestinskii. In 1921 Zinoviev replaced Krestinskii, and in 1922 Rykov and Tomskii were added.

If the setting up of the Politburo was little more than a reassertion of established practice, the formation of the Organizational Bureau (Orgburo) in March 1919 as a second sub-committee of the Central Committee, overlapping in membership with and lower in status than the Politburo, did indeed break new ground. According to Lenin, while no hard and fast rule for assigning matters between the two bureaux was possible, the general principle was that 'the Orgburo allocates forces, while the Politburo decides policy'.[1]

From the beginning the Politburo and the Orgburo supplanted the full Central Committee in a way which confirmed the apprehensions of their critics. The Central Committee met only six times between April and November 1919, instead of the prescribed sixteen times. The Politburo in contrast held 29 separate meetings and 19 meetings jointly with the Orgburo, and the latter met no less than 110 times on its own.[2] In fact, it was soon apparent that it was becoming something like a subordinate Politburo.

Meanwhile, a third sub-committee, as it were, of the Central Committee had emerged. This was the Secretariat. Until 1920 there was only one Central Committee secretary – Sverdlov till his death in March 1919, and then Krestinskii. But in March 1920 two additional secretaries, Preobrazhenskii and Serebriakov, were appointed. Each of

---

[1] *Lenin*, volume XXV, p. 112.
[2] *Izv.Ts.K.*, No. 18, 23 May 1920.

these secretaries became responsible for a group of Central Committee departments, and it became established that matters of sufficient importance to require decision by one of the secretaries but not warranting the attention even of the Orgburo should be settled on the basis of consultation between the three secretaries. Thus the Secretariat became a board. The relationship which evolved between the Secretariat and the Orgburo was in 1921 officially stated to be that 'in the absence of an objection by members of the Orgburo ... the Secretariat's decision is to be regarded as a decision of the Orgburo'.[1] These four intricately interlacing bodies – the full Central Committee, the Politburo, the Orgburo and the Secretariat – controlling as they did virtually all aspects of the country's life – offered great opportunities to the man who could manipulate them and co-ordinate them in pursuit of his clearly defined ends. From 1922 onwards Stalin was the only bolshevik leader who was a member of all four bodies. He made the most of his opportunities.

Of the remaining members of the Politburo in 1922, both Zinoviev and Kamenev, the virtual bosses of Petrograd and Moscow respectively, enjoyed a good deal of local power. Trotsky had no party apparatus at his command, and his reputation was much damaged by the attacks made upon him in the trade unions dispute in 1920 and 1921. He was now, particularly since Lenin's influence was waning, exposed to the full venom of Stalin's and Zinoviev's hatred. Rykov was to succeed Lenin as Chairman of the Council of People's Commissars, and Tomskii was the leading trade unionist. None of these men in 1922 wielded power or influence comparable to that of Stalin. In view of this fact, the subsequent assertion by Trotsky and others that Stalin's rise to power was quite unexpected in 1922 must be treated with reserve.

*　　　*　　　*

The relationship between the bolshevik party and the bolshevik state underwent a radical change in these first few years. Lenin's doctrine of the party as an organization of professional revolutionaries, as the 'general staff' of the revolution, certainly contained the seeds of the later notion of the party as the 'leading and directing force' of Soviet society. Yet the seizure of power did not witness the organic growth of the one from the other. The party appears to have entered upon the revolution without any plan of adapting its structure and

---

[1] *Izv.Ts.K.*, No. 31, 20 July 1921. See also No. 3 (51), March 1923, for a reference to conferences of heads of departments of the Central Committee.

methods from those of a conspiratorial revolutionary party to those of a governing party. Nor was there any attempt to think out in advance what institutional relationships ought to be established between the organs of the party and those of the new Soviet state. This was perhaps merely an aspect of the bolshevik denigration of the importance of institutional forms, reflected in the illusion which Lenin fostered that administration was a trifle which could safely be entrusted to 'any housewife' – provided she were a proletarian.

The result was that early relations between the party and the soviets merely grew out of the conditions and circumstances of the revolution, without being planned or willed by anyone. At the very beginning the party gave a classical performance of its role of 'guiding nucleus'. It was the party which decided upon, planned and directed the 'soviet' seizure of power, the soviets serving merely as 'levers' manipulated by the party. But once the Provisional Government had been over-thrown, and power had been vested in the executive committees of the soviets, both at the centre and locally, all the party's most experienced and authoritative cadres were posted to these executive committees, just as Lenin became Chairman of the Council of People's Commissars. The soviets consequently became the bodies within which important decisions were taken, and the soviet network soon virtually replaced the party network as the main channel through which the central bolshevik leadership controlled the provinces.

In the first months after the October Revolution, strong tendencies towards fragmentation and 'local patriotism' made themselves felt in the provinces. Many village and city soviets resisted all and any authority from outside, and only gradually united with their neighbours to form 'local republics' – such as those of Kazan' and Kaluga which became proverbial for their resistance to centralized authority. By mid-1918 the bolsheviks had in the main overcome these tendencies. But it is important to note that they achieved this more through direct collaboration between bolshevik officials in the soviet organs – the All-Russian Central Executive Committee and the provincial soviets' executive committees – than through the hierarchy of party committees.[1]

As bolshevik power came to be exercised almost exclusively through the soviet apparatus, and the party machinery tended to atrophy, the question arose what function the party organization as such now still

[1] M. Vladimirskii, *Organizatsiia sovetskoi vlasti na mestakh*, Moscow, 1919, pp. 52–3. By December 1919 communists predominated to the extent of 92·8 and 82·2 per cent in the provincial and district soviet executive committees respectively – M. Vladimirskii, *Sovety, ispolkomy i s''ezdy sovetov*, Part I, Moscow, 1920, p. 9.

had to perform. There were even suggestions that the party had now served its purpose, and might be abolished, so long of course as communists predominated in the soviets.[1] The party leaders evidently felt at this stage that the process had gone too far, and Sverdlov (the main power behind the party organization) told the Seventh Congress in March 1918 that much more attention would now have to be devoted to the party organization as such, and that the party must now undertake 'a significant part of the work which has up to now been performed by the soviets'.[2]

For over a year, however, this was to remain little more than a declaration of intention. There were two main reasons for this. The more important was that the secretary of the Central Committee, Sverdlov, who controlled what party apparatus there was, was also the Chairman of the Central Executive Committee of the Congress of Soviets, and thus had at his disposal the large and now centralized apparatus of the soviets. It was not surprising, therefore, that, as the civil war developed, Sverdlov tended to use the existing machinery for controlling the provinces, shelving for the time being the plan of reviving a strong party apparatus. The second factor making for the continued subordination of the local party bodies was their financial dependence upon the soviet executive committees, which 'made difficult the party committees' task of supervising the work of the executive committees'. The result was that, up to 1919, local party committees had next to no full-time staff, their functions were essentially confined to propaganda, and they were wholly dependent upon the executive committees of the local soviets, which themselves were staffed by the leading local communists. Party organizations had thus become, in the words of the Central Committee secretary, merely 'the agitation departments of the local soviets'.[3]

This arrangement was perhaps tolerable and practicable so long as the one exceptional man, Sverdlov, stood at the head of both the party and the soviet hierarchies. But in March 1919, on the eve of the Eighth Congress, Sverdlov died. The cornerstone of the existing structure was gone, and the bolshevik leaders could no longer baulk the question of party–state relations. The results of their deliberations were embodied in a long and confused Resolution on Organizational Questions adopted by the Eighth Congress. The gist of this was that there was to be an end to the integration of party and soviet bodies.

---

[1] See Preobrazhenskii's speech at the Ninth Party Congress, *IX S"ezd*, p. 58.
[2] *VII S"ezd*, pp. 194–5.
[3] *Izv.Ts.K.*, No. 16, 28 March 1920; *IX S"ezd*, pp. 25–6.

Party committees were to maintain themselves in a position to 'guide' and 'control' government bodies through directives given to the party 'factions' inside them, taking care, however, not to take upon themselves the detailed work of administration.[1] But the difficult problem of how in practice to 'guide' and 'control' without at the same time reducing the soviet organs to ciphers was not solved then, and, for that matter, has not been solved since.

There were three essential conditions for the achievement of this programme. First, the party had to be equipped with a large, well-organized staff. Previously the Central Committee had possessed no departmentalized administrative apparatus. Sverdlov had administered the party hierarchy personally, aided by a handful of assistants, who numbered fifteen at the time of his death.[2] It was now resolved to place at the disposal of Krestinskii, the newly appointed secretary of the Central Committee, a properly organized staff grouped into nine departments.[3]

The second condition was that the party machine should be invested with adequate powers to put into effect its 'controlling' function. The most vital consideration here was clearly control over distribution of personnel. Accordingly the Eighth Congress resolved that 'the whole matter of assignment of party forces is in the hands of the Central Committee of the party. Its decision is binding upon all. . . . The Central Committee is charged with carrying on a decisive struggle against local separatism in these questions.'[4] Finally, party bodies had to be freed from their financial dependence upon their soviet opposite numbers. It was not until four or five months after the Eighth Congress that the leaders realized that this continued dependence was obstructing the revival of the party machine. They thereupon decided to finance the local party committees directly through the Central Committee, and the People's Commissariat of Internal Affairs was required to make funds available to the Central Committee for this purpose. Thereafter the network of party officials increasingly supplanted the executive committees of the soviets. By 1921 the secretary of the party committee had replaced the chairman of the soviet executive committee as the leading official at local levels. By

[1] *KPSS v rez.*, volume I, p. 446. In the following year disciplinary control over party 'fractions' and cells was tightened up – see *Izv. TS.K.*, No. 33, October 1921, and *SPR*, No. 2, 1922, p. 42.

[2] *Izv. Ts.K.*, No. 8, 2 December 1919. (According to Krestinskii at the Tenth Congress the staff at the date of Sverdlov's death numbered 30, but this figure possibly included clerical staff – see *X S"ezd*, p. 15.)

[3] *Izv. Ts.K.*, No. 16, 28 March 1920.

[4] *KPSS v rez.*, volume I, pp. 444.

March 1922 the process had gone so far that the Eleventh Congress was forced to resolve that it had become necessary 'to relieve the party of a number of questions of a purely soviet character which it has come to take upon itself in the period just past'.[1]

It was not long before the new central machine of the party began to consolidate its own position. Its first step was to liquidate the autonomy of various party institutions and organizations operating outside the control of the regular machine. Much had already been done along these lines in 1917 and 1918, but autonomous organizations persisted, in the railways, the postal service, the Army and elsewhere, and the Eighth Congress in March 1919 therefore resolved 'gradually to liquidate such organizations, dissolving them in the general communist organization'.[2]

The second step was to bring the local party committees under the full control of the Central Committee. A beginning had been made with this even in 1918, but some idea of the immensity of the task still to be accomplished at the time of the Eighth Congress can be gained from the fact that, while the Central Committee was already in touch with most of the provincial organizations, it had no direct contact with half the district party organizations. There was no regular system of reporting to the Central Committee, and there was the greatest variation both in the structure and in the methods of local party bodies.[3] Krestinskii's staff assiduously set about building up two-way links between the centre and the provinces. The number of reports, minutes of committee meetings and similar documents reaching the Central Committee from the local party organizations, which totalled only 470 in May 1919, averaged over 4,000 per month by the summer of 1920. By December 1919 already the Central Committee had established direct contact with 95 per cent of the district committees. Meanwhile, the number of circulars addressed by the Central Committee to local organizations rose from 71 in the period April–November 1919, to 253 in 1921. During 1920 the Central Committee's dealings with local party organizations were still largely devoted to internal matters. By 1921 it was able to switch its main attention from internal organization, and to extend its control into the fields

---

[1] *ibidem*, p. 600. The integration condemned by the Eighth Party Congress between local party and government organs had not been overcome. All that had happened was that the dominant position within the integrated structures had shifted to the party committees. The personnel of party and government bodies at the local level continued to overlap – see *Izv.Ts.K.*, No. 37, January 1922.

[2] *KPSS v rez.*, volume I, p. 443.

[3] *IX S"ezd*, pp. 22–4.

of personnel and ideology, and over the activities of non-party bodies.[1]

Meanwhile the staff of the Central Committee apparatus underwent an enormous expansion commensurate with the growth of its work. In December 1919 it still numbered only 80, by March 1920 it had risen to 150, a year later it totalled 602.[2] From then on it remained relatively unchanged. The apparatus of these early years deserves some study, since it was then that the problems and their solutions emerged which influenced the form of the apparatus at all later periods.

Of nine departments projected at the time of the Eighth Congress in 1919 five were set up immediately: The Information and Statistics Department (*Informotdel*), of which the task was to extract from the local party committees data on their composition, structure, methods and activities; The Organization and Instruction Department (*Orgotdel*), responsible for working out and establishing the institutional forms of the party apparatus, and supervising their functioning; The Records and Assignment Department (*Uchraspred*), concerned with the collection of statistical and personal data on party members, to serve as the basis for Central Committee appointments and allocations of personnel. In addition, there was a shortlived Travelling Inspectorate, and a General Department, or chancery of the Central Committee.[3] In 1919 two further departments were added: a Rural Department primarily for propaganda among the peasants; and a Department for Work among Women.

In addition to these regular departments of the Central Committee, there were a number of special 'bureaux' and 'groups' responsible for party work among national minorities. Functioning through parallel 'national sections' in the local party organizations, these bureaux were responsible for propaganda, study courses, publishing, conferences and similar activities for both the party members and the 'masses' of the nationalities concerned.[4] At the time of the Ninth Congress in March 1920 the Central Committee contained a Bureau for communists of the East, a Bureau for Jewish sections, Finnish, Polish, Estonian, Lithuanian-Belorussian, Votiak and Chuvash Bureaux, and

[1] *Izv.Ts.K.*, No. 16, 28 March 1920; No. 22, 15 September 1920; No. 8, 2 December 1919; No. 39, March 1922.
[2] *Izv.Ts.K.*, No. 8, 2 December 1919; No. 28, 5 March 1921; No. 3 (51), March 1923.
[3] *Izv.Ts.K.*, No. 8, 2 December 1919; No. 15, 24 March 1920; No. 16, 28 March 1920.
[4] For the functions of the national sections see *SPR*, No. 1, pp. 66–7 and *SPR*, No. 2, pp. 71–2.

German, Hungarian, French, Italian, Czechoslovak, Rumanian and South Slav sections.[1]

In view of the importance attached by the bolsheviks to propaganda, it may seem remarkable that for almost three years after their seizure of power they possessed no central party agency for the ideological activities of the régime. Ideology, 'culture' and propaganda were partly in the hands of a number of semi-autonomous government agencies, partly administered by specialized departments for the Army and the railways, and partly – and this applied particularly to literature and the arts – independent of control. This is not to say that the party, as such, played no part in propaganda activities. The Rural Department, the Department for Work among Women, and the national sections were all primarily concerned with propaganda and agitation. But there was no one responsible for co-ordinating their activities, let alone those of the multifarious free-lance non-party left-wing propaganda agencies.

In September 1920 the Department of Agitation and Propaganda of the Central Committee (*Agitprop*) was set up. Although it did not entirely escape friction with the other agencies already in the field, its initial steps were cautious and modest – as shown by the fact that in March 1921 its staff still totalled only 17.[2] But gradually its jurisdiction was extended and its influence deepened. In the autumn of 1921 it set up a Press Sub-Department (taking over the activities of the Press Bureau which had been formed a few months earlier).[3] In 1922 the Press Sub-Department of *Agitprop* assumed responsibility for the local press. By 1923 (as will be seen below) it was beginning to concern itself with creative literature, which up to this date, in so far as it was not so hostile to the revolution as to engage the attention of the GPU, remained the province of various competing and mutually antagonistic left-wing literary cliques. It should be noted that anti-religious propaganda also formed no part of the responsibilities of *Agitprop* at this date. This activity was also during the early years left to enthusiastic amateurs. The new régime confined its assault on the Church to confiscation of church property, and to the persecution of priests and believers on the grounds of their allegedly counter-revolutionary activity. In 1921 the functions of the Rural Department were also merged in *Agitprop*.

The two key departments, which dominated the party apparatus,

[1] *Izv.Ts.K.*, No. 16, 28 March 1920.
[2] *Izv.Ts.K.*, No. 28, 5 March 1921. For its structure in November 1921 see *SPR*, No. 2, pp. 62–4.
[3] *Izv.Ts.K.*, No. 36, 15 December 1921.

were the Organization and Instruction Department and the Records and Assignment Department (*Orgotdel* and *Uchraspred*). A picture of the activities of *Orgotdel* may be obtained from its correspondence with local party organizations. Of nearly six hundred and fifty letters sent out by *Orgotdel* between mid-April and mid-November 1919, the great majority were concerned with answering enquiries and issuing directions on such aspects of party work as propaganda, the organization of non-party conferences, party work among women, and national minorities.[1] The absorption of the Information Department (*Informotdel*) by *Orgotdel* at the end of 1920 was a logical step, since studying the activity of the local committees obviously needed to be closely integrated with the work of guiding them.

Orgotdel was also constantly being entrusted with other branches of activity which from time to time required special attention from the Central Committee. Such was the work of reconciling and codifying the multitude of resolutions and decrees issued by the central organs of the party. Again, until the setting up of the party Control Commissions in September 1920, which is dealt with below, *Orgotdel*, was made responsible for settling the innumerable disputes which arose between party officials and party organs.[2]

In May 1921 the important function of inspection was added to the responsibilities of *Orgotdel*, and it was provided with a staff of so-called Central Committee Instructors. In visiting a local organization, the Central Committee Instructor had the right to inspect all papers, including secret ones, and to attend all meetings, including closed ones. All communist officials, including police officials, were obliged to present papers for examination upon request. The Instructor had no right to give orders to local officials, except in so far as he was authorized to do so in his credentials, but he was expected to recommend any required changes to the provincial committee, and if the latter disagreed, to take the issue to the Central Committee for decision. Between March 1922 and March 1923, 74 investigations were undertaken by Central Committee Instructors.[3]

In June 1922, two months after Stalin's appointment as General Secretary, L. M. Kaganovich was made head of *Orgotdel*. He immediately undertook a reorganization and restaffing of the

[1] *Izv.Ts.K.*, No. 29, 7 March 1921.
[2] *Izv.Ts.K.*, No. 22, 18 September 1920.
[3] *Izv.Ts.K.*, No. 33, October 1921. (The institution of Central Committee Instructors had already been foreshadowed at the Tenth Party Congress in March – see *KPSS v rez.*, volume I, p. 525.) See also *Izv.Ts.K.*, No. 39, March 1922 and No. 3 (51), March 1923; and *SPR*, No. 3, pp. 108–9 and *Izv.Ts.K.*, No. 9 (45), September 1922.

department. It was given a new establishment of 59, including 19 'responsible Instructors'.[1] This was followed by a further expansion of the influence of *Orgotdel*, which began to show enhanced interest in personnel matters, although these were properly speaking the province of the other main department, *Uchraspred*. These incursions of *Orgotdel* into fields of activity proper to *Uchraspred* appeared to have the blessing of the secretariat itself. In December 1922 a conference was called of provincial and regional *orgotdels*. Personnel questions were one of the main subjects of discussion.[2] The trends were thus already apparent which were to lead to the merging of *Uchraspred* with *Orgotdel* under Kaganovich a little over a year later.

During the civil war there were probably more persons directly assigned to posts by the Central Committee than in any other period of Soviet history. It was not therefore surprising that the Central Committee organ primarily responsible for appointments, the *Orgburo*, should have devolved much of this work upon the apparatus of the Central Committee, and in particular upon the Records and Assignment Department (*Uchraspred*). This devolution was apparent in the very first months of the existence of the apparatus. Already between April and November 1919 *Uchraspred* carried out 2,182 assignments as compared with the Orgburo's 544.[3]

The Central Committee's assignment work falls into two main periods during the first five years of the Soviet régime. In the first, roughly from the Eighth Congress in 1919 to the Tenth in 1921, personnel records were poor, yet enormous demands for party workers were being made upon the Central Committee. Consequently much of its assignment work took the form of 'mobilizations', that is, pin-pointing areas of personnel weakness and drafting all available cadres to these areas, without making any close study of the suitability of individuals for the work entailed. The transition to the second period began towards the end of 1920, but was not completed till the second half of 1922. It was characterized by the replacement of 'mobilization' by more or less careful individual selection on the basis of vastly improved records and techniques, and the devolution of responsibility for more junior appointments upon lower party committees.

In the first months after its formation, *Uchraspred* made an attempt to collect basic data on party members, but had not made much

[1] *SPR*, No. 3, pp. 103–4, and *Izv.Ts.K.*, No. 7 (43), July 1922.
[2] *Izv.Ts.K.*, No. 1 (49), January 1923.
[3] *Izv.Ts.K.*, No. 8, 2 December 1919.

headway before it became bogged down with the work of assigning hundreds of communists sent up by local committees or simply presenting themselves. At one time, the number of party members appearing at *Uchraspred* reached 100 to 150 a day. The work of *Uchraspred* reached its zenith in 1920. Between April 1920 and mid-February 1921 it undertook over 40,000 postings. Over half of these were to the army, but very substantial numbers were also assigned to civilian work.[1] With the end of the civil war in sight, *Uchraspred* could look forward to a situation in which its work would not be geared to 'mobilization', and it began to prepare the ground for suppler and more selective methods.

The first step was to establish a card index of party members. For this purpose all communists were divided into three categories – the 'commanding corps', those in less responsible posts but marked for promotion, and the 'party masses'. In August 1920 requests were sent out to the provincial committees for lists of all responsible workers at their level, and later similar requests were sent to central government agencies. By March 1921 most of this material was to hand and carded, but the majority of provincial committees were not yet carrying out the Central Committee instruction to notify changes. Further procedural improvements to this end were made in the course of 1920 and 1921.[2] The more selective character of *Uchraspred*'s work became apparent after the Tenth Congress. In December 1921 *Uchraspred* assigned only 581 communists, about one-sixth of the average monthly total during 1920. Mobilizations were not yet completely at an end, however. A number were undertaken during 1921, including 13 large ones involving altogether 5,000 to 6,000 communists. Most of these were seriously underfulfilled, owing mainly, according to *Uchraspred*, to the widespread feeling that mobilizations were purely a war-time measure. The 1921 mobilizations led to numerous resignations from the party.[3] By 1923 it was recognized that mobilizations had outlived their usefulness. The new method of individual assignments had come to stay.

Throughout 1921 measures were being taken to build up *Uchraspred*'s records and to regularize procedures. There were already 23,500 responsible officials on the records of *Uchraspred* by November 1921, broken down into groups corresponding to different fields of

---

[1] Details in *Izv.Ts.K.*, No. 28, March 1921, and No. 22, 18 September 1920.

[2] *Izv.Ts.K.*, No. 22, 18 September 1920, and No. 28, 5 March 1921; *SPR*, No. 1, p. 79.

[3] *Izv.Ts.K.*, No. 33, October 1921, No. 37, January 1922, and No. 39, March 1922.

specialization. These were augmented by a census begun in August 1921 of leading officials, covering about 70,000 in all. Data on about 26,000 of these were available by March 1922.[1] Apart from these efforts to build up the new card index of leading officials, *Uchraspred* began to investigate the mass of miscellaneous papers which had accumulated in the personal files of the Central Committee. In the provinces, however, personnel work in 1921 was still in complete confusion, and a number of decisions taken in the latter part of 1921 were aimed at correcting this situation.

By 1922 *Uchraspred* had succeeded in devolving responsibility for junior postings on to the subordinate committees and was able to concentrate its personnel work more and more upon senior appointments. Parallel with this development went a tendency for the Orgburo and especially the Secretariat to take a more direct hand in appointments. About 1,000 appointments were approved by the Secretariat or Orgburo between March 1922 and March 1923, including 42 secretaries of provincial committees.[2] Finally, the party census carried out at the beginning of 1922 made it possible for the first time for the Central Committee to have a personal record of every member in the party. Further improvements in Central Committee records were made in the spring of 1922. For example, a special register was established of leading workers, consisting of senior officials in the provincial and central agencies and some 1,760 'underground' workers. Later in the year all students were placed on the records of the Central Committee, and became subject to assignment by *Uchraspred*.[3]

[1] *Izv.Ts.K.*, No. 36, 15 December 1921, and No. 39, March 1922.
[2] *Izv.Ts.K.*, No. 42, June 1922, No. 43, July 1922, and No. 3 (51), March 1923.
[3] *SPR*, No. 3, pp. 128–30, 133, 137; *Izv.Ts.K.*, No. 7 (43), July 1922.

XIV   Control over the Provinces: Army and Legal Machinery

As described in the last chapter, the party apparatus had established its claim, even during Lenin's lifetime, as the real power controlling the country's destiny. By 1923, at any rate, an effective machine had been built up at the centre. But its success in establishing fully centralized control depended on the extent to which it could subordinate local party organs to central orders. In form, power in the provinces was vested in provincial, city and district party conferences, at which the local committees were elected, and to which they were responsible. But these local party conferences were from the first highly dependent upon their executive organs, and this dependence became more marked as time went by – a fact reflected in changes in the party rules. These required provincial conferences every three months in 1919, every six months in 1922, but only once a year after 1923.[1] Soviet historians make no bones of the fact that 'in the period of the illegal existence of our Party, when party organizations were compelled to have a purely conspiratorial character, party committees were composed from top to bottom by appointment or co-option'.[2] The revolution opened the way for party organizations to elect their officials, but the elective principle was weak in bolshevik tradition, and it immediately ran up against the claim of the Central Committee to dispose freely of the party's human resources. Thus, while local party conferences at this stage often enjoyed considerable freedom in electing their committees, the key local officials, who inevitably dominated the committees, were posted by the Central Committee, and subject to removal by the Central Committee.

As at the centre, the local executive organs of the party took on a two-tier structure, with power progressively passing to the upper tier. The party rules provided for a provincial committee of unspecified

[1] *KPSS v rez.*, volume I, pp. 464–5, 659–60, 729. During the civil war it was of course impossible for conferences to be held with the prescribed regularity.
[2] *Pravda*, 7 December 1952.

size, and a five-man 'bureau' (at first called a 'presidium') of the committee.[1] In 1921, the relationship between the local party committee and its bureau (or presidium) was described as follows: 'The functions of the full committee are purely advisory in character. The presidium carries on current work, reporting to the committee and in especially urgent cases has the right, apart from the committee, to decide [even] matters of principle.'[2] The departmental structure of local party committees at first showed a great variety. It was only in December 1919 that the Central Committee began work to bring order out of this chaos, and by the latter part of 1920 the majority of provinces had adapted their party apparatus to the Central Committee pattern.[3]

For the first eighteen months after the seizure of power, the chief party official in the local committees was usually a communist leader employed mainly in the local soviet, and serving as a part-time chairman of the party committee. From 1919 onwards, with the growth of the new party apparatus, the post of secretary became the dominant one in all local party committees. The party rules adopted in December 1919 made the district secretaryship a full-time post.[4] The emergence of the party secretary as the key figure in the party machine at every level coincided with the establishment of the party machine as the dominant hierarchy in the bolshevik leadership's system of controls. Party secretaries thus came, by 1921, to bear primary responsibility for all that went on in their area. The practice was introduced of calling the provincial secretaries periodically to report personally to the Central Committee. They were also required to make secret written reports every month on the political situation in their provinces.[5] Thus it was that the national network of party committees came to be unified and transmuted into an administrative machine, whose backbone was the hierarchy of party secretaries. The assimilation of the party to a bureaucratic machine became further evident when the Central Committee laid down detailed

[1] *KPSS v rez.*, volume I, pp. 464–5, 659–60.
[2] *Izv.Ts.K.*, No. 32, 6 August 1921.
[3] A study of 40 provincial committees and 300 district committees made in the second half of 1919 showed that no two had the same structure; *Izv.Ts.K.*, No. 24, 12 October 1920.
[4] *KPSS v rez.*, volume I, p. 465.
[5] The practice of summoning provincial secretaries to report in person began in November 1921, and grew steadily: see *Izv.Ts.K.*, No. 36, 15 December 1921, No. 3 (51), March 1923. For instructions on the form of the written reports see *SPR*, No. 2, pp. 79–80. In April 1922, immediately after Stalin had taken over as General Secretary, an instruction was issued that the reports should be sent by the 5th of each month personally to the Central Committee Secretary – *SPR* No. 3, p. 122.

establishments for all subordinate party committees, covering their whole staff from secretaries to cleaners, and divided party officials into five categories corresponding to the five salary grades of government officials.[1]

Indeed, charges and counter-charges of bureaucratization were rife in the party from 1920 on. Where the word 'bureaucracy' was not just a form of abuse, its use often indicated an awareness that the party had suffered a change, but the nature of this change was little understood. It was blamed on the failings of individuals – the arbitrariness of leaders or the 'careerism' of the system, or upon the practice of taking decisions individually rather than in committee. Or again, it was equated with the 'militarization' of the party, and blamed on civil war conditions. No one appeared to appreciate that 'bureaucratization' flowed inevitably from the administrative role allotted to the party, and from the structure which it adopted in order to perform this role. Remedies, therefore, in so far as they were genuine attempts at reform, necessarily attacked the symptoms rather than the disease itself. This was made abundantly plain in 1921 at the Tenth Congress, which called for the universal application of the elective principle and the elimination of 'appointment' (*naznachenstvo*) as a system, yet left the Central Committee's powers over personnel intact; and called for freedom of criticism and discussion in the party while at the same time it clamped down on existing criticism and made any future group of critics vulnerable to charges of 'factionalism'. In these circumstances insistence on the elective principle could mean no more than that the apparatus should see to it that the formality of 'election' should be observed in assigning personnel to elective posts, and that discussion and criticism could concern itself solely with the question whether or not the leadership's policies were being correctly carried out, but not with these policies themselves.

The first five years of bolshevik power were bedevilled with continual factional fights in the local party organizations. To some extent these reflected the struggles within the party leadership and the great issues debated at the party congresses. In the majority of cases, however, they were not concerned with national political issues, but merely grew out of the antagonism of rival groups of local leaders. The forms of this antagonism were many and varied. For example, secondary leaders were often able to mobilize the resentment of the rank and file against the inner group. Again, conflicts took the form of the struggle of district officials against the provincial organization, of

[1] *SPR*, No. 1, pp. 57–8, No. 2, pp. 49–51, No. 3, pp. 110–12.

the working-class element against the 'white-collar' element in the local committee, of disagreement between the soviet and party officialdom, or, in some areas, of strife on national grounds between Russian and national minority leaders.

These squabbles led to inefficiency in the party organizations which was obviously intolerable under civil war conditions, and the Central Committee was therefore able to secure support for the drastic measures it devised to combat them. The standard method used, according to the Central Committee, was to recall from the organization 'those comrades who had taken the most active part in the squabble', and to send 'new workers in their place'.[1] In practice, one faction (usually the weaker), or both, were removed from the organization and the members distributed among various other areas and fields of work, often without reduction in status for the individuals concerned. Though this 'honourable exile' was resented by some of its victims, it was too plainly necessary to be seriously challenged. But once 'honourable exile' became established as the standard method of dealing with group struggles in local party organizations, its potential value as a political weapon became obvious. It seems to have first been used in this way against the Workers' Opposition in 1921.[2] From 1921 on, as the Central Committee Secretariat passed under the domination of Stalin, 'honourable exile' became one of the principal methods of securing control over all local organizations and of breaking up concentrations of supporters of his actual or potential rivals. It must be emphasized, however, that such considerations had played no significant role in 1919 and 1920 when the practice first became established. That it was able to survive and become entrenched, and so become available later as a political weapon, was simply because in the hands of its original users it was so obviously disciplinarian rather than political in intent.

From its inception the party apparatus was entrusted with the investigation of charges made against party members, whether these concerned their personal conduct (immorality, drunkenness, etc.) or their public life (using official position for private ends, violating party discipline, peculation, etc.). Before the Ninth Congress in 1920 there existed in the Central Committee a Conflicts Commission for this purpose, later transformed into a Conflicts Sub-Department. In

[1] *Izv.Ts.K.*, No. 3 (51), March 1923.
[2] The most important instance was that of the Samara organization. This case is described in Robert V. Daniels, 'The Secretariat and the Local Organizations in the Russian Communist Party 1921–1923', *The American Slavic and East European Review,* volume XVI, No. 1, February 1957, pp. 32–49 and pp. 41–2.

the following year over two thousand cases came before this sub-department. Meanwhile in September 1920 the decision had been taken to establish a hierarchy of control commissions, as tribunals for dealing with disciplinary questions. The Conflicts Sub-Department soon adopted the practice of passing its more serious cases to the Central Control Commission for decision. In time it became apparent that these two bodies were duplicating each other's activities, and towards the end of 1921 the work of the Conflicts Sub-Department was wound up.[1]

The control commissions were originally created ostensibly in response to demands for action against the overbearing and 'bureaucratized' party officialdom and it was as independent tribunals that they issued their first appeal to party members.[2] In order to make them independent of the regular party apparatus, the local control commissions were to be elected by the local party conferences and the Central Control Commission by the all-Russian party congress, and no member of a party committee could serve on them. Cases of dispute between a control commission and the corresponding party committees were to go before a joint sitting of the two bodies, and if agreement was still not reached, they were to be settled by the next higher party committee. Disagreements between the Central Committee and the Central Control Commission were to be placed before the party congress.[3] However, as official attempts to define the duties and powers of the control commissions made abundantly clear, the line between their jurisdiction and that of the party committees was not easy to draw. On the one hand the party committees were themselves expected to combat abuses, and on the other hand these abuses were frequently so intimately bound up with the details of day-to-day administration that the control commissions were obliged to keep in very close touch with the practical work of the local party apparatus. These two aspects of the situation were reflected in the fact that members of control commissions were empowered to attend meetings of party committees, without a right to vote, while the party committees were responsible for carrying out the decisions of the control commissions, since the latter had no executive staff of their own.

In these circumstances an attitude of detached independence became virtually impossible, and it was inevitable that the control commissions should be caught up in the internal rivalries and

[1] *Izv.Ts.K.*, No. 39, March 1922.
[2] On 11 November 1920 – see *SPR*, No. 1, pp. 55-6. Cf. *Izv.Ts.K.*, No. 26, 20 December 1920.
[3] *ibidem*, pp. 56-7.

squabbles which bedevilled local party life. There was strong pressure upon them either to become absorbed into the ruling clique or else to join forces with the 'outs' in the local organizations against the 'ins'. As a Central Committee report put it, 'there were also cases where the provincial control commission, instead of settling a conflict, itself joined forces with one of the groups, and adopted a decision expelling the other side from the party.'[1]

The effect of this was to discredit the reputation for independence of the local control commissions. There was pressure to strengthen the vertical links between them, culminating in a decision of the Eleventh Party Congress in March 1922 to the effect that 'the Central Control Commission has insufficiently unified and guided the work of the local control commissions, and . . . the future Central Control Commission . . . should pay more attention to this side of the matter'. At the same time the control commissions were given a small apparatus for conducting their own investigations.[2] The skill with which the members of the Central Control Commission were chosen at the Eleventh Congress in 1922 reveals the mastery over the party apparatus which was already passing into Stalin's control. Only one of the members elected in 1921 was re-elected in 1922, but of the seven elected in 1922, four were to remain in their posts for many years to come. Thus was begun the transformation of the control commissions into a second highly centralized hierarchy, paralleling the hierarchy of party secretaries. From their original conception as a check on the party bureaucracy, they now became an integral part of this bureaucracy, and a powerful instrument in the hands of the party leaders. In the heyday of their early independence, the control commissions had established their right to discipline both party and government officials.[3] This right could now be used as an added weapon to break down local resistance to the central leadership. The majority of the charges coming before the control commissions were ostensibly non-political ('violation of party discipline', 'abuse of position', 'non-communist conduct', etc.). But such formulae were in practice sufficiently elastic to ensure the expulsion, dismissal or reproof of any local communist leader of an independent turn of mind. For all this, some vestiges of the independence of the local control commissions survived to the end of the period now under review, and the control commission hierarchy was far from being the smooth-working and

[1] *Izv.Ts.K.*, No. 3 (51), March 1923; No. 42, June 1922.
[2] *KPSS v rez.*, volume I, pp. 636–9.
[3] For an early instance of such independent action by the Central Control Commission, in the Trade Union dispute in 1920–1, see my *The Origin*, pp. 288–9.

flexible machine it was to become by the mid-20's in the hands of Stalin and his faction.

* * *

Thus, by 1923 the basis for the control by the party over national life had been laid: the perfected system of control over appointments which enabled the central apparatus to place trusted and well-screened nominees in key positions in all the party organizations; strict party discipline, which ensured both that the nominees would obey the centre and that the rank and file members of local party organizations would obey the central nominee; and finally, the establishment of party supremacy over state institutions. The working out of the latter principle presented other features of interest in certain cases, of which the most instructive were the armed forces and the judicial and police systems.

The growth of party control over the armed forces was as haphazard as that of the rest of the party machinery. The bolsheviks from the first realized the importance of creating an organization inside the army, and already by June 1917 a wide network of party cells existed both in front and rear units. The outstanding temper of these organizations was that of extreme revolutionary ardour, which Lenin, for fear of a premature rising, was careful to restrain.[1] In the army, as elsewhere, the bolsheviks were the victims of their own political warfare. Before October 1917 all party effort was directed towards undermining army discipline by encouraging insubordination and 'democratic' demands of the most extreme nature. When, after February 1918, the time came to rebuild an army and to prepare for resistance to the enemies of the bolsheviks, the extreme revolutionary and democratic traditions previously inculcated were to prove a serious obstacle to the formation of the disciplined army now considered necessary. For years thereafter the central party authorities struggled with an anarchical tradition of independence in communist cells within the army which acted as a brake on all efforts to create a centralized disciplined military party machine.

The main architect of the Red Army, Trotsky, was the most determined opponent of these anarchical traditions of the military communists. 'Send me communists who know how to obey', he had wired to Lenin on first arriving at the front in 1918 to take charge of military operations. He did not hesitate thereafter to ensure that the com-

[1] S. E. Rabinovich, *Vserossiiskaia voennaia konferentsiia bol'shevikov 1917 goda,* Moscow, 1931, pp. 10–17, 22, 45–6.

munists learnt this simple lesson – even to the extent of shooting the disobedient. A communist's duties, he wrote later, were 'to watch over the morale of his fellow soldiers', to exhort them hour by hour, to 'keep careful check on their work' and to inspire them by his example.[1] The iron discipline over army communists was justified by results, since it provided a fanatical leaven for the, at best, luke-warm peasant mass of the army. But for the duration of the civil war, and thereafter, it aroused intense opposition, and it was some years before an effective system of centralized party discipline was built up.

Until 1919 there was in practice virtually no central organization in existence. The numerous party cells, most of which had grown up spontaneously, determined their own rights and functions, endeavouring to assert what they claimed as their natural right of superiority both over the non-party ranks and over the ex-officers of the imperial army, who formed the overwhelming majority of all officers. But in the course of 1919 an improvised system of central control gradually took shape. This grew out of the so-called political departments of military and naval formations, which were charged with the supervision and co-ordination of all political activity in the armed forces. These departments were headed by a Central Political Administration (abbreviated to PUR), which though not directly subordinate to the Central Committee, but to the Revolutionary War Council (of which Trotsky as People's Commissar for War was chairman), nevertheless worked closely with the Central Committee Secretariat.[2] This network was given control over all political work inside the army, in particular the right to make all appointments and to enforce all party decisions. It also acquired jurisdiction over the political commissars, who had been appointed from the start as political watchdogs over the former officers of the imperial army now serving with the Red Army and whom the bolsheviks did not trust. The control by PUR over the recalcitrant party cells was greatly facilitated by two factors: first, by the power which it was given to effect transfers, thus enabling it to break up centres of indiscipline. Secondly, by the mass recruitment into the party which took place in the autumn of 1919, whereby the total number of communists in the army rose to 280,000.[3] This had the effect of swamping the obstinate veteran communists with more malleable new recruits. The authority of PUR was further

---

[1] L. Trotsky, *Kak vooruzhalas' revoliutsiia*, Moscow, 1923–25, Volume II, Part II, p. 126.

[2] *Iz.Ts.K.*, No. 8, 2 December 1919.

[3] I. Petukhov, *Partiinaia organizatsiia i partiinaia rabota v RKKA*, Moscow, Leningrad, 1928, p. 26.

strengthened in 1919, when the special detachments responsible for security inside the armed forces were placed under the control of the political commissars, and therefore came under the overall control of PUR.[1]

Towards the end of the civil war, and for some time thereafter, several other attempts to break the stern centralized control were made by the army communists. Thus, in the course of discussions among army communists early in 1921 two demands were voiced by dissidents: the one, that all military party organs should be elected inside the army and not appointed; the other, that the army party organizations should be placed under the jurisdiction of the local civilian party committees.[2] Each of these demands would, if conceded, have destroyed centralized control – the former by admitting oppositionists into the army political apparatus, the latter because the local committees were not at that date yet fully subordinated to the central apparatus. Later, in 1923, demands were also voiced in army communist circles for the complete subordination of the entire army political machinery to the military commanders, by integrating it into the military chain of command.[3] The central apparatus, PUR, was able without difficulty to crush all these demands for autonomy. But though the principle of centralized party control thus became established in the army, it is nonetheless important to bear in mind that up to 1924 PUR still retained some independence of the Central Committee. Its complete subordination would only come about during Stalin's conflicts with Trotsky. Thus, of the two features which have remained distinctive of the pattern of party structure in the army ever since – centralization, and integration with the civilian party apparatus at the top, but not at any lower level – the one grew out of the exigencies of military discipline, the other was enforced for fear that the political apparatus within the army might become an instrument in the hands of a rival for power.

The relation of the party during the first five years of Soviet power to the legal organs and to the organs of repression must also be discussed. It was significant that neither the party, nor the security organs, headed by the *Vecheka*, nor the various tribunals instituted by

[1] See a resolution of the Eighth Party Congress in *KPSS v rez.*, volume I, p. 440. A short time before, on 21 February 1919, these detachments had been placed under the immediate control of the Revolutionary War Council by a decree – see *Sistematicheskii sbornik vazhneishikh dekretov 1917–1920*, Moscow, 1920, p. 55.

[2] Petukhov, *op. cit.*, p. 57. For the party instruction which forbade any interference by the civilian party organizations in the military party organizations see *SPR*, No. 2, pp. 120–1. It was dated 27 July 1921.

[3] Petukhov, *op. cit.*, pp. 70–1.

the revolutionary power, were so much as mentioned in the Constitution of the RSFSR which was adopted in July 1918. This was in part due to the faith of the drafters of the constitution that some of these organs were temporary, and in part to a desire, for propaganda purposes, to disguise the existence of popular opposition to the régime.

For the first few years of the Soviet régime, the ideological foundations of law rested on the few isolated remarks on the subject by Marx and Lenin, who shared a contempt for law and lawyers. For Marx law was essentially a function of the production relations subsisting at a particular epoch. Like the state, law was the expression of the will of the dominant class and of its endeavours to retain power: after the social revolution, when once the transitional dictatorship of the proletariat was over, it would be possible to pass beyond 'the horizon limited by bourgeois law'.[1] Lenin (in *State and Revolution*) similarly regarded law as a temporary, bourgeois survival which would progressively disappear as the means of production became socialized.[2] In one form or another these primitive formulations of the nature of law were to dominate Soviet legal theory until the early 30's.

But although in theory Lenin conceded the survival for some time of bourgeois law, the practice of the party was at no time based on this theory. On the contrary, its immediate effort was directed at destroying the pre-revolutionary system of law, the courts, the judiciary and the Bar. At the same time, a flood of decrees issued from the government, many of which had no hope of being put into effect during the chaotic days of war communism. The practical solution adopted for purposes of daily administration was to leave an almost unlimited margin of discretionary power to the communist judges.

The decree which swept away the existing courts and created new local courts for both civil and criminal matters, and revolutionary tribunals for the trial of cases of counter-revolution, sabotage and other forms of resistance to the 'conquests of the revolution', was published on 24 November 1917. A special revolutionary tribunal for dealing with 'crimes . . . against the people, committed by means of the press' was first set up on 18 December 1917.[3]

Meanwhile there had also come into being the *Vecheka* – the All-Russian Extraordinary Commission for Combating Counter-Revolution, Sabotage and Speculation, with its numerous local

---

[1] *Critique of the Gotha Programme*. The English translation, published in Moscow, misses the whole point by mistranslating *Recht* as 'right' instead of 'law'.
[2] *Lenin*, volume XXI, p. 435.
[3] *Sovetskaia prokuratura v vazhneishikh dokumentakh*, Moscow, 1956, pp. 15–18, 23–4.

sub-commissions (*Cheka*). It appears to have evolved out of a branch of the Military Revolutionary Committee, headed by F. Dzerzhinskii, who also became the first head of the *Vecheka*, when it was established on 6 or 7 December 1917.[1] Originally intended, or stated to be intended, as an organ for conducting investigations only, with a view to handing the accused over if necessary for trial by the revolutionary tribunals, it almost immediately 'acquired' direct powers of executive action, including the infliction of the death penalty.[2] Although the revolutionary tribunals were only first openly instructed to apply the death sentence in June 1918, the *Vecheka*, as Lenin admitted, had been shooting without restraint from the beginning of the seizure of power.[3] Various decrees in the course of the civil war purported to limit the direct executive powers of the *Vecheka* and to ensure some form of trial by the revolutionary tribunals. These decrees did not make very much difference, partly because they were not complied with and partly because the revolutionary tribunals were in practice little more than organs of the *Vecheka*, often presided over by its members and unrestricted in their own discretionary powers.[4] There is no doubt that the *Vecheka* was a law unto itself, little restrained either by decrees, or by the party, whose executive arm it admittedly was.[5]

[1] According to an announcement made on 13 December the *Vecheka* was set up by a decision of the Council of People's Commissars on 7 December. According to a document quoted from the central archives by M. V. Kozhevnikov, *Istoriia sovetskogo suda*, Moscow, 1948, p. 59, the decision was taken on 6 December. Although Soviet historians have subsequently associated Lenin with the original proposal, the only known proposal on the subject emanating from Lenin at the time bore no relationship to the proposal which was adopted, and which apparently came from Dzerzhinskii – see *Lenin*, volume XXII, pp. 126–9, for a letter to Dzerzhinskii dated 6–7 December 1917. Lenin is stated to have first raised the question in the Council of People's Commissars on 6 December – *ibidem*, p. 593 – and there is no doubt that terror was always accepted by him as a necessary means for struggling against counter-revolution. For discussion of the origins of the *Vecheka* see E. J. Scott, 'The Cheka' in *St Antony's Papers, Number 1. Soviet Affairs*. No. 1. London, 1956, pp. 1–23, and Simon Wolin and Robert M. Slusser, *The Soviet Secret Police*, New York, 1957, pp. 3–9, 31–3, 372–3.

[2] Kozhevnikov, *op. cit.*, pp. 59–60.

[3] When the left socialist revolutionaries objected to the official restoration of the death penalty, Lenin, with some justification, taunted them with their inconsistency, since they had hitherto approved 'the shooting in Dzerzhinskii's Commission' – see *Lenin*, volume XXIII, p. 124.

[4] For details of the attempts to curb the *Chekas* and of the conflict between the revolutionary tribunals and the *Vecheka* see Scott, *loc. cit.*

[5] According to a directive of the Central Committee, dated 3 [*sic*] February 1919, the *Chekas* 'were created and exist as organs of the party, and work under its direction and control' – quoted in an anniversary speech by the then head of the security organs, I. A. Serov, in 1957, *Pravda*, 24 December 1957. The date of the directive as given by Serov must be wrong, since the issue of the *Cheka* was only first discussed in the Central Committee on 4 and 5 February 1919 – see *Lenin* (5), volume xxxvii, p. 729.

The emergency revolutionary tribunals, which from the first bore the brunt of all penal jurisdiction in close co-operation with the *Vecheka*, were repeatedly enjoined to base their decisions on 'revolutionary consciousness', or 'socialist consciousness of justice'. Their composition was overwhelmingly communist. The communist lawyers were conscious of the theoretical incompatibility between a wide measure of discretion in practice and any legal system. A decree of 12 December 1919, formulated by the People's Commissariat of Justice (then headed by P. I. Stuchka), claimed that it was now possible to speak of 'uniform measures' of law, and of the 'systematization' in fact of a 'new law'. Lenin also from time to time stressed the need for greater legality. But no legal order can develop without two conditions. One is the existence of a judiciary sufficiently independent of the executive power to be able fearlessly to interpret and apply the law without regard for the immediate aims or wishes of that executive power. The second condition is the submission of the executive power to fixed and definite legal rules – whether the rules be of its own making, or issue from a legislature to which it is itself responsible. The communist party, which from the first set out to make itself the sole repository of all arbitrary executive power, was never prepared to allow either of these conditions to develop. This attitude could be justified by the doctrine that since law was no more than the will of the proletariat in action, and since the will of the proletariat was expressed by its vanguard, the communist party, there could be no room for any fixed legal limitations so long as the communist party was in control. In practice the theory foundered against the increasingly evident truth that the dictatorship of the proletariat was often being exercised as much against the proletariat as against the bourgeoisie. The evolution of Dzerzhinskii's views on the attitude of the *Vecheka* to workers and peasants illustrates the way in which this organ had changed from an instrument of a workers' revolution into the punitive arm of an unpopular state machine. In January 1921 Dzerzhinskii still stressed that much greater leniency should be shown to workers and peasants than to the bourgeoisie: by February 1924 he was radically opposed to 'liberal nonsense', according to which, in dealing with accused persons, less severity was shown in the case of proletarians.[1]

After the end of the civil war both the judicial system and the extra-judicial organs of repression were regularized. Apart from the

---

[1] 'F. E. Dzerzhinskii o revoliutsionnoi zakonnosti' in *Istoricheskii arkhiv*, No. 1, 1958, pp. 3–25.

influence exercised by critical foreign socialist opinion there was now also strong pressure inside the communist party for more normal conditions. Furthermore, the development of commercial relations under NEP of itself created a need for some degree of legal certainty. In 1922 a new system of civil and criminal courts was created (the latter designed to replace the revolutionary tribunals) and codes of law were promulgated for the first time. Since the continued existence of the *Vecheka* could no longer be so easily justified now that communism had achieved victory in the civil war, it was necessary, as Lenin pointed out at the end of 1921, to restrict it 'to the purely political sphere'. At the same time Lenin stressed that the workers' power could not survive without some organization like the *Vecheka* – blaming this fact not on internal discontent but on the efforts of foreign powers to undermine the communist régime.[1] The *Vecheka* was accordingly in February 1922 replaced by the GPU, the State Political Directorate of the People's Commissariat of the Interior, the NKVD.

These formal changes did not alter either the power of the party to control the judicial organs, or the degree of discretionary power available to the party for the purposes of repressing opposition. Hitherto the Central Committee could ensure by direct orders, coupled with threats of expulsion, that the revolutionary tribunals, which were virtually all-communist in composition, should carry out party policy.[2] But in the case of the people's courts, of which nearly half the members were non-communists in 1923,[3] new methods were required. In large measure control could be ensured by the now much-improved party apparatus. Nominees of the party apparatus were in control of the People's Commissariat of Justice, which in turn controlled the election and recall of judges – carefully defending its own monopoly of centralized control against the attempts of local soviet and party organs to interfere with it.[4]

But the principal method of party control over the courts was

---

[1] *Lenin*, volume XXVII, pp. 139–40. A year before Lenin told a visiting Spanish socialist that a very long time, 'perhaps forty or fifty years', would be necessary in Russia for the transitional period of dictatorship – see Fernando de los Rios, *Mi viaje a la Rusia sovietista*, Second edition, Madrid, 1922, p. 63.

[2] For instances of direct party interference in the work of the courts see *Leninskii sbornik*, volume XXI, p. 223, and volume XXIII, p. 238.

[3] Kozhevnikov, *op. cit.*, pp. 130, 143. It should be noted that the chairman and deputy chairman of the provincial courts were all party members.

[4] *ibidem*, p. 128. For a graphic picture of the way in which the local party authorities exercised control over the judges see a memorandum of the Smolensk Province Party Control Commission dated 20 August 1928 quoted from the archives of the Smolensk party organization in Merle Fainsod, *Smolensk under Soviet Rule*, Cambridge, Mass., 1958, pp. 178–9.

through a system of centralized supervision over the activity of all the courts by state procurators. This system, originally instituted by Peter the Great, and virtually abolished after the liberal reforms of the judiciary in the nineteenth century, was revived in May 1922, on Lenin's initiative. In a letter to the Politburo Lenin urged that only if the procuracy were completely centralized, and independent of the control of local soviet organs, would it be possible to remedy the 'sea of lawlessness' into which the state was plunged. The remedy envisaged by Lenin (and adopted) was to create at the centre a procuracy of 'about ten reliable communists' who would work under the supervision of and in the closest contact with the party organs – the Orgburo, the Political Bureau and the Central Control Commission. Responsibility to the party congress would, he thought, be ensured through the latter.[1] Lenin failed to mention in this context the one party organ, the Secretariat, which a very short time after established its control not only over the three other organs but over the party congress as well.

As regards discretionary methods of repression, the GPU retained all the powers of its predecessor to arrest, to banish without trial to the forced labour camps (first set up, under the People's Commissariat of Internal Affairs, in April 1919), and to conduct unrestricted searches and investigations. It was common knowledge that the powers of the GPU included execution by shooting, though no decree conferring this power was ever published. The GPU was in turn succeeded in 1923 by the OGPU, or Unified State Political Directorate, and the growth of this vast apparatus of systematized terror after 1923 will be examined in later chapters.

Discretionary repressive powers were not, under the 1922 reforms, confined to the police organs but were made an integral part of normal criminal law and procedure. Again it was Lenin, ever conscious of the precarious hold of communist power, who insisted on this. It would be deception for the new criminal code to promise abolition of terror, he wrote on 17 May 1922. 'The paragraph on terror must be formulated in as wide terms as possible, since only revolutionary consciousness of justice and revolutionary conscience can determine the conditions of its application in practice.' His rough draft of the paragraph on discretionary power was duly embodied in the Criminal Code (of 1922), and has remained an integral part of criminal justice in the Soviet Union in relation to political charges ever since: 'Propaganda or agitation, or participation in an organization, or co-operation with

[1] *Lenin*, volume XXVII, pp. 298–301.

organizations, having the effect (i.e. the propaganda or agitation) of helping in the slightest way that part of the international bourgeoisie . . . which is endeavouring to overthrow [the communist system] by force, whether by intervention, or blockade, or by espionage, or by financing of the press, or by other means' – is punishable by death or imprisonment.[1] It is difficult to think of any action unwelcome to a government which cannot be brought under this loose definition. Apart from Lenin's contribution, the criminal code embodied several other articles which, by giving wide discretionary powers to the judges to convict even where no offence specified by law had been proved, in effect placed the manipulation of criminal justice in the hands of the judges, and ultimately in the hands of those who in turn controlled them – the party. Thus, by virtue of Articles 2 and 10 of the Code, the courts were given power to punish any 'socially dangerous' act, defined as any act which menaces the stability of the dictatorship of the proletariat, is an obstacle to the development of socialism, or disorganizes social relations, even where such an act is not specifically foreseen by the Code. They were to punish such acts by 'analogy' with those specific crimes foreseen by the Code which were closest to the 'socially dangerous' act. Parallel to this view of individual rights as subject always to the overriding interest of the state, the Civil Code of 1922 by virtue of Articles 1 and 4 made it clear that private rights were only 'granted' by the state (and therefore, by implication, revocable) for the purposes of developing the productive forces of the country, and were only to enjoy protection if they did not contradict their 'social and economic purpose'.

[1] *ibidem*, p. 296.

XV   Conflicts among the Leaders: First Phase[1]

The perfecting of the party apparatus, described in the last chapters, gave Stalin, who could manipulate it at all vital points, a considerable advantage over his colleagues. During Lenin's illness in 1922 the conduct of affairs lay virtually in the hands of Stalin, Zinoviev and Kamenev. All three had had long experience in the party apparatus under Lenin's immediate orders. An even greater bond between them was fear and dislike of Trotsky, a comparative newcomer to the party and an opponent of bolshevik organizational methods before the revolution. Stalin and Zinoviev, moreover, had been in personal conflict with Trotsky since 1918. The need to unite against Trotsky was rendered all the more imperative by Trotsky's qualities as a rival: his great gifts of mob oratory and his undoubted brilliance, which contrasted only too strikingly with Zinoviev's transparent demagogy, Kamenev's pedantry and Stalin's obscurity. Trotsky enjoyed a following among the army communists and among communist youth, he had played as great a part as Lenin in making the bolshevik victory possible in 1917, he was the victor in the civil war and the architect of the Red Army. His rivals now recalled with apprehension Trotsky's overbearing personality, which had manifested itself so strikingly during his period of office as People's Commissar for War. Long habit of drawing analogies from the French Revolution, to which Trotsky himself was particularly prone, perhaps strengthened the fears of Stalin, Zinoviev and Kamenev that here was the natural candidate for a 'Bonapartist' *coup*. Their anxieties were not allayed when in the autumn of 1922 Trotsky succeeded in removing his old antagonist, Gusev, from the Political Directorate of the army and replacing him by his close friend of 1917, Antonov-Ovseenko. (Gusev shortly

[1] I had the advantage in preparing this and the following chapter of using a MS. work by Robert Vincent Daniels, *The Conscience of the Revolution: the Communist Opposition and the Shaping of Soviet Russia.* I am most grateful to Mr Daniels for his generosity in putting this valuable study at my disposal. It was published in 1960 by the Harvard University Press.

afterwards entered the Central Control Commission and became a stalwart supporter of Stalin.)

But though he enjoyed the great advantage of control over the party apparatus, Stalin faced a serious obstacle: Lenin was becoming increasingly critical of his conduct. The immediate cause of Lenin's disquiet, on the evidence at present available, seems to have been the policy pursued towards Georgia by Stalin and Ordzhonikidze. Lenin's Notes on the National Question, dictated at the end of December 1922, have already been described. Apparently Stalin became aware of Lenin's change of front over the Georgian question and attempted to see the sick man. On 23 December 1922 a letter from Krupskaia to Kamenev complained of Stalin's 'rude outburst' when Krupskaia had attempted to shield her husband from Stalin's importunacy.[1] Lenin, although still able to read and dictate, took no action until 5 March 1923. On this date he sent a letter to Stalin, in which he rated him for his rudeness to Krupskaia and demanded an apology. A threat to sever all relations accompanied this demand.[2] On the same day he wrote to Trotsky to ask him to undertake the defence of the Georgian deviationists in the Central Committee.[3] Thus it was to Trotsky, the comparative newcomer, and his opponent for so many years before the revolution, that the dying Lenin now turned in desperation. Trotsky apparently agreed to Lenin's request, because on the following day Lenin forwarded to him the three Notes on the National Question which he had dictated some ten weeks before. On the same day, 6 March 1923, whether because he had insufficient faith in Trotsky or because he hoped thereby to strengthen his hand, Lenin sent a note to the leaders of the Georgian party, headed by Mdivani and Makharadze, giving his support 'with all my heart' against Ordzhonikidze, Stalin and Dzerzhinskii.[4] Stalin now made another attempt to stop Lenin from interfering in party affairs. But four days later a further stroke put Lenin out of action. So far as is known, he intervened in party wrangles no more.

A formidable threat therefore faced Stalin over the question of

[1] This letter, which was first made public by Trotsky in exile, was read to the secret session of the Twentieth Party Congress by N. S. Khrushchev. For the text see *The Anti-Stalin Campaign and International Communism*, A Selection of Documents. Edited by the Russian Institute, Columbia University. New York, 1956, p. 8. And see new Lenin works, *loc. cit.*, pp. 329–30.

[2] Also first made known to the Russian party on the same occasion – *ibidem*, pp. 8–9. It was first published in the Soviet Union in the Fifth Edition of Lenin's works: see *Lenin* (5), volume LIV, pp. 674–5.

[3] Leon Trotsky, *Stalin*. An Appraisal of the Man and his Influence. Edited and translated from the Russian by Charles Malamuth. London, 1947, p. 361.

[4] *ibidem*.

policy towards Georgia which was due to come up for discussion at the forthcoming Twelfth Party Congress, in April 1923. He was rescued by Trotsky, who with all this ammunition in his hands remained inactive. Meanwhile, fortified by the opportune stroke which had removed Lenin from the scene, Stalin had little difficulty in mid-March in securing the routing of Mdivani and Makharadze by an overwhelming vote at the Georgian party conference which preceded the All-Russian Party Congress.[1] Thus the central apparatus was evidently strong enough to ensure the desired result, in spite of Lenin's letter of support addressed to the dissident leaders. Trotsky still kept Lenin's notes to himself, and contented himself with publishing a somewhat colourless article on the national question in *Pravda* on 20 March. A few days later Trotsky, still without revealing Lenin's notes, made a protest in the Central Committee which Stalin succeeded in getting expunged from the record.[2] It was only on the eve of the Twelfth Party Congress, on 16 April, that Trotsky admitted that he had Lenin's notes in his possession, and then only after Lenin's secretary, Fotieva, had, for reasons which cannot on the evidence be explained, forwarded copies of the notes to the Politburo. At the same time Fotieva expressed the view, which she said was backed by Lenin's sister, that Lenin had not had time to revise the notes so as to put them into final form for the printers.[3] Stalin, with the support of the majority in the Politburo (though against the opposition of Bukharin), was thus provided with an excuse for not publishing the notes – much to his regret, as he said in a declaration issued at the time. The declaration also publicly blamed Trotsky for keeping them secret for so long.[4] Thus the Congress opened on 17

[1] *XII S"ezd*, p. 185.

[2] Trotsky's protest about this to the Secretariat dated 28 March 1923 is among his papers in the Library of Harvard University.

[3] Trotsky's letter to Stalin of 16 April 1923 is printed in his *Stalin*, pp. 362–3. Fotieva's covering letter to Kamenev which accompanied Lenin's Notes on the National Question was circulated with other documents to the delegates of the Twentieth Party Congress and printed together with the text of Khrushchev's secret speech to this Congress in a release by the US State Department of 4 June 1956. These and other documents were published in *Kommunist* on 30 June 1956, but the covering letters were omitted from this publication. They are therefore only known from the State Department release, but their authenticity is beyond question. All the documents are conveniently reprinted in translation in Bertram D. Wolfe, *Khruschchev and Stalin's Ghost*, New York, 1957, pp. 257–79, in a slightly amended translation. Fotieva's letters are at pp. 277–8. Fotieva's action is all the more difficult to understand, unless she was subjected to pressure, because she had previously informed Trotsky that Lenin was anxious that his notes should not become known to Stalin before the Congress – *Stalin*, p. 362. Her recently published diaries of this period throw no light on this question – see L. A. Fotieva, 'Iz vospominanii o V. I. Lenine' in *Voprosy istorii KPSS*, No. 4, 1957, pp. 146–67.

[4] Wolfe, *op. cit.*, pp. 278–9.

April with Trotsky exposed either as a coward or as a plotter. The text of Lenin's notes was unknown to the delegates, though rumours about their contents were circulating freely among them. At the Congress, which lasted until 25 April 1923, Trotsky did not utter a word on the national question. He thus failed to use an opportunity, which would never come again, of attacking Stalin and his supporters with the full authority of Lenin.

Lenin's notes were by implication referred to by most speakers in the debates at the Congress. Bitter speeches were made on the national question by the Georgian national communists. But Stalin was well prepared. The Congress was carefully packed with his own supporters, and a victory for his policy was a foregone conclusion. Of the Russians, only Bukharin defended Lenin's views. The Georgian opposition, moreover, was handicapped by the fact that the real object of criticism – the stranglehold of the party over all the life of the country – was something which they themselves had accepted and endorsed many times in the past, and which it was also becoming risky to criticize. But Makharadze was courageous enough to point out that since the single, central party 'in the final resort determines everything for all the republics', to speak of independence was meaningless. Stalin, in a very skilful speech, manœuvred between extreme views, and quoted Lenin's utterances in the past both in support of his own policy and in order to offset the damage done by the three notes – to which he made no direct reference. 'Comrades,' he ended, amidst bursts of applause, 'I must say that I have not for a long time seen a congress so united, so imbued with one idea. I regret that Comrade Lenin is not here. If he were here he would be able to say: "for twenty-five years I have been forging a party, and now here it is, complete, great and strong".' Hypocrisy could go no further. But he was not entirely wrong. The triumph of the apparatus was complete – and it was Lenin who had been its begetter.

The reasons for Trotsky's failure to carry out Lenin's injunctions and to take an open stand against Stalin have been the subject of much speculation. Trotsky himself, in his autobiography written afterwards in exile, says that, while he believed he could have won at the Twelfth Congress, he was held back by the fear that his action would have been interpreted as a move to step into Lenin's shoes, 'of which the very idea made me shudder'.[1] Another possible explanation is that he was afraid of endangering the stability of the party apparatus by the removal of Stalin. There were indeed good reasons in 1923 why

[1] L. Trotsky, *Moia zhizn'. Opyt avtobiografii*, Berlin, 1930, volume II, p. 219.

Trotsky should have hesitated to do anything likely to weaken the party dictatorship. The situation of industry was still catastrophic, and may well have seemed to Trotsky a far more urgent problem than the state of the party, whatever temporary inconveniences this might seem to entail. The grave industrial situation, in turn, was likely to produce a recrudescence of worker opposition to the whole party hierarchy. This opposition had only been driven underground by the Eleventh Congress. Trotsky certainly had no wish for such allies as the Workers' Opposition, for whom he had a withering contempt. Serious doctrinal differences among the party theoreticians (which are dealt with later) were also not very far below the surface. Apart from this, Trotsky did not view the policy of Stalin and Ordzhonikidze in Georgia with the same disfavour as Lenin. Some time before Lenin's notes were forwarded to the Politburo, he had discussed them with Kamenev, and told him that the last thing he wanted was conflict at the Congress. 'I am against removing Stalin,' he said. He seems also to have reached some agreement with Kamenev that policy in Georgia would in some respects be modified and that Stalin would apologize to Krupskaia.[1] But, if so, the breach of this agreement does not appear to have moved him into action.

Lenin, during the few months of 1922 when he was able to work, did not confine his criticism of his colleagues, or limit his views on the future of the communist régime, to the question of nationalities. He also left behind comments on the question of the succession, on the reorganization which he wished to see in the party machine and on the future of economic policy. Since much of the political struggle of the next few years was to centre around these pronouncements of Lenin, it is necessary to examine his views on each of these questions. On 24 and 25 December 1922 Lenin dictated a note which formed one of a series on party reorganization, in which he set down his judgement on a number of his colleagues. In this note he warned that the main threat to the stability of the party leadership lay in the relationship between Stalin and Trotsky. On the one hand Stalin had concentrated 'enormous power' in his hands and was not always sufficiently cautious in using it; Trotsky, on the other hand, 'the most able man in the present Central Committee', was liable to be too self-confident and to be too much attracted by the purely administrative side of affairs. With regard to other leaders, he emphasized that 'the October episode' should not be held against Zinoviev and Kamenev. Bukharin he characterized as 'the most significant

[1] *ibidem*, pp. 222–5.

275

theoretician' in the party, if somewhat scholastic and weak on dialectics, while Piatakov, though very able, was too much given to administrative questions to be reliable 'in a serious political question'. On 4 January 1923, following upon Stalin's attempts to lobby him over the question, he dictated a postscript: 'Stalin is too rude', and this was insupportable in the General Secretary. 'Therefore, I propose to the comrades to think out some way of removing Stalin from this position,' since this apparent 'trifle' might otherwise lead to a split in the party leadership.[1] This note and postscript, which were expressly intended as a directive for the forthcoming party congress, remained secret for over a year from all members of the party, so far as is known, except Krupskaia and the two secretaries to whom they were dictated, one of whom was Fotieva. None of the three, however, revealed the existence of this note, or 'Testament', as it became known.

Lenin's views on party organization and on economic policy were contained in several further notes dictated about the same time, and in two articles which, with some reluctance on the part of the Central Committee, were published in *Pravda* on 25 January and 4 March 1923. So far as the party was concerned, his main preoccupations were his fear of a possible division in the top leadership, and his concern over the bureaucratic, corrupt and incompetent behaviour of those who were employed in party and government organs. The first remedy which he proposed was to increase the membership of the Central Committee to fifty, 'or even a hundred', by the inclusion mainly of workers and peasants. His proposal for obviating bureaucratic tendencies in the party was to elect a new Central Control Commission, also composed of workers and peasants. At the same time he urged that the Commissariat of Workers' and Peasants' Inspection, the vast engine of control which up till 1922 was headed by Stalin, and of which Lenin had for some time past been very critical, should also be restocked with some 300 to 400 employees selected for their high calibre. The two instruments of control should not only work very closely together, but should be organically fused. Moreover, the plenary sessions of the enlarged Central Committee should become something in the nature of party conferences, meeting every two months. The Central Control Commission should participate in its deliberations.[2] His aim was thus twofold: to infuse proletarian and

[1] See *Lenin*, Fourth Edition, volume XXXVI, pp. 543–6. The first three notes together are headed 'Letter to the Congress', and the first line of the first note reads: 'I would very much advise this Congress to undertake a number of changes in our political structure.'

[2] *ibidem.*

peasant blood into the policy-making and inspection organs of the party, and to dilute the influence of the top party leaders. He seems to have shown no awareness of the fact that the real centre of power in the party was shifting to the party secretariat and its network of secretaries.

The keynote of Lenin's last known thoughts on the economic problem was the need to preserve at all costs the union between the peasants and the workers which NEP was intended to bring about. As he repeatedly asserted, if this union failed, the results would be disastrous. The solution for agriculture, he wrote in January 1923, lay in the development of co-operation. Since political power was now in the hands of the workers, co-operation would acquire an entirely different character from that contemplated by Utopians like Robert Owen, who imagined that one could achieve socialism through co-operation without capture of political power by the proletariat. But co-operation in Russia would be possible only after a 'cultural revolution' among the peasants, since the social and political revolution had preceded the cultural transformation of the peasantry.[1] With regard to industry, Lenin had little to say. But in a further series of notes dictated at the end of December 1922 (which remained unpublished until 1956) he suggested that the State Planning Commission (*Gosplan*) which had been set up in 1921, but which had not yet begun to function, should be given legislative powers, subject only to a limited right of the Central Executive Committee to override it.[2] This view went some way towards meeting a suggestion for enlarging the powers of *Gosplan* which Trotsky had been advancing for some time against the opposition of most of his colleagues. Lenin also at the end of his life placed great faith in the electrification of the country as a means of strengthening socialism.

Discussion of changes to be made in the higher party organs began in the Politburo at the end of January 1923, and formed one of the principal subjects of debate at the Twelfth Congress in April. Stalin presented the main report. It was in his interest to support Lenin's plan for the enlargement of the Central Committee and for the subordination of the Politburo to the larger body. For of the seven Politburo members, Lenin was ill, Trotsky was a lone figure, Tomskii had no weight, thus leaving Stalin dependent on the precarious support of Rykov, Zinoviev and Kamenev. In the Central Committee of twenty-seven, moreover, there existed, according to Stalin, a

---

[1] 'O kooperatsii', *Lenin*, volume XXVII, pp. 391–7.
[2] *Lenin*, Fourth Edition, volume XXXVI, pp. 548–51.

'hard core' of up to fifteen who were in danger of becoming the 'high priests of party leadership'. They were, in fact, supporters of Zinoviev. Stalin's proposal to enlarge the Central Committee to forty members and nineteen candidates by the inclusion of 'local party workers' seemed eminently reasonable, as did also the subordination of the Politburo to the Central Committee. It had the advantage, moreover, of coinciding with Lenin's wishes. The Central Control Commission was also enlarged to fifty, and provision was made for the participation of its members in Central Committee plenary meetings. Provision was also made for the integration of the Central Control Commission with the Workers' and Peasants' Inspection.

The enlargement of these organs, mainly to the benefit of officials in the party network who owed their careers to the Secretariat which Stalin controlled, considerably strengthened his supporters. It soon became the normal practice for the enlarged Central Committee and the Central Control Commission to deliberate and vote jointly at plenary meetings. Stalin had thus little cause to fear the 'hard core'. He was also successful in strengthening his position in the Politburo; of the four candidate members, of whom Bukharin now became one, three, Kalinin, Molotov and Rudzutak, were all good 'Stalinists'. Although the resolution adopted on Stalin's report paid lip service to the need to promote workers, in practice the great majority promoted were, as hitherto, intellectuals. Lenin's main proposal had therefore been tacitly ignored. Nor was there any discussion of the organization and powers of the Secretariat. But important reforms went ahead after the Congress. A further step was taken to improve the efficiency of the apparatus by the setting up of a school for the training of local part secretaries – who were still, in theory, supposed to be elected.[1]

Although at the Twelfth Congress isolated voices were raised in criticism, there was scarcely any opposition to all these proposals. Zinoviev lectured potential critics and reminded them that the dictatorship was there to stay for ten years at least. He explained that 'left' criticism had now become 'objectively' the same as menshevik criticism. Trotsky, having failed to fight Stalin on the nationality issue, consistently refrained from expressing any criticism. When one of his supporters publicly voiced his apprehension that Trotsky was being edged out at the top, Trotsky went to great lengths to repudiate the suggestion.

His main concern at the Congress was with the industrial situation, which was indeed becoming serious. At the root of the crisis lay the

[1] *KPSS v rez.,* volume I, p. 729.

fact that while prosperity was reviving in agriculture, industry was stagnating for lack of capital to restore the ravages of the revolution and the civil war. The result was a shortage of goods to supply the peasants' demands, with a consequent fall in agricultural prices and a corresponding steep rise in industrial prices. This economic predicament acquired the name of the 'scissors' crisis – a vivid description used by Trotsky to characterize the lines on a graph which showed agricultural and industrial prices rapidly diverging after August 1922. Trotsky, who made the main report on industry and was received with boisterous applause, had the satisfaction of seeing his Theses advocating a better planned industrial policy adopted by the Congress.[1] Since the policy which they expressed was not in the event implemented this victory was to prove of little worth.

But although the Congress presented a fairly united appearance, there were sufficient indications that the harmony rested on slight foundations. The hope that Lenin would still return to work (and Kamenev, whether truthfully or not, had given the Congress an optimistic prognosis) prevented the very real divisions from causing disunity. A number of delegates felt, and some said so, that the stifling of party criticism, and the practice of appointment instead of election in filling party offices, was having the effect of driving opposition underground, and hence would lead to groups and factions forming. The communists employed in the state economic organs felt uneasiness because economic enterprises were not allowed greater freedom from party interference so that they could develop more efficiency. There was also a fundamental disagreement on economic policy which Trotsky's Theses did little to obviate and which, in a form distorted by the power struggle, was to dominate party discussions until the end of 1927. The basic problem was how to find the capital to restore and develop industry. Zinoviev at the Congress was optimistic about the prospects of developing both foreign trade and loans from foreign capitalists in the form of concessions, but few were convinced of the reality of these expectations.

The view accepted by the official party leaders, Zinoviev, Kamenev and Stalin, and of which Bukharin later became the principal theoretical exponent, was founded on the bedrock principle that nothing must be done to antagonize the peasants. The peasant sector of the economy should be encouraged to prosper, and thereby enabled to provide by its purchasing power the capital for industry. True, this would mean that industry producing goods for the peasants'

[1] *ibidem*, pp. 687–705.

consumption would recover first, but a prosperous consumer goods industry would in turn enable a heavy producer goods industry to expand. Basically this was not very far from the views of Lenin. The left-wing view, of which Preobrazhenskii became the main advocate, was founded squarely on the primacy of heavy industry. According to this view, there was danger in giving the peasants too much freedom of choice in the market, since this could enable them to hold the régime up to ransom. Preobrazhenskii advocated a system of enforced saving, which should be directed at extracting their money from the peasants in order to finance heavy industry. The counterpart of what Marx called 'primitive capitalist accumulation', or the various techniques which capitalist systems used in order to extract capital from the economy, was 'primitive socialist accumulation'. Preobrazhenskii, however, recognized that there was a barrier to socialist accumulation, since the victorious working class 'cannot treat its labour power . . . in the same way as capitalism did'. Trotsky's position was close to the left view, since he also recognized that 'only the development of industry creates an unshakeable foundation for the dictatorship of the proletariat'. He urged the need for an overall planned economy, which would make possible a balanced development of both the free and the socialized sectors.[1]

These divergent theories, though not fully developed at the Congress, were already implicit in the muffled debates which took place. One factor which helped to preserve unity was the existence of continued underground menshevik activity, and of two communist underground movements – the Workers' Truth and the Workers' Group. The latter group had even succeeded in disseminating its covert appeals among the Congress delegates. Against such a threat to their authority the whole party was ready to unite. The Workers' Truth, more intellectual in its composition, was mainly inspired by the ideas of Bogdanov. (Lenin's ally until their quarrel in 1909. Bogdanov had long abandoned active politics, and was now engaged in medical research.) It attacked the 'new bourgeoisie' of party workers, factory directors and the like, whom it accused of exploiting

[1] Trotsky's views appear from the Theses which were adopted. For Preobrazhenskii's views see Alexander Erlich, 'Preobrazhenskii and the Economics of Soviet Industrialization', in *The Quarterly Journal of Economics*, volume LXIV, February 1950, No. 1, pp. 57–8; and Alexander Erlich, *The Soviet Industrialization Debate 1924–1928*, Cambridge, Mass., 1960. See also E. Probrazhensky, *The New Economics*. Translated by Brian Pearce, with an Introduction by A. Nove, Oxford, 1965. Bukharin's views were most fully formulated in his 'The Way to Socialism and the Worker Peasant Bloc', which has only been available to me in the French translation, *Le Chemin du Socialisme et le Bloc Ouvrier-Paysan*, Paris, 1925.

the toiling masses. Its aim was to form cells within party and trade union organizations so as to help the proletariat to acquire the necessary class consciousness to make itself fit to govern.[1] The Workers' Group, which was entirely proletarian in its composition, had been founded by a stormy petrel of the opposition, Miasnikov, after his expulsion from the party for his part in the appeal of the Twenty-Two to the Comintern. This group also attacked the exploitation of the workers by the privileged party bureaucrats. But in addition it advocated freedom for all socialist parties (not for liberals – 'for professors, lawyers and doctors there is only one remedy – to push their faces in'), freedom of discussion, and the election of new soviets centred on the factories. There was much that was likely to appeal to the workers in these vigorous programmes, and the two groups were active in the strikes which took place in the summer and autumn, until they were both liquidated by the GPU in September.[2] No party leader publicly questioned the legitimacy of employing the police against dissatisfied workers, and the majority of the Central Committee expressly approved it.

The harmony which appeared on the surface of the party at the Twelfth Congress did not last long. The Central Committee, which in September 1923 discussed the problem of dealing with the two worker opposition groups, also had three other problems to deal with: the problem of wages, the 'scissors' crisis, and the general discontent inside the party over the disappearance of democracy in party life. Its deliberations, which had the immediate result of precipitating opposition into the open, were also overshadowed by events in the sphere of foreign relations. A sub-committee which dealt with the 'scissors' problem proposed measures which were in the short term successful: but, since they consisted in forcing down industrial prices and at the same time increasing the purchasing power of the peasants, they ran directly counter to the views of the left-wing theorists, who accordingly boycotted this sub-committee.[3] The sub-committee on internal

---

[1] These doctrines of the Workers' Truth derived from Jan Waclaw Machajski, as expounded by him in his pamphlet, *Umstvennyi rabochii*, which was published in 1904 under the name of A. Volskii.

[2] On the views of the Workers' Truth, see their appeal, printed in *Sotsialisticheskii vestnik* (Berlin), No. 3 (49), January 1923, and No. 19 (65), October 1923. On the Workers' Group see V. L. Sorin, *Rabochaia Gruppa (Miasnikovshchina)*, Moscow, 1924 (with a preface by Bukharin), where long extracts from their Manifesto of February 1923 were reprinted from the records of the GPU. See also *Izv.Ts.K.*, No. 9–10, 1923, pp. 13–16.

[3] For details on the work of this sub-Committee and the right-wing nature of its report, see Edward Hallett Carr, *The Interregnum 1923–1924*, London, 1954, pp. 104–17.

party questions, which was headed by Dzerzhinskii, likewise antagonized the left. It tabled a proposal to cure discontent in the party by increased discipline, including a suggestion that party members should be obliged to disclose to the GPU any information in their possession on the existence of factions or groups.[1]

Meanwhile, the alliance between Zinoviev and Stalin, which had already been subjected to some strain when Stalin successfully swamped Zinoviev's supporters on the Central Committee, was again shaken. In the late summer, or early autumn, Zinoviev made a clumsy move to outmanœuvre Stalin. At a meeting in the Caucasus with a group of party leaders which included Bukharin and Voroshilov (who subsequently made the discussions public) and his own close supporters Lashevich and Evdokimov, he discussed measures to prevent the Secretariat from becoming too powerful. Stalin, to whom the gist of these talks was formally communicated, handled the situation in masterly fashion. He first offered to resign, fully confident that his offer would be refused, and that the refusal would demonstrate once again how dependent the party was for its continued survival on his administrative skill. A compromise was then reached, whereby Trotsky, Bukharin and Zinoviev were taken into the Orgburo. It proved of no practical importance, and neither Trotsky nor Bukharin in the event ever attempted to interfere in what to them was an alien sphere, the apparatus. Even Zinoviev only attended two meetings.[2]

On 8 October Trotsky served a declaration of war on the Central Committee and on its *alter ego*, the Central Control Commission.[3] The immediate occasion for it was Dzerzhinskii's proposal in the subcommittee that party members should act as informers for the GPU. But Trotsky's decision to do now what he had not attempted to do at the Party Congress may also have been provoked by an effort to undermine his influence in the army which had been made shortly before, apparently at Zinoviev's instigation. Trotsky's declaration blamed the dictatorship of the Secretariat for the unrest in the party, announced his intention of making his views at long last known far and wide to party members, and hinted that a change of leaders was desirable. He also attributed discontent among the proletariat to faulty industrial policy. A week later the Politburo received the so-called

[1] This appears from Trotsky's declaration of 8 October 1923, to which reference is made below.
[2] These facts were made public at the Fourteenth Party Congress in the following year.
[3] The full text of this letter was never published, and no copy of it is to be found among Trotsky's papers in Harvard Library. Long extracts were published in *Sotsialisticheskii vestnik*, No. 11 (81) of 24 May 1924, and by Max Eastman.

Declaration of the Forty-Six which may have been stimulated by Trotsky's action. This document criticized the 'inadequacy of the party leadership' in dealing with the economic crisis, and the 'completely intolerable' régime inside the party. The dictatorship of one faction of the party, which had been accepted at the Tenth Congress, had now, it was alleged, 'outlived itself', and the signatories demanded a party conference representing all shades of opinion to discuss what should be done. Of the signatories to this declaration, most of whom were to support Trotsky in the struggles which lay ahead, the majority were old left-wingers who had at one time supported either Trotsky's position or that of the Democratic Centralists in the trade union dispute of 1921 – such as Preobrazhenskii, Serebriakov, Osinskii, Bubnov and Sapronov. A great number of them were employed in the higher economic organs of the state.[1] It was a challenge which, unlike Trotsky's, could not be met by allegations of personal ambition.

At a discussion of the two declarations at the end of October at a joint Plenum of the Central Committee and the Central Control Commission, Stalin, sure of his majority, had no difficulty in securing an overwhelming vote condemning Trotsky's move as a 'grave political mistake' and the Declaration of the Forty-Six as a 'factional' move, threatening the party with disunity at a moment of danger.[2] At the same time, Stalin and his supporters pretended readily to accept the need for greater democracy in the party, and during the whole of November a spate of articles, resolutions and reports of meetings discussed the best way to achieve this end. On 5 December the Politburo purported to terminate the discussion by adopting a resolution which seemed to go some way towards meeting the views of the opposition on economic questions; and fully accepted the need to reform the party in the direction of greater democracy.[3] Indeed, almost every criticism put forward by the opposition was incorporated in this resolution, which in its terms recalled the resolutions on party democracy once adopted by the Tenth Congress in 1921, in a similar endeavour to pacify critics.

At this point Trotsky played into Stalin's hands. He had been absent from the October discussions through illness, but the text of the Politburo resolution was discussed with him and approved by

---

[1] There is a copy of this declaration among Trotsky's papers, and another in the International Institute for Social History at Amsterdam, of which a translation by Professor E. H. Carr is printed by him, *op. cit.*, at pp. 367–73.

[2] *KPSS v rez.*, volume I, pp. 767–8.

[3] *Pravda*, 7 December 1923. The resolution was issued in the names of the Central Committee and Central Control Commission.

him – though Trotsky apparently reserved his rights to urge upon the party that the reform must be 'pushed from below'.[1] On 8 December Trotsky wrote a letter entitled 'The New Course', which was published in *Pravda* on 11 December. (It was subsequently also published as a pamphlet.) Although ostensibly a warm endorsement of the pious hypocrisies of the resolution of 5 December, Trotsky's article was plainly directed against the party apparatus and the all-powerful secretaries. The main argument of 'The New Course' was that democracy inside the party would never come about through the efforts of the party machine. The party itself must subordinate the machine to its control, make it the executant of the collective will, and renovate it by clearing out the bureaucrats who were stifling all criticism. There was also a significant appeal to the young generation to keep the old guard on the revolutionary path – significant, because Trotsky enjoyed a good deal of personal following among the young communists in the army and in the universities. 'The New Course' also contained passages calculated to appeal to the communist economists and industrialists, in which Trotsky argued that only party democracy could lead to real party guidance of economic enterprises. The present system of rule by secretaries could only result in inefficiency through inept interference. This was, in substance, the argument of the Forty-Six. What Trotsky did not say in 'The New Course', though he was repeatedly to be accused of it, was that groups or factions should be allowed inside the party.

It was a clumsy challenge, doomed to failure. It could not now hope to carry the party behind it (as a challenge with Lenin's authority behind it might have done eight months previously at the Party Congress) because party decisions could be manipulated by the apparatus which Trotsky could not control. There was little chance that Trotsky, with his reputation for ruthless dictatorship, could have evoked any response from the many discontented proletarians, both inside and outside the party, who saw nothing to choose between him and Stalin. Nor was it likely that Trotsky, who never doubted the need for the communist party to preserve its monopoly of power, would seek to appeal to these workers. An intensive discussion in the press and at meetings (in which Trotsky took virtually no part) followed the publication of 'The New Course'. In this discussion, in spite of Trotsky's considerable following, the dice were loaded in

---

[1] Max Eastman, *Since Lenin Died*, London, 1925, p. 39. (The information contained in this book was for the most part derived from Trotsky, and most of it has subsequently been confirmed from other sources.)

favour of the apparatus, since it could control both the voting at meetings and often what appeared in the party press. The main allegation now made against the opposition was one which was in fact untrue – that they were aiming at setting up a separate group or faction in the party. But this was the time-honoured method of dealing with critics which Lenin had first used with success at the Tenth Congress in 1921.

The discussion culminated in a party conference, the Thirteenth, which met between 16 and 18 January 1924. It was a hand-picked gathering. Trotsky was still absent through illness. The few spokesmen for the opposition, none of whom had a vote, did not conceal that they knew that the defeat of their views was a foregone conclusion. A resolution condemning Trotsky and the opposition was adopted against only three dissenting votes. Stalin, who led the attack, was stoutly supported by Zinoviev and Kamenev. Two ominous warnings to the oppositionists were sounded at this conference. One was the publication, on Stalin's own initiative, of the secret clause in the resolution of the Tenth Party Congress relating to expulsion from the party for 'factional' activity. The other was a sentence in the resolution passed at the conference which prescribed 'decisive measures' against those who circulated 'forbidden documents'. Lenin's 'Testament', with all its explosive implications, was still unknown in the party, though it is a not improbable hypothesis that Stalin was aware of its existence. The resolution on economic policy also represented a rebuff to the left-wing theorists. It emphasized peasant support as the keystone of the proletarian dictatorship. While stressing the need for improved planning, it sought to deal with the economic crisis not by intensive development of heavy industry, but by price control, stabilization of the currency, and the development of agricultural prosperity. This was intended to provide both exports and a market for industrial products, and thus eventually the capital for the building up of heavy industry.[1]

On 21 January, three days after the conference had concluded its labours, Lenin died. There was no immediate problem of succession. The three leaders, Stalin, Zinoviev and Kamenev, were firmly entrenched, and for the time being united. Stalin, now committed to the right-wing course in economic policy, could also count on the support of its main exponent, Bukharin (who was a candidate member), and of Rykov, another right-winger, who replaced Lenin as Chairman of the

[1] *KPSS v rez.*, volume I, pp. 778–802. For the secret clause of the 1921 resolution see *ibidem*, pp. 529–30.

Council of People's Commissars. Trotsky, already discredited by the failure of his attack, was further weakened by the expulsion of his supporters from the student party organizations and from the organs of the Communist Youth Organization, as well as by the removal of his ally, Antonov-Ovseenko, and his supporters, from the political directorate of the army (PUR).

Lenin's death provided Stalin with the opportunity which he required to inaugurate a new cult of 'Leninism'. Its external trappings were in marked contrast to the genuine lack of ostentation which always characterized Lenin – the hieratical oaths of loyalty to his memory, the embalming of his corpse in a mausoleum in Moscow, the renaming of Petrograd. Trotsky's failure to attend Lenin's funeral, whether as he says[1] because he was deceived over the date, or because of paralysis of will, despair and distress, helped Stalin immediately to assume the leadership of the cult. The purpose of the new cult was clear to all: if Lenin was Allah, then Stalin was his prophet. Along with the innumerable portraits and busts of Lenin which the party propaganda machinery flung into circulation, went the familiar photograph (even to the inexpert eye, a composite photograph) of Lenin and Stalin smiling side by side in serene friendship, in the summer of 1922. Those few who knew the true course of relations between Lenin and Stalin wisely kept their peace. But it was indicative of the state of mind of the party that a flood of rumours circulated in Moscow – Lenin had asked for poison, Lenin had revealed before his death that he had been poisoned, Lenin had recovered sufficiently to come to Moscow and pay a visit to his office in October 1923 (this fact at least was true) and had discovered that his papers had been rifled.[2]

The theoretical foundations of Leninism were now also laid. A new journal, *Bol'shevik*, came into existence, with the avowed object of combating 'Trotskyism'. In April 1924 Stalin delivered a series of lectures in Moscow, at the Communist University named after Sverdlov, which under the title 'Foundations of Leninism' became the first canon of Stalinist orthodoxy. Their main stress was on the need for unity and discipline in the party, on the role of the party as leader of the masses, and on the vital need to preserve the support of the peasants for the proletarian dictatorship. All of these points could

[1] *Moia zhizn'*, volume II, p. 250.

[2] In his *Stalin*, which Trotsky did not get time to complete before his assassination in August 1940, Trotsky suggests that Stalin may have poisoned Lenin – see pp. 370–83, where the various rumours in support of this view are collected. Many other rumours of the kind indicated in the text were current at the time in party circles close to the top, and I have also used the unpublished memoirs of N. Valentinov (N. V. Vol'skii).

with justice be described as Lenin's. New and more startling additions would before long be made to the canon as occasion required it. Along with the perfection of theory went improvements in organization (which are described later) – the purging of oppositionists, and the swamping of the party by the admission of over two hundred thousand young new members, who could be relied on to be amenable to the guidance of the secretaries. Another success in the policy of insurance against Trotsky was the appointment in the spring of 1924 of one of Trotsky's main opponents in military questions, Frunze, as Deputy Commissar for War. With virtually no resistance from Trotsky, Frunze became the *de facto* Commissar long before Trotsky's actual removal from this post in January 1925. There was little reason for Stalin to anticipate any serious opposition at the forthcoming Party Congress, the Thirteenth, which was due to meet on 23 May 1924.

A few days before the Congress opened, Krupskaia forwarded to the Politburo the notes which Lenin had dictated between 23 December 1922 and 23 January 1923, including the so-called 'Testament'. She explained that she had suppressed the two notes constituting the latter (some of the other notes had meanwhile already been published) because Lenin had expressed the 'definite wish' that these notes should be submitted to the next Party Congress 'after his death'.[1] A commission of the Central Committee could hardly do otherwise than decide that the notes should be laid before the Congress, but by an adroit manœuvre the notes were in fact only read, with suitable comments, to leaders of delegations to the Congress.[2] Immediately after the Congress Stalin boldly offered his resignation to the Central Committee, in view of Lenin's strictures, but the whole Central Committee, including Trotsky, according to Stalin's account three years later, insisted that he should remain in this post.[3] For the time being embarrassment was avoided (no mention was made of the notes at the Congress sessions), but they were to be heard of again before very long.

The Thirteenth Congress was a model of unanimity. In part this was due to careful organization. None of the opposition speakers

---

[1] See her letter of 18 May 1924, reprinted in Wolfe, *op. cit.*, pp. 258–9. Her statement that Lenin had intended them to be submitted to the next Congress after his death is plainly at variance with the intention expressed in the Notes by Lenin that they should be taken into account by the forthcoming, i.e. the Eleventh Congress.

[2] See L. Trotsky, *The Suppressed Testament of Lenin*, With Two Explanatory Articles, New York, 1935, pp. 11–12, 17. See also Boris Bazhanov, *Stalin. Der Rote Diktator*. Berlin, 1931, pp. 30–4, according to which Stalin was rescued by the intervention of Zinoviev. (Bazhanov was a former official of the Central Committee apparatus, and claimed to have been Stalin's personal secretary.)

[3] *Stalin*, volume X, pp. 175–6.

present was entitled to vote, though a few, including Trotsky and Preobrazhenskii and six other signatories of the Declaration of the Forty-Six, were present as non-voting delegates. But there was also a marked desire for unanimity in face of the shock caused by the loss of Lenin's leadership. This was the keynote of Trotsky's rather weak defence of his position. He made no confession of error, as some demanded he should, but contented himself with a declaration of loyalty: 'My party – right or wrong . . . I know one cannot be right against the party . . . for history has not created other ways for the realization of what is right.' The somewhat bolder Preobrazhenskii was met with a torrent of invective. But even Krupskaia, who had only just seen Lenin's wishes flouted, contented herself with urging moderation in polemics. Evidently Stalin's argument that 'to declare war on the party apparatus . . . means the destruction of the party' was recognized by all as little short of the plain truth.

The Congress made few changes in the party leadership. Bukharin replaced Lenin in the Politburo, and the new candidate members were Frunze, Dzerzhinskii and Sokol'nikov, the Commissar of Finance. The size of the Central Committee was raised from forty to fifty-three members, and from seventeen to thirty-four candidates. Those elevated were mainly men from the provincial apparatus who had proved their loyalty to Stalin. The most spectacular rise was that of Kaganovich, Stalin's right hand in the Central Committee apparatus. He now became a full member of the Central Committee, and a member both of the Secretariat and of the Orgburo. The Control Commission, of which the importance was rapidly increasing, was also trebled in size. The only casualty among oppositionists in the Central Committee was Radek, a known supporter of Trotsky. But he was removed not for his political activities at home but for the failure of the communist uprising in Germany in October 1923, for which he was conveniently blamed.

Meanwhile there was further signs that the triumvirate which had ruled Russia since Lenin's illness was not as united as when they had joined against Trotsky. It was perhaps to conceal the friction that Zinoviev had gone out of his way at the Congress to express his solidarity with Stalin. But Zinoviev had never felt at ease about the way in which Stalin had at the Twelfth Congress successfully counterbalanced his 'hard core' group in the Central Committee. Nor is it likely that Stalin had forgotten Zinoviev's initiative in convening the meeting in the Caucasus in the summer of 1923. Stalin's first hint that the other two members of the triumvirate were inferior in status to himself was dropped in a speech in June 1924. Both Zinoviev and Kamenev were criticized for mistakes in doctrine. Zinoviev, although not named, was censured for the error of identifying the dictatorship of the party with the dictatorship of the proletariat (an identification, incidentally, expressly made in a resolution of the Twelfth Congress a year before). Kamenev had made the mistake of referring to the need of transforming a Russia of 'Nepmen' into a Russia of socialism – thus implying that there was no socialism as yet (although, incidentally, Lenin used a very similar expression in 1922).[1] Apart from these theoretical and quite dishonest niceties, a more concrete move was made by Stalin in the late summer of 1924 when Kamenev's supporter, Zelenskii, the secretary of the Moscow party organization (where Kamenev was chairman of the executive committee of the soviet), was sent off to Central Asia and replaced by Uglanov.

In face of these attacks, Zinoviev, according to his own account, organized a meeting of some fifteen 'bolshevik-Leninists', which condemned Stalin's 'uncomradely' action. Some effort was then made to work out a *modus vivendi* with Stalin which came to nothing. Stalin, secure in his majority both in the Politburo and in the Central Committee, parried the move by branding it as an attempt to undermine collective leadership and replace party democracy by dictatorship.[2] It was evident that a more determined attack by Stalin would not be long delayed.

[1] *Stalin*, volume VI, pp. 257–8. For the resolution of the Twelfth Congress see *KPSS v rez.*, volume I, p. 683: 'The dictatorship of the working class can only be assured in the form of the dictatorship of its vanguard, the Communist Party.' According to Stalin, this formulation crept in by mistake. The argument that the effect of NEP had been to create state capitalism which, so long as political power is vested in the proletariat, is the sure road to socialism, was the main content of Lenin's speech to the Eleventh Party Congress.

[2] According to his own account at the Fourteenth Congress – *XIV S"ezd*, pp. 454–5.

XVI   The Defeat of Trotsky

By the autumn of 1924 relations between Stalin on the one hand and
Zinoviev and Kamenev on the other were nearing breaking point.
But two circumstances prevented a split at this stage between the
members of the triumvirate. The first was the outbreak on 27 August
1924 of a rising in Georgia. It had been carefully prepared, under
menshevik leadership, and was directed against the communist dictatorship which had been imposed by force of arms in 1921 and never
accepted by the population. The rising was easily put down by the
Red Army. It happened opportunely to enable Stalin to rally support
by raising the cry of 'Kronstadt', and also to argue that since the rising
was a peasant rising (a statement which conveniently ignored the fact
that insurrection also took place among the proletariat in the manga-
nese mines), the only policy to pursue in the USSR was the policy of
the 'right' – reconciliation with the peasants at all costs.

But the main saviour of the unity of the triumvirate in the autumn
of 1924 was probably Trotsky. About the time of the seventh anniversary of the bolshevik seizure of power he published a collection of
essays, entitled *1917*, prefaced by an introduction entitled 'Lessons of
October'. In this introduction Trotsky developed, by means of historical analogies, a theme which was to become his main obsession in later
years – the betrayal of the revolution by the 'right'. He drew a parallel
between the failure of the uprising in Germany in 1923 and the
opposition of some bolsheviks, notably Zinoviev and Kamenev, to
Lenin's plan for the uprising in October 1917. In each case the fault
was the same – the 'menshevik' position of those who lacked revolutionary courage. Moreover, by implication the whole 'right' policy
towards the peasants was thus branded as unrevolutionary. Since an
attack of this nature was certain to drive Zinoviev and Kamenev back
into close alliance with Stalin, the publication of 'Lessons of October'
was a political blunder. On the other hand, as Zinoviev later admitted
both to Trotsky and to some of his supporters, 'Lessons of October'
was merely a convenient pretext for Zinoviev and Kamenev, since
they had already decided before its publication that they were going

to utilize Trotsky's old dissensions with Lenin for the purposes of re-opening an attack on Trotsky.[1] That Trotsky's point was a telling one, in a party where traditionally only the most revolutionary could claim to be a good bolshevik, became evident from the avalanche of attacks on 'Trotskyism' which now ensued. Stalin led the attack, and the whole machinery of party propaganda was mobilized to develop it. The pamphlet itself was virtually suppressed, and the opponents of Trotsky enjoyed the advantage of being able to criticize him on the basis of quotations torn from their context. Trotsky, plunged into a fit of depression and despair, made hardly any attempt to answer his attackers – the one reasoned reply which he wrote remained unpublished.[2]

Stalin skated lightly over the sins of Zinoviev and Kamenev, even going to the length of admitting (as was indeed the case) that he too had wavered for a time over the correct policy in March 1917 before Lenin's arrival in Petrograd.[3] Trotsky's appeal to history was a dangerous move, when the 'facts' of history could so easily become what the party leaders wished them to be. Stalin now began the process of denigrating Trotsky's role in the seizure of power and in the civil war. The leading part played by Trotsky in October 1917 had hitherto never been questioned, and had indeed been publicly acknowledged by Stalin in an anniversary article in *Pravda* in 1918.[4] This role, Stalin now alleged, had been greatly exaggerated – Trotsky's contribution to victory was no more than that of any other bolshevik. The real leadership of the rising had been in the hands of a group of five, including Stalin, but not Trotsky, which the Central Committee had set up to maintain liaison with the Petrograd soviet. This travesty of the facts (the group of five, the so-called 'Centre', is not known ever to have functioned at all) was only the first step in the campaign. Before many years the history of October would be progressively rewritten to show that Trotsky had been a traitor already in 1917, and that indeed Stalin was the main architect of victory.

The heresies in doctrine alleged against Trotsky were mainly three. They were not all thought up at the same time, nor all fully developed at once, but in one form or another they provided the basis for attacks

---

[1] *Biulleten' oppozitsii*, No. 9, February–March 1930, p. 32.
[2] The MS. of this article, 'Nashi raznoglasiia', is among Trotsky's papers in Harvard Library.
[3] In a speech on 19 November 1924 – see *Stalin*, volume VI, p. 333.
[4] See *Pravda*, 6 November 1918. Compare this article as reprinted in Stalin's collected works years later where the passage referring to Trotsky as the man mainly responsible for the success of the *coup* was omitted – *Stalin*, volume IV, pp. 152–4.

on 'Trotskyism', so long as this remained an aspect of the struggle for power. The first of these heresies was discovered in Trotsky's adherence in 1905–6 to the doctrine (which went back to Marx) of permanent revolution. Trotsky, it will be recalled, had then argued that the task of the social democrats was not to relax their efforts after the bourgeois revolution had been accomplished, but to continue straight on with their attempts to bring about the next phase, the social revolution. This was in fact precisely the policy followed by Lenin after February 1917. But in 1905 and after, Lenin, mainly for tactical reasons, had attacked Trotsky's views as 'semi-anarchist', and had advanced his own theory of 'revolutionary democratic dictatorship of the proletariat and peasantry'. Raking up the old controversy was designed to show that Lenin and Trotsky were poles apart in 1905.[1] From this it was an easy step to the next heresy – 'underestimating the peasants'. In 1905 Trotsky had argued that the peasants were by nature bourgeois, and would therefore always have to be led by the proletariat. Again, it was obvious that the policy followed by Lenin not only in 1917, but during the civil war and even under NEP, when the economic concessions to the peasants had not been accompanied by any political concessions, was based on the firm conviction that the peasant was an incorrigible bourgeois. But again, in 1905 and after, Lenin had attacked Trotsky's formulation. Dragging up this old dispute now had the great advantage that it enabled Stalin to argue that Trotsky's economic proposals, with their accent on heavy industry, erred in 'underestimating' the peasants, and were therefore contrary to Lenin's views after NEP on the present need to preserve peasant support at all costs. There was, moreover, some justification for the allegation that the views of some of Trotsky's partisans, such

---

[1] How close Trotsky's views on 'Permanent Revolution' were to Lenin's practice in 1917 becomes apparent from the following passage written by Trotsky in 1922: 'This abstruse term represented the idea that the Russian Revolution, whose immediate objects were bourgeois in nature, would not however stop when these objects had been achieved. The revolution would not be able to solve its immediate bourgeois problems except by placing the proletariat in power. And the latter, upon assuming power, would not be able to confine itself to the bourgeois limits of the revolution. . . . The proletarian vanguard would be forced . . . to make very deep inroads not only into feudal property, but into bourgeois property as well. In this it would come into hostile collision not only with the bourgeois groupings which supported the proletariat during the first phases of the revolutionary struggle, but also with the broad masses of the peasants, who had been instrumental in bringing it into power. The contradiction in the position of a workers' government in a backward country with an overwhelming majority of peasants can be solved only on an international scale, in the area of the world proletarian revolution.' (From the Preface to *1905*.) If for 'proletariat' one reads 'Bolshevik party', this would seem to be an accurate description of what happened in 1917, and it is difficult to see what Lenin could have disagreed with in it.

as Preobrazhenskii, ran counter to the doctrine underlying NEP, as conceived by Lenin.

The third and most important heresy alleged against Trotsky was also the one which called for most ingenuity. No communist had hitherto openly questioned the fundamental assumption that the ultimate success of the revolution in Russia must depend upon the help given to it by the outbreak of revolution in other countries, and in particular in the advanced industrial countries of Europe. This assumption runs continuously through Lenin's thought, and it was upon this gamble on revolution in Europe that the seizure of power in 1917 was based. Since then, hopes of further revolutions had been dashed, but confidence that they must sooner or later take place, and that when this happened the temporary difficulties of the communists in Russia would thereby be alleviated, was never officially abandoned. Stalin himself in his lectures on the 'Foundations of Leninism' in April 1924 had expressly asserted the accepted view that the Russian revolution was dependent for the final victory of socialism on international revolution.[1] However, with the prospects of revolution in Europe receding, a revision of the doctrine in favour of one which would make the Russian communist feel that he had only himself to depend on for his survival in power was plainly desirable. Stalin used the opportunity of his polemics with Trotsky to make this revision.

Diligent search in Lenin's works for the right sentences to bolster his new case unearthed a passage in an article written in 1915, which foresaw that in view of the unequal development of capitalism in different countries, revolution might first break out in a few countries, or even in one country. Stalin was little troubled by the fact that Lenin in this article was not referring to Russia, and moreover expressly coupled such a victory in one country with immediate renewed efforts to spread revolution to other countries. This slender foundation enabled Stalin to build his doctrine of 'socialism in one country': while it was true that there could be no guarantee against the restoration of the bourgeois order without the co-operation of the proletariat in several countries, it was perfectly possible to build a complete socialist system in one country alone.[2] The lack of canonical authority

[1] J. Stalin, *Problems of Leninism*. Moscow, 1947, p. 38. These lectures were delivered and published before the attack on Trotskyism got under way. This formulation was revised, as Stalin himself explained, when the dispute over 'socialism in one country' arose in the party – *ibidem*, p. 158.
[2] For the statement of the doctrine in December 1924 see *ibidem*, pp. 94–123. For Lenin's article see *Lenin*, volume XVIII, pp. 230–3, published in August 1915. And see pp. 144–5 above.

was, perhaps, counter-balanced by the fact that in practice many communists were already aware that to stake too much on the prospect of further revolutions in the foreseeable future was unrealistic. The great value of the doctrine of 'socialism in one country', so far as policy at home was concerned, was that it gave Stalin and his supporters a powerful answer to Trotsky's attack: he had exposed them for their lack of revolutionary fire, they could now argue that his hopes of world revolution were merely a symptom of lack of faith in what the communist party could achieve in Russia unaided.

Zinoviev and Kamenev, as might be expected, took a most energetic part in the campaign of vilifying Trotsky, which occupied the latter part of 1924. At a meeting of the Central Committee on 17 to 20 January 1925 they even put forward a demand that Trotsky should be expelled from the party. Stalin resisted this demand. As he explained later, this policy of cutting off heads was dangerous, it was liable to be 'infectious': you cut off one head today, another tomorrow, a third the day after, 'and then what will be left of the party?'[1] He contented himself with securing the removal of Trotsky from his post as nominal head of the army. Trotsky willingly accepted this further demotion, indeed apparently suggested it himself, since as he wrote later, he was anxious to remove any suspicions that he was aiming at a 'Bonapartist' restoration.[2]

With the potential Bonaparte thus left without an army, Stalin was free to concentrate upon a new centre of discontent which was beginning to develop in Leningrad. The conflict with this new threat to his authority occupied the political scene for most of 1925. It began with moves by Stalin to undermine Zinoviev's position, and developed as the result of Zinoviev's attempts to resist this threat to himself. Zinoviev had the advantage of being able to control the powerful Leningrad party organization, which enjoyed some degree of independence as well as the old tradition dating from the early history of the party when Petersburg was the premier committee. The Leningrad communists were moreover proletarians in outlook, if not always by social origin, and therefore the more readily inclined to follow radical, anti-peasant views.

The circumstances in which the communist party found itself provided ample opportunity for genuine doubts about the correct course to pursue. For the party was in truth in a dilemma throughout the

[1] *Stalin*, volume VII, pp. 379–80.
[2] L. Trotsky, *Moia zhizn'*. Opyt avtobiografii. Volume II, Berlin, 1930, p. 261. The removal of Trotsky took place on 17 January 1925 – see *KPSS v rez.*, volume II, pp. 106–15.

whole of the period between the introduction of NEP in 1921 and the collectivization of the peasants in 1929 – a dilemma flowing directly from the attempt to graft Marx's concepts, designed for a proletarian society, upon a society which was still largely peasant. Thus, the party could either return to the traditional bolshevik treatment of the peasants, in other words, exploit them for the advantage of the proletariat, and thus risk another Tambov rising or Kronstadt revolt; or else it could allow the peasants sufficient freedom to till the land in peace and to develop their resources within a more or less free economy, but in such case it ran the risk that the peasants would use their economic freedom to acquire political influence which might in time rival the monopoly of the party. Of course, there were many variants and compromises possible between these two extremes of the dilemma. But in the conditions prevailing in the Russian party, bedevilled as it was by the struggle against Stalin's growing power, by the restriction of free discussion and by the fear that a false step would lead to the overthrow of the communist régime, such a compromise was impossible. There could be no middle way between submission to the Secretariat and rebellion. When Zinoviev came to choose rebellion as the alternative to submission, and annihilation, he naturally enough exploited the doubts about the policy pursued by the party leaders towards the peasants which many radicals in his party organization felt, and were ready to voice. But it would be naïve to see in this move any genuine conversion to more radical views on the part of Zinoviev or his shadow, Kamenev. They had repeatedly in the past, so long as their alliance with Stalin seemed solid, supported the pro-peasant policy. They were only moved to adopt the left-wing platform when their own position was threatened and were prepared to compromise over doctrine, had Stalin been willing to leave their authority intact.

Preliminary skirmishes began almost immediately after the January 1925 plenary meeting of the Central Committee, at which Trotsky was condemned. For the time being the campaign against 'Trotskyism' abated. Early in February Stalin made several moves designed to undermine Zinoviev's authority in the Comintern[1] – it was his first incursion into the field of international communism. A little later he succeeded in removing Zinoviev's supporter from the leadership of the Leningrad Communist Youth Organization, which had attempted to assert its independence of Moscow. In turn, Zinoviev's supporters

---

[1] These moves are described in Ruth Fischer, *Stalin and German Communism. A Study in the Origins of the State Party.* London, 1948, chapters 25 and 26.

were voicing the left-wing point of view in the Leningrad press, and even more forcibly (as Stalin's informers were aware) in private. But there was as yet no open opposition movement. When the Fourteenth Party Conference met on 27 to 29 April, at which agricultural policy formed the main subject of discussion, Zinoviev remained silent, and there was little sign of any opposition. A month later Zinoviev openly praised the conference decisions as a compromise between the several points of view current in the party. This was perhaps true of the resolution on paper.[1] But there had been unmistakable signs that both Bukharin and Stalin regarded the appeasement of the peasants as the all-important aim, and were little disturbed by fear of the rising influence of the more prosperous peasants, the so-called 'kulaks', which caused apprehension to the left-wingers. A few days before the conference Bukharin had made his famous appeal to the peasants: 'Enrich yourselves, develop your farms, do not fear that you will be subjected to restrictions.'[2] Although he formally repudiated this formula later, he continued to publish articles to much the same effect, as did also the members of a group of young economists who were known to be his pupils. At the conference the overall tax on the peasants was reduced by 25 per cent (the difference was unobtrusively made up by a government monopoly of vodka), and the speeches of Rykov and Bukharin belittled the 'kulak' danger. (Stalin did not speak.) The conference of proletarians and bureaucrats decided the fate of the peasants, as usual, in the absence of the peasants. Of 178 voting delegates and 392 without a vote, only 6·2 per cent were classified as of peasant origin.

But by the summer and autumn of 1925 the conflict was becoming more acute. Zinoviev now produced two theoretical works. The possible variations on the true meaning of Leninism had been almost exhausted, so that it was difficult to pick one which had not been already appropriated by either Stalin or Trotsky. But Zinoviev hit on one new idea upon which to found his attack on the right-wing policy: according to true Leninism, he now argued, NEP was not an evolution, but a 'strategic retreat'. By implication, a long-term policy of building up a prosperous, smallholding peasantry was unorthodox: the main reliance should be placed on the proletariat and poor

---

[1] See *KPSS v rez.*, volume II, pp. 145–61. While the resolutions contained no 'left-wing' measures directed at differential taxation of the richer peasants, they did at the same time lay great stress on developing co-operation and also instructed the Central Committee to work out for the next Congress a system of agricultural taxation which would take account of the 'complicated variations of agricultural economy'.

[2] *Pravda*, 14 April 1925.

peasants.[1] His supporters in Leningrad attacked Bukharin's economic theories with much more outspoken vigour. Stalin now began to assail the Leningrad organization – the only one which he did not as yet fully control. He was successful in securing the removal, for an incautious remark, of one of Zinoviev's supporters, Zalutskii. But he failed, for the time being, when he attempted to have his own nominee installed as secretary of the Leningrad Committee.[2] War was thus declared, and upon an issue on which Stalin was unlikely to compromise.

The Fourteenth Congress of the Party was by now, autumn 1925, long overdue. It had been postponed several times, but was eventually fixed for 18 December. From 3 until 10 October an extended plenary meeting of the Central Committee was held. The opposition, in the person of four representatives – Zinoviev, Kamenev, Sokol'nikov (the Commissar for Finance) and Krupskaia, a member of the Central Control Commission – complained that their right to express their views freely on the subject of the right-wing deviation had been obstructed, and they demanded a discussion. (The unhappy Krupskaia, who had accepted in silence the flouting of Lenin's wishes, had joined her two old friends for a last, hopeless attempt.) A compromise was reached by adopting a resolution on agricultural policy which stressed the need for equal vigour both in guarding against the 'kulak' danger and in ensuring the support of the peasants.[3] For the moment all were apparently satisfied.

Zinoviev would at this stage have been willing to abandon further conflict, provided that his dominion in Leningrad was left intact. But Stalin was now determined to force him into the open, so that he could the more effectively rout him. A short time before the Congress was due to meet, the normal eve of congress local conferences were in progress both in Moscow and in Leningrad. The Leningrad party organization elected a delegation to represent it at the forthcoming Congress from which all the candidates whom Moscow had attempted to infiltrate were excluded. The Moscow organization countered by passing a resolution openly attacking the Leningrad organization, and Leningrad replied in kind. An abusive campaign followed in the

[1] Zinoviev's ideas were developed in a book *Leninism*, published in the summer of 1925, and two articles 'The Philosophy of the Epoch', published in *Pravda* on 19 and 20 September.

[2] These moves against Zinoviev in Leningrad, as well as the earlier moves in the spring all appear from the speeches at the Fourteenth Congress.

[3] *KPSS v rez.*, volume II, pp. 180–4. Cf. the appeal to all party members, which was voted at the same time, which spoke of the increasing danger of 'kulak' influence, and spoke of 'loss of nerve' in face of the 'kulak' danger, which threatened the union of workers with the poor peasants (*ibidem*, pp. 188, 189). Such left-wing phrases had been unusual for some time past.

press controlled by the respective organizations. A last-minute attempt by Zinoviev to effect a compromise broke down, owing to the refusal of the Central Committee to guarantee that in return for the Leningraders refraining from further overt opposition, there would be no reprisals after the Congress against any of their number. Nevertheless, when the Congress opened, Zinoviev, with complete certainty of his imminent defeat, showed sufficient courage to claim the right to deliver a minority report to the Congress.[1]

With the exception of the Leningrad delegation which had been hand-picked by Zinoviev, all the other local delegations were hand-picked by Stalin's supporters in the secretariat network. The Leningrad group could therefore at most look to the support of a few isolated individuals like Kamenev and Krupskaia. The Congress marked the lowest ebb of political morality which the party had as yet reached. Zinoviev was anxious to retain his authority in what had hitherto been his undisputed domain, Leningrad. Both he and (with one notable exception) his supporters at the Congress, therefore, contented themselves with comparatively reasoned criticism, and urged that their views should be taken into account in the resolutions finally adopted. Jeers, insults and catcalls were the reply. Krupskaia, who ventured the opinion that the majority was not necessarily always right, and unwisely referred to the Stockholm Congress in 1906 when the bolsheviks had been in the minority and the mensheviks in the majority, caused such an uproar that she was forced to withdraw her remark. The opposition speakers were further handicapped by their own conduct in the past. Having backed, and implemented, the party policy of centralization and discipline, they were now forced to advocate the kind of democracy in the party which they had themselves helped to destroy. There was no easy answer to Mikoyan's taunt (Mikoyan was one of Stalin's rising protégés): 'When Zinoviev is in the majority, he is for iron discipline ... when he is in the minority ... he is against it.' Bukharin retorted to Krupskaia: 'N. K. Krupskaia says truth is that which corresponds to reality, each can read and listen, and answer for himself. But what about the party? Disappeared, as in the magic picture.' This was little short of accepted

---

[1] These events appear from the speeches at the Congress. For the terms upon which Stalin was willing to 'compromise' and which Zinoviev rejected, see *Stalin*, volume VII, pp. 388–9. They involved the acceptance by Zinoviev of the organizational changes which Stalin had tried but hitherto failed to effect in Leningrad, and the disavowal of his two principal supporters. On Zinoviev's willingness, indeed eagerness to compromise, provided he was allowed to remain master of his organization, see especially *XIV S"ezd*, pp. 220, 507, 522–3, 524.

doctrine in the party, and recalled Trotsky's own 'My party, right or wrong'.

One man alone, Kamenev, had the courage to say what was in the minds of all the opposition and maybe of a good many others. In a direct attack on the Secretariat, he said: 'I have come to the conclusion that Comrade Stalin cannot fulfil the role of unifier of the bolshevik general staff. . . . We are against the doctrine of one-man rule, we are against the creation of a Leader.' Uproar, shouts of indignation and demonstrations broke from the assembled delegates, to be carefully recorded for posterity in the Congress stenogram. In the wings Stalin's lieutenants guided the general bedlam into a staged ovation for the General Secretary. It was a measure of Stalin's triumph over the party. The term Leader, applied to Stalin, would before long become the generally accepted title. Stalin took no part at the Congress in the quarrel with the opposition until after they had stated their case. His reply was a defence of collective leadership, which he claimed Zinoviev had all along been trying to undermine. How, he demanded rhetorically, was the party to be led without Rykov, without Molotov, without Kalinin, without Tomskii, without Bukharin? (When the speech was reprinted in his collected works, Tomskii had been driven to his death, and Rykov and Bukharin shot as traitors, so their names were omitted from the revised text.) 'It is impossible,' he concluded, 'to lead the party otherwise than collectively. It is stupid to think about any other way after Lenin, it is stupid to talk about it.'

The opposition was, of course, defeated on the vote. Its defeat was reflected in the new top leadership. Kamenev was removed from most of his posts – the chairmanship of the Council of Labour and Defence (one of the organs of economic policy making), the chairmanship of the Moscow Soviet, and the deputy chairmanship of the Council of People's Commissars. For a short time he held the post of Commissar for Trade, which, however, he soon lost to Mikoyan. Sokol'nikov was demoted from the Commissariat of Finance to deputy chairmanship of the State Planning Commission. Zinoviev remained in the Politburo for the time being, Kamenev was demoted to candidate member. The number of full members of the Politburo was increased to nine by the elevation of Molotov, Kalinin and Voroshilov, three supporters of Stalin. The Moscow secretary, Uglanov, was rewarded for his campaign against Leningrad by promotion to one of the five places as candidate member. In the Central Committee, enlarged to 106, there were only a few casualties, but sixteen promotions from candidate to full membership and twenty-three new candidates further strengthened the number of Stalin's supporters. The Central Control Commission was also increased to 163.

The main blow against Zinoviev was struck after the Congress. On 5 January 1926 a strong team, headed by Molotov, was sent to Leningrad. By intensive work in the local factory organizations, by transfer to other posts of the more recalcitrant party officials, and by the force of their prestige and of the authority of the Congress, Molotov and his commission succeeded by the end of the month in winning over 96 per cent of the votes in all Leningrad organizations. Zinoviev's unpopularity may also have had something to do with this victory. Zinoviev was now removed from his post as chairman of the Leningrad Soviet, and was thus left without any party organization under his control, though one supporter – Evdokimov – still remained in the Secretariat and Orgburo.

When the smoke of battle cleared from the Congress, there appeared to be, in the resolutions which had been passed by it, one passage which represented a compromise with the views of the left opposition. This was a reference to the need to develop the machine and armament industries so as to make the USSR self-sufficient and independent of imports from the capitalist states.[1] This passage among others was later to be much pressed into service to show that Stalin had foreseen the need for rapid industrialization as far back as 1925, and had not merely adopted the programme of the left opposition after removing its members from the scene. But for the time being it led to no change in either industrial or agricultural policy.

Trotsky had taken no part in the events of 1925, and though present at the Congress, did not speak. He followed Zinoviev's manœuvres with detached contempt. His most notable political act during the year had been in connexion with Lenin's 'Testament'. In the course of 1925 Max Eastman – an American writer – published a book entitled *Since Lenin Died* in which, on the basis of information emanating from well-informed foreign communists or from persons who stood close to Trotsky, he not only correctly reproduced long extracts of the 'Testament', but also gave an accurate (as we now know) account of the political conflicts since Lenin's death. Trotsky published in September 1925, as he later claimed under threat from Stalin, an article repudiating the book and casting doubt on the authenticity of the document quoted. The suggestion that any important document had been concealed from the party by the Central Committee was a

[1] *KPSS v rez.*, volume II, p. 195.

'slander', and all talk of concealing or violating a 'Testament' was a 'malicious invention'.[1] A similar denial was also published by Krupskaia. No more valuable weapon could have been placed by Trotsky in Stalin's hands. Trotsky's failure to assume the leadership of the opposition after his fiasco early in 1924 had demoralized his followers, who were still numerous in many sections of the party but were afraid to show their hand. There also still existed inside the party a strong element of proletarian opposition. These worker critics might in the last resort have accepted Trotsky as leader. It was inconceivable that they should have followed Zinoviev. His supporters were confined to Leningrad, and followed him partly from old loyalties, but more often because of their dependence on him.

The first hint that all the groups or trends opposed to Stalin's dictatorship should unite had been dropped by Zinoviev at the Fourteenth Congress, when he proposed that the Central Committee should be enjoined to bring back for active work in the party all members of all former groups. Apart from Trotsky's followers, there were two groups which, though necessarily inactive in the conditions prevailing in the party, held critical views on the dictatorship of the Secretariat. One was the surviving group of Democratic Centralists, of which Sapronov was the leader. The other was the remnant of the Workers' Opposition, led by Shliapnikov. These groups had so far, by avoiding any overt action, escaped major repressions, though victimization of individual sympathizers with their views continued. Shliapnikov later attributed the comparative immunity of his followers during 1925 to the fact that a 'certain' group in the Central Committee (by which he plainly meant Stalin's) had been making repeated attempts to secure him and his followers as allies against the Leningrad opposition.[2]

The idea of union between all communists opposed to the régime of authoritarianism in the party was born out of defeat – and therefore too late to be effective. Nor was the basis for union very solid: the adherents of the Workers' Opposition had not disguised their contempt for the opposition which Trotsky headed in 1923–4. Shliapnikov, in a criticism of Trotsky which he was allowed to publish in *Pravda* on 18 January 1924, pointed out that Trotsky and his followers had all supported the measures against the oppositionists at the Tenth

[1] *Bol'shevik*, 1 September 1925. For Trotsky's subsequent explanation see his letter to Muralov of 11 September 1928 in *The New International* (New York), November 1934, pp. 125–6.

[2] M. Zorkii (editor), *Rabochaia oppozitsiia. Materialy i dokumenty 1920–1926 g.g.* S predisloviem E. Iaroslavskogo, Moscow, Leningrad, 1926, pp. 188–9.

Congress in 1921; their activities now were only aimed at capturing the party apparatus, and there was no reason to suppose that the apparatus would be any different under new management. Lasting improvement could only be brought about by increasing the proletarian element in the party and by allowing free activity to the rank and file.

Again, Zinoviev's sole asset had been the Leningrad party apparatus which he had controlled, and which he had now lost. All that remained to him now was the apparatus of the Executive Committee of the Comintern, of which he was still president, one supporter in the Secretariat and Orgburo, Evdokimov, and another, Lashevich, in the Revolutionary War Council. Trotsky could still hope to rally some supporters in the party to his side, although his failure hitherto to show courage, skill or determination had severely demoralized his followers. Moreover, by allowing himself to be edged out of the command of the Red Army, and by demolishing the force of Lenin's last injunctions to the party, he had already destroyed his two main weapons.

The United Opposition came into existence in the spring and early summer of 1926, and remained active until its final defeat at the end of 1927. It waged an unequal struggle throughout. With the aid of the apparatus of the party which he now firmly controlled, Stalin and his supporters, who rallied in the face of this new threat to their own positions, could not only manipulate the voting in the party organizations, but could also ensure that the views of the opposition should only reach the wider circles of the party in suitably distorted forms. The assistance of the OGPU (the successor of the GPU), now a normal adjunct in the settling of party disputes, was also readily available for dealing with the lesser figures of the opposition. But the practice of using the police arm against leaders of such stature as Trotsky or Zinoviev was not yet accepted in the party. It was this fact which for a time gave the opposition leaders some latitude, though often at severe cost to humbler party members who were courageous enough openly to support them.

The opposition realized that an all-out assault against the stranglehold of the apparatus was doomed to failure, not only because of its inherent strength as an efficient instrument but also because in the last resort the majority of the party would support it. For they knew that their own precarious hold over the country depended upon this apparatus. It was therefore essential to propound a doctrine which, if it could not hope to win over the party at once, would at any rate stand some chance of winning wide adherence in the course of time. The formulation of this doctrine was largely the work of Trotsky. Its content is well known, in spite of the distortions to which it was subjected by its opponents, from Trotsky's later publications in exile, from the papers preserved in his archives, now deposited in the Library of Harvard University; and from occasional publications during the campaign, either illegal, or accomplished with the help of foreign dissident communist sympathizers who were able to utilize the facilities available in the capitalist world.

The opposition was careful not to portray itself as a faction, let alone a rival party, or to attack the principle of party unity. The fear of factions was by this time almost pathological in all sections of the party. There was, moreover, the serious difficulty for Marxists that any faction which set itself up against the 'workers' state', headed by its communist vanguard, was of necessity regarded as 'counter-revolutionary'. Trotsky solved the difficulty by resorting to a parallel with the French Revolution and using the symbol of 'Thermidor', the overthrow of Robespierre and the Terror. In revolutionary tradition (even if the historical facts do not bear it out) the downfall of Robespierre was always regarded as the victory of bourgeois elements over the pure stream of revolution and social reform. So Trotsky argued that in Russia there was a danger that the forces of 'Thermidor', represented by the party bureaucracy, would defeat the revolutionary tradition, represented by the masses. Trotsky did not while in Russia openly assert that 'Thermidor' had already occurred, since to have done so could have amounted to an open call to revolt by the masses. Even so, the mere parallel of 'Thermidor' was explosive in content, in view of the ready response which left-wing slogans could always evoke among the rank and file in the party.

Trotsky proceeded to ascribe all the faults of the current régime inside the party to antagonism between the bureaucracy and the proletariat: repressive measures become necessary and the suppression of party democracy inevitable, once there is a 'divergence between the direction of economic policy and the direction of the feelings and thoughts of the proletarian vanguard. . . . Any other explanation of the growth of bureaucratism is secondary. . . .' The opposition therefore demanded, on familiar lines, a policy which would put an end to the lag in the development of industry, improve the lamentable condition of the industrial workers and counteract the menace to socialism of the growing wealth and power of middle peasants and 'kulaks' in the villages. In the international sphere, the opposition in like manner blamed the lack of revolutionary ardour of the Soviet leaders for the failures of the Comintern. The 'innovation', according to which victory of socialism in Russia, in Europe and in the world at large was not to be regarded as indissolubly one, must be cast aside. So long as the Russian party was not genuinely bolshevik in its internal policy, there could be no hope of a really revolutionary policy in the Comintern. In the course of their attacks on Stalin in the eighteen months which followed, the opposition especially blamed the Russian leaders for the failure of the General Strike in Britain in 1926 and for the severe defeat of the communists in China in 1927.

Before Trotsky and Zinoviev could come to terms, certain old scores had to be wiped out. Trotsky tacitly withdrew his strictures against Zinoviev and Kamenev contained in 'Lessons of October', while Zinoviev admitted that Trotsky's criticisms of 'bureaucratism' in 1923 had been well founded.[1] Agreement between these three was reached by April 1926, but alliance with the other smaller opposition groups took a few months longer. The new allies presented a common front at the plenary meeting of the Central Committee on 6 to 9 April 1926, demanding a programme of more intensive industrialization. They followed this up with a declaration of their full programme on the eve of a further plenary meeting on 14 to 23 July.[2] Stalin immediately responded with organizational measures. Evdokimov was removed from the Secretariat and Orgburo already in April. In readiness for the plenary meeting in July a long indictment was prepared against Lashevich and others, who were alleged, probably rightly, to have been holding secret conspiratorial meetings. All this activity, it was asserted, was linked with dissident foreign communists and was directed by Zinoviev from his position as president of ECCI. At the plenum of the Central Committee in July Lashevich was ousted from his post in the Revolutionary War Council and from the Central Committee, and Zinoviev was removed from the Politburo.[3] His removal from the Comintern was now only a matter of time. Rudzutak replaced Zinoviev in the Politburo, and five loyal pillars of the apparatus were brought in as candidates: Mikoyan, Andreev,

[1] The abuse which each had heaped upon the other in the past provided ample ammunition to Stalin's supporters for attacking what Stalin described as 'an open, straightforward and unprincipled deal' – see *Stalin*, volume VIII, p. 237.

[2] A copy of this twenty-page declaration which, apart from the main protagonists, was signed by ten others including Piatakov and Krupskaia, is among Trotsky's papers in Harvard Library.

[3] See *KPSS v rez.*, volume II, pp. 280–6. Both Lashevich and Evdokimov were signatories of the declaration of July.

Ordzhonikidze, Kaganovich and Kirov. There was as yet no further official condemnation of Trotsky.

Organizational measures were not, however, sufficient. It was not difficult for Stalin now to destroy the oppositionists. But it was necessary to go further and discredit the ideas which they stood for in the estimation of the party, if the hold of the apparatus was to remain secure. Two small blows were struck at the fringes of the opposition before the main blow fell. In July a private letter of a member of the Workers' Opposition, which had been in the hands of the OGPU for two years, was unearthed and published, allegedly with some distortions. This letter, in the form in which it was published, described the foreign communist parties as remittance men of the Russian party, and urged an extensive implementation of Lenin's idea of concessions to foreign capitalists so as to finance heavy industry. This enabled the Politburo to argue that the opposition was in reality a petty bourgeois right-wing deviation, and not left-wing at all – always a powerful argument.[1] A few months later a comparatively unknown communist was demonstratively expelled from the party for an article in which he argued that absolute unity was impossible in the party so long as the country was largely non-proletarian and other parties were prohibited. Trotsky and Zinoviev, while dissenting from this view, with which Stalin was obviously trying to saddle them, and which neither of them had ever held, nevertheless found the courage to protest against the expulsion of a party member without first giving him a hearing.[2]

For the main blow in October 1926 Trotsky and Zinoviev themselves provided the ammunition. In a gesture of despair the leading oppositionists staged a series of demonstrations in factory party cell meetings, demanding a party discussion on the vital issues at stake. The resulting attack from the party machine can easily be imagined. As if frightened by their own boldness, six leaders – Trotsky, Zinoviev, Kamenev, Piatakov, Sokol'nikov and Evdokimov – published a declaration admitting that they had been guilty of violating party discipline, abjuring factional activity for the future, and repudiating both their left-wing supporters in the Comintern and the remnants of the Workers' Opposition, with whom a few months before they had concluded an alliance.[3] Their motives, as they later explained, probably quite truthfully, were a desire to make possible the retention of

[1] Zorkii, *op. cit.*, pp. 158 ff., 170 ff., 190 ff.
[2] The article was by Iu. Ossovskii, and was published in *Bol'shevik*, No. 14, 1926 (September/October). For details of Trotsky's and Kamenev's resistance in the Politburo and Zinoviev's written protest see *XV Konf.*, p. 500.
[3] *Pravda*, 17 October 1926.

some influence inside the party.[1] But their action, which caused consternation among their rank and file followers, was both futile and dishonourable – futile, because it only encouraged Stalin to press still further against weak and discredited enemies, dishonourable, because it made reprisals against their supporters all the more easy to justify. At a plenary meeting of the Central Committee on 23 and 26 October 1926 (as was now usual, sitting jointly with the Central Control Commission) the opposition leaders were given a stern warning, Zinoviev was ousted from the Comintern, Trotsky was removed from his seat in the Politburo, and Kamenev from his position as a candidate member. However, the opposition still pressed for their right to voice their views in the councils of the party and demanded that their statement of policy, which they presented to the Central Committee, should be circulated to the party conference, the Fifteenth, which was due to open on 26 October. Their request was rejected, and the conference was only allowed to see Stalin's interpretation of the opposition views as set out in a number of Theses.

It was thus already as a discredited and somewhat ridiculous band of failures that the opposition appeared at the Fifteenth Conference. Stalin could moreover claim the defection from their side of Krupskaia. She later explained her defection by alleging that the opposition had gone too far in their criticism, which might lead the masses to think that the party and the Soviet government no longer represented their interests.[2] It was the end of Krupskaia's influence on party policy. She had been subjected to continuous persecution since 1922. Before deserting her allies she had, however, arranged for the transmission of Lenin's 'Testament' to foreign dissident communists, and the two notes were published for the first time in full in the *New York Times* a week before the conference opened.[3] The opposition leaders, though present at the conference, were not given a chance to state their case. Jeers, interruptions and obstruction from the chair (Zinoviev's speech, for example, is in parts barely intelligible in the stenogram) made their task difficult. Stalin's Theses, which were adopted unanimously (none of the oppositionists present had a vote), skilfully, if dishonestly, garbled the opposition's case in order to show that they were really speaking the language of menshevism. The

[1] This was the explanation given by Kamenev at the Fifteenth Party Conference, and is borne out by a note, dated 16 October 1926, which is preserved among Trotsky's papers.
[2] In a letter to *Pravda*, 20 May 1927.
[3] On 18 October 1926. For details of how Lenin's 'Testament' reached the hands of foreign socialists and hence publication see the well-informed note in *Est et Ouest*, No. 151, Paris, 1–15 May 1956, pp. 14–15.

central point of the debate was the issue of 'Socialism in one country'. This was Stalin's answer to the left-wing appeal of the opposition platform. By focusing attention on the doubts of the oppositionists regarding the possibility of building socialism in Russia without the help of further revolution, he was able to brand them as weak and faltering, without faith in their own powers, and pinning their hopes on foreign revolutions, the probability of which in the near future was becoming increasingly remote. The resolution which was adopted not only condemned the opposition, but urged that the party should redouble its efforts to make the opposition admit the error of its views. It was not enough for them to submit to party discipline: they must be forced to admit that their views were wrong.[1] This was, after all, Trotsky's own doctrine enunciated in 1924: 'I know one cannot be right against the party.'

The events of the following year were a curious re-enactment of what had happened before. Once again there were half-hearted attempts at defiance, and a move to compromise by the opposition, followed by capitulation and defeat. For a few months the opposition lay low, trying to build up its clandestine organization. Once again it was an event in international communism which precipitated action. In 1926 it had been the defeat of the General Strike in Britain which had led to the first declaration of policy by the opposition; this time, in May 1927, it was the massacre of the Chinese communists by Chiang Kai-shek in Shanghai. The opposition opened a campaign against the party leaders which was of an extremely telling and embarrassing nature. Another comprehensive statement of their case was put before the Politburo in the form of a declaration on 25 May 1927, in which Comintern and domestic failures were linked in an indictment of the whole course of policy pursued by the leaders.[2] But the very telling nature of the opposition indictment made it all the more imperative for Stalin to destroy his opponents if he wished to retain his authority. Events were making their arguments appear more convincing. This was good reason for adopting them – much as Lenin had once adopted the mensheviks' argument for NEP. But before doing so, it was essential to annihilate the opposition.

A new factor was thrown into the scales about this time which both sides tried to exploit – a war scare. In May 1927 the British government broke off diplomatic relations with Russia as the result of a

---

[1] *KPSS v rez.*, volume II, pp. 329–40.
[2] A copy of this Declaration, to which eighty-four signatures were appended, is also among Trotsky's papers in Harvard Library.

police raid on the offices of the Soviet Trade delegation in London, which was stated to have produced evidence of subversive communist activities against Britain. There was never any real danger of war, but inside the USSR both sides in the conflict may well have believed that there was. The opposition argued that for successful defence in the event of a war the present leadership would have to be replaced by leaders who were acceptable to the proletariat, while in the international sphere the Russians should rely on the really revolutionary elements in the various foreign communist parties who were now being branded as deviationists. Stalin and his supporters, on the other hand, could argue with some force that now was the time to close the ranks in the face of the common danger. By the summer the temper in the party was at fever heat, and there can be little doubt that the OGPU would have been relieved to be given the right to arrest prominent members of the opposition. But before this power could be conferred, the culprits would have to be expelled from the party, and according to rumour, a 'right-wing' of the Politburo, consisting of Rykov, Bukharin, Tomskii and Kalinin, was still opposed to this course.[1] Whatever the reason, it was to the Central Committee, where he could always be sure of a majority, that Stalin turned for his next move, as so often in the past when unable to obtain a majority in the Politburo. At a stormy plenary meeting at the end of July and the beginning of August 1927 he was able to put through a resolution expelling Trotsky and Zinoviev from the Central Committee. The occasion this time was a public speech by Trotsky at the railway station when seeing off one of his supporters who had been 'posted' to the Far East. Owing to the conciliatory efforts of Ordzhonikidze (who had by now become chairman of the Central Control Commission), a compromise was reached. The resolution was rescinded, and in return the two opposition leaders made yet another declaration of unconditional submission to the authority of the Central Committee.

As Trotsky realized at any rate by June 1927, the 'extirpation', as he wrote privately, of the opposition was only a matter of time.[2] Though not yet free to arrest them, the OGPU was already using its resources against the members of the opposition. Their skeleton organization was penetrated by agents of the OGPU, provocateurs were employed to trap them into admissions of treasonable activity,

[1] Boris Souvarine. *Staline. Aperçu historique du bolchévisme*, Paris, 1935, p. 414.
[2] In a letter to Ordzhonikidze of 28 June 1927, of which a copy is preserved among Trotsky's papers.

and an organized campaign, sometimes of an anti-Semitic character,[1] was put in hand. It was therefore as a gesture of despair, with full knowledge that their days of freedom were numbered, that the opposition made its final demonstration before the end came. The Fifteenth Congress of the party was already long overdue in the summer of 1927. (The last had met in December 1925, and congresses were supposed to be held annually.) The Congress was repeatedly postponed, in anticipation of a settlement with the opposition, but was finally fixed for 2 December 1927. In preparation for the Congress the opposition drew up in September a further long statement of their policy, the third. In this statement they did not conceal the fact that they were aiming at a complete renovation of the party leadership. They demanded that the Central Committee to be elected by the Congress should be both 'closely related to the masses' and 'independent of the apparatus' – a description plainly inapplicable to Stalin and his supporters. The opposition's statement was submitted to the Central Committee, with a request that it should be printed and circulated to the delegates at the Congress. The Central Committee refused this demand, on the grounds that to do so would violate the decisions of the Tenth Party Congress. This was not an entirely wrong interpretation, and Stalin and his supporters were thus able once again to shelter behind the mantle of Lenin's authority.

The opposition had taken precautions against this refusal to publicize their programme. An underground printing press, under the direction of Trotsky's supporter, Mrachkovskii, had been organized to print it for wide distribution.[2] The OGPU was aware of these arrangements, for within a few days the printing press was seized and those responsible for setting it up arrested. Other arrests followed, and those apprehended were immediately expelled from the party, and thus left at the mercy of the OGPU. The OGPU also spread further rumours that the opposition had been maintaining contacts with a White Guard officer. The opposition leaders now threw caution

---

[1] Among Trotsky's papers there is a record of a meeting held in September 1927 in a party cell to demand the expulsion of Trotsky, which was one of the thousands organized by the Secretariat as part of the campaign. The principal speech stressed that Trotsky's nationality precluded him from being a communist since 'it shows that he must be in favour of speculation' and that Trotsky and his supporters had 'made a mistake about the Russian spirit'. Such remarks by a party member at a time when anti-Semitism was a punishable offence are not likely to have been made without higher authority.

[2] One charred copy of this illegally printed document is preserved among Trotsky's papers. The text of the declaration was later published in translation in Leon Trotsky, *The Real Situation in Russia*, translated by Max Eastman, London, n.d. (1928), pp. 23–195.

to the winds and organized a number of public meetings at which they addressed crowds of workers. Retribution followed swiftly. At a joint meeting of the Central Committee and the Central Control Commission on 21 to 23 October Trotsky made a last defiant speech. For the first time he referred to Lenin's 'Testament' in an attempt to disparage Stalin. It was much too late. Stalin could effectively turn the attack by reference to Trotsky's own denial of Max Eastman's revelations in 1925.[1] It was in any case too late to appeal to Lenin, who had become little more than a legend exploited by both factions for their own ends. Trotsky and Zinoviev were now expelled from the Central Committee.

A fortnight later, on 7 November 1927, the tenth anniversary of the bolshevik seizure of power, the opposition leaders held organized demonstrations in the streets of Moscow and Leningrad. The OGPU was ready for them, and the demonstrations were easily dispersed by the police, or broken up by gangs of ruffians. The proletariat watched with disinterested apathy while the two factions, each claiming to speak in its name, fought out their battles. It was the end of the opposition. Trotsky and Zinoviev were expelled from the party on 14 November and all that remained for the Fifteenth Congress, when it met on 2 December, was to set the seal on their condemnation. The expulsions were duly endorsed, and a further group of opposition leaders, seventy-five members in all of the Trotsky-Zinoviev faction, and eighteen Democratic Centralists, were also expelled. The Congress was a demonstration rather than a deliberative body, and of course completely unanimous. Scores of delegations of workers attended to attest their solidarity against the opposition. In the debates, one small group of oppositionists, present at the Congress 'on the orders of the Central Committee', read their speeches, to the accompaniment of the jeers and catcalls which protocol now demanded, and were then expelled. In the course of the Congress a series of declarations by various other groups of oppositionists protested their intention to remain loyal to the decisions of the Congress, and petitioned either for readmission to the party, if already expelled, or the remission of the sentence if not. Trotsky, who signed several of these petitions, did not, however, sink as low as Zinoviev and Kamenev, who not only petitioned for readmission, but renounced their views as 'anti-Leninist' – only to have their petition rejected. On 19 January 1928 the Press announced, in veiled terms, the 'departure'

[1] For Trotsky's speech see *ibidem*, pp. 3–19; Stalin's reply is in *Stalin*, volume X, pp. 172–205.

from Moscow of a group of some thirty oppositionists, headed by Trotsky. It was the beginning of his exile which was to end twelve years later with a blow from an alpenstock dealt by an agent of Stalin's police.

Reflecting on his defeat ten years later, Trotsky argued that the fact that the opposition was theoretically right, and Stalin wrong, was immaterial. 'A political struggle is in its essence a struggle of interests . . . and not of arguments.' Personalities were also quite irrelevant, as were also such considerations as the greater skill of Stalin. What had occurred was a triumph of the 'bureaucracy over the masses'. In Lenin's time bolshevism was a mass movement, but after the civil war 'the masses were pushed away gradually from participation in the leadership', and the 'bureaucracy . . . conquered the bolshevik party'. Only 'superficial minds' could regard the struggle, which was a social process, as a struggle for power, or political rivalry for Lenin's heritage. As for the suppression of opposition parties in Lenin's times, this was merely an 'episodic act of self-defence', and, like the forbidding of factions in 1921, was only an exceptional and temporary measure.[1]

This analysis is not borne out by the facts. However much more democratic the régime in the party in Lenin's day might appear in retrospect, there was no period in its history when the masses participated in the leadership. The 'bureaucracy' of party secretaries which Trotsky was now attacking was overwhelmingly composed at its higher levels of old bolsheviks who had joined the party before the revolution, and the social composition of the party was not very different in 1921 and in 1927, indeed its proletarian component had increased.[2] As for Trotsky's picture of the policy towards opposition parties and towards factions in the party (which has very largely influenced even historians whose work claims to be objective), the evidence is inescapable that as early as 1917 it was Lenin's firm determination, in which he was fully supported by Trotsky, to destroy the two socialist parties. Again, if it was Lenin's intention in 1921 that the prohibition of factions should only be a temporary measure, not a jot of evidence has come down to us to substantiate this view. It would, moreover, have been quite inconsistent with the views on party organization held by Lenin after 1902, which Trotsky himself had attacked before the revolution. Like Martov before him, Trotsky had

---

[1] Leon Trotsky, *The Revolution Betrayed. What is the Soviet Union and Where is it Going?* Translated by Max Eastman, London, 1937, pp. 87–104.
[2] See below, p. 316–17.

fallen a victim to his faith in Marxist dogma: because each believed in the necessary unity of the party of the proletariat, both men – Martov between 1910 and 1914, Trotsky after 1922 – made the mistake of trying to compromise with an opponent whose sole aim was political annihilation of all who stood in his way. Yet, though it is easy to criticize Trotsky for throwing away his opportunities to rally wide support for the overthrow of Stalin while this was still possible, it is also necessary to remember that this was a course which he could not lightly pursue. For a small minority, ruling by force in the teeth of proletarian and peasant opposition, can ill afford to saw away the only firm branch which supports it – a well-disciplined organization. All communists had recognized the necessity of such a party machine in 1921. It was too late for them to draw back, even when that organization threatened to engulf them.

XVII   Party Composition: Relations with the Government

In the four years between 1 January 1924 and 1 January 1928 the party membership expanded almost threefold – from a total of 472,000 to 1,304,471.[1] These totals include both full and candidate (probationer) members. The latter, who formed between a quarter and a third of the total, did not all necessarily become full members. On 1 January 1925 for example, over 28,000 candidates, admitted in 1921 or earlier, had still not been promoted to full membership.[2] Yet the official probationary period varied from six months, in the case of industrial workers, to two years for those considered less reliable. In some cases candidates lost interest before the time was ripe for their admission as full members. Although the party remained predominantly masculine, the number of women members continued slightly to increase – for example, from 11·2 per cent on 1 April 1925 to 12·8 per cent, totalling about 156,000, on 1 January 1928.[3] The Communist League of Youth (*Komsomol*) also expanded rapidly during this period. Founded at the end of 1918, the *Komsomol* for the first years of its existence, owing to the belated development of party discipline in its organization, reflected in magnified form the opposition and disillusionment discernible in the party itself, and its membership had by 1922 fallen disastrously. Efforts made after 1922 to increase its numbers were rewarded, and at the same time drastic purges and reorganization were undertaken in order to eradicate the left-wing trends among the young, whose sympathies were usually attracted by what seemed to them the more revolutionary opposition. By 1927 the *Komsomol* was two million strong.[4]

The biggest single recruitment drive was the so-called Lenin

---

[1] *BSE*, volume XI, p. 533; *VKP(b) v tsifrakh*, vypusk 8, Moscow, Leningrad, 1928, p. 6.

[2] *Izv.Ts.K.*, No. 28 (103), 27 July 1925.

[3] *Izv.Ts.K.*, No. 22–23 (97–98), 22 June 1925; *VKP(b) v tsifrakh*, vypusk 8, p. 32.

[4] See Merle Fainsod, *How Russia is Ruled*, Revised Edition, Cambridge, Mass., 1963, pp. 284–8.

Enrolment.[1] Although projected in the autumn of 1923, it was only launched after Lenin's death early in 1924, and yielded over 200,000 new recruits. Since most of these were young workers, the new influx affected both the social composition of the party and its average age, and replenished some of the ravages caused in the party after the end of the civil war by disillusionment and the purges. The Lenin Enrolment also provided the Secretariat, at the outset of its battle against the left-wing opposition, with a mass of malleable recruits to counter-balance the more intractable older communists. That the Lenin Enrolment was intended to play its part in the struggle with the opposition became evident when it was disclosed at the Thirteenth Congress in May 1924 that the new recruits, although of course only admitted to candidate status, had nevertheless, in disregard of party rules,[2] been allowed to vote in the election of delegates to the Congress. The Lenin Enrolment was only the first, and most advertised, of a series of drives throughout the period of NEP. The main emphasis of these appeals remained on the recruitment of workers, of whom the proportion in the party had reached its lowest ebb – 41 per cent, according to classification by social origin, in 1921.[3] At the Fifteenth Congress in 1927 the claim was made that between January 1924 and 1 January 1927 no less than 488,000 workers from industry had been admitted to the party.

The main characteristics of the party during the period of NEP were youth, inexperience and a low educational standard. As the 1927 party census showed, a quarter of the members were under twenty-five, over half under thirty and over 85 per cent under forty. The youth of the rank and file was reflected in the relative youth of the party aristocracy, the Central Committee. As elected in December 1927, nearly half of its 121 members and candidate members were under forty, and three-quarters were under forty-five. The party as a whole was inexperienced in the sense that the older bolsheviks, those who had taken part in the pre-revolutionary struggle, in the hectic activity of 1917 and in the civil war, were already a small minority. Death, old age, purges, disillusionment and quite a number of suicides[4] had all taken their toll. At the lower levels of party life the

---

[1] For details on the Lenin Enrolment see T. H. Rigby, *Communist Party Membership in the USSR 1917–1967*, Princeton, 1968, chapter 3. (Cited hereafter as Rigby, *CPSU*.)

[2] See on this *SPR*, No. 5, p. 251.

[3] See p. 238 above.

[4] 14·1 per cent of all members who died in the first quarter of 1925 and 11·9 per cent of all candidate members who died were suicides – *Izv.Ts.K.*, No. 34 (109) of 7 September 1925.

'underground' party man, as those with pre-revolutionary experience were known, was a rarity. For example, among the members of the bureaux of party cells elected in the autumn of 1927 only 1·4 per cent had joined the party before 1917.[1] However, the further up one looked in the party hierarchy the more prominent the 'undergrounders' became. 'Undergrounders' formed 44 per cent of the delegates to the Fourteenth Congress in 1925, for example, and together with civil war veterans still dominated the higher party committees in 1927. Thus, about three-quarters of all senior secretaries were of pre-1917 seniority in 1925, and the 'undergrounders' still formed 71 per cent in 1927; 14 per cent were civil war veterans.[2] All but ten of the Central Committee elected in 1927 had joined the party before 1917. But lower down the scale, for instance among the secretaries of primary cells at the end of 1927, the new generation of communists already formed the majority – over 60 per cent had joined the party after 1921.[3] Thus the picture presented was that the most experienced veterans were in the key positions, but a new generation was gaining experience at the lower levels of the apparatus. These new men owed their advancement to Stalin and the Secretariat.

The census of 1927 disclosed that the educational level of the party was still very low. Less than 1 per cent had completed higher education, less than 8 per cent had received even secondary education, and, apart from about a quarter of the party classified as 'self-taught', over 2 per cent were illiterate. There was, however, a very slight advance in the level of education as compared with 1922, and it was to the credit of the party rank and file that the percentage of those who had made the attempt to educate themselves, in order to make up for lack of schooling, had doubled.[4] An analysis of the educational background of directors of state enterprises made in January 1928 graphically illustrated the lack of technically trained communists. The great majority of the directors, nearly nine-tenths, were party members, but only 2·8 per cent of them had had higher education. As against this, of the non-party directors, 58 per cent had received higher educational training[5].

The social composition of the party during this period is harder to establish. The charge that the party was losing its proletarian character was frequently made by the opposition, thus making the question

---

[1] *VKP(b) v tsifrakh*, vypusk 8, p. 44.
[2] *Bol'shevik*, No. 15, August 1928, p. 19.
[3] *VKP(b) v tisfrakh*, vypusk 8, p. 45.
[4] *Sotsial'nyi i natsional'nyi sostav VKP(b)*. Itogi vsesoiuznoi partiinoi perepisi 1927 goda. Moscow, 1928, p. 41.
[5] *Bol'shevik, loc. cit.*, p. 27.

a political issue. Hence exaggeration and distortion of statistics on social composition were frequent. There is no doubt, however, that the efforts made by the leaders to increase the proletarian component of the party were crowned with some success. But in order to arrive at an accurate estimate of the social structure of the party by 1927 it is necessary to distinguish the classification of members both by their social origin and by their actual occupation, since the two were by no means identical in practice. Many members who were quite properly classified as workers or peasants by social origin had long ceased to work at the bench or at the plough by the time they entered the party, and were fulfilling administrative duties. Moreover, a substantial number of workers and peasants, actually engaged in manual labour at the time of joining the party, were transferred to administrative work after recruitment: an analysis made in the 1927 party census showed that about a third of members who had joined as 'workers' were already in administrative employment, or studying, and about a quarter of the 'peasants' recruited were now working in offices. Hence the recruitment of workers by the party did not necessarily produce a corresponding increase in members actually working at the bench or at the plough.

With these reservations in mind, it is instructive to look at the figures for social composition on 1 January 1928, published by the Statistical Department of the Central Committee. Classified by social origin, the breakdown appears as follows: workers 56·8 per cent; peasants 22·9 per cent; employees 18·3 per cent; 'others' (i.e. those whose social origin cannot be assigned to any of the three groups) 2 per cent. A different picture emerges if one looks at the analysis of actual occupations of party members on the same date. Leaving aside 6·3 per cent who were in the Red Army, only 35·2 per cent were working at the bench as wage earners, and only 1·2 per cent were actually tilling the soil as labourers. A further 9·2 per cent, classified as engaged exclusively in agriculture, were better-off farmers, probably often employing hired labour to supplement their own. Officials of all kinds, including junior and part-time officials, formed 38·3 per cent. If one adds to this figure 9·8 per cent classified as 'others', then apart from the Red Army communists, nearly half the party members were engaged in non-manual occupations.[1]

In terms of social origins, according to official data, it was evident that the more responsible officials tended to be recruited from among those classified as 'employees and others' in origin, rather than from

[1] *VKP(b) v tsifrakh*, vypusk 8, pp. 8–11.

those classified as workers or peasants. Thus, an analysis made in 1925 of nearly two thousand party members posted to responsible positions in 1923–4 showed that 59·7 per cent came from this 'black-coated' category.[1]

The 459,067 worker communists in 1928 represented a substantial proportion of the total labour force. According to a calculation made in 1926, the average percentage of communists in the differing branches of industry was 14·4, and over 20 per cent in three major industries. It was notable, however, that the percentage of communist workers was much higher in the smallest enterprises and decreased progressively in enterprises employing over 500 workers.[2] Quite a different picture was presented by the village, where the communist hold was strikingly weak. At the beginning of 1928 there were fewer than 200,000 communists in the villages with a total rural population of 120 millions, and of those only 15,000 were agricultural labourers.[3] Moreover, an analysis of rural communist cells as at 1 January 1928 showed that 19·8 per cent of their members were industrial workers, 42·8 per cent individual farmers, 44·5 per cent employees 'and others', and 2·9 per cent collective farmers. A survey of 27 village cells conducted by the Saratov provincial committee in September 1927 illustrated the weak influence of communism in the villages. Membership was low, and attempts to increase it had failed: there were virtually no working peasants in the party cells, and the few members who were of peasant origin were officials of one kind or another. In a number of cases the majority of the members of the cell were not even local inhabitants. The cells had virtually no influence on local life, except in mobilizing the voters for elections to the soviets; but the soviets, when once elected, played very little part in village affairs.[4] Beginning with 1927, there was a marked increase in the numbers of workers in rural cells and a corresponding decrease of peasant members. Secretaries of rural cells of worker origin, who already formed 80·5 per cent of all rural cell secretaries in 1927, formed a higher percentage still in 1928.[5]

* * *

[1] *Izv.Ts.K.*, No. 22–23 (97–98), 22 June 1925. See also, on the question generally, Rigby, *CPSU*, chapter 4.
[2] *Bol'shevik*, No. 12, June 1926, pp. 60–71.
[3] *VKP(b) v tsifrakh*, vypusk 8, p. 10.
[4] See *Sostoianie i rabota sel'skoi iacheiki VPK(b) saratovskoi organizatsii*. Sbornik materialov obsledovaniia gubkoma VKP(b). S predisloviem tov. I. M. Vareikisa. Saratov, 1927, *passim* for a detailed picture of the village cell at this time. Cf. Merle Fainsod, *Smolensk under Soviet Rule*, pp. 45–7.
[5] *PS*, No. 11–12 (13–14), June 1930, pp. 31–5.

The Politburo, as elected by the Fifteenth Congress in 1927, after the routing of the left opposition, consisted of nine men, including Stalin. Four of them were virtually Stalin's creatures: Kuibyshev, Molotov, Rudzutak and Voroshilov. The remaining four, Bukharin, Kalinin, Rykov and Tomskii, had supported Stalin against Trotsky and the left opposition not because they were Stalin's creatures so much as because they upheld the policy of the 'right' towards the peasants which Stalin had backed against the attacks from the 'left'. The eight candidate members of the Politburo consisted entirely of younger men, most of whom had made their names as leading party secretaries, and who owed everything to Stalin. They included Kaganovich, Kirov, Uglanov and Mikoyan. Most decisions were made in the Politburo, which in its deliberations now covered the whole range of national life. Controversial questions, and especially those which were interwoven with the struggle for power, were usually transferred for discussion to the plenary meeting of the Central Committee. This had the advantage of giving an appearance of greater democracy, since the decisions of the Plenum, unlike those of the Politburo, were usually published; and, so far as Stalin was concerned, it ensured him the majority which he could not always, before 1927, rely on in the smaller body. According to the declaration of the opposition of July 1926,[1] Stalin had also inaugurated the practice from 1923 onwards of holding private meetings of his supporters in the Politburo, together with the chairman of the Central Control Commission. These meetings, the opposition alleged, fixed the agenda and policy for the official meeting, and sometimes even took decisions which were never placed on the agenda.

The other committee of the Central Committee, the Orgburo, acted in the main as a subsidiary Politburo. Its functions were never very clearly defined, either in relation to the Politburo or to the Secretariat, to which it progressively lost influence. It had responsibilities for the more senior appointments. There were also provisions for the removal of questions of a political nature from the Orgburo for the decision of the Politburo. As constituted in 1927 at the Fifteenth Congress, the Orgburo consisted of thirteen members and seven candidates. These were the five party secretaries and three candidate secretaries, with the addition of a few members of the trade union and economic hierarchy. Although in theory the Secretariat remained subordinate to the Orgburo, the close identity in the membership of the two bodies, the domination of each by Stalin and the controlling power over its

[1] See p. 304, above.

agenda vested in the Secretariat enabled the Secretariat in practice to run the Orgburo.

The main centre of party administration was the Secretariat, headed after 1922 by Stalin as General Secretary. His four assistants included Molotov and Uglanov, who was also secretary of the Moscow party committee. By 1925 the Secretariat had 767 full-time employees on its staff. There was only one major change in its structure after 1923. This was the merger in 1924 of the Assignment Department (*Uchraspred*) and the department for organization and instruction into one department for both organization and assignment (*Orgraspred*). This immediately became the key department of the Secretariat, which concentrated in its hands the entire direction of subordinate party organs and the all-important function of making appointments. Its history is the story of Stalin's success in controlling the party. In addition to *Orgraspred*, the Secretariat included departments for the Press, for work in the villages, for statistics, for administration, for agitation and propaganda (*Agitprop*), for work among women, for accounting, and for Information.[1] There is one reference in soviet sources to the existence already in 1924 of a Secret Section of the Secretariat. This section, of which the existence at a later period of history is not in doubt, was presumably already designed for liaison between the party and the OGPU.[2] By 1924 the Secretariat had itself become a sub-committee, meeting separately from the Orgburo.[3] The secretariats of the subordinate party organizations were planned on the same pattern as the Secretariat in Moscow.

Developments in secretariat practice during the later 20's in the main took the form of improvements on the system already established by 1923. These developments, which played an important part in enabling the Secretariat to consolidate itself as the real centre of power in the country, took place without any direct authorization from the Party Congress, by administrative action behind the scenes. The improvements effected between 1924 and 1927 can be grouped under three heads. First, after the setting up of *Orgraspred* the system of control over the subordinate party organizations was perfected by improving the inspection, guidance and verification of the work of the local committees. This was achieved very largely by the corps of instructors attached to *Orgraspred*, who maintained constant touch with the committees and were invested with full powers. In cases of

[1] Merle Fainsod, *How Russia is Ruled*, pp. 190–1.
[2] See *Proletarskaia revoliutsiia*, No. 6, 1935, p. 130. It was headed by I. P. Tovstukha.
[3] *Izv.Ts.K.*, No. 5 (63), May 1924, p. 43; *SPR*, No. 5, p. 502.

unusual difficulty or importance special delegates were dispatched by the Secretariat in the name of the Central Committee to conduct more thorough visitations. The local secretaries were also summoned to Moscow for periodic conferences.[1] Secondly, the system of maintaining personal records of party members was rationalized. The attempt to keep a central record of virtually all party members, which had been made somewhat ambitiously in the first years, was abandoned. The centre now only kept full records in the case of key men, and delegated the responsibility for other records to the local organizations. The impressions gathered by the instructors provided the centre with material not only for the official personal record, which was, in theory at any rate, open to inspection by party members, but also for the confidential files, which were kept secret. The provincial secretariats in turn maintained similar systems of control and records for subordinate organizations.[2] The whole of this sytem of rational delegation of authority was only made possible by the fact that Stalin had succeeded in placing his trusted nominees at all the vital provincial points, and his conflict with Zinoviev over the control of Leningrad should be viewed, in part, in the light of this fact.

A third change also involved more delegation. The practice of making appointments by the centre was restricted to a limited list of key posts. All appointments in the country, from the highest to the lowest, were listed as being within the competence of some particular organization, or, in some cases, of several organizations which had to concur in making the appointment. Devolution and systematization were thereby achieved. Regulations made in 1926 fixed the number of appointments within the competence of the highest party organs at over 5,500. About a third of these, consisting of the key posts, were variously within the competence of the Politburo, the Orgburo or the Secretariat; another third exclusively within the competence of one of the secretaries of the Central Committee, with right of appeal to the Central Committee; and a third, stated to be 'elective' posts, were to be decided upon by special commissions set up by the Central Committee.[3] Thus it will be seen that, except in the comparatively few cases which had to go before the Politburo, where Stalin was not always sure of a majority, all these key appointments were within the gift of the Secretariat, the Orgburo or the Central Committee, all of

[1] *Izv.Ts.K.*, No. 19–20 (94–95), 30 May 1925; *SPR* No. 6, volume I, pp. 508–10, No. 5, pp. 228–31.
[2] *Izv.Ts.K.*, No. 3 (61), March 1924, pp. 14–25; No. 4 (62), April 1924, p. 52; *SPR*, No. 6, volume I, pp. 341–6 and 528–38.
[3] *Izv.Ts.K.*, No. 1 (122), 18 January 1926.

which Stalin could control. An important development in the making of appointments by the Secretariat dated from the end of 1923 when *Uchraspred* (as it then still was) succeeded in gaining a measure of control over appointments of officials in the government departments, which had hitherto retained autonomy in this matter.[1]

The most important power of the Secretariat was, of course, its control over the vital network of secretaries throughout the country, the 'apparatus'. In theory all these appointments were (and still are) elective. But the tradition of election was never very strong in bolshevik organizations, and, while official resolutions periodically paid lip service to the elective principle, in practice the Secretariat invariably decided who was to be 'elected', or removed, or transferred, and seems to have encountered little difficulty in enforcing its views. Instructions intended for the guidance of party organizations published during this period scarcely conceal that the members of the apparatus were appointed; though, as one instruction puts it frankly, it was desirable that in the case of elective offices the posting should only be made in cases of extreme necessity and should coincide with the election.[2] The practice of appointment to elective posts was constantly criticized by the opposition, which never succeeded in achieving anything more than the publication of official resolutions, in 1921 and again in 1923, reiterating the sanctity of the elective principle. Trotsky's more concrete proposals to modify the paragraphs of the party Rules of 1925, which conferred wide powers on the central organs of 'approving' elections of local committees and officials,[3] were only put forward by him at the Fifteenth Congress at the end of 1927, when it was much too late for any proposal by Trotsky to have any effect.

The number of full-time paid party officials was 15,325 in August 1922.[4] At the time of the Fourteenth Congress in 1925 the ratio of the apparatus to the party as a whole was stated to be one to forty, which gives a total apparatus of about 20,000. Party officials were paid salaries which were up to 50 per cent higher than the scales laid down for comparable government employees, and in addition enjoyed

---

[1] *SPR*, No. 4, pp. 144–6. See also *Izv.Ts.K.*, No. 9–10 (57–58), October–November 1923, p. 43, *ibidem*, p. 34, and No. 1 (59), January 1924. Attention was first devoted to this problem in July and August 1923 – No. 7–8 (55–56), August–September 1923 – but the problem of evolving a rational system of agreeing appointments with all interested parties was not solved within the NEP period – see *Bol'shevik*, No. 8, April 1928, pp. 66–71.

[2] *SPR*, No. 5, p. 257, a circular referring to elective trade union officials.

[3] *KPSS v rez.*, volume II, pp. 248–50. Trotsky's proposal is preserved among his papers in Harvard Library.

[4] *VKP(b) v rez.*, volume I, pp. 676–9. (The figure is an estimate.)

privileges not easily available to others. If there were some who displayed a fanatical austerity and devotion, there were many who were tempted to abuse their privileged position. Evidence of corruption and
dishonesty among party officials abounds. The control commissions
frequently took disciplinary action against the guilty. But often too, so
long as an official was producing results, they turned a blind eye to his
personal failings – until he fell from grace, and the burden of past
misdeeds was then added to the current charge.[1] The financial resources of the party were according to party Rules after 1922 supposed
to come from the dues of members, from subsidies of the higher party
bodies and 'from other income'.[2]

The periodic congresses and conferences ceased after 1923 to be
bodies which deliberated party policy. Their function became to
endorse the policy decided upon by the leaders, or to set the seal of
formal approval on the defeat of an opposition view. Their importance, therefore, was that they provided a public forum from which
authoritative directives could be issued, and where the leaders could
report on their past activity. There was criticism of these reports, to
be sure, so long as any opposition survived. Nor was the criticism
necessarily ineffective because, as will be seen later, much of what the
opposition advocated was in the event adopted – after the opposition
had been eliminated. But the overwhelming majorities which the
party leaders could rely on at all congresses and conferences nullified
any immediate effects of criticism. The great majority of the delegates – 70 per cent at the Fourteenth Congress in 1925 for example –
came from the party apparatus. After the Eleventh Congress in 1922
there was no occasion when the leaders experienced any difficulty in
securing nearly unanimous approval for their proposals. This was
partly achieved by manipulation of the party Rules so as to ensure
that delegates known to be critical were present only in a non-voting
capacity. But in part it was the result of the improved control by the
Secretariat over the selection of delegates, helped by the fact that
delegates connected with the party apparatus, particularly the rising
generation of young secretaries, could be relied on to support the
General Secretary, on whose good-will their future depended.

The main deliberative body, in which all the controversial decisions
were taken during the period of NEP and of the battle against the left
opposition, was Stalin's improvisation – the joint Plenum of the

---

[1] There is ample evidence on this matter in Merle Fainsod, *Smolensk under
Soviet Rule, passim.*
[2] *KPSS v rez.*, volume I, p. 663.

Central Committee and of the Central Control Commission. In this body the ambitious rising generation was well represented, and Stalin could always be sure of a majority in his favour. The Central Control Commission (which it will be recalled was organizationally fused with the People's Commissariat of Workers' and Peasants' Inspection) was primarily an organ of control over party and government. But in relation to the joint Plenum it performed the further function of a general staff. It collected and prepared the data and materials so as to provide the Plenum with the basis upon which to take decisions. The joint Plenum thus became the main originator of government policy.

The main function of the Central Control Commission, and of the local control commissions subordinated to it, remained the maintenance of discipline among party members. Originally this had been interpreted to mean that a control commission should endeavour to maintain high standards of party ethics but should not take sides in any of the party controversies. After 1923, at any rate, no attempt was made to disguise the fact that the control commissions had become the instruments of the central leadership, pledged to maintain party unity by disarming party critics. The regulations promulgated on the functions of the Central Control Commission in 1924, for example, emphasize that the main tasks of the Central Control Commission include 'determined struggle with all kinds of groupings and tendencies towards factions within the party', 'broad, systematic study of unhealthy phenomena in the party in the field of ideology . . .', and 'purging the party of ideologically alien, harmful and demoralizing elements'.[1] During the conflict with the Leningrad opposition the Central Control Commission, with the exception of a few of its members (including Krupskaia), took an open stand against the opposition and acted jointly with the Central Committee in the efforts to rout it. At the Fourteenth Congress suggestions by some of the opposition speakers that it was the duty of the Central Control Commission to act impartially in party disputes were met with derision. The members of the control commissions enjoyed very full powers in their investigations into the conduct of both organizations and individual party members. Although during this period the party, through the control commissions, jealously safeguarded itself from any encroachments by the OGPU, and retained the privilege of purging itself, the Central Control Commission, as its chairman admitted to the Congress, nevertheless maintained very close liaison with the security organs, and did not hesitate to make use of their services in order to obtain the

[1] *SPR*, No. 5, pp. 500–2.

information which it required. The Central Control Commission was headed by Kuibyshev until 1926. He was succeeded by Ordzhonikidze when Kuibyshev moved to head the Supreme Council of National Economy (VSNKh) in succession to Dzerzhinskii. Kuibyshev owed everything to Stalin. Ordzhonikidze as an old bolshevik was no creature of Stalin, but the two men had worked closely together for years, were fellow Georgians, and throughout this period on good terms.

No general purge of the party, comparable to that which took place in 1921, occurred up to 1927. But the exclusion of members considered undesirable, not only for their oppositional views but also for such offences as drunkenness (a very frequent reason), careerism or dishonesty, remained a feature of party life. Since an expelled party member at worst was left to the mercy of the OGPU and at best lost his post and privileges, a system of appeal from local control commissions to the Central Commission was provided. The general incidence of expulsions, rather higher in 1923–4, when the main victims were Trotsky's supporters among the students and in the army, was perhaps 1 per cent of all party members in 1926 and 1927, or a little more. During the time of the battle against the united opposition in 1926 and 1927, the Central Control Commission, in contrast to the Central Committee, appears to have itself become infected with oppositional tendencies or sympathies, or at any rate failed to show sufficient determination in combating them. For no less than 60 of its 163 members elected at the Fourteenth Congress in December 1925 were not re-elected at the Fifteenth Congress in December 1927. But since none of them was expelled from the party it is probable that their fault had been more the failure to control oppositional tendencies among the members of the local control commissions. An important additional function of the control commissions was talent spotting for the Secretariat: they were required to report on individual party officials and to recommend the more promising for promotion.

* * *

During the period 1924 to 1927 the party also made considerable progress in extending its influence over all aspects of life in the country. Although by the end of 1927 the range and depth of this control was still far from total, when compared with later periods of Soviet history, it nonetheless presented a considerable advance from the party's point of view on the fragmentary and often haphazard control of the early years. The evidence leaves no doubt that the progressive extension of control was throughout planned and deliberate, at any rate from 1923 onwards. On the other hand, the timing of the process was often dictated by the current situation. The tightening of party control over the army, for example, was an aspect of the battle against Trotsky. Control over education was, in part at any rate, dictated by the long-term aim to train up communists who could in time replace the large number of non-communist experts on whom the régime still had to rely during the 20's. As against this, progressive assertion of control over industry and agriculture was at all times an inherent part of the doctrine. At no time was there a particular moment which can be pointed to as the one when a decision was taken to pass from less to more control. The onset of totalitarianism was inherent in the determination which the bolsheviks showed from the first to tolerate no rivals for power, and no independent institutions.

By 1923 the party had achieved complete ascendancy over the soviets. Although for purposes of propaganda the soviets were exalted as the most democratically elected bodies in existence, it was no secret that the ascendancy of the party was only maintained by the abuses practised at election time. These were made easy by the loosely drafted electoral instructions, which left a very wide latitude to the electoral commissions to admit or reject candidatures, or returns. The electoral commissions were, of course, composed of party members. At the end of 1924 and in 1925, however, at the height of the 'right-wing' policy of appeasing the peasants, a decided change took place in preparation for the forthcoming re-elections to about half the local rural soviets. The party organizations were chronically weak and without influence in the villages. The aim of the new policy of allowing some freedom of election to these local soviets was frankly stated to be to attract the peasants to take an interest in organs towards which they had hitherto shown complete apathy. As Stalin explained in a speech in October 1924, unless the peasants could be induced to take an interest in the village soviets, 'the political activity of the masses will pass by the soviets, over their heads, and will spill over into dangerous demonstrations like the Georgian rising'.[1] It was now openly admitted by the communist leaders that elections hitherto had not been free, and that if the non-party peasants were to be attracted to co-operate with the party in the soviets they must be allowed greater freedom in electing candidates of their own choice.

In the new electoral instructions issued in 1925, party organizations were instructed no longer, as in the past, to 'impose their list at

[1] *Stalin*, volume VI, pp. 313–20

election meetings'. Nor should voters 'be excluded merely because they have been critical of local soviet authorities'.[1] Though the peasants suspected at first that all this was merely a trick, in the elections of 1926 and 1927 successful communist candidates were usually very much in the minority. For example, after the 1927 elections both in the RSFSR and in the Ukraine nearly nine-tenths of the members of the village soviets and three-quarters of the chairmen were non-party. The Secretary of the Central Executive Committee, Enukidze, at the Fifteenth Party Congress, nevertheless claimed great credit for the percentage of communists elected, 'especially if one takes into account the fact that the methods practised in elections in former years were no longer applied – such as the appointment of candidates, the transfer of electors, a certain amount of pressure, etc.'

How far this experiment in democracy really led to self-government is another matter. At the same congress, for example, it was only modestly claimed that the soviets had 'in fact' become organs of power only 'here and there'. The handful of communists could still impose their will or circumvent the soviets. Moreover, the rural soviets had in practice little influence on administration in the villages, which the peasants managed to keep under their own control. The opposition viewed the new electoral practice with grave suspicion, regarding it as yet another concession to the *kulaks*. The leaders themselves were unhappy about this experiment, which revealed the slender popular support enjoyed by the party, and in some instances led to demands for the formation of rival parties. The party was repeatedly enjoined to remember that 'putting new life into the soviets' certainly did not mean 'the slightest relaxation or softening towards hostile groups', let alone toleration of mensheviks or socialist revolutionaries.[2] In the following year even this modest attempt to make some elections more genuine was quietly abandoned, and it was never repeated.

* * *

The party crust in state undertakings and organs, in contrast to the soviets, was still very thin in 1923. For example, only 5 per cent of the five thousand employees of VSNKh were communists, and they were not in the most important positions. Considerable efforts were made

[1] See *SPR*, No. 5, pp. 294–6, for a Central Committee Directive dated 10 February 1925.
[2] In addition to the information contained in the speeches at the Fifteenth Congress, see also *Sostoianie i rabota sel'skoi iacheiki*, referred to in note 4, p. 317, above, at pp 24, 26, 109.

in succeeding years by the Orgburo and *Orgraspred* to improve this situation. According to figures quoted at the Fifteenth Congress at the end of 1927 the percentage of communists employed in state departments and organizations averaged 20 or more. Considerable progress was also made in staffing the economic organs with communists. It was claimed at the Fifteenth Congress that three-quarters of the staffs of the boards of management of state trusts were party members, and four-fifths of all directors and assistant directors of enterprises. However, the increasing number of party members in government departments and in economic organs did not necessarily lead to greater harmony between the communist technicians and the communists who represented the party apparatus – for example, the secretary of the party cell in individual government departments or organizations. Throughout the period there was constant friction. Party cells and party members were exhorted not to allow 'guidance' to develop into interference, or into an attempt to displace the state organization concerned by doing its work for it. Party relations with the economic organs and state departments illustrated the limitations which throughout the 20's operated as a brake on smooth control by the party. In the first place, so long as party members were not united in their views on fundamental economic questions, the mere placing of communists in key positions in economic organs was no guarantee that the policy of the Central Committee would be willingly implemented. Again, party control was further limited by the factor which led Lenin to describe the Soviet administrative machine as nothing more than the old bureaucratic machine 'lightly anointed with Soviet oil' – shortage of suitably qualified communists.

The borderline between policy and administration is never easy to draw. The party cells in the government machines were supposed to 'guide', but not to 'interfere'. But where does guidance end and interference begin? Besides, 'party guidance' was one thing when it was imposed on bourgeois experts or on bureaucrats of the imperial civil service: for they were outside the illumination conferred by party wisdom, and were expected to give their skill without questioning the superior judgement of the communists placed over them, however technically inexperienced these might be. But 'guidance' raised quite different problems when it was exercised by non-expert important party bosses over expert, but less important, party members. This question already arose at the Twelfth Congress in 1923. Krasin argued that the party should 'render unto Caesar the things that are Caesar's' – meaning that it should leave the government departments

327

alone to get on with their jobs. Zinoviev, with commendable frankness, argued that dictatorship by the party over the whole state machinery was nothing to be ashamed of or concealed, and that the sooner it was achieved the better. This conflict between the 'apparatus' communist and the expert party member was not resolved during the 20's. Indeed, it was not a problem which could be resolved by the mere packing of government organs with an increasing number of communist employees, since the division of communists into technical experts and professional politicians was not thereby removed. It was perhaps a problem incapable of solution so long as the system maintained one set of men to do a job, and another to tell them how to do it.

XVIII Army and Security: Industry and the Peasants

In the last resort the ability of the party to retain its hold over the country depended on the extent to which it could control the armed force available – the army and the security organs. It is therefore essential to glance at the nature of party relations with these two forces.

When the civil war was drawing to a close, in April 1920, the future of the army was discussed by the party at its Ninth Congress. A permanent standing army was against social democratic tradition, and there were demands for transition to a national militia. Trotsky put forward a proposal of some ingenuity, under which the future militia should be built around the industrial centres, so that its leading cadres could be organized in close co-operation between the army and the trade unions, and under the control of the proletariat. This proposal, which amounted in effect to a military 'dictatorship of the proletariat', was approved in principle, but never carried out. The Kronstadt Rising, the peasant rebellion of 1921–2 and the unrest among the industrial workers at the same time all combined to make any thought of arming a national militia too dangerous to contemplate. There was also opposition to a militia on principle, both from some of the professional officers who regarded it as less efficient than a standing army and from Tukhachevskii, the most brilliant communist commander of those who emerged in the civil war, who believed that the RSFR must retain an army capable of offensive action so as to lend support to revolution elsewhere. When the army was reorganized in 1924 the system adopted was universal military training for all socially reliable citizens (the unreliable, such as priests or *kulaks*, were admitted for fatigue duties only) as well as a standing army about half a million strong. Trotsky, though nominally still People's Commissar for War until 1925, had by this date been *de facto* displaced by his deputy, Frunze, another talented civil war commander, and played no part in the reorganization.[1]

[1] On the history of the early development of the Red Army see D. Fedotoff-White, *The Growth of the Red Army*, Princeton, 1944, on which I have drawn freely. See also John Erichkson, *The Soviet High Command: A Military-Political History 1918–1941*, London, 1962.

Trotsky's open emergence into opposition at the end of 1923 also led to an important change in party control over the army. The Central Committee had not hitherto succeeded in asserting complete authority over the political directorate of the army, PUR, which nominally at any rate was still subordinate to the Revolutionary War Council. Its head in 1923 was a friend of Trotsky and sympathizer with his views, Antonov-Ovseenko, and Trotsky could also count on a measure of support from the officials of PUR and from the army communists generally. An article published by Trotsky in *Pravda* on 4 December 1923, in the course of his first open conflict with Stalin, contained a sentence to the effect that younger soldiers ought not to be terrorized by their elders. At the height of the debate in the party between the opposition and the Central Committee, Antonov-Ovseenko, without consulting the Central Committee, issued a circular under the imprint of PUR calling for widespread discussion in the army of the forms of political control. The army communists, among whom resentment against central party control of their political organizations was strong, welcomed with enthusiasm this opportunity of criticizing centralized party discipline. The Central Committee thereupon annulled the order, and dismissed Antonov-Ovseenko, replacing him by Bubnov.[1]

In the course of 1924 the system of political control over the army was reorganized. PUR was now placed under the immediate direction of the Central Committee, operating, as the new party Rules at the end of 1925 described it, 'as the military department (*otdel*) of the Central Committee'.[2] The Central Committee exercised its control through the network of political departments in military districts, and in military and naval formations and units, all hierarchically subordinate to the central organs of the party. The local party organizations had no jurisdiction over the military party organizations, though liaison was maintained between the two. Thus was created a form of party control over the army which was quite independent of the authorities responsible for the military command.

Closely linked with this change was the reform of the system of political commissars. This form of dual command survived from the civil war and was causing considerable friction by 1924. The

---

[1] On this incident see also I. Petukhov. *Partiinaia organizatsiia i partiinaia rabota v RKKA*. Moscow, Leningrad, 1928, pp. 72–3. And see also Merle Fainsod, *Smolensk under Soviet Rule*, pp. 338–42, for the working in practice of the Central Committee Directives of 20 December 1924 and 6 March 1925 on the functions of party cells in the armed forces and on unity of command respectively.

[2] *KPSS v rez.*, volume II, p. 254.

commanders resented the dilution of their authority and consequent loss of efficiency. Many of them were by now party members and could claim that a system instituted in order to safeguard the revolution against the risk of disloyalty by ex-officers of the imperial army, who formed the vast majority of commanders during the civil war, was now no longer applicable. The commissars in turn, many of whom had acquired military experience and a taste for military matters, often felt that they were as well qualified to command as the young communists graduating from the military schools. A compromise was reached in 1925 which favoured the commanders more in appearance than in fact. The commander was given sole responsibility of command, and the commissar was to become his assistant for political matters. But the political assistant maintained direct relations, over the head of the commander, with the political organs next in the hierarchy. In case of dispute between the commander and his assistant the ultimate decision rested with the Revolutionary War Council of the District, where party rather than military members predominated. The problem of relations between the military and political command was certainly not solved during the 20's. The system of single command was only introduced gradually. By March 1928 all corps commanders, less than three-quarters of divisional commanders and a little over half of the regimental commanders (in all cases the figures relate only to commanders who were party members) had achieved undivided command.[1]

Once Trotsky's plan for a proletarian praetorian guard was abandoned, it was inevitable that the army should be overwhelmingly peasant in its composition. In 1926 71·3 per cent of all soldiers were peasants, as against 18·1 per cent workers and 10·6 per cent 'others'.[2] Moreover, the practice of stiffening key troops with an extra dose of proletarian blood meant that in many units the proportion of peasants was even higher. For example, according to an instruction valid in 1925, a minimum of 50 per cent proletarians had to be allocated to armoured and railway troops, and 25 per cent to the troops of the OGPU, while only 8 per cent were allowed for infantry.[3] The army communists therefore had to play an important role in guiding their

[1] Petukhov, *op. cit.*, p. 82. For the documents relating to the various changes made in party control over the army at this time see *SPR*, No. 5: on the establishment of single command (p. 476); on the function of party cells (pp. 479–85); and on the functions of party organizations in the armed forces generally (pp. 493–6).

[2] St Ivanovich, *VKP(b). Desiat' let kommunisticheskoi monopolii*, Paris, 1928, p. 146. In contrast, among the communists in the armed forces the percentage of peasants was only 38·5 – see *VKP(b) v tsifrakh*, vypusk 6, Moscow, 1927, p. 39.

[3] St Ivanovich, *op. cit.*, p. 147.

socially less reliable comrades. The political organization in the army performed a variety of functions: indoctrination, maintenance of morale, welfare and censorship. An important responsibility of the military party organization was also the recruitment and training of new party members from among the annual intakes, with the object of sending them back to the villages to strengthen the weak party network among the peasants.

The total number of communists in the army increased considerably between 1924 and 1928. The main increase was in 1925–6, from 57,000 in 1925 to 72,000 in 1926. By 1927 party members in the army numbered 82,000, and together with 120,000 *Komsomols* made a total with party affiliation of 202,000 – or 37 per cent of the whole army. The party members were organized in relatively small cells, averaging not more than 15 each. The proletarian element was weak among army communists, and was rather lower than in the party as a whole, where by 1927 those of worker origin formed over half of the party. The rapid enrolment of communists in the army meant that the level of political education among new recruits was too low to enable them to take an active part in political guidance. Hence, control over the army party organization gradually passed into the hands of the more experienced communists, and they were for the most part the officers (commanders) of the regular army. In general, the main strength of the party was among the officers, of whom over half were communists in 1927.[1] At the end of 1926, according to PUR, two-thirds of all posts in the military party apparatus were occupied by officers. The *Komsomol* were mainly in the ranks. From the point of view of the army private, the party official responsible for his indoctrination and political guidance was in most cases at the same time his superior officer – a fact which considerably facilitated the development of strict party discipline inside the army along with military discipline.[2]

In addition to control by the party, the army was also subject to a separate form of control by special sections of the OGPU operating inside it, and responsible for security. After 1921, at any rate, these sections were quite independent of any military form of control. The OGPU (The Unified State Political Administration) was set up on 15 November 1923. It had been provided for in the Constitution of the USSR adopted in July 1923, and was to be the successor to the GPU. Unlike the GPU, the OGPU was independent of the NKVD,

---

[1] The ex-officers of the imperial army were fast being replaced by trained communist officers, and by 1930 only 4,500 out of some 50,000 ex-officers were still serving in the Red Army.

[2] St Ivanuvich, *op. cit.*, pp. 149–51.

or People's Commissariat of Internal Affairs. In other respects it inherited the rights and functions of its predecessors, and in the course of time acquired many more. Continuity with the earlier organizations of internal security was symbolized by the fact that Dzerzhinskii, the founder and head of the *Vecheka* and in 1923 People's Commissar for Internal Affairs, became the chairman of the OGPU. He remained its chairman until his death in 1926, although after 1924 his energies were mainly devoted to the VSNKh, when he became its chairman as well, and OGPU matters were left largely in the hands of his deputy, Menzhinskii. Among the functions which the OGPU acquired or extended between 1923 and 1927 may be mentioned censorship of printed matter, plays and films; administration of frontier areas, for which it was allotted a special corps of Border Troops; and the command of an enlarged force of Special Troops to replace the armed detachments over which both the *Vecheka* and GPU had disposed, at any rate after 1918. Although the powers of the OGPU were not fully defined in such decrees as were published, in practice it never lacked power to do whatever it was required to do by the party. Apart from the express powers of banishment, arrest, search and investigation which it inherited from the GPU, it also took over the wide powers recited in the decree of 6 February 1922, under which the GPU was set up, to fufil 'special instructions by the praesidium of the All-Russian Central Executive Committee or the Council of People's Commissars for the protection of the revolutionary order'.

In theory the OGPU was subordinate to the Council of People's Commissars, and also subject to control by the procurators.[1] In practice, since both the Council of People's Commissars and the procurators were in turn controlled by the party, it is impossible to describe the OGPU as anything other than an agency of the party. No serious rivalry for power developed during this period between the OGPU and the party. Dzerzhinskii, a fanatical communist, who believed that all means justified the ultimate end, served Stalin as faithfully as he had served Lenin until his death. Party control meant in effect either Politburo, or more usually Orgburo, Secretariat or Central Committee control. Dzerzhinskii was a member of the Central Committee throughout, a member of the Orgburo from 1921 until 1924, and thereafter a candidate member of both the Orgburo and the Politburo. The Secretariat, or the Orgburo, controlled senior

[1] See a decree of 28 May 1922, reprinted in *Sovetskaia prokuratura v vazhneishikh dokumentakh.* Moscow, 1956, pp. 212–15. There is no evidence of any conflict during the NEP period between the procurators and the OGPU – see e.g. Fainsod, *op. cit.,* pp. 174–7.

appointments to the OGPU, and less senior appointments were coordinated with the local party organization. But the local party organizations had to keep their distance in relations with the local security organs both so far as appointments and all other matters were concerned.[1]

After the rise of serious opposition movements inside the party, the delicate question arose of what the function of the OGPU should be in relation to heretical members of the party. The party zealously preserved its right to deal with its own members,[2] and would not generally allow the OGPU to act against a party member until he had either been expelled, or at any rate until, like some of the members of the Workers' Opposition who suffered at the hands of the OGPU, he had become an outcast. In the case of a senior party member it was accepted – and even Stalin dared not flout the rule – that arrest could only be authorized by the Politburo. On the other hand, both the Secretariat and the Central Control Commission worked very closely with the OGPU, and never scrupled to rely on its co-operation and assistance, at any rate after 1923, in building up the case against oppositionists.

* * *

The position is very different when one comes to look at the nature of party control over industry and agriculture. The conditions of NEP, which tolerated both a free market and free enterprise even if subjected to interference and restrictions, necessarily imposed limits on the extent to which the party could control and direct. It will be recalled that the rapidly growing divergence between industrial and agricultural prices which became apparent in 1923 (the 'scissors' crisis) polarized opinion in the party broadly between the left-wing minority, which looked to expansion of heavy industry as the remedy, and the majority which placed agricultural prosperity and contentment in the forefront for frankly political reasons – fear of a peasant revolt. In the debates of the ensuing years the struggle for power and resistance to the growing influence of the Secretariat dominated the

[1] See *ibidem*, p. 166; see also an instruction of the Central Committee on 25 May 1926 on the procedure to be followed in the making of appointments within the OGPU, which leaves little discretion to the party organization – *SPR*, No. 6, volume I, p. 567.

[2] Fainsod, *op. cit., loc. cit.* A secret decree of the Central Committee of 26 April 1925 required the party to be notified in all cases of arrests of party members, and allowed interventions by the party organs where they were satisfied 'of the actual innocence of a communist and the lack of substance of the accusations levelled against him'.

political scene so much that theoretical differences of opinion acquired subordinate importance. But one result of this intermingling of theory with manœuvring for power was that, although there was a good deal of force in the allegations made by the oppositionists that the national economy was losing its socialist character, it was not until the opposition was routed at the end of 1927 that Stalin was prepared to make changes in the economic policy of the party.

The solution of the 'scissors' crisis largely determined the future course of economic policy for the next few years. It involved in the main three measures. First, the lowering of industrial prices and a consequent effort to lower production costs; secondly, the establishment of a stable currency so as to encourage the peasants to sell their produce in the market; and thirdly, stimulating the peasant to increase his prosperity by his own efforts. The crisis of price divergence was overcome by 1924. But the recovery of ravaged industry proceeded at a much slower pace than that of agriculture, which had attained over three-quarters of the 1913 level of production by 1923, and by 1925 was beginning to approach the pre-war figure.[1] In contrast, total industrial production had barely achieved half of the 1913 level by 1923-4, and only reached the pre-war level by 1926-7 - or, if allowance is made for a drop in the quality of products, even a year later. Moreover, the recovery of light industry was proceeding more rapidly than that of heavy industry.[2] The basic reason for this lag in industry was shortage of capital for investment. Hopes of foreign loans, which were high in the early 20's, soon foundered. No reconciliation was possible between the demands put forward by prospective foreign investors and the concessions that the USSR was prepared to make, and no agreement could be reached on the question of repayment of pre-war foreign loans which the Soviet government had repudiated. Foreign trade, although expanding fairly rapidly (by 1927-8 exports had reached more than half of the 1913 level), still showed an adverse balance throughout the period of NEP.

The leaders of the party stuck to the view that capital accumulation could only result from the increase of the prosperity, and therefore of the purchasing power, of the peasants. The left opposition persisted in urging the need for more forceful methods of extracting capital from the villages. Their argument was for a time considerably

[1] S. N. Prokopovich, *Narodnoe khoziaistvo SSSR*, volume I, pp. 174-5. The pre-war figure for overall production was slightly exceeded in 1926-8, but the increase of population as compared with 1913 meant that the problem of adequate food supply for the whole population still remained unsolved.

[2] *ibidem*, pp. 346-7.

strengthened, so far as their proletarian supporters were concerned, by the fact that they could point not only to the poor economic conditions of the workers, but to the growing prosperity of the peasants. For the standard of living of the workers recovered more slowly than that of the peasants. Real wages of workers in terms of purchasing power were only 69·1 per cent of 1913 level in 1923–4. Thereafter there was a steady rise to 85·1 per cent in 1924–5, to 108·4 per cent in 1926–7, and to 111·1 per cent in 1927–8. Moreover, in the latter years of NEP the worker was eating more than in 1913, and his working day fell from 8½ hours in 1921 to 7·46 hours in 1927–8.[1] There was, however, a problem of unemployment, which at the Seventh Trade Union Congress in December 1926 was stated to exceed a million, although much of this was due to the drift of the chronic excess of rural population to the towns rather than to lack of employment for the regular industrial proletariat.

It was the constant argument of the left-wing theorists, like Piatakov and Preobrazhenskii, that it was impossible to maintain both public and private sectors in the one economy at the same time, and that in the end one must devour the other. The steady increase of state control over industry and trade during the NEP period seemed to bear out their argument. So far as concerned industry, the privately owned sector, which was as much as a third in 1923–4, fell to 20·8 per cent by 1926–7, and rapidly thereafter. The private sector covered almost entirely the small-scale handicraft industries, and was never significant in large-scale industry. As regards trade, foreign trade was from the first a state monopoly. But internal trade was encroached upon by the state even more rapidly than industry. The privately controlled sector, which formed over half of all trade in 1923–4, was progressively squeezed out of existence, and virtually ceased to exist by 1931.

The government policy initiated at the time of the 'scissors' crisis of lowering industrial prices and production costs depended for its success in large measure on the attitude of the industrial workers, and this in turn depended on the trade unions. The party had already established control over the trade unions before NEP, and it retained its dominant position. On 1 January 1927 the total number of communists enrolled in the unions, both members and candidates, was 1,190,200. Since the total party membership was at the same date 1,212,505, it follows that nearly all party members and candidates were enrolled in the trade unions, in spite of the fact that not more

[1] *ibidem*, volume II, pp. 97–8, 121.

than half the party members, if that, were in fact engaged in manual work. The total trade union membership at the same date was 10 millions. Not all of these, however, were manual workers, since according to the principle of soviet trade unionism managerial, technical and white-collar staffs in any particular industry were all organized in the same union as the manual workers. The percentage of communists in trade union organs was very much higher than their proportionate strength in the unions – 11·9 per cent – and especially at the highest points of the trade union hierarchy. For example, the Plenum of the All-Union Central Council of Trade Unions was 100 per cent communist in 1924 and 99·6 per cent in 1926; the members of all the All-Union Congresses were 98·9 per cent communists in 1924 and 87·1 in 1926. Local trade union committees had a percentage of communists around 90: their chairman and secretaries were without exception communist. At lower levels the factory committees were estimated as 25 per cent communist in 1926, and the commissions attached to them for dealing with labour conflicts 22·2 per cent.[1]

The highly centralized party control over the trade unions, which had been a marked feature of the trade unions in the early 20's and the cause of considerable resentment among trade union communists, remained unaltered. It was indeed an inevitable corollary of the highly centralized nature of the party itself. Trade union control was only an integral part of party activity, subject to the same rules and the same overall direction – as trade union leaders, including Tomskii, frequently emphasized. The trade union organs were strictly forbidden to by-pass the party organs: party instructions of 1923–4 ensured that directives from higher to lower trade union party organs should go through the party channel of the Central Committee and the provincial party committee.[2] This was indeed essential if the trade union communist organization was to be kept fully integrated with the ordinary party network. The Central Committee of the party and its Secretariat also soon asserted the sole right to control both the election of trade union organs, and especially of the key officials, and the transfer of officials from one union to another, or from a union to a party organization. The control of the party over the unions gave the party, or more precisely the Secretariat of the party, a powerful instrument for the government of the industrial workers. The party could control the expulsion of workers from the unions, which, in view of growing unemployment towards the end of the 20's, became a very serious

[1] See St Ivanovich, *op. cit.*, pp. 100–1.
[2] *Izv.Ts.K.*, No. 4 (62), April 1924, p. 25.

sanction, since the expelled worker was in practice almost certain to lose his employment. That expulsion was resorted to not only for reasons of factory discipline is evident from the cases recorded in the official trade union newspaper. Reasons for expulsion included not only drunkenness, unpunctuality or hooliganism, but also 'criticism of the work of the union organ', religious observances, or the fact that a worker's wife was engaged in trade.[1]

The functions of trade unions under NEP were laid down by the Eleventh Party Congress in 1922, for which Lenin drafted the resolution. The resolution recognized that one of the main tasks of the unions would be the defence of the class interests of the proletariat in its struggle against capitalism, in view of the fact that a limited revival of private capitalism had now been permitted. In the case of nationally owned undertakings, the duty of the unions was 'undoubtedly' to 'defend the interests of the workers, to promote as far as possible the increase of their material welfare' and to correct the errors of economic organizations which flow from the 'bureaucratic deformity of the state apparatus'. The resolution went on to recognize that so long as both capitalism and 'bureaucratic deformity' survived, the class struggle, in the form of strikes, would have to continue. But, since the object of strikes was no longer the overthrow of class domination but the strengthening of an already established proletarian state, strikes could only be explained by the 'bureaucratic deformity' of the proletarian state, survivals of capitalism and the political backwardness of the working masses. It was therefore the duty of trade unions to do everything in their power to bring about a peaceful solution of disputes 'with the maximum advantage to the groups of workers represented by them', and if, in spite of these efforts, a strike did break out, it was the duty of the trade union to help to promote both a speedy settlement and the removal of the causes which produced the dispute.

The Congress further laid down that the unions were not to attempt to interfere in the running of individual enterprises: their participation in state control of industry was to be strictly limited to the right to nominate and promote the election of their candidates for membership of the state organs. The unions must also do all in their power to promote the closest and most harmonious relations with the specialist technicians whose services were essential for the development of industry. (The last two provisions were a reminder of the conflicts over the syndicalist trend in the unions which was encouraged by the

[1] *Trud*, 14 November, 17 November, 18 November, 2 December, 4 December 1925.

Workers' Opposition, and the hostility to the non-party specialists which had also grown up by the early 20's, and had caused such bitter conflict in the party.) The resolution ended with emphasis on the need for the trade unions to win and maintain the confidence of the masses of workers who were not party members. Their main method should always be that of persuasion, but 'as participants in the state power, they could not refuse to use methods of compulsion'; they must defend the interests of the workers, but could not in their capacity as builders of the new society 'refuse to exercise pressure'. The Congress foresaw that these twin duties would certainly give rise to conflicts and friction, but sought comfort in the hope that these difficulties could be speedily resolved by the communist party.[1] A further resolution of this Congress urged the party organs to undertake a 'renovation' of the leading trade union organs in order to provide them with a complement of suitable communists. It was perhaps significant that this provision, which was scarcely consistent with the resolution on the absolute inviolability of the electoral principle in composing trade union organs, adopted at the previous Congress in 1921, did not appear in Lenin's draft,[2] and was apparently added in Lenin's absence.

The policy laid down by the Eleventh Congress did not prove easy to carry out in practice. In the first place the trade union communists were not always inclined to obey the self-denying ordinance of the Congress which forbade their interference in management. They were not entirely to blame for this tendency, particularly when dealing with non-party managements, in view of the general encouragement which the party gave to its members to behave as a privileged caste in the days when as a small minority it was seeking to assert its control over national life by rough-and-ready means. Criticism by the Central Committee of undue interference by trade union organs in management was made repeatedly during the period of NEP. But the most difficult precept to put into practice was the dual responsibility of the unions, both as protectors of the workers' interests and as participants in a government which was building a socialist order. The need to develop industry with the little capital available to do it necessarily acted as a brake on wages, and stimulated demands for greater production. The union leaders were repeatedly placed in the difficult position of having to side with the management in their capacity as party

---

[1] *KPSS v rez.*, volume I, pp. 603–12.

[2] *ibidem*, pp. 612–13: contrast Lenin's draft of this resolution in *Lenin*, volume XXVII, pp. 147–56.

members, when their duty and often inclination as trade unionists
made them sympathize with the demands of the workers. Although
strikes remained legal, it became impossible for a communist, on pain
of expulsion from the party, ever to support them, though there is
evidence that many communist trade unionists sympathized with the
strikers, and secretly or even openly tried to side with unofficial
strikes. In October 1925 a stern warning that their action would be
followed by disciplinary measures, including expulsion from the
party, was sounded by the secretary of the Moscow party organization, Uglanov.[1]

The trade unionists never succeeded, as the Eleventh Congress had
enjoined, in winning the confidence of the non-party mass of workers.
For the rank and file worker, as repeated official statements acknowledge, the union, the party and the management remained the 'bosses'
– an attitude which was also shared by many rank and file communist
trade unionists. Indeed, the trade union leaders, and in particular
Tomskii, did not conceal the fact that support by the union for the
interests of the management and of production, where this was dictated by party policy, had to take precedence over the immediate
interests of the workers. Yet many of the trade union leaders, including Tomskii, still had the interests of the industrial workers at heart.
That they were able to give loyal service to the party in the way in
which they did was due both to their faith that they were thereby
helping to build socialism for the future, and to the fact that wages and
work conditions did, however slowly, improve. But the improvement
was due much more to the policy of the party and the government
than to any efforts by the trade unions, which were rapidly becoming
little more than an important instrument for party control over labour.
A very different situation would arise after the end of NEP when a
policy of rapid industrialization, bringing quite new hardships to the
working class, was embarked on.

The picture of party control is in no way comparable when one
turns from industry to the villages. Individual farming was almost the
universal pattern: state and collective farms together in 1927 supplied
less than 2 per cent of the total grain crop, and covered little more than
1 per cent of the total land under cultivation. Since the charge that the
rich peasants, or *kulaks*, were becoming an exploiting class was
repeatedly made by the opposition, and would before long become the
official doctrine, it is necessary to examine the social composition of
the peasant population in 1927. No one ever asserted that the richest

[1] *Pravda*, 4 October 1925.

peasants were more than a small minority. According to official data, proletarians formed 8·2 per cent of the village population, poor peasants 21·1 per cent, middle peasants 66·8 per cent, and *kulaks* 3·9 per cent. These categories were never clearly defined, but an approximation can be made by looking at the size and distribution of holdings. There were no longer any estates of large size comparable to the pre-revolutionary landlords' estates. By the middle 20's, holdings exceeding 27 acres formed two-fifths of all land, and farms of between 15 and 27 acres about half. The remainder, one-tenth, consisted of holdings of less than 15 acres.[1] The poor peasants were those whose holdings were insufficient to keep a family. The middle peasants, the backbone of the farming system, owned at any rate some animals and farm equipment, and could make a living off their land.

The term *kulak* was never defined, if only because for political reasons it was convenient to keep the category vague, and different meanings were attached to the word by different factions in the party. The traditional meaning of the term, which literally means 'a fist', was the richest peasant in the commune who often held the rest of the commune members in fee by acting as money-lender and mortgagee. In Soviet classification up to 1928 the term was most usually applied to the well-to-do peasant who owned one of the larger holdings, draught animals and some equipment, and who was in a position to hire labour and to acquire land by lease from among the poorer peasants. But the Soviet *kulak* no longer engaged either in money-lending or mortgaging, both of which were forbidden, but himself worked the land with his family. In plainer terms, the 3·9 per cent *kulaks* were usually the more industrious and skilful farmers whose enterprise in bettering their own position had since 1922 been encouraged by the party. Both the hiring of labour and the leasing of land had been authorized in 1925, accompanied by exhortations to 'enrich themselves' and by their industry to benefit the national economy.

The strength of the *kulaks* lay neither in their number nor in the proportion of the total yield of grain which they produced. In 1927 just over 85 per cent of total grain production came from the middle and poor peasants, and only 13 per cent from those classified as *kulaks*. According to figures supplied by Molotov to the Fifteenth Congress

[1] In Smolensk province in 1927 five per cent were classified as *kulaks*, 70 per cent as middle peasants and 25 per cent as poor peasants – Fainsod, *op. cit.*, p. 238. See also Otto Schiller, *Die Kollektivbewegung in der Sowjetunion. Ein Beistand zu den Gegenwartsfragen der russischen Landwirtschaft.* Berlin, 1931, pp. 9–10; Maurice Dobb, *Soviet Economic Development since 1917*, London, 1948, p. 209.

in 1927, over half of the commodities reaching the villages was distributed by the communist controlled co-operatives, and nearly two-
thirds of all produce from the land was marketed through the
co-operative organizations. But in many ways the well-to-do peasant
remained the pivot of village social organization, and all the efforts of
the party had failed to supplant him. The traditional village communes survived with little change right up to the collectivization in
1929 much as they had emerged from the uncompleted Stolypin
reforms,[1] and affected the lives of about three-quarters of the peasants.
The new households had grown up around these communes (now
called 'land associations'), which in many places remained the centres
of village administration much more than the soviets or the co-operatives. Again according to figures supplied to the Fifteenth Congress,
the 2,300 village soviets had a total budget of about 16 million roubles,
while the budgets of the land associations and other informal peasant
organizations totalled 80, or according to one estimate, even a hundred
million. These figures may well have been exaggerated, just as the
influence of the well-to-do peasants certainly was at different times for
political purposes. But a detailed survey carried out in 1928 under the
auspices of the Communist Academy enables us to obtain some picture of the real influence of the *kulaks* – though allowance should be
made for the political motive at that date to overstate it. It is plain that
the better-off peasants, as the traditional leaders of village life, were
the natural rivals of the soviet administration which the party was
endeavouring to build up. The 'secret meetings' which the survey
refers to appear on closer investigation often to be mere gossiping at
the village mill, or on the way from market. But it was the kind of talk
that the 'middle' peasants were likely to listen to much more than the
speeches of townsmen in the guise of secretaries of a rural cell, and the
talk was not likely to be pro-communist. The attempt at winning the
peasants over to the soviets left behind it a heritage of peasants disenfranchised as *kulaks* by the electoral commissions, and their natural
resentment found expression at these informal meetings.

None of this was in any sense a political movement. But to a party
for which its own monopoly of power had by now become an obsession, the danger that here was the beginning of national peasant

[1] As late as 1926–7 the communal form of land tenure accounted for 64·8 per cent
of all arable land in Smolensk province – see Merle Fainsod, *op. cit.*, p. 46. For the
structure and powers of the 'land associations' see I. I. Evtikhiev, *Zemel'noe pravo*,
Moscow, Leningrad, 1923, pp. 127–8, 108, and also Paragraphs 42–64 of the Land
Code of 1922, which gave official recognition to these traditional forms of agricultural associations.

movement which might grow strong enough to threaten it may have seemed real enough.[1] The failure of communism to take root in the countryside was also reflected by increased religious activity. According to the same survey there were said to be twice as many organized religious communities as in 1922-3. Organized dissenters were said to number nearly a million, while in the RSFSR alone over 11,000 groups of believers were registered; 560 new communities of orthodox believers were said to have come into existence in 1928 alone. The influence of religion was particularly strong in the Ukraine, where there were said to be more priests than before the war, and the proportion of those with some religious allegiance was estimated as at the lowest 20 per cent, and very much higher in some districts.

By the time that the Fifteenth Congress met at the end of 1927 there were unmistakable signs that a change in policy which would vitally affect both industry and agriculture was under way. Although presented in a guarded form, it was plainly a departure from the 'right' policy which had hitherto been so steadfastly defended against critics from the 'left'. Yet no ripple of dissent appeared among the main upholders of the right-wing view, such as Bukharin or Rykov, at all events on the surface. There were, however, two reasons which may have made a switch in policy more acceptable to all. One was the fact that the left opposition was now routed, and therefore the adoption of part of its policy involved little risk of the return to power of political rivals, with heavy scores to pay off for their past treatment. The second fact was the serious fall in grain supplies to the market, which threatened the towns with shortages, the effects of which could already be felt at the end of 1927. The total quantity of grain produced in 1926-7 was somewhat above the total production for 1913. But the proportion which found its way to the market had fallen. The reason was not far to seek. Where before the war the bulk of produce for the market had come from landowners and *kulaks*, it now came from middle and poor peasants, and they were living better and eating more, thus leaving less for the market. In figures, their total production had increased by 62 per cent, but the quantity they sent to the market had only increased by 26·3 per cent.[2] This was not quite the same as what the oppositionists meant in their repeated warnings that

[1] A. Angarov, *Klassovaia bor'ba v sovetskoi derevne*, Moscow, 1929, *passim*. The whole subject of the peasantry on the eve of collectivization is exhaustively studied in Moshe Lewin, *La Paysannerie et le Pouvoir Soviétique 1928–1930*, Paris and The Hague, 1966, chapters i–viii. An English translation of this important study appeared in 1968.
[2] S. N. Prokopovich, *Narodnoe khoziaistvo SSSR*, volume I, pp. 175–6.

the *kulaks* would before long hold the Soviet régime up to ransom. There was no political motive behind the middle peasants' growing appetite. Nevertheless, the imminent food shortage certainly seemed to bear out the truth of the opposition's case to many who were not likely to analyse its cause with very great precision.

The proposals made at the Fifteenth Party Congress in December 1927 resembled closely many of the points vainly advocated by the opposition in the past few years. The principal decision of the Congress was to issue a directive to the Central Committee to work out in readiness for the next Congress of Soviets a Five Year Plan for the development of the national economy. The directive, which had been approved in the Central Committee in October 1927, laid special stress on the need to develop both the heavy industry required for increasing the output of means of production and the basic industries needed for purposes of defence. (The latter was a repercussion of the war which had swept the party in the summer of 1927.) The directive contemplated that the capital required would have to come from the peasants, but, as if in answer to a charge that the Central Committee had stolen the opposition's clothes, was careful to stress that whereas in 1924 or 1925 a policy of extracting more capital from the villages would have been perilous, now that the firm union between the workers and the poor and middle peasants was assured, the policy was correct.

The decisions of the Congress on agricultural policy and the speeches made in support of them by Stalin and Molotov foreshadowed a very different attitude towards the well-to-do peasants from that pursued hitherto. Taxation of the wealthier peasants was to be increased, the leasing of land severely restricted, and the competition of the communal organizations with the village soviets was to be brought to an end. Above all, there was to be a drive for the formation of agricultural producers' co-operatives – hitherto co-operation had mainly been developed for marketing and for the supply of consumer goods to the peasants. But it was stressed that there would be no compulsion of the 'middle' peasants to force them into the new co-operatives, and individual farming would remain the basis of agriculture for 'a considerable time to come'. As Molotov expressed it at the Congress, anyone who attempted to force the middle peasant into larger scale farming units was 'an enemy of the workers and peasants' since he would be destroying the alliance between them. Stalin also emphasized the need for larger units of agricultural production, to be formed not by pressure but by persuasion. The need in Russia for co-operative farming was indeed evident, if only to undo the effects which the break-up of the large grain-producing estates had had upon the market. The extraction of more money from the *kulaks* and the restriction of their activities were socialist measures to which in principle not even the 'right' could object – even if it was upon the basis of the assurances, encouragement and promises of the right-wing leaders that the more industrious and prosperous peasants had acquired the modest wealth of which they were now to be deprived. For the moment therefore no rift appeared between Stalin and his allies of the 'right'.

XIX Intellectual Life:
the Party at Home and Abroad

By 1927 the party could claim to have achieved almost complete mastery over the mechanism of the state and a large measure of control over the sinews of industry. But it had made little progress with agriculture, and had not yet achieved systematic control over intellectual life. It will be recalled that the party lacked university educated members, who formed less than 1 per cent as late as 1927. Throughout the 20's, and for some time thereafter, the party relied in large measure on non-communist intellectuals who were prepared to co-operate. There were a few writers and professors in the communist party, but large numbers of Russian intellectuals repudiated the communist régime, and many of them emigrated while it was still possible to do so, or joined the White side during the civil war. But there were also many who, without accepting communism, were prepared loyally to co-operate with a communist government. Their motives were mixed. Patriotism and the desire to help to rebuild their ruined country were often stronger than political differences. Many no doubt hoped that the excesses which they disliked in communist rule would in time be eradicated, as the régime became more certain of itself and more solidly established. The long tradition of the Russian intellectual of pursuing his life of the spirit in a state of permanent alienation from the government also played its part. The subsequent elimination, and often vilification, by the communists of the intellectuals who co-operated with them in the early years must not be allowed to obscure the fact that, while it lasted, this co-operation was loyal and unstinted.

There were two policies open to the party in establishing relations with the intellectuals outside the party. One was the application to the intellectual sphere of the policy inherent in NEP: a policy of genuine co-operation with non-communists, which recognized both mutual interests and differences, but which aimed ultimately at winning over the entire intelligentsia to communism by the persuasive appeal of its sterling qualities – much as the peasants, according to the theory of NEP, were to be won over to communism by the proof which it would eventually offer of its superiority as a system by catering for their interests. This was always the view of the right wing in the party, and their support of Stalin was based upon the belief that he too shared this view. The other policy was to make do with non-party supporters so long as there was no alternative, but to replace them at the first opportunity by communists and non-communists prepared to accept full communist discipline. It was to become clearly apparent by about 1930 that the latter had become the chief aim of the party, but it could not be implemented before then.

An intensive policy of educating party members was pursued during the 20's.[1] By 1927–8 there were over forty thousand party schools, study groups and organized courses of all kinds in existence, and the number enrolled in them was over three-quarters of a million. The schools were intended to train not only party members but also potential recruits to the party, and of the total number of students in 1927–8 only 62·2 per cent were already members. The development of party schooling during the 20's was such that there was always a substantial proportion of communists who had been through some kind of training, and a number who passed from the more elementary party schools to the higher schools. Party schooling soon came under the control of the Secretariat, and therefore provided it with a valuable instrument for training up the kind of loyal officials which it required, and for indoctrinating them against 'Trotskyism'. Nonetheless, although the teaching in the party schools was necessarily strongly angled towards such subjects as 'Leninism' and party history, the general training which they provided went some way to offset the lack of education from which so many party members suffered.

The problem of the universities was tackled by the party in two ways. Since it was unable to restock them with communist staff, it had to content itself with infiltrating them with individual communist teachers, or with attempting to exercise some kind of control through the party cells formed inside them. But this was necessarily a make-shift method. As a longer term programme, a series of 'communist universities' were built up during the 20's, side by side with existing universities, with the aim of producing a future generation of communist university teachers, and of supplying an alternative to bourgeois

[1] For details on party schooling, on the communist universities and the Communist Academy I have drawn freely on the doctoral dissertation in the University of London on 'Soviet Party Schools' by my former student Dr Zev Katz.

higher education. An important step in this direction was the establishment in 1921 of the Red Professors' Institute, which specialized mainly in the social sciences, history and philosophy. With the defeat of the 'left' theoreticians in the 20's, it was natural enough that the Red Professors' Institute should have become the stronghold of the right wing, many of its members being followers of Bukharin's views. The other 'communist universities' were conceived of more as schools for the training of the highest level party theoreticians and officials. By 1924 there were ten such 'communist universities' in existence, with over six thousand students, and by 1928 there were nineteen universities and 8,400 students. In addition, the party exercised strict control over the posting of all party members who had completed their education in the normal universities. For this purpose the Secretariat set up in 1926 a commission on which all interested departments and institutions were represented.

A similar policy was pursued with regard to the Academy of Sciences, as the Imperial Academy of Sciences was renamed. A parallel body was set up, known first as the Socialist, and later as the Communist Academy which became the centre of party intellectual activity. Although a completely official body, subordinated to the Central Executive Committee, the Communist Academy nevertheless retained until 1927-8 a large measure of aloofness from the strife going on in the party. The Praesidium elected in January 1927, for example, included Preobrazhenskii and Riazanov, as well as Bukharin, and Piatakov's works on economic theory were published by the Academy as late as 1926, although his views were by then already considered very heretical. The intellectual activity of the Academy during this period was the golden age of Marxist thought in the USSR. A number of stimulating works appeared under the auspices of the Academy, in which the leading Marxists of the party, writing from different points of view, attempted to develop the principles of Marxism in the conditions applicable in Russia. Very few of these intellectuals were destined to survive the more rigorous control which would be applied to the Academy after NEP had been abandoned.

Thus, in the academic sphere, although the problem remained unsolved, the outlines of the future solution were already discernible. In the case of literature, however, the party came up against the difficulty of reconciling its desire to control creative activity with the equally strong desire of the creative writer to retain his freedom. The intervention of the party in the field of literature could hardly be related to existing Marxist doctrine. Marx and Engels had conventional views on literature and art and did not incorporate them into their system. Lenin's tastes in literature were also conventional, and in private conversation he did not conceal his dislike of the modern experimental schools in literature which sprang up after the revolution, regarding it as the duty of writers to be intelligible to the masses. His only written pronouncement on the subject would later be much canvassed as authority for complete party control over all literature, and became the foundation of the communist theory of literary control. This was an essay written in 1905 urging that literary effort should be subordinated to party aims. From its context it apparently related only to 'literature' in the limited sense of party political writings.[1] It is true that in 1920 Lenin intervened sharply against a modernist group *Proletkul't* which claimed to lead a movement of new, truly proletarian art and literature, which would serve to unite and rally the forces of the proletariat as a class. *Proletkul't*, however, claimed that as a movement it should be free from party controls, and at this point Lenin insisted that it should be brought under the general control of the People's Commissariat of Education.[2] But this sole intervention can easily be explained by the fact that *Proletkul't* was inspired and led by Lenin's old antagonist Bogdanov, whose views he detested.

This incident apart, for some years various contending groups of communist and non-communist littérateurs pursued their feuds, usually with no more interference from the party than censorship by the OGPU. Few of the leading literary figures adhered to the new régime; most of them emigrated, and some like the poet Gumilev fought against the bolsheviks and paid with their lives. Alexander Blok, possibly the greatest poet of the time in Russia, supported the bolshevik revolution, to the dismay of his friends, but was almost immediately disillusioned and died in 1921 of disappointment or remorse. The most talented writers who remained in Russia formed a group known as the Fellow Travellers: these writers were the counterpart in literature of the ex-officer in the Red Army or of the non-party technician in the state factory. They accepted the régime, without subscribing to the official doctrine, and while quite ready to concede

---

[1] This article, 'Partiinaia organizatsiia i partiinaia literatura' was written in November 1905 and was prompted by the practical consideration that as the result of the revolutionary events of that year the party could now publish openly inside Russia and not only illegally or abroad, and would therefore be entering into relations with private publishers. At one point Lenin specifically says that he is only dealing with political and not creative 'literature'. There are however some passages which can lead to the inference that creative literature too should be subordinated to party aims. See *Lenin*, volume VIII, pp. 386–90.

[2] *Lenin*, volume XXV, pp. 409–10, 637.

the need for censorship as a protection against subversive writings, wished to remain free to write as their vision and imagination impelled them. The Fellow Travellers were the constant object of attack by various extreme experimental left-wing groups of writers, who claimed to be creating a new form of 'proletarian' art, which would replace the art of the 'bourgeoisie' and become a weapon in the class struggle, but whose political zeal in general rather outpaced their talents.

The party for a time remained neutral in this contest, though from 1923 onwards the officials of *Agitprop* began to take a close interest in the activities of the literary groups – recording writers, studying the literary journals and bringing the publishing houses under close control. Throughout the period of NEP, however, small independent publishing firms survived precariously, and it was still possible for Russian writers to publish with émigré firms abroad. In 1925 however, the Central Committee intervened in the literary quarrels with a resolution dated 18 June. Reported to have been drafted by Bukharin, this resolution certainly embodied the philosophy of the 'right' wing. Though siding in principle with the left-wing proletarian writers, the resolution stressed that their claim to drive all others from the field was premature and their methods undesirable. Their task was to win over the Fellow Travellers by persuasion and example, and by closer co-operation. The resolution also, while stressing that literature should aim at being comprehensible to the masses, urged the need for the free competition of different styles.[1] The freedom inaugurated by this resolution was to prove short-lived. The defeat of the opposition and the end of NEP were to usher in an entirely new kind of party approach to literature. Even during the period of comparative freedom, however, the party was never at a loss if it wished to prevent a writer from publishing. One of the most talented of early Soviet writers, E. Zamiatin, who eventually emigrated, claimed in a letter written to Stalin in 1931 that he had been virtually prevented from publishing in Russia after 1920 as a reprisal for an article in which he had complained that excessive heresy-hunting was stifling all creative work.[2]

Thus in matters of education and literature, the party, as in agriculture, tolerated, if unwillingly sometimes, forms of activity which ran counter to its doctrines. It remained confident that it would in the fullness of time, by persuasion and example, win over those who were

[1] Reprinted in *Izv.Ts.K.*, No. 25–26 (100–1), 13 July 1925.
[2] E. Zamiatin, *Litsa*, New York, 1955, pp. 277–82.

not yet prepared to accept the doctrine in its entirety. The position was different as regards the social structure, where direct intervention by legislation and by administrative action was more readily possible. Early attempts to break up the family as a centre of social cohesion may be cited as an example of such intervention. This movement probably owed much less to Lenin, whose views on marriage as on literature were conventional, than to left-wing hotheads, of whom Alexandra Kollontai was typical. Soviet family law, as enacted in the Family Codes of 1918 and again in 1926, was squarely aimed at breaking up the family as a unit. Both marriage and divorce were reduced to simple registration, no distinction was made between legitimate and illegitimate children, or after 1926 between registered and unregistered *de facto* marriages, the rights and duties of both partners were equalized, and no relationship was in law recognized as subsisting between the husband's kinsmen and the wife's.

In contrast, the attack on the Church and on religion was always fundamental to Lenin's policy. Marx's famous dictum that 'religion is the opium of the people' did not in the context mean that the people should be forcibly deprived of their opium after the revolution, but that social conditions should be so improved that they would no longer need it. Lenin's militant materialism went rather further than this. Already in 1905 he had stressed the need for the party to struggle against religious obscurantism, and his reason for not including atheism as compulsory doctrine in the party programme was, as he explained, only because many potential followers might be repelled by such an article of faith.[1] No attacks were made on religion during the months before the seizure of power. Even after that the party, well aware of the fact that religious practice was deeply ingrained in Russian life, preferred to leave anti-religious activity to the *Vecheka*, and to amateur efforts by enthusiastic communists. Legislation was confined to expropriation of Church property, the persecution of priests, the prohibition of religious instruction to persons under 18, and the refusal of legal recognition to church marriages. The Constitution of 1918 recognized freedom of both religious and anti-religious propaganda as the right of every citizen, but in practice the Church was from the start placed under a handicap, since it was the *Vecheka* which in the last resort had the power of determining what was 'religious propaganda' and what was 'counter-revolutionary propaganda'.

In spite of the advantages which the party enjoyed, its assault on

[1] *Lenin*, volume VIII, pp. 419–23.

religion made little progress during the NEP period. The party could persecute priests and preach atheism, but the communists were soon to discover that religion thrives on persecution. By 1923 two methods which had been used in the endeavour to break the hold of the Church had failed: a staged trial and condemnation of fifty-four high dignitaries of both the Orthodox and the Roman Catholic Churches (1922); and an attempt about the same time to create a new subservient so-called 'Living Church', to draw allegiance away from the Orthodox Church. New methods therefore had to be tried. The main new effort adopted during the period was the formation in 1925 of the Militant League of the Godless. The League received more support from the party apparatus which sponsored and ran it through *Agitprop*, than it did from the population who were urged to join it: by 1928 its total membership was only 123,000.[1] Its propaganda was of a crudely blasphemous nature, which repelled more people than it converted. Other administrative measures included forbidding the sale of Christmas and Easter foods and decorations. It was perhaps owing to the failure of this anti-religious drive that a compromise was reached with the Church. On 19 August 1927 the last acting Patriarch to survive at liberty, his predecessors in office having been successively imprisoned, after negotiation with the government announced on behalf of all members of the Church that he had assured the government of their 'sincere readiness to be fully law-abiding citizens' and to remain aloof from all political parties seeking to harm the Soviet Union.[2] If the Church thereby to some extent compromised its integrity in admitting by implication that it had hitherto been supporting counter-revolution, it at the same time removed, so far as the government was concerned, any justification for action against it. The compromise was not destined to last beyond 1928.

* * *

It will be recalled that policy towards the national minorities was shaped at the Twelfth Party Congress in 1923, when Stalin had succeeded in winning support for more centralized control than Lenin had thought desirable. Opposition to his policy from some of the national communists, chiefly the Ukrainians and the Georgians, had

[1] For details see N. S. Timasheff, *Religion in Soviet Russia 1917–1942*, London, 1943, Chapter ii. On the failure of the League of the Godless in Smolensk province during the NEP period see also Merle Fainsod, *Smolensk under Soviet Rule*, pp. 432–4, based on the archives of the Smolensk party organization.
[2] Matthew Spinka, *The Church in Soviet Russia*, New York, 1956, chapter ii For some further and more recent literature on religion in the Soviet Union see Bibliographical Note, Appendix I.

received guarded backing from the right wing of the party, notably Bukharin, but had been easily routed. Shortly after this Congress Stalin took several steps to consolidate his victory over the national opposition. Some of those who had spoken against him at the Congress, for instance Rakovskii, a leading communist in the Ukraine, were posted out of harm's way – Rakovskii became the first Soviet envoy to Britain.

But it was the case of Sultan-Galiev which caused most stir in the party. Sultan-Galiev was leader of the Tatar communists, and was at one time a faithful protégé of Stalin. Disillusioned in the dictatorship of the proletariat, but still a convinced communist, he had been advocating 'the establishment of the dictatorship of the colonies and semi-colonies' over the industrial metropolis, and the setting up of a Colonial International. More concretely, he also demanded the re-establishment of the former autonomous Moslem Communist Party, which the Central Committee had disbanded in 1918. Stalin evidently decided to make an example of Sultan-Galiev. With the aid of the GPU he obtained incriminating 'evidence' against Sultan-Galiev, and, armed with this 'evidence', Stalin succeeded in persuading the other members of the Politburo to have the Tatar leader arrested – at any rate, Zinoviev and Kamenev later admitted that they had reluctantly given their consent, and none of the other members is known to have remonstrated. Since Sultan-Galiev was still a member of the party, and a leading member at that, this was a dangerous precedent for the future role of the GPU in inner party disputes. A special party conference was called in June 1923 to discuss the case. Stalin now produced what he described as evidence that Sultan-Galiev was a traitor in league with anti-communist nationalist movements, and asserted that Sultan-Galiev had confessed. (Sultan-Galiev was of course not present or given an opportunity to defend himself.) Although not all the members of the conference were convinced, Stalin obtained his majority, and Sultan-Galiev was expelled from the party.[1]

Sultan-Galiev was apparently at some time released from arrest, for at the end of 1929 he was once again stated to have been arrested, and thereafter he disappeared. His case was a warning to other would-be nationalists that the step from the advocacy of autonomy for the national parties to treason was a short one, and it had its effect. During the NEP period there were few significant signs of nationalism among

---

[1] See A. Benningsen, 'Sultan-Galiev, l'U.R.S.S. et la révolution coloniale', *Esprit*, April 1957 (Paris), pp. 641–59. For Stalin's speech in 1923 see *Stalin*, volume V, pp. 301–12.

the communist leaders of non-Russian nationality. The Georgian rising in 1924 was, of course, openly anti-Communist. There were other reasons for this besides Stalin's action against Sultan-Galiev. One was the improved mechanism of the central party apparatus, which could make free use of transfers of any potential trouble makers, and of appointments of reliable emissaries from Moscow to dominate the local parties in the national minority areas – of Kaganovich, for example, as First Secretary of the Ukrainian party. Another was the comparative tolerance and laxity of central government administration during the period of NEP, which may in part have been due to Rykov's occupancy of the post of Chairman of the Council of People's Commissars.

Considerable efforts were made throughout this period to make the leading party officials and functionaries in the national republics and territories 'more native', though not with very great success. This is indicated by the figures for the national composition of delegates to party congresses, who represented the party élite of the whole country. For example, in May 1924, at the Thirteenth Party Congress, Russians formed 60·8 per cent of all delegates, and Jews formed another 11·3 per cent. The Turko-Tatar peoples who were at that date almost 11 per cent of the whole population of the country, were represented by only 1 per cent of all delegates. The Ukrainians had 4·7 per cent of delegates. Yet, according to the census figures of 1926, Ukrainians formed over 21 per cent of the total population, and Russians just under 53 per cent. At the Fifteenth Congress in December 1927 the Turko-Tatar group of delegates had only risen to 1·6 per cent and the Ukrainians to 9·8 per cent, while some other national delegations had slightly decreased as compared with 1924. The Russian delegates formed 62 per cent. The figures for the party as a whole in 1927 show that the national minorities were still often under-represented in the party in proportion to their total numbers. Thus Ukrainians still formed under 12 per cent as compared with 65 per cent Russians. The under-representation of Muslim peoples was still very marked. For example, the Tatars formed 1·37 per cent of the party and 2 per cent of the population, the Uzbeks 1·19 per cent of the party and 2·65 per cent of the population, and for the Bashkirs the comparable figures were 0·21 and 0·49 per cent. As against this, the Georgians, Belorussians and Armenians were represented fully in proportion to their total populations, or even a little more.[1]

[1] Figures for nationality of congress delegates will be found in the relevant congress reports. The figures for 1927 are based on the party census of that year –

Progress was however made with the training of communists from the national minority parties. From the early 20's onwards a number of universities and institutes existed for the various nationalities at which both Russians and native communists were trained for service in the national parties. The foundations were thus being laid for the emergence of a corps of communists of the native nationalities, but properly assimilated, indoctrinated and disciplined, who could be used to strengthen the as yet very thin stratum of native communists in the local party machines. But so long as they lacked the necessary native leaders, properly schooled, the leaders in Moscow were careful, by concessions to national sentiment and to cultural tradition, not to alienate too much those older native communists on whose services they still depended. Thus they were successful in preserving the loyal co-operation of many of the native communists who were to fall as oppositionists of one kind or another in the 30's.

*   *   *

The history of the relationship of the USSR with foreign countries and with their communist parties is at all points closely interwoven with the events inside Russia which have already been described. Criticism of the foreign policy pursued by the party after Stalin and his allies had established their supremacy over it became the stock in trade of the opposition, with consequent exaggeration by both sides. The opposition alleged that Stalin and the 'right' wing had betrayed the cause of world revolution: the threat of a 'Thermidor' inside Russia explained, according to them, the decreasing tempo with which revolution abroad was being encouraged. Stalin, in turn, sheltered behind the mantle of Lenin, showing much ingenuity in claiming Lenin's authority for particular tactical moves which Lenin could not in his time have anticipated. Yet, allowing for all this exaggeration, it was the case that the policy of retreat from world revolution, in the sense that from a tactical first priority it became an ultimate strategic aim, was already well established before Lenin's career ended. It

---

see *Sotsial'nyi i natsional'nyi sostav VKP(b). Itogi vsesoiuznoi partiinoi perepisi 1927 goda*. Moscow, 1928. The under-representation of some nationalities to the benefit of others was illustrated by figures which were given by Ordzhonikidze to the Fifteenth Congress in 1927 on the national composition of organs of the state apparatus. In Moscow and Leningrad, as might be expected, the employees of state institutions were overwhelmingly Russian and Jewish – with a rather large Jewish percentage (11·8 and 9·4 respectively). In the national republics, Russians predominated (from two-thirds to three-quarters) over natives in the Central Asia republics, in Georgia Russians were a small minority among those employed, while in the Ukraine Russians and Jews occupied about a fifth each of all posts, and about a third each of all posts in the capital – *XV S"ezd*, pp. 399–401.

stemmed less from any change of theory than from the practical recognition that the hope of further immediate revolutions was vain, and that the most concrete step towards encouraging them in the future was the consolidation of the communist régime in Russia. This was after all the reasoning by which Lenin justified the peace of Brest-Litovsk in 1918. Long before Stalin began to play any part in decisions on foreign policy it was well established that in some circumstances it might be more advantageous, both for Russia and for ultimate world revolution, if Russia were to consolidate a diplomatic gain even at the expense of a foreign communist party. Alliance with Turkey, to the detriment of the Turkish communists, was one such instance. The subordination of the Chinese communists to the Kuomintang was another. Moreover, in the latter case, the agreement between Russia and Sun Yat-Sen in 1923 was concluded by Ioffe, a close and lifelong friend of Trotsky, and there is nothing to indicate that Trotsky, who was later so critical of the consequences of this agreement, had any misgivings at the time.

It was, of course, true that Stalin used developments in the Comintern in order to help him in his struggle against his rivals, especially Trotsky and Zinoviev, who until the middle 20's played a leading part there. His struggle against Trotsky also provided him with a good excuse to ensure the removal from the Comintern, and from their own parties, of left-wing foreign communists who were known to sympathize with Trotsky. But it is easy to exaggerate this aspect of the matter, especially if it is seen, as is often the case, through the eyes of the defeated oppositionists. From the end of the civil war, at any rate, the Russians were pursuing two parallel policies which were on the face of it incompatible. One was the furthering of world revolution through the Comintern, the other was the consolidation by normal diplomatic means of trade relations and alliances with the capitalist powers. The incompatibility was perhaps more apparent than real. Neither Stalin nor those mainly responsible for foreign policy during the 20's believed that the capitalist powers would be so blind as to fail to discern the contradictory nature of the two aspects of Soviet policy. It is unlikely that they expected the capitalists to be so naïve as to be deceived by the frequent denials made by the Soviet Union that it was fomenting revolution, or by its assertions that revolutionary activity was unconnected with official Soviet policy, but was the action of private individuals, whom the Soviet authorities, as the government of a democratic state, were unable to restrain. The Russian communist leaders believed that there were objective reasons which would, whatever their inclinations, force the capitalist powers into alliances and relations with the Soviet Union, however much those alliances or relations might benefit the Soviet Union more than themselves. One was the desire to secure Soviet trade. Another was the rivalry between the capitalist powers, which, in spite of temporary stabilization, the communists always believed was never far below the surface. A third was the support which they hoped they could win among the workers of the capitalist powers and among the anti-imperialist populations of the colonial and semi-colonial countries.

The communist leaders were also aware of the advantage which they could derive from the fact that the powers with which they were principally concerned during the NEP period – Britain, France and Germany in Europe, and the USA – were democratic powers with a free party system. There was therefore the possibility of exploiting the political party in opposition against the party temporarily in power. In all this complex and subtle policy the Comintern necessarily had an important role to play. But it was not the kind of policy which could be left to the individual parties composing the Comintern to work out in free debate: the only condition for its success was to impose it ruthlessly from above. This reason alone, apart from any natural authoritarianism in the traditions of the Russian communist party, would have dictated the increasing subordination of the foreign parties to strict rule by the Russian party.

These basic principles of communist foreign policy during the NEP period are best illustrated by the cases of Germany, Britain and China. In the main, the policy pursued towards Germany was con-solidation of the advantages gained in 1922 at Rapallo. Germany was an outcast, with serious grievances against the peace settlement imposed upon her at Versailles. This, together with the opportunity which, under the terms of the secret agreements, Russia offered to Germany to rearm in breach of the Versailles Treaty, helped to bind Germany to Russia. With the recovery of Germany's economy new possibilities for trade were also opened up. Even after the admission of Germany to the League of Nations, agreed on by the Western European powers at Locarno in October 1925, the Soviet Union, which regarded the League with deep suspicion and boycotted it, was still able to retain diplomatic ascendancy over Germany. The USSR was successful in negotiating a Neutrality and Non-Aggression Treaty with Germany on 24 April 1926 which effectively cut Germany out of participation in any forcible action by the League under the terms of its Covenant.

Thus Russia appeared to have more to gain from stability in Germany than from any attempts to sponsor revolutionary upheavals from within. Nevertheless, tempted by the ferment caused in Germany by the occupation of the Ruhr by French and Belgian troops, the Comintern encouraged and promoted a communist rising inside Germany in October 1923. It was an immediate and complete failure, as could indeed have been foreseen. Both Trotsky and Zinoviev had given the adventure their full support, Stalin had privately advised caution, but he had played no public part in the affair. When the aftermath of recriminations set in, Stalin, quite uncompromised by the failure, was the one who gained most. The fiasco was blamed on Radek, who, like Stalin, had advised caution.[1] This incidentally gave Stalin the advantage of the withdrawal from active politics inside Russia of a man who in matters of home policy was a supporter of Trotsky. Radek was reprimanded, became rector of one of the communist universities for national minorities, and was dropped from the Central Committee at the Thirteenth Congress in May 1924. The main result of the incident, so far as Russian policy was concerned, was to confirm Stalin in his view that left-wing adventures were not likely to be as advantageous as a more subtle, long-term policy of communist expansion; and to bring about a reversion in Comintern policy from promoting direct revolution to the United Front tactics of penetrating and utilizing the mass workers organizations of the 'bourgeois-democratic' countries, which was advocated by Lenin in 1920.

In its diplomatic relations with the outside world, the Soviet Union now entered on what was at first called the 'breathing space' during a temporary stabilization of capitalism, and a year later, in 1925, would be described as 'a long period of so-called peaceful co-existence between the USSR and the capitalist countries'.[2] The elaboration of this view of foreign policy was closely related to the development by Stalin, in the course of polemics with Trotsky, of his doctrine of 'socialism in one country'. Both Stalin, and Bukharin who preached the new gospel to the Comintern, were careful to insist that building 'socialism in one country', during a period of 'peaceful co-existence' did not mean the abandonment by Russia of the main aim – promoting world revolution. Yet, there was often a slight difference of emphasis discernible between the formulations used by Stalin and by Bukharin. For Stalin, prospective revolutions in other countries were more

---

[1] For a detailed account of the fiasco in Germany see E. H. Carr, *A History of Soviet Russia, The Interregnum 1923–1924*, London, 1954, Chapter ix.
[2] *KPSS v rez.*, volume II, pp. 194–5.

usually related to what for him was their primary function – bolstering the communist régime in the USSR. Bukharin saw the growing strength of the USSR as a 'mighty lever of the international proletarian revolution'.[1]

For a time diplomatic successes in relations with Britain seemed to prove the validity of the new policy. In January 1924 the first Labour government was returned in Britain, and shortly after taking office recognized the Soviet Union *de jure*. Britain's example was soon followed by Italy and many other governments, though not by the USA. Stalin attributed this diplomatic triumph 'above all' to the growing popularity of the Soviet Union among the masses in the capitalist countries. Opportunities for the development of trade with Britain, now appeared to be good. Discussions were initiated in an attempt to settle the question of British claims against the USSR as the basis for an agreement on loans from Britain to Russia. But the Labour government fell in October 1924. The Russians, confident in the support which they believed they now enjoyed among the working masses in Britain began to overplay their hand. In the midst of the election campaign in Britain a letter, containing instructions for subversive activities and allegedly signed by Zinoviev as chairman of the Comintern, was made public in the British press. Whether genuine or not, and the Russians strenuously denied its authenticity, the letter differed little from what Zinoviev had been saying in the Comintern in the past months.[2] The victory of the Conservatives in the elections in Britain soon led to a deterioration in Anglo-Soviet relations. But the Soviet leaders, while continuing to voice their contempt for the British Labour Party leaders, intensified their policy of winning the support of organized labour in Britain. Friendly relations were established with the British trade union movement, and a joint Anglo-Russian Trade Union Committee was set up in 1925. In May of the following year the General Strike which broke out in Britain was openly supported by the Russian party, to the extent of an offer of funds from the communist-controlled Soviet trade unions.

The Conservative government in Britain had meanwhile been taking steps to reverse the policy of its predecessor. The negotiations inaugurated by the Labour government were not pursued, and there

---

[1] Compare, for example, Stalin's speech to the Fifteenth Party Conference in *Stalin*, volume VII, pp. 246–66, with Bukharin's Report to the Seventh Enlarged Plenum of the Executive Committee of the Comintern, in November–December 1926, quoted in extract in X. J. Eudin and Harold H. Fisher, *Soviet Russia and the West 1920–1927*, A Documentary Survey, Stanford, 1957, pp. 336–7.

[2] Eudin and Fisher, *op. cit.*, pp. 301–7.

were repeated protests over Soviet subversive activities both inside Britain and in the territory of the British Empire. In May 1927 a raid on the premises of the Soviet Trade Delegation in London was alleged to have produced evidence of extensive Soviet espionage and subversive activity in Britain conducted through the Delegation, diplomatic relations were suspended and the Trade Delegation was expelled. Yet all was not lost. Commercial relations were still maintained, and the Soviet leaders had the satisfaction of knowing that the action of the Conservative government was strongly disapproved by the Labour opposition. Nevertheless, the rupture of relations with Britain created inside Russia a credible fear of war, when viewed in relation to other events. A dispute with France was in progress over the activities of French communists inside the country. In March Italy ratified a multi-lateral Convention of 1920 guaranteeing the secession from Russia of Bessarabia, which the RSFSR had never recognized. In Poland the Soviet ambassador was assassinated in June while discussions on a proposed non-aggression treaty were in progress. About the same time the British Trade Union Council dissolved the Anglo-Russian Trade Union Committee. The exploitation of the war scare both by Stalin and by the opposition has already been dealt with, as well as its immediate repercussions on home economic policy.[1] The other effect, the entry of the Soviet Union into the field of international disarmament discussions, belongs to a later chapter.

The opposition had bitterly criticized the 'right' for entering into relations with the British labour and trade union movements, branding this as a betrayal of the pure, revolutionary ideal. Yet the sober truth was that, from the Soviet point of view, Russian policy in Britain had been, if anything, too revolutionary. The opposition were on stronger ground in their criticism of policy in China. The alliance between the Chinese communists and the non-communist Kuomintang had been steadfastly pursued. It was true that alliance with a 'bourgeois nationalist' movement for national independence in a semi-colonial country was in accordance both with Lenin's views and with the decisions of the Second Comintern Congress in July 1920. But the Comintern had at the same time stressed that communist parties should retain their identity. They must 'give the peasant movement as revolutionary a character as possible, organizing the peasants and all the exploited, wherever possible, in Soviets'. This was the policy which the opposition urged should have been pursued in China, and which the 'right' refused to adopt, placing its faith in what it believed

[1] See pp. 307–8 above.

were the more solid prospects of victory under the wing of the Kuo-mintang. Whether or no the policy of direct insurrection could have succeeded, the policy of alliance with the Kuomintang proved an evident and disastrous failure. Although the country was on the edge of revolt, expropriation of the landlords on the Russian model was not what many Kuomintang leaders wanted, and the ill-assorted partner-ship could only be maintained by restraining communist attempts to provoke a peasant uprising. Theoretically, using the favourite analogy of Russian experience, the Kuomintang became the *kadets*, but unlike the *kadets* they had played as Bukharin explained, an 'objectively revolutionary role', and therefore it was correct for the communists to support them.

However, there were limits to the degree to which the Chinese communists, or the Russian communists who were their constant mentors, could be expected to follow passively a bourgeois pro-gramme in the hope of a socialist victory in the distant future. The communists in China, as once in Russia, tended to interpret 'support' of the Kuomintang in their own way. In June 1927 a secret telegram from Moscow to the Chinese communists, urging direct action in defiance of and against the Kuomintang leadership in order to freshen and reinforce it and to 'liquidate the dependence upon unreliable generals immediately' fell into the Kuomintang's hands. The com-munists were promptly expelled from the Kuomintang and many arrests followed. Since the Chinese '*kadets*' had now become 'counter-revolutionary', direct action against them was considered justified. Two communist insurrections accordingly took place in September, in Swatow and in Hunan, but both failed. The Chinese débâcle was rendered all the more embarrassing to Stalin by the fact that it came at the last stage of his conflict with the opposition. Everything that they had predicted in China now appeared to be coming true. It was a measure of the importance of control over the party apparatus, when compared with questions of doctrine, that Stalin's position was not more shaken.

Subsequent events showed that Stalin was still very sensitive to opposition criticism of his policy. For even after the opposition had been completely routed, an insurrection in China was organized by two Comintern emissaries, the German Heinz Neumann and the Georgian Besso Lominadze, apparently at Stalin's personal instiga-tion. The insurrection took place in Canton on 11 December 1927, but was suppressed by 14 December. In February 1928 the Executive Committee of the Comintern duly blamed Neumann as partly responsible for the failure. But in spite of valiant attempts by Stalin and the Comintern to prove that the policy they had advocated in China had been throughout doctrinally completely sound, the plain fact remained that the influence of Moscow on the Chinese revolutionary movement had suffered a very severe set-back.[1]

In the last attack on Stalin's leadership of the party which Trotsky attempted to make in October 1927, at the joint Central Control Commission and Central Committee Plenum which expelled him from the Central Committee, he laid special stress on the betrayal of the international revolutionary movement. Yet, if the events of the past years had proved one thing, it was that left-wing revolutionary adventures did not pay. In contrast, the patient consolidation of the Soviet Union; negotiations aimed at extending trade with the capitalist world; diplomacy designed to frustrate a threat of war against the USSR by exploiting the divisions between the individual powers; and above all, developing all the support which the Soviet Union could hope to win among the populations of the outside world by its propaganda – all these seemed to hold out much better promise for the ultimate triumph of 'world revolution'. Trotsky taunted Stalin with the fact that the bourgeois press, from the *New York Times* downwards, was congratulating him on his 'statesman-like intelligence' in suppressing the left-wing advocates of world revolution.[2] He did not realize that the illusion of the Western world that suppression of the left wing meant abandonment of the ultimate revolutionary objective was one of Stalin's main assets.

[1] For a summary of the complex events in China between 1925 and 1927 and for a selection of documents see X. J. Eudin and Robert C. North, *Soviet Russia and the East 1920–1927*, A Documentary Survey, Stanford, 1957, pp. 288–310 and 347–96. On Neumann's relations with Stalin see his widow's memoirs, Margarete Buber-Neumann, *Von Potsdam nach Moskau*, Stationen eines Irrweges, Stuttgart, 1957, pp. 174–94.
[2] Leon Trotsky, *The Real Situation in Russia*, Translated by Max Eastman, London, n.d., p. 169.

PART THREE

The Third Revolution

XX The Defeat of Bukharin

Not even the shrewdest observer at the Fifteenth Party Congress in December 1927 could have concluded that the Soviet Union was on the eve of a new social revolution which would plunge the country into virtual civil war. It was true that the resolutions adopted by the Congress foreshadowed more determined measures to reduce the influence of the *kulaks* than had been resorted to at any rate for the past few years, and stressed the need to develop industry, and especially heavy industry. Taxation was now to fall more heavily on the well-to-do peasants, the leasing of land was to be restricted, and the rivalry of the land associations with the local soviets in the matter of village administration was to be brought to an end.[1] But there was no suggestion by anyone at the Congress that there was to be an abandonment either of NEP, or of its cardinal principle, so much emphasized in Lenin's last writings, that the sole hope of the survival of the communist régime lay in preserving a close alliance between the peasants and the proletariat. Nor was there any hint of an intention to 'pump' resources out of the peasants on the lines of the left-wing theorists' methods of 'primitive socialist accumulation'. Indeed, one resolution of the Congress stressed that the only correct source of capital was to be found in the savings of a prosperous agriculture.[2]

It is not possible on the evidence to say when Stalin formed the decision to enforce the collectivization of agriculture at all costs, and with the minimum of delay, and to develop industry at a rapid pace on the basis of capital extracted from the peasants. It is probable, however, judging from the course of his political manœuvres during 1928, that he had already formed this decision by the time of the Fifteenth Congress, while taking every precaution to conceal it. It is certain that the decision was formed outside the councils of the Politburo, since the support upon which he relied there in his conflicts with the left opposition depended upon complete acceptance of NEP, with all its implications for both agricultural and industrial policy. Of the

[1] *KPSS v rez.*, volume II, pp. 470–88.
[2] *ibid.*, p. 456.

nine full members of the new Politburo elected after the Fifteenth Congress, at least three – Bukharin, Tomskii and Rykov – could certainly not be relied on to endorse any policy which did not accept NEP as its basis. The support of at least one other member, Kalinin, was doubtful. Nor could Stalin, as hitherto, be sure of such un-questioning backing by the lower ranks of the party as would enable him to follow his usual practice of appealing from the Politburo to the Central Committee, or to his own 'Parliament', the joint Central Com-mittee and Central Control Commission Plenum. The power of the Secretariat was, of course, undiminished. But Stalin had built up his following by advocating a policy of caution, prosperity and gradual-ness against the bolder, more intransigent and revolutionary measures, both at home and abroad, associated with the left opposition. To reverse this policy and yet to retain sufficient support below in order to offset the certain opposition which he would have to face in the Politburo called for considerable political skill.

By the end of 1927 the drop in grain supplies to the towns was assuming alarming proportions, and in the second half of December two instructions were issued by the Central Committee urging local party workers to take energetic measures to extract grain from the peasants. The instructions were of little effect, apparently, because at the beginning of January 1928 the Central Committee was threatening party members with disciplinary action if they did not bring about an improvement in grain supplies.[1] In February an extensive purge of local party members took place.[2] The local communists were hardly to be blamed if, after years during which they had been abused for Trotskyist leanings if they showed any excessive zeal in harassing the better-off peasants, they were slow in falling in with the changed party line and, as Stalin put it, 'do not understand the basis of our class policy in the villages'.[3] However, emergency measures to deal with a sudden crisis did not of themselves suggest that a complete swing in policy was impending. Rumours that the abolition of NEP would now follow upon the routing of the left opposition were indignantly denied. It was true that in February, at a meeting of the Comintern Executive, it became evident that a change of policy was contemplated for the forthcoming Comintern Congress: the policy of united action with non-communist parties, for which Stalin had been so bitterly attacked by the left, was now plainly going to be abandoned.[4] But

[1] *Stalin*, volume XI, pp. 1–9, 11.
[2] *ibid.*, p. 235; *Pravda*, 18 April 1928.
[3] *Stalin*, volume XI, p. 13.
[4] *10 let Kominterna v resheniiakh i tsifrakh*, Moscow, 1929, pp. 271–80.

there was as yet no open sign of any rift between Stalin and those who had hitherto been his allies in home affairs. The Joint Plenum of the Central Committee and Central Control Commission, which met on 6 to 11 April 1928, passed its resolutions unanimously. While angrily denouncing 'malicious rumours' that NEP was to be reversed, the party leaders agreed on a number of drastic measures for pumping food out of the peasants.

The Plenum also dealt with another matter, of far-reaching importance. A month before, the OGPU had claimed to have uncovered a counter-revolutionary plot by non-communist specialists working in the Donets Basin, at Shakhty. The discovery, soon to be followed by the trial and condemnation of the accused, was made the occasion for a call for greater vigilance with regard to the bourgeois specialists and for more energetic measures for training up communist technicians.[1] The ten-year alliance between the party and the non-communist experts who had helped it to survive was coming to an end.

Immediately after this Plenum, at a meeting of the Central Executive Committee of the All-Union Congress of Soviets, Stalin showed his hand and, apparently for the first time, let his allies see that something much more radical than temporary measures against recalcitrant peasants was in the air. The draft of a new land law, introduced without warning at the last minute, proposed to deprive the peasants of their unrestricted right to the use in perpetuity of land cultivated by their own labour; to confine this right to peasants who joined an existing or a new collective farm; and virtually to deprive all those declared by the electoral commissions to be *kulaks* (a very fluid category) of all right to any land. The draft ran into immediate opposition, and was hastily withdrawn ostensibly for the purpose of further extensive discussion.[2] This draft law disclosed one feature of future policy – rapid collectivization of the peasants. Its other aspect – industrialization at break-neck speed – was brought into the open in the following month, in May.

In accordance with the directives of the Fifteenth Party Congress, the economists of the State Planning Commission (*Gosplan*) were working on a comprehensive plan for the development of industry. Their work was based on the underlying assumptions which had dominated policy hitherto, that industrial expansion must be limited by the speed with which it was possible to accumulate capital as a result

---

[1] *KPSS v rez.*, volume II, pp. 492–510.
[2] *Izvestiia*, 25 April 1928.

of the expanding prosperity of agriculture. But by May the head-quarters of economic administration, VSNKh, headed by Kuibyshev, had entered the planning field and dumbfounded the economists of *Gosplan* by proposing an expansion of 130 per cent in industry in five years. It soon became apparent that the two organizations were no longer working on the basis of the same premises. What for *Gosplan* was an economic impossibility was for VSNKh a fortress to be stormed, an achievement to be won by bolsheviks for whom nothing was impossible, and the like. The faith of the VSNKh planners had already been well expressed in an article by one of the leading econo-mists of the Stalin era at the end of 1927, in phrases which were later to become familiar in Stalin's own speeches: 'Our task is not to study economics, but to change it. We are bound by no laws. There are no fortresses which bolsheviks cannot storm. The question of tempo is subject to decision by human beings.'[1] Stalin at the end of May sounded the new call to party members: the only solution was collec-tivization of agriculture and the rapid development of heavy industry – the alternative was suicide.[2] There was no longer any talk, as hitherto, of collectivization as a long-term aim, and on a voluntary basis.

Since, in the absence of any other source of capital, the investment for industrial expansion at the high rate contemplated could only come by forcible extraction from the peasants, it must have been evident by now to the orthodox right-wing theorists, like Bukharin and Rykov, that a complete volte-face was on the way. They made no overt move, however, to forestall the plan. Their hesitation need cause no surprise. Any illusion that an appeal to the wider ranks of the party against a policy supported by the General Secretary could have any chance of success had been shattered by the abysmal failure of Trotsky only a few months before. Their only chance may have seemed to them to lie in outvoting Stalin and his supporters in the Politburo and in the Central Committee.

The burning questions of the day came up again for discussion at a meeting of the Central Committee which lasted from 4 to 12 July 1928. The official account of the resolution adopted on the grain situation, as published at the time in the press, suggested that out-

---

[1] S. G. Strumilin, in *Planovoe khoziaistvo*, No. 7, 1927, p. 11; for an account of the debate on the plan see M. Dobb, *Soviet Economic Development since 1917*, London, 1948, chapter x. Strumilin, though a *Gosplan* economist, became the exponent of the VSNKh point of view. And see, for a definitive study of the whole period 1928–52, Naum Jasny, *Soviet Industrialization 1928–1952*, Chicago, 1961.
[2] *Stalin*, volume XI, pp. 87, 93.

standing differences had been resolved by compromise. It stressed that individual small and middle-sized households must for 'a considerable period' remain the basis for grain production, though voluntary co-operatives of producers should be encouraged. The 'extraordinary measures' against the *kulaks* ordered by the Central Committee in December 1927, which it was stressed had only been temporary, were repealed, and the 'administrative arbitrariness' and 'breaches of revolutionary legality' in which they had resulted were condemned. NEP was once again reaffirmed (reinforced by a quotation from Lenin) as the only basis for the construction of socialism, and all talk of its repeal was branded as 'counter-revolutionary chatter'.[1] But Stalin's speeches at this meeting, only published many years later, disclosed that debate had been fast and furious, and that Stalin had urged a very different policy. He told the meeting quite frankly that in order to industrialize it was necessary to exact a temporary 'tribute' from the peasants so as to provide capital for speeding up the tempo of industrialization. It was an 'unpleasant business', but bolsheviks cannot shut their eyes to things merely because they are unpleasant. Since the Soviet Union had no colonies or weaker countries to plunder, and would, indeed, never plunder, even if it could, there was no alternative. It was the essence of NEP, that so far from being a policy of retreat from socialism, it was in its nature an attack on capitalism. In fact, NEP was a 'distinct form of and a weapon of the dictatorship of the proletariat', and would entail an ever-increasing sharpening of the class struggle against resistance by capitalist elements. Stalin urged the need for 'gradual' collectivization, but significantly omitted the usual proviso that this should be a voluntary process.[2] Ample quotations from Lenin could scarcely conceal the fact that the policy now urged by Stalin was a good deal nearer to the views of Preobrazhenskii than to those of Lenin or Bukharin.

We know from another source that the session of the Central Committee and the meeting of the Politburo which preceded it, had witnessed an open clash between Stalin on the one hand and Bukharin, Rykov and Tomskii on the other. Shortly before the end of the Central Committee session, on 11 July, Bukharin called unannounced on Kamenev and gave an excited account of the situation. It is perhaps surprising that Bukharin should have chosen as his confidant the man whom he had done his best to ruin. But it is clear that Bukharin feared

[1] *KPSS v rez.*, volume II pp. 511–17.
[2] *Stalin*, volume XI, pp. 144–87.

that Stalin would now seek to re-establish an alliance with Zinoviev and Kamenev, who had recently been readmitted to the party, and hoped to outbid him for their support. Kamenev preserved an account of the conversation, which is now in the Trotsky Archives. It was subsequently clandestinely printed in Moscow by Trotsky's supporters.[1] Stalin's policy, said the frenzied Bukharin, was ruinous for the revolution. He was an unprincipled intriguer who changed his theories at will in order to get rid of whomever he wished. He had now made concessions only in order to ruin Rykov, Tomskii and Bukharin. His policy could lead only to terror, civil war, bloodshed and famine.

The picture of the support that the three champions of the right could reckon with, as painted by Bukharin, was not optimistic. Yagoda, the deputy chief of the OGPU, Bukharin claimed was behind them, and so originally were Kalinin and Voroshilov. But the latter two had changed sides at the last moment – evidently (according to Bukharin) Stalin had some kind of hold over them. Ordzhonikidze had also first abused Stalin and then voted with him, and the Central Committee as a whole seemed unaware of the impending peril. The Secretary of the Moscow organization, Uglanov, was in full agreement with the opposition, but Stalin was already working to have him replaced by Kaganovich. According to Bukharin, the intention of the opposition was to lie low, to publish articles, and thus to open the eyes of the party to the grave danger which faced it. Kamenev does not seem to have been convinced of Bukharin's prospects of success against Stalin, since he decided 'to wait calmly for signals from the other camp'. Bukharin's incautious, or desperate, act substantially contributed to his rapid defeat, since the subsequent publication of the details of this interview (if it was not already known to the OGPU) eventually provided Stalin with valuable ammunition.

It may well have been the existence of strong opposition to Stalin's policy in the important Moscow organization which determined Stalin to avoid for the time being any open breach with Bukharin. No public admissions of dissensions were made, and rumours of a split in the party leadership were sedulously denied. Particular care was taken to avoid parading any internal disunity, so soon after the convulsions caused by the conflict with Trotsky, before the eyes of foreign communists. The Sixth Congress of the Comintern was meeting about

[1] The clandestine leaflet (of which a copy was made available to me by the late Mr B. I. Nicolaevsky) was dated 20 January 1929. The account of the conversation was also reprinted in *Sotsialisticheskii vestnik*, No. 6, 22 March 1929, and No. 9 of 4 May 1929.

this time in Moscow, and sat from 17 July until 1 September. Rumours of new disagreements among the Russian leaders were rife among the delegates. They were officially denied in a statement addressed to the Comintern signed by all the members of the Politburo, including Bukharin.[1] Stalin himself went out of his way to deny the rumour to the more important delegates,[2] but at the same time a whispering campaign was conducted among the foreign delegates in an endeavour to discredit Bukharin, who was still the chief Russian spokesman at the Congress.[3] Moreover, Bukharin's prestige was somewhat demonstratively undermined at the Congress. Several amendments to the draft of the main resolution prepared by him were insisted upon by his colleagues on the Russian delegation, which included Stalin – a clear indication that his authority was no longer to be regarded as infallible.[4]

The Russian party now carried out one of those reversals of policy which characterized its leadership of the Comintern, and reflected the extent to which this organization was utilized as a battlefield for Russian domestic quarrels. The right-wing policy of alliance with non-communist parties, which had brought Stalin under such heavy fire from Trotsky both with regard to China and to Britain, was now jettisoned. The more moderate elements in the foreign parties, who had served their turn as the supporters of the campaign against Trotsky, now became the chief enemies, with whom before long Bukharin would be coupled. The resolutions of the Congress recognized that a new revolutionary upsurge was on the way. The main enemies of the communists were now the right-wing reformists inside the communist parties and also the social democrats, and in particular the 'left' social democrats who pretended to be in favour of unity with the communists but in reality betrayed them and were 'the most dangerous enemies of communism and of the dictatorship of the proletariat'.[5] The main effort must now be directed against them and against the right wing within the several communist parties. Bukharin faithfully carried out an assignment with which, as he privately admitted, he was not in sympathy. In his view the best interest of the

---

[1] *KPSS v rez.*, volume II, p. 557.

[2] To a meeting of the top people of each important party – e.g. Lovestone and Foster of the American Communist Party. (Private information from another US delegate, Mr Bertram D. Wolfe.)

[3] Benjamin Gitlow, *I Confess*. The Truth about American Communism. New York, 1940, p. 507.

[4] La Correspondance Internationale, *VIe Congrès de l'Internationale Communiste* (17 juillet–1er septembre 1928), Compte-rendu sténographique, pp. 1661–3.

[5] *ibidem*, pp. 1700–10.

communist lay in alliance with the socialist parties against the mounting danger of fascism.[1]

The relation of these changed tactics in the Comintern to Russian conditions became apparent when *Pravda*, after the conclusion of the Congress, drew the moral on 18 September 1928 that the fight against right-wing pro-*kulak* elements was just as vital inside Russia as elsewhere. Meanwhile, the veil which had shrouded the stormy disputes in the party leadership was partly lifted by Uglanov, the Secretary of the Moscow organization and Bukharin's ally. Apparently against Bukharin's advice and wishes, he showed his hand at a Plenary meeting of the Moscow party organization held between 11 and 15 September, and revealed that the right-wing view enjoyed considerable support among the Moscow communists. The Moscow communists made no open attack on Stalin's policy, but the tenor of their speeches, and in particular that of Uglanov himself, left little doubt where their sympathies lay. Speaking in the language of 1927, Uglanov stressed the dangers of Trotskyism, and quoted the resolutions of the Fifteenth Congress as the bedrock of policy.[2] On 30 September Bukharin himself brought the dispute into the open by means of an article in *Pravda*, of which he was still nominally the editor.

This article (which was reprinted as a pamphlet), entitled 'Notes of an Economist', is the only complete statement of the views of the right-wing opposition to Stalin's policy which has been preserved. Bukharin began with a review of the achievements of the past three 'years of reconstruction', claiming that solid gains had been made. Industry was growing rapidly. The production of agricultural machinery in particular was three times the pre-war level, and was beginning to effect a technical transformation of the village. The socialized sector of agriculture was rapidly increasing – the capital of the state-run co-operative sector of agriculture had risen by 14 per cent. The share of investment assigned to industry showed, he claimed, the rapid pace of industrialization: from 12 per cent in the first of the three years of reconstruction it had risen to 23 per cent. But the strength of industry depended on the strength of the peasant market. The American example showed that well-to-do farmers, unburdened by excessive rents, could create an enormous internal market for industry. The mistake of the Trotskyists had been that

[1] From a private letter from Bukharin to the Swiss right-wing communist, Humbert-Droz, quoted in Robert Vincent Daniels, *The Conscience of the Revolution: Communist Opposition in Soviet Russia,* Cambridge, Mass., 1960, pp. 335–6, from the Humbert-Droz papers.
[2] *Pravda*, 13 and 21 September 1928.

their plan of pumping the maximum amount of capital out of the peasants would have had the effect of a regression to the economic pattern of pre-revolutionary Russia – exploitation of the peasants by the state – when what was now needed was to develop the country on the American pattern.

Coming to the crisis caused by the shortage in grain supplies, Bukharin denied that this had been due to wilful withholding of produce from the market: every child knew that the story of millions of tons of grain withheld by *kulaks* was a 'fairy tale', and no one believed it. The real cause was the dispersed nature of agriculture. Its 'attendant phenomena' were an increase in the supplementary income of the peasants from non-agricultural work, an inadequate supply of goods to the villages, inadequate increase in taxation of the *kulaks*, and hence their growing influence. The remedy lay in the limitation of the *kulak* sector, in the development of co-operation and in a correct price policy. Planning for industrialization was necessary. But over-centralized planning would defeat itself in an economy in which agriculture was still subject to the private market and the laws of supply and demand; while over-ambitious planning for the growth of industry, which took no account of resources and did not keep pace with the development of agriculture upon which these resources depended, would become a 'parasite' on agriculture instead of the means of its transformation. Industrialization must proceed at the maximum possible speed, but the tempo set must be one which could be maintained. To this end the most important factors were the increase of the efficiency of production methods and the lowering of costs so as to increase the capital available for investment.[1]

Stalin now dealt first with the second rank of dissidents. Kuibyshev, his main lieutenant in putting through high industrialization targets, sounded an immediate warning that 'all available measures' would be used by the party to nip 'pessimism and lack of confidence' in the bud. On 11 October three of Uglanov's most important subordinates were removed, including a certain Riutin, of whom more will be said later. Uglanov himself was for the time being left in his post. A week later Stalin spoke of the right-wing danger in the party to the Moscow organization, at the same time emphatically denying that there were any disagreements on policy inside the Politburo.[2]

In spite of these protestations, dissension inside the Politburo was

---

[1] A slightly abridged translation of the article will be found in Bertram D. Wolfe, *Khrushchev and Stalin's Ghost*, New York, 1957, pp. 295–315.

[2] *Stalin*, volume XI, pp. 222–38.

reaching fever heat. Stalin was clearly determined to go ahead with his new policy. On 3 October the agenda for the forthcoming session of the Central Executive Committee included the new land legislation which had run into opposition at the previous session, and on 4 November a further directive of VSNKh was published in *Pravda* increasing proposed industrial norms over and above the originally very high figures published in the late summer. Bukharin and Tomskii now attempted some action. As we know from further conversations which took place at the beginning of 1929 between Bukharin and Kamenev, and were made public by the Trotskyists abroad,[1] Bukharin and Tomskii, while still determined to maintain a public front of unity, attempted in the Politburo to force a change of leadership by the removal of the main supporters of Stalin. Stalin temporized, agreed to the demands, but did nothing to implement them. When faced by Bukharin, Rykov and Tomskii with a threat of resignation, he apparently succeeded in patching up the breach by agreeing to a series of compromise resolutions on policy at a Plenum of the Central Committee which met between 16 and 24 November 1928.[2] As Bukharin admitted later to the somewhat astonished Kamenev, a denunciation of the, as yet anonymous, right-wing deviation in the party included in these resolutions was drafted by Bukharin himself. Stalin in his speech to the Central Committee, published in the press at the time, once again dismissed rumours of dissension inside the Politburo, and even went out of his way to describe Bukharin's 'Notes of an Economist' as a justifiable, if abstract, point of view.[3] His main attack was concentrated on a relatively minor critic, Frumkin, whose views bore considerable resemblance to those of Bukharin.

In their desire to preserve party unity the right leaders had thrown away any chance they might have had of rallying the party around themselves against Stalin. In spite of their potential strength on the Politburo, their nerve had failed them when it came to taking decisive action against Stalin. As so often before, fear of the overthrow of unpopular communist rule had acted as a powerful deterrent against any move which might shake the régime to its foundations. Armed with the declarations of solidarity to which the right-wing leaders had subscribed, Stalin could now brand as 'factionalism' any open disagreement with his policy. As for the rank and file supporters of the right, betrayed and bewildered they were an easy prey to reprisals by

---

[1] *Biulleten' oppozitsii*, No. 1–2, July 1929, p. 15.
[2] *KPSS v rez.*, volume II, pp. 525–40.
[3] *Stalin*, volume XI, pp. 245–90 (p. 260).

the apparatus. But the three leaders themselves could not now long survive unscathed. The weak Rykov was the least serious opponent. Bukharin, formidable if only because of his reputation as a theorist, had jeopardized his position both by compromising and by his conversations with Kamenev – now made public by the Trotskyists, probably with this very object in view. Tomskii, the trade union leader, was from Stalin's point of view a particularly important target. During NEP his leadership of the trade unions, if unyielding on matters of party discipline, had at any rate served the workers by ensuring rising living standards. But the enforced tempo of industrialization now contemplated could scarcely fail to lower these standards, and a new type of trade union discipline would be called for which Tomskii could be expected to oppose.

In his speech to the Central Committee in November 1928 Stalin laid the theoretical foundations for what would shortly become the accepted new policy. He argued that the victory of socialism could only be ensured by 'catching up with and overtaking' the capitalist countries in industrial and economic development. Nor could security and independence be assured without creating an industrial basis for national defence. Both these considerations demanded a high tempo of industrialization. Moreover, without industrialization it was impossible to build up a prosperous agriculture, since this depended on mechanization. With skill, if inaccuracy, he caricatured both the right and the left. Both were wrong. If the right say 'Leave the *kulak* alone, let him develop freely' (which Bukharin did not say), the left say 'Smash the middle peasant as well as the *kulak*.' If the right say 'We have run into difficulties, let us fold our hands and give in', the left say 'What do we care about difficulties, let us rush forward without giving them a thought.' Thus did Stalin follow the time-honoured method of appearing to avoid deviations to either side of the true, middle course, while at the same time making a turn of 180 degrees from hitherto accepted policy.

Preparations for the new policy went ahead step by step. On 27 November 1928 Uglanov, in spite of full admission of his errors, was dismissed from the Moscow organization, and a further purge of subordinate organizations was carried out. During its session in the first fortnight of December, the Central Executive Committee adopted the new land law, which removed such guarantees as remained to the individual peasant land-holder. The Eighth Trade Union Congress, which met at the end of December, voted approval of the ambitious targets for industrialization proposed by Kuibyshev.

Although no conflict with Tomskii appeared on the surface, the ground was well prepared for his removal. The resolution adopted by the Congress stressed the need for democracy in the unions. There was to be no stifling of criticism, and 'bureaucratic' officials, whatever their status, were to be removed. Every kind of opposition to democracy in the unions must be rooted out 'wherever it was to be found'.[1] This charter of liberty would serve in due course as a pretext for the removal of Tomskii, who certainly could not be said to have encouraged democracy in the unions. The new masters of the trade unions, however, would rule the workers with a severity which Tomskii had never dreamed of. Significantly, the newly elected Praesidium of the Congress Plenum included five prominent Stalinist supporters, among them Kaganovich, whose reputation as a trouble shooter was by now well established, and another trusted agent of Stalin who was not even a member of the Plenum.[2] Tomskii attempted to resign, but his resignation was not accepted.[3] He apparently took no part in trade union activities up to his removal six months later.

Bukharin made a last attempt to warn the party of what he regarded as a false course. On the anniversary of Lenin's death, 21 January 1929, he made a long speech subsequently published in *Pravda* and as a pamphlet, with the explosive title 'Lenin's Political Testament'. It was a courageous action, because by this time Bukharin was being shadowed by the OGPU, his contacts with Kamenev were known, and his position as editor of *Pravda* had been undermined by the appointment of a subordinate to spy on him. In this pamphlet Bukharin analysed Lenin's views at the very end of his life on the basis of his last five articles. To many of his readers Bukharin's pamphlet could not fail to call to mind the other 'testament' which could, of course, not be openly discussed. (A resolution of the Fifteenth Party Congress that it should be printed as an annex to the stenogram had been disregarded.)[4] Without naming Stalin, Bukharin quoted from Lenin's article 'On Co-operation' a passage which ran directly counter to what Stalin had been urging for some time: 'We are compelled to recognize a radical change in the whole of our view of socialism. . . . Formerly we placed . . . the central emphasis on political struggle. . . . Now the central emphasis . . . must be trans-

[1] *Pravda*, 29 December 1928.
[2] Akulov, who subsequently became an important official in the OGPU; see *Pravda*, 25 December 1928.
[3] See his speech at the Sixteenth Party Congress, *XVI S"ezd*, p. 144.
[4] The text of the 'Testament' had in fact been published in the Bulletins of the Fifteenth Congress, distributed to delegates, but not reprinted in the stenographic report published subsequently.

ferred to *peaceful organizational and cultural work.*' (The italics are Bukharin's.) He added the comment that this meant that there should be no 'third revolution'.[1] Yet Stalin, since his speech to the Moscow organization on 19 October 1928, had been emphasizing that the essence of NEP lay precisely in the intensification of the class struggle. An open clash could not long be delayed.

Matters were apparently brought to a head in February 1929 by a summons to the right-wing leaders from the party Control Commission to answer for their offence in making the approach to Kamenev. The three leaders addressed a protest to the Politburo, of which the content is only known from quotations by their opponents. They complained of one-man decisions, and of the substitution of control by one man for collective control. They also, according to Stalin, demanded a reduction of the tempo proposed for industrialization, an end to the formation of collective and state farms, the restoration of private trade, and the abolition of extraordinary measures against *kulaks* which were leading to 'military feudal exploitation of the peasants'. In terms strongly reminiscent of every previous opposition movement in the party, they also complained of 'bureaucratization' and of a policy which was leading to the liquidation of the Comintern. It is unlikely, in the light of the views expressed by Bukharin in 'Notes of an Economist', that this represents an accurate summary of what was said in the Politburo. But the formulation enabled Stalin to portray Bukharin and his supporters as the defenders of the hated and despised *kulak*, and therefore as only one step removed from anti-Marxists, or even counter-revolutionaries. The Politburo, with the aid of the Central Control Commission Praesidium, investigated their conduct, condemned them for their views, for their conduct in making contacts with Kamenev while pretending to be in agreement with the policy of the Central Committee, for tendering their resignations and for the arch sin of forming a separate faction.

This indictment was duly approved by the Central Committee in April 1929, when Stalin delivered a very long attack on Bukharin and his group which was, however, not published until many years later.[2] Trenchant criticism was now poured on views which Bukharin had expressed as far back as 1925 in a pamphlet entitled 'The Way to Socialism'. This pamphlet, written mainly as an answer to the theories of the 'left', had argued the case for the gradual winning over to, or

[1] N. I. Bukharin, *Politicheskoe zaveshchanie Lenina*, Second edition, Moscow, 1929, pp. 9–10. The passage quoted from Lenin will be found in *Lenin*, volume XXVII, pp. 396–7.
[2] *Stalin*, volume XII, pp. 1–107.

'growing into', socialism of the non-socialized sector of the economy, and especially agriculture, by holding out the attraction of the greater advantages which socialism would offer. It was the classical theory of NEP, and followed logically from Lenin's last writings. It had also been the official theory of the party during the whole of its campaign against Trotsky and other left-wing critics. But according to Stalin, the crux of Bukharin's mistake then and now was his failure to realize that intensification of the class struggle was the only way to preserve socialism from disaster. To talk, as Bukharin and his supporters did, of exploitation of the peasants was to play into the hands of the counter-revolutionaries.

As if to combat the argument that the new party line was simply a revival of the left-wing economist Preobrazhenskii's 'primitive socialist accumulation', Stalin argued that collectivization on a large scale had only now become possible because the great mass of the peasantry were 'longing' for it. Trotskyism, he said, differed as much from the present policy as the policy of the right: the Trotskyists denied the need for any kind of union with the peasants, while the right wing stood for union with the peasants whoever they were, including the *kulaks*. The only correct policy was that of union with the middle and poor peasants against the *kulaks*, and that was the policy now being pursued. Attacks on Bukharin as a theoretician followed, reinforced with ample quotations from Lenin's old polemics with Bukharin in Switzerland during the war. Stalin ended with warning threats to the right leaders, but nonetheless opposed the suggestion of 'some comrades' (unnamed) that Bukharin and Tomskii should be expelled from the Politburo. The Central Committee resolution sternly condemned the right leaders, and further recommended that Tomskii and Bukharin should be removed from all posts occupied by them. Rykov, who was still Chairman of the Council of People's Commissars, was, however, not removed from his post.[1]

Although not made public at the time, the resolution of the Central Committee was circulated throughout the party, and the breach in the party leadership could not for long be concealed. The right leaders were now in a very weak position. Complaints about 'bureaucracy' and the dictatorial régime in the party came very ill from the men who not long before had been in the forefront of the attack on Trotsky and his allies for making the very same complaints. They had played

---

[1] For the information available on this incident see the article referred to in note 1, p. 374; *KPSS v rez.*, volume II, pp. 549–67; *Stalin*, volume XI, pp. 318–25, and volume XII, pp. 2–10. See also Rudzutak at the Sixteenth Congress, *XVI S"ezd*, pp. 201–2.

into Stalin's hands by accepting a compromise and by voting for resolutions proclaiming unanimity in the leadership. These could now be used against them to accuse them of double dealing. The approach to the disgraced left-wingers was a blunder, which was bound to be either betrayed by the Trotskyists, who had little reason to love Bukharin, or discovered by the OGPU, or both. They had given Stalin the time he needed to prepare the ground for their downfall. Now that a condemnation for factionalism by the Central Committee was recorded against them, any further overt move which could be interpreted as criticism of official policy could only lead to expulsion from the party organs, or even from the party. The only course now open to them was to avoid such expulsion, in the slender hope that so long as they remained inside the party they could at any rate influence policy, or even in time win sufficient support in the Politburo and Central Committee to bring about the removal of Stalin.

Stalin was fully alive to this situation, and quite determined that the downfall of at any rate Bukharin and Tomskii should be complete enough to prevent any hope of their rehabilitation. This was particularly necessary in view of the fact that Stalin's own position as undisputed leader of the party was not completely secure. There was apparently still some wavering in the Politburo in some cases, notably that of Kalinin, whom Stalin handled with great care – so much so that he was allowed to make plainly right-wing speeches with impunity.[1] Had Kalinin and one other member voted with the three right-wing leaders on a straight division, Stalin's majority would have been at an end. Lower down there may have been opposition from the deputy chief of the OGPU, Yagoda, whose views are likely to have been due less to ideology than to fear that an over-rapid policy of collectivization would create a security problem beyond the powers of the OGPU to handle.

For some time after the April Plenum of the Central Committee the breach with the right still remained little publicized, and there was no criticism of the three right-wing leaders by name. Of the three men, Rykov seems either to have come nearest to capitulation, or at all events to have concealed his real views better than the other two. Immediately after the Plenum, between 23 and 29 April 1929, the Sixteenth Party Conference met to adopt the new industrial and agricultural policy which had caused so much dissension in the course of preparation. The views of Kuibyshev and VSNKh were by now

[1] See e.g. *Pravda*, 23 September 1928; *XVI Konf.*, pp. 142, 209 (April 1929).

established as official, and the more cautious planners of *Gosplan* completely discredited – a number of them were eventually to figure as defendants in some of the trials of 'wreckers' and 'saboteurs' during 1930 and 1931. Both the ambitious five-year plan and the plan for rapid collectivization of agriculture were adopted unanimously, and, in spite of rumour to the contrary, the conference does not appear to have been the scene of very violent conflict. The resolution on the five-year plan was indeed adopted on the proposal of Rykov, whose speech in support of it reads like a model of Stalinist orthodoxy. Bukharin and Tomskii, if they did not overtly support the new policy, at any rate did not openly oppose it, though Bukharin soon after published in *Pravda* a somewhat incautious review of a German book in which scarcely veiled criticism of Stalin's policy was evident.[1]

Having won this support for his policy at the conference, Stalin now felt confident enough to make some moves against the principal opposition leaders. Immediately after the conference Uglanov was removed from his position as candidate member of the Politburo and from the Secretariat. On 2 June 1929 Tomskii was removed from his position as head of the trade union organization and eventually replaced by the drab N. M. Shvernik, who was to remain a loyal party boss of the unions for many years to come. A month later, on 3 July, Bukharin was removed from the Praesidium of the Executive Committee of the Comintern.[2] The publication of this resolution of the Comintern Executive in *Pravda* was the signal for an open press campaign against Bukharin, who was no longer in a position to reply. There was no talk now of a theoretical difference of opinion. Bukharin was accused of 'collaboration with capitalist elements' and of an attempt to form a bloc with former Trotskyists – two very serious charges, of which one, the latter, had the additional force of being true. In the spate of denunciations which followed in the press, full rein was given to imagination, with all the advantages enjoyed by an attacking side which feared neither reply nor contradiction of its more glaring inaccuracies.

Completely discredited, the right leaders were finally required to make public admissions of their sins. Uglanov and his supporters, formerly of the Moscow organization, signed a declaration repudiating Bukharin and his group in the necessary grovelling terms which was published on 18 November 1929. Bukharin, Rykov and Tomskii made

---

[1] See *Pravda*, 30 June 1929.
[2] Text of the resolution, which among other things blamed Bukharin for his review in *Pravda*, is in *SPR*, volume VII, Part II, pp. 35–6.

an unsuccessful attempt to salvage something of their human dignity. In a declaration addressed to the Central Committee, which was once again in session from 10 to 17 November 1929, they expressed their acceptance of the decisions of the Central Committee, but apparently failed to repudiate their opinions in sufficiently abject form. The Central Committee rejected the declaration, expelled Bukharin from the Politburo and severely warned Rykov and Tomskii of the consequences of the 'slightest attempt' to renew their struggle against the party line.[1] Shortly afterwards, on 26 November 1929, the three leaders published a declaration in the required terms, They admitted that the Central Committee was right, and that 'our views . . . have proved erroneous'. They pledged themselves to carry on a decisive struggle against all deviations from the party line in the future.[2] Stalin's victory was for the time being complete. With the brakes on his revolutionary policy thus removed, he told a meeting of Marxist agricultural experts on 27 December 1929 that the party had now moved on from 'a policy of limiting the exploiting activities of the *kulaks* to a policy of liquidating the *kulaks* as a class'.[3] On 5 January 1930 the Central Committee resolved that in place of 20 per cent of farmlands which were to be collectivized within the five-year plan period, as approved by the Sixteenth Conference of the party and by the Congress of Soviets subsequently, the 'enormous majority' of peasant households would be so collectivized.[4] It was an eloquent comment on the small significance in party practice of the decisions of official party or soviet organs when compared with the determined will of one strong leader.

[1] *KPSS v rez.*, volume II, pp. 662–3.
[2] *Pravda*, 26 November 1929.
[3] *Stalin*, volume XII, p. 166.
[4] *KPSS v rez.*, volume II, pp. 664–7; in fact the Sixteenth Party Conference had only approved collectivization of 17·5 per cent of farmlands – *ibid.*, p. 571.

XXI   The Third Revolution

The social revolution upon which Stalin embarked in 1929 was a watershed in the history of the party. Stalin's conflict with the leaders of the left opposition had been basically a power conflict, as was evident from the fact alone that no sooner were they defeated than he adopted their policy, though in a much exaggerated form. In contrast the issue between Stalin and Bukharin was one of principle, however much Stalin may have utilized it in order to advance his own influence. Bukharin, Rykov and Tomskii were not sentimentalists, and could have had few illusions as to the nature of communist rule, and in particular as to its dependence for survival on a considerable degree of force. But they accepted limits to the amount of human suffering that they were prepared to impose, at any rate on peasants and workers. Once the experiment of war communism had been recognized as a failure and NEP inaugurated, a return to the civil war methods seemed to them inconceivable. Bukharin was right in arguing that Lenin had conceived of NEP as an evolutionary road to socialism and industrialization, in which the socialized sector of the bipartite economy would gradually overtake and oust the private sector by its example – its greater efficiency and its better results. No doubt history might need an occasional push – it is not, for example, recorded that any one of the three right leaders protested against the suppression during the 20's of ostensibly legal private enterprise in favour of state enterprise. But so forcible a 'push' as to necessitate, as Bukharin had foreseen in July 1928 in conversation with Kamenev, terror, bloodshed and the possibility of the collapse of Soviet rule, was neither a risk which they were prepared to take nor a price which they felt justified in exacting.

Stalin felt no such scruples and recognized no self-imposed limits to what he was prepared to risk in order to achieve his plan of transforming the country on his own model; nor did he hesitate as to the amount of suffering which he was ready to inflict on the population. If he is to be condemned for his inhumanity, he must at all events be given credit for his courage. Yet the very enormity of the task upon which he now embarked in some ways insured him against opposition from within. For nearly five years to come the communist party was to be engaged in open war against a terrorized, hostile and desperate people. As the terror gathered momentum, so did the score of hatred and dreams of revenge mount. There were few party members who did not realize that it was too late to turn back, and that however burdensome Stalin's rule might be, it was preferable to the vengeance which would break out against the whole party if, through disunity, it should once lose its controlling power. Hence, after the defeat of Bukharin at the end of 1929 it was no longer likely that any organized opposition would arise within the party. The story of resistance to Stalin inside the party, so far as it can be conjectured, unfolds as one of improvised plots, cautious intrigue at the top, and finally a last desperate protest drowned in a bloodbath.

That Stalin's decision to abandon NEP commanded a good deal of support in those sections of the party which had never been reconciled to NEP became evident from the reaction of the left oppositionists. Many thousands of them had been exiled after the defeat suffered by Trotsky, Kamenev and Zinoviev at the Fifteenth Party Congress in December 1927. Trotsky himself had remained in exile for about a year, until January 1929, when it was decided to expel him from the Soviet Union. Once outside Russia, he became a magnet around which all anti-Stalinist communists could gather. But if his exile was, from this point of view, a disadvantage to Stalin, it also provided him with a formula for dealing with his political opponents, who could now, whatever the grounds of their opposition, be conveniently accused of plotting with Trotsky for the overthrow of the Soviet régime. Zinoviev and Kamenev, readmitted to the party since June 1928, seem to have entertained hopes that with the attack on Bukharin now well under way they would be fully rehabilitated. Rumours that a deal between them and Stalin was pending were certainly rife during 1928, but there is no evidence to suggest that they were well founded. For the time being Zinoviev and Kamenev remained in obscurity, enjoying humble appointments. The supporters of the left opposition remained in exile or in penal camps, and their number increased during 1928 and 1929 as the tempo of arrests and purging in the ranks of the party increased. Several thousand of them were thus estimated to be in captivity early in 1929.[1]

As the change in policy became apparent, numbers of more or less prominent left oppositionists sought to make their peace with Stalin.

[1] Boris Souvarine, *Staline*, Paris 1935, p. 452.

The first to capitulate was Piatakov, as early as 29 February 1928, soon to be followed by Krestinskii and Antonov-Ovseenko. In the following year, on 14 July 1929, a group headed by Radek and Preobrazhenskii petitioned for readmission to the party. Of the prominent left oppositionists, the one who held out longest was Rakovskii, who, in spite of the increasing hardships to which he was subjected, resisted until 1934. The capitulators were usually readmitted to party membership, and in many cases given posts of relative responsibility. At the Sixteenth Party Congress, in the summer of 1930, Stalin claimed that Trotskyism was no longer of any importance; its followers had either broken with the movement and renounced their views, or had become 'petty bourgeois counter-revolutionaries', acting as an information bureau on the affairs of the Russian communist party for the capitalist press.[1] Yet virtually all former Trotskyists were in the end either executed or exiled at the end of the 30's, and none is definitely known to have survived. The reason, from Stalin's point of view, is not far to seek. In the conditions which developed after 1930, where the rigid pattern of conformity and obedience imposed on party members of necessity habituated them to lie freely about their real opinions, there was little reason to trust any communist's professions of loyalty. Since all the former oppositionists had good reason to hate Stalin, they were naturally enough first on the list for elimination when the turn came for the severe purges of the older bolsheviks.

The case of Piatakov, even if not typical (it will be recalled that Lenin in his 'Testament' had praised Piatakov for his abilities, but had doubted his political acumen), is revealing of the attitude of mind of the left oppositionists after 1928. A social democrat of long standing, who was neither a communist nor a menshevik at the time, who worked with Piatakov in VSNKh until the late 20's, recorded a remarkable conversation with Piatakov in 1928, in the course of a visit to Paris, where Piatakov was then trade representative. Piatakov's capitulation had appeared in *Pravda* shortly before this conversation.[2] In the course of their talk Piatakov provoked his former colleague by the suggestion that he lacked courage. The latter replied somewhat heatedly with a counter-charge to the effect that Piatakov, by capitulating almost immediately after his expulsion from the party (in December 1927) and by repudiating opinions which he had held until so short a time ago, had shown his own lack of moral courage.

[1] *Stalin*, volume XII, p. 343.
[2] *Pravda*, 29 February 1928.

Piatakov, in a state of great emotional excitement, replied with a long tirade. The essential Lenin, he said, was not to be found in the creator of NEP and in the leader's last articles, which were not only in his, Piatakov's, view but in that of many members of the Politburo the product of weariness and sickness. The real Lenin was the man who had had the courage to make a proletarian revolution first, and then to set about creating the objective conditions theoretically necessary as a preliminary to such a revolution. What was the October revolution, what indeed is the communist party, but a miracle? No menshevik could ever understand what it meant to be a member of such a party. The essential characteristic of this party is that it is bounded by no laws, it is always extending the realm of the possible until nothing becomes impossible. Nothing is inadmissible for it, nothing unrealizable. For such a party a true bolshevik will readily cast out from his mind ideas in which he has believed for years. A true bolshevik has submerged his personality in the collectivity, 'the party', to such an extent that he can make the necessary effort to break away from his own opinions and convictions, and can honestly agree with the party – that is the test of a true bolshevik. There could be no life for him, Piatakov continued, outside the ranks of the party, and he would be ready to believe that black was white and white was black, if the party required it. In order to become one with this great party he would fuse himself with it, abandon his own personality, so that there was no particle left inside him which was not at one with the party, did not belong to it.[1]

There is no reason to suppose that Piatakov's views on the party were unique. Trotsky had said something very similar at the Thirteenth Party Congress in 1924.[2] Perhaps it was this faith in the wisdom of a collective party will which prevented so many bolsheviks for so long from seeing that what they believed to be the will of 'the party' was rapidly becoming the personal whim of one man. Piatakov did not live to reap the reward of his devoted service to bolshevism. Reinstated after his petition, he returned to Russia and served for a time as Chairman of the State Bank, and then under Ordzhonikidze as Deputy Commissar for Heavy Industry. He played a vital role in the realization of the first five-year plan. In 1936, in spite of Ordzhonikidze's efforts to save him, he was arrested, accused of treason, made the confessions required of him, and in 1937 he was shot.

[1] N. Valentinov (N. V. Vol'skii), 'Sut' bol'shevizma v izobrazhenii Iu. Piatakova', *Novyi zhurnal* (New York), No. 52, 1958, pp. 140–61; also based on my conversations with the author.
[2] See p. 288, above.

Trotsky himself, in his exile abroad, followed a different evolution. Although more extreme than Trotsky's policy, Stalin's new course had so many features in common with what Trotsky had for so long advocated while he was still in the party that it was not always easy for him to find theoretical justification for further opposition to Stalin. Rakovskii, from his distant banishment, provided a doctrinal basis which became the main argument used by Trotsky and his supporters against Stalin. Rakovskii argued that the proletarian state had under Stalin become in essence a bureaucratic despotism. The most active workers had simply become bureaucrats, enjoying considerable economic advantages in return for their service to the leadership. In turn, the party leadership had become authoritarian, elevating to the dignity of communist dogma what was nothing more than a method of command and compulsion. The opposition had therefore been right in 1923–4 when it had made its attack on the suppression of democracy in the party.[1]

All communists were agreed in principle in 1928 on the urgent need to develop industry. But there was disagreement on the question of tempo – how fast was it possible to do it? – and its corollary – the extent to which it was permissible to do it at the expense of the peasants. That the peasants would in the end have to provide the capital for investment was obvious, in the absence of any hopeful prospects of attracting foreign capital or of increasing foreign trade. Even Bukharin's policy of providing the necessary capital out of increased agricultural prosperity would in all probability also have necessitated helping on economic processes by employing some force. Bukharin and his supporters never indeed denied the need to apply restrictive measures of some kind to the *kulaks*, and experience had already shown how flexible in practice this category was. Yet it is inconceivable that they would have been prepared to unleash the kind of war against the whole population which Stalin found necessary. Those who argue that in the end any Soviet government would have been forced to extract capital for industry at machine-gun point ignore the fact that Bukharin's policy for industrialization was not conceived in isolation from foreign policy. If he stood for a period of peaceful development at home, he also believed in co-operation against the rising forces of reaction abroad. By a combination of these two factors – a lull in the 'class war' at home and co-operation with

---

[1] *Biulleten' oppozitsii*, No. 25–6, pp. 9–32. The argument that the communists had become a 'new exploiting class of bureaucrats' was also used in February 1930 by the group of Democratic Centralists in captivity – *ibid.*, No. 11, p. 35.

democratic states abroad – foreign capital might well have been induced to flow into the Soviet Union, as Lenin certainly had hoped.

Stalin's motives for the timing of his decision to industrialize the country at high speed, regardless of the consequences, may well have been compounded of various factors. There was, of course, the attractive prospect which a change of course always offered for getting rid of serious political rivals. Less convincing, and much canvassed after the German invasion in 1941, is the argument that rapid industrialization was a far-sighted policy designed to meet the threat of war by creating the basis for a defence industry. There was little prospect of any kind of invasion in 1928. If the ravages created by over-rapid industrialization and collectivization are taken into account, it would not be very rash to conclude that at least the same degree of industrial development could have been achieved by 1941 with less drastic means. A more probable motive, if the importance which Stalin attached to control by the party apparatus is taken into account, was his wish to put an end to the relative independence from all control by the party which the peasants enjoyed under NEP. It will be recalled from an earlier chapter[1] that by 1927 it was apparent that the party and soviet organizations in the villages were quite powerless to assert their authority over the peasants. The familiar bogy of 'the *kulak* holding the state up to ransom' was no doubt, as Bukharin called it, a fairy tale. But to an autocrat as suspicious as Stalin even such comparatively harmless institutions as the traditional village communes may well have appeared as dangerous rivals to the party organizations. Finally, with his instinct for the right way of holding on to power, Stalin may well have realized that to unleash a war of each against each far and wide throughout the country was the most certain way of making sure of his own survival at the helm. In conditions of comparative peace and harmony, Stalin's unpopular organizational talents might well seem no longer so essential to the party for its own survival in power, and other leaders might then come to the fore.

The subjugation of the peasants was ruthless and chaotic, and was accomplished at breakneck speed. At the same time rapid development of industry was pursued, with heavy industry, especially iron and steel, as the main objective. The task of effecting the revolution in the villages fell to the party members. By a decree of the Central Executive Committee the executive committees of the local soviets were given the power to apply 'all necessary measures in the struggle

[1] See pp. 341–3, above.

387

against the *kulaks*, including total confiscation of their property and their banishment beyond the confines of the relevant regions and provinces'.[1] The confiscated property was to become part of the common and indivisible fund of the collective farms, supposedly representing the capital brought into the collectives by the poor and landless peasants. The decree neither defined *kulak*, nor specified that the formation of collectives was to be a voluntary process. In order to strengthen the political nerve of the local village communists, 25,000 'workers with adequate political organizational experience' were dispatched from the towns, and they were followed by many more. In view of the punitive measures which had been taken in 1928 and 1929 against local communists who showed insufficient determination in applying the emergency measures designed to extract grain from the *kulaks*, it was perhaps not to be wondered at that the first wave of collectivization was accompanied by excesses. Even so, party members could not always be relied on to stomach the task that was now imposed upon them under the guise of 'war against the *kulaks*', which turned out to be a war against the whole peasantry. The brunt of the operation fell upon the OGPU, whose officials participated in every one of its grim phases. The speed with which the process was attempted alone gives some indication of the ferocity which accompanied it. The beginnings of collectivization had already been made in the second half of 1929, and the percentage of collectives rose from 4·1 per cent of households in October 1929 to 21 per cent on 20 January 1930. By 10 March 1930, 58 per cent of all farms were collective. Over half the total peasant households had been collectivized in five months.[2]

The resistance of the peasants showed itself in an immediate catastrophic fall in the numbers of cattle and horses, which were slaughtered in tens of thousands. The government decided on a retreat. In an article published on 2 March 1930, Stalin wrote that it was 'stupid and reactionary' to form collectives by force, and blamed the excesses which had been taking place on 'giddiness from success'.[3] The resolution of the Central Committee issued shortly afterwards threw some official light on these excesses. Those treated as *kulaks* had 'sometimes' included poor and middle peasants – in some instances up to 15 per cent of all peasants had been thus 'dekulakized'. (No official estimate had ever suggested that *kulaks*, even in the loosest definition

---

[1] Decree of the Central Executive Committee of 1 February 1930, quoted in S. N. Prokopovich, *Narodnoe khoziaistvo SSSR*, volume I, p. 189.
[2] *ibid.*, p. 191.
[3] *Stalin*, volume XII, pp. 191–9.

of this term, had exceeded 4 per cent of the peasants.) This resolution also revealed the frenzied nature of the 'class war' in the villages and confirms laconically the harrowing picture recorded at the time by a number of observers. Peasants, stated the resolution, were being forcibly deprived of all their property under the guise of collectivization, and churches were being closed, ostensibly by popular demand, but in fact by administrative force.[1]

The relaxation after March 1930 had immediate effects. Within six months, by September 1930, the percentage of collectivized farms dropped from 58 to 21.[2] The respite was only temporary. The Sixteenth Party Congress, held in June and July 1930, stressed that the *kulak* had not yet been beaten, and could be expected to display 'savage resistance'. A long and determined struggle was necessary in order to complete collectivization.[3] By the following year, 1931, the percentage of collectivized farms was once again 52·7, and by 1934 nearly three-quarters of all farms had been collectivized.[4] Contrary to the lavish promises contained in the Plan, agricultural production was lower in 1933 than in 1928, and the number of cattle was only somewhat over half the 1928 total.[5] In 1932 a famine struck the villages which lasted into 1933. The cause of this famine was not drought. It was the disintegration of the peasant economy, resulting from the peasants' resistance both to collectivization and to the government's policy of forcibly depriving them of their produce at compulsorily low state prices. The famine was an artificial one: the quantity of grain actually available was comparatively little diminished, and the government insisted on maintaining procurements at the same level, while the peasant starved. Thus, the amount of grain which the government extracted from the peasants in 1932–3, at the compulsory state price, was less than one-fifth lower than in 1931–2, and substantially higher than in 1929–30.[6] From the point of view of the government this ruthless policy not only enabled it to maintain, as far as possible, both the standard of living in the towns and the level of grain export; it also served as a salutary lesson to the peasants that resistance to collectivization did not pay.

[1] *KPSS v rez.*, volume II, pp. 668–71.
[2] Prokopovich, *op. cit.*, p. 193.
[3] *KPSS v rez.*, volume III, p. 61. At the same time, this Congress went out of its way to stress that collectivization could only be carried out on a voluntary basis, without indicating how it was to be achieved, in the face of the resistance of the peasants, except by force.
[4] Prokopovich, *op. cit.*, p. 204.
[5] *ibid.*, p. 206.
[6] *ibid.*, p. 213.

The government also reacted to the peasants' recalcitrance with reprisals. A number of decrees in the late summer and autumn of 1932 strengthened the arm of the government against the peasants. The death penalty was authorized to be applied for theft of grain, peasants leaving the collective farms were denied the right to any land, except from the, in practice non-existent, free land fund of the state, and the penalties against speculation were increased. There were also mass deportations, and to the casualties suffered as the result of famine were added the losses suffered at the hands of the OGPU. The total loss to the peasants in life and liberty between 1929 and 1933 has been variously estimated by Western economists, and the number of the deported alone was believed by some to have been as high as five million families.[1] According to Stalin himself, in conversation in later years with Sir Winston Churchill, as many as ten million peasants were dealt with during this period, and 'the great bulk were very unpopular and were wiped out by their labourers'.[2]

Important first-hand evidence has now become available on the role of the party in collectivizing the peasants. During the Second World War the records of the party organization of the Smolensk region fell into German, and subsequently into Allied hands, and have now been made public. Smolensk was a mainly agricultural region and its experience may be regarded as typical of what went on in many other places. Two facts emerge beyond any doubt from the party and OGPU reports of the Smolensk region for the period 1929–33. First, that in spite of occasional attempts to restrain excesses, a vast, disorganized campaign of arrests, deportations and confiscation was unleashed against rich, middle and poor peasants alike who resisted the attempt to force them into the new collectives. As the local OGPU reported on 23 February 1930, middle and 'even' poor peasants were being arrested by 'anybody' in any way connected with collectivization. Secondly, that what was perhaps originally intended as an orderly reform, at any rate by some of the more responsible party officials, very soon turned into an orgy of wholesale looting. As the OGPU reported on 28 February 1930, the slogan of many 'dekulakization' brigades was 'drink, eat – it's all ours'. If it was true that the more conscientious party officials tried to restrain this all-round anarchy and licence, it was also plain that such efforts as they made met with no success so long as Stalin himself did not intervene.

[1] See e.g. L. E. Hubbard, *The Economics of Soviet Agriculture*, London, 1939, pp. 117–19.
[2] W. S. Churchill, *The Second World War*. Volume IV: *The Hinge of Fate* London, 1951, pp. 447–8.

Finally, Stalin did intervene, in a secret circular signed by himself and Molotov, dated 8 May 1933, addressed to all party, OGPU and judicial organs. This complained of a 'saturnalia of arrests' by 'all who desire to, and who, strictly speaking, have no right to make arrests'. It ordered that these indiscriminate arrests be 'immediately stopped' and that arrests in future should only be made in cases of 'active struggle' or 'organized resistance'. Maximum deportation quotas were laid down for certain regions. The struggle was not yet over. But the period of licensed anarchy was at an end.[1]

It was not to be wondered at that the shock of the experience of collectivization, and its attendant famine, should have made a profound impact both upon the rank and file and upon the leaders of a party of which the members were seldom more than one remove from the soil. Many carried out their grim duties with zeal, but there were also many who were repelled by their experience. In studying the effects upon the leading party members it is also necessary to take into account the process of rapid industrialization which was the concomitant of collectivization. The first thing to be borne in mind is the way in which the First Five Year Plan was made acceptable during 1928 and 1929 to the party at the time of Stalin's conflict with his right-wing opponents and with the more moderate economists of *Gosplan*. There had been no promise of 'blood, sweat and tears', no call to accept sacrifices for the sake of a distant, better future. On the contrary, Stalin and his supporters had always emphasized that the plan, with its optimistic promises of rapid advance and improved all-round prosperity, was attainable, that it only required true bolshevik courage for all to be well. Such ultra-revolutionary appeals were always sure of some response – it will be recalled with what skill Stalin had launched his policy of 'socialism in one country' as an alternative to Trotsky's revolutionary demands, with the very aim of outdoing him in revolutionary zeal. Hence, at the outset, industrialization evoked a good deal of enthusiasm.

As the years wore on, to an ever-mounting crescendo of self-congratulation from the party leaders, exaggerated claims of success, faked statistics and exhortation to yet greater efforts, the more sober realities of the situation produced a corresponding depression. In place of the promised plenty, there was food shortage, accompanied by strict rationing, especially marked during the famine year of

[1] These Smolensk party records, which contain a great mass of authentic evidence on the life of the party and of the country in general for the period 1920–39 are admirably analysed in Merle Fainsod, *Smolensk under Soviet Rule*, Cambridge, Mass, 1958. On collectivization see Chapter xii, *passim*, and pp. 185–8.

1932–3. The rapid influx of peasants from the villages into the towns, which were unprepared to receive them, contributed to the lowering of the standard of living, which had made so substantial an advance by the end of NEP. Absenteeism among workers was soon followed by repressive measures, direction of labour and strict factory discipline: by November 1932 one day's absence was a ground for instant dismissal; in December the internal passport was introduced.

By itself, discipline would not necessarily have led to disillusionment in the communist party, which always had strong leanings towards authoritarian methods, and which could argue that works discipline where the workers' state is the factory owner is very different from the discipline imposed by the capitalist. The same could conceivably have been argued about the introduction of piecework rates for time rates, which became widespread by the end of 1932. Although as a system it was generally accepted as favouring the employer rather than the worker (Marx, for example, had branded it as a weapon of capitalist exploitation) it could still be claimed that where the beneficiary was the state there could be no question of exploitation. But these theoretical considerations did not disguise the fact that a marked change was taking place in relations between workers and management which even observant visitors could note, and which was therefore apparent to party members. The worker under NEP, when something of the early egalitarianism and revolutionary élan still survived, could comfort himself in face of the economic hardships which he suffered with the sense that he was one of the privileged revolutionary class. By 1931 or 1932, whatever might be said in theory, the relationship between workers and management was undergoing a change which was uncomfortably reminiscent of the picture of exploitation associated with capitalism – even if no one dared say so. All this might have caused little stir had the Plan been successful in achieving its aims. But the results of the First Plan fell far short of the aims which had been set.[1] By 1933 no communist could have been blamed for doubting whether Stalin and his supporters were really the best men to lead the party.

These changes of party mood were only gradual, as the situation altered in the course of these few years. When the Sixteenth Party

[1] L. E. Hubbard, *Soviet Labour and Industry*, London, 1942, pp. 60–2, 58. The percentages of fulfilment there given are: coal 86; pig iron 62; steel 57; crude petroleum 13; cotton textiles 58. See also N. Jasny in *Sotsialisticheskii vestnik*, December 1956, pp. 243–5; and Naum Jasny, *Soviet Industrialization 1928–1952*, Chicago, 1961, pp. 64–9.

Congress met from 26 June to 13 July 1930, the credit of the right-wing leaders seemed to have reached its lowest ebb. Bukharin, who was not present at the Congress, was spared the humiliation which fell to the lot of Rykov and Tomskii. Each of these two leaders made avowals of his errors in the most abject terms. But, in spite of the fact that all three right-wing leaders were re-elected to the Central Committee, there was no question of their rehabilitation. Speeches and resolutions stressed the need for unremitting struggle against the right-wing 'opportunists' who, it was asserted, were now adopting a new trick: in place of open opposition they were now formally acknowledging their past errors and formally expressing their agreement with the party line, but this in reality only meant that they had passed from open opposition to hidden opposition and were waiting for a more favourable moment to renew their attack on the party.[1] The implication of this general charge of conspiracy against past opponents of Stalin's policy was that police methods were now to be adopted for dealing with political opponents.

Rumours were current at the time of stormy conflicts behind the scenes, but there is no evidence of them in the official transcript of the Congress proceedings. The particularly servile obedience which marked this Congress, as reported, could to a large extent be explained by the stern disciplinary measures which had for some time past become normal in the party. In April 1930 Kaganovich had been put into the Moscow organization as First Secretary to clean it up. The fall of Tomskii from his position in the trade union hierarchy had been followed by wholesale expulsions of trade union communists. In approving these measures in the trade unions, the Sixteenth Congress recorded that these 'opportunist' trade union communists had been showing 'trade unionist tendencies' and had not only 'failed to understand the tasks of the proletarian dictatorship during the reconstruction period', but had also shown resistance to the party in its attempts to 'reconstruct' the nature of trade union activities.[2] In plainer language, they had attempted to defend the interests of the workers against the all-embracing claims of the state.

The official party handbook for 1930 records repeated instances of the committees of entire party organizations being removed and replaced. There was, however, another reason, apart from fear of disciplinary reprisals, which may have rallied the party at this date against the right-wing critics. There was open war in the villages, and

[1] *KPSS v rez.*, volume III, p. 21.
[2] *ibid.*, p. 64.

the desperate peasants did not hesitate to kill any communists, regarding them as their natural enemies. It followed, in the minds of many communists, that to side with the right, and therefore with the peasants, was to side with those who were killing communists, and therefore with counter-revolution. At the Sixteenth Congress one of Stalin's group of provincial plenipotentiaries, Sheboldaev, effectively pointed this moral. He described the emergence of an opposition group in the Lower Volga region, and quoted from a speech or statement of an old bolshevik member of the group in which, after making a number of criticisms of collectivization on lines which closely followed Bukharin's 'Notes of an Economist', this oppositionist went on to say that it was necessary to work for a change of leadership, if need be by force of arms. The statement quoted may very well have been the record of an OGPU interrogation, and therefore little related to truth. But the moral was clear, and the Congress delegates by their interruptions showed that they had understood. From right-wing views to a plot to overthrow the leadership, and therefore to counter-revolution, was only a step.[1] It was probably not very far from the truth that only a forcible overthrow of Stalin could have made it possible for any view other than his to be given a hearing. But this was a prospect fraught with great risk to the survival of the whole communist régime.

The ensuing years were, however, to show that there were some limits to the support which Stalin could rely upon from his colleagues at the summit of the party. The Politburo elected after the Sixteenth Congress requires attention, because while on the face of it it seemed to herald an outright victory for those who had backed Stalin to the hilt, it included several men who were later to pay the penalty for opposing him. Bukharin and Tomskii were of course gone, and so was the candidate member Uglanov. The full members were: Voroshilov, Kaganovich, Kalinin, Kirov, Kossior, Kuibyshev, Molotov, Rykov, Rudzutak and Stalin. Rykov, retained for the time being, was removed by the end of the year and replaced by Ordzhonikidze. The candidates were: Mikoyan, Chubar', Petrovskii, Andreev and Syrtsov. The latter two only remained as candidates for a short time; Syrtsov fell into disgrace, and Andreev left upon his appointment to the Central Control Commission. The views and actions of these men in the years 1931 to 1933, with which we are now concerned, must in the absence of clear evidence remain largely conjectural. Nevertheless, some light has now been thrown on the whole question by the information

[1] *XVI S"ezd*, pp. 135–6.

disclosed in 1956 to the Twentieth Party Congress by the First Secretary of the party, N. S. Khrushchev.[1]

Bukharin's turn to make an abject renunciation of his views came at the Seventeenth Party Conference, held from 30 January to 4 February 1932. Rykov, after his resignation from the Chairmanship of the Council of People's Commissars, remained People's Commissar for Posts and Telegraph, Bukharin was for a time in charge of the research department of the Commissariat of Heavy Industry, which was headed by Ordzhonikidze after it came into existence in 1932, and later became editor of the government paper *Izvestiia*. Discredited by having repudiated their views, the right leaders were less likely to be able to rally support among the more violent, if less prominent, oppositionists who for several years, between 1930 and 1933 at any rate, were attempting to form conspiratorial groups in the party.

It is probable that a number of minor groups of this nature existed, but our information only makes it possible to be certain of three – one at the end of 1930, the other two in the second half of 1932. The first of these groups, that of Syrtsov and Lominadze, was mainly remarkable for the fact that its leaders had hitherto been outstanding for their loyalty to Stalin. Syrtsov had for many years been an important official of the Secretariat, and had been elected a candidate member of the Politburo a few months before. Lominadze, it will be recalled, had organized the Canton rising in December 1927 for Stalin's special benefit. Both were alleged to have formed factions or groups inside the party, and to have acted as focal points for counter-revolution, with a platform expressing the 'panic-stricken' views of the right wing. Syrtsov is supposed to have referred to the great successes in industry as 'eye-wash', and to the announcement of the setting up of the Stalingrad tractor factory as a 'Potemkin village'. Lominadze is alleged to have referred to the 'lordly, feudal attitude to the needs of

---

[1] This information was disclosed in secret session to the Twentieth Congress on 24–5 February 1956. The text of the speech has not been published in the USSR, though its existence has been repeatedly referred to in official documents. The only text available to us is the one published by the US State Department on 4 June 1956, though extensive summaries of the speech appeared in communist papers in various countries. The US text appears to be a version prepared for the information of foreign communists by the Russian party, and therefore presumably differs somewhat from the speech as delivered. The State Department text has been tacitly accepted as authentic by communist parties all over the world, and has never been formally repudiated by the Russian leaders, except somewhat casually on one occasion, and there can be no possible doubt of its authenticity. The text is reprinted in *The Anti-Stalin Campaign and International Communism*. A Selection of Documents, edited by the Russian Institute, Columbia University, New York, 1956, pp. 1–89. (Cited hereafter as *The Anti-Stalin Campaign*.)

the peasants'.[1] Both were expelled from the Central Committee in December 1930, but it does not appear that any further repressive measures were taken against them. Lominadze at any rate seems to have remained at liberty, a bitter and disappointed man, until his suicide in 1934.[2]

Two groups are known to have been active in the second half of 1932, the darkest moment in these years of upheaval. One, headed by Riutin, the former ally of Uglanov in the Moscow organization, is reliably reported by at least two sources, whose testimony has been in many respects corroborated by events, to have circulated a secretly duplicated programme which included an attack on Stalin in very bitter terms.[3] Another group also circulated a secretly duplicated manifesto, which was officially stated to have been 'similar' in its views to Riutin's.[4] Unofficial rumours of the contents of this manifesto reported that it demanded a reduction in the amount of capital investment, the disbanding of the collective farms, and a change of the top leadership. It also was said to include an attack on Bukharin for having abandoned the struggle.[5] Riutin, the leaders of the other group (Eismont, Tolmachev and others) and some other former oppositionists such as Zinoviev and Kamenev, who were reportedly in sympathy with their programmes, were all rounded up and sent into penal exile early in 1933. Since political prisoners still enjoyed a comparative degree of privilege at this date, this must be regarded as a punishment of some leniency.

It is possible that a clash took place between Stalin and his colleagues on the issue of the fate of these people, with Stalin demanding

---

[1] *Pravda*, 2 December 1930.

[2] On the last years of Lominadze see Margarete Buber-Neumann, *Von Potsdam nach Moskau*, Stationen eines Irrweges, Stuttgart, 1957, pp. 413–15.

[3] W. G. Krivitsky, *I was Stalin's Agent*, London, 1939; *The Letter of an Old Bolshevik*, A Key to the Moscow Trials, London, 1938. In spite of these lurid titles, both these sources are accepted by the consensus of scholarly opinion outside the USSR as containing substantially accurate accounts. The former is by an officer of Soviet Military Intelligence, the latter, published anonymously in *Sotsialisticheskii vestnik* in 1936–7, is apparently based on information supplied from an oppositionist high up in the party hierarchy. Both sources have been repeatedly confirmed by official information released long after they were published. Krivitsky met his end in Washington in 1941 in circumstances which raise strong suspicion that he was done to death by agents of the Soviet police – further confirmation that his disclosures were considered damaging by Stalin. (Since the first edition of this book was published in 1960, the fact that the late B. I. Nicolaevsky was the author of *The Letter of an Old Bolshevik* has been made public; and the source of his information at the time has been disclosed to have been Bukharin when on a visit to Western Europe in 1936. See Boris I. Nicolaevsky, *Power and The Soviet Elite*, New York, Washington, London, 1965, pp. 3–25. *The Letter of an Old Bolshevik* is reprinted *ibidem*, pp. 26–65.)

[4] *KPSS v rez.*, volume III, p. 199.

[5] *Biulleten' oppozitsii*, No. 31, p. 23.

the sternest measures against the leaders of these groups. Three independent accounts published in the 30's, each by a witness who was in a fairly good position to know, refer to this clash.[1] But the best evidence of it is now to be found in the disclosure by First Secretary N. S. Khrushchev to the Twentieth Congress of the Party in 1956 of the text of the telegram in which Stalin appointed Ezhov to head the security service in place of Yagoda, and thereby inaugurated the purges of 1936–8. In this telegram, dated 25 September 1936, or about four years after the period with which we are now concerned, Stalin accused the OGPU of being 'four years behind' in the matter of dealing with the menace of counter-revolution.[2]

If the composition of the Politburo in 1932 be examined, it does indeed look as if Stalin, when once he made clear his intention to unleash a wave of police terror inside the party itself, came up against some opposition. Of the nine full members, apart from Stalin, only two, Molotov and Kaganovich, can be stated with certainty to have at all times given Stalin their full and unswerving support in all his measures. Two, Voroshilov and Kalinin, were known to be lukewarm supporters, who had at one time sympathized with Bukharin. Of the other five, four – Ordzhonikidze, Kossior, Rudzutak and Kirov – were quite probably opponents of Stalin's terrorism, and possibly a fifth, Kuibyshev, may have resisted the use of terror against members of the party. The evidence for this view appears from the subsequent fate of these men, all of whom (unless Kuibyshev's death allegedly from heart failure in 1935 was really due to natural causes) were to become victims of Stalin's vengeance.

If the Politburo members did display these scruples in the autumn of 1932, they were apparently limited to safeguarding members of the communist party. For several years past all these leaders had tolerated, and presumably approved, the condemnation and execution, with or without trial, of groups of non-communist technical specialists of all kinds, on charges of sabotage and wrecking. On the occasions when trials were held the evidence was, to say the least, unconvincing. Notable among such trials was that of a group of former mensheviks held in early March 1931, on charges of setting up a counter-revolutionary organization aimed at the restoration of capitalism. These former mensheviks, who included the historian of the revolution,

[1] Krivitsky, *op. cit.*, p. 203; *Letter of an Old Bolshevik*, pp. 16–21; A Ciliga, *Au Pays du Mensonge Déconcertant*, Paris 1950, pp. 163, 219. (Ciliga spent a number of years in camps for political prisoners and met many of the oppositionists who found their way there.)

[2] *The Anti-Stalin Campaign*, p. 26.

Sukhanov, and such noted economists as Groman, had worked for years in important posts in the economic organizations of the state. They were all duly condemned and sentenced to long terms of imprisonment, which none of them is known to have survived. Nevertheless, the menshevik trial cannot be regarded as a success for the OGPU, in spite of the full confessions which its skilled officers succeeded in extracting from these elderly and mostly infirm intellectuals. The essence of the charge was that the conspiracy had been formed during an alleged secret visit to Russia by the menshevik leader in exile, Abramovitch. The mensheviks in exile had no difficulty in showing, and in supporting their case by published photographs, that at the very time when he was supposed to have been secretly visiting Russia Abramovitch was in fact taking part in deliberations of the Socialist International in Brussels.

But these 'trials', if unconvincing, served a propaganda purpose. They provided an excuse for failures in the achievement of economic targets by attributing them to sabotage. Even more important, by beginning to eliminate the old non-communist technicians upon whom the régime had hitherto relied, and to whom it owed its economic development, they prepared openings for the new class of communist technicians whom the party was fast training up. The menshevik 'trial' also heralded the fall of that stormy petrel, Riazanov. Riazanov, always an individualist, the wittiest man in the party and far and away its best Marxist scholar, had been a thorn in the flesh of the more practical politicians since as far back as 1901, when he clashed with *Iskra*. Riazanov never concealed his contempt for the tactical vagaries of policy which took place in the name of Marxist theory. 'They don't need any Marxist in the Politburo,' had been one of his typical interjections at the Sixteenth Party Conference, in April 1929. The menshevik trial was made a convenient occasion to implicate Riazanov and to expel him from the party by alleging illicit contacts between him and the mensheviks. He disappeared during the purges, and died in 1938.

From Stalin's point of view, the fact, if it was a fact, that the Politburo was not prepared to support him in the policy which he considered necessary to terrorize the party into submission must have had the result of diminishing the freedom with which he could use the ordinary apparatus of the party and security organs. Since ultimately the apparatus of the party and police was subject to the control of the Politburo, which could be expected to be suspicious of any attempts to use it for personal ends, alternative means had to be found. Little evidence is available to show how Stalin succeeded in overcoming this real difficulty. But we know, from the disclosures made by Khrushchev in 1956, that Stalin did succeed in the course of time in circumventing the normal machinery of the party and of the police by the skilful use of personal agents within this machinery, upon whom he could rely as completely loyal to himself. There are a few pointers, in the course of 1933 and 1934, in the moving into key positions by Stalin of three men on whom he would eventually rely for accomplishing the decimation of the party which he considered necessary. One of these was N. I. Ezhov, an official of the Secretariat. At the beginning of 1933 the Central Committee decreed that a complete verification and purge of party membership was required. When after some delay the purge commission was appointed, one of its members was Ezhov.[1] If, as later developments suggest, Stalin was beginning to build up Ezhov as a man of confidence, no better appointment could have been selected, since membership of the purge commission gave him access to the fullest information on the entire membership of the party, as well as valuable experience in organizing a purge. At the elections to party organs held immediately after the Seventeenth Congress, on 10 February 1934, Ezhov became a member of the Orgburo. These were to be his first steps in a rapid rise up the party ladder in the following two years.

Another key figure during these years was A. N. Poskrebyshev, whose whole career was spent in the central party apparatus until his disappearance after Stalin's death. Poskrebyshev became the head of Stalin's personal secretariat, possibly in 1931. The functions of this body, of which the very existence is only casually mentioned in Soviet sources, but which apparently existed by 1924, if not earlier, are far from clear. But from the fact that an obituary of Poskrebyshev's predecessor in office in the personal secretariat was signed not only by the heads of the departments of the Secretariat but also by Yagoda and several deputy heads of the OGPU, it is a fair inference that, among other things, it maintained close relations with the police.[2] The third key figure who emerged into prominence in 1933 was A. I. Vyshinsky, a former menshevik, and professor of law at, and later rector of, Moscow University. Vyshinsky became deputy state procurator, and not long after, in 1935, chief procurator.

These initial moves by Stalin probably did not escape the notice of

---

[1] *Izvestiia*, 29 April 1933.
[2] *Pravda*, 10 August 1935; see also *Proletarskaia revoluitsiia*, No. 6, 1935, pp. 129–31.

his colleagues on the Politburo. Perhaps the hope of the more moderate elements in the Politburo was to ease Stalin out of the Secretariat, or at any rate to counter-balance the key men whom Stalin was advancing by men in whom the 'moderates' felt more confidence. According to one circumstantial account, the candidate of the moderates whom they hoped to build up against Stalin was S. M. Kirov, the secretary of the Leningrad organization.[1] There was little in Kirov's career up to 1933 to suggest that he was a 'moderate'. He had been a protégé of Stalin against Zinoviev, to whose office he succeeded. He was to all appearances a wholehearted supporter of collectivization and of the Five Year Plan. There is also little, if anything, in his published speeches to suggest the moderate, except, perhaps, a much greater emphasis upon practical matters than upon the traditional right- or left-wing bogies; and at times a remarkable absence of the customary fulsome eulogies of Stalin at every appropriate or indeed inappropriate occasion. Kirov certainly had three advantages over Stalin – he was youthful, good-looking and a Russian, and even the official stenograms of party gatherings make it clear that the public acclamations which he received were second only to those accorded to Stalin. If the Politburo 'moderates' were looking for a suitable candidate to oppose to Stalin they certainly could hardly have picked a better man than Kirov.

If reports at the time are to be believed, at any rate by 1933 or 1934 Kirov was beginning to voice the private opinion that the time had come to put an end to strife in the country. If so, this was the direct contrary of what Stalin was saying – that now was the very time to intensify the class struggle, and that talk of its dying down was 'counter-revolutionary'. It is possible that the readmission of Zinoviev and Kamenev to the party (after their arrest in connexion with the opposition scandal at the end of 1932 and early in 1933) was due to Kirov's influence. At all events, whether Kirov's rumoured reputation for moderation was deserved or no, it is quite clear that in the course of 1933 and 1934 his advance to the top of the ladder paralleled and indeed outstripped that of Ezhov, over whom, as a Politburo member and the second most prominent regional party secretary, he had a considerable advantage. When the purge commission was set up in April 1933 Kirov also became a member of it. The composition of this body bears some marks of a compromise. Its chairman was Rudzutak, subsequently to be done to death by Stalin, and therefore quite possibly a 'moderate' at this date. But Stalin's nominees –

[1] *Letter of an Old Bolshevik, passim.*

Kaganovich, Ezhov, Iaroslavskii and Shkiriatov – outnumbered Kirov and the two 'old bolshevik' members, Stasova and Piatnitskii.

However, it was at the time of the Seventeenth Party Congress, which met in Moscow from 26 January to 10 February 1934, that signs of compromise between Stalin and the more 'moderate' members of the Politburo became most evident. This Congress assumed the name of the 'Congress of Victors', though the claim to victory was only in part justified. The situation in the villages was, it is true, showing some signs of improvement. Gross agricultural production and stocks of cattle were very slowly beginning to rise. But, in spite of the paeans of praise at the achievements of industrialization, the sober fact that the ambitious targets in industry had not been reached was known to all, if none dared openly to admit it. The standard of the workers' living was falling steadily, housing conditions were appalling, food was still rationed, and rigorous works discipline was in force to drive the men to ever greater effort. At the same time there were two factors which helped to spread a feeling in the party that the time had come for reconciliation and peace rather than for further strife. The grimmest feature of Stalin's revolution, the war against the peasants, was behind them. It had been terrible while it lasted, its victims had been innumerable, but at any rate collectivization had been achieved. There could be no question now of turning back. Abroad, the victory of Hitler in Germany, which many within the party may have been tempted to attribute in part to the policy of an all-out campaign against the social democrats which Stalin had unleashed in 1928, cast an ominous shadow of war. Outwardly, the 'Congress of Victors' showed a measure of consideration for the defeated opposition which had not hitherto characterized party congresses. A number of prominent oppositionists – Bukharin, Zinoviev, Kamenev, Lominadze, Preobrazhenskii, Piatakov, Radek, Rykov and Tomskii – were allowed to appear and speak, without the usual accompaniment of catcalls and derision. Each acknowledged his past errors, but with some measure of dignity. The ritual reference at the end of each speech to the greatness of Stalin's leadership earned each penitent speaker a measure of applause, recorded in the stenogram.

But behind the ritual of self-congratulation, fulsome praise of Stalin and enthusiastic condemnation of deviation both to the right and to the left, the realities of compromise were nevertheless discernible. One such significant sign was the adoption, on Ordzhonikidze's proposal, of a somewhat more modest rate of industrial growth for the forthcoming Second Five Year Plan than that proposed in the draft resolution submitted to the Congress.[1] But it was the composition of the party organs which proved most revealing of the fact that Stalin was not having things all his own way. The Central Committee elected at the Congress included Piatakov among its members, and Bukharin, Rykov and Tomskii among the candidate members. At the Central Committee Plenum, which met immediately after the Congress, a new Politburo was elected consisting of Stalin, Molotov, Kaganovich, Voroshilov, Kalinin, Ordzhonikidze, Kuibyshev, Kirov, Andreev and Kossior as full members, and Mikoyan, Chubar', Petrovskii, Postyshev and Rudzutak as candidate members.[2] Of the nine full members, apart from Stalin, at least three, Ordzhonikidze Kirov and Kossior, might perhaps be expected to oppose any attempt by Stalin to unleash terror on the party, and all but two of the remainder (Molotov and Kaganovich) could not, on their past record, necessarily be relied on to support Stalin in his most extreme policies. Of the five candidates, only one, Mikoyan, was a completely reliable 'Stalinist'. The re-election of Kirov, who had received an ovation at the Congress according to the stenogram and according to reports current at the time an ovation equal to that accorded to Stalin, was a victory for the 'moderates' – if it was the case that they were grooming Kirov as eventual successor.

The new Secretariat consisted of Stalin, Kaganovich, Kirov and Zhdanov – the latter a new figure who was coming into prominence as secretary of the important Gorky organization. There was one notable fact about the laconic announcement of this election which appeared in the press. Stalin, who since 1922 had invariably been described as 'General Secretary', was now described only as 'Secretary'. Such points of formal title are always a matter for scrupulous care in Soviet practice. Any question of error in Stalin's title is quite inconceivable, and it was plain to all that some diminution of authority was thereby intended. Stalin's special *homme de confiance*, Ezhov, was not yet apparent at the summit of the party. But he was elected a full member of the Central Committee and, in addition to joining the Orgburo, was appointed at the Congress second in command of the Party Control Commission (as the Central Control Commission was now renamed), which was headed by Kaganovich. The pieces were thus displayed on the board. But it was to take a further two years of manœuvre before Stalin was in a position to make the move which gave him final victory.

[1] *XVII S"ezd*, pp. 435–6.
[2] *Pravda*, 11 February 1934.

XXII   Stalin's Victory over the Party

For a time after the 'Congress of Victors' had concluded its labours some signs of normality and peace were discernible. The harvest of 1933 had been good, and the worst of the famine was over. The gathering war clouds which accompanied Hitler's rise in Germany gave a sense of urgency to the desire for unity and solidarity inside the party. Before long it seemed as if the modest victory which the more moderate elements appeared to have won at the Congress was bearing some fruit. Former prominent oppositionists were quietly allowed to resume honourable, if humble, employment. According to one account, the 'moderates' were successful in 1934 in restraining Stalin's demands for drastic action – this time against some members of the *Komsomol* who had been showing an unhealthy interest in the study and discussion of the exploits and methods of the terrorists of the early revolutionary movements.[1] Indeed there even seemed to be some indications that the powers of the OGPU were being curtailed. In July 1934, after a wave of trials for sabotage and conspiracy, designed to find scapegoats for industrial and agricultural shortcomings, Vyshinsky, the deputy state procurator, ordered his local procurators to halt the policy of indiscriminate prosecution of engineers and directors.[2] By a series of decrees, of which the first was dated 10 July 1934, the OGPU was absorbed in a reorganized People's Commissariat of Internal Affairs (NKVD), which now took over all the functions of police and security, including the administration of the rapidly growing forced-labour camps and the exploitation of their inmates for industrial schemes. A Special Board with delimited powers of inflicting punishment by administrative action replaced the former Judicial College of the OGPU which in the course of time had acquired virtually unlimited powers of life and death.[3]

The benefits of the new course were also extended to the peasants, at a Plenum of the Central Committee which met from 25 to 28

---

[1] *The Letter of an Old Bolshevik*, London, 1938, pp. 29–30.
[2] Merle Fainsod, *How Russia is Ruled*, p. 432.
[3] See Simon Wolin and Robert M. Slusser, *The Soviet Secret Police*, pp. 46–8, for details of the decrees.

November 1934. This Plenum adopted in principle three measures, two of which signified some relaxation of the rigours which had been imposed during the first Five Year Plan. It decided to abolish bread rationing; and it adopted the draft of a new Model Statute for the collective farms which substantially increased the existing very limited rights of their peasant members to cultivate their small plots of private land.[1] This Plenum was attended by Kirov, who travelled from Leningrad to Moscow for the purpose. No replacement for Kirov had yet been appointed to the Leningrad organization, and he returned to Leningrad after the Plenum meeting.

Three days later, on 1 December 1934 in the evening, a young communist, L. Nikolaev, fired at and fatally wounded Kirov in his office at the party headquarters in Leningrad. The true explanation for this murder, for which tens of thousands, if not more, paid with their lives, is still shrouded in mystery. Official accounts, which blamed it successively on foreign powers, on the Zinovievites, on Trotsky and on the right opposition, are not convincing. Unofficial accounts by those who appear to have been well informed tell yet another story.[2] According to these accounts, Nikolaev was a young romantic revolutionary, disillusioned with the inhuman and bureaucratic forms which the party seemed to have assumed, and inspired by the example of the terrorists of *Narodnaia Volia*. His motives were said to have been revealed by his diary, which clearly showed that he had neither accomplices nor any organization behind him. The official published account of the trial of Nikolaev, which was held in secret (if it was held at all), does indeed refer to such a diary, but states that it was a forgery, designed to create the impression that the killing was not part of a careful conspiracy, but merely a protest against 'unjust treatment of individuals'.[3] Unofficial accounts further suggested that the security organs knew that the assassination was being contemplated some time in advance, but connived at it, on Stalin's instructions. This allegation was to some extent supported by the fact that the security officers who were put on trial for their negli-

---

[1] *KPSS v rez.*, volume III, pp. 256–65; S. N. Prokopovich, *Narodnoe khoziaistvo SSSR*, volume I, pp. 252–5.

[2] A good deal has been written on the murder of Kirov by those who were close enough to the events to speak with some degree of authority. The best accounts are probably those contained in *The Letter of an Old Bolshevik, passim*; and in Elizabeth Lermolo, *Face of a Victim*, London, 1956. Both have been confirmed in several respects by N. S. Khrushchev's secret speech to the Twentieth Party Congress. The background to the murder was reassessed by B. I. Nicolaevsky in *Sotsialisticheskii vestnik*, October and December 1956. See also Robert Conquest, *The Great Terror : Stalin's Purge of the Thirties*, London, 1968, Chapter ii.

[3] *Pravda*, 27 December 1934.

gence in failing to guard Kirov effectively were, for Soviet conditions, given strikingly mild prison sentences. In his account of the assassination given to the Twentieth Party Congress in 1956, N. S. Khrushchev, who presumably had had access to the relevant records, hinted, without naming Stalin, that the circumstances of Kirov's death were very suspicious: the NKVD officer personally responsible for Kirov's safety had been killed in an obviously staged accident before he could be interrogated, and other officers had subsequently been shot presumably 'to cover the traces of the organizers of Kirov's killing'.[1]

But whether Stalin organized it or not, Kirov's death gave him the opportunity for which he had been waiting. On the day of the assassination a decree issued by the Central Executive Committee virtually deprived those accused of terroristic acts of any rights of defence. A secret party directive issued the same evening ordered the speeding up of the cases of those accused of the preparation or execution of acts of terrorism: investigation was to be followed by immediate execution; no time was to be allowed for an appeal for mercy. As Khrushchev later told the Twentieth Party Congress, this directive 'became the basis for mass acts of abuse against socialist legality. During many of the fabricated cases the accused were charged with the "preparation" of terroristic acts; this deprived them of any possibility that their cases might be re-examined, even when they stated before the court that their "confessions" were secured by force, and when, in a convincing manner, they disproved the accusations against them.'[2] It should be noted that this directive, though apparently issued by Stalin on his own authority in the first instance, was subsequently approved by the Politburo. The decree remained in force for some time after Stalin's death.

This charter of lawlessness was at first applied to non-communists, described as 'White Guards', batches of whom were executed for alleged 'preparation of terroristic acts' in various cities in the USSR. There was no suggestion that these men had had any connexion with the Kirov assassination.[3] But before long blame for the murder was laid on the former members of the Zinovievite opposition and on Trotsky. On 30 December Nikolaev and thirteen alleged accomplices

---

[1] *The Anti-Stalin Campaign*, pp. 25–6. For another hypothesis, which by implication rejects the theory that Kirov was by 1934 an opponent of Stalin, and which suggests that Stalin merely connived at what was intended to be an unsuccessful attempt on Kirov's life to provide himself with an excuse for mass repressions, see *Biulleten' oppozitsii*, No. 42, 1935, p. 7.

[2] *ibidem*, p. 25; the decree is in *Pravda*, 5 December 1934.

[3] e.g. *Pravda*, 6 and 8 December 1934, but there were many other such mass executions.

having allegedly been tried in secret, were sentenced to death and immediately shot. The accomplices were said to have been 'Zinovievites', and reprisals against oppositionists followed. Thousands of former oppositionists, who had long ago recanted and had been re-admitted to the party, were now expelled again, arrested and deported. Zinoviev and Kamenev were among the first to suffer.[1]

But Stalin was determined to press the advantage which the panic caused by Kirov's death offered in order to begin the kind of assault on the party which he had contemplated at least since 1932. On 16 January 1935 an announcement signed by Vyshinsky, as deputy state procurator, disclosed that Zinoviev, Kamenev and other ex-oppositionists were to be tried for maintaining a secret centre of opposition in Moscow, for deceiving the party by their false declarations of repentance, and for indirectly influencing Kirov's assassin by 'ideological' means – no direct complicity in the murder was suggested. Zinoviev, Kamenev and others were tried in secret and sentenced to imprisonment.[2] This trial may be regarded as a milestone in the history of the party, because it was the first occasion (apart from the case of Sultan-Galiev in 1923 – see page 353 above) on which political opposition by communists, inside the communist party, was made the subject of an open criminal charge. Since this grave step could not have been taken without the approval of the Politburo at least, it must be assumed that the more moderate members either approved it or were unable to oppose it effectively. In either case, their action sealed their own fate. It is possible that Kuibyshev in the Politburo and Maxim Gorky outside it made some efforts to restrain Stalin. The fact that Yagoda was later charged with poisoning these two men raises at any rate the hypothesis that either he did in fact do so, on Stalin's instructions, and was then accused of having done so in order to be removed as a witness who knew too much; or that he was forced to confess to these crimes as part of an endeavour to divert suspicion from the real culprits. The sudden death of Kuibyshev announced on 26 January 1935 and the fact that literary attacks on the hitherto sacrosanct Gorky were allowed to be published about this time[3] lend some credence to the hypothesis. Gorky died on 18 June 1936.

A possible sign that something in the nature of a compromise between Stalin and his close supporters on the one hand and the more moderate elements in the party leadership on the other was being

---

[1] *Pravda*, 22 December, 27 December, 30 December 1934, 10 January 1935.
[2] *Pravda* 16 and 18 January 1935.
[3] See e.g. *Pravda*, 28 January 1935, for an attack by the novelist Panferov.

reached appeared at the Central Committee Plenum on 1 February 1935, when additional members and candidate members of the Politburo were elected. Of the two new full members, one Mikoyan, was a stalwart Stalinist, but the other, Chubar', was perhaps a moderate. The candidate members were Stalin's right-hand man, Zhdanov, who took over Kirov's post in Leningrad; and another possible 'moderate', and future victim of Stalin's vengeance, Eikhe.[1]

Nevertheless, a number of moves soon showed that Stalin was still steadily increasing his own ascendancy over the party. Ezhov, who had been appointed a secretary of the Central Committee in succession to Kirov on 1 February 1935, was shortly afterwards also made head of the Control Commission of the party in place of Kaganovich, whose talents were called on to restore discipline in the People's Commissariat of Transport.[2] The appointment of Khrushchev as First Secretary of the Moscow party organization, prominently featured in *Pravda* on 9 March, completed the placing of Stalin's henchmen in key positions. The two main party organizations, Leningrad and Moscow, were now in reliable hands. Ezhov was not only installed in the Secretariat, but was also in control of the main organ responsible for discipline and orthodoxy in the party. Lower down the hierarchy, a rising young man, G. M. Malenkov, who had for some time been employed in the Secretariat, and was now assistant director of the, as yet unpublicized, Cadres Department of the Secretariat, became Ezhov's right-hand man in the business of purging the party.[3] Poskrebyshev still controlled the personal secretariat, and possibly also the Special or Secret Department of the Secretariat concerned with the security forces.[4] Vyshinsky, another trusted henchman, was the key man in the procuracy, of which he soon became the head.

But although the machine for launching the terror was thus complete in 1935, Stalin moved with considerable caution. Screening and purging of party members went on throughout the year. A great

[1] *Pravda*, 2 February 1935.
[2] *Pravda*, 1 March 1935.
[3] The *Directorate* of Cadres was only officially set up in 1939. But a Department of Cadres seems to have already been in existence at this date, since two Central Committee circulars in the Smolensk party records refer to Malenkov as assistant director of the Cadres Department of the Central Committee. They are signed by Ezhov as Secretary of the Party, and dated 8 July and 10 August 1935.
[4] A Secret Section of the Secretariat was set up in 1930 (though it may have already existed before – see page 319 above), and a Special Section, presumably its successor, was created in 1934. The relationship between this section which dealt with the police, and Stalin's personal secretariat is obscure, and the two may in fact have become identified.

many members were expelled, and many arrested. Nevertheless, the assault on the party during this year was moderate compared with what was to come.[1] At the end of 1935 a Plenum of the Central Committee declared the general mass purge at an end and decreed that those sections of the party which had not yet been subjected to it should be exempt.[2] But in the middle of 1935 there had been two portents of things to come. On 25 May the Society of Old Bolsheviks was wound up, and a month later the Society of Former Political Prisoners and Exiles was also disbanded. These associations of revolutionary veterans were in each case stated to have been dissolved at their own request, and the commissions set up to take over their assets and records included in the one case Malenkov and Shkiriatove, and in the second Ezhov.[3] The principal inquisitors of the party were thus put in possession of all materials relating to the generation of old bolsheviks against whom Stalin's main blow would fall in 1936 and after. It was about this time too that a drastic reorganization of the *Komsomol* was carried out on Stalin's personal initiative with the aim of eliminating 'enemies of the party'.[4]

An incident in the course of this year illustrated the way in which Stalin was prepared to use his extraordinary powers to eliminate opponents and gratify his own vanity. It also showed that his colleagues in the Politburo or Central Committee were either prepared to support him in such an action or at any rate unable to restrain him. On 7 June 1935 the Plenum resolved, on the basis of a report by Ezhov, to exclude A. Enukidze, one of the old Georgian bolsheviks, from the Central Committee and from the party. The Central Committee gave no reason for this quite sudden action (Enukidze had been Secretary of the Central Executive Committee of the Congress of Soviets since 1918 and wielded considerable administrative power), beyond the allegation that he was 'politically degenerate'. Zhdanov and Khrushchev, who were charged with explaining this action to Leningrad and Moscow party members respectively, alleged that Enukidze had been guilty of 'liberalism' in employing nobles, former princesses and 'Trotskyists'.[5] But an equally possible explanation is that Stalin had taken the opportunity to revenge himself on Enukidze for the latter's memoirs of the early days of party activity in the Caucasus which did not portray Stalin in a sufficiently prominent role.

[1] For figures see chapter 24.
[2] *KPSS v rez.*, volume III, p. 288.
[3] *Pravda*, 26, May and 26 June 1935.
[4] *Pravda*, 28 June 1935.
[5] *Pravda*, 8, 13, 16 and 19 June 1935.

At any rate, it was very soon after Enukidze's downfall that a new supporter of Stalin, L. P. Beria, an NKVD official then in office as First Secretary of the Georgian party organization, sprang into prominence by publishing a revised version of the hitherto accepted history of the bolshevik party in Transcaucasia. Stalin now appeared in a much more important role than before. Enukidze and another Georgian, Orakhelashvili, were blamed for distorting the true facts.[1] (Enukidze and Orakhelashvili were shot after a secret trial on 16 December 1937.[2]).

In spite of these incidents, the hope persisted that a period of comparative peace was in sight for the party. The reaction to the murder of Kirov seemed to be coming to an end. Material conditions in the country were slowly improving, and food supplies by the autumn of 1935 were sufficiently adequate to permit the abolition of such rationing as still remained in force. Output of the main materials required for the building up of the means of production was beginning to show a steady rise, as compared with 1932 and 1933.[3] Throughout the country, in the new industries which were fast springing up, all ranks of the party were throwing themselves with enthusiasm into a new campaign – the 'Stakhanovite' campaign – designed to urge the workers to yet greater effort in building the new socialist order. If there was still fear, there was also some hope.

One factor which led the more sanguine to hope that the worst was over was the decision to adopt a new constitution. The preparations for the new constitution and discussion of the proposed draft occupied most of the two years 1935 and 1936. The question of revising the constitution was, so far as was made public, first discussed at the Central Committee Plenum in February 1935, when Molotov was instructed to suggest to the Seventh All-Union Congress of Soviets certain changes in the constitution. These were to be directed towards 'further democratization of the electoral system' and towards making the constitution correspond to the new class relations which had been

---

[1] *Pravda*, 29 July 1935 and following issues. Beria's history was subsequently printed in book form, and went through many editions. The reference to Enukidze and Orakhelashvili is in L. Beria, *K voprosu ob istorii bol'shevistskikh organizatsii v Zakavkaze*, Ninth edition, Moscow, 1952, p. 7. And see Bertram D. Wolfe, *Three Who Made a Revolution*, Chapter xxiii.

[2] *Pravda*, 20 December 1937. But according to more recent reference books, Orakhelashvili 'died' in 1940 – see, e.g. volume LI of the *Bol'shaia sovetskaia entsiklopediia*, p. 218.

[3] e.g. pig iron: 12·5 million tons in 1935, 6·2 in 1932; steel 12·6 million tons in 1935, 5·9 in 1932; coal: 109·6 million tons in 1935, 64·4 in 1932; cement: 3,478,000 tons in 1932, 4,488,000 in 1935. *Narodnoe khoziaistvo SSSR, statisticheskii sbornik*, Moscow, 1956, pp. 62, 63, 67, 79.

brought about by the defeat of the *kulaks* and by the establishment of socialist ownership of industry and collective farming as the basis of Soviet society.[1] The Congress set up a Constitutional Commission, with Stalin as chairman, but including Bukharin and Radek among its members – as if to symbolize the reconciliation of all political antagonists in the work of preparing the new constitutional order.[2] By June 1936 the draft was ready for the approval of the Central Committee. In addition to the changes proposed in February 1935, it also contained a new chapter setting forth the rights and duties of citizens. A nation-wide discussion of the draft took place on a very extensive scale, under the direction and guidance of the party. This discussion (which had little effect on the final form of the draft) served to invest the new constitution with the appearance of popular mass support, and thus to set the seal of legitimacy upon the social order which it symbolized. On 5 December 1936 the new constitution was unanimously approved by the Extraordinary Eighth All-Union Congress of Soviets. The voting of the constitution was made the occasion for the personal triumph of Stalin, who presented the main report. In the words of *Pravda*, he was the 'genius of the new world, the wisest man of the epoch, the great leader of communism'.[3]

The formulations contained in the new constitution raised certain questions of doctrine, such as the nature of the state and of law in a society in which it was claimed that socialism had been achieved and class antagonism abolished. These questions will be considered in a later chapter. The decision to alter the electoral system from indirect to direct election, from a limited to a universal franchise, and from open to secret voting, was a measure of the confidence of the party in its ability to ensure the return of candidates of its own choice without the restrictions formerly considered necessary. The guarantees of civil freedoms which the constitution offered raised some interesting problems in a state in which the monopoly of political power had long been the preserve of the communist party, itself above the law. The relevant articles of the constitution were drafted with this well in mind. Thus Article 125, which guaranteed freedom of speech, freedom of the press, freedom of assembly and freedom of street demonstrations, was prefaced by the qualification that these freedoms were accorded in order that they might be exercised 'in conformity with the interests of

---

[1] *KPSS v rez.*, volume III, p. 266.
[2] *Pravda*, 8 February 1935. Bukharin was in fact Secretary of the Commission, and mainly responsible for the draft of the constitution. I am indebted for this information to the late Mr B. I. Nicolaevsky.
[3] *Pravda*, 25 November 1936.

the working people and in order to strengthen the socialist system'. Official comment, when the draft was first published for discussion,[1] stressed that these rights were accorded only to those who submitted to party leadership, and not to those who wished to criticize it. The guarantee of freedom from arrest, except with the sanction of the court or of a procurator, was likewise of little practical value where both the judges and the procurators were usually party members, and always under party control.

The new constitution differed strikingly from the old in that it recognized the existence of the party. Article 141 mentioned the party as one of the organizations which had the right to nominate candidates for election to public offices. Article 126 recognized that 'the most active and most politically conscious citizens in the ranks of the working class and other sections of the working people unite in the Communist Party of the Soviet Union (Bolsheviks), which is the vanguard of the working people in their struggle to strengthen and develop the socialist system and is the leading core of all organizations of the working people, both public and state'.

Thus, a careful scrutiny of the draft of the new constitution showed that it left the party's supreme position unimpaired, and was therefore worthless as a guarantee of individual rights. Indeed, it may be doubted how far it was possible to provide for any system of established legal rights so long as the party was intent on preserving its own unchallengeable position against the rest of the population. As in 1921, by denying rights to others, the party member at the same time unavoidably placed himself at the mercy of arbitrary rule. But those reared in the communist system are seldom skilled in constitutional analysis, and there is no doubt that the mere fact that the new constitution with its paper guarantees was imminent raised the hopes of many party members that the era of lawlessness was at an end. Moreover, one of the main objects of the constitution was to persuade the world outside the USSR of the democratic nature of the Soviet system. At this time the Soviet Union was seeking to win over socialist and liberal opinion in the Western world; it was urging collective security and trying to organize an alliance against Hitler. Stalin's speech to the Eighth Soviet Congress showed that he was fully alive to this aspect of the new constitution. It was, he said, 'the only thoroughly democratic constitution in the world'. Its international significance could 'hardly be exaggerated' when the 'turbid wave of

---

[1] See e.g. *Pravda* of 22 June 1936: 'We shall not give a scrap of paper nor an inch of room for those who think differently (from the party) . . .'

fascism . . . is besmirching the democratic strivings of the best people in the civilized world'.[1] The reactions of even enlightened opinion outside the USSR to the new Soviet constitution showed that Stalin had not overestimated the credulity, ignorance or willingness to be persuaded of his foreign audience.

Whatever hopes the prospect of a new constitution and other signs of moderation might have raised in the course of 1935, the year 1936 opened ominously. In spite of the decision that the purge was at an end, a new purge was launched on 14 January 1936, in the guise of a Central Committee order that all party documents were to be exchanged for new ones. The object of this exchange of documents was stated to be the elimination of 'passive people, who do not justify the lofty title of party member'. This operation, by which many were expelled, went on until May. No sooner was the exchange completed, than the Central Committee dispatched on 29 July 1936 a Top Secret letter to all party committees down to the lowest territorial level entitled 'On the Terrorist Activity of the Trotskyite, Zinovievite Counter-revolutionary Bloc'. It was a demand for 'vigilance' in exposing hidden enemies and for a renewed screening of party members. It was followed by a wave of denunciations, expulsions and arrests.[2]

On 19 August 1936, while the discussion of the constitution was still in full swing, sixteen leading ex-oppositionists, headed by Zinoviev, Kamenev, Evdokimov and I. N. Smirnov, were arraigned for public trial on capital charges. They were accused of organizing a 'terrorist centre', under the direct instructions and guidance of Trotsky from his exile. This centre, it was alleged, had been in existence since 1932, and had as its object the organization of terrorist acts against Stalin and other leaders – including Voroshilov, Kaganovich and Zhdanov, but curiously enough excluding Molotov. (The exclusion of Molotov suggests that Molotov was at that time out of favour, but this has not been confirmed by any other evidence.) The assassination of Kirov was now squarely laid at the door of this 'terrorist centre'. The evidence adduced consisted solely of the preliminary examinations and admissions of the accused, all of whom, except I. N. Smirnov, publicly admitted their guilt in court. All were sentenced to death, and were immediately shot.

The arraignment and execution of prominent old party leaders as terrorists came as a bombshell to the great majority of party members.

[1] J. Stalin, *Problems of Leninism*, Moscow, 1947, p. 567.
[2] Merle Fainsod, *Smolensk under Soviet Rule*, 1958, pp. 232–7.

Moreover, the nature of the evidence left no doubt whatever that this was to be only the first of many trials, and that Stalin was preparing nothing less than a complete elimination of all former oppositionists, both of the left and of the right. Bukharin, Tomskii and Rykov were implicated in the course of the trial, while Kamenev's testimony involved Sokol'nikov, Radek and Preobrazhenskii in the conspiracy. Another of the accused implicated Putna, then Military Attaché in London.[1] In the course of the trial Vyshinsky, who conducted the prosecution, issued an announcement that he had given orders to institute an investigation against Rykov, Bukharin and Tomskii in view of the evidence disclosed at the trial.[2] This was immediately followed by a series of resolutions demanding their blood, ostensibly passed by workers' organizations.

There is some evidence that the plan for the wholesale extermination of all oppositionists – for that is what it was – met with some unexpected if belated resistance. On 10 September 1936 an announcement was published in the press to the effect that the investigations into the charges made against Bukharin and Rykov had disclosed no 'legal basis' for any accusation against them, and that the investigation had been terminated.[3] The suicide of Tomskii, shortly after the investigation had been ordered by Vyshinsky, may have had the effect of reminding some party members of their responsibilities to old revolutionary comrades. A number of accounts suggest that Ordzhonikidze was one of the principal opponents of this new form of political struggle, and that in particular he fought to save his deputy in the Commissariat of Heavy Industry, Piatakov. There is some evidence to support these rumours. Ordzhonikidze was to die suddenly, allegedly of heart failure, on 18 February 1937. But according to what N. S. Khrushchev told the Twentieth Party Congress years later he was 'forced to shoot himself'.[4] Moreover, although on 23 January 1937 Piatakov was charged jointly with Sokol'nikov, Radek and Preobrazhenskii, it was significant that his name had not been mentioned along with those of the other three in the first trial. Piatakov had also been allowed to publish a letter in the press applauding in the customary manner the trial and condemnation of Zinoviev, Kamenev and the rest – a certain sign that at the time, at any rate, he was still officially not in disfavour.

[1] People's Commissariat of Justice of the USSR, *The Case of the Trotskyite-Zinovievite Terrorist Centre*, etc. Moscow, 1936, pp. 58, 67–8, 116.
[2] *Pravda*, 21 August 1936.
[3] *Pravda*, 10 September 1936.
[4] *The Anti-Stalin Campaign*, p. 69.

There may also well have been opposition to Vyshinsky's plans from the legal profession. At any rate, the Deputy Commissar for Justice, and the leading legal theorist, E. Pashukanis, was about this time, January 1937, severely criticized, and later presumably shot.[1] There were doctrinal reasons for the attacks on Pashukanis, to be sure, which will be considered in a later chapter.[2] But Pashukanis, of the many lawyers who were criticized was one of the very few to be additionally branded as a 'wrecker' and 'enemy of the people', which suggests that more than differences on legal doctrine lay behind his fall. Indeed, there can be no doubt that one reason which sealed Pashukanis's fate at a time when Stalin was intent on his policy of unrestrained terror, was the fact that he was the author of a draft of a new criminal code for the USSR, as provided for in Article 14 of the draft of the new Constitution. The new draft criminal code apparently, among other provisions, excluded the death penalty. Although unpublished, Pashukanis's draft was stated to have had considerable influence inside the Institute of Soviet Constitution and Law of the Communist Academy, of which he was director.[3] The succession of Vyshinsky to this post, after the fall of Pashukanis, soon put an end to these 'liberal' trends, and the criminal code was to remain unrevised for twenty-two years.

While the trial of Zinoviev and Kamenev was in progress in the summer of 1936 Stalin was on holiday at Sochi, on the Black Sea, in company with Zhdanov. Evidently he thought that the unleashing of the mass terror could be safely left in the hands of Ezhov and Vyshinsky. It is possible that the exoneration of Bukharin and Rykov indicated to Stalin that something had gone wrong with the master plan. At any rate, on 25 September 1936 the two leaders addressed a telegram to 'Kaganovich, Molotov and other members of the Politburo' to the effect that it was 'absolutely necessary and urgent that Comrade Ezhov be nominated to the post of People's Commissar for Internal Affairs. Yagoda has definitely proved himself incapable of unmasking the Trotskyite-Zinovievite bloc. The OGPU is four years behind in this matter'.[4] The Politburo seems to have been ready to comply, or

---

[1] For the first attack, mainly on doctrinal grounds, see an article by Iudin in *Pravda* of 20 January 1937. For a further attack by Vyshinsky, which refers to Pashukanis's 'wrecking' activities, links him with Bukharin, and speaks of him as 'the double dealer who has now been exposed' see *ibidem*, 9 April 1937.

[2] See pp. 471–5, below.

[3] This appears from the report of a meeting subsequently held in the Legal Section of the Academy. See *Sotsialisticheskaia zakonnost'* (Moscow), Nos. 10–11, 1937, pp. 10–17.

[4] *The Anti-Stalin Campaign*, p. 26.

to have overruled any who objected, because on the following day the appointment of Ezhov was approved. Yagoda became People's Commissar of Posts and Telegraph – a post hitherto occupied by Rykov and apparently reserved for those whose next destination was prison.[1] The fall of Yagoda was followed by wholesale changes in the upper ranks of the security service. The old Chekists, who had spent their lives in the machine of terror, no doubt, as they persuaded themselves, in the service of 'the revolution', were replaced for the most part by newcomers who, like Ezhov himself, had mainly served in the apparatus of the party. Thus, of the six top security officers immediately below Yagoda in rank, only one is known to have survived the change of chiefs. It is notable that this one alone, Zakovskii, had seen no service in the civil war. Possibly he was believed to be less likely to show loyalty to the veteran bolsheviks who were not to be immolated.[2]

The second show trial took place in the last week of January 1937. Piatakov, Radek, Sokol'nikov and Serebriakov now headed a group of seventeen defendants. The second trial was organized with greater psychological subtlety than the first. Once again Trotsky was portrayed as the real master mind behind the scene. But the first trial, by limiting the charges to a plot against the party leaders, had restricted its popular appeal to the somewhat questionable extent of the popularity which these leaders could be supposed to enjoy. The second trial sought to arouse the more certain emotion of patriotism. For the charges were now expanded to include a plot to dismember the USSR at the behest of and for the benefit of Japan and Germany. The importance of the inclusion of Piatakov among the defendants became evident from the use that was made of it. His position in the Commissariat of Heavy Industry was exploited to make more plausible the charges of sabotage and wrecking. Thus not only was a convenient explanation provided for shortcomings or disasters which could well have been due to inefficiency in planning or direction, but an additional degree of odium was attached to the defendants by blaming them for past disasters which were known to have caused loss of life and limb.

Like the first, the second trial foreshadowed further trials to come. Bukharin and Rykov, as well as the dead Tomskii, were once again fully implicated by the evidence, in spite of the fact that the first two

[1] *Pravda*, 27 September 1936.
[2] For the biographical details of Yagoda's six deputies see *Pravda* of 27 November 1935. Zakovskii was referred to by N. S. Khrushchev as active in the NKVD under Ezhov – see *The Anti-Stalin Campaign*, pp. 35–6.

had been officially exonerated after an investigation. Radek, who gave his evidence with the zest of an artist playing an imaginative part, also implicated Putna, and went out of his way to bring in the name of the Commander in Chief, Tukhachevskii – a clear indication of what lay in store. This time there were no unseemly denials of guilt. All the defendants confessed, and all but four were sentenced to death. Among those whose lives were spared were Radek and Sokol'nikov. Radek had plainly earned his remission by the readiness with which he was prepared to give evidence of any fact required of him by Vyshinsky, who was again in charge of the prosecution. Sokol'nikov may possibly have owed his life to the fact that he had been ambassador in London. He had made friends in British left-wing circles, notably with Sydney and Beatrice Webb, whose book on the USSR had done much to portray the Soviet Union as an essentially free and democratic country. An act of apparent clemency towards him might have been calculated to make the trial more acceptable to foreign opinion. Both died in camp in 1939.[1]

Sometime at the end of 1936 or the beginning of 1937 a number of party leaders apparently made a belated, and desperate, stand, in an attempt to stop the holocaust of arrests and executions which had been launched against the party. The opponents of Stalin's plans were now in a hopeless position. They had supported, or at any rate failed effectively to oppose, the successive steps by which he had built up his ascendancy over the party – the advancement of Ezhov and Vyshinsky, the first trial of Zinoviev and Kamenev in 1935, the purge of 1936, the trial of August 1936 and the ousting of Yagoda. Ezhov's purge of the NKVD had provided Stalin with an obedient instrument of terror which he could use against any party member, however powerful, if need be behind the back of the normal party organs. The sudden and mysterious deaths of Kuibyshev and Ordzhonikidze were warnings to those in the know of what could happen even to the mightiest who ventured to oppose Stalin. Although the evidence is far from clear, it seems probable that some attempt was made by the Central Committee members to put a stop to the terror in the party before it was too late. Credit is due to them for an act of courage and honesty. But for the predicament in which they found themselves their own conduct over the years was to blame.

Matters came to a head over the question of the fate of Bukharin and Rykov. The two leaders of the former right opposition were

[1] This appears from several Soviet sources, e.g., *Lenin* (5th edition), volume XLV, pp. 648, 652.

probably arrested in January or February 1937.[1] At a Plenum of the Central Committee held between 23 February and 5 March 1937 the 'question of the anti-party activity of Bukharin and Rykov was examined and it was decided to exclude them from the ranks of the party' – so far the official announcement, published at the time.[2] Shortly afterwards Stalin's supporters, the Secretaries of the Moscow and Leningrad organizations, Khrushchev and Zhdanov, were entrusted with explaining this new development to party members. Both delivered attacks on the two fallen leaders. From Khrushchev's speech it is plain that Bukharin and Rykov attended the meeting of the February–March Plenum – possibly they were brought there from prison. But, added Khrushchev, 'they came to the Plenum to deceive . . . they did not tread the path of repentance'. He concluded that the party was now entitled to deal with them 'as is required by the interests of the revolution', since they were 'enemies of the party and of the working class'. Zhdanov in his speech openly identified them with Trotsky.[3]

Some evidence that the members of the full Central Committee at last attempted to oppose either this renewed persecution of Bukharin and Rykov or the further extension of the terror which had been launched against party members is to be found in the fact that the majority of its members were arrested and shot, for the most part in the course of 1937 and 1938. According to the statement made by Khrushchev at the Twentieth Party Congress, of the total of 139 members and candidates elected at the Seventeenth Congress in 1934, 98, or 70 per cent, were thus eliminated.[4]

Khrushchev's account to the Twentieth Congress was naturally somewhat guarded, because while repudiating some of Stalin's policy of terror during the period 1936–8, Khrushchev was embarrassed by the fact that he himself, and a number of his colleagues who were present, had survived the holocaust, and could therefore be presumed to have supported Stalin in the Central Committee at the time. According to Khrushchev, it was at the February-March 1937 Plenum that 'many members actually questioned the rightness of the established course regarding mass repressions under the pretext of combating "two-facedness".' The doubts were most ably expressed, according to

---

[1] At his trial in March 1938 Bukharin said that he had been under arrest for over a year, and his name appeared on the masthead of *Izvestiia* as editor until 16 January 1937.

[2] *Pravda*, 6 March 1937.

[3] *Pravda*, 17 March and 21 March 1937.

[4] *The Anti-Stalin Campaign*, pp. 22–3.

Khrushchev, by Postyshev, the Secretary of the Ukrainian party organization. He quoted some of Postyshev's words, presumably from the unpublished transcript of the meeting. 'I personally do not believe that in 1934 an honest party member who had trod the long road of unrelenting fight against enemies, for the party and for socialism, would now be in the camp of the enemies. I do not believe it . . . I cannot imagine how it would be possible to travel with the party during the difficult years and then, in 1934, join the Trotskyites. It is an odd thing. . . .' It was either on this, or on another occasion, that Stalin, possibly genuinely surprised that Postyshev, who like so many members of the Central Committee had hitherto supported him in his policy, should now turn against him, rounded on him: 'What are you, actually?' – 'I am a Bolshevik, Comrade Stalin, a Bolshevik', replied Postyshev.

Khrushchev only mentioned by name a few of the many who according to him paid with their lives for attempting to thwart Stalin in the Central Committee – Postyshev, Rudzutak, Eikhe, Chubar', Kossior, Kosarev. But he made it plain that after study of the materials relating to charges made against members of the Central Committee, the evidence showed that the cases against them had been fabricated, and that where confessions had been obtained, they were obtained by torture: indeed, 'lengthy and documented materials pertaining to mass repressions against the delegates to the Seventeenth Party Congress and against members of the Central Committee elected at that Congress' had shown that 'many' party, Soviet and economic officials who were branded as enemies, spies or wreckers in 1937–8 had been falsely charged. They had only confessed to 'all kinds of grave and unlikely crimes' when 'no longer able to bear barbaric tortures'. Khrushchev also revealed what happened to those who did not confess to the charges fabricated against them: they were shot after secret trials, and their protests addressed to Stalin or the Court were suppressed. Khrushchev quoted two such protests – from Eikhe and from Rudzutak. Both had confessed under torture, both retracted their confessions at the trial, which was held in secret. Eikhe's plea to Stalin ended with the words: 'I will die believing in the truth of party policy as I have believed in it during my whole life.' Rudzutak's only request was that the Central Committee be informed that there existed within the NKVD 'an as yet unliquidated centre which . . . forces people to confess'.[1] The loyalty of these men and of many like them to the idea of 'the party', which recalled that of Trotsky and Piatakov,

[1] *ibidem*, pp. 22, 29, 34–5, 82.

and which could even survive the inhumanities to which they had been subjected by its leaders, was in the last resort the main reason for Stalin's victory.

Thus, some tentative, if belated, opposition of nearly three-quarters of the Central Committee members and candidates to Stalin's policy of mass repression is, at any rate, not excluded.[1] There was an oblique reference, perhaps, to this opposition in Stalin's speech to the February–March Plenum which was published in *Pravda* on 29 March 1937. He criticized the party for its lack of vigilance in dealing with spies and saboteurs, in spite of repeated warnings, and spoke of the two secret instructions by the Central Committee, on the subject of vigilance, dated 18 January 1935 and 29 July 1936 (to which reference was made above). Stalin offered some excuse for the delay in dealing with all the spies and wreckers with whom the party was riddled. It had been necessary first to educate tens of thousands of technicians before the technical backwardness of the country could be overcome. Now the danger was no longer lack of technicians, but 'political lightheartedness'. As if to emphasize the point that an apparently good technician was not necessarily immune from suspicion, he attacked the 'rotten theory' that a man who did good work was necessarily loyal. On the contrary, the real wrecker must show success at his work from time to time in order to divert suspicion. The 'chatter' which was going around that measures taken against wreckers would weaken the fulfilment of the plan, said Stalin, must be stopped.

Stalin also showed some practical concern for the dislocation of the party apparatus which his mass repressions were bound to bring about. He outlined a new scheme of intensive courses for party officials, of which the main emphasis was on the training up of replacements. Second and third secretaries were to be rapidly trained, so that they could take their immediate superiors' places. Zhdanov, whose speech at this Plenum was published a little later, laid particular stress on the need for much greater democracy in the party. A number of speakers at the Plenum, all of whom were among the victims of the blow which fell soon after upon the Central Committee, were criticized by him for their failure to appreciate the finer points of party democracy.[2] A Central Committee Instruction, published in *Pravda*

---

[1] There is perhaps some doubt about the date when it was first voiced. An account by a former highly placed party member, published in 1951, places the revolt of the Central Committee in the autumn of 1936. See A. Ouralov, *Staline au Pouvoir*, Paris, 1951, pp. 34–41.

[2] Such speeches at this Plenum as were published were reprinted in *O perestroike partiino-politicheskoi raboty. K itogam plenuma Ts.K.VKP(b) 1937 g.*, Moscow, 1937.

on 21 March 1937, called for free and open nomination and discussion of candidates for party offices, election by secret vote and other democratic safeguards. There was little danger, in the conditions of universal fear which by now prevailed in the party, that any election could take place which was not in accordance with the directives of the higher party instance. But this time-honoured exercise in hypocrisy was presumably designed to persuade the rank and file of the party that the mass repressions now in progress were solely designed to remove the more dictatorial among the party secretaries. If this was the object – and it will be recalled that similar tactics were adopted before Tomskii was removed from the trade union party hierarchy – it is, to say the least, improbable that many were convinced.

The mass attack on the party, in which tens if not hundreds of thousands of party members were arrested, began towards the end of 1936 and lasted until the end of 1938. Stalin's concern for the effects of his policy on the party apparatus were understandable enough, if one looks at the ravages in the upper ranks alone of the party. The Central Committee elected in 1934 consisted of 71 full members and 68 candidate members. Of these 139, ten at least were by the spring of 1937 already dead or in prison. According to Khrushchev, 98 were arrested and shot, 'mostly' in 1937–8. (Khrushchev may have been exaggerating when he said that all were shot, since at least one of those arrested, G. I. Petrovskii, reappeared after Stalin's death.) But it would seem that at the very least 90 top party leaders were eliminated in one way or another after the February–March Plenum of 1937. Between them they represented a considerable concentration of power within the party apparatus, in the national economy, in the government apparatus and in the army. They included, for example, the two leading secretaries of the Ukrainian Central Committee, the Chairman of the Council of People's Commissars of the Ukraine and the Chairman of the Executive Committee of the Ukrainian Soviet Congress (S. V. Kossior, P. P. Postyshev, V. Ia Chubar' and G. I. Petrovskii); a number of leading regional (*oblast'*) secretaries, on whom Stalin had hitherto principally relied for putting through his policy (such as M. M. Khataevich of Dnepropetrovsk or B. P. Sheboldaev of the North Caucasus); several People's Commissars in the USSR and RSFSR; the Secretary of the *Komsomol*, A. V. Kosarev; and a number of prominent military figures. These were, among the full members of the Central Committee, Gamarnik, the head of the Political Directorate of the army and Iakir, Commander of the Ukrainian Military District; and among the candidate members,

Marshal Bluecher, Commander-in-Chief in the Far East, Marshal Tukhachevskii, the Commander-in-Chief Land Forces, two other leading commanders, Egorov and Uborevich, and Gamarnik's deputy, Bulin. Stalin's two close friends and comrades who survived all the purges, Voroshilov and Budennyi, the former a full member and the latter a candidate member of the Central Committee, presumably supported Stalin.

The effects of the terror upon the composition of the party are dealt with in a later chapter. But some idea of the disorganization caused by arrests and executions during 1937 and 1938, and of the consequent turnover, can be derived from two figures alone. The first, which was revealed to the party in 1956 at the Twentieth Congress by Khrushchev, shows the extent to which delegates to the Seventeenth Party Congress, who represented the party and soviet hierarchy of officials, were affected. Of a total of 1,961 voting and non-voting delegates, no less than 1,108, or more than half, were arrested on charges of counter-revolutionary crimes.[1] The other figure was given by Stalin to the Eighteenth Party Congress in 1939. Over 500,000 party members, according to Stalin, were promoted to leading party and state positions between 1934 and 1939.[2] Not all of these necessarily stepped into dead men's shoes, since some of the promotions were no doubt due to the expansion of the administrative and party machine as the result of industrial development. Moreover, the period referred to by Stalin includes 1935 and 1936 as well as 1937 and 1938, and repressions against and expulsions of party members were already taking place on quite a substantial scale in the first two years of this four-year period. The total of those eliminated in the first two years was, however, moderate when compared to the more hazardous years 1937 and 1938. According to Khrushchev, for example, 'the number of arrests based on counter-revolutionary crimes grew ten times between 1936 and 1937',[3] though apparently in this instance Khrushchev was referring to non-members of the party as well as to party members. All in all, the turnover of party and Soviet officials during the main years of Stalin's campaign against the party, 1937 and 1938, can probably be reckoned in hundreds of thousands.

[1] *The Anti-Stalin Campaign*, p. 23.
[2] *XVIII S"ezd*, p. 30.
[3] *The Anti-Stalin Campaign*, p. 30.

XXIII   The Climax of the Purge

In the last resort, the survival of the communists in power during the
critical years of Stalin's 'third revolution' would have been impossible
without the support of the armed forces. Indeed, the régime's retention during the period of collectivization of the allegiance of the army,
in spite of its large peasant component, must be credited as one of
Stalin's major achievements. The strength of the party inside the Red
Army grew markedly during the period of the Five Year Plan, and by
the end of it all senior commanders and 93 per cent of divisional
commanders were party members. There is no evidence to suggest
that opposition among the army communists ever became a serious
problem to the authorities during this period. The figures alone
illustrate this assertion. For example, in 1929 only 3·5 per cent of the
military communists were purged as compared with 11·7 per cent for
the party as a whole. In 1933 expulsions from the army communist
organizations were only 4·3 per cent, while the civilian organizations
during the same year were purged to the extent of 17 per cent.
Shkiriatov, of the Central Control Commission, even went out of his
way to praise the exemplary orthodoxy of the army communists. Of
course, these figures may be misleading, in the sense that Stalin may
have decided not to tamper with army morale by successive small
purges, but to reserve his main blow for a later date. All that can be
said is that if any serious convulsions were shaking the political temper of the army between 1929 and 1934 no reliable information about
them has so far been revealed.

But if the army thus remained loyal to Stalin after 1929, it was also
one of the main beneficiaries from his policies. Among the material
benefits were important concessions to soldier collective farmers and
their families. Of greater interest to the officer were the concessions on
housing facilities and on supplies of consumer goods, together with
substantial pay increases. Equally if not more important was the
increase in prestige. The reintroduction of ranks in September 1935
swelled the pride of the serving officers; it also led to a vast influx of
students to the military schools. At the same time a rapid expansion of

the army was taking place after 1934. Before long a large officer corps of young, newly trained, mainly proletarian officers had arisen in the army. By May 1937 it was calculated that three-quarters of all officers were such young Red commanders, who owed their position and new prestige entirely to Stalin and his policy. The remainder were veteran officers of civil war experience, and all mainly occupying the higher commands. It is easy to imagine the pressure for promotion which this situation created.

Apart from pressure from below there was also friction at the top. This was due to the system of political control, which remained in essence the same compromise system as that evolved during 1925 which has already been described.[1] From 1929 to 1937 the Political Directorate of the army was headed by Jan Gamarnik. Gamarnik had every quality likely to render him unfit for the generation of communists which Stalin was seeking to elevate – Jewish origin, intelligence, internationalism, honesty, and sincere belief in the communist mission. The humdrum junior political instructors whom his machine turned out in large numbers rubbed along well enough with the Red commanders at the lower levels. But at the higher levels, where the civil war veterans were mostly in command, the senior and more intellectual political officers consorted ill with the often uneducated, if militarily distinguished, civil war veterans. These two factors – pressure for promotion and friction at the higher levels between military and political officers – created sufficient dissensions inside the army for Stalin to exploit when he decided that the time had come to strike at the army command.

By early 1937 signs were multiplying that the next victim of the purge would be the army. In January 1937 two army leaders were mentioned at the trial of Piatakov and Radek. At the February-March Plenum of the Central Committee Stalin had dropped a very strong hint when he spoke of the harm which a few spies on the staff of the army could do. By April the Commander-in-Chief, Tukhachevskii, was being openly cold shouldered, and on 10 May the system of political commissars was reintroduced. On 11 June 1937 the press announced that a group of military leaders had been arrested and would be tried the same day in secret. The officers named were

---

[1] See above, pp. 330–1. Except where otherwise indicated, the facts on the Red Army in the preceding and following paragraphs are taken from D. Fedotoff-White, *The Growth of the Red Army*, Princeton, 1944, which gives an excellent account of the subject; the fullest treatment of the army purge of 1937–8 is in John Erickson, *The Soviet High Command: A Military-Political History 1918–1941*, London, 1962, Chapters xiii–xv.

Tukhachevskii, Iakir and Uborevich, commanders of military districts, Primakov, deputy commander of a military district, Kork, head of the War College, Feldman, Eideman and Putna, the former military attaché in London. Gamarnik was stated to have committed suicide on 31 May when faced with arrest. No specific charges were ever formulated against these officers – indeed there is no evidence, other than the press announcement, that any trial was ever held – but a spate of accusations followed, in the usual manner, in the press. (These were further added to in March 1938 at the trial of Bukharin.) These accusations included espionage on behalf of Germany and Japan; engaging in a conspiracy to carry out a *coup d'état* in favour of the leaders of the right-wing and Trotskyist oppositions; and plotting the dismemberment of the USSR in favour of Japan and Germany, in return for the military support of these states.

Waves of arrests now followed and continued throughout 1937 and 1938. The arrests in the army, which fell with equal severity on both military and political officers, affected the higher command much more heavily in proportion. The great majority of the civil war veterans were removed, though there were exceptions – Konev was one. The total number of victims, according to Japanese intelligence estimates, was: 35,000 in all, or about half the total officer corps; three out of five marshals; 13 out of 15 army commanders; 57 out of 85 corps commanders; 110 out of 195 division commanders; 220 out of 406 brigade commanders; all eleven Vice Commissars of War; 75 out of 80 members of the Supreme Military Council, including all the military district commanders. The air force, navy and all but one of the fleet commanders were eventually eliminated. In percentages of ranks: 90 per cent of generals and 80 per cent of colonels. Purged officers below the rank of colonel were estimated at 30,000.[1]

Arrests were continuous throughout 1937 and 1938. So far, however, as the higher command was concerned, the purge appears to have taken place in two waves. Thus a number of important commanders survived until after mid-1938. Of the 14 commanders of military districts on 11 June 1937 six had gone by January 1938; but between January 1938 and the middle of the year eight more changes were made. The most likely explanation of this method was that the delay was needed in order to complete the training and preparation of the new officers of the future. This is to some extent borne out by the

[1] See Raymond L. Garthoff, *How Russia Makes War*. Soviet Military Doctrine. London, 1954, pp. 220–1.

fact that certain officers who were later to win renown emerged only in the later phase of the purge. Extensive military manœuvres were held in all military districts in the autumn of 1937 which Voroshilov attended. They may have been designed to enable the younger men to show their paces.

The most significant move had been the reintroduction, on the eve of the purge, of the dual command political commissar system – with the commissar counter-signing all military orders instead of acting as political deputy – which had been progressively scrapped since 1925. Its revival was probably regarded as an emergency measure, even though Voroshilov, at the Eighteenth Party Congress in 1939, laid great emphasis on the commissar's military importance and foretold how the commander and commissar would both together lead their units and formations into battle. The absurdity of this notion from the point of view of military efficiency was to be amply demonstrated in the first phase of the Finnish campaign in 1939.

The last major reorganization was that of the *Komsomol*, in August 1937, following upon the elimination of its leader Kosarev.[1] With the defeat of his critics, even in the secret conclaves of the Politburo and the Central Committee, Stalin could claim in effect to be master not only of the destinies of the country but of the interpretation of the past. As is the privilege of despots, he now devoted himself to the rewriting of history.[2] He could even claim to control the data themselves. Thus, the results of the census held in January 1937, which presumably disclosed something of the losses caused by the executions, deportations and famine of the 30's, were simply annulled and suppressed.[3] At the end of 1937 the results of the first elections held under the new constitution were heralded as conclusive evidence of the enormous popular support enjoyed by Stalin and the party leadership; 96·5 per cent of the electorate voted. Of about 94 million votes cast, only about 135,000 had crossed off the sole candidate's name from the ballot paper, and only 62,000 voting papers were invalid[4]. Meanwhile, just rewards were handed out to the men who had made Stalin's victory possible. Vyshinsky's Order of Lenin was announced on 21 July 1937. Ezhov was similarly decorated about the same time, on the occasion of the opening of the Moscow-Volga Canal which had been built by the forced labourers of the concentration camps under

[1] *Pravda*, 29 August 1937.
[2] The growth of party control over history and cultural matters generally is discussed in a later chapter.
[3] *Pravda*, 26 September 1937.
[4] *Pravda*, 15 and 17 December 1937.

his command.[1] In October 1937 Ezhov became a candidate member of the Politburo.[2] In January 1938 another stalwart supporter of Stalin was rewarded, the First Secretary of the Moscow organization, N. S. Khrushchev, who now became First Secretary of the Ukrainian party organization. He replaced the turbulent Postyshev as a candidate member of the Politburo.[3]

In the first fortnight of March 1938, with all opposition now finally routed, the last act of the drama was staged. Bukharin, Rykov, Yagoda, Krestinskii, Rakovskii and sixteen others were put on public trial. Most of the charges followed the familiar pattern. Once again, Trotsky was portrayed as the real power behind the conspiracy now called the 'Anti-Soviet Bloc of Rights and Trotskyites'. The accused were charged with sabotage, with a conspiracy to overthrow Stalin and his close colleagues, with espionage on behalf of Germany and Japan and with a plot to dismember the USSR in favour of these powers in return for their support. The officers who had been shot in June 1937 were also stated to have been parties to this plot. There were, however, also some novel features. Yagoda was additionally charged with having poisoned Maxim Gorky, Kuibyshev and his former chief in the OGPU, Menzhinskii, and several distinguished physicians were in the dock alongside of him. Bukharin, no doubt with the object of countering any popularity which he still enjoyed, was additionally accused of having plotted with the left socialist revolutionaries to arrest and kill Lenin, Stalin and Sverdlov as far back as 1918. Except on this last charge, which Bukharin denied to the end, the evidence adduced consisted almost entirely of the admissions made at their preliminary interrogations by the accused. On the charge of plotting to kill Lenin in 1918, several witnesses were called. These were former left socialist revolutionaries and left communists – ghosts from the past, who were themselves in the hands of the police.

Once again, the accused confirmed in court the evidence which they had given under interrogation. But there were several hitches in the proceedings. The first came when Krestinskii went back on the confession which he had already made. He withdrew his retraction after a further twenty-four hours spent in the hands of the NKVD, and then made the necessary admissions in open court. But Vyshinsky, who was again in charge of the prosecution, was less successful with one of the witnesses, Boris Kamkov, called to substantiate the allegation

---

[1] *Pravda*, 5, 15 and 18 July 1937.
[2] *Pravda*, 13 October 1937.
[3] *KPSS v rez.*, volume III, p. 306.

that Bukharin had plotted against Lenin's life in 1918 with the left socialist revolutionaries. This courageous socialist revolutionary terrorist defied the communist procurator, much as he had defied the henchmen of another despotism in the past. He denied repeatedly that there had been any plot or conspiracy against Lenin in 1918. Kamkov was already a prisoner in the hands of the NKVD, and nothing is known of his subsequent fate except that Soviet sources record his 'death' in 1938. It can be easily surmised. All but three of those accused were sentenced to death. The three sentenced to imprisonment included one of the doctors and Rakovskii – another former ambassador to London.

The three show trials of 1936–8 have formed the subject of much discussion both at the time and since, and they certainly raise important questions for the historian. The first question is: was the evidence adduced at them, or any of it, true? There are certainly very good reasons for dismissing the whole of it as the product of the imagination of the NKVD and Vyshinsky. The bulk of it, with exceptions of no significance, consisted of the admissions of the accused, made under interrogation during their confinement in the hands of the NKVD. We know now from the statements made by Khrushchev to the Twentieth Party Congress that the officers of the NKVD were empowered to and did use torture, both mental and physical, in order to extract admissions.[1] Moreover recent official history of the party published by the Soviet authorities no longer suggests that Zinoviev, Kamenev, Rykov or Bukharin were traitors. It contents itself with saying that their views were 'mistaken', that as a result of persisting in their mistakes they became opponents of the party and therefore 'objectively' a part of the anti-Soviet forces, and, in Bukharin's and Rykov's cases, 'agents of the *kulaks*'.[2]

Apart from these considerations, wherever it has been possible to check the evidence used at the trials against known facts, it has been found wanting. Trotsky made particular efforts to clear himself of the charges which had been made against him, and was successful in establishing before an independent commission of enquiry the falsity of the allegations wherever they could be tested.[3] It proved easy to

[1] *The Anti-Stalin Campaign*, pp. 31–42.
[2] See e.g. Bol'shaia sovetskaia entsiklopediia, Second edition, volume 50, Moscow, 1957, pp. 258, 263.
[3] See *The Case of Leon Trotsky*, Report of Hearings on the Charges made against him in the Moscow Trials. By the Preliminary Commission of Inquiry, John Dewey, Chairman, etc. London, 1937; *Not Guilty*, Report of the Commission of Inquiry into the Charges against Leon Trotsky in the Moscow Trials etc., New York and London, 1938.

expose a number of errors of the kind that one would expect to find in a case which had been invented in the office of Vyshinsky. For example, an hotel where a vital meeting had taken place, according to the evidence, was shown to have been destroyed before the First World War and never rebuilt. Again, the evidence at one trial laid stress on a clandestine meeting with Trotsky which one of the alleged conspirators was supposed to have attended in Norway by plane. It was possible to show that no aircraft had landed at the airfield alleged on or near the date alleged. The great mass of new material which has emerged since the defeat of Germany in 1945 has produced some evidence of conspiracy between the NKVD and the Gestapo, but none of any contacts between the Germans and the oppositionists. Finally, wherever the evidence adduced at the trial related to past events, the distortion and falsification to which these events were subjected by the prosecution can easily be exposed by anyone in possession of the sources available to the historian. One such instance was the charge made against Bukharin of plotting to kill Lenin and others in 1918, where well-known facts relating to this period were falsified beyond recognition in order to bolster an accusation for which there was no foundation.[1]

The question of the army's attitude is of especial importance. Was there an army conspiracy in 1936 or 1937? All the internal evidence is against it. The time for a conspiracy to oust Stalin and to put Bukharin in power was 1929 or 1930, not 1936 or 1937. We do not know how Tukhachevskii and other military members of the Central Committee voted in the Plenum of the Central Committee of February-March 1937 which expelled Bukharin and Rykov from the party and left them to their fate. If they voted against Stalin, they were prematurely showing their hand. If they voted for him, it certainly did not save them. In any case, the normal way of dealing with a conspiracy is by a sudden swoop, without warning. The arrests of June 1937 were nothing of the sort, since they had been preceded by a series of warning signs ever since the beginning of the year.

Emigré accounts of a conspiracy are conflicting, scrappy and unconvincing; they are, moreover, often coloured by the version of the 'conspiracy' given at the trial of Bukharin which is least likely to be the correct one. There is, it is true, some slight evidence to be found in support of the view that a *coup d'état* had been planned in the fact that the first wave of arrests fell with particular severity on the

[1] I have dealt with this incident in detail in my *The Origin of the Communist Autocracy*, pp. 143-5.

commands of the Moscow garrison, on the command staffs of the key western frontier districts of Kiev and Belorussia and in the isolated Far East. But this too could be explained in terms of simple caution. Not one scrap of evidence has emerged from the hearings at the War Crimes trial at Nuremberg of any contacts between the Germans and the executed officers. But there are very circumstantial accounts, both before the war by Krivitskii, and after the war by Hoettl who worked in the Gestapo, which suggest that evidence against Tukhachevskii and others was faked by the Gestapo in conspiracy with the NKVD, and then fed back into Russia through Czechoslovakia by Soviet agents in Paris. The part played by Czechoslovakia is confirmed by Sir Winston Churchill's account of what Benes told him.[1] Moreover, even the Soviet authorities no longer accept the view that the officers executed in 1937 were enemy spies. The names of Tukhachevskii and of several of those shot with him have been restored to the list of commanders who distinguished themselves in the civil war. It is also admitted that the purge of 1937–8 was unjustified and undermined the efficiency of the army as a fighting force until new commanders emerged – a judgement which is scarcely consistent with the view that those who were eliminated were German spies.[2]

Thus, the only possible conclusion on the evidence at present available is that the facts which the prosecution sought to prove at the trials were at any rate to a very large extent false, and that if any of the facts adduced were true there is no means of distinguishing the true from the false. For example, it is possible that some of the defendants discussed the removal or even the assassination of Stalin and possibly of some of his chief supporters. It is perhaps a matter for surprise that the army leaders in particular, who, unlike Bukharin or Zinoviev, had weapons at their command, should have waited patiently for months to be arrested after the first indications that they were to be next on the list of victims. But these are mere conjectures which must remain such until further evidence becomes available. One thing is certain: had there been a conspiracy which involved the army, the leading party organs and the police on the scale and to the extent to which the trials and the terror taken together purported to make out, it is beyond the bounds of all probability that such a conspiracy should have failed.

[1] See Wilhelm Hoettl, *The Secret Front*, The Story of Nazi Political Espionage. London, 1953, pp. 79–87 (the later memoirs of Walter Schellenberg, to the same effect, are presumably based on the same knowledge, or rumour); W. G. Krivitsky, *I Was Stalin's Agent*, Chapter vii; W. S. Churchill, *The Second World War*, volume I, London, 1948, p. 225.

[2] *Bol'shaia sovetskaia entsiklopediia*, Second edition, volume 50, Moscow, 1957, pp. 419, 424, and many subsequent sources.

The second question is, why did the defendants confess? The first point of importance to note is not that those who were put on public trial confessed, but that it was those who confessed who were put on public trial. Khrushchev gave the Twentieth Party Congress the names of a few brave men who were tried in secret or shot without trial because they did not confess – Rudzutak, Eikhe, Kossior, Postyshev, Chubar', Kosarev. There were many, many more – all the army officers without exception, and Karakhan, Enukidze, Preobrazhenskii, to name only a few. Yet those who did confess were also for the most part brave men, old revolutionaries who had faced the hazards and hardships of conspiracy, prison and exile with courage and determination. It may be that the mental and physical torture which was applied to them is sufficient explanation. History affords only too many examples of the ways in which the most powerful man can be broken and reduced to clay in the hands of a determined torturer. No one who has not himself experienced the hopelessness of isolation in the hands of an enemy, without prospect of martyrdom or expectation of mercy, with anonymous death and subsequent execration as the only alternatives to compliance with the tormentor's will, has the right to judge these men.

Since they were all revolutionaries, victims of a new order which they had worked to build, and in which they all still believed, it is little wonder that each reacted in a different way to his predicament, trying as best he could to save something of his faith and human dignity. For not all the confessions were alike, as even the published records reveal. Some of the defendants, Piatakov for example or Rykov, repeated their story without any attempt to resist or without much need of prompting, as if determined to go through with a last irksome duty and to obtain release in death. Others, notably Radek, entered into the part with zest, dominating the stage, embellishing the story, weaving improbability upon impossibility, actors to the last. It is even possible that in some cases these men had persuaded themselves that in making the required confession they were doing a service to the cause to which they had given their whole lives. A reliable witness, Krivitskii, whose memoirs have already been quoted before, has left an account of the way in which one of the defendants, Mrachkovskii, was persuaded to confess to the wild crimes of which he was accused because 'the party' required it of him. Mrachkovskii was the son of a revolutionary, a bolshevik since 1905, a follower of Trotsky in the 20's, and one of the first to suffer imprisonment for distributing an illegally printed programme. For a long time he resisted both the attempts of his interrogator to break him and Stalin's personal offer to spare his life if he confessed. In the end the interrogator won. 'I brought him to the point where he began to weep,' this interrogator told Krivitiskii. 'I wept with him when we arrived at the conclusion that all was lost, that there was nothing left in the way of hope or faith, that the only thing to do was to make a desperate effort to forestall a futile struggle on the part of the discontented masses. For this the government must have public confessions by the opposition leaders.'[1]

Bukharin was probably another such case. Although he had spent over a year in isolation in the hands of the NKVD, Bukharin's evidence and last plea do not read like the words of a broken man. He readily confessed to the crime of counter-revolution of which he was accused, but resolutely denied the charge that he had plotted against Lenin's life or that he had been an agent of a foreign power. There was no more truth in the one charge than in the other. But to confess to a plot against Lenin meant to trample upon the whole of the revolutionary ideal for which he had lived. To confess to 'counter-revolution' was another matter. No one knew better than Bukharin that in the idiom of the party, which he had helped to power, truth was only relative – to oppose the party leaders in any way was very readily interpreted as 'objectively' to serve the cause of counter-revolution. With the menace of Hitler growing ever greater, Bukharin may well have persuaded himself that his death would not be in vain if it served to strengthen the first socialist state for the ultimate, inevitable conflict with the forces of fascism which he foresaw.

From Stalin's point of view the trials served an important purpose. By focusing attention on an enemy outside – Trotsky, in alliance with Germany and Japan – they helped to divert attention from discontent at home. They provided an explanation for the economic hardships and industrial shortcomings. Above all, they painted a picture, in colours sufficiently lurid for the simplest mind to understand, in which any opposition to Stalin was clearly identified with treason. Much of the credit for this achievement must go to Vyshinsky. For he succeeded in keeping out of the trial any suggestion which any defendant tried to make that his opposition had been in any way ideological, or that there was any mass support behind the opposition. The defendants were portrayed as traitors and common criminals, not as ideological opponents.

The only disadvantage which Stalin faced as the result of the trials was the risk of antagonizing Western opinion, especially socialist

[1] W. G. Krivitsky, *I Was Stalin's Agent*, pp. 219–25.

opinion, at a time when he was intent upon cementing a 'popular front' of all left-wing parties as an insurance against the possibility of an attack by Germany. But the risk was worth taking, since he could be sure of two powerful allies: ignorance of Soviet conditions and hatred of Hitler, which readily led even some non-communists in the West to treat the trials as genuine. Even so sober an observer of the Russian scene as Sir Bernard Pares could regard the wrecking activities as 'proved up to the hilt', and the rest of the evidence as 'convincing'.[1] Communists and pro-communists acted as advocates with skill and enthusiasm – sometimes with more enthusiasm than frankness. The German author, L. Feuchtwanger, for example, not only gave a false description of the trial of Piatakov and Radek to his Western readers, but clearly showed in writing for his Russian readers that he himself knew it was false. Thus, in an account written for non-Russian readers, 'the whole thing was less like a criminal trial than a debate carried on in a conversational tone by educated men who were trying to get at the truth . . .' Yet even the drab pages of the stenograms of these three trials immediately belie this description. Rarely can there have been such a spectacle of human degradation as that presented by the conduct of these prosecutions by Vyshinsky. He used every art, and his considerable talents, to tear the last shred of dignity from the broken semblances of men to which the defendants had been reduced during the long months of their torment. That Feuchtwanger knew that he was writing to deceive his non-Russian readers is evident from the fact that while in Russia, during the progress of the trials, he was at pains to advise the Russians that 'abusive epithets and noisy indignation' were not the way to explain what was happening to the West.[2]

The three show trials were only the most dramatic aspect of the greater process of Stalin's two-year assault on the party and on the population at large – the *Ezhovshchina* as the Russians called it, after its main executant, Ezhov. The question must be posed why Stalin found it necessary to inflict this blow. Explanations which seek the answer in parallels with the more degenerate Roman emperors and in Stalin's mental derangement do not convince – except to the extent that any man who is ready to sacrifice millions of lives in order to execute his policy should be regarded as insane. Stalin was certainly

[1] Quoted in M. Muggeridge, *The Thirties 1930–1940 in Great Britain*, London, 1940, p. 246.
[2] L. Feuchtwanger, *Moscow 1937*, London, 1937, p. 145; contrast his article in *Izvestiia* of 30 January 1937. I am indebted to an unpublished study of Bukharin's trial by Dr G. Katkov for this and for other illuminating sidelights.

of a vengeful nature, and vain to the point of unbalance. But the assault on the party showed too much careful preparation, planning and system for madness to be the explanation. It is easy, perhaps tempting, to blame the cruelties and injustices of those years upon the aberrations of one man – this, for example, was to be the explanation put forward by the party leaders in 1956, when Stalin's death was eventually followed by a reassessment of his reputation. But it is an explanation which neither makes allowance for the circumstances in which that man found himself nor illuminates the reasons which enabled one man to impose his will on so many millions. Viewed from Stalin's point of view, there was a certain inexorable logic which led to the holocausts of the late 30's.

It was not ambition alone which had led Stalin in the 20's to amass his great power over the party. The survival in power of the party was at stake during those years, and few communists ever doubted that for the party to retain its monopoly of power was the first and foremost aim of all policy. But this survival required centralized discipline inside the party, and Stalin was probably the only man who could ensure it. The backing which he received during his conflict with the left opposition was primarily due to the realization of this fact. Even Trotsky himself wavered in his opposition for fear of upsetting the whole structure of party rule. But the control over the party which Stalin built up in the 20's was only a prelude to the social revolution which he effected in the early 30's. Leaving aside the question whether the timing of this revolution was wise or the methods used for effecting it necessary, there is no doubt that in carrying it through Stalin had a considerable measure of support from the party. But since this revolution meant an all-out war by the communist party against the majority of the population, the peasants, it was unavoidable that Stalin's personal power over the party should have increased in the process: the reasons which had helped his power to grow in the 20's were increased a hundredfold when the campaign against the peasants began.

By 1934 Stalin's revolution had been successfully accomplished, at any rate to the extent that the point of no return had been reached. The collectivization of agriculture was a fact, and industrial development was at last beginning to show signs of an upward trend. Two courses were now open to the party. One was peace, a halt to purges, a relaxation of discipline, a resting upon the laurels of success. Something of this kind may have inspired those (if there were such) who looked to Kirov as the embodiment of a new outlook. To Stalin such a course may well have appeared disastrous. He may have feared that the end of the corybantic drive which had so far carried the party to victory would bring a dangerous relaxation which would also spell the end of the party's monopoly of rule. He may also, and rightly, have foreseen that in conditions of peace within the party there would be no room for him. For it is seldom that the man who has ruled by terror can himself survive when once that terror comes to an end. Too many passions and hatreds have been aroused, too many voices are raised calling for vengeance for past wrongs. The Riutin programme in 1932, if accounts of it are authentic, placed the removal of Stalin in the forefront of its demands – a fact which Stalin is not likely to have forgotten in 1936. Thus Stalin was led to choose the second course, terror. But terror is useless, indeed dangerous to those who apply it, if it stops halfway and does not render harmless all who might, if left alive or at liberty, harbour thoughts of revenge. With the thoroughness which always characterized him Stalin did not stop half-way: he carried out a complete renovation of the party by the elimination of the generation which had made the revolution and won the civil war, and the raising up of new men who owed everything to him. Thus, Stalin's revolution in agriculture and industry and his assault on the party which consummated this revolution must be seen as integrated parts of one and the same process.

The question whether Stalin's achievement in transforming the country outweighs the loss and suffering he inflicted upon it is meaningless: it depends in turn on another question, to which no answer is possible, whether the same, or better, results might not have been achieved by different men with different methods. But for Stalin his success and his personal despotism were one and the same, and it was to the consolidation of this personal despotism that the terror made an essential contribution. Its main effects were three. It was first of all prophylactic, since it eliminated all who might conceivably be expected to rival or oppose him. It was secondly constructive, since it restocked the entire élite of the country with men who owed everything to Stalin and who knew that their continued survival depended on conformity to his wishes. Third, and perhaps most important, both inside the ranks of the party and outside them, it broke up, effectively and for a long time to come, all possibility of cohesion or solidarity. For the purge of the party was accompanied by a much more extensive terror against all important sections of society. No one, in any walk of life, who had for some time past become entrenched in a position of authority and had surrounded himself with compliant subordinates or congenial colleagues remained unscathed.[1] In the wave of panic, denunciation, hypocrisy and intrigue which was unleashed, no one could trust his fellow or feel secure in the protection of any institution or individual on whom he had hitherto relied. The 'atomization' of society, which some have seen as the most characteristic feature of totalitarian rule, was completed in the years of the terror.

The end of the terror came suddenly and quietly. But throughout 1938 there were indications that the party leadership was apprehensive that arrests and expulsions were beginning to threaten the very survival of the party as a machine. In the atmosphere of fear and indecision which the purge engendered, it was becoming increasingly difficult to restock the party and administrative apparatus with replacements, made necessary by the many removals. One reason for this was the natural caution, much criticized in the party press, of the party members who had survived the purge so far in taking the responsibility for recommending new recruits. As one party member frankly said, when asked why he never proposed a new candidate for membership, 'Suppose something happens to him, then I will have to answer.'[2] A number of steps designed to remedy this growing shortage of party members were taken in the course of the year. The Central Committee Plenum issued a stern order to party organizations in January 1938, warning them against exaggerated vigilance resulting in expulsion from the party for no adequate reason, and calling upon them to set about hearing appeals from those who claimed that they had been penalized without cause. The blame for these malpractices was, of course, laid on the local party committees and on 'traitors' who had penetrated these committees and abused the purge for their own ends – for all the world as if the *Ezhovshchina* had never existed.[3] The situation was somewhat slow to improve – not surprisingly, because the powers of the police remained unchanged, and the party organizations were torn between fear of arrest if they did not expel everyone who could be remotely regarded as suspect, and fear of party discipline if they did. Other measures were adopted to meet the serious situation caused in the party apparatus by the ravages of the purge. Non-party members were, for the first time for many years,

---

[1] For an interesting example of this aspect of the purge see the case of the removal of Rumiantsev who had for years ruled the Smolensk regional party organization with exemplary loyalty to Stalin, in Merle Fainsod, *Smolensk under Soviet Rule*, pp. 58–60.

[2] Quoted in Zbigniew K. Brzezinski, *The Permanent Purge*, Cambridge, Mass. 1956, p. 120.

[3] *KPSS v rez.*, volume III, pp. 306–15.

allowed to take up leading posts in government and economic organs,[1] and provision was made for accelerated recruiting to the party.[2]

The leaders of the party were indeed in a dilemma. On the one hand sheer practical necessity dictated the restoration of some semblance of normal conditions in the ranks of the party. But on the other hand, to suspend the terror too precipitously was to court disaster where so much hatred and injustice had been bred for the past years by the NKVD. They accordingly proceeded with caution. In July 1938 L. P. Beria, whose career had hitherto been confined to Georgia, first in the OGPU and then in the party apparatus, was appointed as assistant to Ezhov. By the end of the year Ezhov had been quietly edged out. On 8 December 1938 the press announced that he had been relieved of this post in the NKVD, but retained that of People's Commissar of Water Transport – a post to which he had been appointed in March or April 1938. His successor as People's Commissar in the NKVD was Beria. Ezhov disappeared into the obscurity from which he had been raised by Stalin and was never heard of again. According to one rumour, he died insane.[3] Mass arrests now came to a sudden stop, and innumerable cases in which investigations were pending were dropped and the suspects released. A number of NKVD officers were arrested, and prisoners in the camps had the unusual experience in many cases of meeting their former interrogators as fellow prisoners. At least one security officer was tried and executed for extracting false confessions. There was some amelioration in prison camp conditions.[4] But there was no change in the powers and privileges of the NKVD, nor in the system of forced labour which it administered. There was no repudiation of the terror or rehabilitation of its victims. Although past excesses were now freely admitted, the blame for them was laid squarely on traitors and enemies, such as Trotskyites, who had succeeded in worming their way into the security organs. There had been some mistakes – and the party was now, as always, taking the credit for putting them right.

In March 1939, after an interval of over five years, a Congress of the party gathered once again, the Eighteenth. It was a cowed and

---

[1] *PS*, No. 6, March 1938, p. 62, resolution of the Central Committee of 4 March 1938.

[2] *PS*, No. 23, 1 December 1938, p. 43; resolution of the Central Committee of 14 July 1938. See also the next chapter, and Brzezinski *op. cit.*, pp. 119–28.

[3] Ezhov was given no mention in the re-edition of the official *Short History* of the party published in 1939, and has since, in volume 50 of the Soviet Encyclopedia, published in 1957, p. 424, been described as an 'enemy of the people', in company with Yagoda and Beria.

[4] See Merle Fainsod, *How Russia is Ruled*, pp. 442–3.

servile assembly. There was no debate, no criticism, no discussion. Speaker after speaker obediently echoed the line laid down by the authors of the main reports – Stalin, Molotov and Zhdanov. Orators vied with one another in ingenuity to devise some novel form of praising the greatness of Stalin – the stenogram bristles with little poems, culled by delegates from all corners of the Soviet Union in honour of the Leader. Both Stalin and Zhdanov referred to some of the events which had shaken the party in the past few years. According to Stalin, the purge had been accompanied by 'grave mistakes', indeed 'more mistakes than might have been expected. Undoubtedly,' he went on, 'we shall have no further need of resorting to the method of mass purges. Nevertheless, the purge of 1933–6 was unavoidable and its results, on the whole, were beneficial.'[1] It was thus an oblique promise that the *Ezhovshchina* was over. But his listeners could not have failed to realize that by limiting his remarks to the period of 1933–6 he had in fact omitted all reference to the two main years of the terror, 1937 and 1938.

Zhdanov was rather more explicit. With the cool cynicism of which he was a master, he rated the local party organizations for their 'mistakes', citing instance after instance of the kind of pathological suspicion which had prevailed in the party: evidence had been faked, the exclusion of one 'spy' had been followed by the expulsion of everyone who could possibly at any time have had even the remotest contact with him, in one instance 64 per cent of a local party organization had been expelled, and so on. Zhdanov scolded the local organizations soundly for their stupid excess of zeal.[2] The resolution voted by the Congress went a little further in its assurances. It recognized that mass purges of the party had proved ineffective. On the one hand they had failed to eliminate the real enemies of the party who had wormed their way into it and were deceiving the party. On the other hand, the mass method excluded the individual approach to each member's case 'and in practice often leads to the restriction of the rights of party members'. In order to ensure that members' rights should not henceforth be so restricted, the party Rules adopted by the Congress made some new provisions safeguarding the right of appeal against expulsion from the party.[3]

Thus it was cold comfort at best that party members were offered at this Congress. Stalin had emerged victorious once again. There was

[1] J. Stalin, *Problems of Leninism*, Moscow, 1947, p. 625.
[2] *XVIII S"ezd*, pp. 519–24.
[3] *KPSS v rez.*, volume III, pp. 368, 375.

no trace of an opposition. The Politburo was reinforced. Two faithful lieutenants of Stalin, Zhdanov and Khrushchev, were elected full members. Every man in the Politburo was now a tried, and proved, follower of the leader who could be relied on to support him through every turn and twist of policy. The police was in the hands of a trusted servant, who had proved his worth as far back as 1935 in the rewriting of the history of bolshevism in Georgia to Stalin's taste. Below the Politburo nothing counted: no one was likely to raise his voice for some time to come. Abroad, war clouds were gathering. Before long the loyalty of Stalin's supporters was to be put to a further test – the pact with Germany of 23 August 1939. Events had already been moving for some time past towards this sudden reversal by the party of its avowed foreign policy.

XXIV Composition and Structure: 1929-1941

On 1 January 1928 the total strength of the party, members and candidates, was over a million and a quarter.[1] In the next few years recruitment continued at a steady rate, and by 1 January 1933 the total strength was just over three and a half million members and candidates. This rapid expansion, which was prompted by the growing administrative requirements of the period of the First Five Year Plan, was necessarily reflected in the quality of membership. In particular, many of those who joined the party in the flush of enthusiasm which was generated by the launching of the First Five Year Plan proved unequal to the demands on their loyalty which the stern years of enforced collectivization of agriculture exacted. Two purges were mainly directed against such weaker elements. The first, ordered by the Sixteenth Party Conference in April 1929, resulted in over 116,000 expulsions by the time of the Sixteenth Party Congress in June–July 1930. A further 14,000 left voluntarily. Thus the total loss suffered by the party as the result of this purge was over 130,000 members, or 11·7 per cent of all communists submitted to a check. The reasons stated for expulsion were 'passivity', 'lack of discipline' (about one-fifth of all those expelled), drunkenness, 'bureaucratic attitude to work' and 'alien elements'. Expulsions fell most heavily upon peasants, and more heavily upon intellectuals than upon workers. Very few old bolsheviks were expelled.[2]

On 12 January 1933 a more drastic purge was ordered, and recruitment was suspended.[3] Over 800,000 were expelled in the course of 1933, and a further 340,000 were expelled during the following year. The instructions for this purge showed that the main edge of it was to be directed against those whose firmness of purpose was inadequate for the tasks which the party now demanded, or whose sympathies lay

[1] 913,221 members, 391,250 candidates, total 1,304,471. See *VKP(b) v tsifrakh* vypusk 8, Moscow, Leningrad, 1928, p. 6.
[2] *KPSS v rez.*, volume II, pp. 605–14; *PS*, No. 10 (12), May 1930, pp. 14–19.
[3] *KPSS v rez.*, volume III, p. 198.

with the 'kulaks'. The first results already showed that the principal victims were those who had joined in 1932, and the next in order to suffer a high rate of expulsion were those who had become members in 1927–8. By 1 January 1935 the party totalled only slightly over 2,350,000.[1]

Recruitment was not resumed until the end of 1936. Meanwhile, the assassination of Kirov on 1 December 1934 gave a decidedly political turn to the next phase of the purge, which continued uninterrupted throughout 1935. By 1 January 1937 total membership, including candidates, stood at just under two million, from which a figure for expulsions for the two years 1935–7 of over 350,000 can be inferred.[2] In order to estimate the total impact of the Ezhov purge on the party, the figures for total membership, including candidates, before its inception in 1936 and after its conclusion in 1938 must be compared. This gives a difference of about 445,000, which does not, however, represent the total number of victims. Recruiting had been resumed after November 1936, and can be estimated at roughly 410,000 for the whole period. The net loss in membership, added to the number of new recruits, gives an approximate figure of the total purged – about 850,000, or 36 per cent of the party.[3] Thus, if the comparatively modest, numerically speaking, consequences of the assassination of Kirov be set aside, there were two major assaults upon the party: in 1933–4, and in 1936–8, accounting respectively for over a million and for 850,000 members. The objects of the two attacks were, however, quite different. The first was mainly aimed at eliminating new recruits who had not stood up to the test of experience. The second, which in contrast to the first was not an official purge decreed by the Central Committee but an operation privately launched by Stalin and Ezhov, almost behind the back of the Central Committee, effected a complete transformation of the party

[1] *SPR*, No 8, p. 293; *Bol'shevik* No. 15, August 1934, p. 9.
[2] Fainsod, *op. cit.*, p. 249.
[3] Based on the calculation in Zbigniew K. Brzezinski, *The Permanent Purge*, pp. 98–9. The real figure of expulsions is probably not known even to the Soviet authorities. Dr Rigby gives a somewhat lower figure for expulsions for the years 1935, 1936 and 1937: around 600,000 (see Rigby, *C.P.S.U.*, pp. 209–14). Assuming that expulsion was almost invariably followed by arrest, the overall figure of 850,000 purged in 1936–9 may be an underestimate. Thus, Academician A. D. Sakharov, who may well have had access to the official figures released to high party members in 1956, gives a figure of over 1,200,000 arrested in the years 1936–9, of whom only 50,000 were eventually freed – see his clandestinely circulated pamphlet *Razmyshleniia o progresse, mirnom sosushchestvovanii i intellektual'noi svobode*, Frankfurt a/Main, 1968, p. 24. But it is, of course, possible that party members *arrested* in the period 1936–9 had in fact been *expelled* from the party in one of the purge years before 1936.

and especially of its top echelon, into an élite of Stalin's own making.

The overall effects of the purges became clear when Malenkov gave the Eighteenth Party Congress in March 1939 an analysis of the 1,589,000 full members of the party according to the date on which they joined the party. Only 8·3 per cent, or 132,000 persons, had joined the party earlier than the end of 1920. Since there were 733,000 members and candidates at the beginning of 1921, it followed that less than a fifth of them remained party members in 1939. Twenty-two per cent, or 250,000, of the 1939 members, according to Malenkov, joined during the years 1921–8. Since we know that the party grew by about 1,100,000 during this period, it follows that less than a quarter of these recruits had survived the purges. Finally, 70 per cent, or over 1,100,000, of the full members in 1939 had joined after 1929. Now, of the 410,000 who joined the party after recruitment was resumed in November 1936 at most 200,000 could have already become full members by 1939. It can therefore be inferred that some 900,000 had joined between 1929 and 1933 when recruitment was suspended. Since the number of those who joined during this period, 1929–33, was about two million in all, it would seem that less than half of this total had survived the purges.[1]

The social composition of the party had also undergone a profound change, which was in the main the result of deliberate policy in recruitment. For some years after the launching of the First Five Year Plan official policy still followed the traditional preference for working-class recruits to the party. The avowed aim was to increase the proportion in the party of workers actually engaged in production, and this aim was achieved. A Central Committee directive of 7 January 1929 required that 90 per cent of all recruits in industrial areas and 70 per cent in rural areas should be workers in production. On 1 April 1930 workers actually engaged in production were stated to form nearly half the party (48·6 per cent), a rise from 40·8 per cent in January 1928.[2] The party Rules of 1934 still prescribed that preference should be given to workers in recruiting new members to the party, but since recruitment was suspended at the time, and for two years thereafter, this provision was of little practical importance.

When recruitment was resumed after November 1936, and especially during 1938 when an effort was being made to repair the ravages

[1] *XVIII S″ezd*, pp 148–9. See also T. H. Rigby, *The Selection of Leading Personnel in the Soviet State and Communist Party.* Unpublished Ph.D. Thesis in the University of London, 1954. (Quoted hereafter as *Rigby Thesis*.)

[2] *PS*, No. 11–12 (13–14), June 1930, pp. 14, 19.

caused by the purges in the ranks of the party, it became apparent that a new policy was being pursued. The need for a reassessment of the traditional preference extended to manual workers was obvious. After 1928 the party was progressively building up its own technical intelligentsia to take the place of non-communist technicians upon whom it had hithero relied. Stalin in June 1931 told a conference of executives that just as no ruling class hitherto had managed without its own intelligentsia, so the working class of the USSR must also build up its own industrial and technical specialists. These, according to Stalin, were to be trained from among the sons of workers and peasants.[1] During the next years thousands of young men, many of them party members, were trained as specialists to serve the growing industry. They were not all sons of peasants and workers: in fact, few peasant children found their way to the higher educational institutions, and the number of students who were children of 'salaried employees and specialists', already half that of the children of manual workers in 1934, exceeded half by 1938.[2] The Soviet Union was beginning to look for talent wherever it could find it and to abandon the doctrinal pre-eminence of manual labour. Very many of these new technicians became party members: by 1936 already 97 per cent of plant managers, 82 per cent of chiefs of construction and 40 per cent of chief engineers were communists.[3]

It was obviously impossible to keep this new class of technicians, trained up by the Soviet régime, outside the ranks of the party. It would, moreover, have been a short-sighted policy, since most of them were likely to support a régime which had given them both prospects of advancement and a sense of pride in participating in the transformation of their country. When recruitment to the party was resumed at the end of 1936 the technical specialists were welcomed as members. While no figures of the social composition of the party as a whole were published at the Eighteenth Congress in 1939, figures relating to recruitment in two of the republics after the purge, when compared with recruitment in 1929, show that recruits from the 'intelligentsia' and 'office worker' categories formed 42·8 and 44·5 per cent, as compared with 1·7 per cent in 1929.[4] Both Stalin and Zhdanov, in their speeches to the Eighteenth Congress, criticized the

[1] J. Stalin, *Problems of Leninism*, Moscow, 1947, p. 369.
[2] Figures quoted from Soviet statistical sources in Gregory Bienstock, Solomon M. Schwarz and Aaron Yugow, *Management in Russian Industry and Agriculture*, New York, 1944, p. 112.
[3] *ibidem*, p. 30. For figures published much later, and therefore less likely to be reliable, see *Kommunist*, No. 11 (1958), pp. 52–65.
[4] *XVIII S"ezd*, pp. 544, 577; *BSE*, volume XI, p. 534.

survival of bigoted hostility to the admission of intellectuals to the party, and the new party Rules gave recognition to what was now an established policy by abolishing preferential categories for candidates for admission to the party and throwing membership open to all 'conscious and active workers, peasants, and intellectuals, loyal to the cause of communism'.[1]

Recruitment figures published in the years following the Congress showed how well-rooted was the new policy: more than 70 per cent of recruits, where figures are available, came from the new intelligentsia.[2] Two other characteristics of the party which emerged after the purges must also be noted. It was now a young party: among the delegates to the Eighteenth Congress, for example, there were scarcely any over fifty, about half were under thirty-five, and well over three-quarters under forty.[3] This youthfulness was of course a result of the elimination of the older bolsheviks and of the restocking of the party. Secondly, the party was still predominantly male: as late as 1941 women formed only 14·9 per cent of the total membership – a slight decline from 15·9 per cent in July 1932.[4]

The trends which were apparent by 1939 in the party as a whole, especially its youth and recent admission to membership, were even more marked in the case of the party élite – the secretaries, the committee men and the holders of responsible positions in government and industry. In 1930 and 1934, for example, the great majority of delegates to the party congresses, who formed a fair representation of this élite, had joined the party before the end of the civil war: 82·4 and 81 per cent respectively. In 1939 this generation of recruits formed only 19 per cent. Analysis of the Moscow and Leningrad regional conference delegates about the same time shows that this near elimination of the older bolsheviks from positions of responsibility in the party was not confined to the higher party posts.[5] As might be expected, the heavy purge had had the effect of producing a very high turnover in the party committees throughout the country. In elections to the committees held in 1938, for example, the percentage of members elected for the first time varied from 35 in the lowest organizations to 60 in the highest. The overwhelming majority of secretaries by 1939 were under forty and had joined the party not earlier than 1924.[6]

[1] *KPSS v rez.*, volume III, p. 382.
[2] Fainsod, *op. cit.*, pp. 263–4; *Rigby Thesis*, chapter iv.
[3] *XVIII S"ezd*, p. 149.
[4] *Bol'shevik*, No. 1, 1951, p. 11.
[5] *Rigby Thesis*, chapter v.
[6] Fainsod, *op. cit.*, p. 196.

Another marked trend in 1939 was the improvement in the education of delegates to the Congress, which reflected the rising educational standard in the party as a whole. Over a quarter of delegates to the Eighteenth Congress had completed higher education, and a further quarter secondary education. In 1930 the equivalent percentages were 4·4 and 15·7.[1] Available evidence does not make it possible to assess with any accuracy the social composition of the party élite. The latest figures published on the social origins of delegates to the Party Congress relate to 1934: workers 60 per cent, peasants 8 per cent, white-collar workers 32 per cent. At the same date the percentages of workers and peasants actually engaged in production were 9·3 and 2 respectively. Since the purges of the 30's made such considerable inroads upon the older bolsheviks, among whom the greatest proportion of members of middle-class origin were to be found, it may safely be asserted that the predominances among the élite of those who came from the working class, or to a lesser extent the peasants, continued to grow after 1938.[2] Thus, by 1939 the leading role in the party was being increasingly played by young men, recruited after 1929, who owed their education and advancement to the acceptance without question of Stalin's leadership and for whom the revolution and the civil war were little more than a legend.

*   *   *

Whatever other objects Stalin may have pursued in effecting this transformation of the party, one of them was to ensure his own supremacy. By 1939 this was virtually unchallengeable. The Politburo had not emerged from the purges unscathed. Of the ten full members elected in 1934, only six were still there in 1939: Stalin, Molotov, Andreev, Kalinin, Kaganovich and Voroshilov. They had in the meantime been joined by three new men: Mikoyan, Zhdanov and Khrushchev. Four full members were gone: one of them, S. V. Kossior, was purged and shot, three had died in circumstances which were, to say the least, suspicious – Kirov, Kuibyshev and Ordzhonikidze. Four of the five candidates elected in 1934 – Chubar', Petrovskii, Postyshev and Rudzutak – had been, or were shortly to be, purged, and all but Petrovskii were in the end executed. Eikhe, who became a candidate member in 1935, was shot in 1940; Ezhov, who became a candidate in 1937, had by 1939 sunk into obscurity. Besides, although the purge had come to an end, the instrument of terror was

---

[1] *Rigby Thesis*, chapter v, where the Soviet sources of this information are listed.
[2] *Rigby Thesis*, chapter v.

intact: under Beria's command, it remained as effectively under Stalin's personal control as it was in the days of Ezhov. The elimination from the Politburo of anyone who was prepared to challenge Stalin made of this supreme policy-making organ a committee where the views of one man were quite certain to prevail. Indeed, it became as easy for Stalin to put through the policy without convening the Politburo as it had been for him to launch the purges of 1936–8 in spite of opposition from perhaps as many as three-quarters of the members of the Central Committee. At the Twentieth Congress in 1956, Khrushchev gave a description of the way in which Stalin could manipulate meetings of the Politburo by excluding at will anyone whom he wished from any particular deliberations.[1] While his description related apparently to the latter years of Stalin's life, there is no reason to suppose that the position was any different in 1939, when Stalin had revealed the lengths to which he was prepared to go in dealing with opponents.

The Central Committee elected at the Eighteenth Congress in 1939 was convened periodically, at any rate until 1941, though it is unlikely that it met as often as the three times a year prescribed by the party Rules of 1939. But there was little reason to fear any independence of mind from this Central Committee. Its members were renewed at the Eighteenth Congress to the extent of nearly four-fifths – eloquent evidence of the effects of the purge, if one recalls that between 1919 and 1934 the percentage of renewal had varied from 21 to 7. One-third of all members and candidates were regional party and government officials, about a fifth were army and police officials, and the remainder were mainly central party and government officials. The party Congress, which was now required by the party Rules to meet every three years, was not in the event destined to meet again until 1952. The effective sources of authority in the party must be looked for in the individuals closest to Stalin in the top leadership, and in the party apparatus.

If the leading eighteen men and one woman[2] in the party and

---

[1] *The Anti-Stalin Campaign*, pp.83–4.
[2] Stalin: Secretary of the Central Committee.
Molotov: Chairman, Council of People's Commissars.
Kalinin: President, Supreme Soviet Praesidium.
Kaganovich: PC Transport and Fuel Industry.
Voroshilov: PC Defence.
Mikoyan: PC Foreign Trade.
Andreev: Chairman, Commission of Party Control.
Zhdanov: First Secretary Leningrad, Head of Agitprop.
Khrushchev: First Secretary Ukraine.
Beria: PC NKVD.

government machinery are examined, it will be seen that they fall roughly into two groups. In one group are those who, while unwavering in their support of Stalin throughout, nevertheless had already reached prominence in the party before Stalin had achieved his victory. These can be described as the 'Old Stalinists'. In the second group are those who owed their advancement in the party entirely to Stalin, and indeed only came into prominence in the course of the purges. These can be described as the 'Neo-Stalinists'. In the Politburo, as constituted after 1939, it was the 'Old Stalinists' who predominated: Molotov, Kaganovich, Voroshilov, Kalinin, Mikoyan, Andreev and Shvernik – apart from Stalin himself. But the 'Neo-Stalinists' were represented by three: Zhdanov, Khrushchev and Beria. The two groups were more evenly distributed in the Orgburo and the Secretariat. In the Orgburo four 'Old Stalinists' – Kaganovich, Andreev and Shvernik (in addition to Stalin himself) – were balanced by five 'Neo-Stalinists' – Malenkov, Zhdanov, Mekhlis, Mikhailov and Shcherbakov. Similarly, in the Secretariat, Stalin and Andreev were balanced by Zhdanov and Malenkov. The Council of People's Commissars was firmly under the control of Molotov. But of the six deputy chairmen of the Council of People's Commissars only Mikoyan and Kaganovich represented the old guard. Bulganin, the Chairman of the State Bank, Voznesenskii, the Chairman of *Gosplan*, and Vyshinsky all owed their advancement to the purges. The sixth, the only woman in the top leadership, Zemliachka (although an old bolshevik and an early supporter of Lenin in his fight against *Iskra* in 1904), had only re-emerged into prominence in 1938, when she became Chairman of the Soviet Control Commission (the successor of *Rabkrin*) in place of the purged Kossior, and was in this sense a 'Neo-Stalinist'.

It cannot, of course, be suggested that the old and new Stalinists fell into water-tight compartments. Nevertheless, it was only to be expected that this difference of background would in time play a part in the rivalries and intrigues for favour and power which were to become increasingly important as Stalin advanced in years. It will be

---

Shvernik: First Secretary, Trade Union Council.
Malenkov: Head of Cadres Directorate, C.C.
Mekhlis: Head of PUR (Military Political Directorate).
Mikhailov: First Secretary *Komsomol*.
Shcherbakov: First Secretary Moscow.
Bulganin: Chairman, State Bank.
Voznesenskii: Chairman, *Gosplan*.
Zemliachka: Chairman, Soviet Control Commission.
Vyshinsky: Deputy Premier, Chief Procurator.

seen later that the classification attempted helps to illuminate some of the conflicts which took place. Particular attention must be paid to the four secretaries, who probably wielded more power than anyone else. Kaganovich was no longer among their number. Stalin, though since 1934 simply described as 'Secretary', was of course in general control. Andreev had overall responsibility for agriculture. Zhdanov, in addition to being First Secretary of the Leningrad organization, was mainly responsible for ideological matters, on which he had been the spokesman of the Central Committee since 1934. Malenkov was the expert on appointments, or cadres. But after 1939 he also assumed supervisory responsibility for industry and transport,[1] thus encroaching on what had hitherto been the preserve of Kaganovich. However, Malenkov, not yet a member of the Politburo, was in a weaker position in this respect than the other three secretaries.

One further point must be noted. The victory of Stalin over his opponents in the party leadership had resulted in the elimination of almost all those of middle-class origin who had once formed the great majority of the party leaders. All the 'Old Stalinists', with the exception of Molotov, were of working-class or peasant origin. This humble origin was less evident among the 'Neo-Stalinists': both Malenkov and Zhdanov, for example, were of middle-class background, and so probably was Beria. But if the top leadership of the party alone be looked at, it was true to say that Stalin's victory had been ensured by men of those social classes in the name of which the revolution had been made.

The territorial pattern of party organizations remained in substance unchanged from what it was in the the 20's. It was set out in the party Rules in 1934, and with little difference of substance again in 1939.[2] Several layers of party administration were designed to parallel the territorial subdivisions of the USSR. Within the RSFSR party organizations existed in the several territories (*krai*) or regions (*oblast'*). Within the regions themselves there were city and district (*raion*) organizations, and the larger city organizations were also subdivided into districts. Each territorial organization was hierarchically subordinate to the next highest organization – the district or city to the autonomous republican, territorial or regional organization, and the latter in turn to the Central Committee and the All-Union Congress. In every Union Republic, other than the RSFSR, there

[1] This is evident from the speech of the delegate from Molotov Oblast' at the Eighteenth Party Conference in 1941.
[2] *KPSS v rez.*, volume III, pp. 236–42, 385–93.

was a republican party organization, some of them successors of the national parties of the 20's; in the larger republics there were regional organizations as well. In the case of the largest republic, the RSFSR, no central republican party organization was provided for, and the party network was directly subordinated to the All-Union organization. The Rules provided for a Central Committee and a periodic congress in the republics; for territories or regions there was a territorial or regional committee, as the case might be, and a periodic conference. The distinction in the case of the republics was one of name only, no doubt with the national susceptibilities of the republics in mind – functions and powers were identical. The local committees, in turn, were to elect an 'executive body' and 4 to 5 secretaries. City and district organizations likewise were to hold periodic conferences, to elect a committee, and a smaller 'bureau', and three secretaries.[1]

The party rules also provided for a network of 'primary party organizations' (hitherto known as 'cells') in all factories, collective farms, all military and naval units and all institutions where there were at least three party members. These primary organizations were normally to be subordinate to the city or district committees, but the Rules envisaged an exception: the Central Committee was given power to take over party control over backward sectors of industry, or in other special cases, and in such event to by-pass the territorial party organizations by means of special 'political departments'. In such cases the primary party organizations would be directly subordinate to the Central Committee. Described in the Rules as the 'foundation of the party', the primary organizations were to 'mobilize the masses' in the undertaking or farm concerned, in order to ensure the fulfilment of the plan, the 'strengthening of works discipline', and the development of socialist competition. They were made responsible for the work of agitation among the masses, and were to take an active part in the economic and political life of the country. They were also to attract new members to the party and to be responsible for their first steps in political education. Furthermore, the primary organizations in all institutions, except the government departments, were given the right of 'control over the administration of the undertaking'.[2] It was a charter of considerable powers. Primary organizations over fifteen

---

[1] The 1939 party Rules, re-enacting the 1934 Rules, also made provision for party organizations in the circuits (*okrug*). These intermediate administrative areas, in between the republican regions and the districts, were already nearly obsolete in 1939, having been abolished in 1930, except for a few national *okrugs*.
[2] The meaning of the word *kontrol'* is perhaps closer in meaning to 'supervision' or 'verification' than 'control'.

members strong were to elect a bureau, and all organizations elected a secretary, or several secretaries in the case of the larger organizations. But full-time paid secretaries were only provided for by the Rules in the case of organizations over a hundred strong.[1]

The backbone of this hierarchy was formed by the full-time paid secretaries and other officials of the party organizations at all levels. Integration was achieved by ensuring in practice that subordinate secretaries and officials should be represented on the next higher committee and its bureau or executive organ – officials of lower organizations in many cases formed a quarter of the membership of regional committees, or republican central committees. The total number of these secretaries in 1939 can only be estimated. In 1927, according to Stalin, the 'leading forces' of the party, its 'generals, officers and non-commissioned officers' numbered between 133,000 and 194,000,[2] and the higher of the two figures is probably a fair estimate for the size of the apparatus of the party in 1939. This would mean about one official for every twelve party members and candidates. No information is available on the amount of salary paid to these secretaries. It will be recalled[3] that already in the 20's the salaries of party officials were somewhat higher than those paid to the corresponding ranks and responsibilities in other walks of life. It is very unlikely that this position should have changed by the end of the 30's, when egalitarianism in earnings was very much in disfavour.[4] The source of party funds is likewise a matter for conjecture. According to the Rules they were to be derived from 'members' dues, party undertakings and other sources', and since the party is not known ever to have been short of funds for its purposes one can only assume that adequate allocations from state funds[5] were made whenever necessary to the party.

The party Rules stressed that all secretaries were to be elected. In practice, as is evident from frequent admissions in the party press in the 30's, as in the 20's, election was a formality, since the Secretariat could always ensure the election of its nominees. Even the Rules recognized this state of affairs by the provision that the election of

---

[1] This provision was frequently violated in practice.
[2] Quoted in Fainsod, *op. cit.*, pp. 205-6.
[3] See pp. 321-2, above.
[4] In 1957 the salary of a secretary of a primary party organization was apparently 1,400 roubles a month, which was about double the average wage in industry. See *SPR*, 1957, p. 441. This invaluable source book on the party, suspended after 1934, resumed publication in 1957.
[5] No indication of such allocations appears in the budgets, but they could be covered under the general heading of 'administration'.

secretaries required the 'confirmation' of the next highest party organization – city and district secretaries by the territorial, regional or republican committee or central committee, and territorial, regional and republican secretaries by the Central Committee in Moscow. Indeed, it is clear that the practice of nomination by the central organs extended also to the 'election' of members of party committees, bureaux and executive organs. At the end of 1936 and early in 1937, against the background of mounting terror, there were frequent references in the party press to violations of party democracy during elections. New Central Committee instructions on elections, dated 30 March 1937, purported (as so often before) to remedy some of these violations. These provided for free discussion of candidates' qualifications before election took place, and for a secret vote. However, almost immediately after these new instructions were published, articles began to appear complaining that local party leaders had misinterpreted the instructions, and had failed to exercise 'guidance' over elections, to challenge unsuitable nominations, or to prevent excessive discussion of the merits of candidates. It was made clear that party leaders should attend meetings of subordinate party organizations and not absent themselves for fear of violating party democracy. In March 1938 open voting for party secretaries was restored.[1]

The position was not very different as regards free discussion. The Rules stressed the right of all party members to participate in 'free and business-like discussion' of all 'practical questions of party politics'. But apart from the obvious limitation contained in these words, the days were long past when any party member would dare to venture any criticism which he thought was likely to draw unwelcome attention to himself, let alone any criticism of a policy approved higher up. The Rules also contained severe limitations on the right to initiate the kind of discussions on a wide scale which had characterized the early years when opposition could still arise inside the party. These limitations were ostensibly designed to prevent 'anti-party elements' from abusing party democracy, or to make it impossible for an 'insignificant minority' to 'impose its will on the great majority of the party'. Presumably, the 'great majority' was expected to know that it was right so long as it accepted the party leaders' views; but was not trusted to be sufficiently certain in its convictions not to be swayed by an 'insignificant minority'.

[1] *P.S.*, No. 4, February 1937, pp. 58–9; No. 6, March 1937, pp. 3–4; No. 8, April 1937, pp. 50–4; No. 10, May 1937; pp. 22–30; No. 8 April 1938, pp. 3–7, 62–3.

The functions of the Orgburo were never clearly defined. According to the party Rules, it exercised 'general direction over organizational work'. But whereas in the 20's it had concerned itself mainly with party matters, in the early 30's it was widely concerned with questions of industry, agriculture and labour.[1] It seems that it replaced the Central Control Commission both as the general staff office of the Politburo and as the administrative arm of the Secretariat. The Central Control Commission was thereby enabled to devote itself exclusively to its increasing disciplinary preoccupations. Renamed the Commission of Party Control in 1934, it lost such vestiges of independence as still survived up to that date. The rule that members of the Central Control Commission could not at the same time be members of the Central Committee was dropped – in 1934 its chairman, Kaganovich, and some of its members, such as Ezhov, were also members of the Central Committee. Its organization was strengthened, its powers were increased and its structure was completely centralized: in particular, the Commission of Party Control now acted through plenipotentiaries in the republics, territories and regions,[2] in place of local control commissions as hitherto. In 1939, at the Eighteenth Congress, a further change was made, though of a formal nature: the Commission of Party Control was no longer to be elected by the Congress, but to be directly appointed by the Central Committee. The difference between the two methods had for long been only one of name.

The Secretariat remained the real centre of authority in the party. Its importance during the 20's in the control of the distribution of communists within the party machine and the government departments has already been stressed. But with the launching of the First Five Year Plan the tasks of distributing party talent and of supervising the agricultural revolution and the growing industry, along with the related problem of organizing the necessary propaganda in favour of the new policy, increased very considerably. From 1930 until 1941 the party experimented with two broad variants of departmental structure for the Secretariat: the one, which assumed overall control of the distribution of all party members, but did not attempt to exercise daily control over industry and agriculture from the centre; the other,

---

[1] See the plan of work for the Orgburo for 1931 printed in *SPR*, No. 8, pp. 280–7. See also Aleksandrov (no initials), *Kto upravliaet Rossiei : Bol'shevistskii partiino-pravitel'stvennyi apparat i Stalinizm. Istoriko-dogmatischeskii analiz.* Berlin, n.d., pp. 316–20. This is in many respects still the best, most detailed and accurate analysis of the party and government machine for the period up to 1932.

[2] *SPR*, No. 9, pp. 247–9.

according to which the Secretariat became responsible not only for distribution of party cadres (as they were called) but for constant, daily control from the centre over each branch of the national economy. The former system was the tradition before 1930. The key department of the Secretariat was the Organization-Assignment Department (*Orgraspred*), formed in 1924, through the efforts of the energetic Kaganovich, out of the fusion of the two separate departments, for Organization and Instruction, and for Assignment. All appointments of party members went through *Orgraspred* or were under its ultimate supervision. It also controlled and checked the activities of all party organizations in the country. The other main department up to 1930 was that for Agitation and Propaganda.[1]

A severe strain was placed on both these key departments by the increased demands made upon them as a consequence of the developments in industry and agriculture after 1929. Anxious, indeed often forced to intervene in these developments, the Secretariat possessed no machinery for direct control over industry and agriculture. This control was exercised by the party through its network of local secretaries, its subordinate organizations and the party cells in enterprises and in the government departments. In 1930, at the Sixteenth Party Congress, a complete reorganization was announced by Kaganovich. He stated that the existing apparatus of the party was quite unable to fulfil the demand for cadres which had increased as the result of the Plan. A great deal of 'confusion and chaos' had resulted, and *Orgraspred* had been deluged with demands which it was unable to fulfil. He accordingly advocated decentralization within the Secretariat of the responsibility for placing cadres. The solution adopted was to split *Orgraspred* into two departments: Organizations and Instruction, and Assignment. The Organization and Instruction Department was made responsible only for the distribution of party workers within the actual apparatus of the party, and for the supervision of the local party organizations. The Assignment Department was subdivided into eight sections covering the various branches of the national economy such as heavy and light industry, transport, agriculture, finance, planning and trade. Each section was to specialize in the assignment of personnel within its own field. The Agitation and Propaganda

[1] See pp. 317–18, above. The following is a complete list of departments of the Secretariat up to 1930: Organization-Assignment, Press, Work in the Villages, Statistical, Administration of Affairs, Agitation and Propaganda, Work among Women, Accounting, Information. There was also the Special or Secret Department, of which the existence was not officially acknowledged before 1930, which is believed to have maintained relations with the OGPU, and may have been identical with or closely linked with Stalin's personal secretariat.

Department was also split into two: a Department for Agitation and Mass Campaigns, and a Department for Culture and Propaganda. This doubling of the propaganda effort reflected the new demands made upon the central apparatus to extend control over opinion and over cultural activities in general. This Congress also set up a Department for Administration of Affairs, and the existence of a Secret Department, which presumably served for liaison with the OGPU, was made public for the first time.[1]

But while this reorganization relieved the problem of cadres to some extent, it still left the Secretariat ill-equipped to establish the direct control over industry which it increasingly sought to exercise. The Assignment sections could deal with the posting of party members within their area of competence; but they were not given the powers to deal with all aspects of party control over the particular branches of the national economy as a whole. Mass persuasion, for example, was the responsibility of the Agitation Department, verification of the carrying out of party instructions was the responsibility of the Organization and Instruction Department.[2] A bold attempt to concentrate all party activity and control in one department for each of the main branches of production was made at the Seventeenth Party Congress in 1934. Once again it was Kaganovich who argued the need for a change. He made it plain that the method of dividing up the work of the Secretariat by functions performed rather than according to branches of the economy controlled had prevented the central party organ from exercising the kind of control over the national economy which it thought desirable. The Central Committee, it was said, had often obtained less information from its own departments than from other organizations. The Secretariat was accordingly reorganized into nine departments. Four of them covered the national economy: Agriculture; Transport; Industry; and Planning, Finance and Trade. Each of these departments was now to be made responsible for every aspect of party work: the supply of cadres, control over subordinate party organizations, the checking on the fulfilment of party instructions and mass agitation. The new Department for Culture and Propaganda of Leninism would now only deal with ideological and cultural control, but no longer with mass agitation campaigns. A new Department

[1] See Fainsod, *op. cit.*, pp. 190–200 for an admirable treatment of the whole question of the reorganization of the Secretariat between 1930 and 1939, and for good charts.

[2] See *SPR*, No. 8, for the structure of this latter department in 1932. It included sections for party work in agriculture, in industrial undertakings, in transport and in the universities, in addition to its main Instructor Groups for dealing with the supervision of local party organizations – its primary purpose, officially.

of Leading Party Organs (ORPO) was to concern itself solely with the assignment of officials to the party organizations. The reorganization was completed by the setting up of two administrative departments, and of a Special Department. No mention was made at the Congress of the functions of the latter.[1]

The effect of this organization was to concentrate control over the entire national economy in the central apparatus to an extent which had not hitherto been attempted. The system did not, however, work out as intended. Before very long the department for Leading Party Organs, ORPO, was beginning to take over responsibility not only for the posting of party officials, but for all cadres work – in other words, there was a return to the old practice. This development took place in the first instance in Leningrad under the influence of Zhdanov, the First Secretary of the Leningrad organization who had become a Secretary of the Central Committee in 1934. It is probable that the same development took place in the Central ORPO in Moscow, which from 1934 to 1939 was headed by Malenkov.[2] Though no doubt there were administrative reasons for this return to the old method of concentrating personnel selection in one department, it is possible that part of the motive underlying it was a desire on the part of the ambitious Zhdanov, and of Malenkov, a fellow Neo-Stalinist who at the time worked closely with him, to sap some of their powers from the new industrial departments of the Secretariat which were under the overall control of Kaganovich.

At any rate, at the Eighteenth Party Congress in 1939 a further reorganization of the Secretariat took place, this time on Zhdanov's proposal. Malenkov benefited from the change which followed; in contrast, Kaganovich was excluded from the Secretariat. Both Zhdanov, and his deputy in Leningrad, Shtykov, argued at this Congress that the industrial departments of the Secretariat had outlived their usefulness. The main arguments adduced were that these departments created confusion by competing with one another for party talent; and furthermore that they usurped the functions of the economic and the soviet organizations, and were becoming a 'peculiar kind of people's commissariat of a people's commissariat'. Instead of concerning themselves with the state of party political work within

---

[1] *XVII S"ezd*, pp. 532–3, 672.

[2] For Leningrad see the statement of Zhdanov's deputy, Shtykov, at the Eighteenth Congress in 1939 – *XVIII S"ezd*, pp. 571–3; that the same development was taking place under Malenkov in Moscow is suggested by the reorganization of ORPO in September 1935 to include sections for industrial and agricultural cadres – see *PS*, No. 17, October 1935, pp. 73–8.

industrial enterprises, they took upon themselves the actual work of management, and thus undermined the independence and sense of responsibility of the managers. The Secretariat was accordingly reorganized. All personnel matters were now concentrated in a Cadres Directorate (which was higher in status than a department), and all Propaganda and Agitation matters in a Propaganda and Agitation Directorate. Malenkov became head of the former, and Zhdanov, the ideological expert of the party, of the latter. Two departments on the 1934 pattern were, however, preserved: one for Schools and one for Agriculture. The remaining departments set up in 1939 were the Special Department, a department for administrative matters, and an Organization and Instruction Department for the supervision of subordinate party organizations. A parallel organization was laid down for the local party committees.[1]

One of the objects of the reorganization was to encourage greater initiative and responsibility on the part of managers of industry. But the plan did not make allowance for the complete sapping of initiative or of readiness to take responsibility which the purge had universally brought about. The result of the change was immediate chaos. The enterprises, suddenly left without the party control upon which they relied, were said to be going from bad to worse.[2] No formal return to the 1934 system in the Secretariat was attempted. But informally, centralized party control was reasserted by setting up in various party organizations in the regions and cities *ad hoc* industrial sections equipped for overall supervision over industry. Presumably, though evidence is lacking, general control over these local sections was exercised at the centre by Malenkov's Cadres Directorate, which was already equipped with sections for the various branches of industry. At the Eighteenth Party Conference in February 1941, on Malenkov's proposal, formal recognition was given to a practice which had already informally been put into effect in many parts of the country. All subordinate party organizations were now required to appoint *several* secretaries, who were to concern themselves exclusively with the industrial and transport problems within their areas, and to exercise regular supervision and control.[3] This abandonment of the experiment

[1] *XVIII S"ezd*, pp. 507–44; 570–5; *KPSS v rez.*, volume III, pp. 376–7.
[2] This was the theme of the leading article in *PS* in September 1939, of which Malenkov was at the time editor. It remained the leading theme in the party press until the outbreak of war.
[3] *KPSS v rez.*, volume III, pp. 433–5. The tasks of one such section were described as 'to correct faults in good time, and to help party organizations and managerial staff in a concrete fashion in the leadership of production' – *PS*, No. 21, November 1940, pp. 53–7.

of liberating industry from too much party control was no doubt dictated by practical considerations. But the effect of the change was once again to increase the powers over industry of the Cadres Directorate of the Secretariat, controlled by Malenkov, which alone was equipped to act as the central supervisory department over the new local network of industrial secretaries. And, as once before, Malenkov's gain in influence meant a corresponding loss for the Deputy Premier most concerned with industry, Kaganovich. The 'Neo-Stalinists' were thus successfully asserting themselves. But the complex problem of the relationship between the party and industry was far from solved when the outbreak of war with Germany, four months after the Eighteenth Conference, temporarily eclipsed it.

XXV   The Party and the Nation
(the State: Agriculture and Industry: Culture: Doctrine: Religion)

As far back as 1926 Stalin had formulated his interpretation of the relationship between the party and the state. The 'guiding directions' of the party combined with the carrying out of those directions by the 'mass organizations of the proletariat' together constituted the dictatorship of the proletariat. Stalin went on to say that the 'party exercises the dictatorship of the proletariat' and 'in this sense ... governs the country'. But it does this through the soviets. Although 'in essence' the dictatorship of the proletariat means the dictatorship of the party, the two are not identical.[1] When in 1936 the new constitution for the first time openly admitted the existence of the party and its role in the state, Stalin was careful to point out that the formulation he had made ten years before was still valid: the aim of the new constitution, he said, was to preserve unchanged the dictatorship of the 'working class' and 'the present leading position of the communist party'.[2] In practice this meant that the party, whose leaders laid down policy at the highest level, looked in some measure to the network of soviets and other parts of the state machinery to implement policy. But in order to prevent the soviets from rivalling its authority, it was essential for the party to ensure control over them.

There proved to be no difficulty in achieving this in the elections held after the new constitution came into force. Although both the constitution (Article 141) and the electoral regulations appeared to envisage the possibility that several candidates might be nominated in one constituency, in practice in elections which took place after 1937 only one candidate was nominated in each constituency. It may be presumed that the local party organization had the deciding voice in

[1] J. Stalin, *Problems of Leninism*, Moscow, 1947, pp. 136–44.
[2] *ibidem*, p. 557.

the selection of this single candidate.[1] An examination of the published reports of so-called pre-election conferences held in 1937, at which the candidates who had already been nominated submitted themselves for final approval, showed that in every case the candidate was approved unanimously, and no alternative name was in any single case submitted.[2] When it came to the election itself, there seems to have been little difficulty in ensuring that the overwhelming majority of voters cast their votes for the approved name, in spite of the provisions for secret voting. For in practice the voter was faced with the choice of either dropping his voting paper unmarked into the ballot box, or of drawing attention to himself by entering one of the voting booths, in the full view of party representatives present, in order to cross off the name of the sole candidate printed on his voting paper. In the conditions of nervous apprehension created by the terror there were, not unnaturally, few who were prepared to take this step.

The practice in the 1937 elections, and in local elections held thereafter, was to ensure a majority of party members in the Supreme Soviet, the republican soviets and the more important city soviets. In 1937, for example, the percentages of party members in the Soviet of the Union and in the Soviet of Nationalities were 81 and 71 respectively. In the republican soviets in 1938 the percentage was around 75. In a selected number of local soviets in 1939 the percentage of party members varied from 18·4 per cent in the village soviets to around 50 and 70 per cent respectively in the city and district soviets.[3]

The percentage of party members was considerably higher in certain other organs, notably in the courts of law. In spite of the insistence of the constitution (Article 112) that 'Judges are independent and subject only to the law', this provision was never interpreted to mean that there should be judicial independence from party control. The official view is well summed up in the standard Soviet history of the Soviet judicial system: 'It must be borne in mind that the independence of the judges and their subordination only to the law does not mean independence from the state, or independence from the policy of the party and the government, because the court is an organ of power, and

---

[1] A decree of the Central Committee of 22 January 1957 directs party organizations when putting forward candidates for elections to the soviets to agree them first with workers and peasants at meetings, and then, after hearing all views, to put forward a single candidate – see *SPR*, 1957, p. 457. This is the first published instruction on the role of the party in selecting candidates for official nomination. By implication, the practice of agreeing candidates before nomination had not been followed hitherto. Ample evidence of the control by the local party over elections to the soviets will be found in Fainsod, *Smolensk Under Soviet Rule*, pp. 93–5.
[2] *Rigby Thesis*, chapter ii.
[3] *ibidem*.

its function is one of the functions of state control.'[1] In 1931 nearly all judges were already party members, and only about a third of them had received any legal training. The proportion of party and *Komsomol* members among the judges was still about the same in 1938 as in 1931 – 94·8 per cent.[2] The number of judges with university legal training remained low, according to figures published for 1941 (about a quarter), but over half of the remainder had received some instruction in law.[3] There was thus little risk during this period that the courts would present any serious obstacle to the putting through of party policy. Moreover, as the historian already quoted remarks with reference to the period 1935–41, 'the completely unfounded privileged position of the organs of state security reduced the role and activity' of the courts.[4]

In its efforts to direct the national economy of the country, the primary concern of the party was, of course, with agriculture and industry. The history of agricultural developments in the 30's falls into two periods. During the first, of which the main features have already been sketched in a previous chapter, the party virtually waged war against peasant resistance to the transformation of farming. It was only after 1934 that the peasants, broken by famine and terror, accepted the new system as inevitable and began to make the best of it. During the turbulent years when collectivization was under way it is scarcely possible to speak of any established form of rural party organization. It was a period of improvisation and make-shift experiment. In the first place, the existing rural organizations of the party were weak and quite inadequate for the task demanded of them. Although intensive efforts were made to increase the peasant component of the party – the rural membership increased from 400,000 to over 800,000 between 1930 and 1934 – the party leaders, as often happened, seem to have overestimated the support which they would find for their new policy in the villages. At any rate, the impact of the purge of 1933 and 1934 fell with particular severity on those who had been newly recruited to the rural organizations. Between 1933 and 1935 the number of collective farm party organizations was halved, and the number of territorial rural organizations dropped by a third.

---

[1] M. V. Kozhevnikov, *Istoriia sovetskogo suda, 1917–1956 gody*, Moscow, 1957, p. 277.

[2] 84·8 per cent party members, 10 per cent *Komsomol*, according to the P.C. for Justice, quoted in Julian Towster, *Political Power in the USSR, 1917–1947*, Oxford, 1948, p. 302, note 13.

[3] Kozhevnikov, *op. cit.*, pp. 264–5, 319.

[4] *ibidem.*, p. 234. Needless to say, this sentence does not figure in the edition of this work published in 1948.

The result was that many collective farms and rural areas had no party organizations at all, or at most only a single communist. As late as the Eighteenth Congress in 1939 there were only 12,000 primary party organizations for 243,000 collective farms, with a total membership, including candidates, of 153,000.[1] The great majority of these rural party members was not engaged in farming, but occupied administrative positions.

Since, therefore, the rural organizations were either non-existent or weak and unreliable, the task of transforming the village fell to the proletarians. Between 1930 and 1934 some fifty thousand of such proletarian missionaries *in partibus infidelium* were drafted to the villages to carry out the party assignment.[2] Large though this number was, it was still quite inadequate for the purpose of building up an effective territorial network of rural cells. The missionaries were accordingly used at key points – in the state and collective farms, and in the Machine Tractor Stations (MTS) – to build up nuclei of party control, all of which were directed from the centre. In January 1933 local control over agriculture was vested in newly created organs – the political departments of the MTS, which were to be under the direct control of the Central Committee. The resolution of the Joint Plenum of the Central Committee and Central Control Commission which set them up began by stressing the unreliable nature of existing village party organizations: they not only lacked the necessary vigilance against hostile elements, but also at times fell under the influence of the enemies of collectivization. The new political departments in the MTS were to have full powers of political control over agriculture: they were not to be afraid of waging a struggle inside the collective farms to expel 'anti-social, anti-collective farm elements, under the mistaken idea that such a struggle might wreck the unity of a collective or state farm'. They were also to play their part in purging the party organizations in the villages. The heads of the MTS political departments were to be appointed directly by the Central Committee.[3]

This system lasted nearly two years. In November 1934 the hated political departments of the MTS were abolished and a somewhat

---

[1] *XVIII S"ezd*, p. 109, p. 227. Cf. *PS*, No. 20, October 1939, p. 53, which shows that in Smolensk district in 1939 only 135 out of 9,428 collective farms had either party organizations or candidate or *komsomol* groups. On 1 July 1932, the latest date on which data on the social composition of the party were published, 26·9 per cent of all communists were classified as peasants by social origin, but only 18·3 per cent were at the time actually engaged in agriculture – Merle Fainsod, *How Russia is Ruled* Revised Edition, p. 252.

[2] *XVII S"ezd*, p. 558.

[3] *KPSS v rez.*, volume III, pp. 187–98.

more normal system of party control set up. This consisted of making the regional party organization the main centre of local party control over the farms. These were now equipped with agricultural sections, which paralleled the Agricultural Department set up in the Central Secretariat in the reorganization of 1934. The MTS political departments survived, however, in a modified form. They retained their functions as party organizations, each under a deputy director of the MTS for political matters,[1] and if only by reason of the fact that they were the party organization in closest physical proximity to the farms, they continued for years to rival the weak and often remote district (*raion*) party organizations. The 25,000 urban communists who headed the political departments for these two years, 1933 and 1934, played a vital role in putting through collectivization. It is of interest to note that these officials, who played so important a part in the revolution in agriculture, were overwhelmingly drawn from among those old bolsheviks who were eventually to suffer severely in the purges: of over ten thousand such officials in 1933, 82·6 per cent had joined the party before 1920.[2]

Quite apart from their political influence, the MTS were by the end of 1934 already in a position to exercise a considerable economic influence on agriculture by virtue of their monopoly of mechanical power. By the end of 1934, the 3,500 MTS controlled a force of 281,000 tractors and other mechanized appliances upon which the 240,000 collective farms depended,[3] and the mechanization of farming made further, if chequered, progress during the 30's. The first and possibly main object of collectivization, the supply of labour for industry, was thus achieved, since mechanization led to a drop in the manpower required on the farms. By 1937 workers and employees formed 36·2 per cent of the population, and peasants (including 5·9 per cent individual peasants) 63·8 per cent. In 1928 the percentage of workers and employees to the total population had been less than half this figure.[4]

Some improvement in agricultural production was also registered in the course of the 30's. During the first years of enforced collectivization the growing needs of the towns had to be satisfied in the teeth of peasant resistance, and the methods adopted to extract food from the peasants differed little from those of the years of war communism. Compulsory deliveries, under the guise of 'contracts', were enforced,

[1] *KPSS v rez.*, volume III, pp. 260–5.
[2] *PS* No. 13–14, July 1933, pp. 62–4.
[3] *KPSS v rez.*, volume III, p. 261.
[4] *Narodnoe khoziaistvo SSSR, Statisticheskii sbornik*, Moscow, 1956, p. 19.

often at machine-gun point, with little regard to the actual capacities of the farms to produce. But after 1933 deliveries to the state were based on the acreage planted – or supposed to be planted. The prices paid by the state for such deliveries were extremely low, but at any rate some incentive to produce was thereby created. Production began to improve and some form of order began to appear. The total income from agriculture in the USSR, having dropped by about 25 per cent between 1928 and 1932, was by 1937 some 15 per cent above the 1928 figure, and probably remained slightly above the 1928 figure up to the eve of the war in 1941. Grain production in the late 30's was on an average 15 per cent higher than in 1928, most of this increase being accounted for by an increase of over ten per cent in the sown area.[1] Agriculture did not, however, recover during this period from the effects of the slaughter of their cattle by the peasants in the early days of collectivization. The total number of cattle, sheep and goats was still below the 1928 total ten years later.[2]

The collective farms formed the mainstay of agriculture throughout the 30's. The few remaining individual peasants were gradually forced out of existence by taxation and administrative discrimination. The small number of state farms (*sovkhoz*), in which the members worked for wages as direct employees of the state, were as yet of comparatively little significance in the total agricultural effort.[3] The collective farm (*kolkhoz*) was not in theory regarded as a completely socialized form of undertaking. While the land which was tilled in common was state owned, the members of the collective farms were regarded as the owners in common of the livestock, implements and buildings. The land was secured to them in perpetuity by the state. When the form of this farming co-operative became stabilized in the early 30's, it was recognized that private enterprise also had a part to play in collective farming. As Stalin emphasized in 1935, it was essential 'in present conditions' to take account of the individual interest of the collective farmers as well as of their communal interest. 'Without this it is impossible to place the collective farms on a sound basis.'[4] This principle had to some extent been recognized from the first, but was only placed on a regular footing in 1935. As embodied in the Model

[1] Based on the calculations of Dr Jasny. See Harry Schwartz, *Russia's Soviet Economy*, New York, 1950, pp. 305–13, where they are summarized and discussed.
[2] Otto Schiller, *Die Landwirtschaft der Sowjetunion 1917–1953*, Tuebingen, 1954, p. 63.
[3] In 1937 collective farms occupied nearly 116 million hectares, and state farms just over 12 million – S. N. Prokopovich, *Narodnoe Khoziaistvo SSSR*, volume I, p. 243.
[4] Quoted in Prokopovich, *op. cit.*, pp. 252–3.

Charter for collective farms which was enacted that year, the harmonization of private and community interests took two forms. In the first place the remuneration of the members of the collective farms was made dependent upon total production. Each member was to receive, after deduction made for the compulsory state deliveries, the remuneration in kind of the services of the MTS and the amounts set aside for capital costs, a payment and an allocation from the residue of the produce proportionate to the skill and the effort which he had contributed. Secondly, each peasant household was allowed to have, for its own personal exploitation, a plot of ground varying in size from $\frac{1}{4}$ to $\frac{1}{2}$ an hectare, or in some districts up to one hectare; and to own a limited number of cattle and sheep (one cow in the case of grain-producing farms) and an unlimited number of poultry and rabbits. (This right, of great importance to the peasant, was guaranteed in Article 7 of the 1936 Constitution.) The produce from the private plot could be marketed in the free market, which was allowed to survive.

This combination of socialist and private enterprise in one farm was intended to encourage the peasants to develop co-operative farming by allowing them to retain a subordinate interest in private enterprise. It did not work out like that in practice. The very low prices at which the state purchased the produce which the farms were compelled to deliver seemed unattractive when contrasted with the very much higher prices obtainable in the free market. The high quotas of delivery fixed centrally by the state, often in disregard of local conditions, made the certain profit from the private plot a much more tempting prospect for the peasant than his precarious share in a problematic surplus from the collective produce. He put his energies, and his heart, into his private plot, and did as little as he safely could for the collective. A few figures will show how remarkable was the development of the productivity of these tiny plots when compared with the very modest growth of the production of the collective farms. In 1938, for example, the collective farmers, whose private plots formed only 3·3 per cent of the total cultivated area, owned privately, upon these plots, no less than 55·7 per cent of all cows in the country, and 40 per cent of all sheep.[1] In spite of the enormous disparity in area, and in spite of the advantage of mechanized power which the collective farms enjoyed, the production of the peasants on their private plots in 1937 was 21·5 per cent of the total agricultural production of the country. The share of the collective farms was 63 per cent.[2] Such

[1] Quoted in Prokopovich, *op. cit.*, p. 256.
[2] *ibidem*, pp. 267–8.

was the power of survival of the peasants' instinctive preference for private enterprise, and the attraction of the free market.

It was only to be expected that the party should have viewed this situation with apprehension. In the course of 1939 and 1940 a number of measures were adopted designed to redress the balance in favour of the collectivized sector of agriculture. These measures were aimed at putting an end to the peasants' practice of surreptitiously enlarging their private plots at the expense of collective farm land; at enforcing greater works discipline so as to ensure that peasants put in at least a minimum of work on the collective farms; and at altering the basis of computing the amount of crop deliveries to the government in a manner which favoured the government. At the same time greater incentives were offered to those farms which exceeded their planned output. Party utterances left no doubt that an all-out assault was being planned on 'the instinct of petty private property', in which party members were, as once before, to be called upon to play a leading role.[1] The outbreak of hostilities on 22 June 1941 interrupted this new campaign against the farmers before it had got properly under way. But it left its mark on the peasants, who did not forget that on the eve of a war which was to make such severe demands on their endurance the party had declared its own private war against them.

During the ten years spanned by the first two Five Year Plans, from 1929 until 1937, the Soviet Union achieved an astonishing rate of industrial development. In 1928 the pre-war level of production had been reached, or even exceeded. By 1937 total production was nearly four times higher than in 1928. The main expansion had, as might be expected, taken place in the production of the means of production rather than of consumer goods. This economic expansion continued until interrupted by the war.[2] It is self-evident that the driving force behind this rapid industrial development was the party. It is also self-evident that, while disagreement might be possible, so long as any disagreement was tolerated, as to the pace of development, there was no party member who did not endorse the view that industrial expansion was in itself a desirable aim. The sacrifices which the rapid pace chosen by Stalin entailed called for quite exceptional measures of leadership by the party. But the nature of this leadership differed in

[1] See *Pravda* of 27 May, 3 June and 19 June 1940; the three main resolutions of the Central Committee on the subject are printed in *KPSS v rez.*, volume III, pp. 396–424.

[2] This estimate is based on the detailed calculations in Donald R. Hodgman, *Soviet Industrial Production 1928–1951*, Cambridge, Mass., 1954. The official figures claimed an even higher rate of increase, but there is general agreement among economists outside the USSR that these figures were exaggerated.

the two periods with which we are now concerned. For support of the first plan the party could rely on a certain amount of enthusiasm not only from its members, but from the working class generally. Like the period of war communism, to which it bore much outward resemblance, it was a bold fight against superior odds. For all the hardships which it entailed, the very magnitude of the enterprise fired the imagination and evoked something of the old revolutionary bolshevik enthusiasm which the relatively prosperous years of NEP had damped.

The second period was very different in character. By 1934 the worst hardships were over, and the war against the peasants had been won. In the country at large, as in the party, there was a sense that the time had come to relax, and to reap some reward for the sacrifices which had been made. Stalin feared this relaxation more than anything else. His efforts to counter it inside the party, which were only crowned with success in 1938, have already been described. So far as the working class and the new rising class of Soviet-trained technicians were concerned, new methods were called for to sustain enthusiasm. The second plan was more modest in its targets than the first and the targets were not all achieved. But they were very much more nearly achieved in the case of the basic means of production than in the case of consumer goods: the output of the latter, though it increased very considerably over the output of 1933, still fell far short of the plan in many instances.[1] More goods were available for the consumer: but prices were high.

The policy of the party was now more than ever to ensure that the share in those scarce and expensive consumer goods should be strictly proportionate to the effort made by each towards the expansion of the national economy. The last traces of the egalitarianism which had characterized the early period of communist rule now disappeared, to give way to a society in which rewards were carefully graded and comfort and privileges were strictly proportionate to rewards. Analysis of the distribution of the earnings of wage and salary workers and employees in 1934, three years after the main assault on wage equality began, shows that the difference between the highest and the lowest paid was over 29 to one, and that workers in heavy industry were earning substantially more than those engaged in producing goods for the consumer.[2] Piece-rate methods of payment predominated in industry, and output norms were based on the output of the best

[1] Leonard E. Hubbard, *Soviet Labour and Industry*, London, 1942, pp. 280–1.
[2] Harry Schwartz, *op. cit.*, pp. 464–5.

workers and not on that of the average workers. By this means the rates of payment were kept down with two advantageous results from the point of view of the state: more capital could be ploughed back into industry, while at the same time restriction on purchasing power kept down pressure for the scarce consumer goods. An enormous propaganda effort, the so-called Stakhanov movement, was initiated in 1935, in order to encourage high output efforts by individual workmen – to the benefit of the individuals who could attain outstanding results, but to the detriment of the average workers. For their basic norms rose, since enterprises were urged to base production quotas for all workers upon the average of the best, and not upon general average performance.

This policy would not have been possible without the support of the trade unions. They were required to support wholeheartedly and at all costs increased production rather than to obtain a fair reward for all their members. The complete control which the party had achieved over the trade unions after the ousting of Tomskii in 1929 had been essential as a preliminary to forcing the unions to accept this new role. The Sixteenth Party Congress in 1930 stressed that the 'primary' task of the trade unions now was to mobilize the masses for the building of socialism. They must make these masses understand that rapid industrialization and the reconstruction of agriculture were 'the only correct way' to achieve radical improvement in the working-class standard of living.[1] It is possible that the unpopular Stakhanov movement (there were frequent instances of the murder of Stakhanovites by their fellow-workers) also infected some of the trade union communists with oppositional feeling in the second half of the 30's. Tomskii's successor as head of the trade unions, Shvernik, told the Eighteenth Party Congress in 1939 that since 1934 the composition of trade union committees in factories had been changed to the extent of 70–80 per cent, and that of the central committees of trade unions to the extent of 96 per cent. But the evidence does not reveal whether this purging of the trade union communists was due to their opposition to the party's policy or whether it was merely part of the systematic purging of all leading officials which took place in 1936–8.

One effect of this policy of the party, of which the primary intention was to increase the means of production, was to create a society in which wealth, privilege and position were becoming the monopoly of a minority. An experienced observer of the economy of the USSR noted on a visit to the country early in 1937 the emergence of what he

[1] *KPSS v rez.*, volume III, p. 63.

called a 'bureaucratic élite'. As compared with 1934, the rich were becoming richer, and the poor were becoming poorer. The outward symbols of class distinction (such as habits of dress, or different forms of address from superiors to inferiors and vice versa), which the revolution had swept away, had reappeared and a 'ruling class was crystallizing out of the mass'.[1] Many members of this élite fell victims to the purge in the years 1936–8.[2] But the new men who stepped into their shoes inherited their predecessors' class characteristics along with their privileges.

The source of capital for the rapid development of industry was the labour of the peasant and the worker. The peasants made the greatest contribution. That the peasants often lived at starvation level during these years is attested to by many witnesses who have since left the USSR. According to the calculations of one moderate and balanced expert, the peasants went hungry in 1932 and 1936, were half fed in 1933 and 1935, and had enough to eat in 1934, 1937 and 1938.[3] The workers, other than the well-paid minority, did not fare very much better. Again only an approximate calculation of real wages is possible, since official data on wages do not take account of the rise in prices after 1928. According to one calculation of real wages, in terms of the food price index, the workers' overall earnings were about half the 1928 level in 1936 and 1937, a little over half in 1938, and half again in 1940.[4]

The USSR was also in a position to exploit the labour of the in-mates of the corrective labour camps administered by the NKVD. Although not of a productive nature, this labour had the advantages that it was unpaid, that it required very little expense to feed and house, and that it could be used for construction and other work in remote areas in conditions of hardship that might have led free labour to revolt. Calculations of the total size of this labour force at different periods made by experts outside the USSR (no official figures have ever been published) vary from a few million to twenty million. The

[1] Hubbard, *op. cit.*, Chapter xix.
[2] For details of the effects of this purge on the technical and industrial élite see Z. Brzezinski, *The Permanent Purge*, pp. 87–91.
[3] For a detailed investigation of the effects of collectivization on the peasants see Naum Jasny, *The Socialized Agriculture of the USSR*, Plans and Performance, Stanford, 1949, *passim*, and especially at pp. 692–3, 697–8; Prokopovich, *op. cit.*, volume I, p. 274.
[4] Harry Schwartz, *op. cit.*, p. 461. Cf. Prokopovich, *op. cit.*, volume II, p. 121, who calculates wages in terms of food-baskets as follows: 6 in 1928, 5 in 1932, 2·24 in 1936 and 2·18 in 1941. In contrast, Hubbard, *op. cit.*, p. 165, concludes that real wages in 1937 were about the same as in 1913, which is rather more than half of those obtaining in 1928. But all these calculations are admittedly only approximations.

NKVD, as the contractor of forced labour to the government, was responsible for the construction of major projects like the White Sea-Baltic Canal in 1931–3, the Moscow-Volga Canal in 1932–7, and the Baikal-Amur railway, started in 1934. Whole towns and administrative areas were erected by the NKVD in remote parts of the USSR, of which the largest was Dalstroi in the Far East, mainly for the exploitation of the gold and other precious metal deposits. Of eighty electrical power stations listed in the 1941 State Plan, nine were under the direction of the NKVD, and therefore built by forced labour.[1]

Foreign trade played initially no part during the period under review as a source of investment capital. Very high targets had been set in the First Five Year Plan for the development of foreign trade, but they were realized only to the extent of about a quarter. Between 1933 and 1937 the USSR was successful in achieving a favourable balance of trade, but this balance was little more than sufficient to offset the unfavourable balance of the preceding years.[2] The pattern of Soviet foreign trade reflected the continued emphasis on the development of the means of production and the extent to which the government was prepared to exact sacrifices from the population to this end. In 1937, for example, the proportion of imports of goods for consumption to imports of means of production was about one to ten – as compared with three to seven in 1913, or 12·5 to 86·4 in 1927–8.[3]

*   *   *

The pace and violence of political and social developments during the 30's called for control over the minds of the population on a scale which had not been necessary in the easier years of NEP. Enthusiasm had to be whipped up, shortcomings glossed over, successes exaggerated. This was the function of 'mass agitation' – the practical implementation on the ground of the general propaganda lines laid down by the party leaders. But in addition to engaging in its routine functions of agitation and propaganda on a very much increased scale, the party further succeeded during the 30's, largely under Stalin's personal direction, in achieving virtually total control over all intellectual life. Some idea of the scope of the activity of the party in the intellectual field may be gathered from an examination of the

---

[1] *Gosudarstvennyi plan razvitiia narodnogo khoziaistva SSSR na 1941 god*, Baltimore, n.d., pp. 80–4, 9–10. The percentages of the NKVD's share in production of chromium and timber respectively were 40 and 12. For the most thorough and balanced study of forced labour see David J. Dallin and Boris I. Nicolaevsky, *Forced Labor in Soviet Russia*, New Haven, 1947.

[2] Prokopovich, *op. cit.*, volume II, pp. 202, 205.

[3] *ibidem*, p. 219.

structure of the Culture and Propaganda Department of the Central Secretariat in 1932. (It will be recalled that at that date there still existed a separate Department for Agitation and Mass Campaigns, that the two functions were amalgamated in one department in 1934, and this department expanded into a Directorate in 1939.) In January 1932 the Central Committee enjoined the Culture and Propaganda Department (*Kul'tprop*) to provide 'systematic guidance of work in the field of theory' and in the registration, selection and education of learned and scientific 'cadres'. The structure of this department, as approved by the Orgburo on 7 May 1932, showed that it was fully equipped for these tasks. Its establishment had been increased by some 35. It was divided into twelve sections: for party books and political literature; for party schools; for mass propaganda (subdivided into numerous sub-sections for the national minority areas, Moscow and Leningrad, and the main areas of the RSFSR); for schools; for scientific research establishments; for technical propaganda; for newspapers (similarly subdivided into sub-sections); for culture among workers and collective farmers; for journals, including the journals concerned with party history; for scientific literature; for creative literature; and for the fine arts, including the cinema.[1]

The party machine was thus adequately equipped for the task which it undertook during the 30's – the creation of an official theory, from which no deviations were to be tolerated, on such matters as philosophy or law, the bringing under control of the creative activity of writers or historians, and the rewriting of the history of the party. The major part in all this was played by Stalin himself, who after 1930 began to intervene personally in these intellectual fields, and became the established authority on questions upon which his competence had not hitherto been suspected. Stalin's fiftieth birthday, on 21 December 1929, was the starting point for an intensification of the cult of the Secretary of the party as the supreme leader and genius in every branch of art, learning and science, which was to continue until his death in March 1953. Since by 1929 Stalin had already achieved a position of supremacy in the leadership of the party, it is to say the least improbable that this cult could have been launched and continued except as the result of his personal orders. Theoretical justification for this new role of the individual leader in a system which claimed to be founded on the scientific principles of Marxism was provided at the outset in the official journal of the party in January 1930.[2]

---

[1] *SPR*, No. 8, pp. 288–90.
[2] See K. Popov, 'Partiia i rol' vozhdia' in *PS*, No. 1, 1930, pp. 3–9.

Stalin's first excursion into the intellectual field was in the realm of philosophy, in a speech on 27 December 1929. The philosophers were successfully brought to heel by the end of 1930.[1] In 1932 creative literature was disciplined into obedience to the party line. Already in 1928 two party decrees had defined literature as 'a tool in the organization of the masses' and had summoned writers to play an active part in propaganda for the new tasks upon which the party was now embarking. But exhortation was not enough. For some years the Russian Association of Proletarian Writers (RAPP), although sympathetic and loyal to the communist régime, tenaciously fought to defend the creative independence of the writer from direct party control. It was a losing battle. In 1932 the more or less independent RAPP was abolished and replaced by the 'monolithic' and party controlled Union of Soviet Writers.

Stalin is said to have formulated, in conversation with writers, his doctrine of the kind of truth which a communist writer should seek to portray, to which he gave the name 'Socialist realism'. This is officially defined as a doctrine which, 'being the basic method of Soviet artistic literature and literary criticism, demands of the artist a truthful, historically specific depiction of reality in its revolutionary development'. Moreover, the artist must combine his picture of truth 'with the task of ideologically remaking and re-educating the toilers in the spirit of socialism'. The writer's 'truth' therefore must be dialectical: he must portray reality as seen by the party, by seeing with the eyes of party policy the seeds of the future which, even if barely discernible today, will be visible tomorrow. He must also inculcate in the masses those ideas which the party desires to inculcate, or, to use another of Stalin's phrases, quoted by Zhdanov, become an 'engineer of human souls'.[2] The Union of Soviet Writers did not lack means to ensure that only those writers who were prepared to accept these principles should be able to publish their works. Moreover, the purges of 1936–8, during which a number of prominent writers of the early period of Soviet literature disappeared, served as a warning that from creative literary freedom to charges of counter-revolution was only a short step. It is perhaps a matter for admiration that Soviet literature

[1] For an account of the subjugation of the philosophers and for a summary of the views of the schools of philosophers see Gustav A. Wetter, *Der Dialektische Materialismus, Seine Geschichte und sein System in der Sowjetunion*, Freiburg, 1952, pp. 147–200. (An English translation of this work was published in London and New York in 1959.)

[2] Quoted in Robert M. Hankin, 'Soviet Literary Controls' in *Continuity and Change in Russian and Soviet Thought*, edited by Ernest J. Simmons, Cambridge, Mass., 1955, p. 448.

of the 30's, while it cannot stand comparison with the literature of the 20's, is still not totally devoid of all literary merit.

The impact of party control on legal theory and on the theory of the state during the 30's was of special interest, in view of its connection with the constitution of 1936. Marx and Engels drew no distinction between the state and law, regarding each as necessary only so long as antagonistic classes survived, and each as destined to wither away when once the proletariat achieved power and liquidated the exploiting class. This doctrine of the withering away of the state after the revolution is fundamental to Marxist analysis, because if the mechanism of the state survives the revolution, in spite of the fact that the proletariat is supposed to be in power, this throws doubt on the validity of the claim of those who are at the helm of the state to represent the proletariat: for why should a victorious class in power need instruments of oppression in order to rule over itself? Lenin, on the eve of the bolshevik victory in 1917, reconciled both theory and practice in his *State and Revolution* by postulating that the state would have to survive, but only for the intermediate period while the proletariat was establishing itself in power; at the same time he asserted that the state would begin to wither away progressively from the moment the revolution took place.

Increasingly preoccupied with concrete responsibilities after the seizure of power, the practical-minded Lenin grew ever more impatient of Utopian talk of 'withering away', and even clashed with the more doctrinaire Bukharin as early as 1918 (at the Seventh Party Congress) on the subject of including the time-honoured formula in the party programme. But no one during the 20's ever questioned the place of the formula in orthodox Marxist doctrine. To the legal theorists of the 20's it was the keystone of the arch. They regarded law as an essentially bourgeois phenomenon, appropriate as a survival of the old order in the conditions of NEP, when private enterprise and a free market continued to operate, but destined to wither away when once socialism had been fully established. Pashukanis, the most influential as well as the most outstanding legal theorist to emerge after the revolution, went even further. He maintained that it was impossible even to conceive of 'socialist' or 'proletarian' law. Law was essentially the product of a social system based on commodity exchange, and must therefore disappear under socialism. It would be replaced by a system of administration in which social principles would take the place of the outmoded juridical principles. Meanwhile, in so far as law still survived, it was bourgeois law, while the rules which emanated from the new dictatorship of the proletariat did not partake of the nature of law at all. Pashukanis's main work was published in 1924, and was reissued in several editions, the last being that of 1927.[1]

The situation changed radically when in April 1929 Stalin delivered an all-out attack on Bukharin at a Plenum of the Central Committee, and criticized in particular statements made by him in the past on the withering away of the state. Stalin emphasized that so far from the state withering away, the country was now entering upon a period of intensified class struggle.[2] The following year, 1930, at the Sixteenth Party Congress, Stalin reiterated that the correct Marxist formula was that the state would first have to develop itself to the highest extent 'in order to prepare the conditions for its withering away'. In face of such supreme authority, Pashukanis could do no less than retract. But while he repudiated his views on the withering away of the state, he continued to maintain that in the Soviet system law was subordinate to policy: 'I may say that for us revolutionary legality is a problem which is 99 per cent political.'[3] In spite of this frank, if true, admission, Pashukanis retained his dominant position in the Communist Academy until the end of 1936, and his post as Deputy People's Commissar for Justice.

The problem of the withering away of the state assumed a new importance after 1934. The 'kulaks' had been liquidated, there were theoretically no more antagonistic classes left, and therefore no doctrinal justification remained for the continued existence of the state, which according to Marx, Engels and Lenin exists solely for the purpose of preventing antagonism between the exploiting and exploited classes from erupting into violence. For the many who hoped that the new constitution would usher in a period of peace after the turbulent war in the villages, the Marxist abstraction about 'withering away' provided a convenient formula for expressing the longing for a calmer life which they felt, but did not openly dare to reveal. It has been suggested in a previous chapter that it was precisely against such hopes that Stalin's sudden blow in August 1936 against the party and the country was directed, and that he had been held back for some years by resistance in the top leadership. The sudden attack on

---

[1] It is entitled *The Theory of Law and Marxism*, and was published by the Communist Academy. It is printed in an English translation in *Soviet Legal Philosophy*, translated by Hugh W. Babb, with an introduction by John N. Hazard, Cambridge, Mass., 1951, pp. 111–226.
[2] *Stalin*, volume XII, pp. 369–70.
[3] *Soviet Legal Philosophy*, p. 280.

Pashukanis,[1] without any previous warning, at the beginning of 1937, more than six years after his recantation, must be seen as a part of this process. Vyshinsky, who led the attack and succeeded Pashukanis as the leading lawyer after the latter's elimination, was of course also one of Stalin's principal instruments in launching the terror in 1936.

Shortly after the fall of Pashukanis, Vyshinsky formulated a new theory of law which avoided the dangerous Marxist concept of the withering away of law under socialism, and at the same time was consistent with the acceptance of a state and legal system as a permanent feature, which was implicit in the new constitution. According to Vyshinsky, all law must be regarded as the expression of the will of the ruling class, backed by force. In the bourgeois state law is the expression of the will of the exploiters. In the Soviet socialist state it expresses the will of the proletariat: indeed, since the peasants and the intellectuals are solidly behind the proletariat, the will of the worker class merges with the will of the entire people and accordingly Soviet law is an 'expression of the will of the whole people'.[2] (Vyshinsky did not state whether the several million Soviet citizens herded in the concentration camps were also to be regarded as a part of this general will.) This new formula, if little related to Marxism, had the practical advantage of emphasizing the permanent nature of law, and thus of excluding dangerous speculation about the withering away of the state. A year later, in 1939, at the Eighteenth Party Congress, Stalin returned to the subject. Engels's proposition that the state withers away when there are no longer any antagonistic classes required modification, according to Stalin. It was only true when once the revolution had triumphed all over the world. In the capitalist encirclement in which the USSR found itself, the state would continue to exist even in the present stage, where socialism had been achieved, and no antagonistic classes, let alone exploiters, remained. Indeed, the state would continue to exist even after the USSR had progressed to the next and higher phase, communism, so long as capitalist encirclement was a fact.[3]

The distinction between socialism and communism drawn by Stalin in 1939 was traditional in Marxist theory. Marx had asserted in 1875 that the transition from capitalism to communism would require an intermediate phase, socialism. In this phase inequality of reward for different degrees of talent and productivity would still survive. But, in

---

[1] See p. 414, above.
[2] *Soviet Legal Philosophy*, p. 339.
[3] *Problems of Leninism*, pp. 631–8.

the 'higher phase of communist society', when 'all the springs of co-
operative wealth flow more abundantly' then the 'narrow horizon' of
bourgeois law would be crossed, and the principle established: 'From
each according to his ability, to each according to his needs.'[1] When in
1918, at the Seventh Party Congress, the name 'communist' was
adopted by the party, Lenin reminded his listeners of the two phases.
But, unlike Stalin, he maintained that whereas talk of withering away
of the state was premature during the first stage, it would come about
in the second stage.[2] In 1936, when Stalin only claimed that the first
stage, socialism, had been achieved, but that the second stage, communism, still lay ahead,[3] his assertion that the time had not yet come
for the state to wither away was at any rate consistent with Lenin's
views, even if his warning that it would have to increase in power was
not. In contrast, his statement in 1939 that the state would survive
even under communism was consistent neither with the views of
Marx nor with the views of Lenin, at any rate as expressed in his
writings.

There were therefore good reasons for eliminating Pashukanis, if
only because he was the most persuasive theorist of the withering
away of the state. The accusation that he devised his legal theory with
the intention of weakening the Soviet state, and was therefore a traitor,
is not worthy of consideration – indeed since 1956 it has been officially
admitted in the Soviet Union that, while his views were mistaken, the
criminal charge against him was trumped up, and he has been posthumously rehabilitated. It is, of course, possible that Pashukanis,
and some of the other lawyers who were purged when he fell, had
tried in 1936 to obstruct Vyshinsky's plans in their endeavour
to preserve some legality. There is also an obstinate integrity in
Pashukanis's insistence that policy predominated over law in the
Soviet Union.

Pashukanis belonged to that school of old Marxist theorists who still
survived in the Communist Academy and the Red Professors'
Institute, so long as these bodies were allowed to exist. They were the
heirs of the days of relatively free discussion of Marxist problems
which characterized the 20's. Such discussion came to an end at the
beginning of the 30's. The Communist Academy was transformed,
under party direction, from a seat of learning into a training centre for

[1] Karl Marx and Frederick Engels, *Selected Works*, volume II, Moscow, 1951,
p. 23, 'Critique of the Gotha Programme'.
[2] *Lenin*, volume XXII, p. 365.
[3] J. Stalin, *Problems of Leninism*, Moscow, 1947, p. 548, Speech of 25 November
1936 on the draft Constitution of the USSR.

party officials: as its staff and activities rapidly expanded, so scholarship declined. Control over the Communist Academy passed to reliable party hacks. But most of the older type of scholars survived precariously until the purge of 1936–38. A number of them succeeded in the early 30's in publishing learned works which to the ever-suspicious party may have appeared, and may even have been intended, as veiled criticisms of the régime. Such, for example, was a study of the Jacobin terror published in 1930 by an historian, Staroselskii, for which Pashukanis wrote a preface.[1] Pashukanis's own ambiguous recantation in 1930 may well have appeared to contain such veiled criticism of the decay of legality in the Soviet state. The Communist Academy was eventually in 1936 closed down and merged in the Academy of Sciences, which by then had become completely dominated by the party. The Red Professors' Institute, and the old communist universities, such as the university named after Sverdlov, quietly ceased to exist.

Stalin's most important achievement in effecting control over thought was in the writing of party history. The history of the party had of course been used from the beginning as an instrument by rival factions – Lenin himself had not been above rewriting historical events when it suited his argument. But until 1931 the production of learned works on the history of the party had remained in the hands of scholars who, however strong their pro-bolshevik bias, nevertheless usually retained some respect for the facts. Much of the historical work on the development of the party published before 1931 is of value, and some of it is outstanding. At the end of 1931 a letter from Stalin appeared in the journal of the Commission for the Collection and Study of Materials for the History of the October Revolution and History of the Russian Communist Party which had been set up by the Central Committee. This letter contained an attack on the editors for allowing the publication of an article which had attempted to examine, with the objectivity hitherto customary in this journal, a question of bolshevik policy towards the German social democrats on the eve of the First World War. The crude terms of Stalin's letter left no doubt that in future there was to be no room in the writing of party history for 'archive rats', who preferred objective facts to the version of his-

[1] Ia. V. Starosel'skii, *Problema iakobinskoi dikatury*, s predisloviem E. B. Pashu-kanisa, Moscow, 1930. This work is so rare that no copy of it is to be found in the libraries of Britain or USA – presumably it was withdrawn after publication. I have been able to use a copy in private possession, which was surreptitiously presented by the author in 1934 (he was by then already living under a cloud) to a visiting pro-communist professor. Several works on Nechaev, published about the same time, may also fall into this category of 'aesopian' criticism of Stalin's régime.

tory which suited the current policy of the party.[1] It was the end of any work on party history worthy of the name.

However, the task of even the most subservient of party historians was not easy because of the absence of any authoritative ruling on the particular version of history acceptable to Stalin. Such histories of the party as were produced in the 30's were rapidly overtaken by events, as the heroes of yesterday became traitors, or as an hitherto accepted theory was altered to fit new circumstances. It was not until 1938 that an authoritative history could be produced – the famous *Short Course on the History of the All-Union Communist Party (bolsheviks)*. Although ostensibly the work of a commission, Stalin was certainly responsible for its final shape, and indeed its gnomic style bears all the marks of his pen. Its terse chapters summarize the grotesque version of the history of the party which it was now desired to perpetuate as true. In issuing it the Central Committee stressed in a resolution that its twin aims were to provide an authoritative history of the party; and to liquidate the 'dangerous cleavage in the sphere of propaganda between Marxism and Leninism which has appeared in recent years', as a result of which Leninism had been taught as something different from Marxism. It is not clear to what this refers, though plainly, for those who were bold enough to say so, 'Leninism' (which by 1938 meant 'Stalinism') and Marxism were far from identical. Confirmation of the fact that after 1938, at any rate, publication of works on, and memoirs concerning, Lenin was 'virtually' prohibited is to be found in a decision of the Politburo of 5 August 1938, the existence of which was only made public some twenty years later.[2]

It was also significant that during the purge of 1936–8 the vast network of party schools (there were four and a half million students studying in these schools in 1934) appears to have been very largely closed down, at any rate at the lower levels. It is possible that it was feared that the party schools might become centres of unwelcome discussion while the purge was in progress. Now, with the publication of the *Short Course*, an entirely new system of party schools at all levels was set up by the resolution of the Central Committee already referred to. The main basis of their work was to be the *Short Course*, which was to be studied with different intensity at different levels.[3]

[1] *Stalin*, volume XIII, pp. 84–102.
[2] *SPR*, 1957, p. 364.
[3] The Central Committee resolution on the *Short Course* and on the reorganization of party education is in *KPSS v rez.*, volume III, pp. 316–32. For information on the Communist Academy and on party schools I have used the 1957 Ph.D. Thesis in the University of London on 'Party Schools in the USSR' by my former student, Dr Zev Katz.

For years thereafter it was to remain the main, if not the only, subject of study for communists in training, replacing not only other histories but the sources of Marxism as well. As a means of propaganda it could scarcely have been excelled. It became the basis for the training of a generation of communists who, while little tempted to think for themselves, need never be at a loss for the official answer to every problem. No one understood better than Stalin that the true object of propaganda is neither to convince nor even to persuade, but to produce a uniform pattern of public utterance in which the first trace of unorthodox thought immediately reveals itself as a jarring dissonance. Apparently it had proved easier for a totalitarian power to control men's tongues and actions than to gain dominion over their minds.

No new features appeared during the 30's in the policy of the party towards religion and the Church. The party leaders continued to waver between direct attack on the Church and the more indirect method of administrative persecution. The failure of direct attack in the early 20's did not discourage a further attempt to use this method in 1929 as part of the policy of mastering the peasants. The lack of success of this campaign, which took the form of the compulsory closing of churches and which led to frequent armed clashes with the peasants, was virtually admitted by the Central Committee in a decree of 14 March 1930. As was usual, those who had merely carried out the orders of the party leaders were blamed for practices which 'bear no relationship to the policy of our party' – the closing of churches 'without the consent of the overwhelming majority of the villagers', and mockery of religious beliefs.[1]

But if direct attack was once more abandoned, indirect attack was renewed. A number of administrative measures were adopted, of which the aim was to restrict the activities of the Church to organized worship, and to prevent any form of social or educative activity. An amendment of the earlier constitution, adopted on 22 May 1929, permitted freedom of religious *worship* and of anti-religious propaganda, in place of the freedom of both religious and anti-religious *propaganda* proclaimed in the original constitution. The same restriction on religious propaganda was re-enacted in the constitution of 1936 (Article 124). Meanwhile, the League of Militant Atheists expanded, and in the early 30's was confidently looking forward to the complete extermination of religion. An enormous propaganda effort in favour of atheism was launched, and anti-religious teaching was introduced in the schools. For a time after 1934 there was something

---

[1] *KPSS v rez.*, volume II, pp. 670–1.

of a lull, during which the Church and believers benefited from the general relaxation of pressure with which the Second Five Year Plan opened. In August 1937 a further sudden assault was launched on the Church. Churchmen were arrested in large numbers and treason trials were staged. Many of the remaining churches were closed down. The result of all this effort was from the point of view of the party disappointing. The figures of the census of 6 January 1937, which included a question on religious belief, were suppressed. But an estimate published by the head of the League of Militant Atheists, E. Iaroslavskii, suggested that two-thirds in the villages and one-third in the towns, or about 45 per cent of the population, were believers. Two years later the estimate was still the same.[1]

[1] Quoted in N. S. Timasheff, *Religion in Soviet Russia 1917–1942*, London 1943, p. 65, from the official publications of the League of Militant Atheists. For abundant evidence of the failure of the League of Militant Atheists during the 30's in Smolensk province see Merle Fainsod, *Smolensk under Soviet Rule*, pp. 437–40.

XXVI The Non-Russian Peoples: Foreign Relations

How far was the party, as leader of a multinational state, representative of the several nationalities? What developments took place in the policy of the party towards non-Russian peoples? It will be recalled that at the end of the NEP period the national composition of the party still left many of the non-Russian groups under-represented in proportion to their size.[1] Since virtually no data on national composition have been published for the 30's, no accurate estimate of the change in this respect can be made. Such evidence as there is suggests that the proportion of non-Russian communists in the leading positions in the party was slowly rising. If, for example, the national composition of delegates to the Sixteenth Party Congress in 1930 is compared with that of delegates to the Fifteenth Congress in 1927, it appears that Russian delegates had dropped from 62 to 57·4 per cent. But the non-Russian delegates were still far from representative of the strength of their nationalities in the country as a whole. Some non-Russians were over-represented, for example, the Georgians and Armenians, with 1·8 and 2·3 per cent of the delegates as compared with a share in the total population of 1·24 and 1·07 per cent; and most of all the Latvians, who formed only 0·09 per cent of the population, but provided 4·3 per cent of all delegates. As against this, Ukrainians (8.6 per cent of delegates, 21·22 per cent of the population), Kazakhs (1·3 per cent of delegates, 2·7 per cent of the population) and Uzbeks (1·3 per cent of delegates, 2·65 per cent of population) were under-represented in the party élite.[2]

But efforts were being made to draw natives into the local party organizations, at any rate in the early 30's. The Kazakh party, for example, increased its Kazakh membership from 37·9 per cent to 52·3 per cent between 1928 and 1932; and an analysis of the percentage of local nationals in 21 national party organizations published in 1930

[1] See pp. 354–5, above.
[2] *PS*, No. 13–14, July 1930, p. 30.

showed that in nine of them natives varied from 55·5 (Belorussian) to 89 per cent (Armenian), and in a further nine from 35·2 per cent (Volga German) to 48·5 per cent (Uzbek).[1] By 1935 the proportion of natives had risen somewhat in three parties of Central Asia – the Uzbek, Tadjik and Turkmen parties. No data for the 30's are available for others.[2]

The effects of the great turnover during the later 30's on national composition can only be guessed at. In so far as names are a reliable guide, the list of the delegates to the Eighteenth Party Congress in 1939 seems to contain a higher proportion of Ukrainian and Central Asian names, and far fewer Jewish names, than appeared in the list of delegates to the Congress in 1934. A comparison of party strength and population ratio in certain regions and national republics in 1939 suggests that the Ukraine was still slightly under-represented, and Belorussia, Uzbekistan, Tadjikistan, Turkmenistan and Kazakhstan strongly under-represented. But the party was strong in Georgia, Armenia and Azerbaidjan.[3] If these tentative data can be taken as a guide, they would seem to reflect the events which had left their deepest scars upon the whole country – the purges of 1936-8. The Jews, who formed a high proportion of the old bolsheviks, had suffered particularly severely.[4] The Transcaucasian republics, though as much affected by the purge as any other republics, were still capable of producing an adequate flow of replacements. The Central Asian republics, where the supply of the new type of recruit demanded by the party – the technician or intellectual – was necessarily more limited, had not yet recovered from the blow.

The policy of the party towards the non-Russian nationalities during NEP can be summarized as centralized control of the national parties, comparable to the type of control which was maintained over the subordinate party organizations of RSFSR; and at the same time the building up of local party cadres from among the native population, composed of men who were ready to sacrifice their local national interests to the general All-Union policy of the party. Within these limitations, the party was anxious to avoid exacerbating local national sentiment by any undue assertion of Russian predominance. The Sixteenth Congress in 1930 reiterated the time-honoured warning against the two deviations in policy: 'Great Russian chauvinism' so

---

[1] *PS*, No. 19-20, October 1932, p. 70; No. 19-20, October, p. 21.
[2] Merle Fainsod, *How Russia is Ruled*, Revised edition pp. 266-7.
[3] *ibidem*.
[4] The question of the policy towards the Jews acquired special importance during and after the war, and will be dealt with in a later chapter.

far as the Russians were concerned, and 'local nationalism' so far as the non-Russians were concerned. The resolution did, however, stress that of the two, the former was the greater danger.[1]

In practice in the succeeding years the main blows were directed against local nationalism. The reason for this was plain enough. The rigours of collectivization, the increasingly centralized control imposed from Moscow in the interests of industrial planning, and the general hardship which resulted from the new policy inevitably revived national and anti-Russian feeling among many of the local communists, who had been prepared to accept Moscow's lead in the easier conditions of NEP. Agricultural Ukraine and Belorussia, where resistance to collectivization was strong, were severely affected by the first wave of purges, between 1933 and 1936. In the Ukraine, for example, during 1933 alone over half of all regional party secretaries were purged.[2] The suicide of an old Ukrainian bolshevik, Skrypnik, in protest against the purge, symbolized the change which had taken place in the attitude of many native communists to Moscow. For Skrypnik, although an opponent of the centralization imposed on the national republics in 1923, had nevertheless loyally co-operated with the leaders in Moscow throughout the NEP period.

This first assault on the party organizations in the non-Russian areas, which was mild when compared with the main blow launched in 1937, did not succeed in eliminating all local national loyalties. There is no reason to credit the wild accusations which were made against non-Russian communist leaders during the years of the Ezhov purge – they were no more credible than the accusations made against many other party members at the time, the falsity of which has since been admitted. Nor was national consciousness, let alone separatism, very strongly developed in most of the non-Russian areas – apart from Ukraine and Transcaucasia. But there were at least two reasons which contributed to the development of nationalist, or at all events anti-Russian, feelings among the non-Russian communists in the 30's. One was economic. The system of centralized planning paid little heed to the particular needs of local areas. If it was more rational and economical to grow industrial crops, such as cotton in Uzbekistan, in place of food for local consumption, the plan exacted it. From the point of view of the local area the system, however rational, was unwelcome, because it made such an area dependent for the

[1] *KPSS v rez.*, volume III, p. 21.
[2] The course of the purges among the non-Russian party organizations during the 30's is admirably summarized and analysed in Z. Brzezinski, *The Permanent Purge*, pp. 77–82, and 180–9.

food which it required on the precarious supplies directed from the centre.

The second cause of growing nationalism was one which all colonial powers have lived to experience. The new native communist cadres, raised from a state of backwardness and educated for service as administrators of the colonizing power, grew more conscious of their national pride and began to find the continued tutelage of the Russian communists irksome. This feeling became particularly accentuated in the later 30's, when the practice became established in most of the non-Russian party organizations that while first secretaries might be natives, the second secretaries must be Russians. Since the second secretaries invariably tended to become more important inside the organizations, there was obvious room here for friction.

About the middle of 1937 a co-ordinated assault was launched on all the national parties. In discussing the Ezhov purge there has been occasion to note that it often betrayed a planned and deliberate character. This was particularly clear in the case of the attacks on the national parties. Each was systematically developed according to a fixed pattern, which excluded any possibility of coincidence, and showed that what was intended was not a security operation, but 'social engineering'. In each case the assault began with violent criticism of the local leaders for nationalist deviation. This was then followed by the removal, and usually trial and execution, of the leaders – a number of the leaders of the national parties figured in the show trial of March 1938 along with Bukharin. The elimination of the leaders was then followed by decimation of the party organizations, and by mass arrests both of party and non-party members. All the attacks were launched at about the same time.

When the smoke of battle lifted the pattern of the operation became discernible. Most of the old native leaders who still survived in 1937 had now disappeared. But below them considerable inroads had also been made into the network of subordinate secretaries, the men who had been trained up during the 30's. In the Ukraine, for example, in 1938 nearly half of the secretaries of party organizations were once again replaced.[1] In Georgia, between early 1937 and early 1939, 260 out of a total of less than three hundred first, second and third secretaries of local party committees were replaced,[2] as well as several

---

[1] *Pravda*, 16 June 1938; according to statistics cited by Zhdanov to the Eighteenth Congress, in the mid-1938 elections to party committees the percentage of those replaced varied from 35 in the primary party organizations to 60 in the regional, territorial and republican committees.
[1] *Pravda*, 21 March 1939.

thousand other party officials. It was a salutary lesson to those who wished to rise in the party that nothing less than complete subordination of national interests to the interests of the USSR, as decided by the party leaders in Moscow, would be accepted. On the other hand, for those non-Russians who were prepared to accept this condition, the opportunities to rise were increasing and the prizes high. If the party exacted obedience from and imposed hardships upon the native populations, there was perhaps comfort in the reflection that the unprivileged majority of Russians were little better off. But the years which followed were to show that the bitter feelings, which an essentially Russian party had aroused among some of the populations whom it was seeking to weld together into one state, had not been forgotten.

*   *   *

By 1928 the Soviet Union had emerged from its isolation and had become a force in international relations. It is not possible to trace here the entire course of Soviet foreign policy during the 30's. But it is necessary to point to some aspects of Russian relations with the outside world which illustrate the effects of the domination of Stalin and of the party and its doctrine over Russian foreign policy. Much of Soviet foreign policy from 1928 until the outbreak of the second world war was, of course, unconnected with communism, and represented the ordinary efforts of a growing power to protect its interests in the world around it. But there were three assumptions underlying the foreign relations of the USSR which had been evolved during the 20's and which still coloured most of its decisions. The first assumption was that since conflict between the capitalist states and the USSR was sooner or later inevitable, the only ultimate hope of salvation lay in the furthering of revolution both inside the capitalist states and in their colonial and semi-colonial dependencies. As an immediate aim the policy of exploiting to the full the dissensions between the capitalist states should be pursued. The second principle, already well established by 1928, was that the strength and continued survival of the USSR were the most important factors in the furthering of such revolutions, and that all international revolutionary policy must be subordinated to these immediate objects. The third basic assumption from which the Soviet Union proceeded was that the nature of the capitalist states was such that an avowed policy of subversion directed against them by the USSR did not preclude the maintenance of some semblance of normal relations, and particularly the extended development of trade relations.

Since from Stalin's point of view the preservation of his own position in the party against those who sought to challenge it and the preservation of communist rule in the USSR were one and the same, it followed logically enough that the Comintern should once again, as in the 20's, have become a battle-ground for internal Russian feuds. The change of policy at the Sixth Congress of the Comintern in the summer of 1928, from co-operation with foreign socialist parties to all-out war against them, to which reference has already been made,[1] clearly served to prepare the ground for the elimination both of Bukharin and of those foreign communists who were likely to give him any kind of support. Expulsions of dissidents or potential dissidents soon followed in the various parties of the Comintern, and many of those expelled who were unfortunate enough to find themselves in the USSR during the 30's fell victims to the successive purges. Foreign communists were to learn the lesson during the 30's that there was no middle way for them between subservient acceptance of Moscow's orders and a charge of being agents of the capitalist police.

But the change of policy in the Comintern, in addition to serving the interests of Russian internal struggles, also reflected a growing exasperation with the European socialist parties. Officially the change was justified by the existence of a new revolutionary upsurge. In this revolutionary upsurge, it was argued, the social democratic parties would betray the cause of the proletarian dictatorship. The party of the proletariat, therefore, must work alone for a direct seizure of power, not by the peaceful way of winning a parliamentary majority, but by 'the violent abolition of the power of the bourgeoisie, the destruction of the apparatus of the capitalist state . . . and its replacement by new organs of proletarian power which are, above all, instruments of repression designed to break the resistance of the exploiters'.[2] The unhappy experience with the Kuomintang in China, the fiasco of the Anglo-Russian Trade Union Committee, and continuing strained relations with the German social democrats, who in 1926 added to their unpopularity in the eyes of the Soviet communists by exposing Soviet military co-operation with the German army, offer a more likely explanation. The imposition by the USSR of increasing discipline over the communist parties in Europe to some extent defeated its own purpose. For the more obvious it became that they were little more than the mouthpieces of Moscow, the harder it

[1] See pp. 370–72, above.
[2] *VI Congrès de l'Internationale Communiste (17 juillet-1er septembre 1928). Compte-rendu sténographique.* Paris, 1928, pp. 1597 ff.

became for them to adapt their policies to the internal conditions of their own countries, and consequently to win any mass support.

The rise of national socialism in Germany made no immediate difference to the tactics of the Comintern. The social democrats still remained the principal enemy against whom the efforts of the German communists were to be directed. This policy, which on a number of occasions actually involved co-operation by communists with the national socialists against the social democrats, caused considerable friction among the German communists,[1] and may be presumed to have caused a good deal of private heart-searching among the communis's in Russia as well – open criticism of the policy was of course identified with the 'right' heresy, and was therefore impossible. If there existed at any time the possibility of a socialist victory in Germany as an alternative to a victory for Hitler, the policy of Moscow effectively precluded it. The tactics of the Comintern were officially defended on the grounds that a victory of national socialism in Germany could only be a prelude to a proletarian revolution, a view which was maintained even after Hitler had achieved power in 1933.

However, this comforting illusion could not be kept up indefinitely. According to one circumstantial account, the view that Hitler had come to stay was firmly established in Stalin's mind after Hitler's massacre of his political rivals on 30 June 1934, the 'Night of the Long Knives'.[2] Stalin may even have suffered a pang of jealousy at the thought that his fellow-dictator had succeeded so shortly after coming to power in carrying out the very operation that Stalin was anxious, but as yet unable, to perform. The nationalist resurgence of Germany created a security problem for the USSR. Though the immediate fury of the Third Reich appeared to be directed against the Versailles powers in the West, Hitler's writings left no doubt, for those who troubled to read them, that Russia was no less an object of German territorial ambitions. There was also the probability that Germany would ally herself with Japan for the purpose of a joint assault on the USSR. Moreover, viewed from the communist angle, there was always the possibility to be reckoned with, and therefore at all costs to be prevented, that Germany would in the end join forces with the other 'imperialist' powers for an all-out assault on 'socialist' USSR. This dictated the need for following one of two alternative, and mutually

[1] Margarete Buber-Neumann, *Von Potsdam nach Moskau*, Stationen eines Irrweges, pp. 283–4, 287–93.

[2] W. G. Krivitsky, *I Was Stalin's Agent*, p. 29 – where the date is wrongly given as 13 June 1934.

exclusive, courses – alliance with Germany, or alliance with the Versailles powers, and particularly with France. Logically there should have been no distinction from a communist point of view between an alliance with Germany and an alliance with any other 'capitalist' power. All were assumed to be equally bad, unreliable and ultimately hostile, and the question of an alliance was purely one of expediency, in the interests of strengthening by tactical means the position of the USSR. As Stalin pointed out at the Seventeenth Party Congress in January 1934, the existence of a fascist régime in Germany was no more of an obstacle to good relations between the USSR and Germany than the Italian régime, which had not precluded 'the most excellent relations'.[1]

But logic is not always the sole factor in determining judgement, even where communists are concerned. There is no doubt that for communists of the type of Bukharin, and for the many older bolsheviks who thought like him without daring to say so, the idea of an alliance with a power as openly predatory and barbarous as national socialist Germany was much more abhorrent than a policy of alliance with the more orthodox 'imperialists'. At the same Congress Bukharin, who, in the atmosphere of comparative conciliation with the opposition which then prevailed, was allowed to make a penitent speech, devoted much of his time to an attack on Hitler, reinforced with quotations from national socialist writings.[2] The contrast in tone with Stalin's references to Germany was striking. There can be no doubt that a policy of alliance with Germany would have met with considerable resistance in the party so long as any of the older, more traditional type of revolutionaries survived inside it. Conversely, it is not too fanciful to suppose that Stalin's victory over the old bolsheviks, their surrender even, in some cases, was in part assured by the fact that at the time when it took place the Soviet Union was in the forefront of the fight against Hitler, and the need for unity to defend socialism against the forces of darkness was felt to be paramount. It was not an accident that the last article which Bukharin was allowed to publish in 1936 was a bitter attack on German fascism.[3]

[1] *XVII S''ezd*, p. 13.
[2] *ibidem*, pp. 127–9. It will be recalled that in 1928 Bukharin had already been privately opposed to the Comintern policy of all out attack on the social democratic parties – see p. 372, above.
[3] See 'Marshruty istorii', *Izvestiia*. 6 July 1936. It is arguable that Bukharin, in this article, while outwardly contrasting the merits of the Soviet constitution with the defects of Nazi Germany, was inwardly aware that the parallel between the two countries was closer than the contrast, and that the article was therefore an act of cryptic opposition.

From Stalin's point of view, an alliance with Germany offered certain advantages over an alliance with the Versailles powers. There were first of all the traditional ties established since 1922 in the Treaty of Rapallo, which the USSR was certainly reluctant to break. There was the important link of trade – during the period of the First Five Year Plan Germany was far and away the largest single source of Russian imports, and second only to Britain as a customer for Russian exports. Finally, a deal between two dictators always presents certain attractions with which democracies cannot compete – absolute secrecy, freedom from interference by public opinion, a greater lack of scruples over the rights of other states which may be affected by the deal – in short, all those aspects of diplomacy to which the term 'realism' is euphemistically applied by dictators of the right and left alike. But whatever hopes Stalin may have had of an alliance with Germany were rebuffed by Hitler. On 26 January 1934 an agreement between Poland and Germany aroused Soviet suspicions that these two powers were contemplating a deal at Russia's expense. Shortly afterwards, on 14 April 1934, Germany rejected a Russian proposal for a joint Russo-German guarantee of Finland and the three Baltic states. The USSR was naturally anxious to consolidate its relations with the states bordering upon its frontiers by stronger means than the pacts of non-aggression by which it was already bound to its neighbours. But these states, which had formed part of the Russian Empire, were equally naturally suspicious of any Soviet guarantee to which no other great power was a party, for fear that it might be used as a pretext for reabsorbing them into the USSR. In the case of Poland there was the additional apprehension that the USSR would not remain content with the present frontier, which left a number of Ukrainians in Poland, and which Poland had been able to exact from a weakened Russia in 1920 only as a result of military victory.

Since there were no prospects of better relations with Germany, the consolidation of relationships with the other Western powers, and particularly France, was a natural development in Russian policy. An important step in this direction had already been made at the end of 1933, when the United States recognized the Soviet Union. Negotiations with France which began in the spring of 1934 culminated with the entry of the Soviet Union into the League of Nations in September 1934, and a Franco-Soviet Treaty of mutual assistance, signed on 2 May 1935. A fortnight later a mutual assistance pact in similar terms was also signed between the Soviet Union and Czechoslovakia. But it contained the stipulation that the provisions for mutual assistance should only come into force if and when France came to the aid of the signatory which was the victim of an attack.

Hitherto the Soviet Union had been an implacable opponent of the League of Nations. It had, it is true, participated after 1928 in the negotiations for disarmament conducted under the auspices of the League. Its far-reaching proposals for universal disarmament were admittedly[1] designed for purposes of propaganda, in order to expose the lack of serious intention on the part of the leading members of the League to reach agreement on disarmament – a not very difficult task. But after 1934 Soviet intentions were different: to help to make the anti-Axis alliance which the League represented, after the departure of Germany, Italy and Japan, into an effective bulwark against the aggressive ambitions of these three powers. In this respect the record of the USSR as a member of the League was neither better nor worse than that of other members, and in some instances the Soviet Union was prepared to go further than other powers. The Soviet Union had, however, little use for much of the mechanism of co-operation which the League was trying to develop, and no use at all for arbitration or judicial settlement.[2]

The entry of the USSR into the League inaugurated a halcyon period in relations with other states. Efforts were now made to wipe out the impression left in the minds of the non-communist powers that the USSR was an outcast planning to subvert the rest of the world. In this new role a considerable share of the success belonged to M. Litvinov, the People's Commissar for Foreign Affairs, whose detestation of Hitler's régime was not in doubt, and who, aided by his British-born wife, made a favourable impression on the representatives of the powers with whom he came into contact at Geneva. The USSR now put itself forward as the leading champion in the resistance to Hitler. The menace of German aggression was growing, and, as it grew, so did the number of those who were prepared to be convinced that the Soviet Union was a vital factor in keeping it in check.

When the Seventh Congress of the Comintern met in July and August 1935 it endeavoured to exploit this new situation, without at the same time abandoning the ultimate aim of revolution. In yet another of its characteristic swift turns of policy the Comintern now called for 'a united front with the social democratic workers' or a 'broad people's front with those labouring masses who are still far

[1] E.g. in the resolution on this subject of the Sixth Congress of the Comintern, *VI Congrès de l'Internationale Communiste*, p. 1,724.
[2] See my 'Soviet Participation in International Institutions', *Year Book of World Affairs*, volume III, 1949, pp. 205–40.

from communism, but who nevertheless can join us in the struggle against fascism . . .'. Communist parties were blamed for having in the past treated every bourgeois party as identical with the fascists; the working class was now enjoined to preserve bourgeois, parliamentary democracy, until such time as it could be replaced by 'proletarian democracy'. Communist parties were to join with other parties, if need be, but they must (rather like the social democrats in the Duma) constantly expose their treachery to the working class, and remember that the ultimate object was still proletarian leadership.[1]

The Soviet Union thus endeavoured to promote the immediate tactical aim of organizing resistance to Germany without abandoning its ultimate objectives. It was not an easy task. Internal developments inside the USSR, in spite of extensive propaganda woven around the new constitution, and in spite of the almost unlimited credulity of the intellectuals in many countries outside the USSR, were a stern reminder that 'proletarian democracy' meant something very different from what the terms might imply in their normal, non-communist usage. The Moscow-dominated communist parties in the various European countries faced an uphill task in their new role of political parties claiming to serve the best national interests of their own country. The inconsistency in the position of the Soviet Union remained – that of claiming to be a loyal member of a community of non-communist states, while at the same time maintaining an organization of which the avowed aim was the subversion of the Western democratic system of government. Far from admitting any past intentions to promote world revolution, Stalin now blandly denied that the Soviet Union had at any time ever entertained such an idea. 'If you think,' he told an American press correspondent on 1 March 1936, 'that the Soviet people want to change the face of surrounding states, and by forcible means at that, you are mistaken.' When the correspondent asked him if that meant that the original plans and intentions of bringing about a world revolution had now been abandoned, Stalin retorted: 'We never had such plans and intentions.'[2] But two years later, in February 1938, he wrote that 'the political assistance of the working class in the bourgeois countries for the working class of our country must be organized' as a defence against capitalist encirclement.[3] Thus, if Stalin during the later 30's was

---

[1] See the resolutions of the Congress printed in *VII Congress of the Communist International*, Abridged Stenographic Report of Proceedings, Moscow, 1939, pp. 565–603.
[2] Interview with Roy Howard, *New York Times*, 6 March 1936.
[3] In *Bol'shevik*, No. 2, February 1938.

prepared to allow Litvinov to attempt to build up a genuine coalition against Germany, he was, to use a phrase of Lenin's 'keeping a stone up his sleeve'.

Nor did Stalin during that time abandon his endeavours, now conducted in the greatest secrecy, to pursue his original plan of an alliance with Hitler. In July 1934, while the negotiations for the Franco-Soviet pact were in progress, the French claimed to have reliable information that the Russians were also sounding out the possibility of a pact with Germany.[1] Secret negotiations, as we now know, were also conducted by the Soviet trade representative in Berlin, Kandelaki, at the end of 1936 and the beginning of 1937, though once again without success.[2] If it was true that the European powers never fully trusted communist USSR or welcomed her as an ally, it was also true that the Soviet Union never regarded her closer relations with the West as more than a tactical step towards the ultimate objective: the consolidation and expansion of Soviet power.

Given this atmosphere of mutual distrust, the policy of collective security against German expansion stood little chance of success. By 1928, when Hitler's demands on Czechoslovakia brought Europe to the verge of war, relations between the USSR on the one hand and Britain and France on the other were strained and distant. Stalin's part in the Spanish civil war (for this was essentially Stalin's policy, and not Litvinov's) did not improve the standing of the Soviet Union as an ally against fascism. It soon became evident that the Soviet Union, for all its professions of solidarity with the republican cause, was less concerned to ensure victory over the insurgents and their German and Italian allies than to establish its own control over the government of Spain. In the midst of a life-and-death struggle, the NKVD went about its bizarre business of trials, executions and purges of Trotskyists and other dissidents who abounded in the motley Spanish and volunteer left-wing organizations. Within the republican government itself, those members who enjoyed the confidence of the USSR, and were indeed its agents, intrigued and plotted against the others. Many illusions on the nature of Russian communist rule were

---

[1] *Documents on British Foreign Policy 1919–1939*, Second Series, volume VI: 1933–34, London, 1957, pp. 875–7.
[2] These very secret negotiations were first disclosed by Krivitsky, *op. cit.*, pp. 37–9. That they in fact took place is now confirmed in a personal dispatch from Neurath to Schacht, dated 11 February 1937, from which it is clear that Kandelaki, in the name of Stalin and Molotov, put out feelers for an agreement with Germany but was rebuffed by Hitler. The document is among the files of the German Foreign Ministry which fell into Allied hands during the Second World War. I am indebted to Professor John Erickson for a copy of this document. See also Schacht to Neurath, dated 6 February 1937, *ibidem*.

shattered in the Spanish civil war. Moreover, confidence in the value of the Soviet Union as a military ally had been undermined by the execution of the leading members of the Red Army command in June 1937 and the extensive purging of the army.

Thus it was perhaps understandable that Britain and France should have preferred to meet the Czech crisis of 1938 alone. The agreement with Germany at Munich in September 1938, which left Czechoslovakia at the mercy of the Germans, was arrived at without the participation of the USSR. This is not the place to discuss the wisdom, or the ethics, of the Munich agreement. But it is probable that Stalin drew from it the conclusion that the Western powers were leaving Germany a free hand against the USSR. If so, he was wrong, because the German intention was to attack first in the west. For this Germany required assurance that her rear in the east would not be in danger of attack. The Germans rightly drew the conclusion that the collapse of the system of collective security, as shown by the Munich agreement, raised the prospects of 'a more positive attitude on the part of the Soviet Union towards Germany',[1] but waited for the USSR to make the first move. For Germany, having rebuffed several advances by Stalin in the past, could not be sure that the USSR would not use negotiations with Germany merely as a lever for exerting pressure on Britain and France. The first tentative approach was made by the Russian ambassador in Berlin on 17 April 1939. On 3 May Litvinov, the architect of the policy of collective security, was replaced by Molotov, Stalin's close associate.

During the spring and summer of 1939 the Soviet Union simultaneously conducted negotiations with Germany, and with Britain and France. So far as the negotiations with the Western powers were concerned, there was little enthusiasm for an alliance on either side. Britain, at any rate, was unwilling to join with the USSR in guaranteeing the Baltic states, as the Russians demanded, without the consent of those states. Plainly, to have done so would have amounted to giving the Soviet Union a free hand to annex them. Poland was unwilling to grant the Soviet Union right of passage for the Red Army. In an article published in *Pravda* on 29 June 1939 Zhdanov accused Britain and France of using the negotiations merely as cover for making a deal with Germany. The description was perhaps more applicable to the attitude of the USSR. A fortnight before this article appeared the Soviet Union had conveyed to the Germans that

---

[1] On 3 October 1938 – see *Documents on German Foreign Policy*, Series D (1937–1945), volume IV: *The Aftermath of Munich*, London, 1951, pp. 602–3.

although Russia was negotiating with Britain and France, a rapprochement with Germany was closest to her desires.[1] Negotiations now proceeded simultaneously, publicly with Britain and France in Moscow, and secretly in Berlin. On 22 August 1939 it was announced that the German Foreign Minister, von Ribbentrop, was on his way to Moscow, and on the following day a Treaty of Non-Aggression was signed between the Soviet Union and Germany. By the terms of a secret protocol annexed to the Treaty, the three Baltic states and about half of the territory of Poland were recognized as being within the sphere of influence of the USSR 'in the event of a territorial and political rearrangement'. Germany also declared her 'complete political disinterestedness' in Bessarabia.[2]

In retrospect such events as the appointment of Molotov or Zhdanov's article may look like pointers to the impending change of Soviet policy towards Germany. At the time the secrecy of the negotiations with Germany was such that the Treaty of 23 August came like a bombshell. No one could doubt that it was the prelude to war. On 1 September 1939 Germany invaded Poland, and on 3 September Britain and France declared war on Germany in fulfilment of a guarantee to Poland which had been given the previous March. For the communist parties both in Russia and in Europe, particularly in Britain and in France, the Russian change of front was a supreme test of discipline. The Soviet Union had changed overnight from foremost champion against the German aggressors into an ally, even an accomplice, of Hitler. The communist parties came out of the test with flying colours. The British and French parties in particular showed that they were steadfast enough not only to put Soviet interests before those of their own countries, but indeed to remain unaffected by the vital peril in which their countries now found themselves. They denounced their governments as aggressors, and, echoing Molotov, ridiculed the suggestion that an ideology such as national socialism could be destroyed by force, or by a 'senseless and criminal war . . . camouflaged as a fight for "democracy"'.[3] Inside the USSR not a ripple of dissent or question appeared within the cowed and silenced party. Stalin's methods of remoulding the party, if stern, had at any rate been thorough.

[1] *Nazi-Soviet Relations 1939–1941*, Documents from the Archives of the German Foreign Office, edited by Raymond James Sontag and James Stuart Beddie, Washington D.C., 1948, pp. 20–1.
[2] *ibidem*, pp. 76–8.
[3] See Molotov's speech of 31 October 1939, reprinted in Jane Degras (editor), *Soviet Documents on Foreign Policy*, volume III, Oxford, 1953, pp. 388–400.

XXVII The War: Party Control over the Army

Peace for the USSR had been secured by the German treaty. Stalin's ambition of a pact with Hitler, which would leave the USSR immune while war was unleashed on the Western powers, was now, after years of patient effort, crowned with success. But the territorial advantages which Stalin had secured involved the Soviet Union in immediate military commitments. The expansion of Soviet territory which now took place followed the pattern which had been apparent in the eve of war negotiations with the Western European powers, who had refused to concede to the Soviet Union the kind of security for its frontiers which it demanded.

About a fortnight after the German invasion of Poland, the Red Army moved in to occupy the Polish territory which fell to the Soviet sphere by agreement with Germany. It was no temporary military occupation: the territories overrun were incorporated in the Soviet Union, communist party rule was extended over them, and elections on the Soviet model were held to confirm the political change. Shortly afterwards pacts of military assistance were concluded with the three Baltic states, Latvia, Lithuania and Estonia, which were now isolated and unable to expect any support from Germany's enemies. As the Baltic states had always feared, the military pacts were, in June 1940, followed by Soviet-sponsored political *coups* inside each of the three countries and in each case incorporation into the USSR as a Union republic resulted. In the same month a claim was made to Rumania for the return of Bessarabia, which the RSFSR had been forced to cede to Rumania in 1918. A demand was made at the same time for the cession of the adjoining province of Northern Bukovina, although this had never been part of the Russian Empire, and had not formed the subject of any agreement with Germany in August 1939. Rumania was unable to resist these demands, and shortly afterwards Bessarabia and Northern Bukovina were also incorporated into the USSR.

In contrast to the Baltic states and Rumania, Finland resisted

Soviet demands. Negotiations broke down in November 1939, both sides mobilized, and the Red Army attacked on 30 November. In spite of the disparity of forces on the two sides, the stubborn resistance of the Finnish troops, the difficulty of the terrain, the disorganization of the Red Army as a consequence of the purge and the reluctance of the Soviet troops to fight a war of invasion with which they had little sympathy, all combined to extend the campaign for four months.

The attack on Finland embittered Soviet relations with the Western powers. But the impotent gesture of expelling the Soviet Union from the League of Nations – a sanction which the League had never dared apply to other aggressor states like Japan or Italy – infuriated the Russians without helping the Finns. Meanwhile relations between the two dictators were also showing signs of strain. The annexation of Northern Bukovina, the sovietization of the Baltic states and continued Soviet interest in the Balkans alarmed Hitler, while German military moves in territories closely bordering on the Soviet Union caused anxiety to Stalin. On 13 November 1940 Molotov travelled to Berlin for conversations with the German Foreign Minister. He was offered an extensive, if vague, share in the assets of the British Empire, of which the imminent liquidation was assumed, at any rate on the German side, but received little satisfaction on the more concrete problems of Finland, Bulgaria and the Turkish Straits which preoccupied the Soviet Union. Five weeks later, on 18 December 1940, Hitler signed the directive for 'Operation Barbarossa', according to which the 'German Armed Forces must be prepared to crush Soviet Russia in a quick campaign, even before the conclusion of the war against England'. Thereafter Hitler sidestepped all approaches by the Soviet Union aimed at resolving mounting tension by diplomatic means.[1]

It was therefore in conditions of increasing stress in its foreign relations that the party tackled its problems at home during the two years' respite purchased by means of the pact with Germany. After 1939 the party was engaged in extending its control over both agriculture and industry. In agriculture its main aim was to wean the peasant from his attachment to his private plot and to encourage him to increase production on the collectivized sector. At its Eighteenth Conference, which met in February 1941, the party took general stock of its relations with economic enterprises. It resolved that party organizations

---

[1] See on this period *Nazi-Soviet Relations 1939–1941*, Documents from the Archives of the German Foreign Office, edited by Raymond James Sontag and James Stuart Beddie, pp. 247 *et seq.*

had been concentrating their efforts on agriculture to the detriment of industry. Local party organizations, it was stated, had been tending to leave the actual control over industrial enterprises to the industrial commissariats, in the mistaken belief that it was the commissariats and not the party organizations which were responsible for such supervision.

Party organizations were also enjoined to play their part in ensuring the strict enforcement of the twin principles which had become cardinal in Soviet industrial policy since the 30's: differential payment for work and the undivided authority of the factory director. Party bodies were also told to see to the strict enforcement of the severe code of works discipline which had been enacted on 26 June 1940 (when the eight-hour day was also introduced in place of the seven-hour day guaranteed by the constitution). The discussions and decisions of this conference once again illustrated, but did not resolve, the difficulty which must necessarily arise under a system which maintains two parallel organizations of party and state machinery for purposes of administrative control. The conference also touched on another perennial problem – the hostility of the factory director to party propaganda discussion meetings which from his point of view wasted valuable working time without contributing anything of immediately apparent use. Party organizations were now ordered to conduct their political activities outside working hours.[1]

The invasion of Soviet territory by the Germans on 22 June 1941 found the country quite unprepared, both militarily and industrially. Industrial undertakings were hastily evacuated eastwards as the Germans advanced rapidly into the country, and there was naturally a delay before they could be made ready for the production of the vital arms and supplies.[2] After Stalin's death, his successors attempted to lay the blame for Russia's unpreparedness upon his improvidence in ignoring repeated warnings from his military advisers and from diplomatic representatives abroad of the impending German invasion.[3] The subsequent recovery by the country of its powers of resistance is correspondingly laid to the credit of 'the party'. Notwithstanding the undoubtedly vast degree of personal control which Stalin exercised during these years, this view would seem to be an over-simplification.

---

[1] *KPSS v rez.*, volume III, pp. 425–36.

[2] Some 1,300 plants were thus evacuated from an area which in 1940 was responsible for about a third of all industrial production – Harry Schwartz, *Russia's Soviet Economy*, pp. 203–4.

[3] See e.g. N. S. Khrushchev's speech at the Twentieth Party Congress in 1956, *The Anti-Stalin Campaign and International Communism*, pp. 43–6.

For, in the first place, the failure to prepare for the possibility of war with Germany was less the failure of Stalin than an inherent feature of a totalitarian régime: having switched the machinery of mind control to the task of making the surprise pact with Hitler acceptable, it was not possible at the same time to prepare the country for a war which the wisdom of its rulers was hitherto supposed to have averted. And secondly, even if the failure was due to the improvidence of this one man, then 'the party' could scarcely avoid the responsibility for having committed its destinies in this manner to a dictator whom it could not control.

The shock of the German invasion was immediately reflected in the forms which party government now assumed. The gravity and suddenness of the emergency compelled a streamlining of the dictatorship, and the cautious intrigues of the second-rank leaders which had hitherto gone on under Stalin became subordinated to the overriding needs of efficiency.

It will be recalled that after the Eighteenth Congress in 1939 a division was discernible in the party leadership between the two groups which were described as the old and the neo-Stalinists, with the older Stalinists still in the leading positions, and the newer men still in the lower ranks of the leadership, but pressing fast on their heels.[1] We shall hereafter mainly be concerned with Molotov, Kaganovich and Mikoyan among the older established, and with Malenkov, Beria, Voznesenskii and Khrushchev among the newer men. Zhdanov, though perhaps not so readily classifiable, may none the less be counted as a new Stalinist, and was by 1939 already a full member of the Politburo; Khrushchev was also a full member; Beria was a candidate member. The period between the Eighteenth Congress and the outbreak of the war in June 1941 had witnessed the rapid rise in the hierarchy of both Malenkov and Voznesenskii. Malenkov, who as one of the four secretaries of the Central Committee Secretariat was in charge of the all important Cadres Directorate, entered the Politburo as a candidate member in February 1941, along with two fellow 'new Stalinists', Shcherbakov and Voznesenskii. (Shcherbakov died in 1945.) Voznesenskii, a specialist in economic planning, had risen rapidly to prominence during the purge years as a protégé of Zhdanov. He had been chairman of *Gosplan* since 1938, and a deputy chairman of the Council of People's Commissars since 1939, in charge of defence industry. At the same time, in February 1941, Beria became a deputy chairman of the Council of People's Commissars,

[1] See pp. 445–7, above.

presumably to act as co-ordinating commissar for security, which was now split into two commissariats – for Interior Affairs (NKVD) and for State Security (NKGB).

The rise of Malenkov and Voznesenskii, the one a specialist in the manipulation of the party apparatus, the other an industrial planner, may have been part of a deliberate policy on Stalin's part to maintain the balance between the generations while allowing new blood to come to the fore both in the party and in the government machines. At any rate, up till the outbreak of war a parallel balancing of old and new Stalinists was discernible in the two machines. In the Secretariat Malenkov and the much senior Andreev were, next to Stalin, in charge of all day-to-day work. Malenkov, in charge of cadres, was at the same time in overall charge of all industry, since the industrial committees of the local party organizations were subordinated to his department at the centre.[1] Andreev's sphere of activity was agriculture, for which in one capacity or another he was to retain responsibility until his sudden eclipse in 1950. The fourth secretary, Zhdanov, was mainly active in Leningrad, where he was to remain right through the war until the end of 1944. He was succeeded soon after the Eighteenth Congress as head of the Agitation and Propaganda Directorate by G. F. Aleksandrov, though he may have retained overall responsibility for this work in the Politburo.

On the government side, the parallel economic machine up till the war was the Economic Council attached to the Council of People's Commissars (*Ekonomsovet*). Its chairman was Molotov, but next in importance to Molotov, as becomes evident if one examines the decrees issued by this body and the signatures appended to them, were Mikoyan and Bulganin – an 'old Stalinist' and a new. Voznesenskii was a member of *Ekonomsovet*, which also included three men, all under forty, who belonged to the new class of technically trained party members, who had risen rapidly in the course of the purges – Malyshev, Pervukhin and Kosygin. *Ekonomsovet* was given enormous powers. It acted as an inner cabinet co-ordinating the whole economy – producing annual and quarterly plans, reporting and checking on fulfilment, dealing with prices, wages and labour questions. Its decisions were obligatory on all central and local government organs. Since the party Secretariat, in the persons of Malenkov and Andreev, was likewise given overall responsibility for the whole economy, the one for industry by virtue of his control over personnel, the other for agriculture, it is to say the least probable that this dual form of control

[1] See pp. 455–6, above.

gave rise to friction. That the system was workable at all was no doubt due to the concentration of a great deal of decision making in Stalin's hands.

However, the outbreak of war produced an immediate rationalization of this dual system of government. On the eve of the war, on 6 May, Stalin had assumed the post of chairman of the Council of People's Commissars in addition to that of secretary of the party. It was the first time in the history of the country that the party and government apparatus were thus openly fused. On 30 June 1941, after the outbreak of war, the State Committee of Defence, or GOKO, was set up, consisting at first of Stalin, Molotov, Voroshilov, Malenkov and Beria. This committee was given absolute power and authority over all party, government, military and other organizations throughout the country.[1] The whole system of balance between the party organizations on the one hand and the Soviet and economic organizations on the other, which it had been found necessary to maintain, however imperfectly, even in gravest emergencies in the past, was thus swept aside. Malenkov and Beria had been promoted to the innermost centre of policy making over the heads of much more experienced men, including six who, unlike themselves, were already full members of the Politburo: Kaganovich, Mikoyan, Andreev, Kalinin, Khrushchev and Zhdanov. Outside GOKO Voznesenskii became the main figure in economic administration – again over the heads of his older colleagues like Mikoyan and Kaganovich. This is evident from the fact that until late 1942 Voznesenskii's signature appeared on all decrees relating to economic matters which were not signed by Stalin himself. The balance between the more senior and the newer men was somewhat redressed in February 1942 when both Kaganovich and Mikoyan were co-opted into GOKO, along with Voznesenskii. Thereafter its composition remained unchanged, except that in 1944 Bulganin, who had been successfully carrying out political duties at the front, succeeded Voroshilov, at the same time becoming deputy to Stalin in the Commissariat of Defence. Kaganovich's return to prominence after 1939 was completed when he was made a deputy chairman of the Council of People's Commissars in December 1944.

The keynote of wartime administration was rationalization. One sign of this was the bringing back into highest prominence of the men whom Stalin had hitherto allowed to drop to secondary positions, but whose experience was now required. Another was the complete fusion

[1] *Pravda*, 1 July 1941.

of the government and party machines which until the war Stalin had maintained as separate and competing administrations, presumably with considerations of power in mind, but to the sacrifice of efficiency. The individual members of GOKO assumed responsibility for the principal branches of production, irrespective of the place which they occupied in one or other administrative machine.[1] Moreover, the principal conflict between the party and industry, the selection of personnel, was resolved in favour of industry: the Cadres Directorate now became an overall supervisory body, which no longer, as hitherto, acted as an executive body interfering down to the lowest levels both in the selection of personnel and in the running of industrial undertakings, but allowed much greater initiative to enterprises acting in co-operation with the local party organizations.[2]

The impact of the war on the relations of the party with the population over which it ruled was enormous. Of course, the sense of common danger made the people readier to accept the even more stringent control which the new system implied. But the control exercised by the party was administrative rather than ideological, at any rate during the most critical period of the war. It was significant that while the danger was gravest, when even the issue of survival hung in the balance, party and socialist slogans virtually disappeared from official propaganda and were replaced by patriotic and nationalist appeals. Thus, a programme of lectures designed for nation-wide propaganda in July 1941 by the party propaganda organs included not one single reference either to the party or to socialism: the stress was entirely on the fatherland, on national defence, on the heroism of the people, on the partisans and on similar themes.

When, however, the tide of defeat began to turn, at the end of 1942 and the beginning of 1943, party and socialist themes began to reappear in propaganda, and party organizations were rated for having neglected such subjects hitherto. Stalin's wartime speeches reflect this change. His first speech after the German invasion, on 3 July 1941, following nearly a fortnight's ominous silence by the Leader during which panic and speculation were rife, called upon his 'Brothers and sisters' to resist the invader in the name of the fatherland. In November 1943, in contrast, the entire stress was upon the party as the

---

[1] Molotov for tanks, Beria for armaments and munitions, Malenkov for aircraft, and Mikoyan for food and fuel. This appears from the citations to the awards of decorations made to them in September 1943.

[2] See an article by N. N. Shatalin, Malenkov's deputy and, after March 1946, successor in the Cadres Directorate, in *PS*, October 1943: cf. *ibidem*, December 1943, an article by N. Semin.

organizer of the armed struggle and the inspirer of the victory which was now in sight. 'During the war,' Stalin asserted, 'the party has still further cemented its kinship with the people.'[1]

This assertion was perhaps more significant as heralding the revival of the traditional view of the party than as a statement of fact. The complex and ambivalent relations between the party and the population during the years of trial and hardship spanned by the war do not lend themselves to any simple formula. Some more detailed analysis of the question must be attempted, since it is of immense importance for the understanding of all subsequent developments in the party. The historian, moreover, can draw not only on information published in the Soviet Union, but on the great material contained in official German documents, and on the testimony of tens of thousands of Soviet citizens who fled from, or were displaced from, Soviet territory during the war and who did not return.[2]

The failure on the Soviet side to prepare enabled the German attack against numerically superior forces to achieve a rapid success. No plans for withdrawal by the Red Army had been made, vast numbers of troops were encircled and enormous quantities of material and equipment captured and destroyed. Over two million prisoners were taken in the first four months of the war, and Soviet losses in tanks were estimated by the Germans at 17,500. The inference that this very large number of prisoners in the initial stages of the campaign was entirely due to mass surrenders would be erroneous: numerous German accounts not intended for publication stress the stubborn resistance of the Soviet troops. Mass surrender, where it did take place, was often due to encirclement, disorganization and isolation. Indeed the Germans, who had calculated on widespread disaffection among the troops facing them, were themselves taken by surprise. By the end of 1941 the Red Army was fighting stubbornly and well: the command had recovered from its initial disorganization, reserves were coming up, and morale was reinforced by reports of German atrocities

---

[1] *Pravda*, 4 July 1941 snd 8 November 1943; for analysis of war-time propaganda see David J. Dallin, *The Changing World of Soviet Russia*, Oxford, 1956, pp. 197–203.

[2] The literature on Soviet Russia under occupation is enormous. Among the more important recent works which are of relevance may be mentioned: Alexander Dallin, *German Rule in Russia 1941–1945*, A Study of Occupation Policies, London, 1957; George Fischer, *Soviet Opposition to Stalin*, A Case Study in World War II, Cambridge, Mass., 1952; Juergen Thorwald, *Wen sie verderben wollen*, Stuttgart, 1952; Leon Gouré and Herbert S. Dinerstein, *Moscow in Crisis*, Glencoe, Illinois, 1955; D. Karov, *Partizanskoe dvizhenie v SSSR v 1941–1945 gg.*, Munich, 1954; John A. Armstrong (ed.), *Soviet Partisans in World War II*, Madison, Wisconsin, 1964.

filtering back from the occupied areas of Russia. The early disasters suffered by the Red Army were due to failure of leadership as much as to loss of morale.[1]

While it is fair to blame the party for this failure, since it had long assumed the monopoly of all leadership in the country and ousted all rival authority,[2] in a party as centralized as the Soviet communist party the blame must fall primarily on the top hierarchy. Lower down, party members tackled a desperate situation with ruthlessness, but with courage and determination. Both the political and the security networks played a big part in restoring morale inside the army. But the Germans themselves made no small contribution towards strengthening the morale of their adversaries. They had embarked on the campaign without any clear plan for the future of the Soviet Union after conquest, let alone any policy designed to wean the allegiance of the civilian population from its government. For Hitler, confident of rapid victory, the sole aim was the subjugation of the country by his occupying forces for the better exploitation of resources and with no regard for the population. Whatever sufferings the Soviet population had been forced to bear under its communist rulers, it soon learned that the invader's rule was in no way preferable. No preparation of any kind had been made by the Germans for the reception of the numerous prisoners who fell into their hands. They did not need them in the early stages of the war and were content to leave them to rot. Between two and three million prisoners out of a total of over five million either died or were exterminated in the course of the war.[3] News of their sufferings travelled from the occupied areas across the front line and helped to stiffen the morale both of the troops and of the as yet unconquered civilian population.

This brutal conduct of the Germans was also politically shortsighted. There was enough discontent and resentment among the population of the Soviet Union which a more intelligent, more humane and less avaricious conqueror could have exploited. During

---

[1] See on this question Raymond L. Garthoff, *How Russia Makes War*, Soviet Military Doctrine, pp. 423–36; and see also Malcolm Mackintosh, *Juggernaut: A History of the Soviet Armed Forces*, London, 1967, chapters vii and viii.

[2] The question whether there had been failure to prepare for the possibility of a German attack was the subject of acrimonious debate between spokesmen of the army and of the party apparatus point of view in 1956. The army view was that the retreat in the first stages of the campaign in 1941 had been unplanned and forced upon the army by lack of any adequate preparation. The party spokesmen at first contested this view – not unnaturally, since it was upon the party that responsibility for failure to make adequate preparation primarily fell – but in the end were forced to concede that the view of the army spokesmen was correct. See *Voennyi vestnik*, April 1956, and *Krasnaia zvezda*, 9 May and 3 August 1956.

[3] A Dallin, *op. cit.*, pp. 426–7.

the first weeks, while the Germans were advancing through territory which until 1939 or 1940 had formed no part of the USSR, they were received with open welcome. But even in territory which had experienced over twenty years of Soviet rule, the attitude of the bulk of the population varied from hopeful friendliness to cautious but passive expectation.[1] A study of the behaviour of the population of Moscow, when German occupation appeared imminent in October 1941, reveals that passive inertia was the mood of the majority. For a few days all seemed lost, and authority seems to have broken down at the top. In this crisis a minority looked forward to the imminent entry of the Germans as an unmixed blessing. Another minority, mainly consisting of young men in the factories, evinced enthusiastic support for the threatened Soviet régime. But the great majority passively accepted the prospect of collapse of the régime, and hoped for the best under German rule. There was no open hostility to communism, except in a few instances, no sign of any underground movement or spontaneous organization as an alternative to communism, let alone of revolt. When once the party leaders had recovered from their panic, the population once again obeyed them. As for the party officials, no signs of wavernig in their support of the régime appeared among them. Whether this loyalty was due to conviction or to fear of the treatment which the Germans were known to mete out to party officials was, from the point of view of the régime, immaterial.[2]

The attitude of Moscow was probably a fair index of the temper of the population in the areas inhabited by Russians. There was certainly none of that love for or confidence in the party which was the stock theme of party propaganda. When faced with an imminent alternative to communist rule, the population showed no inclination at all to fight to the last ditch for communism, readily accepted its demise, and looked with hope to what the new rulers would offer. But aside from the party there was no organization and, with a few exceptions, no leadership. The position was different in the newly incorporated areas – the Baltic States and Western Ukraine – and in many parts of Central Asia and the Caucasus. Here vigorous anti-communist resistance movements sprang up, many of which were to continue their underground struggle for years after the war had ended.

The party, and especially the NKVD, played an important and vital

[1] *ibidem*, p. 65.

[2] On Moscow see the careful and moderate study by Gouré and Dinerstein, referred to in note 2, page 500, which is based on the accounts of many eyewitnesses.

role in organizing the partisan movement in the territories occupied by the Germans. The partisan movement during the war re-enacted on a small scale the course of the revolution and the civil war – an anarchical mass revolt against authority was largely disciplined, canalized and moulded into a purposeful whole, often against its will, by a communist organization. In spite of assertions to the contrary by both belligerents, the Soviet authorities had apparently made no preparations before the outbreak of war for partisan activity in the event of enemy occupation. Indeed there was little partisan activity at all in the first six months of the war. But by the end of 1941, as a combined reaction both to the breakdown of control by the central party authority in the unoccupied territory and to the behaviour of the German occupation authorities, a sizeable number of partisan bands had spontaneously sprung up. Though patriotically opposed to the invader, these bands were often far from enthusiastic in their attitude to the Soviet authority. With more hope than political realism they took to the woods, and while harrying the enemy with their raids, were equally determined to enjoy the unwonted sweets of freedom from restraint for as long as they could. This mood seems to have predominated even in some cases where the leaders of the bands were old party members with partisan experience in the civil war.

The party leaders, not unnaturally, regarded this movement with suspicion until such time as they were able to assert control over it. The lower level party organizations in the territories overrun by the Germans had been instructed to go underground. They attempted to form partisan bands on their own. But in the absence of central leadership and support, during the months before contact could be established, their efforts to extend control over the few existing partisan bands made comparatively little progress. Their main task was to prevent collaboration between the civilian population and the occupying authorities by means of terrorist acts against both – an activity which considerably helped to break down German morale, but also served to remind the Russian population that communist rule was not yet a thing of the past.[1] Although the question of organizing partisan warfare was discussed in the Politburo as early as 18 July 1941, it took over a year for the central machinery to go into action. On 30 May 1942 a Central Partisan Staff was set up, but only at the end of August 1942 was the first central conference of parti-

---

[1] One of the best descriptions of such an underground party organization is A. F. Fedorov, *Podpol'nyi obkom deistvuet*, Moscow, 1950.

san band leaders held. Voroshilov became partisan Commander-in-Chief.[1]

The main aims of this central staff were to train commanders for partisan bands, to supply bands with arms and instructions, to subject them to central discipline and to set about ensuring their political reliability – not so much as enemies of the Germans, in which they required little encouragement, but as supporters of communism. Some three thousand such commanders (including commanders of the special diversionary units which were NKVD trained and quite independent of the partisan bands) were trained in the course of 1943 and 1944.[2] The creation of a disciplined, centrally controlled force designed to co-operate with the army and the party was not achieved without friction. Nor, in spite of honour and publicity bestowed on individuals, did the party ever completely trust the partisans. After the reconquest of any territory on which the partisans had been operating, the members of the bands were not incorporated in the Red Army, but screened and sent back to the rear for 're-training'. (Trotsky had followed exactly the same policy with regard to partisans operating in the Ukraine in the civil war.) Much bitterness and disappointment was engendered by this action.[3] But in terms of efficiency it was the party, with the help of the NKVD, which made the anarchical partisan movement into a military arm which pinned down very considerable enemy forces. Yet its total size, about 200,000, was small when compared to the total population of the occupied territory.[4]

But if it was true that in occupied Russia the party proved a loyal instrument, this was not necessarily true of individual party members when once they had lost all contact with the party network. Once he had broken the umbilical cord of organization which bound him to the central machine, even a senior party member was ready to jettison his years of indoctrination and to yield to the longings for a freer and more just order, as he conceived it, and indeed to fight for a new régime in the Soviet Union. This was revealed by the German-sponsored move-

---

[1] The dates vary in different accounts. I have taken them from Iu. P. Petrov, 'Kompartiia – organizator i rukovoditel 'partizanskogo dvizheniia' in *Voprosy istorii*, No. 5, 1958, pp. 23–42, which is stated to be based on party archives. For detailed summaries and discussion of the evidence, see John A. Armstrong (ed.), *op. cit.*, pp. 73–139.

[2] Karov, *op. cit.* p. 38; cf. also Garthoff *op. cit.*, chapter xxiii.

[3] On this see a pamphlet published during the war by the Vlasov movement, based on the interrogation of Captain A. D. Rusanov, captured by the Vlasov troops, entitled *Pravda o 'partizanskom dvizhenii'*, n.p., n.d.

[4] For a full and comprehensive study of the partisan movement, based on an enormous mass of captured German material, see John A. Armstrong (ed.), *Soviet Partisans in World War II*, Madison, Wisconsin, 1964.

ment which bears the name of Vlasov. The leaders of this Russian Liberation Movement formed from among Russian prisoners of war were for the most part senior army officers, party members of long standing who had enjoyed privileged positions under the Soviet régime. Vlasov himself had been a party member since 1930, won distinction in the defence of Moscow in 1941, and at the time of his capture in July 1942 was a lieutenant-general who had commanded an army. The movement which promised the Russian population liberation from communism in return for its refusal to support the war effort was, so far as Hitler was concerned, merely a propaganda trick. So far as Vlasov and his colleagues were concerned, it would seem that they were sincerely, if naïvely, persuaded, or deceived into believing, that the Germans would accept their services on terms of equality, in return for the military value which they were convinced their appeal to their fellow countrymen represented. Moreover, the German officers with whom they were directly concerned were for the most part convinced opponents of what they regarded as Hitler's blindness in failing to exploit discontent in the Soviet Union, and mostly opponents of the Nazi régime.

Because of Hitler's opposition the Liberation Movement never acquired any serious reality as a military force. But its simple programme of liberation from communist rule, which closely resembled the programme of the Kronstadt rising in 1921,[1] must have appeared to the party inside the USSR a dangerous temptation to the Soviet population. A tour of occupied Russia by Vlasov, organized behind Hitler's back, evoked enthusiastic response from the local population. The Soviet authorities, who did not know the extent to which the Vlasov movement was a sham, were seriously alarmed. Apart from propaganda designed to discredit Vlasov, several unsuccessful attempts were made by emissaries of the NKVD to murder him. To counter the attractions of his programme, rumours were spread (and were widely believed) that the collective farms would be dissolved after victory, and that other defects in the system would be put right.[2]

There were three conclusions which the party leaders could validly have drawn from their experiences of the war. The first, that nothing but an effective grip by the party organization over the life of the country could handle a breakdown or forestall anarchy at any moment

---

[1] Text in Fischer, *op. cit.*, pp. 59–60.
[2] See Alexander Dallin and Ralph S. Mavrogordato, 'The Soviet Reaction to Vlasov' in *World Politics*, April 1956, pp. 307–22. On the Vlasov movement generally see the fully documented accounts in Fischer, *op. cit., passim*, and A. Dallin, *op. cit*, chapters xxvi–xxviii.

of crisis. Secondly, that the party machine could only operate in a loyal and disciplined manner so long as the nexus between the central organizations and the individual member or committee was preserved intact: left to himself, the party member was as liable to fall a prey to his grievances against the régime as any other citizen. And the third, that the bonds which bound 'the masses' to the party were very slender indeed among wide sections of the population, and especially the peasants. The war, with its appalling hardships and suffering, brought to the surface a freedom of thought which years of terror had effectively kept down. So long as party propaganda had dealt in appeals and assertions which were to a large extent fictitious, outward conformity became a means of concealing true thought, and the strength of the party lay less in the conviction it could create than in the discipline it could enforce. But during the war, when the party laid most stress on patriotic slogans, which all in fact believed and accepted, the party, paradoxically, lost in strength. There were many who felt that they did not need the party (which, incidentally, had so often in the past boasted that Soviet territory was inviolable) to teach them their duty as patriots which they were only too eager to fulfil. And, as must always happen, with loss of respect, went loss of fear.

* * *

It was during the war that the system of party control over the army, which has remained in essence the same, was developed and perfected. After a series of panic measures, the party authorities attempted with some success to place party surveillance of the army on a more rational basis, and to eliminate some of the friction between the party doctrinaires and the professional soldiers which had so often bedevilled relations in the past. It will be recalled that the system of dual command was revived in 1937 in preparation for the purge of the army.[1] Dual command was put to the test in action in the Finnish campaign, and did not prove satisfactory. The commissars and the political personnel assumed responsibility for military questions during action, the authority of the commander was undermined and both discipline and efficiency suffered. It was not therefore surprising that when other radical reforms of the army were undertaken with the object of strengthening military discipline after the conclusion of the Finnish war, the system of dual command was also abolished. On 12 August 1940 the political commissars were replaced by deputy commanders

[1] See p. 423 above.

for political matters. The system which had been progressively developed between 1925 and 1937 was thus reverted to. Undivided authority for all military decisions was vested in the commander, but his political deputy was made responsible for political indoctrination and leadership among the troops. After the German attack in June 1941 the old dual system was reintroduced. But this seems to have been a panic measure, considered appropriate to conditions of emergency and disorganization caused by a surprise attack, and it did not survive when once the tide of defeat had turned. On 9 October 1942 unity of command was restored, and the commissars were once again replaced by deputy commanders for political matters.

Unity of command, with the representatives of the party ranking as deputies of the military commanders, may therefore be regarded as the system which was, and is, considered appropriate to normal conditions. In its essentials, the system evolved after 1942 still remains in force today (1969). Unity of command did not, however, mean that the political and military hierarchies were fused. The political network still remained independent of the military in the sense that it was subject to its own discipline, and conflicts which arose between the commander and his political deputy could be carried to a higher level by the political deputy. The party recognizes the need for military discipline. But at the same time the Soviet army is avowedly a political army; the party leaders therefore look to the political machine within the army to indoctrinate the men who pass through its ranks, to train those who are returning to civilian life in loyalty to the régime and, in peace as well as in war, to prepare the army for such tasks as the party may call upon it to carry out. The commanders, on the other hand, although the overwhelming majority of them are party members, are like all professional soldiers primarily interested in the efficiency of the troops under their command. They are therefore apt to become impatient if too much time is spent on political activity to the detriment of training, or if political discussions threaten at any time to undermine their own authority.

During the war this problem receded into the background. There was little emphasis in party propaganda on doctrinal themes, and the patriotic appeals which the party organizations launched as well as the interest shared by commanders and political deputies in increasing military efficiency and discipline more often than not created a bond between the two hierarchies. But with the end of the war when the party began to reassert its interest in more dogmatic matters of doctrine, which were no longer strictly related to the immediate military task, the friction became more acute. Stalin's personal jealousy of the reputation of some of the more outstanding commanders of the war may have had something to do with this. But events as late as 1957, four years after Stalin's death, were to show that the problem of harmonious relations between the commanders and their political deputies had not yet been solved.

Control of political work in the army is vested in the Chief Political Administration, which is at one and the same time a part of the USSR Ministry of Defence and a department of the Central Committee. This central organization co-ordinates all propaganda work in the army and controls the activities of the network of subordinate officers and of the party and *Komsomol* organizations inside the army through which these officers operate. A political officer, directly subordinate to the Chief Political Administration, is to be found in every department and directorate of the Ministry of Defence, and in the General Staff, each with his own large department. Every military district has a political member of general rank on its military council. Very senior party members, such as Khrushchev and Bulganin, occupied these vital political posts during the war. The political member of the military council appoints the heads of political departments at corps, divisional, regimental and company level.[1] The main political officer in practice is the regimental deputy commander for political matters (*Zampolit*). In the carrying out of his task he has the assistance of the regimental party bureau, with its secretary (nominally elected, in practice appointed and sometimes even brought in from outside the regiment) around whom a hard core of devoted communists is formed, designed to extend its influence throughout the rest of the unit.

In addition there are the regimental *Komsomol* organization, propagandists and advisers in subordinate units. Political activity is mainly of two kinds; political lectures, normally twice a week, on the more theoretical subjects; and daily political information, designed to keep the soldiers informed on the party interpretation of current affairs.[2] As will be seen later, considerable effort was made during the war to broaden the base of the party in the army by intensive recruiting. After the war the pace of recruitment naturally abated, but party representation in the army remained very high. On the eve of the war more than half of the military were communists and members of the

---

[1] The political deputy at company level was abolished in 1943, but restored again in 1949 or 1950.
[2] See Merle Fainsod, *How Russia is Ruled*, pp. 489–95, and J. M. Mackintosh in *The Soviet Army*, edited by B. H. Liddell Hart, London, 1956, pp. 228–33.

Komsomol.[1] In October 1952 86·4 per cent of all officers were stated to be members of the party or *Komsomol.*[2]

It should be noted that yet a further check on the loyalty of the army was, and is, maintained in the form of the special security sections which are to be found at all levels in all parts of the armed forces. The commanders of these sections are completely independent both of the military commanders and of the political deputies, and are subordinated to the head of the state security service. These officers are career security officers, and although they are put into military uniform and given appropriate ranks while on service with the forces, usually have no military experience at all. Their presence among the military is presumably accepted as an unpleasant necessity. In contrast, the political deputies, who are for the most part trained in military matters as well as in party doctrine, are often able to achieve some degree of comradeship with their military colleagues and do not form so completely alien a body in military society.

[1] D. Fedotoff-White, *The Growth of the Red Army*, p. 410.
[2] *Pravda*, 10 October 1952 (A. M. Vasilevskii).

XXVIII   The Aftermath of the War
(Industry: Agriculture: Party Composition)

The hopes of relaxation which the party thought it expedient to encourage while the war was still in progress stood little chance of realization when once victory was assured. The threatening cleavage between party and population, which the party leaders had perforce to tolerate while the emergency was at its height, had now to be bridged. Moreover, there was much to be done to restore ruined industries and to secure the supplies of food. The early disasters of the war had shaken Stalin's sense of security, and perhaps his nerve. But in 1945 this crisis was long behind. With the full apparatus of propaganda now once again under his control he could confidently proceed to build himself up as the saviour of his country. His wisdom and foresight in building industry at breakneck speed and in ridding the country of its fifth column – for thus were the events of the decade before the war now portrayed – made his personal position even more impregnable than before.

As a result of the war Stalin's position as head of both the party and the government machines was enhanced. When after the war GOKO was abolished, Stalin remained Chairman of the Council of People's Commissars (Council of Ministers, after 1946) as well as the First Secretary of the party – in fact, if not in name. This enormous concentration of authority in the hands of one man was reflected in the decline of the functions of the higher party organs. No All-Union Congress or Conference was to meet until October 1952, and even the Plenum of the Central Committee was hardly ever in fact summoned, though decisions were occasionally issued in its name. It is not even certain that the full Politburo met regularly or at all. Master of both administrative machines and in addition of the machinery of terror, the security service, Stalin could manipulate all of them at will with the aid of his personal secretariat, and, as in 1936–8, by personal agents selected to carry out his designs. One consequence was that the party lost something of its privileged position and became merely one of the several instruments of personal despotic rule. The ministerial bureaucracy, for example, became at least as important as, if not more important than, the party apparatus of secretaries. Legislative enactments now issued from the Council of Ministers. In the administration of the nationalized industry the party apparatus, working parallel to the government apparatus, could no longer with the same ease assert its unquestioned superiority when once the Leader was at the apex of both machines.

Reports of the party Congresses held in the Union republics in September 1952 revealed that the relationship between party and government organs at lower levels was far from smooth. Party organs were blamed both for neglect of administrative problems and for encroaching on the work of the industrial departments of the executive committees of local soviets – though it is difficult to see how they could have avoided one or other of these courses. This tension was in practice being resolved with increasing frequency by appeals to the centre or by the dispatch of a party emissary from a higher organization.[1] The problem of friction between the two administrative hierarchies was not new. But it was probably being exacerbated by the fact that the party organization on the spot no longer enjoyed the unquestioned authority which it had been able to assert in the past. In the case of agriculture, the continued absence of adequate party organizations on the collective farms (to which reference is made below) inevitably threw the lion's share of administrative responsibility on to the government organs.

Before examining more closely the developments in the party after 1945, it is necessary to take account of personal rivalries among the top leaders which exercised some influence on them. So long as Stalin was alive there was no questioning his supremacy. None the less, though inhibited by fear from making any move which could be interpreted as opposition by a hyper-suspicious autocrat, the second-rank leaders of the party manœuvred as they could for Stalin's favour, and against their fellows. Stalin, in turn, was presumably content to encourage rivalry among his immediate lieutenants, well aware that such rivalry presented less threat to himself than would a solid band of men who saw eye to eye.

Malenkov's ascendancy continued for most of the war. In August

---

[1] Based on the reports of the republican congresses printed in the Russian language newspapers published in the various union republics in the course of September 1952.

1943 he became chairman of the Committee on the Rehabilitation of Liberated Areas. The members were Beria, Mikoyan, Voznesenskii and Andreev. Of his efficiency as an administrator at a time when the country was in direst need there can therefore be no doubt. Nevertheless, towards the end of the war there were signs that the rivalries between the most powerful individuals under Stalin were once again reviving. The return of Zhdanov early in 1945 to Moscow, and to the Secretariat, may have been the beginning of a clash with Malenkov, who had hitherto shared the running of this vital apparatus with Andreev. After March 1946 Zhdanov as secretary ranked third in the list headed by Stalin and Malenkov.[1] The subtle and energetic Malenkov could have had little difficulty in dominating a weak man like Andreev. Zhdanov was a very different personality to deal with – hard, dogmatic, ambitious, perhaps embittered by the fact that Malenkov, not he, had been singled out for highest prominence during the war. Whatever the cause, it seems that a bitter rivalry now sprang up between the two men.

At the end of 1944 the Council of People's Commissars had set up a committee to deal with the dismantling of German industry in payment of reparations of the Soviet Union. Its chairman was Malenkov. The rough and ready methods adopted by the committee in the chaotic conditions immediately after the war not unnaturally led to a good deal of wastage of valuable material, while competition for equipment led to friction between departments. But, as had often happened before, a real administrative problem was also exploited for political ends. According to circumstantial and apparently reliable accounts by several former employees of this committee, an attack was launched on Malenkov's administration, largely at the instigation of Zhdanov and his protégé Voznesenskii, as a result of which an investigating commission headed by Mikoyan recommended an end to dismantling and its replacement by the setting up of Soviet-owned corporations in Germany to make goods for the Soviet Union. Mikoyan's plan was adopted, in spite of support for Malenkov from Kaganovich and Beria, each of whom was interested in the supply of equipment for the enterprises he controlled – Kaganovich for building material enterprises, Beria for the economic enterprises of the NKVD.[2] Whether for this or for other reasons, Malenkov's fortunes

---

[1] *Bol'shevik*, No. 6, 1946, p. 3.
[2] *Soviet Economic Policy in Post-War Germany*. A Collection of Papers by Former Soviet Officials. Research Program on the USSR, New York, 1953. This study was published some years before other evidence became available to corroborate the alignments between the various leaders there described.

now began to wane. He ceased to be listed as a secretary of the Central Committee in 1946. In June 1947 G. F. Aleksandrov, whose close association with Malenkov became evident from what happened years later,[1] lost his post as head of *Agitprop* and was replaced by M. A. Suslov. (This change was the result of one of the series of assaults conducted by Zhdanov between 1946 and 1948 on artistic, intellectual, academic and scientific activity which will be described in the next chapter.)

However, Malenkov was soon able to restore his damaged fortunes. By 20 July 1948 he had returned to the Secretariat. On 31 August 1948 Zhdanov quite suddenly died. Soon after there followed a ruthless purge of his associates and supporters, though Zhdanov himself was never posthumously vilified. Voznesenskii disappeared from the Politburo and from public life. A secretary of the Central Committee (A. A. Kuznetsov), the chairman of the RSFSR Council of Ministers,[2] M. I. Rodionov, and the secretary of the Leningrad organization, P. S. Popkov, were dismissed, and, as was later disclosed by Khrushchev, executed along with Voznesenskii on trumped-up charges.[3] All were closely associated with Zhdanov in their careers, either in Leningrad or elsewhere.

The blame for trumping-up this 'Leningrad Case', as it became known in current rumour, was much later laid by Khrushchev on the head of the security service at that date, Abakumov, who was executed for this crime in 1954, and later still on Malenkov. No doubt the police played their part in faking the necessary charges. It is inconceivable that they could have done so without Stalin's approval. But Malenkov's complicity in the affair as well is suggested by the fact that V. M. Andrianov, who succeeded Popkov as First Secretary in Leningrad, and subsequently carried out a purge of the Leningrad organization, was closely linked to Malenkov in his career, and disappeared from public life after Malenkov's fall in 1955. What induced Stalin to initiate or tolerate this extermination of valuable administrators can only be conjectured, and no conclusive information has come to light. It is possible that Stalin's ever-present suspicion that

---

[1] Aleksandrov was in no way disgraced in 1947, but remained prominent in academic life, until his appointment as Minister of Culture in March 1954, while Malenkov was still Chairman of the Council of Ministers. But almost immediately after Malenkov's fall from office in 1955 he was violently attacked and ignominiously dismissed – see *Pravda*, 13 and 21 March, 1955. A spate of attacks on every aspect of his academic activity followed thereafter.

[2] The Council of People's Commissars was renamed Council of Ministers in 1946.

[3] *The Anti-Stalin Campaign*, pp. 58–9.

Leningrad might be seeking to recapture some of its traditional independence of outlook played some part.[1]

*   *   *

The resumption by Malenkov of control over the party apparatus in 1948 was a signal for its radical reconstruction, which in turn was associated with the complex problems of industry, created by wartime destruction. As always, the central question was the degree and nature of party control over industrial enterprises. It will be recalled that the system associated with Zhdanov, instituted at the Eighteenth Party Congress in 1939, was designed to ensure that the focal point of day-to-day control over industrial enterprises should be the primary party organizations on the spot, and that the central apparatus of the Secretariat should confine itself to overall supervision in the matter of distribution of personnel. But this system broke down almost immediately in practice, and while the formal structure of the Secretariat remained unchanged, various devices were introduced in 1940 and 1941 under Malenkov's management to make the Cadres Directorate into an instrument for more active and detailed central control.[2]

Some months after Malenkov's return to the Secretariat and Zhdanov's death it became apparent that significant changes had taken place in the structure of the Secretariat, which amounted in substance to a return to the system associated with Kaganovich in 1934, namely some measure of decentralization in the selection of personnel for industry, but greater centralization of day-to-day control over industry. These changes, which bore the imprint of Malenkov's ideas, took place without any formal announcement, and with some measure of secrecy. Their nature can only be inferred from isolated references in the party press. The main change was the abolition of the Cadres Directorate and the redistribution of its functions among a number of departments responsible for the supervision of the various branches of production. Thus, departments were set up for Heavy Industry, Planning, Finance and Trade, Light Industry, Transport, and probably for a number of other branches. A new Foreign Department was set up to deal with the choice of personnel for service abroad, for relations with foreign communist parties, and possibly for other duties in the sphere of foreign policy. Otherwise the main

[1] In one of the letters which preceded the Soviet–Yugoslav break in 1948, dated 4 May 1948, there is a strong hint that Yugoslavs had been intriguing against Moscow with the Leningrad party organization. See *The Soviet–Yugoslav Dispute*, Royal Institute of International Affairs, London and New York, 1948, pp. 40–1.

[2] See pp. 454–6 above.

structure remained relatively unchanged. The departments for Agriculture and for Administration remained as before, as well as the Special Section for police matters.

Control over cultural and propaganda matters remained centralized in a Propaganda and Agitation Department, which however now bore a slightly reduced status as compared with the Propaganda and Agitation Directorate set up by Zhdanov in 1939. In general, it would seem that the policy of enhancing the status of certain departments by elevating them to directorates was abandoned at this time. Thus, the old Organization and Instruction Department, which in 1946 (in Malenkov's absence) had been replaced by a Directorate for Checking Party Organs, was now once again reduced to department status, with the title of Department of Party, Trade Union and *Komsomol* Organs. Its functions were the supervision of all subordinate party organs, the checking on the fulfilment of party decrees and the placing of party functionaries within the party administrative network.[1]

It was significant that the adoption of this production branch system of the division of work in the Secretariat took place at two turning points in the history of the development of Soviet industry: in 1934 and in 1948. In 1934, after the convulsions and the relative failure which characterized the period of the First Five Year Plan, the party was embarking upon the relatively more stable and more productive period of the Second Five Year Plan. In 1948 again the country had reached the point where it was beginning to overcome the ravages which wartime destruction had inflicted upon it. The recovery after 1947 was indeed remarkable. In 1947 overall industrial production had still not attained the level of 1940. By 1948 it had already exceeded it, and by the last year of Stalin's life, 1952, exceeded it two and a quarter times. In accordance with well-established policy, the main advance was in the production of the means of production: thus, in 1952, production in this category was more than two and a half times that of 1940, whereas production of consumer goods had only increased by slightly over one and a half times. The standard of living of

---

[1] See Merle Fainsod, *How Russia is Ruled*, Revised edition, pp. 198–200. Professor Fainsod's reconstruction of the new pattern of division of work in the Secretariat after 1948 is confirmed by a study of the accounts of the republican party congresses held in September 1952, as reported in the relevant provincial party newspapers. The following departments of republican secretariats (which always closely parallel the central model) were referred to: Propaganda and Agitation, Party, Trade Union and *Komsomol* Organs, Agriculture, Light Industry, Heavy Industry, Transport, Planning, Finance and Trade, Administrative, Work among Women, Schools, Sciences and Higher Education Institutions, Literature and the Arts, and, in some instances only, Engineering, Building Materials, Timber and Paper, Oil and Fishery.

the majority of the population still remained very low, and the housing situation was particularly acute.[1] No doubt there were many factors which contributed to this rapid rebuilding of industry. But among them the enhanced central party control adopted in 1948 must also have played its part.

Next to industry, the main preoccupation of the party in the post-war years was with agriculture. Its most immediate concern was to restore discipline in the collective farms over which the party grip had been weakened during the war. Encouraged by the hope that after the war the collective farms would be dissolved, the peasants had in many instances enlarged their private holdings without waiting for official sanction. During the German occupation some of the collective farms had been disbanded, though in the main the Germans preserved the system as the most convenient method of maximum exploitation of the peasants.[2] On 19 September 1946 a joint resolution of the Council of Ministers and of the Central Committee attempted to restore some order in what had obviously become a chaotic situation. The resolution was in the first instance directed towards recovering for the collectives the land and equipment which had been plundered from them by the peasants. But other abuses were also castigated. Local party and government officials were accused of exploiting farm property and produce for their own private gain, and it was asserted that inflated administrative staffs of farms were battening on national property. Violations of the democratic principles of management laid down in the farm model charter were also alleged. Collective farm meetings were no longer taking place, and matters had reached 'such a degree of outrage that chairmen of collective farms were appointed and replaced by the party and soviet organizations of the district (*raion*) without the collective farmers even being aware of it.'[3]

To remedy this state of affairs a Council on Collective Farms was set up, under the chairmanship of Andreev, who had borne the main responsibility for agriculture throughout the war. The Council, which included important party officials and agricultural administrators, was

---

[1] *Narodnoe khoziaistvo SSSR*, statisticheskii sbornik, Moscow, 1956, pp. 46–7. The official figures may be exaggerated – for minor criticism see Naum Jasny, *The Soviet Statistical Handbook 1956*. A Commentary. East Lansing, Michigan, pp. 55–9 – but all Western experts agree that the rate of industrial recovery after 1947 was remarkable. According to the view of Jasny (pp. vii, 150), the standard of living of workers and peasants remained below the standard prevailing in 1928 until 1955.

[2] Otto Schiller, *Die Landwirtschaft der Sowjetunion 1917–1953*, Tuebingen, 1954, p. 43; A. Dallin, *German Rule in Russia 1941–1945*, pp. 310 ff.

[3] *KPSS v rez.*, volume III, pp. 495–501.

given very wide powers, and operated mainly through its own officials, with the co-operation of the secretaries of the regional (*oblast'*) organizations. It achieved success in rounding up the stolen acres,[1] and to a lesser degree in reducing the size of the administrative staffs of farms. But efforts to regularize the methods of party administration were less successful. The root of the problem was the fact that party representation inside the collective farms remained very thin. Hence, unwilling to trust the implementation of its policy to collective farmers who remained independent of the control exercised by a party group in their midst, the party leaders were forced to rely on central direction through a multiplicity of agencies. One such agency was the network of MTS, with its deputy directors for political affairs, who in 1947 were once again strengthened with an infusion of communists dispatched from the towns. Another was the Ministry of Agriculture, functioning through the republics and regions and the agricultural committees of the executive committees of the local soviets.

Considerable efforts were made immediately after the war to improve this situation, and some progress was recorded. The main aim of the party seems to have been twofold: to step up recruitment among collective farmers and to distribute communists in the rural districts in such a way as to make it possible to form primary party organizations in the maximum number of farms. (According to the party Rules, as approved in 1939, a minimum of three communists was required in an enterprise, including a collective farm, before a primary party organization could be formed.) By early 1948 already a third of all collective farms had their own primary party organizations, and there were many districts in which the percentage of farms with their own organizations was considerably higher. But their membership was often very weak: the number of organizations increased very much more rapidly than the total number of their members. In the Ukraine, for example, the number of party organizations increased fourfold between 1941 and 1949, but their total membership only doubled. Apparently the increase was due more to distribution of available rural communists than to increased recruitment of peasants.[2] Greater success was achieved by a more radical reform after 1950 which will be examined below.

[1] On 19 September 1947 *Pravda* claimed that some 14 million acres of misappropriated land had been restored to the collective farms.
[2] T. H. Rigby, 'Social Orientation of Recruitment and Distribution of CPSU Membership. Recent Trends', *American Slavic and East European Review*, October, 1957, pp. 275–90.

The recovery and progress of agricultural production did not keep pace with the strides made in industry. The keynote of the procurement policy remained as before the war: the compulsory delivery by the collective farms of fixed quotas to the state at very low prices. A combination of penalties and rewards within the farms attempted to provide more incentives to collective farmers to spend greater effort on work in the collective enterprise. But the main incentive of profit was lacking, and the farmers still obstinately persisted in their attachment to the private plot which yielded proportionately much greater returns on the tolerated free market. To counteract this trend, increases in taxation were decreed on the income farmers derived from their plots, and owners of cows, sheep and poultry were further required to deliver quota from their private produce to the state. This policy towards the peasants not only resulted in a very low standard of living on the farms, where the poorer peasants were often near starvation level, but failed to achieve any substantial increase in agricultural production.

While Stalin was alive the evident failure of the agricultural policy was dissembled in confident claims of success and by the suppression of statistics. Thus, in his report to the Nineteenth Party Congress, which met in October 1952, Malenkov boldly claimed that agricultural prosperity had been restored after the ravages caused by the war, and that the grain problem, in particular, had been solved 'definitely and finally'.[1] After Stalin's death, figures were published which revealed a very different story. Thus grain production by 1950 was still below a good pre-war year, after adjustment made for the increased area of the USSR. The stocks of cattle presented an even more alarming picture. For cattle as a whole, the figures showed that total stocks were even by the beginning of 1953 still well below the total for 1928, before collectivization had got under way – again after adjustment made for the change in frontiers. In the case of cows, the figure at the beginning of 1953 was even lower, by some 13 per cent, than the total for 1916 – again, with allowance made for change in frontiers.[2] To see the full significance of these figures it must be remembered that the

---

[1] *Current Soviet Policies.* The Documentary Record of the Nineteenth Communist Party Congress and the Reorganization after Stalin's Death. New York, 1953, p. 109.

[2] Figures for grain production for 1950 are from Schiller, *op. cit.*, p. 92; figures for grain production after 1950 and for cattle are from *Narodnoe khoziaistvo SSSR*, pp. 101 and 118. The true state of agriculture was first openly admitted by the Soviet leaders in September 1953, and this admission was followed by intensive efforts, largely successful, to remedy the situation by radical changes in policy.

population of the USSR had increased by some 25 per cent, or over forty million, since 1928.[1]

In such conditions it was not surprising that agricultural policy should by 1950 have given rise to sharp differences of opinion between the party leaders. What was more surprising was that, considering the conditions of secrecy and outward unanimity which had been maintained for years, these disputes should have been allowed to come into the open. It may be that Stalin, well knowing that agriculture was the most pressing and least soluble problem facing the party leaders, was content to encourage open rivalries on this issue among his lieutenants. The party leaders principally concerned were Andreev, Malenkov, Beria and Khrushchev. The entry of Malenkov and Beria into the Politburo as full members in 1946 was the signal for the beginning of their interest in agricultural questions alongside of Andreev, the sole spokesman hitherto.

At the end of 1949 Khrushchev was posted to Moscow as a Central Committee Secretary and as Secretary of the Moscow *Oblast'* Committee. He had since 1938 been the Stalin of the Ukraine, especially during the crucial period of reconquest and reconstruction after the war, from 1944 to 1947, when, like Stalin, he combined the offices of First Secretary of the party and Chairman of the Council of Ministers. The rise of this powerful ruler of the second most important republic of the Union had not escaped the attention of his colleagues in Moscow. Several moves had been apparently directed at breaking his growing power, though without success. In 1946 the Central Committee launched an attack on cadres work in the Ukraine, which was, of course, Khrushchev's direct responsibility. It is possible that Malenkov may have inspired this attack (although there is nothing to suggest any rivalry between him and Khrushchev at this date), since even if he was no longer in the Secretariat, his successor in the Cadres Directorate in Moscow, N. N. Shatalin, was closely linked in his career with Malenkov, and was to disappear from public life soon after Malenkov's fall. This attack on Khrushchev was followed by the dispatch in March 1947 to the Ukraine of the Politburo's main trouble-shooter, Kaganovich, who took over from Khrushchev as Secretary of the party, leaving Khrushchev as Chairman of the Council of Ministers only. However, Khrushchev weathered this attack, and on the departure of Kaganovich at

---

[1] No population figures are available for either 1928 or 1952. The population was 147 million in December, according to the census of 1926. In April 1956 the official estimate was 200,200,200, according to *Narodnoe khoziaistvo SSSR*, p. 17.

the end of 1947 he once again resumed his post as party First Secretary.

The arrival in Moscow of this energetic man, with distinctive views on the management of agriculture with which he had already experimented in the Ukraine, was the signal for the coming into the open of disputes over agricultural policy which may have been smouldering beneath the surface for some time. The first victim was Andreev. On 19 February 1950 an unsigned article in *Pravda* condemned Andreev for his advocacy of the so-called 'link' system on the collective farms. In substance, the link system meant the utilization of labour on the collective farms in small units, or 'links', in preference to larger units, or 'brigades'. This system, which was widely advocated, not only by Andreev, in 1939 and thereafter had the advantage of making work on the farms more individual and therefore of encouraging personal incentive, especially where, in the absence of a high degree of mechanization, large-scale farming was not practicable.

The sudden reversal in policy may have been due to the increase in the degree of mechanization which had been achieved by 1950 as compared with ten years before. There was, no doubt, room for disagreement on the proper moment to make the change. But, from the point of view of party control, the brigade system had considerable advantages over the link system, since it was easier with the slender resources of party personnel in the villages to find a small number of reliable brigadiers than to exercise party supervision over more individualistic smaller units, often consisting of only one family. Andreev, as a result of this attack, ceased to play any important part in political affairs, but was not disgraced. He was allowed to publish a recantation of his erroneous views – in itself a sign of favour – and no action was taken against him. At the Nineteenth Party Congress, two and a half years later, he was dropped from the Politburo's successor, the Praesidium, but remained a member of the Central Committee.

The campaign against the link was not openly led by Khrushchev, though he can be presumed to have supported it. But the related and much more fundamental reform which was embarked upon about the same time was openly launched in his name. This was a plan to amalgamate the collective farms into a smaller number of larger units.[1] The amalgamation was accomplished with considerable rapidity. By the end of 1950 the 252,000 collective farms had been reduced to 121,400;

[1] *Pravda*, 8 March 1950.

by the end of 1952 there were only 94,800.[1] According to Khrushchev, the amalgamation would have the effect of facilitating mechanization, reducing administrative expenses and increasing production. But an equally important result, if not the main object, of the reduction of the number of farms by nearly two-thirds was to make the problem of party control more manageable. The smaller number of farms made possible an increase in the proportion of farms with party organizations of their own, while the reduction in the number of farm chairmen made it easier to fill these posts with party members or persons considered reliable by the party. But the problem of inadequate party representation on the collective farms still remained serious. By the time of the Nineteenth Congress in October 1952, 76,355 collective farms had their primary party organizations, but this meant that some 18,000 still had no party organization. Besides, even where party organizations existed they were weak: only about five thousand of them had over 25 members.[2]

It is probable that much of Khrushchev's policy on agriculture ran into opposition from the two men who to some degree shared with him the responsibility for agriculture in the Politburo (after the departure from the scene of Andreev) – Malenkov and Beria. There is evidence of the opposition of Beria at any rate to the amalgamation policy, since one of Beria's close associates, the party secretary in Azerbaidjan, Bagirov, who was to be executed soon after Beria, criticized excessive haste over amalgamation in May 1951. There is also clear evidence that one at least of Khrushchev's more fantastic ideas was opposed by both Beria and Malenkov. This was his proposal that in the new enlarged collective farms the peasants should be housed in urban conditions, in so-called 'agro-towns' (which they would be expected to build themselves), and should till their private plots on the outskirts. Anything more calculated to arouse the fierce hostility of the peasants would be difficult to imagine, and it is evident that many party leaders felt misgivings about it. It is not surprising that Beria, who retained overall responsibility for security, should have been among the opponents.

The proposal was first made by Khrushchev in a speech in January 1951 which was only published in *Pravda* weeks later, on 4 March.

[1] *Narodnoe khoziaistvo SSSR*, p. 131; the process continued – by the end of 1954 the number was to be 87,100.
[2] These data were given by Aristov to the Twentieth Congress in 1956. Even in 1956 over 7,000 collective farms were still to be without their primary party organizations, and nearly 11,000 of the existing organizations consisted of 3–5 members only. See *XX S"ezd*, volume I, p. 236.

The following day *Pravda* announced that 'owing to an oversight' an editorial note had been omitted to the effect that Khrushchev's article was published only as 'material for discussion purposes' – in other words, was not intended to be authoritative. The scheme was subsequently publicly criticized by two close adherents of Beria – Bagirov, and the secretary of the Armenian party organization, Arutiunov,[1] but for the time being by no one else. But at the Nineteenth Party Congress in October 1952 Malenkov strongly criticized the proposal, which he attributed to 'some of our leading officials', without naming Khrushchev.[2]

There can be no doubt that the decisive factor in all these differences of opinion on agricultural policy was the view of Stalin, since it is inconceivable that any party member at that date would have ventured to criticize another in public without first being certain that his criticism had Stalin's backing. Nevertheless, the association of particular leaders with a particular view may reasonably be taken as an indication that this was the view for which that leader had canvassed Stalin's support, and therefore represented his own view on policy. When, shortly before his death, Stalin made his own views on the future of agriculture known, it became evident that he was contemplating reducing still further the incentive to peasants to produce. In the first place, he decisively rejected a proposal which had apparently been made by two economists to permit the collective farms to buy the mechanical equipment which was under the control of the MTS. This step, Stalin argued, would make the collective farms the only owners of their own means of production in a society in which such means of production were nationalized, and would be a step backward from communism and not a step towards it. On the contrary, the solution of the problem of raising the status of collective farms to the level of national property (which the collective farms had not yet attained, since they were theoretically co-operative and not state enterprises) lay in the abolition of the private market, and of a commodity system generally. Instead of selling his surplus produce in the free market, as at present, the peasant should exchange his surplus produce, by a system of barter, with the state.[3]

*　　*　　*

[1] For Arutiunov's criticism see *Kommunist* (Organ of the Communist Party of Armenia) 21 March 1951; for Bagirov's speech see *Bakinskii rabochii* 26 May 1951. Arutiunov, like Bagirov, fell into disgrace after Beria's downfall, but, unlike Bagirov, was not, so far as is known, executed.

[2] *Current Soviet Policies*, 1953, p. 111.

[3] *Bol'shevik*, No. 18, September 1952, pp. 45–50.

On 5 October 1952 the Nineteenth Party Congress met in Moscow. It was the first Congress to be held for over thirteen years, and had been preceded by congresses in the Union republics. Stalin, who was by then nearly 73, although present at the Congress took no direct part in the debates, beyond making a short closing statement. But although the Leader thus appeared to be husbanding his failing strength, there could be no doubt of his continuing domination over the political scene. His appearances at the Congress were greeted with the traditional clamorous ovations, all speeches ended with the customary invocations to his name, and press publicity was careful to make him the centre of attention. Moreover, with his great gift for self-presentation, he had arranged to publish on the very eve of the Congress a new work, entitled *The Economic Problems of Socialism in the USSR*, in which he had distilled his latest reflections on both domestic and foreign problems.[1] As a natural consequence of this, virtually all discussion at the Congress was already predetermined by the propositions contained in the Leader's latest pronouncement.

Although the question of ultimate succession to Stalin could not of course be discussed, it is unlikely that many failed to realize that Stalin might not live much longer. Looked at solely in terms of the amount of power which, after Stalin and with Stalin's support and approval, each could wield, the most likely candidates for the succession, apart from Molotov, appeared to be Malenkov and Beria, and possibly also Khrushchev – all three 'neo-Stalinists'. Malenkov was still the most important of the secretaries after Stalin, and therefore controlled the party machine. The second was in overall control, at any rate nominally, of the security machine, the MGB, and of the Ministry of the Interior, the MVD. Control over the latter gave him additionally the command of a considerable force of internal security troops and the management of a substantial portion of the national economy, including the development of atomic energy. Khrushchev, although not so powerful a secretary as Malenkov, had, in spite of a set-back, achieved a considerable status since his arrival in Moscow. It was an indication of his growing importance in the Secretariat that by some date in 1952 (probably after the Congress) the Department of Party, Trade Union and *Komsomol* Organs, which controlled all important appointments in the network of party organizations, was headed by his nominee and

[1] It was first published in *Bol'shevik*, in the issue referred to in the preceding Note, which was signed off for the printers on 1 October 1952. It was reprinted in full in *Pravda* of 3 and 4 October.

close associate, A. B. Aristov.[1] Of the three younger men, it was Malenkov who, after Stalin, was given the greatest publicity and the most vociferous reception. He presented the main report of the Central Committee in place of Stalin. But Khrushchev was entrusted with presenting the report on the new party Rules.

It was not to be expected that this Congress would be the scene of any real discussion or would depart from what was now the customary unanimity of such gatherings. But it provided some new information on the size and composition of the party, foreshadowed future policy, and made significant changes in the structure of the party. It is with the latter alone that we are for the present concerned. The main change took place in the leading organs of the party. The Politburo and Orgburo were abolished and replaced by a greatly enlarged Praesidium. No explanation was offered by Khrushchev for this innovation, beyond the fact that the new title was more in accord with the functions of the Politburo, and that experience had shown that it was expedient to concentrate organizational work in the Secretariat.[2] It was perhaps the case that the Orgburo had for some time past outlived its usefulness, and had been superseded by the Secretariat. It was also the case that Malenkov was a member of the Orgburo, and Khrushchev was not.

The twenty-five full members and eleven candidate members of the Praesidium between them represented the high command of party and government administration. They included ten Central Committee secretaries and thirteen vice-chairmen of the Council of Ministers of the USSR, as well as a number of regional party leaders, the heads of the trade unions, two ideologists, the first secretaries of the Ukraine and Belorussia and the Ministers of State Security and Foreign Affairs. Eighteen of the twenty-six who now together with the ten members of the Politburo formed the new top leadership of the party had joined the party in 1924 or later.[3] The bringing in of this new blood could be interpreted, in the light of what had happened in the 20's, as an indication that Stalin was contemplating changes at the top level of the party and was bringing up his reserves in preparation for them. This was in fact the interpretation placed upon this move by Khrushchev four years later when he told the next party Congress

---

[1] See the entry on Aristov in *Politicheskii slovar'*, edited by B. N. Ponomarev, Moscow, 1958. Aristov rose rapidly together with Khrushchev after Malenkov's decline, but fell into disfavour, and lost his posts in the Praesidium and in the Secretariat in 1961, and became Ambassador to Poland.

[2] *Current Soviet Policies*, 1953, p. 137.

[3] See Fainsod, *op. cit.*, pp. 326–34, for a full list and detailed analysis of the Praesidium elected in 1952, and see Appendix III for names.

that the enlargement of the Praesidium by Stalin 'was aimed at the removal of the old Political Bureau members and the bringing in of less experienced persons so that these would extol him in all sorts of ways'.[1] Meanwhile, a Praesidium of thirty-six was obviously too unwieldy for policy making, according to Soviet practice, and a smaller Bureau was secretly set up (its existence was only revealed after Stalin's death[2] and its composition can only be surmised).

The Central Committee of 236 members and candidate members was nearly twice the size of the Central Committee elected in 1939. Analysis of its composition revealed two facts of interest. First, the greater stability among the leading party members when compared with the turbulent years of the late 30's: 61 per cent of its members had been members of the previous Central Committee elected in 1939. This contrasted strikingly with the 22·5 per cent of the full members of the Central Committee elected in 1934 who alone had been re-elected to serve in 1939. Secondly, the representation of regional party secretaries was strongly increased: they now formed nearly half of the full members as against a little over a fifth in 1939. There was also a decline in 1952 of the representation of central government officials, who in 1939 had formed two-fifths of full members, a slight decline in the number of ideologists.[3]

No information was disclosed on the structure of the Secretariat of the kind which had been given in detail in 1939, and no new light was thrown on the changes which had taken place after Zhdanov's influence had ceased. The new Rules merely stated that the main functions of the Secretariat were the checking of the fulfilment of party decisions and the selection of cadres. The personalities of the ten secretaries appointed suggested that Stalin might have been anxious to balance influence inside the Secretariat between Malenkov and Khrushchev – his two most powerful lieutenants in the Secretariat. Apart from Stalin, Malenkov, Khrushchev and Suslov, who still headed *Agitprop*, they consisted of Aristov, L. I. Brezhnev, N. G. Ignatov, N. M. Mikhailov, N. M. Pegov and P. K. Ponomarenko. The first four were probably already associated with Khrushchev, since they were to advance steadily in their careers as Khrushchev rose to greater power in succeeding years. The last two, in contrast, were to suffer decline in their fortunes along with the decline of Malenkov, and were therefore possibly already associated with Malenkov. The

[1] *The Anti-Stalin Campaign*, pp. 84–5.
[2] *KPSS v rez.*, volume III, p. 606.
[3] For a further analysis see *Rigby Thesis*, chapter vi.

Commission of Party Control was, as in 1939, appointed by the Central Committee for disciplinary functions and as a court of appeal against expulsion from the party decreed by republican or regional committees (but not by the Central Committee). A new provision in the Rules equipped the Commission of Party Control with its own plenipotentiaries in the republics and regions, but this was merely official enactment of what had long been established practice.

A number of new provisions in the party Rules adopted by the Congress must be briefly noted. The name of the party was changed to Communist Party of the Soviet Union. The traditional name, bolshevik, symbol of the historic struggle of the two factions, had hitherto been preserved in parenthesis – All-Union Communist Party (bolsheviks). It was now dropped, thus symbolizing the break with the traditions of the past. In the list of the duties of party members the duty of preserving the unity of the party was now placed first. The duty to study in order to acquire the fundamentals of Marxism-Leninism, which occupied first place in 1939, now dropped to fourth place. There was also increased emphasis in the new Rules on the need for fearless self-criticism, party members who attempted to stifle criticism were condemned, and stress was laid on the need for the same party discipline for all, from the highest to the lowest members. This latter provision was aimed at directors who were endeavouring to cut across the red tape of over-centralized control by convenient, but illegal, short-cuts. Malenkov in his speech to the Congress developed these themes at some length.

Another new provision of importance was the enactment relating to the expulsion from the party of members of the Central Committee or of the Central Committees of republican and other subordinate party organizations. Such members could no longer be expelled or removed from the ranks of the committee on which they served without a two-thirds vote of the plenary meeting of the appropriate committee, or of the All-Union Congress in the case of members of the All-Union Central Committee. A member thus expelled was to be automatically replaced by the candidate member next in the line. So far as members of the All-Union Central Committee were concerned, this rule had existed since 1921, though it had certainly been violated in 1937 and 1938, and probably on other occasions. Finally, the interval between party congresses and between Central Committee plenary meetings was increased: congresses were to meet every four, and not as hitherto provided, every three years; and plena were to meet once in six

months, and not as provided in the 1939 Rules, every four months.[1]
The Congress also set up a commission to revise the party programme,
which dated from 1919. Its members included Stalin, Beria, Kaganovich, Malenkov and Molotov, and four of the leading party ideologists.
It is not known if the commission ever met before Stalin's death put
an end to its activities.

*   *   *

It is now time to take stock of the changes which had taken place in
the membership of the party between the Eighteenth Congress in 1939
and the Nineteenth Congress in 1952. The most notable change was
the increase in size. Recruitment continued steadily after the
Eighteenth Congress: by the time of the Eighteenth Conference in
February 1941 the total membership, including candidates, had increased by over a million and a half, to 3,876,885. The war gave a new
impetus to recruitment. The party was anxious to broaden its base,
especially inside the armed forces, and early in the war relaxed the
conditions of admission to the party so as to encourage mass recruitment. About two million were admitted in 1942 alone.[2] By 1 January
1945 membership totalled 5,760,369. Thereafter it continued to expand at a somewhat slower rate: to 6,300,000 by September 1947, and
to 6,882,145 by 1 October 1952. The party membership had suffered
considerable losses through casualties during the war. There was also
an attempt after the war to weed out recent recruits who had proved
unreliable or unworthy. Even so, a very large proportion of the post-
war membership consisted of those who had joined during and after
the war – about half of the total, for example, as at September 1947.[3]

A similar policy was pursued in recruitment to the *Komsomol*, which
grew to 15 million in October 1945, or about half of all those eligible
for membership. This rapid growth seems to have been due primarily
to patriotic motives, which did not survive the mood of the war.
There was a sharp drop in membership after the war. By March 1949
membership totalled a little over 9 million, the pre-war figure. No
doubt disillusionment with a return to the old ways of government
after the war, as well as memories of the violent purge of the *Komsomol*
in the late 30's played their part. However, an intensive recruitment

---

[1] The 1952 Rules are printed in *KPSS v rez.*, volume III, pp. 579–94.
[2] See *PS*, No. 8 April 1943, p. 25.
[3] Fainsod, *op. cit.*, pp. 269–70, where sources will be found. No figures are available for expulsions between the end of the war and the Nineteenth Congress for the
party as a whole. In Georgia and Azerbaidjan they amount to 8 and 10 per cent
respectively – *Rigby Thesis*, Chapter iv.

campaign made good progress among the new post-war generation, and by August 1952 membership had reached 16 million.[1]

Thus the broadened base of the party, though originally dictated by the desire to restore lost confidence in the party among the mass of the population and the army after the outbreak of war, was retained as a permanent feature after the war. The new recruitment policy inevitably involved changes in the social composition of the party. Although detailed official information on this question has not been made public, certain indications enable us to gauge the broad features of the changed social structure of the party by the end of Stalin's life. It will be recalled, that after 1936, when recruitment was resumed, the party abandoned its traditional preference, at any rate in theory, for proletarian and peasant members, and concentrated on drawing into the party representatives of the new intelligentsia. When mass recruitment inside the armed forces began during the war this policy naturally could not be maintained, nor was it desirable to maintain it when what was then aimed at was a mass party rather than a party of the élite. The increased number of peasant communists after the war, brought about by the return of demobilized communist soldiers to their villages, was one result of this new policy. But workers actually engaged in production were also being recruited into the party in increasing numbers, as is illustrated by the fact that in 1949 there were five times as many communists actually engaged in production as in 1940.[2] The process seems to have continued, at any rate in some areas. Of the new recruits in Belorussia in the first six months of 1952, for example, over half were workers or collective farmers,[3] and even in Moscow workers formed 34 per cent of those recruited in 1949–51.[4]

However, available evidence suggests that these worker and peasant communists were very largely engaged in positions of authority in their factories or farms. Thus, an analysis of collective communists published in 1948 shows that over half of them were farm chairmen, brigade leaders, administrators, or otherwise in authority.[5] In sum, after allowance is made for the increased scale of recruitment after 1941 of workers and peasants engaged in production, there can be no

---

[1] Fainsod, *op. cit.*, pp. 290–91. This rapid turnover seems to be a normal feature of the *Komsomol*. Thus, figures disclosed at the *Komsomol* Congress in April 1958 show that no fewer than 11 million, or some 58 per cent, had left and were for the most part replaced since 1954 – *Pravda*, 16 April 1958. Only a very small proportion of this number can have become party members or candidates, and the majority probably drift away as they grow older.

[2] *Moskovskii bol'shevik*, 2 February 1949.

[3] *Sovetskaia Belorussiia*, September 1952.

[4] *Moskovskaia pravda*, 31 March 1951.

[5] *Partiinaia zhizn'*, No. 5, 1948, p. 21.

doubt of the predominance of the white-collar intelligentsia in the party membership in 1952. The only figures published at the time, those relating to Georgia and Kirgizia, both predominantly agricultural republics, gave percentages for this class as 58·9 and 41·4 respectively. It is certain that the percentages were higher for the party as a whole.[1]

The party membership in 1952 was predominantly young, and of recent recruitment. A fairly conservative estimate suggests that about three-quarters of the members had joined the party since the outbreak of the war in June 1941, and that between a third and a half were aged under 35, and about three-quarters under 45.[2] There is no doubt that the educational level of members had improved. A fifth of all party members had completed secondary education in 1947 as compared with 14·2 per cent in 1939: while by the time of the Nineteenth Congress 11·8 per cent of all members and candidates were said to have received either complete or incomplete higher education.[3] The number of women in the party also increased – from 14·9 per cent in 1941 to 19·2 per cent in October 1952.[4] But although women were to be found in increasing numbers in the middle ranks of the party hierarchy, such as secretaries of subordinate party organizations, none was elected to the Praesidium in 1952, and only two out of the 125 full members of the Central Committee were women – the Minister of Health, and the historian Pankratova.

More information can be gleaned about the party élite from a study of the delegates to the All-Union, republican and regional party congresses. The social background of these delegates shows a fairly constant pattern. No list of delegates to the Nineteenth Congress was published and no analysis of their occupations is therefore available. At the Eighteenth Congress in 1939 party officials made up the largest group of 42 per cent, with administrative, trade union, police and army officials next, making up 28 per cent. The remainder represented industry, transport, agriculture, science and culture. If the three congresses of the Ukrainian party held between 1940 and 1952 are

---

[1] *Zaria vostoka*, 18 September 1952; *Sovetskaia Kirgiziia*, September 1952. For a careful analysis based on all available Soviet sources of the social composition of the party in 1957 see T. H. Rigby's article referred to in note 2, page 517. This analysis shows the white-collar element to be no less than 68 per cent (assuming that 10 out of the 14 per cent of communists in the armed forces and police are in positions of command, which is, if anything, an underestimate).

[2] *Rigby Thesis*, Chapter iv.

[3] *XX S'ezd*, volume I, p. 237 (Aristov). According to *Partiinaia zhizn'*, No. 20, 1957, p. 88, in 1956, as at 1 January, 11·2 per cent of all party members had received higher education, and 25·6 per cent unfinished higher or secondary education.

[4] *Bol'shevik*, No. 1 1951, p. 11; *XX S''ezd*, volume I, pp. 238–9 (Aristov).

examined it will be found that there had been a slight decline in the number of party officials among the delegates and a corresponding increase in the number of representatives of agriculture, culture, science and the arts,[1] and it is reasonable to assume that the same trend was evident among the delegates to the All-Union Congress in 1952. But even assuming this reduction in the professional party officials among the delegates to the Nineteenth Congress, party officials were still enormously over-represented in proportion to their total number, which probably did not much exceed 220,000.[2]

Data are available on the delegates to a number of republican congresses held after 1948. Taking the delegates to party congresses to represent the élite of the party as a whole, the following picture emerges of their social and educational background, age and seniority in the party. White-collar employees formed some 60 per cent of the delegates,[3] and again there is no reason to suppose that the proportion was different at the Nineteenth Congress, since the figure corresponds at this Congress very closely to the 58·5 per cent of voting delegates who were stated to have received higher education.[4] It should be noted that all these data refer to occupation. Information on the social origins of party members has not been published for over twenty years, but if biographies of leading party personalities are a reliable guide, peasant and worker origin in the case of the men of the post-purge generation, in other words the great majority, is the rule rather than the exception. The age of delegates to the All-Union Congress in 1952 revealed that comparatively few of those who formed the great

---

[1] Figures and sources in *Rigby Thesis*, Chapter v.

[2] Fainsod, *op. cit.*, pp. 205–6, estimates officials in 1952 at 194,000 – but this seems rather low. The following is a rough calculation:

CC Secretariat staff and staffs of 14 republican secretariats	–	3,000
170 *obkoms* and *kraikoms* at 70 each – – – –	–	12,000
6,500 subordinate city and district committees at 30 each	–	200,000
About 350–400,000 primary party organizations, of these say		
10,000 to 20,000 only with full-time paid secretaries –	–	10,000–20,000
		225–235,000

(On 1 January 1941 the total number of primary party organizations was 184,238; on 1 January 1956 the number was stated to be 'over 350,000'. See *Partiinaia zhizn'*, No. 20, 1957, p. 89.) But the number of paid secretaries of primary organizations may have been higher than 20,000 in 1955, since according to a CC decree of 21 May 1957, printed in *SPR*, 1957, p. 440, the number of these paid secretaries had been increasing inordinately – five times between 1940 and 1957, while during the same period the total number of primary organizations only doubled. (A group of visiting Italian communists in 1957 was told that the number of paid secretaries of primary organizations was 29,000 – see *Problemi e Realtí delí URSS*, Rome, 1958, pp. 44–5. But the number was probably smaller in 1952.)

[3] *Rigby Thesis*, Chapter v.

[4] *Current Soviet Policies*, I, 953, p. 94.

majority of the mass membership, those under 45, had yet reached the higher levels of the party. More than three-quarters of the delegates were aged 41 and over: in 1939 over four-fifths were under 40.[1] Evidently opportunities for rising rapidly to the top were more restricted than they had been in 1939 immediately after the wave of promotions for which the purge had made way. This becomes particularly evident when the party seniority of the congress delegates is examined. Only one-fifth of all delegates to the Nineteenth Congress had joined the party during or after the war: the great majority had joined either between 1921 and 1930 (36·4 per cent) or between 1931 and 1940 (35 per cent).[2] Yet, in the party as a whole the wartime and post-war recruits formed the overwhelming majority.

Further evidence that opportunities for rapid promotion were slower and fewer in 1952 than in 1937-9 is suggested if one examines the rate of turnover in party committees for the two periods. Only 22·5 per cent of the Central Committee members elected at the Eighteenth Congress in 1939 had served on the Central Committee elected at the previous Congress, in 1934. In 1952 the comparable percentage was 61 – and this notwithstanding the long period of thirteen years which had elapsed between the two Congresses and the losses among party members caused by the war. A similar picture is revealed if one looks at the Moscow City Committee over the same interval of time. In 1940 the percentage of members who had not served on the committee before was 73: in 1952 it was only 40. (The difference was less marked in the committee of the Moscow region, where the comparable percentages were 66 and 58.[3]) In general, after allowance has been made for particular districts or organizations where violent purges took place, the overall picture in the party network after 1946 is of relative stability in the higher ranges, and of great mobility below. For example if the appointments of the 73 first secretaries of the largest territorial organizations of the RSFSR are examined for the years 1946 to 1952, it will be found that the number of changes in these key posts varied from 11 in 1947 and 1950 to 20 in 1949, averaging 15 a year over the seven years, or 19 per cent. This turnover was in part due to the elimination of secretaries who had fallen from grace, and in part to promotion of the most capable

---

[1] *ibidem*, and *Pravda*, 15 March 1939. But the percentage of under forties was higher among the delegates to the republican congresses – *Rigby Thesis*, Chapter v.

[2] *Current Soviet Policies*, 1953, p. 94.

[3] Based on the comparison of lists, as published in the press. For details see *Rigby Thesis*, Chapter v.

men. At lower levels and in some of the republican party organizations the turnover during the same period was very much higher.[1] In sum, opportunities were not lacking for the younger men to rise at the lower levels of the hierarchy. But at the top the coveted posts of power were firmly in the hands of the older and more experienced party members.[2]

[1] Data on the RSFSR first secretaries are based on an analysis of appointments as announced in the central and local press during the years 1946–1952. The following table shows the number of changes recorded over a number of years, with the figure in parenthesis showing those who subsequently did not reappear in other appointments, and who were therefore in some cases purged, and in some cases possibly sent to a party school for retraining:

1946: 13 (9)
1947: 11 (7)
1948: 17 (8)
1949: 20 (11)
1950: 11 (4)
1951: 16 (15)
1952: 15 (9)
1953: 9 (5)

More recent figures are appended for comparison:

1954: 10 (1)
1955: 15 (1)

For details of changes in the smaller republics and at lower levels see Brzezinski, *The Permanent Purge*, pp. 137–47.

[2] The conclusions drawn by T. H. Rigby and myself on the party élite correspond very closely to those reached by John A. Armstrong – see his *The Soviet Bureaucratic Élite. A Case Study of the Ukrainian Apparatus*, New York, 1959 which is a detailed study of the party élite in the Ukraine.

XXIX Intellectual Tribulations
Stalin's Death

Three problems with which the party dealt after the war arose from similar causes: ideological orthodoxy, relations with non-Russian communities inside the USSR and relations with communist parties abroad. In each case the war had shattered the kind of control which, so long as the Soviet Union was isolated from the outside world, the party leaders had built up. The war, with its new contacts, its solidarity in the common fight against Hitler in which new loyalties competed with the old, inevitably weakened the party hold which terror and isolation had helped to strengthen. Intellectuals who during the war had been allowed some relations with fellow intellectuals of the countries allied to Russia showed a natural reluctance after the war to return to the conformity prescribed at home. In the newly acquired territories which were incorporated in the USSR, the Baltic states and Western Ukraine, anti-Russian as well as anti-communist feelings ran high. Among some of the non-Russian nationalities which had long formed part of the Soviet Union dormant nationalist feelings had been awakened during the war, in part under the influence of German propaganda. The Jews had been stirred to new hopes by the birth of the state of Israel in 1948.

The war also had repercussions in the foreign communist parties. In some countries they had drawn strength from the fact that they had played a big part in the resistance to German occupation after June 1941, and in a number of countries of Eastern and Central Europe communist parties had been put into power with the active or tacit support of the Soviet army. So long as they had been small, conspiratorial parties with little mass following in their own countries, they had been perforce content to accept the kind of domination over them upon which Moscow insisted. Once in power, thoughts of hitherto undreamt-of independence began to stir.

It is clear therefore that for the Soviet party leaders there was much mending of fences to be undertaken after 1945 before they could feel

533

secure of their control. The threefold campaign which now unfolded was in essence a reassertion of the predominance of the party which the war had done so much to shatter. But it leaned heavily on the strong upsurge of patriotic emotion which the war had evoked. If the Russian intellectual was now told to despise Western achievements in science and the arts for their inferiority to the achievements of Russia, the Central Asian Muslim was taught to recognize the progressive features of his absorption into the Russian Empire, while the Rumanian or Polish communist was reminded that the Russian party was the inspiration and model for all socialist progress.

The assault on the intellectuals took place mainly between 1946 and 1950, and virtually no sphere of creative or learned activity was left unscathed. The party with equal authority pronounced on literature, philosophy, music, biology, philology, or physiology. Many authorities who had hitherto enjoyed the highest reputations and positions were arrested, or at any rate discredited, and in some instances even executed. A few examples must suffice to illustrate the general pattern.

Broadly, the various ideological campaigns can be classified under three heads. The first type was directed almost exclusively at eradicating Western influences or leanings and at reasserting party control over intellectual and creative activity. The successive attacks on literature were typical of this class. The opening move of this drive to restore the ideological leadership of the party apparatus over intellectual and creative activity was the publication in August 1946 of a new party journal, *Partiinaia zhizn'* (Party Life), intended for wide distribution (unlike previous party journals which were intended more for the party élite). The first number of this journal published a decree of the Central Committee on 2 August 1946 on the reorganization of party education. This decree laid particular stress on the need to remedy the 'serious shortage' of party members capable of filling the leading posts in the universities, the learned institutions and the learned periodicals.[1]

The decree was followed almost immediately by another decree containing an attack on two literary periodicals published in Leningrad (*Zvezda* and *Leningrad*). The burden of this complaint was that these periodicals had been publishing works which portrayed Soviet people in a slanderous manner as 'primitive, uncultured, stupid, with vulgar tastes and habits'; works which contained no educational or ideological message, but represented 'art for art's sake', and yet

---

[1] *Partiinaia zhizn'*, No. 1, August 1946.

others which revealed 'servile adulation of contemporary bourgeois Western culture'. The stories of the satirist Zoshchenko and the poetry of Akhmatova were singled out for particular vilification. One of the journals, *Leningrad*, was closed down on 14 August 1946, the other was allowed to survive under the new editorship of the deputy director of the Directorate of Propaganda of the Central Committee.[1] Party attacks of this nature on literature continued thereafter. After 1949, attacks on literature began to show signs of linking up with the mounting anti-Semitism which was beginning to appear in official policy. A series of attacks was launched against authors and critics mostly of Jewish origin for their 'rootless cosmopolitanism'. In order to underline the 'un-Russian' nature of their outlook, the attack was concentrated on Jewish authors who had adopted Russian pen-names. They were not openly criticized as Jews, but care was taken to reveal their original obviously Jewish names in the course of the campaign against them.[2]

The campaigns against the philosophers and the philologists may be cited as examples of a somewhat different objective – the breaking up of academic cliques which the party may have feared would grow strong enough to escape its control. The position of the philosophers may have appeared particularly suspect because the same group of men was entrenched not only in the universities and the Academy of Sciences, but also in the very organ which existed for the purpose of exercising ideological control over them – the Central Committee Directorate of Propaganda. The philosophers were castigated in a public discussion held in June 1947 presided over by Zhdanov. That the primary object was to break up the monopoly position which they had built up for themselves is suggested by the fact that the philosophers who were the object of criticism did not suffer any disgrace and did not lose their academic appointments, but were dislodged from their posts in the Directorate of Propaganda.

In the case of the attack on the philosophers the suggestion was indeed made that they had shown excessive admiration for Western philosophers (which, in the virtual absence of Russian philosophers, it was perhaps difficult for them to avoid). But no such feature could be discerned in the sudden attack on the philologists, which broke in 1950, and which was mainly notable for the fact that Stalin made one of his rare personal interventions. For the most part these ideological battles

[1] *KPSS v rez.*, volume III, pp. 485–8.
[2] E.g. Iasnov-Finkel'stein, Zhadanov-Lifshitz, Sanov-Smul'son – *Komsomol'skaia pravda*, 6 March 1949; *Literaturnaia gazeta*, 9 March 1949.

were conducted in the name of the Central Committee as the final arbiter on all questions of science and the arts, though Stalin's personal interest in these questions was not in doubt. For example, a long-drawn dispute between two rival schools of geneticists culminated in July–August 1948 in the victory of the botanist T. D. Lysenko at an open session of the All-Union Academy of Agricultural Sciences. As Lysenko himself pointed out in his report, whereas formerly the followers of his view had been in a minority in the Academy, the 'situation in the Academy has now sharply changed, thanks to the interest taken in it by the Party, the Government and Comrade Stalin personally'. The situation had indeed changed. No less than twelve of the leading professors and academicians were dismissed as a result of this 'interest', for their refusal to adapt the conclusions of scientific research to an eccentric biological theory favoured by the party.

But theories of genetics can have practical results for agriculture, and in the controversy over Lysenko the party, however mistakenly, may have hoped to advance production by a somewhat clumsy attempt to force the scientists to take Lysenko's views seriously. No such motive could be discerned in the case of the controversy over the Marxist interpretation of linguistics. Nothing is to be gained from an analysis of the tedious and academically worthless debate. The importance of the controversy was its effect in dislodging from control of university and academic posts of the followers of the hitherto accepted school of philologists, that of N. Ia. Marr, who died in 1934. In May and June 1950 a public controversy raged, mainly in the pages of *Pravda*, between the supporters of Marr's views and their opponents. On 20 June Stalin put an end to the controversy by coming out against the views of Marr, and more particularly by an all-out attack in very sharp terms against the 'Marrists' who had entrenched themselves in the academic field. As in the case of the philosophers, one aim of this intervention was to shake academic circles out of their sense of security and comparative freedom from party control. The only important ideological pronouncement which fell from Stalin in this dramatic and unexpected intervention was an assertion with regard to the true nature of superstructure and base in Soviet society – incidental to his general argument that language should not be regarded as a part of the superstructure. The superstructure, Stalin argued, was much more than merely the reflection or projection of the base. 'On the contrary, having come into existence, the superstructure becomes the greatest of active powers . . . and takes all steps to help the new order to finish off and liquidate the old base and the old classes.'[1] It was a reassertion in a different form of the view propounded by Stalin in the 30's of the need for the state to survive and not to wither away, the reassertion of the primacy of politics over economics. But virtually the same view had been expressed, or at any rate authorized by Stalin in 1938 when in the *Short History* the agricultural reforms of 1929 onwards were described as a 'revolution from above'.

In the case of the controversies sketched above, the purpose was perhaps administrative rather than ideological: to put an end to any latent admiration for the cultural achievements of the non-communist world, and to undermine the independence of intellectuals. In contrast, the disputes on questions of economic theory which took place between 1947 and 1950, and which were only given authoritative solution by the publication on the eve of the Nineteenth Party Congress of Stalin's *Economic Problems of Socialism in the USSR*, contained some elements of a genuine search for the correct scientific solution to urgent practical problems. The controversy began soon after the publication in late 1946 of a book by the veteran communist economist, E. Varga, on changes in the economy of capitalism as the result of the war. The book was systematically attacked, and the Institute of World Economy and World Politics of the Academy of Sciences which Varga had directed for many years was abolished. But Varga was not disgraced and retained sufficient authority not to recant his views in their entirety, at any rate until after the publication of Stalin's pamphlet in 1952. One of the main opponents of Varga's views was Voznesenskii, to whose sudden fall in 1949 reference has already been made. Since, however, Voznesenskii's fall did not lead to a rehabilitation of Varga's authority, it would seem that Voznesenskii's removal must be attributed to political intrigue unconnected with his views on the capitalist economy.

The views of Varga which were subjected to criticism can be summarized as follows. The capitalist world would escape a serious economic crisis for at least ten years from the end of the war, the countries of Europe had a good chance of achieving reforms of a socialist nature without the forcible overthrow of existing state machinery, colonial territories would continue to move nearer to independence and the outbreak of either anti-Soviet or inter-imperialist wars was no longer to be regarded as inevitable. Varga's opponents argued that the general crisis of capitalism had been intensified by the world war. Moreover, the balance of power between the 'capitalist' and 'socialist' portions

---

[1] I. Stalin, *Marksizm i voprosy iazykoznaniia*, Moscow, 1954, p. 7.

of the world had altered in favour of the latter: People's Democracies had been established in a number of countries, the communist parties in the capitalist countries were stronger and the class struggle was intensifying, and the colonial peoples were struggling for their independence. The USA, in particular, though temporarily more powerful, would be faced with a severe economic crisis in the immediate future, while her drive for world hegemony would intensify the rivalry between the USA and the other capitalist powers. The implications for foreign relations of this controversy, in which the views of Varga came increasingly under fire, are obvious: if Varga was right, the correct policy for the USSR was co-operation with the non-communist world and abandonment of the pursuit of revolution, since its benefits were attainable without such violent means; if his opponents were right, then, on the contrary, the correct policy was implacable hostility to the non-communist world and the promotion of revolution in the confident expectation that it would attain final victory in the imminent economic crisis of capitalism and in internecine wars among the 'imperialist' powers.

Whatever silent support there may have been among the Soviet leaders for Varga's views (none of them ever openly supported him), Stalin's pronouncements finally settled the issue in favour of Varga's opponents in his pamphlet which was published on the eve of the Nineteenth Congress. Stalin's pamphlet was related to and contained references to a discussion among economists which had been taking place at a high level in connection with the preparation of a new textbook of economics. It was therefore in form not so much a reasoned exposition as a series of forceful answers to views expressed in the course of the discussion with which he disagreed. But two of the opinions expressed by Stalin left no doubt as to where he stood in the dispute over the views expressed by Varga. In the first place Stalin came down categorically on the side of those who regarded the crisis in the capitalist world as imminent. The temporary stabilization of capitalism, which he had himself expounded before the world war, had now no longer any validity, he contended. The Marshall Plan, the war in Korea and the armaments race were merely straws clutched at by the doomed imperialists. He also argued that, in spite of the antagonism between the 'imperialist' and the 'socialist' powers, war was more likely to break out between the imperialists than between them and the Soviet Union. This was due to two reasons: first, because war with the Soviet Union would be more dangerous for the 'imperialists' than internecine war, since it would jeopardize the very survival of capitalism; and secondly because the 'imperialists' knew that there was no danger of attack from the Soviet Union in view of its well-known peaceful policy. But only the destruction of imperialism could permanently obviate the danger of wars.

* * *

The problem which faced the party in its dealings with the intellectuals after the war was not very dissimilar from the difficulties which faced it in its relations with the national minorities. The loosening of controls during the war had reawakened dormant national feelings or given rise to new aspirations which did not exist before. There were in addition two new factors after the war which coloured party policy towards the national minorities. One was the reincorporation into the Soviet Union, after the expulsion of the German occupants, of the territories first annexed on the eve of the war. Among the populations of these territories passive and even armed resistance to Soviet authority continued for many years.[1] The other factor was the encouragement given to Russian, as distinct from Soviet, patriotism during the war. The appeal to Russian history and tradition had proved a powerful factor in evoking an emotion of national loyalty and solidarity which appeals to the Soviet tradition were evidently not so well able to achieve. Stalin was anxious to continue to draw on this source of strength after the war. In a speech at the end of the war he singled out the Russian people as 'the most outstanding nation of all the nations within the Soviet Union', and as the 'guiding force' of the Soviet Union.[2] This view was however in contradiction with the national traditions of some of the minority peoples, who gloried in their past struggle against Imperial Russia, and had hitherto been taught to believe that their association with the Russian people within a communist system was on the basis of equality and a common Soviet patriotism.

The problem was tackled by a combination of administrative repression and an attempt to extend the base of the party among the non-Russian peoples of the Soviet Union. In the course of the war seven nationalities were deported *en masse* from their homes and dispersed in Siberia and Central Asia – the Volga Germans, the Crimean Tatars, the Kalmyks and four small Caucasian nationalities – the

---

[1] There were official references to such armed resistance by underground groups for many years after the war – e.g. in the Ukraine in 1954 – *Pravda Ukrainy*, 24 March 1954; in Latvia in 1953 – *Pravda*, 15 March 1953; in Lithuania in 1956 – *Sovetskaia Litva*, 11 November 1956.
[2] *Pravda*, 25 May 1945.

Chechens, the Ingushi, the Karachai and the Balkars. Their total number exceeded a million. Official announcements accusing these nations of disloyalty were made in some instances, in the case of the others the fact of their deportation only became known when it was observed that all mention of them had disappeared from official publications. After Stalin's death it would be admitted that the deportations were not justified by military or security considerations so far as five of these peoples were concerned, and it is extremely unlikely that the case of the other two was in any way different.[1] After the reoccupation of Western Ukraine and the three Baltic republics there were also extensive deportations to forced labour from these territories of those suspected of even potential disloyalty.

The new enhanced status accorded to the Russian people had repercussions among the intellectuals of the non-Russian republics and territories, including intellectuals within the non-Russian communist parties. The historical view of their resistance to Russian conquest which the peoples of Central Asia and the Caucasus had been encouraged by the party to take, at any rate since the end of the 30's, had made some concession to their national pride: annexation of their territories by Imperial Russia was recognized to have been an evil thing, since it was a part of the oppressive colonial policy of Russia; but it was to be regarded as the 'lesser evil', when compared with the alternative of absorption by other imperialist states. After the war the tendency was for the 'lesser evil' to become an absolute good in official party pronouncements: annexation by Imperial Russia was now portrayed as a beneficial and progressive event. Since this view directly clashed with many national traditions which glorified as heroes persons who had fought against the Russians, it became necessary for these heroes to be vilified as agents of the Western imperialists. The effect of this new chauvinism was to cause considerable unrest among intellectuals in the Caucasus and in Central Asia. In the newly annexed parts of the Ukraine and in the Baltic republics, on the other hand, difficulties were caused by resistance to the policy of rapid collectivization of the farms – thus reproducing in miniature the experience which had shaken the Russian party in 1929–33.

Failings among party members on one or other of these grounds,

[1] See *Anti-Stalin Campaign*, p. 57. Five of the nations, it was stated in 1957, would be resettled in their old homes by 1960. No mention was made of the Volga Germans or the Crimean Tatars. (The Volga Germans had been settled in Russia for nearly two hundred years: their vote in favour of the official list in the elections to the Supreme Soviet in 1937 was stated to have been 99·7 per cent.) For a detailed study of the whole course of the deportations see R. Conquest, *The Soviet Deportation of Nationalities*, London, 1960.

comprehensively labelled 'bourgeois nationalism', figured very largely in the reports of the republican party congresses which were held in September 1952.[1] But there were no indications that the turnover of senior officials in the republics had been going on at a much higher rate than in the RSFSR. Thus, the average rate of turnover among the *oblast'* and *krai* secretaries of the RSFSR for the period 1946–52 can be calculated on the basis of changes which took place each year as 15 out of 73 a year, or 19 per cent. If the rates of change are examined for the national republics in the case of the full and candidate members of their central committees, we get the following picture: in three years since their last election, full members, i.e. the highest party and soviet officials, changed at an average rate of 20 per cent, while the candidate members, or the next level of officials, changed at the rate of 25 per cent. These figures do not suggest any exceptional incidence of purging in the republican party organizations. Indeed, as events were to show, much of the purging still lay ahead.[2]

The republican congresses also laid great stress on the efforts which were being made to increase the native representation in the local parties. But such figures as are available suggest that native representation was still low in 1952 in many of these parties – excepting the Caucasian parties, in which there had always been a strong indigenous membership. In the case of five republics for which figures were published, it appeared that from 40 to 60 per cent of delegates were natives, which suggests that about half of all leading officials in the Central Asian and Baltic republics in 1952 were of local nationality. For the party as a whole the proportion was probably lower: thus, in the Moldavian party, the only case where a figure was published, only 24·7 per cent of all members were Moldavians, while in the case of Tadjikistan it was stated that only 38 per cent of all recruits to the party since 1948 had been Tadjiks.

Two general qualifications are however necessary to the picture suggested by these incomplete figures. In the first place, in view of the considerable influx of Russian nationals into many of the republics, particularly the Baltic and Central Asian republics, the low percentage of native party members is not entirely due to their under-representation. Secondly, the comparatively high proportion of native officials

---

[1] The information on these congresses in this paragraph is based on the reports printed in the 15 republican Russian language newspapers concerned during the last fortnight of September 1952. Detailed references are omitted for considerations of space.

[2] For the period 1952–6 the average turnover among higher party and state officials in the national republics was 33 per cent, as compared with only 13 per cent for the RSFSR *oblast'* and *krai* secretaries.

does not necessarily give a correct picture of the extent of responsibility entrusted by the party to natives. For example, certain key posts in the non-Russian republics, such as the head of the security service, are almost invariably held by Russians or Ukrainians. Again, while the first secretary of a republican party is usually a native, the second secretary is in the great majority of cases a Russian, and it is the Russian second secretary who has the greater responsibilities. Thus, while it was true to say that the party was promoting loyal second rank, and occasionally first rank, leaders from among the non-Russian populations, it was not true to say of these populations, with the exception of the Caucasians, that they had by the end of Stalin's rule attained a position of equality with the Russians. The following figures of the nationality of specialists of all kinds with secondary or higher education, published in 1957 but relating to 1954, illustrate the continuing under-representation of non-Russians in this important group, many of which can be presumed to be party members. For comparison, the percentage figure of the population of the republic concerned to the total population of the USSR is shown in brackets.

Ukrainians:	15·1 per cent	(20·3)
Georgians:	2·3 per cent	(2·0)
Armenians:	1·6 per cent	(0·8)
Uzbeks:	0·8 per cent	(3·65)
Kirgiz:	0·2 per cent	(0·95)
Latvians:	0·7 per cent	(1·0)[1]

Special mention must be made of the Jews. No figures of Jewish membership of the party as a whole are available for any year later than 1927. Since Jews formed a large proportion of the 'old bolsheviks', they suffered accordingly in the purges of the late 30's, and no evidence is available to show to what extent the losses were made up by subsequent recruitment.[2] The extent of representation of Jews in the party is, however, perhaps of little relevance to party policy towards the Jews, since in general Jewish party members were as much if not more opposed to the fostering of Jewish nationalism and to Zionism than non-Jewish members. For a short time during the

[1] The figures for these specialists are in *Dostizheniia sovetskoi vlasti za sorok let v tsifrakh*. Statisticheskii sbornik. Moscow, 1957, p. 261. The population percentages take no account of the admixture of Russian settlers. The under-representation of natives may therefore not be so high in some cases as the figures suggest.

[2] In the Ukrainian party in 1940 Jews formed 13·4 per cent of the membership – a high component in relation to what was then the proportion of the Jewish population to the total in the Ukrainian SSR – about 5 per cent. See John A. Armstrong, *The Soviet Bureaucratic Élite*, New York, 1959, p. 17.

war Jewish nationalism was encouraged and stimulated, but solely for the purpose of mobilizing Jewish opinion in the Western world for the fight against Hitler. The short-lived policy was abandoned after the war. Meanwhile two causes had contributed to the growth of nationalist feelings among Soviet Jewry: the sufferings of the Jews at the hands of the Nazis; and the increase of anti-Semitism (never far below the surface in Russia) which became apparent during the war, and which the party did not think fit to discourage. Observers after the war noted that a policy of unofficial discrimination was being pursued against Jews in admissions to the universities and to certain professions. Though Jews remained well represented in intellectual and scientific life,[1] virtually no Jewish names were to be found after the war in the higher ranks of the party – with the notable exception of Kaganovich. This tolerated or unofficial anti-Semitism received a great impetus after the emergence in 1948 of the state of Israel. For many Jews in the Soviet Union this event was the signal for a new hope of escape to a better life. From the point of view of the party it meant that a part of the Soviet population could now be suspected of a rival allegiance. Jewish culture, hitherto tolerated if not encouraged, was now severely repressed: all publications in Yiddish and the Yiddish theatre were closed down in the course of 1949. Anti-Semitism grew more pronounced. In 1952 virtually all the leaders of Jewish culture were shot, and it is possible that deportation of all Jews may have been in contemplation. By the end of the year, according to some reports, mass arrests of Jews were taking place.[2]

* * *

The story of the foreign relations of the Soviet Union during and after the war is beyond the scope of this book. But some aspects of the impact of these relations upon the party must be considered in outline, if only for their relevance to the developments which have been described in preceding pages. After the defeat of Germany and Japan relations between the Soviet Union and her non-communist allies, which had attained in the course of the common struggle a degree of

---

[1] Of a total of 223,893 higher scientific specialists in 1955, Jews numbered 24,620 as against 144,285 Russians and 21,762 Ukrainians. Yet Jews, by that date, after the massacres by the Germans, formed at most 1 per cent of the population. See *Kul'turnoe stroitel'stvo SSSR*. Statisticheskii sbornik. Moscow, 1957, p. 254.

[2] On the position of Jews in Soviet life generally see the well-documented study: Solomon M. Schwarz, *The Jews in the Soviet Union*, Syracuse, 1951. For the abortive attempt to create a Jewish National Home in Birobidjan after 1928, see *ibid.*, chapter xiii: and see also for a more recent survey of the main facts known, Zvi Giterman, 'The Jews', in *Problems of Communism*, Washington D.C., Sep./Oct. 1967, pp. 92–101.

comparative harmony never known before, rapidly deteriorated. Whatever may have been the causes of this deterioration, there were certain factors on the Soviet side which made the prospect of continuing good relations unlikely. One was the morbid fear betrayed by the party of contamination through contacts with the non-socialist world. The ideological battles which began soon after the end of the war were symptomatic of this fear. The revelation during the war of the slender nature of the bond which bound the population to the Soviet system; the effect upon the army of contact with the outer world; and the apprehension that knowledge of foreign conditions of life, of which the true nature had hitherto been carefully concealed, might lead to more general questioning of party assertions may all have played their part. Besides, a totalitarian system, which has to mobilize propaganda on a scale and with a thoroughness which has no parallel in other forms of government, knows no half-way house between total enmity and total friendship: it must either abuse or embrace. And if it dare not embrace, it has no alternative but to abuse.

There was another factor which overshadowed Soviet relations with her allies from the end of the war onwards. The USSR was anxious to establish her influence over Poland and the other countries of Eastern and Central Europe which were of strategic and economic interest. The allies of the USSR were prepared to concede this interest of the Soviet Union. But events soon showed what a gulf of misunderstanding lay between the Western powers and the USSR when the time came for wartime agreements to be put into practice. The Western powers may well have believed that by such phrases as 'democratic', 'freedom loving', or 'democratically elected' governments they had exacted a promise from the USSR that the ordinarily accepted Western form of free government would be tolerated in these countries, so long as they remained in friendly alliance with the USSR. But the USSR may equally well have been genuinely dismayed to find that these time-honoured circumlocutions for communist party domination and rigged elections should be interpreted in their normal sense. Hence, the progressive establishment of communist régimes in all the countries within the Soviet sphere of influence[1] (with the striking exception of Finland), together with friction over the joint administration of Germany, rapidly led to strained relations. The Soviet Union claimed to see in Western resistance to its

[1] For an account of the establishment of communist régimes in the countries of Eastern Europe see Hugh Seton-Watson, *The Pattern of Communist Revolution,* A Historical Analysis, London, 1953, chapter xiii.

domination over Eastern Europe a hypocritical going back on wartime bargains and capitalist fear of the extension of socialism. The Western powers interpreted Soviet policy as a sign that the Soviet Union was preparing further aggression.

The existence of a number of states in which the communist party was or soon hoped to be the ruling party raised an entirely new problem for the Soviet party. Moreover, both in France and in Italy large communist parties had emerged after the war with substantial representation in the legislature. Before the war the Soviet party had successfully established through the Comintern its domination over all other communist parties, with the possible exception of the Chinese party. By a combination of purging and the realization of the fact that the USSR was the main base for the extension of communism, these parties had been prevailed upon to accept not only Soviet leadership, but also the principle that furthering the interests of the Soviet Union was the best way of furthering the cause of world communism. But the Comintern no longer existed – it had played little part after the Spanish Civil War, and was dissolved in 1943. The position was very different in Europe after the war. In Yugoslavia the communists were in power with a good deal of popular support, and owed little to the Red Army. In the other countries of Eastern Europe where communist parties were in power or on the way to power, it was true that they owed their position almost entirely to Red Army support. But once in power, with problems and prospects of their own to consider, it was natural enough that they should begin to look to their own interests first, and perhaps even to question the wisdom of being governed by Moscow in all their actions. In France and Italy the communist parties were exposed to the temptations of 'parliamentary cretinism', in other words of being diverted from their task of revolution by the prospect of yet greater parliamentary successes. There was therefore urgent need to re-create some kind of unifying organization.

Steps to create such an organization were taken in September 1947 when the Communist Information Bureau (Cominform) was set up at Szklarska Poreba in Poland. Unlike the Comintern, the Cominform was not a world organization, but limited to the communist parties of the USSR, of the countries of Eastern and Central Europe which fell within the Soviet sphere, and, significantly, of France and Italy. Its purpose, as appears from a note of its transactions published many years later by one of the participants, was twofold. In the first place it aimed at consolidating the communist bloc in Eastern Europe by asserting Soviet control over the various parties concerned. This was particularly necessary in view of the temptation to stray from the fold which had recently been held out to them in the form of the Marshall Plan for economic aid. But the second object of the Cominform was to extend communist power wherever possible within the range of the parties represented. Steps were discussed for the consolidation of communist party rule in those countries, like Czechoslovakia, where it had not yet been achieved, and the French and Italian parties were severely censured for their failure hitherto to achieve a revolutionary victory.[1]

The attempt to consolidate the communist block in Eastern Europe was not an unqualified success. Within a few months a quarrel had broken out between the Soviet and Yugoslav parties, and when the Cominform met for the second time, in June 1948, it was for the purpose of denouncing the Yugoslav party and expelling it from its ranks. The reason for the quarrel was the refusal of the Yugoslavs to submit to the kind of economic domination which the Soviet Union was successfully imposing upon the more dependent parties of the other countries within the bloc; and their reluctance to model their internal policy in such matters as collectivization of land on the Soviet model. There was also some suspicion on the Soviet side, possibly not ill-founded, that the Yugoslav party leaders had been taking the first steps towards building up a bloc of communist states in Eastern Europe which would be independent both of Moscow and of the West.[2]

The excommunication of Tito was a severe blow to communist solidarity. One of its immediate effects, for example, was to cause dissensions in the Greek communist party, which contributed to the defeat of the communists in the civil war in Greece in 1949. But the main damage which it did was to create for the first time a new phenomenon: a party which called itself communist, which to all intents and purposes spoke the language of Marxism, and which did not accept the authority of the Soviet Union. In the case of China, after the Chinese

---

[1] Eugenio Reale, *Avec Jacques Duclos au Banc des Accusés à la Réunion Constitutive du Kominform à Szklarska Poreba* (22–27 septembre 1947), traduit de l'Italien par Pierre Bonuzzi, Paris, 1958. Reale represented the Italian party, which he left in 1956, and this book consists of the full note of the unpublished speeches which he took at the time.

[2] For the texts of the correspondence between the two parties and of official statements issued at the time see *The Soviet-Yugoslav Dispute*, published by the Royal Institute of International Affairs, London and New York, 1948. On Tito's attempts to build up an independent bloc see my 'The Post-War Treaties of the Soviet Union', *Year-Book of World Affairs*, 1950, pp. 130–49; and cf. Vladimir Dedijer, *Tito Speaks*, London, 1953, pp. 309 ff.

communists had achieved power at the end of 1949, the Soviet party was more successful in maintaining solidarity, even though it had no means of controlling the Chinese. The common interest which bound the two parties was further cemented after the invasion of Southern Korea by communist-controlled Nothern Korea in June 1950, in which China and the Soviet Union co-operated.

Thus, the post-war period served to underline that new circumstances had brought little change in the Soviet party's basic attitude to its foreign tasks. The fact that Varga was able to take so novel a line showed at any rate that there were some members of the party who were capable of a reassessment of the situation. That his argument failed to make any impact suggests that the old rigid ways of thought were too fixed to be altered. By the time of the Nineteenth Party Congress in 1952 the Soviet Union had reached an impasse in its foreign relations. Prospects of revolution had receded in France and Italy. For all his heresies, Tito was secure in Yugoslavia. The useless Korean war had been dragging on for two and a half years without any prospect of victory. A solid defensive organization had come into existence among the Western powers in the form of NATO. The well-tried methods of propaganda which the communist party had used for years were no longer proving as successful as hitherto. The various forms of 'peace fronts' which had been set up in an attempt to camouflage communist organizations as neutral were now being countered by propaganda directed against the Soviet Union. The secrecy with which the USSR had been able to surround itself had broken down, largely as the result of the testimony which thousands of Soviet citizens who had been displaced during the war, and who did not return, were able to provide. For the first time serious academic study of Soviet history, politics and economics was providing the non-communist countries with a basis for countering Soviet propaganda claims about itself. From the point of view of the Soviet party the time had come for a reassessment of its tactics, if it was to make further inroads in a world which was now largely split into two hostile blocs. Stalin's contribution to foreign policy on the eve of the Congress did not hold out any hopes that he at any rate was capable of producing any new and original thought on the problem.

* * *

The Nineteenth Party Congress took place at the end of a period of mounting tension. One ideological battle had followed upon another. Arrests, purges and executions were becoming usual, normal occurrences once again. The execution of the leaders of Jewish culture, though unpublicized, was widely known and struck a new note of horror. A glazed pall of official prevarication could scarcely hope to disguise the ruinous condition of the peasants of which all were aware. Abroad, the threat of war seemed to be coming nearer as the non-communist powers rallied in defence against Stalin's ever more openly aggressive policy. The Congress itself offered little consolation. In his *Economic Problems of Socialism in the USSR* Stalin foreshadowed even more stringent restrictions on the little liberty of action still left to the peasants. His comforting assurance that war was more likely to break out between the 'capitalist' powers than between the USSR and the non-communist world was perhaps less convincing than he hoped. Malenkov in his speech to the Congress went out of his way to lavish praise on the wise policy which had resulted in the purges and the trials of the 30's. Fear was in the air.

Three months after the Congress had ended its deliberations, the press announced the discovery 'some time ago' of a terrorist group of doctors. These doctors had allegedly confessed to the murder of Zhdanov, and to having plotted to put out of action a number of leading military figures with the object of weakening the defence of the country. The doctors were among the most distinguished medical specialists in the country. Seven out of the nine named were Jews. The announcement further alleged that some of the accused doctors were agents of the American intelligence service, with which they were said to have established contact through an American-sponsored Jewish philanthropic organization. The openly anti-Jewish character of the allegations was perhaps a novel feature. In other respects the disclosure of this 'conspiracy' bore every resemblance to the accusations which became familiar in the later 30's. The charges had, of course, been invented from beginning to end, and the confessions obtained by torture – this was officially admitted after Stalin's death in an announcement published in the press on 4 April 1953. (The arrested doctors were later released – all but two, whose names were missing from the list of those released when compared with the list of those arrested. It is to be presumed, in the absence of explanation, that they had died as a consequence of ill-treatment in prison.)

There can be little serious doubt that the intended 'trial' of the accused doctors would have been the starting point for further accusations, arrests and purges. The extent of the intended purge and its objects are still a matter for conjecture. In his secret report to the Twentieth Party Congress in 1956 Khrushchev suggested that a purge of the older members of the Politburo was being prepared before Stalin died, and he mentioned by name as intended victims Molotov, Mikoyan and Voroshilov.[1] Several facts suggest that Beria was one of the intended victims of the plot. First, that although he was accused after his fall in 1953 of almost every crime committed during Stalin's rule since the mid-thirties, it was never suggested that he had been in any way responsible for fabricating the case against the doctors. Secondly, that in November 1951, long before the doctors were arrested,[2] but conceivably at a time when the plot was already being prepared, widespread arrests took place in Georgia of a group of political leaders, all of them Mingrelians, and all close to Beria, who was himself a Mingrelian. All the arrested, who were accused of complicity in a Mingrelian nationalist plot, were rehabilitated after Stalin's death, only to disappear once again after Beria's fall. In the light of subsequent events the Mingrelian 'plot' looks like something in the nature of a dress rehearsal in preparation for an accusation against Beria. Thirdly, the linking of the 'doctors' conspiracy' with international Jewry could have been used to implicate Beria, since it was he who after the outbreak of war was responsible for organizing an international Jewish appeal committee, in an endeavour to enlist Jewish support in the United States against the Germans and in support of the USSR. One of the members of the committee organized by Beria (Mikhoels) was a relative of one of the accused doctors.

It is also possible that the trial of the doctors would have been the signal for an extensive purge in the party, in government organizations and in industry. Attention has already been drawn to the pressure for promotion among the more recent recruits to the party created by the fact that the older men were firmly in control of the top jobs. In 1937–8 Stalin had consolidated his position by the rapid promotion of a new generation of party members who owed everything to his patronage. It is not impossible that his intention in 1952–3 was to repeat the operation. Two circumstances may be cited in support of this hypothesis. The first was the emphasis which the press began to give immediately after the Congress to the need to pick out and promote new men for senior appointments. The words used by *Pravda* in its leading article of 10 December 1952, when the doctors were already under arrest and the plot all ready for launching, are reminiscent of Stalin's boast at the Eighteenth Party Congress that the purge had made

[1] *The Anti-Stalin Campaign*, pp. 84–5.
[2] The date of the arrest of most of the doctors can be conjectured from the fact that up till about November 1952 articles by a number of them continued to appear in the medical journals.

possible the promotion of half a million new men: 'At the helm of the leadership in industry and agriculture, in the party and state apparatus, there should stand people who are devoted to the cause of communism, who know their work well, are capable of introducing a fresh flow and of supporting all that is advanced and progressive. . . . There are plenty of people answering these requirements, and it is only necessary to know how to pick them out in time, and advance them to the leading posts.' The second suggestive fact was the inclusion, without any explanation, of a charge of contravening Article 58 subsection 7 of the Criminal Code in the indictment on the basis of which a security official, Riumin, was charged after Stalin's death with improperly fabricating the 'Doctors' Plot', and executed.[1] Now this article imposes penalties for undermining the national economy with treasonable intent. But fabricating charges against a group of distinguished elderly doctors cannot in any sense be described as undermining the national economy. The inclusion of this article in the indictment against Riumin therefore suggests the possibility that those who framed it were aware that the charges fabricated by him would not have been limited to the doctors, but were part of a grand design eventually to launch a more far-reaching purge which would embrace industry.[2]

The question of responsibility for launching the abortive plot is also largely conjectural. There can be little doubt that Stalin was the prime mover in the whole affair, since it is inconceivable that a step of this gravity could have been taken without his initiative. Nor can there be very much doubt about the vital role played by Poskrebyshev, who, so far as is known, remained throughout the post-war years in the all-important post of Stalin's personal secretary and head of the Special Section of the Secretariat. In this capacity it is a fair assumption that he had special responsibilities next to Stalin in controlling the security organs, probably over the heads of those officers who were nominally in command of them. Poskrebyshev disappeared without trace immediately after Stalin's death. At the Twentieth Congress Khrushchev raised a laugh among his listeners by referring to him as Stalin's 'loyal shieldbearer'.[3] It was the first public reference to him for three years.

The persons who were made to suffer for fabricating the charges were a group of police officials, headed by Riumin, who were executed in 1954, allegedly after trial. These subordinate officials paid a much

[1] *Pravda*, 23 July 1954.
[2] This argument is advanced by B. I. Nicolaevsky in an article 'Rasstrel Riumina' in *Sotsialisticheskii vestnik*, No. 8–9, August–September 1954.
[3] *The Anti-Stalin Campaign*, p. 55.

heavier penalty than those whose orders they were carrying out. The Minister of State Security, S. D. Ignatiev (who was a career party official seconded to this post), was merely demoted to a provincial party post, and remained a member of the Central Committee. According to Khrushchev, Stalin had threatened to 'shorten him by a head' if he did not obtain the required confessions in a case which was 'fabricated from beginning to end'.[1] But it is difficult to see by what logic he escaped the consequences of issuing orders for the execution of which a subordinate was shot. Some, at any rate, of the secretaries of the Central Committee must have been privy to any plans which were afoot to launch a new purge which was certain to have widespread repercussions in the apparatus under their control – certainly the two senior secretaries, Malenkov and Khrushchev. One of the subordinate secretaries, Aristov, who headed the department responsible for appointments within the party network, and would therefore have been particularly closely concerned with any purge, was temporarily demoted to a provincial post after Stalin's death, but not disgraced.[2]

The contrast between the lenient treatment of highly placed party officials and the severe victimization of subordinate police officials may indicate that the party leaders close to Stalin, while not daring to oppose him while he was alive, were none the less reluctant to start a new blood-bath in the party. Their reluctance is easy to understand. The Ezhov purge had shown that when once such an operation is launched no one can foretell where it will end, and not even the highest placed in the party can be sure of remaining unscathed. Stalin's death on 5 March 1953 from a haemorrhage of the brain halted in its initial stages whatever new assault on the party may have been in contemplation. He was no longer young, and had already been showing some signs of strain at the time of the Nineteenth Congress. In the absence of firm evidence it is fruitless to speculate whether his death was wholly due to natural causes. Of one thing there is no doubt: for many members of the party, both highly placed and less eminent, the death of the Leader came only just in time.

[1] *The Anti-Stalin Campaign*, p. 64.
[2] He was like Ignatiev, elected a member of the Central Committee.

PART FOUR

Since Stalin Died

XXX The Rise and Fall of Khrushchev

Six main features could be distinguished in the party as it appeared to an observer in 1952. It had in the first place become a mass party, yet at the same time selective. It was no longer, as it had been in Lenin's lifetime, a small band of zealots, but an assembly of the nation's élite in all walks of life. It sought talent where it could find it, having long freed itself from the doctrinal preference for proletarian membership, to which in theory it owed its origin and indeed the very reason for its existence. While seeking to broaden its base by admitting worker and peasant members, it consisted predominantly of persons who were in positions of authority at various levels. It aimed to gather into its fold the great majority of men and women in the highest positions. It was probably to this view of the function of the party that the disproportionate predominance of Russians over some of the non-Russian inhabitants of the Union was due. So long as Russians were considered more reliable or more fit for administrative tasks, no considerations of equality of representation were allowed to colour the party's national composition. It was possibly in part, at any rate, for similar reasons that the highest administrative party posts were still in the hands of the older and more experienced men.

The second feature was the predominance within the party of the apparatus of officials and secretaries, who formed a small minority of around three per cent. By virtue of the authority which they had acquired in the course of years, not without bloody conflict, these officials could dominate elections, discussions and decision inside all party organizations throughout the country. The overt efforts which the party leadership made from time to time to stimulate greater democracy in the party rank and file, whether genuine in intention or not, had repeatedly come to nothing. The members of the party had learned from experience that the only safe course was to follow the lead which came from above: to vote for the list which the leaders of the party organization proposed; to criticize only those who had already been censured from above, and then to criticize with vigour; and to vote without question for proposals which came from those in authority, and only for such proposals. The shrewder member knew that whatever calls for greater democracy and initiative might be issued from time to time, the last thing the party leaders in Moscow wanted was members who thought for themselves.

The third feature of the party was the centralization of the apparatus itself. At the top of the hierarchy of secretaries and officials were the secretaries of the Central Committee, controlling through their subordinate officials the several departments of the Secretariat. Experiments in administrative devolution had always proved short-lived. The party had repeatedly returned to the form of administration which left the threads of control firmly in the hands of the central Secretariat. In some cases, for example in the control of agriculture in so far as it was exercised through the political departments of the MTS, the centre acted directly through its own emissaries. But even where there was devolution of party administration through the regular network of subordinate organizations, as in the case of industry, the Secretariat at the centre always found it necessary to retain machinery for day-to-day control.

This centralization of the apparatus, which was observable at the time of Stalin's death, was not a new feature – indeed, much of it derived directly from Lenin's conception of the party, even if in Lenin's lifetime complete centralization was not attained. But the personal ascendancy of Stalin – the fourth feature in order of those now under examination, but probably the first in importance – gave a particular character to traditional forms. Stalin was a great deal more than leader of the party. He could govern either through the party or without it, as he thought fit. The secretaries who controlled the apparatus were faithful executants of his policy, when and if he required it. But he was powerful enough to go outside the normal party channels when he thought it necessary. He could, and did, ignore the formal party organs when he chose – he summoned no Congress for over thirteen years, allowed meetings of the Central Committee but rarely, and even apparently avoided summoning the full Politburo. The powerful security force seems to have been under his direct and personal control, through his personal secretariat. That he needed others to carry out his will is obvious. But he was in a position to mobilize for action now one lieutenant, now another, without any formal discussion or decision, in an atmosphere of intrigue, conspiracy and fear.

This personal ascendancy of Stalin over the party gave rise to the fifth feature which was discernible in the last years of his life: a corresponding decline in the influence of the party.[1] The reason for this decline was that the party apparatus was faced with the competition of the expanding government apparatus, deliberately fostered in the interest of the safety which the dictator sought in the duplication of his instruments of control. So long as he himself stood at the apex of each hierarchy, and in addition wielded, when required, the arm of the security forces, there was little reason for him to fear this enhanced status of the government machinery. At the lowest level of the primary party organizations the competition of the two administrative networks was a fertile source of conflict which could be resolved, if at all, only by increasing central interference: the primary organizations were by the party Rules endowed with the power of 'control', and were expected to exercise it. Within the government departments at the centre, however, the primary party organizations were by the Rules expressly restricted in their powers of control: here at any rate the administrative machine could pursue its tasks unhampered by daily interference – though of course always subject to the policy laid down by the Politburo, or by the dictator acting in its name.[2]

To some extent, moreover, the inconvenience of this dual system of administration was mitigated by the existence of a common pool from which officials of both party and government machines were drawn. It was frequent, indeed usual, for state officials – such as republican ministers, or chairmen of the executive committees of the soviets at the various administrative levels – to be drawn from among those who had served in the party apparatus. To a lesser extent this was also true in reverse: a number of party officials were drawn from among those who had previously served in the state machine.[3] But while it was obviously an advantage that an official in the one machine should have had experience in the other, and consequently an understanding of its problems, interchange by itself could not solve the conflicts which continually arose in day-to-day administration.

The sixth feature of the party at the time of Stalin's death was one which had become firmly established and progressively developed at any rate since the 30's: the interpenetration by party members of all institutions and activities within the state. The process of achieving this had been far from uniform. In one important sphere, the collective farms, as late as 1952 party control was still remote and somewhat

---

[1] The implications of this important, and usually neglected, fact in the study of totalitarianism, are discussed in the Epilogue below.

[2] This provision dated from 1939 – see *KPSS v rez.*, vol. III, p. 392. It was re-enacted in 1952 – *ibidem*, p. 592.

[3] See *Rigby Thesis*, Chapter ix for details.

haphazard because of the continued lack of party organizations in many individual farms. This was a circumstance which the party could not view with equanimity. The fear that agricultural institutions might develop some independence and compete with the political and economic order as determined by the party was endemic among the party leaders at all periods of the party's history – it will be recalled that in an earlier chapter it was suggested that fear of the competition of the old village communes may have been one of the factors which determined the policy of rapid collectivization in 1929.[1] The absence of a fully developed party organization on the farms right up to the end of Stalin's life may in part have been the cause of the completely arbitrary methods by which it was sought to ensure control over the farmers. Only one leader, Khrushchev, so far as is known, had shown some energy in dealing with the problem, when, by amalgamation of the collective farms, he made possible the creation of a more fully developed network of rural party organizations.

*   *   *

Such, in outline, was the party when Stalin's death on 5 March 1953 removed the linch-pin from the machine. The first and immediate concern was to restore this linch-pin in the person of Malenkov. The keynote of the party and government reorganization announced on 7 March was the desire to ensure continuity of leadership and unity in order to prevent what was described as 'disorder and panic'. Both party and government leadership were streamlined and reduced in size. The Council of Ministers was now also to be headed by a Praesidium, consisting of the Chairman of the Council of Ministers, Malenkov, and four First Vice-Chairmen – Beria, Molotov, Bulganin and Kaganovich. Beria became Minister of the Interior, combining within his ministry the security forces and internal affairs, which had hitherto been under separate ministers. Molotov became Foreign Minister, Bulganin Minister of Defence.

The Bureau of the Praesidium of the Central Committee of the party was now abolished (its very existence since October 1952 had remained secret) and the Praesidium itself reduced in size: its members, in the order as published which was neither alphabetical nor by seniority, had been: Malenkov, Beria, Molotov, Voroshilov, Khrushchev, Bulganin, Kaganovich, Mikoyan, Pervukhin and Saburov. There were also three changes in the Secretariat, which included the bringing into this vital organ of Shatalin, Malenkov's

[1] See Chapter 18 above.

deputy for many years in charge of party cadres. Malenkov thus combined, like Stalin, the posts of senior secretary and head of the government machine.[1] For about a week the press proceeded to build up Malenkov in the manner reminiscent of its treatment of Stalin, including the publication in *Pravda* of a faked photograph.[2]

It soon became evident that this appointment of a new Stalin was only a temporary measure. On 14 March the Central Committee 'granted the request' of Malenkov and released him from his post as Secretary. The Secretariat now consisted of Khrushchev, Suslov, Pospelov, Shatalin and Ignatiev, the former Minister of State Security.[3] Party and government machines were now once again divided, as they had been up to May 1941. But there was an important difference. Lenin as Chairman of the Council of People's Commissars had easily dominated both party and government machines, though it was true that the party machine had not been developed to its full powers during his active lifetime. After Molotov had replaced Rykov in this office in 1930, at any rate, Stalin had easily asserted the predominance of the party. But Molotov had been content to remain Stalin's shadow. Now two energetic rivals confronted each other, each in control of a powerful machine. That the object of this division of power represented a common desire among the party leaders to prevent the re-emergence of a new dictator with powers comparable to those once wielded by Stalin was suggested by the emphasis which was now laid in party utterances upon the importance of 'collective leadership'. It is a matter of conjecture whether Malenkov was forced out of the Secretariat by his colleagues, or whether, faced with the choice of relinquishing one of his two offices, he chose to retain the government post in the belief that the government machine had now become the more influential.

The next few months were occupied with reversing the 'Doctors' Plot' and with conflicts between the party leaders and the security and police apparatus. On 10 July 1953 the arrest of Beria was suddenly made public. (He had been arrested about a fortnight before; the rising of 17 June 1953 in East Germany may have served as a

---

[1] *Pravda*, 7 March 1953. The changes were announced as a joint decision of the Plenum of the Central Committee, the Council of Ministers of the USSR and of the Praesidium of the Supreme Soviet: see *KPSS v rez.*, volume III, pp. 603–7.

[2] The photograph bore the caption 'Greatest Friendship', and was a montage designed to show Malenkov alone, though somewhat larger in size, with Stalin and Mao Tse Tung. It was in fact based on a group photograph taken in 1950, from which several intermediate figures had been excised – see *Pravda* of 15 February 1950 and 10 March 1953.

[3] *Pravda*, 21 March 1953.

convenient pretext.) Some of the charges levelled against him (including an accusation that he had worked for the British intelligence service for over thirty years) were no more credible than the kind of charges that Beria's officers had so often in the past made up against others. The real significance of the fall of Beria was more clearly revealed in a memorandum privately circulated by the (party) Praesidium for the information of senior party members. This suggested, among other things, that Beria had used the security apparatus in an attempt to assume for himself powers independent of and against the other members of the Praesidium.[1] But whether this allegation was true or not, there is no doubt that the elimination of Beria put an end to the position of the security organs as a state within a state which they had acquired under Stalin.

Beria's successor was no longer a member of the Praesidium, and the status of the security machine was further weakened by its subdivision once again in March 1954 into a Ministry of Internal Affairs (MVD) and a Committee of State Security (KGB). The Ministry of Internal Affairs was progressively stripped of its vast economic empire, and the enterprises formerly controlled by it brought under the management of the normal economic ministries. A purge took place of senior security officials, and in a few important cases posts hitherto occupied by members of the security service were given to military men. A number of party officials were also put into key posts in the security machine. The fall of Beria could also conveniently be used to throw the blame for past irregularities upon this one man, and thus to exonerate Praesidium members for their own share of responsibility in supporting Stalin's actions.

Within four years this collective oligarchy had given way to a system in which the First Secretary of the party (the title was officially conferred on Khrushchev in September 1953), having eliminated from the Praesidium all but three of its original members, had become, if not an autocrat like Stalin, at any rate to all appearances the unchallenged leader of policy. The reasons why the experiment in oligarchy proved short-lived can at present only be conjectured. There were genuine disagreements on policy between Khrushchev and the rivals whom he defeated, and it is conceivable that his victory over them was due to real support for his views which he could muster in

[1] An account of the contents of this memorandum was given by a senior Polish communist, who saw it in the course of his duties – see *Hearings before the Sub-Committee of the Judiciary*, United States Senate, Eighty-Fourth Congress, Second Session on Scope of Soviet Activity in the United States, June 8, 11 and 29, 1956, Part 29, Washington, D.C., 1957, pp. 1,556–7.

the Central Committee. Some allowance must be made both for the personal ambitions of an energetic man and for the fact that in a system where policy is largely formulated independently of public opinion and where genuine representative organs for resolving differences of view between several leaders of equal status do not exist, a dictatorship of one man offers the advantages of efficiency and convenience. Above all, it is important to remember that the victory of Khrushchev over rivals like Malenkov both symbolized and in fact was the reassertion by the party of its predominance over the government machinery, which under Stalin it had to some extent been losing.

*   *   *

In the course of the first four years after Stalin's death there were at least four major issues upon which divergences of views between members of the Praesidium were evident from such information as was made public. The first was the perennial question of the relative importance to be attached to the production of means of production and to the production of consumer goods. Malenkov's administration was launched to the accompaniment of promises of an increase in consumer goods production. The promise was fulfilled, at any rate to the extent that the rate of growth of production of consumer goods in 1953 for the first time in many years exceeded that for heavy industry.[1] This departure from communist orthodoxy, no doubt dictated by a desire to make the new government more popular, found its theoretical champions,[2] but was subsequently attacked by other economists, and with particular violence by the editor of *Pravda*, Shepilov, on 24 January 1955. This attack appeared on the eve of a plenary meeting of the Central Committee at which it may be presumed the decision was taken to remove Malenkov from his post as Chairman of the Council of Ministers. But the beginning of his decline in influence could be dated much earlier – certainly no later than June 1954, when the method of listing Praesidium members was changed: thereafter they were listed in alphabetical order, and not, as before, in order of importance, with Malenkov heading the list.

On 8 February 1955 at a session of the Supreme Soviet Malenkov was replaced as Chairman of the Council of Ministers by Bulganin,

[1] This can be calculated from the percentage rates of growth in each category of goods in relation to 1940, as printed in *Narodnoe khoziaistvo SSSR*, Statisticheskii sbornik, Moscow, 1956, p. 47. The relative rates for the increase in 1953 of producer and consumer goods were 11·6 and 12 per cent.

[2] See e.g. an article by Ia. A. Kronrod in *Kommunist* No. 16, November 1953.

ostensibly at his own request. In a statement read on his behalf (Malenkov, though present, did not open his mouth), he pleaded his inexperience of administration as the reason for his resignation and admitted his responsibility for the unsatisfactory state of agriculture. Bulganin was succeeded as Minister of Defence by the war hero Marshal Zhukov, who had been appointed deputy Minister of Defence after Stalin's death, and had before then been kept in comparative obscurity. The fall of Malenkov was immediately followed by the disgrace of one of his supporters, the Minister of Culture, Aleksandrov, and by the eclipse of another, Shatalin. There were also later changes in the regional network of first secretaries, which would in due course be reflected in the composition of the Central Committee.[1]

The unsatisfactory state of agriculture, which was a heritage of Stalin's régime, had been revealed in considerable detail in September 1953 in a report made by Khrushchev to the Plenum of the Central Committee. Henceforward the First Secretary became the spokesman for agricultural policy. The plans which he initiated bore the stamp of his more realistic approach to the problem of making collectivized farming a success in face of peasant resistance. But it is not unlikely that his policy raised apprehensions in the minds of the more conservative party leaders, including the older and more rigid communists reared in Stalin's school, like Kaganovich and Molotov, that the collective farms might grow powerful enough to hold the government up to ransom. The main features of this policy, as it developed progressively in the next few years, may be summarized as follows: considerable increases in material incentives to the collective farms to produce; a simplification of the multiple system of central control over the farms, and a decentralization of production planning, so as to allow a measure of local initiative to the individual farms; and a considerable streamlining of the system of party control over the farms,

---

[1] According to some competent observers, the fall of Malenkov was primarily due to his lack of aggressiveness in foreign policy. This view is supported by three pointers: the fact that Malenkov was the first Soviet leader to concede publicly that a nuclear war would destroy all civilization, and not only the capitalist world; that his fall was preceded by a visit of Khrushchev, Bulganin and Mikoyan to China, and followed by the period of four years, before the break between the Soviet Union and China, when relations between the two countries were closest; and by an attack on Malenkov in *Kommunist*, No. 4, 1955, for his 'weak nerve', and for allowing himself to be frightened by the Western imperialist powers. The fact that Khrushchev adopted all of Malenkov's views on foreign policy after the fall of the latter, does not, of course, invalidate the argument. Incidentally, if the fall of Malenkov was in any way due to his resistance to building up China's war potential, then Malenkov may one day be seen as having tried to serve his country better than Khrushchev, whose policy in 1954–5 led to China becoming a nuclear power.

which strengthened the role of the party at the expense of government agencies. (This aspect of the new agricultural policy is further discussed below.)

In addition, a great campaign for producing grain from hitherto virgin territory in Kazakhstan and elsewhere was launched in the spring of 1954; and finally in the spring of 1958 the most revolutionary proposal of all was made public – the transfer of the means of mechanical power to the ownership of the farms, and the abolition of the Machine Tractor Stations. The fact that Khrushchev's measures[1] were to a large extent successful in reviving agricultural prosperity contributed to the prestige and power of the First Secretary, and therefore of the party. When announcing his proposal for the abolition of the MTS Khrushchev was able to claim that the average income of the collective farms which was 111,000 roubles a year in 1949 was now 1,247,000 roubles. Taking a graphic illustration from his own native village, he claimed that the collective farm centred there had increased its production of grain nearly fourfold since 1953, and its income ninefold.[2] These figures were undoubtedly exaggerated, and the collective farm chosen as an illustration far from typical. But whatever his audience may have thought of Khrushchev's figures, there was undoubted evidence of a rise in agricultural prosperity and in living standards.

The decline of the influence of Kaganovich, the most experienced of the older communists on questions of industry, seems to have coincided with the eclipse of Malenkov. The only First Chairman without departmental responsibilities in the Council of Ministers, as reorganized after Stalin's death, he acted as 'overlord' for the whole planning of industry. But in March 1955 three new First Deputy Chairmen were created – Mikoyan and the two planning experts, Saburov and Pervukhin – and Kaganovich soon after became Chairman of the State Committee on Labour and Wages and, after September 1956, Minister of Building Materials Industry. He was thus relegated from a position of policy making to the more practical daily administrative sphere. His successor as the dominant figure in planning was Pervukhin, but Pervukhin's ascendancy was short-lived. At the Twentieth Congress in February 1956 ambitious targets for industrial

---

[1] In their overall results. The 'virgin lands' campaign in the end proved a failure.

[2] *Pravda*, 28 March 1958. A more sober estimate of the increase in collective farm income was given by Khrushchev to the Plenum of the Central Committee on 15 December 1958: as compared with 1952, the total income of all collective farms was rather more than double in 1957 – see *Plenum tsentral'nogo komiteta kommunisticheskoi partii Sovetskogo Soiuza, 15–9 dekabria 1958 goda*, Stenograficheskii otchet, Moscow, 1958, p. 62.

achievements by 1960 were set. The high point of Pervukhin's influence was the Plenum of the Central Committee in December 1956. But by this date investment resources were severely strained, and there were many indications that the industrial targets set by the Twentieth Congress were unattainable. (They were in fact tacitly abandoned in 1957.)

The Plenum sought the solution of the problem in improvement of the central planning mechanism, while at the same time maintaining intact the traditional, centralized control over industry. Pervukhin now became chairman of a considerably strengthened State Economic Commission – a body of recent creation, which had been split off from *Gosplan* for the purposes of current, as distinct from long-term, planning. *Gosplan* was correspondingly downgraded. That Pervukhin was intended to become something in the nature of an 'overlord of overlords' was evident from the fact that nearly all the existing First Vice-Chairmen and Vice-Chairmen of the Council of Ministers were transferred to the State Economic Commission. But there were three notable exceptions: Malenkov, a Deputy Chairman of the Council of Ministers since his resignation in 1955, and Molotov and Kaganovich, both First Deputy Chairmen. (A further Deputy Chairman, probably also in disfavour, Tevosyan, was shortly afterwards appointed Ambassador to Tokyo, and posted away from the centre.)

Two months later, at the Plenum of the Central Committee which met in February 1957, it became evident that quite different ideas were afoot on how to improve the situation in industry. According to the resolution of this Plenum it was now necessary to 'rearrange the work of the State Economic Commission', which should not conflict with *Gosplan*,[1] thus foreshadowing a departure from the policy agreed on the previous December, when *Gosplan* had been relegated to the background in favour of its sister body, and its chairman, Saburov, criticized. Six weeks later, on 30 March, the publication of the Theses which Khrushchev proposed to submit to the forthcoming Supreme Soviet showed that the First Secretary was planning a system of widespread decentralization of control over industry which was diametrically opposed in principle to the system of improved centralized control foreshadowed in the reforms of December 1956. The subdivision of the country into a number of economic regions, each headed by a council of national economy was now proposed. The councils of national economy were to be responsible for the running of the industries within their area, under the overall supervision of a much

---

[1] *Pravda*, 15 February 1957.

enlarged *Gosplan*, which would co-ordinate without however destroying the initiative of the councils of national economy in planning their own output. The central industrial ministries, on the other hand, would no longer be necessary and would disappear.

There is no doubt that this revolutionary proposal evoked a good deal of opposition, much of which did not come out into the open. Even so, the public discussion to which the Theses of 30 March were submitted, though controlled, was sufficient to indicate that opposition to the scheme came mainly from the factory directors and industrial planners. When the Theses came to be debated at the session of the Supreme Soviet in May 1957, not one of the directors or planners present in the hall took part in the debate: if not allowed to oppose, they were not prepared to support. The new law as enacted did indeed make some concessions to the criticism which had been advanced in the press discussion. For example, eight All-Union industrial ministries, of the type which under Khrushchev's original proposal would have been abolished, were (for a time) allowed to survive – they were mostly ministries connected with defence. Even so, no less than ten All-Union ministries and fifteen union-republican ministries of an economic character were abolished.[1] Pervukhin himself became minister of one of the surviving ministries, that of Medium Machine Building, which is responsible for atomic energy. Important as this appointment was, it removed him from any policy-making position. The enhanced role of the party, especially at regional level (which is discussed below), was well symbolized by the appointment as head of *Gosplan* of I. I. Kuz'min, whose career had been mostly spent in the party apparatus.[2]

Thus Malenkov, Kaganovich and Molotov, as well as the planners Pervukhin and Saburov, had lost most in influence by the spring of 1957. Molotov's position had also been severely shaken by his opposition to Khrushchev on foreign policy, culminating in a conflict over relations with Yugoslavia. In May 1955 a delegation from the Soviet Union, headed by Khrushchev, but not including the Foreign Minister, Molotov, visited Yugoslavia. (Tentative steps had already been taken somewhat earlier for the resumption of relations which had been broken off in 1948.) Khrushchev expressed 'sincere regrets' for

[1] *Istoriia sovetskoi konstitutsii*, sbornik dokumentov, 1917–57, Moscow, 1957, pp. 512–19. For a discussion of the problems raised by this industrial reorganization see Philip E. Mosely, 'Khrushchev's New Economic Gambit', *Foreign Affairs*, July 1958.
[2] For his career see the entry in *Politicheskii slovar'*, edited by B. N. Ponomarev, 2nd edition, Moscow, 1958.

the past deterioration of relations, blaming the 1948 rupture conveniently on Beria. The mission of peace ended with a joint declaration which, among other things, stressed the right of each country to pursue its own form of socialism. This Canossa had been throughout opposed by Molotov. In July 1955, however, matters came to a head. Molotov's view was carried for discussion to the Plenum of the Central Committee, where Molotov found no support and was forced to repudiate his opinions.[1] It is likely that there were conflicts on other issues of foreign policy as well (including policy towards Austria), for Shepilov succeeded him as Foreign Minister in 1956.

But Khrushchev's position was to be somewhat shaken by the repercussions of the momentous Twentieth Party Congress, which met in Moscow from 14 to 25 February 1956. The gradual relaxation of tension which had been allowed since Stalin's death, the impact of the curbing of the powers of the security forces which had followed upon Beria's disgrace, and the fact that the Congress was meeting somewhat before its appointed time all lent an air of expectancy to the proceedings. Khrushchev's main report, with which the proceedings opened, did not however produce any very startling surprises. The First Secretary was a man of practice rather than theory, and those among his audience who expected new light to be thrown on the foundations of Marxism-Leninism as a result of new experiences were either doomed to disappointment, or left to read their own interpretation into what he said. There was indeed a certain robust common sense about the speech: the old formulae were all there, but it was clear that no question of doctrine was to be allowed to interfere with the practical issues that mattered – the increase of production at home, the preservation and advancement of communist power abroad. In his short discussion of ideology he repeatedly emphasized that theory was of no use without practical application: the transition to communism, now in progress, was not a matter of propaganda, or of fantastic theories, but of hard work, in order to overtake the productive capacity of more advanced countries. He listed three main tasks in the ideological sphere: preservation of the unity and authority of the party and, above all, of the principle of collective leadership; harnessing the directing activity of the party towards practical tasks; and

[1] This part of the Plenum proceedings was not published, and is only known from the account of the record of the meeting as seen by the Polish communist referred to in Note 1, p. 560, at pp. 1,562–3 of the report there cited. But the fact that the debate did take place at this Plenum was confirmed in June 1957 in the official communiqué dealing with Molotov's expulsion from the Central Committee – see *SPR*, 1957, pp. 121–6.

increase of vigilance in ideological work in order to overcome the influence of bourgeois ideology.

It was when he dealt with the relations of the Soviet Union with foreign countries that Khrushchev made two assertions which were, probably erroneously, widely interpreted to mean startling departures in Soviet policy. In the first place he contended that, although the existence of imperialism still meant that there was always a risk that the imperialist powers would start a war, it was no longer necessary to hold the view that war between the socialist and capitalist states was inevitable. This was interpreted in some circles to mean that the Soviet Union was now prepared to maintain relations of real peace with the non-communist states. But he went on to give his reasons for the change: the 'social and political forces' which favoured peace inside the capitalist states were now strong enough to prevent the imperialist powers from unleashing an aggressive war. This suggested that what Khrushchev had in mind was that war could be prevented by the timely victory of communism, and the 'social and political forces which supported it', in other words, that he now saw a prospect of achieving peacefully the universal victory of communism which hitherto it had been believed could only be achieved by force. He also stressed that the forms of socialism varied with different circumstances, and that there was no single formula applicable to all, making a specific reference to Yugoslavia. There is no doubt that some of the countries of Eastern Europe interpreted this to mean that the USSR would show greater tolerance than hitherto to the desire for independence felt by some of their communist parties. It is unlikely that Khrushchev foresaw, let alone intended, the explosive consequences which his remarks were to have.[1]

On the third day of the Congress, Mikoyan's speech electrified the audience by its open criticism of Stalin. Hitherto, although there had been a considerable decrease in the amount of praise showered on Stalin, and although some of the events of his period of rule had been obliquely criticized, even if the blame for them was thrown on Beria, no one had as yet publicly called in question the dead leader's perfection. Mikoyan now frankly asserted that for the past twenty years 'we have in fact had no collective leadership', but had been living under the 'personality cult' which Marx had condemned. He went on to criticize Stalin's *Economic Problems of Socialism in the USSR*, and even criticized the *Short Course* on the history of the party.[2] The real

[1] *XX S"ezd*, volume I, pp. 34–41, 111–18.
[2] *XX S"ezd*, volume I, pp. 302–3 and 322–5.

bombshell came on the morning of 25 February when the Congress went into closed session to hear a second speech by Khrushchev, 'On the cult of personality and its consequences'.[1] Frequent references have already been made to this secret speech in previous chapters, and reasons advanced for accepting as substantially genuine the only text available, which was published by the US State Department.[2]

In an atmosphere which was tense and emotional, according to accounts circulated at the time by correspondents of foreign communist party papers in Moscow, Khrushchev dramatically tore away the veil in which Stalin's reign of terror had hitherto been conventionally shrouded. With a frankness which had long disappeared from party life he sketched Lenin's conflict with Stalin at the end of his life and retold the long forgotten story of the 'Testament'. He described, with full facts and figures, the assault which had been made during the period of Ezhov's office on party members and leaders, forced by torture to confess to crimes which they had never committed. Khrushchev did not tell the whole story – he neither vindicated Trotsky and Bukharin, for example, nor told of the holocausts which had been wrought on the peasants in the guise of a war against the 'kulaks'. He said nothing of the part played by himself and his colleagues who had survived Stalin's onslaught.

Yet this secret speech, which rapidly became widely known (the text was circulated to communists inside, and to some outside, the USSR), had an enormous effect. To close students of communism outside the communist world it contained little that was not already familiar, if only from numerous reports of refugees from the Soviet Union. But to communists who had dismissed all such reports as slanderous, the official admission that they were substantially true undermined for a time their faith in their leaders. There were serious defections in many parties. In two of the countries of Eastern Europe, Poland and Hungary, the revelations ignited or helped to fan the flames of discontent with the severity of the government of their own communist leaders. Indeed, both the reconciliation of the USSR with Yugoslavia and what Khrushchev said in public at the Twentieth Congress on the subject of different roads to socialism all helped to raise hopes among some of the communists of Eastern Europe that they would now at any rate be able to replace some of the most hated

[1] *XX S"ezd*, volume II, p. 402.
[2] See above, p. 395, note 2.

leaders imposed by Moscow with leaders of their own choice. In Hungary these hopes led in October 1956 to a national uprising of workers and students, which the Soviet Army repressed by force. In Poland an uneasy compromise was reached by the acquiescence of the USSR in considerable changes in the nature of the régime, and in the dismissal of the more unpopular leading communists, including the former Soviet Marshal Rokossovsky. It was not an exaggeration to say that by October 1956 the communist bloc was facing the threat of disintegration.

It is easy to see that this, the greatest threat which communist rule had faced since the Kronstadt rising of 1921, gave powerful ammunition to Khrushchev's opponents, who could argue with some justification that he had placed the whole régime in jeopardy by his revelations at the Twentieth Congress. The drastic economic reorganization of May 1957, which aroused opposition among powerful classes of Soviet society, came on top of the shock caused by the revolts in Hungary and Poland. It is therefore not a matter for surprise that the final settlement between Khrushchev and his opponents in the Praesidium should have come in June 1957. Khrushchev, having been outvoted in the Praesidium and threatened with removal from the Secretariat, succeeded in summoning an extraordinary meeting of the full Central Committee in which he could rely on adequate support. A number of accounts suggest that the Minister of Defence, Marshal Zhukov, played an important part in the crisis both by facilitating transport for the members of the Central Committee and by a show of military force.

On 29 June 1957 a communiqué was issued which stated that an 'anti-party group' consisting of Malenkov, Kaganovich and Molotov, with the support of Shepilov, had tried to bring about changes in the composition of the leading organs of the party by 'anti-party, factional methods' (which presumably meant that they had tried to secure the removal of Khrushchev); that they had disagreed with the party line on a number of issues, including the economic reorganization, the policy on agriculture and the reconciliation with Yugoslavia; and that they had been expelled from the Central Committee (and hence automatically from the Praesidium) by a unanimous vote of the Central Committee in a full session of members, candidate members, and members of the Central Revision Commission,[1] with one absten-

---

[1] This mainly honorific body has the duty of supervising the activities of the central party-apparatus and the finances of the Central Committee (see *KPSS v rez.*, III, p. 587).

tion, that of Molotov.[1] Since however these opponents, Malenkov, Kaganovich and Molotov, were given no opportunity of stating their case publicly (they were presumably given a chance to speak in the Central Committee) there is no way of determining whether, as alleged in the official communiqué, it was they who precipitated the crisis, or whether it was engineered by Khrushchev in order to put an end to the political influence of opponents who were now supplied by events with a powerful argument against himself. Until June 1957 Khrushchev's three opponents remained members of the Praesidium. As elected at the Twentieth Congress with some later additions it also included, apart from himself, Bulganin, Voroshilov, Kirichenko, Pervukhin, Mikoyan, Saburov and Suslov. Thus, out of eleven members in June 1957, five – Malenkov, Kaganovich, Molotov and the two planners, Saburov and Pervukhin, were fairly certain to vote against Khrushchev, and it only needed one vote, that of Bulganin, to turn the scales against him. (Khrushchev had at least four supporters among the seven candidate members, but it is not certain that a candidate member can vote, except probably in the absence of a full member.) Having weathered the attack in June, or perhaps successfully provoked it, Khrushchev was able to place his support in the Praesidium on a sounder basis. After June 1957 it consisted of fifteen full members. Marshal Zhukov, now the Minister of Defence, became one of the new members (he had only been a candidate until then), and so did all the other five candidates, except the disgraced Shepilov.

Khrushchev's industry in securing the promotion of his supporters as candidate members of the Praesidium was rewarded: of the fifteen members, six apart from himself were secretaries of the Central Committee, that is to say his immediate subordinates in the daily administration of party rule.[2] A further change took place by the end of the year. A conflict with Zhukov arose which may have been due, as officially alleged, to Zhukov's inattention to political indoctrination inside the army, or more probably to Khrushchev's sound instincts as an autocrat which led him to remove even a potential rival who had troops under his command. For Zhukov, who had for the past years been backing Khrushchev against all political opponents, had as a result

---

[1] *SPR*, 1957, pp. 121–6. Much light was cast on these events by many of the speeches at a Plenum of the Central Committee at the end of December 1958 of which the proceedings were published – see Note 2, p. 563; and at the 21st Extraordinary Congress in January 1959.

[2] The full members were: Aristov, Beliaev, Brezhnev (all secretaries), Bulganin, Voroshilov, Zhukov, Ignatov, Kirichenko, F. R. Kozlov, Kuusinen (secretary), Mikoyan, Suslov (secretary), Furtseva (secretary), Khrushchev (secretary), and Shvernik.

been steadily advancing up the ladder of political pre-eminence. Zhukov was now quite suddenly relieved of his military post, showered with abuse and expelled from the Central Committee. Zhukov's successor as Minister of Defence was a man who had worked closely with Khrushchev during the war.[1] He was replaced on the Praesidium by the Uzbek Mukhitdinov. At the same time Mukhitdinov and two other members of the Praesidium were appointed secretaries of the Central Committee, but one secretary, Beliaev, was posted to Kazakhstan.[2]

The position in the Praesidium in December 1957, therefore, was that out of fifteen full members, nine (ten, if Beliaev still for a time retained his office in Moscow) were also full-time secretaries of the Central Committee. Of the remaining five full members, three were weak and unimportant personalities (Bulganin, Shvernik and Voroshilov) and two (F. R. Kozlov and Mikoyan) were reliable supporters of Khrushchev. The planners were now at most represented by one candidate, Pervukhin, the lowest on the list of eight, and an ex-planner at that. The contrast with the Praesidium elected in March 1953, upon which Khrushchev was the sole representative of the central party apparatus, and the planners had two full members, was very striking. It was of course a personal triumph for Khrushchev, who had thus made certain of a comfortable majority for all contingencies, since his subordinate secretaries over whose careers he could freely dispose were not very likely to oppose him. But, more important, it was the complete vindication of the status of the party in relation to the government machine. For the nine secretaries, who according to custom established in the 20's, were meeting, probably daily, as a board to co-ordinate the administrative departments of the Secretariat through which all administration of the country was controlled, could now also dominate the Praesidium on issues of policy making. The government machine had been largely emasculated as a result of the industrial reorganization. Even so, within a few months Khrushchev had added the office of Chairman of the Council of Ministers to that of First Secretary, thus completing the victory both of himself and of his party machine. It was no exaggeration to say that in five years he had created what to all appearances looked like the most solid and reliable basis for securing his own continuance in power that any party autocrat could wish for. And yet, within little

[1] Marshal Malinovskii, one of the three military members of the Stalingrad Military Council.

[2] His relinquishment of the office of Secretary of the Central Committee was not published until 12 November 1958.

more than six years, Khrushchev had been suddenly ousted from power, and reduced to that status of living ghost which he himself had devised for defeated political opponents.

*   *   *

The six years or more which elapsed between the time when Khrushchev consolidated his supremacy over both party and government and his fall are in some respects the most colourful in the history of the party. He had effectively rendered harmless his overt opponents: they included both those originally named as the 'anti-party group' – Malenkov, Molotov, Kaganovich and Shepilov – and those whose support of the 'group' was only revealed subsequently – Pervukhin, Saburov, Voroshilov and Bulganin. But the danger was eventually to come from an unexpected quarter – his friends, if friends there be in the jungle of the totalitarian polity. The personal impact of this remarkable, if eccentric, man grew ever more evident in his policies: the sense of security which his firm control over the apparatus seems to have given him right up to the sudden moment of his fall only served to conceal the apprehension and resentment which were building up in the hearts of his closest associates. His policies made enemies in many sections of society. He antagonized the security organs by curtailing their almost unlimited powers, and by exposing their bloodstained past. The party apparatus, many of whom lost their jobs under the impact of his, often impetuous, demands (over half of the secretaries of the provincial party committees were replaced between January 1960 and October 1961) resented the assault on their own authority which public criticism of Stalin after 1956 necessarily entailed. Khrushchev's attempts to remodel the provincial committees at the end of 1962 diminished the status of many of the first secretaries affected. The reform of agricultural control in the course of the same year left several thousand district secretaries looking for other employment; while the setting up in 1963 of the new Party-State Control Committee, under the chairmanship of a former KGB Chairman, A. N. Shelepin, raised apprehensions that party officials would soon face even more exacting disciplinary control. These matters will be dealt with in the next chapter. Besides, the party apparatus had little reason to be grateful to Khrushchev for the fact that some semblance of institutional life had been restored in the party: small as the signs of incipient democracy in the party may have been, and for the most part at the lowest levels at that, they were not welcome to officials who were more used to implicit obedience to their directives. Besides, while Khrushchev never tired of stressing the need for party secretaries to exercise the fullest control over all aspects of life of the country, he was both ruthless and demanding in results, and sudden and unpredictable in exacting the penalty for failure – often, it would seem, on the basis of very hasty and subjective judgements. He never hesitated to make his subordinates pay for the failure of those policies of his own which were quite incapable of implementation. So far as the harassed apparatus man was concerned, life may, in the rosy glow of retrospect, have seemed less hazardous even under Stalin (except during the great purge years) than under Khrushchev. The period of Khrushchev's office is littered with the political corpses of men in high position who fell from grace – suddenly, and without any discernible cause: Beliaev, Mikhitdinov, Spiridonov, Shcherbitskii, and Kozlov – to mention only a few.

Khrushchev cannot but have been aware of the enemies he was making in the apparatus of the party and of the security service. But it would have been natural enough for him to reason that so long as he retained control over this apparatus (which he did until the end) its enmity presented little danger. After all, had not the party been firmly controlled from the top almost since its inception, and certainly since the advent of Stalin? What the ebullient First Secretary did not foresee was that some of his own close associates in the Praesidium of the party would be moved by his policies (which they could do comparatively little, from the nature of the Soviet system, to modify or restrain) to combine with the apparatus in order to thrust him out.

There is little reason to surmise that the hearts of the men who put their heads together to oust Khrushchev from power (Brezhnev, Kosygin, Podgorny, Suslov and Shelepin, among others) bled for the plight of the party secretaries or security officials. But they were sufficiently antagonized by Khrushchev's conduct of affairs in other respects to risk the hazardous conspiracy. There were certain aspects of Khrushchev's policy which aroused apprehension and even antagonism among his immediate colleagues – as can be inferred not only from the evidence available at the time, but more particularly from the actions of his successors when once power was in their hands.

The first such aspect was the condemnation of Stalin which Khrushchev had initiated at the Twentieth Congress in 1956. As he disclosed five years later, he had been faced with opposition to this course from some of his colleagues – Molotov, Kaganovich, Malenkov, Voroshilov 'and others'.[1] It was indeed an operation fraught with risk, since it inevitably raised the question of the complicity in Stalin's misdeeds of the present leaders, including Khrushchev himself. Moreover, one consequence of the condemnation of the period of 'the cult of personality' had been to open the floodgates of criticism of the past – in historical writing, in creative literature and in memoirs. The frightened men of the party apparatus, whose long experience was of the police state in which both history and literature had for years (under the guise of 'socialist realism') carefully avoided even veiled hints at the awful truth of reality, knew quite as well as the avid readers of the new, heady books and articles that denunciation of the present was, as often as not, implied in the condemnation of the past. It was too late to stem the flood; but at all events they wanted to keep the waters under control. In particular they feared, and with some justification, that if once an attempt were made to exact penalties, whether by expulsion from the party, or, even worse, by criminal proceedings, from those who had supported Stalin in his destruction of innocent victims, a chain of events and actions would be started, of which no one could foresee the end.

Khrushchev's persistence, in the face of resistance, in making his party colleagues face some of the reality (never the full reality) of the past may in fact be explained as a move in the political game against his main rival, Malenkov. For after all Malenkov had been personally and fully involved in the great purges of 1936–8, Khrushchev had not to nearly the same extent, except in the Ukraine. Yet, perhaps some credit is due for what was the first attempt for many years to introduce an element of principle into Soviet politics; and it is only fair to recall that it was in part, at all events, Khrushchev's persistence in attacking Stalin that led to his downfall. The whole question came as near to the surface as possible in Soviet conditions at the Twenty-Second Congress of the party which met in Moscow from 17 to 31 October 1961. To the surprise of outside observers, the question of guilt and retribution for Stalin's crimes was the dominant theme in the debates. The Congress agreed to the removal of Stalin's embalmed corpse from the mausoleum where it had lain by Lenin's side. It proved less severe to the living. It was not prepared to follow the lead of Khrushchev and exact party, let alone criminal, penalties from those denounced for their complicity in Stalin's misdeeds. The debate was cautious, and the terms used were veiled. But the difference of outlook

[1] *XXII S"ezd*, volume II, p. 583.

between Khrushchev and some of his supporters on the one hand, and those who did not wish to go so far on this vital issue on the other, was plainly discernible.[1]

It would be naïve to see Khrushchev as a 'liberal' politician on account of his attitude to Stalin's holocaust. Khrushchev remained throughout an arbitrary and unpredictable ruler. Repression of the Orthodox Church and of religion generally increased markedly under his rule; and, while writers were not made to stand trial for their critical works (as was to happen under the rule of his successors), they occasionally ran the risk of certification as lunatics by the psychiatrists of the KGB, or of exile by administrative action on the accusation of being 'parasites', and were in any event constantly subjected to the First Secretary's homely but sharp abuse. Similarly, although no 'liberal' in his foreign policy, Khrushchev was apparently sufficiently alarming to his colleagues to cause apprehension in their minds, and to cause them to put his policies into reverse when once they had overthrown him. However, their fears may have been more aroused by the rash and idiosyncratic manner in which Khrushchev pursued his ploys, than by the policies themselves. Such escapades as the rash attempt in 1962 to install offensive missiles in Cuba, followed by withdrawal when the ruse was discovered and the bluff was called, did little to enhance Soviet prestige. But, as the time of his fall approached, Khrushchev seemed also to be offending against two cardinal principles of Soviet foreign policy of the nuclear age: the support of 'wars of liberation'; and resistance to the 'export of counter-revolution' and the maintenance of the solidarity of the Socialist camp. Thus, he made it clear that he was anxious to disengage from all commitments in South East Asia, including the war in Vietnam; and allowed hints to get abroad that he was prepared to negotiate on the future of divided Germany. This apparent desire by Khrushchev for disengagement in subordinate areas of conflict may have been occasioned by the widening of the split with China, and its first public recognition at the Twenty-Second Congress in 1961 when Albania, the satellite of China, was openly attacked. It was also consistent with Khrushchev's policy, first formulated in January 1960, to reduce substantially the numbers of the armed forces, and to place greater reliance on modern technical weapons, including nuclear power. But this policy had caused fierce resentment in the army, and had in any case proved

---

[1] For a close analysis of the debates at this Congress see Michel Tatu, *Power in the Kremlin: From Khrushchev's decline to Collective Leadership*, London, 1969, pp. 141–64.

impossible to maintain. Nor was reduction of conventional forces consistent with a growing potential threat from China to disputed areas on the Sino-Soviet border. The military, in the person of Marshal Zhukov, had been prepared to rescue Khrushchev in June 1957: it is more than likely that they witnessed his departure in October 1964 without any regret.

Khrushchev also came into conflict with the planners and with those responsible for the management of the planned economy whose task became more complex as the demands of the consumer were increasingly taken into account. The dominant role which he was determined to forge for the party apparatus in this as in other spheres was indeed unrealistic, in view of the highly technical nature of modern planning. This policy was stressed in 1961 in the new party Programme,[1] and became increasingly evident in practice in the following years. Khrushchev believed that this way of doing things could be justified by the improvement in the technical education of the apparatus men on which he insisted. But in truth the amount of technical knowledge which a full-time official in the apparatus could ever hope to wield was bound to remain at best inadequate when confronted with the experience of a full-time technician, scientist, manager, planner or economist. Conflict was therefore inevitable. Yet, the planners were able to hold their own: in the end, a very different structure of industrial control emerged, early in 1963, from the one announced (it would be unreal to say 'proposed') by Khrushchev to the Plenum of the Central Committee in November 1962. An entirely new organ emerged in March 1963 endowed with supreme powers over all industry without exception. No mention had been made of this super-organ at the November 1962 Plenum. This was the Supreme Council of National Economy (SCNE). It was headed by D. F. Ustinov, who now became First Deputy Prime Minister, along with Mikoyan and Kosygin, and was closely associated in his past career with Kosygin. There can be little doubt that SCNE was forced against Khrushchev's opposition. Ustinov was not elected to the Praesidium at the Plenum of June 1963, and was at least once publicly slighted by Khrushchev. Moreover, the prompt disbanding of the SCNE after Khrushchev's fall suggested that its function had been to act, under Kosygin and Ustinov, as a counterweight to the party apparatus, and that it was no longer needed in the conditions of collective leadership. There were also other substantial differences between Khrushchev's avowed intentions and the machinery which

[1] The Programme is discussed in the next chapter.

emerged. In particular, the roles of the main economic organs were reversed. Khrushchev had designed a Council of National Economy for the USSR (which was a new name for the existing State Planning Commission, or *Gosplan*) to deal with short-term planning, and a new *Gosplan* to deal with long-term planning. In the event, the new *Gosplan* took over all planning, while the Council of National Economy of the USSR was left only with the supervision of plan fulfilment.

Perhaps the most pressing reason to remove Khrushchev, as it appeared to his colleagues on the Praesidium, was the increasingly personal nature of his leadership. After the death of Stalin lip service was usually paid to 'collective leadership': it became ever less evident in practice. The ascendancy of Khrushchev after 1958, when he assumed the office of Chairman of the Council of Ministers in addition to that of First Secretary of the party, in itself ill accorded with the denunciation of the 'cult of personality' after 1956. His actions after 1958 showed increasing disregard of his colleagues: both in home and in foreign affairs he tended to act first and then to face his colleagues with a *fait accompli*. He was not always successful in putting through his policies, and some of the policies which he did put through, especially in matters concerning agriculture, which he tried to run almost single-handed, were abject failures. His colleagues, many of whom had narrowly escaped the hazards of a new purge by Stalin in 1953, could have been forgiven for fearing that their own positions could be at risk if Khrushchev continued in office much longer, and became a complete personal dictator. His fall came suddenly, unexpected by most outside observers, and by Khrushchev himself. The circumstances of his ouster are unknown. His replacement as First Secretary of the Central Committee by Brezhnev was announced on 15 October and his replacement as Chairman of the Council of Ministers by Kosygin on the following day. The actual ouster in the Central Committee probably took place on 13 or 14 October. At no time was Khrushchev allowed to make any public statement in his defence, nor was any official account of what happened in the Central Committee ever published. It cannot even be stated with certainty that he was present when the Central Committee met – he could have been under house arrest. But two facts can be asserted with confidence. First, that by the time the Central Committee met Khrushchev's ouster had already been effected: the experience of June 1957, when Khrushchev turned the tables on his opponents in the Praesidium by appealing to the Central Committee, had not been forgotten. And secondly, that some important part in the affair was played by the KGB: the promotion of A. N. Shelepin to full membership of the Praesidium in November 1964 (he had not even been a candidate member) is clear evidence of this. For Shelepin had been Chairman of the KGB from 1958 until 1961, and continued to retain considerable influence in that body through his successor as Chairman, V. E. Semichastny, who was his close associate.[1]

*　　*　　*

The most paradoxical aspect of Khrushchev's fall was that it occurred at a time when, to all appearances, his hold over the party at all levels was complete. The importance of appointments as an index of the relative power and influence of the top leaders has been repeatedly evident throughout this story. There are very strict, if secret, rules relating to the appointment (among many others) of all officials throughout the party at all levels. These rules are set out in lists called *nomenklatura*, in which the persons whose concurrence is needed in the making of particular appointments at all levels, and in all areas of activity, are set out. The secrecy with which the party *nomenklatura* is guarded is explained by the fact that the great majority of the offices within the party which are covered by it are in theory elective. However, certain basic principles relating to the more important offices can be discerned from practice, and a reconstruction of the *nomenklatura* for the more important party offices has been made by a former senior party member.[2] Thus, for example, the Plenum of the Central Committee must concur in the appointment of Secretaries of the Central Committee – and in practice this means a prior decision in the Praesidium; the Secretariat must concur in the appointment of heads of departments of the Secretariat, among a host of other vital appointments in the party apparatus; and heads of certain departments of the Secretariat exercise appointing power over a considerable range of offices – for example, the Department of Administrative Organs does so in relation to the officials of the Security Service. Thus, he who can influence the appointment of the Secretaries who control the important departments can ensure control over a great and vital area of the party apparatus. Of course, this only represents a fragment of the whole picture, since Praesidium, Secretariat and Heads of Departments

---

[1] For the best summary of the evidence relating to the ouster of Khrushchev and analysis of its causes see Peter Reddaway, 'The Fall of Khrushchev', in *Survey*, No. 56, July 1965.
[2] See A. I. Lebed', 'Podgotovka i raspredelenie rukovodiashchikh kadrov SSSR', in *The Bulletin of the Institute for the Study of the USSR*, No. 3 (189), Munich, 1965, pp. 100–117 (reproduced for private circulation only).

likewise participate in appointments at various levels of the government machine. Now, it is usually quite easy, on the basis of timing of promotions or demotions, past associations, or areas of service, to discern the probable allegiance to individual members of the Praesidium or to individual senior secretaries of officials for whose appointment concurrence of the Praesidium or Secretariat is required. Hence, even making all allowance for error, it becomes possible by the study over a period of changes in appointments to discern the rise or fall in influence of the various party leaders.

This method is particularly illuminating for the period of Khrushchev's tenure of office: it shows beyond any reasonable doubt the complete ascendancy of Khrushchev in the matter of appointments. At the time of his fall he was still the only member of the Praesidium with more than one function: he was First Secretary of the Party, Chairman of the Council of Ministers, Chairman of the Praesidium, Chairman of the RSFSR Bureau, and Commander-in-Chief of the Armed Forces. The Central Committee, in which a two-thirds vote is required for vital decisions like the expulsion of a member, included among its 175 full members 73 members of the party apparatus of whose appointments Khrushchev had directly or indirectly approved, 14 military members who were his old associates from the time of the war and 12 close personal supporters – such as his son-in-law and general factotum Adjubei. Thus, all that he required was a further 19 votes from among the incumbents of the state apparatus, the scientists and the ambassadors – not a very difficult task. If one examines the list of the full members of the Praesidium elected on 31 October 1961[1] together with the very few replacements which took place in the following three years, one can find nothing to suggest that Khrushchev was in any danger of failing to secure a comfortable majority at any time. The missing factor, not discernible at the time, was that a number of his close supporters and even protégés – Brezhnev, Kosygin, Podgorny and Polianskii among others – would decide to turn against him.

An examination of the changes in the vital secretariat during the last four and a half years of Khrushchev's period of office reveals an interesting story of a different kind: an attempt, which failed, to install a successor. This was F. R. Kozlov whom, indeed, Khrushchev described on several informal occasions as his designated successor. The Plenum of 4 May 1960, at which Kozlov was appointed Secretary, drastically curtailed the number of secretaries by the removal of the

[1] See Appendix III.

three men (four, if Brezhnev's appointment as Chairman of the Praesidium of the Supreme Soviet be taken into account) who could conceivably rival Kozlov.[1] Within eighteen months, however, something had gone wrong with Khrushchev's plan to clear the decks for Kozlov. One can only conjecture that Kozlov had either shown impatience to succeed as First Secretary or had otherwise proved a disappointment. No doubt the truncated secretariat also proved weak as an administrative machine. At all events, between October 1961 and June 1963 no less than ten new secretaries were added, every one of whom could be identified as a protégé or associate of Khrushchev. (A timely stroke effectively removed Kozlov from the scene in April 1963.) The experiment of grooming a successor had failed: but the First Secretary's control over the Secretariat appeared to be unimpaired right to the end.

It may well be supposed that those who replaced Khrushchev drew the moral from their own success: that the time-honoured system of packing key posts with supporters, friends and associates was not necessarily a safe basis for keeping oneself in office. No assessment of the first years after the fall of Khrushchev can be attempted at so short a distance in time, though some speculations on possible developments in the future will be found in the Epilogue. The new leaders lost little time in reversing virtually all that Khrushchev had done. His elaborate restructuring of the party was swept away, and the novel system of controlling industry through local Councils of National Economy replaced by the more traditional hierarchy of central government departments and subordinate administration. There were changes in policy both at home and abroad. There was no serious reversal of the trend which had existed since Stalin's death of paying more heed to the demands of the consumer. Indeed, some advance was made in 1965 in furthering plans, already under discussion while Khrushchev was in office (associated with the name of Professor Liberman), of giving more initiative in planning their production to individual enterprises; and of making both prices and profits in some degree dependent on efficiency, and on consumer demand. Time was to show that the traditions of overcentralization remained a serious obstacle to the full and successful operation of these new experiments.

But in other respects small trace remained of the imprint of Khrushchev on party policy, and indeed doctrine. By the time the Twenty-Third Congress of the party met at the end of March 1966

[1] See Appendix IV for changes in the Secretariat which illustrate this story.

the Programme of 1961[1] was a dead letter. It had also become apparent long before then that denigration of Stalin was going to be stopped. Stalin's military genius was applauded during the anniversary celebrations of victory in World War II in 1965; while the Theses prepared by Brezhnev for the anniversary of the October Revolution in 1967 followed the now accepted formula of brushing aside the grim events of the Stalin era as 'temporary set-backs and errors'. Along with this 'rehabilitation' of Stalin went increased persecution of literary and intellectual figures. Lastly, Khrushchev's policy in foreign affairs was largely reversed – though, like Khrushchev in the case of Hungary in 1956, Brezhnev and Kosygin were in 1968 to find it necessary to pursue an escaping satellite, Czechoslovakia, with an invasion of tanks and troops. So much in Soviet foreign policy is constant. But in virtually all other areas a new, more vigorous and more expansionist, policy than the one formed by Khrushchev was embarked on: substantial aid was supplied to North Vietnam, military and naval budgets were expanded, and new and large-scale support was provided to the Arab states in their conflict with Israel.[2]

The most important immediate change was the assertion of 'collective leadership'. This much-overworked phrase has been given a variety of meanings in the course of Soviet history. Its practical meaning in 1964 was a resolution by the Central Committee on 13 or 14 October, when Khrushchev was removed, that in future it was undesirable that the offices of First Secretary of the Central Committee and Chairman of the Council of Ministers should be combined in one man.[3] And indeed the intention in the first years of the new régime seems to have been to keep the spheres of First Secretary and Prime Minister distinct, at any rate at the top level. The fact that the two offices were filled by men each of whom was important as a leading political figure in his own right (in contrast, for example, to the situation between 1955 and 1958 when a nonentity like Bulganin was Prime Minister) lent reality to 'collective leadership': decisions of the Praesidium (or Politburo as it became in 1966) required concurrence of all its members, or at all events of its most important members; and no one member enjoyed obvious pre-eminence. For example, there was no evidence, in the first few years at any rate, that Brezhnev, unlike Khrushchev, was the permanent Chairman of the Praesidium, or Politburo.

---

[1] See the next chapter for a description of the Programme.
[2] These matters are also dealt with in the next chapter.
[3] The only known reference to this resolution is in P. A. Rodionov, *Kollektivnost' – vysshii printsip partiinogo rukovodstva*, Moscow,19 67, p. 219.

There were relatively few changes among top leaders in the first few years of 'collective leadership'. The startling elevation of Shelepin to the Praesidium has already been commented on; but he was destined before very long to suffer a slight decline in eminence, particularly in 1965 when his party/state control committee was abolished and he himself lost his seat in the Council of Ministers. No doubt both Brezhnev and Kosygin could concur on the need to prevent a third, and ambitious, leader from wrecking the harmony of their duumvirate. Ustinov eventually and belatedly attained candidate status in the Praesidium, in March 1965. His elevation coincided with his transfer to the Secretariat: it was perhaps not too fanciful to discern in this entry of the top technical expert on the defence industry, closely linked in his career with Kosygin, into the citadel of the party apparatus an attempt to keep its interference in the world of industry and planning down to a minimum. Two of Khrushchev's nominees – V. N. Titov and L. F. Ilyichev – were removed from the Secretariat and from positions of authority in the course of 1965. Ilyichev, the expert on propaganda, was replaced by P. N. Demichev, who became a candidate member of the Praesidium almost immediately after the fall of Khrushchev. Perhaps the most interesting change of all was the election in June 1967 of Yu V. Andropov, who had shortly before replaced Semichastny as Chairman of the KGB, as a candidate member of the Politburo. In one sense this move symbolized the growing status of the KGB – no security chief had attained Praesidium status since Beria. But it could also be interpreted as a further assertion of collective leadership: the presence of the head of the security service on the Politburo could well have the effect of reducing the personal influence over that service of the General Secretary (as the First Secretary was known after the Twenty-Third Congress) through his subordinate in the Secretariat, the head of the Department of Administrative Organs. Only time would show whether collective leadership was going to last. But by the end of 1968 it had at any rate withstood the shock of the invasion of Czechoslovakia on 21 August of that year.

XXXI Internal Developments: Ideology and Policy, 1953–1966

The composition of the party did not undergo any very fundamental changes in the first five years after Stalin's death. Its total size increased by only 4·8 per cent between the Nineteenth and Twentieth Congresses – from 6,882,145 to 7,215,505, including candidate members.[1] The increase was proportionately greater in some of the republics, notably in the Ukraine (15·1 per cent), in Belorussia (13·3 per cent) and in Kazakhstan (11·0 per cent). By January 1959 the total membership of the party was 8,239,131 members and candidates, representing a growth of about 14 per cent.[2] The rate of growth in some republics, at any rate, was even higher. Thus, the membership in the Ukraine increased by some two hundred thousand between 1956 and 1958, or by about 25 per cent, and comparable increases occurred in some other republics.[3] The position with regard to *Komsomol* membership was less satisfactory.[4]

Little information is available for this period on the age of party members as a whole, but it is likely that it remained low. In the case of the Ukraine, for example, in 1958 nearly a fifth of all members were under thirty, and over a third between thirty and forty; a fifth were over fifty.[5] (Admission to the party is open under the Rules from the

---

[1] *XX S"ezd*, volume I, p. 98.

[2] *XXI S"ezd*, volume I, p. 259.

[3] E.g. Moldavia – 17 per cent; Armenia – 10 per cent; Kirgizia – 13·5 per cent. For Ukraine see *Partiinaia zhizn'*, No. 12, 1958, pp. 58–9. The figures for the other republics, and all data on the republican parties unless otherwise indicated which are given in the text hereafter, are taken from the reports of the republican congresses as printed in the Russian-language newspapers published in the republican capitals. No details were revealed in 1958 of the party strength in the Baltic republics.

[4] Membership in 1954: 18,825,327 (*Pravda*, 1 March 1954). Add to this: 10,000,000 enrolled between 1954 and 1958 – *Komsomol'skaia pravda*, 16 April 1958 = 28,825,327. Take away from this an annual wastage of 1,000,000, since one million was the wastage given for 1956–7 – *Komsomol'skaia pravda*, 25 July 1957. This makes 24,000,000 for 1958, also allowing for the 735,000 who transferred to the party – *Komsomol'skaia pravda*, 16 April 1958. Yet membership in 1958 was only 18 million – *ibidem* – i.e. 6,000,000 short.

[5] *Partiinaia zhizn'*, *loc. cit.*

age of eighteen, though persons up to the age of twenty are required to seek admission to the party through the ranks of the *Komsomol*.) The bulk of party members were recent recruits – in the case of the Ukraine, as at the beginning of 1958, one-third had joined between 1941 and 1945, and about two-fifths had joined after the war.[1] Such evidence as there is suggests that the social composition of the party did not undergo much striking change between the two Congresses – the white-collared occupations continued to predominate in the membership. This is also borne out by the fact that the educational standard of members continued to rise. In 1956 14·7 per cent of all members and candidates had received complete or incomplete higher education, as compared with 11·8 per cent in 1952; 22·2 per cent had completed secondary education.[2]

After 1956, however, greater stress was laid on the need to recruit workers and farmers, and by 1958 some change may have become apparent. In the Ukraine, in 1958, workers formed 22·5 per cent and collective farmers nearly 15·5 per cent of all members; workers and farmers were stated to have formed 65 per cent of all recruits in 1957. In Moldavia in 1956–7, 78·3 per cent of all recruits were said to have been workers and peasants. In Azerbaidjan, worker and peasant recruits between 1956 and 1958 made up 60·6 per cent of the total, in Tadjikistan 49 per cent and in Turkmenistan 53·2 per cent.[3] No detailed information exists to show the extent to which the non-Russian nationalities had succeeded in increasing their representation in the party in those cases where they still remained under-represented. In 1956 a number of the republican parties were still under strength in proportion to their total populations – notably the Central Asian and Baltic republics, the Ukraine and Belorussia.[4] The only

[1] *ibidem.* No figures are available for the other republics. T. H. Rigby, *Thesis*, chapter iv, calculates seniority as at 1954 for the party as a whole as follows: 9·3 per cent up to 1933, 15 per cent between 1936 and May 1941, 46 per cent wartime recruits, and the remainder, about 30 per cent, post-war.

[2] *XX S"ezd*, volume I, p. 237. At this date one-third of the total of 15,460,000 technical specialists were party members, i.e. 5,150,000 intellectuals out of a total membership of 7,215,505, or over 70 per cent – see *Kommunist*, No. 11, 1958, pp. 62–3. At the Twenty-First (Extraordinary) Congress in January 1959 it was stated that the number of party members with higher education had increased by 632,993 or 23·9 per cent since the Twentieth Congress – *XXI S"ezd*, volume I p. 260.

[3] Figures for the Ukraine from *Partiinaia zhizn'*, *loc. cit.*, for the other republics from congress reports. It is not known how how far the trend has been general, but at the Twenty-First Congress it was stated that nearly two-thirds of those now admitted to the party are workers and collective farmers – *XXI S"ezd*, volume I, p. 112.

[4] For the whole of the USSR the party membership in 1956 represented 3·55 per cent of the total population. Comparable percentages for some of the republics were: Armenia – 4·33; Georgia – 4·63; Azerbaidjan – 3·52; Kirgizia – 2·54; Uzbekistan – 2·6; Lithuania – 1·44; Ukraine – 2·25; Belorussia – 1·8.

information available for the period up to 1960 on the proportion of native communists in any single republican party is once again the Ukraine, where in 1958 Ukrainians formed 60·3 per cent, Russians 28·2 per cent and others 11·5 per cent.[1]

More information exists on the party élite, as represented by the Union and republican central committees and by delegates to congresses. The older and more experienced party members continued to predominate among the élite, and promotion was comparatively slow for the younger members of recent standing in the party, at any rate to the higher posts. Thus, 65 per cent of delegates at the Twentieth Congress had joined the party before 1941, and only 13·4 per cent had joined since the war.[2] In the party as a whole the percentage of those who had joined since the war was certainly very much higher. Moreover, in spite of the youthfulness which characterized the party as a whole, and which had, if anything, become more marked since 1952, the proportion of more mature delegates had actually increased by 1956 as compared with 1952 – nearly 89 per cent of them were over forty, as compared with 76·4 per cent in 1952.[3] At the republican Congresses, however, this predominance of older delegates was becoming less marked.[4]

The entrenchment in positions of influence of the older and more experienced members appears most marked when one examines the top leadership of the party, the Praesidium. An analysis of the background of the ten full members who had emerged as the real rulers of the country by December 1957, the ten Secretaries headed by the First Secretary, shows the predominance among them of those who were earlier described as the 'neo-Stalinists', the men who only came to prominence under Stalin, and with his support. Of these ten, one, Kuusinen, an old man of seventy-six, could probably be discounted, especially as his intellectual gifts did not suggest that he was the 'éminence grise' of the party. The sixty-three-year-old First Secretary,

---

[1] *Partiinaia zhizn', loc. cit.* More information on this question became available in later years. See below.

[2] *XX S"ezd*, volume I, p. 238. (At the XIX Congress 80 per cent of delegates had joined the party before 1941.)

[3] *XX S"ezd*, volume I, p. 238; *Current Soviet Policies, II.* p. 94. At the Twenty-First (Extraordinary) Congress in January 1959, 78·8 per cent of voting delegates were over forty. But in spite of this continuing maturity of delegates, the number of newcomers to the party élite had increased: 21·1 per cent of voting delegates had joined the party since the war, and only 57·7 per cent had joined before 1941 – *XXI S"ezd*, volume I p. 261.

[4] In 1958 at the congress of the Lithuanian party nearly 50 per cent of delegates were under forty, and 32 per cent between forty-one and fifty. At the Moldavian Congress the figures were almost the same. At the Kirgiz and Tadjik Congresses the age levels were slightly higher.

a party member since 1918, and a member of the Central Committee since 1934, was a typical neo-Stalinist.

Of the remaining eight, two, the Uzbek Mukhitdinov and the first woman to reach the Praesidium, Furtseva, represented the younger generation. Mukhitdinov, aged forty in 1957, had only joined the party in 1942. Furtseva, seven years older and a party member since 1930, only began to emerge into prominence in the Moscow party organization in 1950, after Khrushchev had returned to Moscow. The other six were in their fifties, had all joined the party between 1921 and 1930, and had all only achieved prominence after the purges of 1937–8, and as a result of them. They were the cream of the 500,000 whom Stalin boasted that he had promoted as the result of the *Ezhovshchina*. They were all men who had learned in the hard school the need for implicit submission, for discipline and for ruthlessness if their power was to be preserved. All ten were of peasant or worker origin.[1] Under the energetic leadership of the First Secretary they had broken the influence of the older generation as represented by Kaganovich and Molotov and had made inroads on the generation of neo-Stalinists to which they themselves belonged. They were of the generation for whom Lenin, the revolution and the civil war were little more than legends. But they did not represent the generation for whom collectivization and the purges were already no more than a grim memory for which they need feel no personal responsibility.

Such data as were revealed on the nationality of delegates to republican congresses suggest that Russians still maintained a fairly dominant position. Thus, to take the several republican congresses held in 1958: in Lithuania, the Lithuanians formed 79 per cent, Russians 15; at the Moldavian Congress Russian delegates formed nearly a third; at the Kirgiz Congress Russian delegates made up 29·3 per cent as against 50·7 per cent Kirgiz; and at the Turkmen Congress there were 26 per cent Russian delegates to 62 per cent Turkmen. (The remainder was, in each case, made up of various other nationalities.) As usual, the percentage of Russians in the élite of the Caucasian parties was very small. Judging by the evidence of names alone, which is not entirely reliable, the percentage of Russians in the central committees of the three Baltic republics and of the republics of Central Asia was about a third in 1954 and in 1956 – except in Kazakhstan, where there is a very large Russian population, and where the proportion of Russians and Ukrainians in the central committee was nearly

[1] Biographical details are based on the entries in *Politicheskii slovar'*, edited by B. N. Ponomarev, Moscow, 1958, 2nd edition.

two-thirds. However, in the central committee selected in 1958 the proportion of Russian names dropped noticeably, and this may have been a sign of a new trend. But outside the Ukraine and the Caucasian republics Russians still continued to occupy certain key posts, notably that of Chairman of the Committee of State Security, and of either First or Second Secretary of the Central Committee.[1]

Some idea of the rate of turnover among the party élite can be obtained from examining the composition of the central committees. Thus the All-Union Central Committee as elected in 1956 was new to the extent of nearly a third so far as its full members were concerned, and more than half so far as candidates were concerned. Roughly a third each of full members and candidates elected in 1952 had disappeared without trace. But this represents changes over a period of three and a half years. The republican central committees have since 1952 been re-elected every two years. Comparison of the republican central committees as elected in 1958 and 1956 shows that approximately a fifth to a quarter of members were not re-elected. Turnover seems to have remained high at lower levels, and the Central Committee criticized an annual turnover of party secretaries of 26 per cent in one region as 'too great'.[2]

The Twentieth Congress also provided members with some information on party finance. Party income, according to the Rules, is derived from members' dues, party enterprises and other sources, unspecified.[3] In 1956, as a result of a reduction in the amount of dues payable, party income from this source had fallen from 85 per cent of the total income to 73 per cent. In contrast, income from party publications, the 'enterprises' foreseen in the Rules, had considerably increased. There was virtually no income (0·7 per cent of the total budget) from the unspecified 'other sources'. To compensate for the fall in income from members' dues, it was proposed both to increase publishing activities and to reduce the permanent staffs of party organizations, and it was stated that the staff of the Central Committee apparatus had already been reduced by 24·7 per cent.[4] No accounts have been published by the party since the revolution.

---

[1] Key Russians are sometimes appointed even in the Caucasian parties.
[2] *Partiinaia zhizn'*, No. 9, May 1956. It is not clear what turnover is considered normal – perhaps 20 per cent. Turnover seems to have been very much higher at the lowest level, among secretaries of primary organizations, than at the higher city and district levels.
[3] *KPSS v rez.*, volume III, p. 395.
[4] *XX S"ezd*, volume I pp. 121–5. Dues in 1952 were fixed on a sliding scale varying from 3 per cent for those earning above 500 roubles a month to 0·2 per cent for those earning less than 100 roubles a month.

Formally, the finances of the party are subject to control by the Central Revision Commission, which is elected at the Congress along with the full and candidate members of the Central Committee. In practice effective control rests with the Administrative Department of the Central Committee Secretariat. The responsibility for drawing up the party budget, in which allocations are made to local party organizations from the one central fund controlled by the central organs, is however vested in the Minister of Finance.

Statistical information on the membership of the party released in the course of the 1960's enables us to describe its composition for the period which elapsed between the Twentieth Congress in 1956 and the Twenty-third Congress in 1966. Although Khrushchev stressed in 1961 the need to guard against over-zealous recruitment, there was in fact no reduction in the pace of growth of the party until after his fall. By 1965 party membership had risen from 7,843,196 in 1958 to 11,758,169, i.e. at the average rate of approximately 560,000 a year. Two years later, on 1 January 1967, the total stood at 12,684,133 – an average increase of 460,000 a year.[1] There were also other signs which indicated that a more cautious recruitment policy was now to be followed. There were some signs of tightening up membership: thus, the rate of expulsions in 1966 was more than double what it was in 1964, and only a little more than half of the candidate members were accepted as full members, as compared with 1964.[2] Some changes in the Rules, referred to later, were also aimed at more restricted membership.

The party remained young and male: but a very slight rise in the percentage of women communists between 1957 and 1967 (from 19·7 to 20·9 per cent) may conceal a slight improvement in the chances of a woman entering the party owing to the normalization of the ratio between men and women in the population as a whole.[3] In 1967 over half of all party members were under 40: 5 per cent were 25 or younger, 46·5 per cent aged 26 to 40, 25·6 per cent aged 41 to 50, and 22·9 per cent over 50. Nearly half of all members had been in the party for less than ten years, and a further 20·8 per cent for eleven to twenty years.[4] In other words, up to three-quarters of all party members had joined since the war; and more than half since the death of Stalin. However,

[1] See tables of party membership as on 1 January of each year in T. H. Rigby, *Communist Party Membership in the USSR, 1917–1967*, Princeton, 1968, pp. 52–3. (Cited hereafter as *Rigby*.)
[2] *ibidem*, p. 322.
[3] *ibidem*, pp. 361–2.
[4] See *Kommunist*, No. 15, October 1967, pp. 89–103.

the post-war generation was as yet, in 1967, very sparsely represented in the top leadership of the party: the predominant generations there were the men over 60, who joined the party before 1933, and the men over 50, who joined the party after recruitment was resumed in 1938, or during the war. Thus, an examination of the careers of the 360 members of the Central Committee as elected in 1966 (which is a fair sample of higher officialdom) shows their average age as 56, and their average length of service in the party as 29 years. The older and middle generations contributed about 90 per cent of all members: the post-war generation of party members is represented by a mere 39 out of 360 members. The average age of members of the Politburo in 1967 was a little over 58: the post-war generation was represented neither among the full nor among the candidate members, and the youngest in age was 49.

Some statistics made available in the sixties suggest that the national composition of the party showed a tendency towards the narrowing of the contrast between the better and the more poorly represented nationalities. For example, in 1965, as compared with 1961, the number of communists per thousand of the national group had increased so far as the Ukrainians (36 to 44) and Belorussians (35 to 44) were concerned. There were also some increases in other national groups, but the disparity of representation among many of the smaller nationalities still remained high, and very substantially below the 58 per thousand figure for the Russians in 1965.[1] Since no figures are published on the matter, the proportion of Jews in the party is difficult to calculate, though some indications suggest that it may be quite high, though very much lower than it was before the war.[2] Be that as it may, there are very few Jewish names to be found in party committees at any level, or in the membership of Soviets at any levels, and there can be little doubt that this is due in some measure, at all events, to an official policy of discrimination.

Official statistics showed a slight rise during the period 1956–67 in the percentage of party members described as 'workers' (from 32 per cent to 38·1 per cent) and a slight decline of 'white-collar workers and others' (from 50·9 per cent to 45·9 per cent).[3] But long experience has shown how flexible the term 'workers' can be in party statistics. A more realistic picture is perhaps provided by the percentage breakdown of party members by occupation. As one would expect, the

[1] See table reproduced in *Rigby*, p. 378.
[2] *ibidem*, pp. 383–8.
[3] *ibidem*, p. 325.

major categories are industry (25·2 per cent), science, education and culture (13·7 per cent), collective farms (10·5 per cent), government and party officials (7·4 per cent) and the armed forces (7·0 per cent).[1]

Khrushchev's policy of restoring some institutional life to the party promised many marked contrasts to what had happened for many years with Stalin. The Twentieth All-Union Congress met in 1956 within the four years laid down by the Rules, the Twenty-first, which was an Extraordinary Congress, in 1959, and the Twenty-second in 1961. Republican congresses were held at regular two-yearly intervals. The 1952 Rules had laid down an interval of eighteen months between republican congresses, but this was evidently found impracticable, and the period was formally increased to two years (four years in the case of Ukraine, Belorussia, Kazakhstan and Uzbekistan) by the Twentieth Congress.[2] In spite of this greater regularity than in earlier years, congresses did not become centres of real debate, except perhaps for the Twenty-second, to which reference has been made. Policy, as hitherto, was laid down in the speeches of the major leaders and accepted without modification, or at most with formal amendment, by unanimous vote. Even the All-Union Twentieth Party Congress, with its very outspoken criticism by such leaders as Mikoyan of past irregularities, did not give rise, at any rate at the public sessions, to any greater freedom of debate than in the past. In short, congresses remained what they had been for years: public assemblies of the party and government leaders at all levels at which directives for the main lines of policy, which would become the keynote of party propaganda and activity throughout the country, could be handed down from above.

The All-Union Central Committee likewise met in plenary session with much greater frequency than had been the practice for many years during the lifetime of Stalin. In the four years between 1954 and 1957 the Plenum never met less than twice, and in some years rather more frequently – five meetings, for example, in 1957. Important legislative changes were usually made in the form of joint decrees of the Council of Ministers and of the Central Committee. It is also very probable that, aside from formal sessions of the Plenum, informal consultation takes place between the permanent staff of the Secretariat and local officials and party representatives before decrees are issued

---

[1] *ibidem*, p. 348.
[2] *XX S''ezd*, volume II, p. 429.

in the name of the Central Committee.[1] In this way the party leaders can be kept informed of the opinions of the party bureaucracy throughout the country before formulating their decisions, if they so desire. Available information does not suggest that the Central Committee uses its own initiative to bring influence to bear upon the Praesidium leaders. Legally there is nothing to prevent it from doing so. But the authoritarian traditions of the party and the great power vested in the central Secretariat of making and marring the careers of party members proved effective obstacles to such independence of action.

The emergence after Stalin's death of a Praesidium in which for a time the will of no one member was any longer certain to prevail raised the question whether, in the event of disagreements arising among the members of the Praesidium, the Central Committee would become a kind of appeal court to which such disagreements could be carried for solution. Two occasions are known on which questions were thus removed from the Praesidium to the Central Committee, to which reference has already been made – the question of a disagreement over Yugoslavia between Molotov and other members of the Praesidium in July 1955, and the clash which resulted from what was apparently an attempt to remove the First Secretary from his post in June 1957. In each case the view supported by the First Secretary of the party won approval in the Central Committee and in each case unanimously (though Molotov broke with tradition and abstained in June 1957 on the question of his own expulsion). Reasons have been advanced in the last chapter for suggesting that the Plenum at which Khrushchev's deposition was approved was no exception to the rule. Unanimous voting of resolutions is a tradition of long standing in the Central Committee, and does not necessarily indicate that there was no voice raised against the views of the First Secretary during discussion.

But the influence which the First Secretary can wield over decisions in the Central Committee is considerable. In the first place it seems probable that, although by the party Rules the membership of the Central Committee can only be altered by a vote of the Congress (apart from cases of formal votes to expel members), the First Secretary can at any rate influence membership between congresses by removing members from the posts by virtue of which they are entitled to their seats on the Central Committee. This seems to have

---

[1] A delegation of Italian communists was so informed on a visit to the USSR by a high official of the Central Committee – see *Problemi i realtà dall'URSS*, Rome, 1958, pp. 44–55.

occurred between November 1953 and February 1954 when ten first secretaries of regional committees, all of whom were members of the Central Committee, were replaced, and in one instance, that of Andrianov of Leningrad, publicly disgraced by a personal intervention of Khrushchev. None of these ten was re-elected to the Central Committee in 1956. They did not figure in the list of congress delegates, and so far as is known were given no further appointment. It is very probable that they had all ceased to sit upon the Central Committee long before 1956. Since these men had been appointed to these vital posts in the party apparatus at a time when Malenkov controlled the appointments machine in the Secretariat it is not unlikely that this group of important officials represented potential supporters of Malenkov in the Central Committee who were removed by Khrushchev as a step in his struggle against his rival.

As elected at the Twentieth Congress, after the defeat of Malenkov, the Central Committee contained a large number of party officials whose careers depended upon the First Secretary and who could therefore be expected to support him: 53 per cent of all full members, 31 per cent of candidate members and 40 per cent of members of the Central Revision Commission fell into this category. (It is important to consider all three categories since in the event of a vote to expel a member of the Central Committee – the issue which arose in June 1957 – all three groups exercise the right to vote, in accordance with the rule established at the Tenth Congress in 1921, and a two-thirds majority is required.[1]) Khrushchev's supporters were not however limited to these officials. For example, among the military members of the Central Committee elected in 1956 there were a number of senior officers who had served with Khrushchev during the war on the Military Council of the Stalingrad Military District, but whose presence upon the Central Committee would not otherwise on past practice have been justified on the grounds of the military appointments held by them at the time.[2] Many of the government officials

---

[1] For the 1921 rule see *KPSS v rez.*, vol. I, pp. 529–30. This rule was expressly relied on in June 1957 – see *SPR*, 1957, pp. 121–6 – but the members of the Central Revision Commission voted in place of the members of the Central Control Commission, as provided in 1921. Presumably this was in view of the completely altered character of the modern Committee of Party Control, which is an appointed, not an elected, body.

[2] The three military men concerned were Marshals Eremenko, Chuikov and Malinovskii. (The last named succeeded Marshal Zhukov as Minister of Defence in November 1957.) The two remaining members of this military council – Doronin, First Secretary of Smolensk Regional Organization and Kirichenko, First Secretary of the Ukrainian organization – were both elected to the Central Committee. Kirichenko had been since July 1955 a member of the Praesidium.

represented on the Central Committee no doubt also supported the First Secretary, either out of conviction or out of fear of the adverse influence he might exercise upon their careers if they opposed him. In June 1957 his total support among the three categories of members, candidates, and members of the Central Revision Commission amounted to at least 215 out of 309, or nearly 68 per cent.[1]

The 'production branch' system of dividing up work among the departments of the Central Committee remained unchanged until 1963, when a very substantial reorganization, which was to prove short-lived, was effected by Khrushchev. This is described below. A visiting group of Italian communists was given in 1957 the most complete picture of the party central staff which had been made public for many years, in an interview with a very senior member of that staff. Fourteen departments at any rate existed at the centre in 1957: the Department for Party Organs, which had replaced the Department for Party *Komsomol* and Trade Union Organs; for Agitation and Propaganda; for Culture and Science; for Higher Education and Schools; for Agriculture; for Transport and Communications; four departments for the main branches of industry; a department for administrative organs; for trade, finance and planning organs; a foreign department; and an administrative department. These departments require little comment, since the distribution of functions among them does not substantially differ from the position as established after 1948. The absence of any Secret Department must however be noted. There has been no evidence to suggest that either this department or anything resembling Stalin's private secretariat has reappeared after his death. Party control over the security organs is effected by the Department for Administrative Organs. The Department for Party Organs maintains general supervision over subordinate party organizations, including the allocation of cadres and the control over the appointments of officials. For this purpose it is divided into four territorial sections, each covering a group of republics (excluding the RSFSR), and four functional sub-sections: for membership cards; for cadres; for organization and rules questions; and for trade unions, *Komsomol*, and soviets.[2]

[1] This is suggested by the fact that according to F. R. Kozlov, then First Secretary of the Leningrad regional party organization, this number of members, and candidate members of the Revision Commission, put down their names to speak against the 'anti-party group' at the June Plenum. See *Leningradskaia pravda*, 5 July 1957. And see chapter xxx above for the extent of Khrushchev's support in the Central Committee on the eve of his fall.

[2] *Problemi i realtà dall'URSS*, loc. cit. The position is now (1968) very similar. See Appendix IV for list of departments.

The total number of paid party officials in 1957–8 can be fairly estimated at around 240,000 – after allowance has been made for some 25 per cent reduction in staffs actually made or contemplated at the centre, in the regions and in the republics, and assuming the number of paid secretaries of primary party organizations at 29,000, the figure given to the Italian delegation.[1] There is no evidence on which to base any closer approximation to the size of the apparatus for the period 1958–68. There is no reason to suppose that it has been reduced in size.

A novel feature of the administrative apparatus of the party under Khrushchev's rule was the introduction of a measure of decentralization through the creation of separate departments for the RSFSR and for the Union republics. This process, which began some time before 1956, was regularized in 1956 when a so-called Bureau of the RSFSR was set up, thus for the first time in the history of the party creating a separate party administration for the RSFSR. The decree setting up this Bureau listed the departments through which it would operate. These may well have corresponded to already existing departments of the Central Committee for the RSFSR which were now to be co-ordinated: for party organs, for propaganda and agitation, for science, schools and culture; for industry and transport; an administrative department; and a department for trade and financial organs.[2] It was however plain that the process of administrative decentralization within the party thus adopted was not to be allowed to go too far. Effective co-ordination at the centre was ensured by providing in the first instance that the First Secretary of the Central Committee should also be the Chairman of the RSFSR Bureau. Moreover,

---

[1] See pp. 529–30. above. Allowing for the reductions we get the following approximate figure for 1958:

Central Apparatus and republics – – – – – – –	2,250
Regional, etc., Committees – – – – – – – –	9,000
City and District Committees – – – – – – –	200,000
Full-time secretaries of primary party organizations – – –	29,000
	240,250

The regional and republican committees were ordered to submit plans for the reduction of their staffs by 25–30 per cent on 24 March 1956 – see *SPR*, 1957, p. 406 – and it has been assumed for the purposes of this estimate that this had been carried out by 1958. The reports of republican congresses held early in 1958 provide some evidence that reductions in the size of the apparatus had in fact taken place. Cf. *Partiinaia zhizn'*, No. 12 of 1956, No. 23 of 1957 and No. 19 of 1958. For steps taken to reduce the number of full-time paid secretaries of primary party organizations and for a scheme for part-paid secretaries see *SPR*, 1957, pp. 440–1.

[2] *SPR*, 1957, p. 127. However, the Bureau of the RSFSR had general governmental administration responsibilities and was not an exclusively party organ.

although separate departments for party organs were now to exist for the Union republics, including the RSFSR, only one central register of party members (upon which the posting of personnel depends) was maintained – in the Department of Party Organs of the Central Committee.[1]

The budget of the party also remained centralized, though the powers of republican central committees were substantially enlarged in August 1957, especially in matters concerning propaganda and party education.[2] The Central Committee, in the person of its apparatus, also retained its right to intervene in the affairs of the republican parties when it considered it necessary, either by summoning its leading officials to the centre or by sending out emissaries to deal with the situation on the spot.[3] Thus the reform seems to be in keeping with the general enlargement of the sphere of responsibility of the republics, always subject to overall central control, which took place after 1954. Another aspect of this same process of remedying excessive centralization was the abolition of the special political departments – not only those of the MTS but also those which had existed for many years in transport organizations or in the militia, and which were responsible directly to the centre, thus cutting out the territorial party organizations. As is noted below, some measure of re-centralization of the party organs took place in the last years of Khrushchev's period of office – in line with the increased reversion to centralization in the control over industry.

The regularization of the whole party machinery which took place and the revival of the functioning of the normal party organs led to some slight development inside the party of the democratic process which had been stagnant for many years and was never very strong. The radical reforms of industry and of agriculture, to which some reference has already been made, were preceded by public discussion which, if the acceptance of the principles of the proposal emanating from on high was a foregone conclusion, nevertheless influenced the formulation of important detail. There was constant exhortation to party organs and members, in the party press and in public utterances, to extend the democratic process to all levels: to elect freely the members and officials of local organizations, to criticize and debate in a more uninhibited fashion, and to stimulate greater participation in

---

[1] *Problemi i realtà, loc. cit.*
[2] *SPR*, 1957, pp. 441–2.
[3] *Problemi i realtà, loc. cit.*

party life of the *bureaux* – the equivalent at city and district level of the All-Union and republican central committees.

The party leadership was, no doubt, genuinely concerned to shake party members out of the disciplined lethargy into which they had been plunged under Stalin's terrifying rule. But the traditional fear of spontaneity and respect for authority died hard, and such development in the direction of democracy as took place seems to have been modest. An article in the authoritative central party journal on the meaning of freedom to criticize illustrates the difficulty which faces the ordinary party member in deciding what he can or can not properly, and safely, say in debate. Freedom of criticism is there stated to be subject to certain limits. A party member is entitled to have his opinion, and to express it. Lenin is quoted as authority for the view that any repressions against party members because their views differ from the views adopted by the party are 'inadmissible'. However, criticism must not be aimed at 'undermining the foundations' of the party or of its decisions. It must never be 'criticism for the sake of criticism', but must be 'businesslike in character', and 'imbued with concern for improvement'.[1] The distinctions are fine. Since, moreover, in the last resort it is the top party leaders who decide what is and what is not permitted criticism, the ordinary member cannot be blamed if he errs on the side of caution.[2]

Another such article shows that the position is very similar when one examines the question of the election of party organs and officials. Elections under the Rules are by secret ballot, in which each member of the particular organization votes for a list of candidates. The ballot is preceded by an open discussion of the candidatures on the list, and the party Rules stress the right of every member to criticize all candidates placed upon the list and to remove any name proposed for inclusion on the list if they so decide. It is the invariable practice for the representative of the next highest party organization (usually one of its secretaries) to be present at this discussion. He is enjoined on the one hand never to 'impose' his list of candidates upon the meeting of the lower organization; yet at the same time he must 'direct' the

[1] See *Voprosy partiinoi raboty*, Moscow, 1957, pp. 50–7. This volume consists of reprints of authoritative articles from the party press. (For instances of attacks on the nature of criticism at party meetings for such faults as 'petty bourgeois anarchism and indiscipline', followed by expulsions or other disciplinary measures, see e.g. *Kommunist Armenii*, 26 January 1958; *Pravda*, 5 April 1956 (one of the instances following upon the XXth Congress), and *Pravda*, 21 January 1957.)

[2] Authoritarian tradition in the party dies hard. In 1966 a party official, F. Petrenko, was still lamenting the fact that discussions at party meetings are largely a sham – see *Pravda* for 20 July 1966.

election, since 'democracy has nothing to do with spontaneity, when any chance result can emerge'. This direction by the emissary from the higher party organization takes the form of helping the meeting to compile the list of candidates. That his help is in practice successful is evident from the fact that in the 'great majority' of elections the number of candidates on the list prepared under his direction and the number of vacancies to be filled is the same.[1] Thus it is clear that the vital stage in most cases of these elections will be not the secret ballot but the open discussion, in the presence of the representative of a higher party organ which precedes it. Nevertheless, the party press records a few instances at the lowest level of party organizations in which the meeting has successfully insisted on its own candidate, in opposition to the view of the emissary from above. Even this would hardly have been conceivable in the latter part of Stalin's lifetime. Some of the stirrings of party members became evident in the discussion which preceded the revision of the party Rules in 1961.

The Party Rules, as adopted in 1952, remained substantially unchanged until they were revised by the Twenty-Second Congress in October 1961, in accordance with a resolution of the Plenum of the Central Committee of 10 January 1961. Considerable discussion of the draft, which was approved by the Central Committee on 19 June 1961, took place. It does not appear that the discussion had very much practical effect: at the Congress Kozlov, who piloted the discussion of the new draft Rules, simply summarized proposals made for amendment, accepting or rejecting them as he thought fit, and the delegates accepted his views unanimously. In the event no important amendments were made to the draft: 30 in all, of which 26 were grammatical. But the discussion in the party press did reveal that there was a strong desire in the rank and file of the party for greater freedom in the election of officials and delegates. With characteristic communist tactics Kozlov insisted that the new Rules should provide for secret voting, and castigated as undemocratic those who had urged a change to open voting. However, when the Central Committee's instructions on voting were issued after the Congress, they contained provisions for open voting by show of hands, in the case of all the more important party offices – thus ensuring the time-honoured system of indirect pressure of the delegate from the higher party organization whose representative is inevitably present at the election.[2]

[1] *Voprosy parliinoi raboty*, pp. 27–32.
[2] For text see *S.P.R.*, volume 4 1963, pp. 482–8

The changes made can be divided into three categories: declaratory changes, changes relating to the position of members, and institutional changes. To the first category belongs the revised description of the party as the 'vanguard of the Soviet people'; and (Art. 58) a new, long moral code for party members, embodying ideals of conduct which often bear little relation to the reality. Both these provisions are taken from the new party Programme, also adopted at this Congress, and reflected Khrushchev's philosophy of the party. There were also a number of declaratory provisions, strengthening, on paper, the rights of party members to freedom of discussion and freedom of criticism. The second category of changes related mainly to the provisions for expulsion, which in their new formulation gave more protection to the individual member than before. However, the new Rules, like the old, made no provision for any independent authority to which the member expelled can appeal. The most important change in the third category was a provision (Art. 25) for compulsory, systematic renewal of the composition of all party organs. In the case of the Central Committee and its Praesidium no fewer than a quarter of the members were to be newly elected at each party Congress; in party organs down to and including the regional committees, one-third of the membership was to be renewed at each election; and in organs at the lower levels one-half of the membership. There was, however, a safeguard: a party worker of exceptional organizational or political ability could be elected for an unspecified 'longer period', provided that two-thirds of those present concurred.[1]

Amendments to the new Rules were made, after the fall of Khrushchev, at the Twenty-Third Congress, in April 1966. One group of amendments made admissions to the party slightly more difficult -- in line with the new policy of more restricted recruitment. More significant, perhaps, was the repeal of the provision for compulsory renewal of party organs enacted in 1961. This was consistent with the policy of Khrushchev's successors of conciliating the older members of the apparatus, with whom the provision for rotation had been unpopular. Another amendment provided that all union republican congresses are to be held at intervals of two years, and the provision of a four-year interval in the case of Ukraine, Belorussia, Uzbekistan and Kazakhstan was repealed. Finally, the Bureau of the Central

---

[1] The 1961 Rules are reprinted in the *Proceedings* of the Twenty-Second Congress. For a more detailed discussion of the Rules see Leonard Schapiro, 'The New Rules of the CPSU', in Leonard Schapiro and Albert Boiter (editors), *The USSR and the Future*, New York, London, 1962, pp. 179–94.

Committee for the RSFSR was abolished. It was the last survival of the many new organs created by Khrushchev.[1]

Some reference has already been made to the extensive transformation of the party organs which Khrushchev attempted. Since none of them survived his departure, and, in so far as they were implemented, lasted only a very short time, they can only be briefly described. The Bureau of the Central Committee for the RSFSR had already embodied one of Khrushchev's favourite notions: that it was desirable to fuse party and state officials into one organ, so that the party, while retaining its predominant influence, would nevertheless not become detached and alienated from the administration which it existed to supervise. In the course of 1962 and 1963 he tried to apply this principle to party control of agriculture. Until 1962 the main organ responsible for party control over agriculture was the district committee, of which there were nearly 4,000. Most of these district committees were swept away in the course of 1962 and 1963 (it is an understatement to say that the measure was not popular with the party apparatus). In their place party committees were set up inside the new administrative organs designed for the control of agriculture – the Kolkhoz-Sovkhoz (or Sovkhoz-Kolkhoz in some areas) Administration Directorates.[2] It does not appear that the methods of work of the new Committees were very different from those of the former district committees, as many complaints in the press showed.[3] The district committees were restored in November 1964.

An even more extensive reorganization of the party machinery was announced by Khrushchev to the Central Committee Plenum in November 1962. New organs were created at the centre – Bureaux for Chemical and Light Industry, for Agriculture and for Industry, for Central Asia and for Transcaucasia; an Ideological Commission; and a Commission for Party Organizational Questions. It is not clear what they all did – indeed some of them, like the Bureau for Transcaucasia, remained on paper. Two other innovations were of more importance. One was the division of party committees at all levels, down to and including the all-important regions, into two: an agricultural committee and an industrial committee. The ostensible aim

[1] The amendments are reprinted in the *Proceedings* of the Twenty-Third Congress. The Rules, as amended, are freely available in English translation in an official Soviet edition.

[2] A few district committees survived: the total of party committees, and surviving district committees, in 1963 was 1,711 as compared with 3,743 district committees previously – see an article by G. Shitarev in *Kommunist*, No. 7, 1963.

[3] See e.g. *Sovetskaia Rossiia*, 8 March 1963 and 29 May 1963; *Kazakhstanskaia pravda*, 14 June 1963.

was to make party control over these two branches of the national economy more effective, less formal, less spasmodic and less remote. But the garrulous Khrushchev also made it quite clear that one of his aims was to reduce the status of some of the regional secretaries who had built up powerful empires for themselves. The other innovation was the Party-State Control Committee (headed by Shelepin at the centre and, with isolated exceptions, by a party secretary at all levels). This engine of control over all aspects of life, was given enormous powers of investigating, reprimanding and dismissing officials throughout the length and breadth of the country: on paper, at all events, its powers extended to party as well as state officials.

There is no doubt that, in spite of the customary paeons of praise which greeted Khrushchev's proposals in the Central Committee, his novel ideas aroused considerable apprehensions. All his innovations disappeared after his fall – and may indeed have been one of the reasons for his fall. They were chaotic in conception, in many cases, and hard enough to implement, even given good will. But the evidence suggests that their implementation (along with the implementation of his reforms in planning, to which reference has been made) ran into considerable obstruction. For example, it became quite clear, even long before it was abolished in December 1965, that the Party-State Control Committee was exercising no jurisdiction at all in the disciplining of party members: the party, as hitherto, was jealously guarding this right for itself. When the hybrid organ of control was abolished the old pattern was reverted to of a separate Committee of Party Control: and of a system of State Control (on lines traditional since the days of *Rabkrin*), now renamed People's Control. More interesting still, perhaps, was the relative failure of the experiment in divided regional party committees. In practice fewer than two-thirds were divided. Moreover, since only the Industrial Committee retained an Administration Organs Department in its Secretariat, and therefore retained sole control, at its own level, over police and security, it may be presumed that it remained in most cases the more important committee of the two.[1] The divided Committees were reunited in November 1964. The Congress also adopted two changes in nomenclature. The title of First Secretary reverted to the form used by Stalin – General Secretary; and the supreme policy-making Praesidium of the Central Committee became once again known as the

---

[1] These little known facts appear, so far as is known, only in one source, an official pamphlet explaining the new system: M. P. Karpov i V. M. Zasorin, *Po proizvodstvennomu printsipu: Novoe postroenie partii*, Moscow, 1963 (July).

Politburo – its title until 1952. Nervous observers at the time interpreted these changes as a sign of reversion to 'Stalinism': the more likely reason for them was the desire to obliterate the memory of the era of Khrushchev's rule.

* * *

The most important development affecting the party during the period of Khrushchev's office was its changed relationship to the government, to agriculture and to industry. The rivalry between Khrushchev and Malenkov which ended in the victory of Khrushchev was in a sense as much a conflict between the party machine and the government machine, in which the party machine won, as a pure struggle for power. The predominance of the party secretaries in the highest councils of the party, the policy-making Praesidium, achieved by 1957, symbolized the fact that the party had now asserted its primacy and would not tolerate rival counsels. The decline in authority of the Council of Ministers and the assumption by the First Secretary of the post of Chairman of the truncated Council of Ministers were merely the final touches in a victory already achieved.

The constitutional theorists of the party kept pace with the practical developments. An officially approved text-book of constitutional law, published in December 1955, describes one of the functions of the highest party organs as being to give directives to the government organs in the working out of legislative proposals. One form of this direction by the party, it stated, was the joint decree of the Central Committee and the Council of Ministers. By this method the 'unchallengeable' authority of the party ensures that the decree will be given the 'wide support of the Soviet people'.[1] Some authors went further than this and maintained that one of the functions of the party was to lay down what the work of the state organs should be in the light of the policy of the communist party. This included the right of party organs to issue direct instructions to the soviets and to their executive committees.[2] The familiar injunctions on the relations of the party to government organs were still issued: the party was to guide these organs, but not to seek to take over their functions. The old conflict between 'guidance' and 'usurpation' still remained. But after

[1] See M. P. Kareva, S. F. Kechekian, A. S. Fedoseev, G. I. Fed'kin, *Teoriia gosudarstva i prava*, Moscow, 1955, pp. 290–2. (Text-book approved for university use by the Ministry of Education.)

[2] Ts. A. Iampol'skaia, *Organy sovetskogo gosudarstvennogo upravleniia v sovremennyi period*, Moscow, 1954, pp. 71, 76–7.

1955, at any rate, there was no longer any doubt where, in case of conflict, authority really lay.

The enhanced role of the party was brought into relief by the far-reaching reforms of agriculture and industry to which some reference has already been made.

The decision to allow the collective farms to dispose over their own mechanical power, apart from its enormous economic and political importance (Stalin, it will be recalled, described the proposal to make this change in 1952 as 'a step back from communism rather than a step towards it')[1] involved a radical change in the mechanism of party control over the collective farms. Up to 1953 party and government control over the collective farms was little less than chaotic. The individual farm was liable to receive orders from the political departments of the MTS, from central party emissaries of all kinds, from the regional and district party secretaries, from the regional soviet executive committees, and from the representatives of the Ministry of Agriculture – among other officials. There was confusion and lack of responsibility, tempered, or made worse, by the occasional energetic interference of the local party secretary. In September 1953 the political departments of the MTS were abolished, and the task of close and effective supervision over the farms was laid upon the district party secretaries. The *raikom* (district party organization) was reorganized in such a way that its first secretary was placed at the head of a group of 'secretaries for the MTS zone'. Each of these latter secretaries was to control a network of 'instructors', whose duty it was to work in close contact with the MTS brigades, and with the farms which fell within the area served by the MTS. At the same time the powers of the MTS as organizers of production on the farms, under the overall control of the Ministry of Agriculture, were greatly increased.

It is possible that this system of control, which relied so much upon the MTS, was intended to be only temporary, until such time as the party organization inside the farms could be improved. At any rate, in addition to the efforts made to strengthen the primary party organizations inside the farms, many thousands of party members, mostly from the towns (30,000 in 1955), were sent out to take up posts as chairmen of collective farms. As party organization on the spot improved so increasing decentralization was permitted: the functions of local party officials increased as those of the central officials diminished, while from 1955 onwards the MTS and collective farms were permitted to

[1] *Bol'shevik*, No. 18, 1952, pp. 48–9.

draw up their own detailed plans of production for central approval and co-ordination instead of as hitherto receiving minutely detailed instruction from the centre. The last stage of the process was reached in 1958 when the decision was made to abolish the MTS. As a result the farm was to become an independent planning unit, with the district party secretary as the focal point of party control, and as the watch dog who would reconcile the interests of the overall national plan for production with the aspirations of individual farms. It is too early to make any forecast of the probable results of this radical change. But the fact that the change was made at all was some evidence that the development of party organizations on the farms was considered far enough advanced for the local party organizations, in conjunction with trusted farm chairmen and strengthened primary party organizations, to exercise the control which for over twenty years had been vested in the MTS as proletarian outposts in the ever suspect agricultural hinterland.

The agricultural reforms were accompanied by the progressive development of the kind of normalization of party control over the collective farms for which the foundations were laid by Khrushchev in Stalin's lifetime when he inaugurated the amalgamation of the collective farms into larger units. Normalization of party control over the collective farms entails control by the territorial party organizations, the district committees but working inside each collective farm through an adequate party primary organization, which can in turn extend its influences over the rest of the members of the farm. In 1956, over 7,000 of the 87,500 collective farms were still without a primary party organization, and in over 10,000 farms primary organizations were only three to five members strong.[1] By 1958 the position was much improved. The total number of collective farms had by then dropped to about 78,000,[2] as the result of further amalgamations; there had been intensified recruitment among collective farmers for enrolment in the party; and thirdly, the decision taken at the beginning of 1958 to disband the machine tractor stations and to incorporate the majority of their personnel in the collective farms released a large number of party members to swell the party organizations of the collective farms. 'Nearly all' collective farms now had primary organizations.[3] In 1962 a new revolution in the form of party control was

[1] *XX S"ezd*, volume I, p. 236.
[2] *Pravda*, 28 March 1958.
[3] According to what Khrushchev told the Central Committee in December 1958, the organizations averaged 20 members each, and totalled 1,350,000. See *Pravda*, 16 December 1958.

embarked on by Khrushchev (reference has already been made to it). It was too short-lived to leave its mark, and the more traditional form of party control was immediately reverted to by Khrushchev's successors.

The reorganization of industry, which led to such serious and continuing conflicts among the party leaders, also had the effect of strengthening and regularizing the system of party control. At the lowest level the powers of the primary organizations in industry remained unaltered. But the fact alone that the increase in the number of paid full-time secretaries was by 1957 causing concern to the authorities was a sign that the enhanced status of the party was resulting in increased activity. There was no indication that the perennial conflicts which spring from the existence of dual authority had been resolved, though the growing number of party members with technical training was making it possible to ensure in an increasing number of cases that the responsible party official was equipped with some knowledge of the skills of those whom he controlled. At higher levels the diminution and devolution of the authority of the All-Union Council of Ministers brought a corresponding increase in the influence of the party.[1] Within the areas of the councils of national economy the party could exercise control through the powerful regional first secretaries. It was of significance that the number and areas of authority of these councils as finally adopted corresponded very closely to the areas already controlled by these regional first secretaries, even in cases where economic considerations might have suggested a subdivision of an area, or a different grouping of resources and enterprises.[2] Evidently it was not considered politic to interfere too much with a well-established network of authority. It was upon these secretaries, working directly to the appropriate departments of the Secretariat in Moscow, that the task of ensuring that local interests did not conflict with the overall policy of the party primarily fell. Primary party organizations were also set up within each council of national economy. But their powers were assimilated to those of primary organizations within ministries, and therefore did not extend, as in the case of primary organizations in individual industrial enterprises, to controlling its activities.[3]

[1] However, the chairmen of the councils of national economy have in the majority of cases (58 as against 15, where information exists on their previous careers) been drawn from the ranks of ministerial or technical officials – see A. Poplujko, 'The Sovnarkhoz Chairmen' in *Bulletin of the Institute for the Study of the USSR*, Munich, May 1958, volume V, No. 5, pp. 14–19.

[2] See an article by A. Nove in *Problems of Communism*, No. 6, volume VI, Nov.–Dec. 1957, pp. 19–25, 'The Soviet Industrial Reorganization'.

[3] *Partiinaia zhizn'*, No. 11 June 1958, p. 16.

Thus the general trend of the five years 1953–8 could be described as a great increase in the authority of the party achieved by some measure of decentralization and a large degree of rationalization of the methods of control. The personal, arbitrary and over-centralized despotism and the endless conflict of authority which characterized Stalin's rule were gradually being replaced by a system in which the machinery of government was subordinated to the party. If the business of administration was on the whole left to the machinery of the state, there was no doubt that the direction of policy, the preservation of the central plan from encroachment by local interests and the day-to-day control over the way in which government organs and economic enterprises did their work, fell upon the shoulders of the party. At the apex of the system stood the secretaries of the Central Committee, who after the end of 1957, if not before, could control in the party Praesidium the formulation of all policy at the highest level, and whose leader, the First Secretary, after April 1958, had also assumed formal leadership of the government machine. If the existence of this dual system of administrative control continued to give rise to conflicts, there was no longer any doubt that the party had the last word. This was the system which, for the last years of his term of office, Khrushchev struggled to maintain in being. The extent of resistance which he provoked among the planners and technicians, and probably in the army, has already been referred to in the last chapter. It will also be recalled that he was far from successful in putting through his own scheme for the control of planning and the running of the economy, and had been forced to swallow substantial modifications imposed on him by the planners.

In assessing the career of this extraordinary man one is forced to ask the question: was his policy merely a hotch-potch of unrelated 'hare-brained schemes', as his successors were to suggest? Or was there some coherent and connected view of the nature of what communist society should be like at the back of all Khrushchev's policies? In so far as this question can be answered, the answer must lie in the party Programme adopted in October 1961, at the Twenty-Second Congress, which was indeed primarily convened for the purpose of adopting it. It is true that the limelight at this Congress was largely stolen by the debates about Stalin and what was to be done (or not to be done) to his accomplices; it is also true that the Programme of 1961 passed into oblivion almost as soon as did its predecessor of 1919.

Nevertheless, the Programme bears the imprint of Khrushchev in every line, it was debated, glorified and voted before his authority entered on its decline (in 1962 and 1963) and it is in the Programme that the record of his political faith is to be sought.

Immensely long, repetitive, verbose and boastful, the Programme ranges over the past and future, covering all aspects of Soviet ambition, both at home and abroad. The central theme of Part Two, which deals with 'The Tasks of the CPSU in Building a Communist Society', is the imminent approach of the higher phase of communism in the Soviet Union, in which the principle 'From each according to his ability, to each according to his needs' will be implemented. The current decade (1961–70) is to be occupied in building the material base for this happy event: in the following decade, by 1980, Soviet society will be approaching communism, 'a communist society will in the main be built in the USSR'. The bulk of the seven chapters which make up this second part is taken up with discussion of the increasingly important role which will be played by the party in all stages – including the stage of full-scale communist construction, due to start in 1980. Khrushchev's theory of the nature of the party was his main contribution to ideology. His first innovation was the claim that the party had already become a party or vanguard of the whole people, and no longer, as hitherto, the party or vanguard of the ruling class, the proletariat. This novel view is somewhat difficult to reconcile with anything that Marx wrote: if there are no longer any classes, but only a whole people, there can, according to Marx, be no place for any kind of party, or indeed any kind of state or government at all.[1] Khrushchev was not apparently alive to the inconsistency of the survival of a 'party' in circumstances which are described as communism: indeed, the Programme at no point in the future envisages the disappearance of the party, and constantly stresses the need for the party to play an increased role in the future communist stage. But what Khrushchev did achieve, however clumsily, in his Programme was some kind of answer to the theoretical problem of the 'withering away of the state' as class conflict becomes a thing of the past. Stalin, it will be recalled, had relegated the 'withering away' of the state to the far-off day when capitalist encirclement would have ceased to exist: in the meanwhile he stressed in theory (and proved in practice) that the state, so far from withering away, would grow ever stronger. Many foreign communists were perturbed less by the

[1] The views of Marx on 'The Free State', 'The People's State' etc. are best set out in his 'Critique of the Gotha Programme' – see Karl Marx and Frederick Engels, *Selected Works*, volume II, London, 1950, pp. 13–45.

thousands of victims which Stalin's theory devoured than by the inconsistency of his views with the doctrines of Marx. Khrushchev, if in somewhat primitive a fashion, did at any rate try to provide a guide to this thorny question for the perplexed communist. The state, he asserts in the Programme, will indeed progressively wither away, in the shape of its institutions. In practice this would mean that various functions carried out by government organs would be taken over by 'public organizations'. This process made some headway under Khrushchev: some functions of the militia were taken over by bands of 'volunteer' vigilantes, extensive use was made of 'volunteer' services in many branches of administration, some of the functions of the law courts were taken over by comrades' courts in the factory and by Soviet meetings organized for the hounding and exiling of those described (in an all-embracing definition) as parasites. Behind all this medley of bigoted, crude, amateur bungling and injustice stood the goad of the party official. It was a far cry from the utopia of Marx. But it corresponded to some vision that Khrushchev carried in his heart of a society in which force would give way to a process of self-organization – except that the 'self' would be replaced by the high-minded, incorruptible, morally pure and devoted members of the party of the future. It was a naïve enough vision; but was it so much more naïve than Lenin's dream in *State and Revolution*?[1]

The first part of the Programme dealt with the future of international communism, and was out of date almost before it was printed. Although by October 1961 the dispute between the Chinese and Soviet parties was in full spate, convention still required official reticence on the subject. It was for this reason that Khrushchev's public attack on China's satellite Albania at the Twenty-Third Congress was rightly interpreted as an attack on China. In succeeding years the momentous cleavage in the world movement became apparent for all to see. The dispute between the two parties came into the open, couched at first in ideological verbiage about 'co-existence', 'revisionism', 'dogmatism', 'cult of personality', and the like, and before long descending to vulgar abuse, which suggested a deep personal antipathy between Khrushchev and Mao Tse Tung. But in truth the Sino-Soviet split far transcended personal animosities: it soon became evident that what was at stake was a contest for the leadership of the world revolutionary movement, and that the split

---

[1] The text of the Programme is reprinted in Leonard Schapiro and Albert Boiter (editors), *The USSR and the Future*, New York, London, 1962, pp. 253–312.

between the protagonists was having momentous repercussions in communist parties all over the world. The story of this dispute, which is as yet (1970) far from resolved, is outside the scope of this book. Personal animosity on the part of Khrushchev may have played a part in exacerbating it: after all, it was Khrushchev who in 1954 had drawn China in as an ally in his internal conflict with Malenkov and had indeed for some five years thereafter helped to build up China as an industrial and nuclear power. There was therefore cause for personal rancour at being spurned by the Chinese party leader. Yet, Khrushchev's successors fared little better than he: after an initial attempt at reticence and even reconciliation, they too found themselves engaged in as bitter polemics and hostility as Khrushchev and were desperately trying both to shore up the shattered remnants of communist unity, and to project themselves as leaders of world revolution. Only time would show what could be saved from the wreckage of the unity of those parties which still nominally accepted Soviet leadership; and what progress China could make as leader of a new type of revolution of the 'poor and the blank' against all established order, which in its formulations recalled Bakunin more than it did Marx.

*   *   *

The leaders of the party had graphically summed up their own view of the state of popular feeling towards the party when, immediately after Stalin's death, they spoke of the need for measures to prevent 'disorder and panic'. Evidently they had reason to fear that, once the stern hand of the Leader was removed, they could not rely too confidently upon the population rallying behind the surviving lieutenants. No doubt there was also uncertainty as to which individual lieutenant could hope to command the allegiance of the party apparatus. As once in an earlier period of crisis, in 1921, the party set about to win the support of the population by a policy of concessions and by a determined effort to improve material conditions. The history of the next five years was a record of successive steps to improve the lot of the farmers and of the workers, and to provide more material benefits to absorb the spending power of the more privileged members of society. The party certainly called for sustained effort to increase production in all fields. But, in contrast to what happened under Stalin, it saw to it that these efforts did not go unrewarded by material benefits, and tried moreover to ensure that available material goods should be spread among wider sections of the population than had been the case for many years past.

One of the most important measures taken by the party in the course of cleaning up after Stalin was an improvement in the observance of the law. The complete disregard for legal safeguards and the arbitrary and almost universal practice of terror under Stalin were now freely admitted, though care was taken to blame this upon individuals such as Beria, and upon the 'cult of personality' which it was said Stalin had in his latter years improperly encouraged. Any suggestions that this illegality might have been the result of the privileged position above the law which the party always arrogated to itself and of the absence of a judicial service enjoying independence were derided, and sternly silenced. Whatever had gone wrong in the past, the party was not to blame: and the fact that efforts were now being made by the party to right the wrongs proved, according to the party leaders, that it was not the party which had been at fault in the past.

Indeed, the practical measures taken to create an improvement in observance of the law and to remove past injustices were of considerable significance. There were several amnesties, an extensive review took place of persons confined in the forced labour camps, and many were released. There were a number of rehabilitations, most of them posthumous, of prominent communists sentenced or eliminated in the past as traitors of one kind or another. (Among those rehabilitated in this manner was the former Deputy People's Commissar of Justice, Pashukanis, of whom it was now stated that although his opinions had been erroneous, the charge that he was a traitor had been false.)[1] Extensive reorganization of the forced labour system was started. A number of riots in the camps after Stalin's death (reported outside the USSR by former inmates) may have helped to speed up the reform. The MVD was progressively stripped of its vast economic enterprises, which were now placed under the control of the appropriate industrial ministries. The living and working conditions of the penal labour force, now very much reduced in numbers, were considerably improved. It was planned to reorganize all the camps into 'colonies', and the newly formed colonies, as well as the surviving camps, were placed under the jurisdiction of the MVD jointly with the local soviets. Both the local soviets and the procurators were made respon-

[1] The entire evidence on both the purges and the subsequent rehabilitations will be found in Robert Conquest, *The Great Terror: Stalin's Purge of the Thirties*, London, 1968.

sible for the supervision of conditions in these camps, or colonies. A decree of 5 November 1934, which had empowered the People's Commissariat of Internal Affairs to sentence to deportation by administrative action persons regarded as 'socially dangerous', was stated to have been repealed – though the decree of repeal has not been published.[1] In 1955 a statute was passed giving the procurators detailed powers of supervision over arrests, over places of detention, over the preliminary investigation of criminal charges both by the militia and by the security organs, as well as over the observance of legality generally in the courts and in administrative actions.

Although it cannot be stated with certainty that these provisions were in fact observed,[2] there is no doubt that a significant improvement in legal practice took place. Writers on law were much occupied with the discussion of further improvements, in preparation for new legal codes of criminal law and procedure, which were eventually enacted in December 1958. All these developments were no doubt much welcomed by the population. Yet certain reservations remained. Whatever wide powers the courts and procurators enjoyed on paper, they still remained powerless in any case of conflict with party policy. The party always retained its right to ride roughshod over the law if considerations of policy demanded it: it was constantly reiterated that the legally fundamental independence of the procurators and judges did not mean independence from control by the party, to which they were all subject. And, with this limitation, powers conferred by legal enactment lost much of their practical validity, since they could be exercised only for so long as the party chose to tolerate them. During the period of the greatest disregard for the law, for example in 1937 and 1938, the procurators were by the terms of the

---

[1] See *Sovetskoe gosudarstvo i pravo*, January 1956, p. 3; the date of the repeal was later stated to have been September 1953 – see *Partiinaia zhizn'*, February 1957, No. 4, p. 68. See *ibidem*, pp. 66–8, for an official summary of what has been done to strengthen legality, and cf. an interesting account of personal conversations, as well as published information, in Harold J. Berman, 'Soviet Law Reform – Dateline Moscow 1957' in the *Yale Law Journal*, volume 66, No. 8, July 1957, pp. 1,190–1,215.

[2] For example, a statute of 24 May 1955 gives the procurators stringent powers of control over arrests and over all preliminary investigations of criminal charges, including, presumably, since they are not expressly excluded, investigations conducted by the security organs. Nevertheless, in the Codes of Criminal Procedure of the RSFSR and of the other Union republics, as republished in October 1957, the annotations which state that powers of control over actions of the security authorities are governed by special (unpublished) regulations, are reprinted without comment. See *Ugolovno-protsessual'noe zakonodatel'stvo SSSR i soiuznykh respublik*. Sbornik. (Osnovnye zakonodatel'nye akty). Edited by D. S. Karev. Moscow, 1957, pp. 57, 108, 156, 193, 199, 200, 255, 260, 277, 383, 376. The statute of 24 May 1955 is on pp. 31–7.

legislation then in force entitled to exercise control over the organs of state security, and theoretically required to countersign every order for arrest. These powers had proved of little avail when once the party was determined on its lawless course; they might prove of little avail once again. Perhaps the position was best summed up by a remark made by the Deputy Procurator General to a visiting American professor of law: 'If it becomes necessary we will restore the old methods. But I think it will not be necessary.'[1] Slender as the gains of the law and legality may have been while Khrushchev was at the helm, there were at any rate no major retrograde steps to record in this sphere. The foundations of criminal law and procedure adopted by the Supreme Soviet on Christmas Day 1958 and the Union Republican Codes which were passed in accordance with these foundations thereafter, though not perfect, were still a great advance on any of the law which had existed in the Soviet state since its inception. The same cannot be said of Khrushchev's successors, whose first years in office witnessed a steady increase of the role of the KGB in the manipulation of the legal process. The powers of the security officials were increased, among other things, by considerably increasing the range of the type of offence which they were entitled to investigate. Khrushchev had claimed, perhaps not quite truthfully, that there were no longer any political prisoners in the USSR: under the rule of his successors the number during their first four years of rule ran into tens of thousands. On 16 September 1966 the Supreme Soviet of the RSFSR adopted an amendment to the Criminal Code which was aimed at putting a stop to any form of criticism of the existing order – by word, deed, or demonstration – and laid down a penalty of up to three years' imprisonment for violation of the new articles.[2] Perhaps the most graphic illustration of the attitude of the new régime to the law was the posting in October 1967 of a career KGB officer and Deputy Chairman of the KGB, S. G. Bannikov, to the Supreme Court of the USSR.

*   *   *

Although the question of the foreign relations of the Soviet Union after Stalin's death is a subject which cannot be treated here, there is one respect in which Khrushchev's attempt to win greater adherence from the public was reflected in foreign policy which must be briefly

[1] Berman, *loc. cit.*, p. 1,215.
[2] Now articles 190¹, 190² and 190³ of the Criminal Code of the RSFSR.

noted. Stalin had not hesitated in his relations with the non-communist world to bring the Soviet Union to the brink of war: at the time of his death fruitless negotiations were being dragged out to end hostilities in Korea, and his policy in the last few years of his life had had the effect of bringing into existence an armed alliance of states who feared for their own independence. Although it was unusual for Soviet leaders to admit this possibility (which was clearly at variance with the messianic character of the Marxist view of history), the development of nuclear weapons made it increasingly likely that any war between the Soviet Union and the United States would inflict deadly damage on each belligerent. The foreign policy of the Soviet Union therefore began to reflect, much as did its policy at home, the need to persuade a population which feared another war that its leaders could be trusted to preserve the peace. The agreement for an armistice in Korea soon after Stalin died was probably due to such considerations.

However, it was not with the pursuit of a policy of diplomatic compromise, or with limited agreements on disarmament, international inspection or arbitration that the party leaders sought to win the confidence of those over whom they ruled – such a policy would indeed have signified a complete break with the traditions established over many years. The keynote of the new policy was well described by the First Secretary to the Twentieth Party Congress when he stressed that wars between the socialist and non-socialist powers were now no longer to be regarded as inevitable, since the 'forces of peace' inside the non-socialist countries could be mobilized in order to restrain the governments of the imperialist powers from unleashing another war.

Translated into more concrete terms, this meant the intensification of an energetic campaign to portray the Soviet Union as the champion of peace and the non-communist countries as the supporters of war. Much of this appeal was directed not only at communist sympathizers inside non-communist countries, but at ordinary men and women whom it was hoped to persuade that the only obstacle to peace was the intransigence of the governments of the non-communist countries in refusing to reach agreement with the Soviet Union. This was a very different policy from that once pursued through the Comintern. It was an appeal to a much wider following than the communist parties in Western Europe or the USA, at any rate, had ever been able to win. Indeed, in some instances the Soviet Union was quite content to by-pass or jettison a communist party if it saw greater opportunity of winning over supporters who might be repelled by the traditional communist party. This policy of seeking wider support than mere propagation of communism could hope to achieve was pursued with particular determination in the former colonial territories of Africa and Asia, where the Soviet Union hoped to appeal to growing nationalism and to the unpopularity of the Western powers.

That the aim of this policy was the ultimate triumph of communism on a world scale was at no time denied – to have denied it would indeed have been inconsistent with the fundamental Marxist view of history. What was denied, with emphasis and repeatedly, was that the Soviet party had any intention of assisting the inevitable processes of history by subversion or by force. At the Twentieth Party Congress the First Secretary stressed not only that it was right for each country to pursue its own road to socialism, but that it was possible for the transition to socialism in some instances to take place without a civil war or violence. But other speakers, notably Mikoyan, quoted instances of what was meant by peaceful transition to socialism – namely the Baltic countries and the countries of Eastern Europe. Yet in all these instances communism had come to power either as a result of Moscow organized subversion and direct threat of military action by the Soviet Union or as the consequence of the presence of Soviet troops. Evidently support of this nature given by the USSR to a communist *coup d'état* was not, in the view of the party, to be regarded either as subversion or as violence.

But if the party leaders were thus anxious to convince their followers within the party and outside it that they were pursuing a policy of peace, there was one respect in which they showed that they were prepared to use force – the preservation of communist rule in the countries in which these parties had established themselves in power as a result of the advance of the Red Army. In East Germany in June 1953, and on a larger scale in Hungary in October 1956, Soviet troops went into action in order to defend communist rule against revolt which, while characterized as 'counter-revolution' by the Soviet Union, appeared to an uncommitted observer (a commission of the United Nations in the case of Hungary) to be a popular mass revolt against communist rule, but not an attempt at restoring any form of reactionary government. Evidently in these instances the danger of allowing the collapse of any communist government was considered to outweigh both the loss of prestige and the inconsistency with peace-loving protestations implicit in military action directed against workers and students. (Much the same could be said about the invasion of Czechoslovakia in August 1968 by his successors.) Moreover,

Khrushchev did not hesitate, in 1962, to take his country to the brink of nuclear war, when he attempted to install missiles in Cuba. Whatever talk there was in Soviet publicity about 'peaceful co-existence', it was repeatedly stressed that this did not extend to 'ideological co-existence': here a bitter and relentless struggle must continue. The purpose of détente, therefore, was to safeguard the USSR against nuclear war: but at the same time to push forward as much as possible with political warfare. The changes introduced by Khrushchev's successors were more changes of style than substance. Bolder in some respects than Khrushchev, less anxious to neutralize areas of conflict (Vietnam, the Middle East, Germany), they nevertheless, during the early years of their stewardship, pursued the same basic aim: maximum advantage to be gained from limited military and unlimited political warfare, and avoidance of nuclear confrontation.

* * *

The release of tension after Stalin's death led to a ferment and an impatience with the old methods of party control, both inside the USSR and in the communist-controlled countries outside the Soviet Union. This caused serious concern to the party leaders in Moscow. The party ideologists, with more regard perhaps for convenience than for historical accuracy, condemned such impatience under the comprehensive term of 'revisionism' – thus identifying it with the theories which Bernstein had advanced in 1899 in criticism of Marx's and Engels's insistence on the need for a violent revolution before socialism could be attained. The identification had the advantage that Lenin's strictures on Bernstein and his Russian followers of nearly sixty years before could be pressed into service against modern malcontents. Revisionists, says a recent authoritative handbook, declare that Marxism-Leninism is 'out of date', deny the historical necessity for a proletarian revolution and for the dictatorship of the proletariat during the transition from capitalism to socialism, 'deny the leading role of the Marxist-Leninist party' and the 'principles of international socialism', repudiate democratic centralism and demand the 'transformation of the communist party from a fighting revolutionary organization into something like a discussion club'.[1]

But the new spirit was alive among the intellectuals. Cautious, and at times quite bold, voices were raised among the writers (many of them party members), calling for sincerity in literature, for freedom

[1] *Politicheskii slovar'*, pp. 474–5.

for the artist to write what he saw and not what was demanded of him, and in some cases even criticizing the party straitjacket. Such voices had not been heard since the early 30's. The party leaders reacted to this new mood with apprehension, which became more marked after the attempted revolution in Hungary in October 1956, in which writers and intellectuals played a leading part. There was, so far as is known, no return to the methods of terror which Stalin had never hesitated to use in order to silence his critics. But the party admonished, cajoled and criticized: in the last resort, since it controlled the Union of Writers upon whom every author's right to have his work published depended, it could effectively exert economic pressure on the bolder spirits. The party did not either discourage all criticism or demand that nothing but panegyrics of its own achievements should be written. But it insisted upon two things. First, that all creative art must be consciously directed towards the furthering of the aims for which the party stood – there must be no 'art for art's sake'. And secondly, that while criticism might be directed at individual abuses within the system, there must be no criticism of the system itself, no exacerbation of any existing tensions in society. Loyalty to party policy and party control must always be emphasized.

Greater liberty was also allowed in other intellectual fields. In particular, scientific research was no longer subject to the dead hand of Stalin's personal whims and bigotry, and accordingly made remarkable progress. But there remained one field of research upon which the party continued to show extreme sensitiveness – the history of the party. Mikoyan's strictures on the *Short History* at the Twentieth Congress did not open the road to any objective assessment of past events. In his speech to the Twentieth Congress in closed session Khrushchev had been careful to emphasize that his strictures on Stalin applied only to the last years of his life: Stalin's battle with the followers of Trotsky and with the right opposition had been quite correct in principle, even if there had been some exaggerations in practice. The party leaders now sought to find authority for their own policy in reinterpretation of Lenin's thought and action. As a result, further layers of myth were added to the legends with which the history of the period of Lenin's rule was already encrusted. An article on the remote past, dealing with bolshevik policy in March and April 1917, before the arrival of Lenin in Petrograd, in which the facts were, for the first time in many years, stated with some measure of objectivity, led to the break-up of the editorial board of *Voprosy istorii*

(Problems of History), the dismissal of the chief assistant editor and author of the article, and a reprimand to the editor, Pankratova.[1] Several editions of a concise history of the party and several volumes of a large six-volume history did nothing to dispel the view that the CPSU leaders are unable to face the light of real historical scholarship when their past is concerned.

Thus, the determination of the party to retain its grip over the population remained as great as it had ever been before: the party might listen more than before to the voice of the 'masses', but it held to its conviction that it must lead them, and, whenever necessary, try to force its will upon them. For all that, a profound difference in the relations between party and population could already be discerned five years after Stalin's death. The population may have remained outwardly docile, and as little conscious of the possibility of exercising any control over its rulers as it had been for the past seven centuries. But it was no longer cowed by terror as it had been for long periods under Stalin. No one could be sure that terror would not return, and even without terror the severity of the ordinary law and its flexible interpretation by the courts offered a sufficient deterrent to would-be rebels. Nevertheless, a population which had seen Beria humbled and had heard of Khrushchev's devastating criticism of Stalin, at any rate at second hand, was bound to feel that some of the magic power with which Stalin had surrounded himself had worn thin.

The position of Khrushchev when faced with the new tide of unwonted intellectual freedom was necessarily somewhat ambivalent. On the one hand, a man bred in the party apparatus and in the traditions of Stalin was hardly likely to welcome even the most circumscribed freedom of criticism. On the other hand, Khrushchev had identified himself with the denunciation of Stalin and could not go back on that without playing into the hands of his enemies. Thus, however much the intellectuals may have been bullied and harried by Khrushchev and his ideologists, two great conquests remained. In the first place writers and scholars were free to criticize Stalin and his era – even though the implication often followed that much that applied in 1936 still applied in 1956, or for that matter in 1964. (It was Khrushchev who personally authorized in 1962 the publication of the most shattering and moving picture of the concentration camp ever penned, *One Day in the Life of Ivan Denisovich*, by A. Solzhenitsyn.)

---

[1] For the article (by E. N. Burdzhalov) see *Voprosy istorii*, No. 4, 1956, pp. 38–56; for the decree reconstituting the editorial board and *inter alia* criticizing the article see *SPR*, 1957, pp. 381–2.

And secondly, that it was the party that dealt with the intellectuals, and not the KGB.

In both these respects there was a marked change after Brezhnev and Kosygin had taken over. Criticism of Stalin and his age was severely restricted, and even completely halted. (Solzhenitsyn's subsequent major works on the Stalin era remained unpublished in the USSR, though the manuscripts found their way out of the country, and were published abroad.) Above all, the powers of the KGB and of the militia were steadily increased, and the KGB was given an active part to play in the persecution and bringing to trial of writers, religious leaders and students. Khrushchev had gone so far in 1962 as to abolish the Ministry of Internal Affairs (MVD) which controls the militia, at the All-Union level, and renamed it the Ministry for the Protection of Public Order. The local MVD officers were even subordinated to the Executive Committees of the regional Soviets. In July 1966 the All-Union Ministry for the Preservation of Public Order was restored (its new incumbent, Shchelokov, was a close associate of Brezhnev) and in November 1968 the old name of dreaded memories, MVD, was also revived. The powers of the security organ, the KGB, were progressively stepped up from 1965 onwards, and the KGB entered upon what was to prove an active campaign of persecution of dissident intellectuals: it began in the Ukraine in the summer of 1965. The writers Siniavsky and Daniel were arrested in September 1965, and tried and sentenced at the beginning of the following year.

Much of this internal tightening up was, no doubt, due to increased crime, drunkenness and hooliganism with which the Soviet Union was afflicted for reasons not dissimilar to those which have led to the same results in non-communist countries. But one phenomenon was new, and, in the eyes of the communist leaders, very alarming: the growth of a movement of dissent, spread over wide sections of society, and showing signs of organization. The movement embraced both the Baptist community and the Orthodox Church: in each community courageous and forceful groups voiced discontent with their officially recognized leaders, and demanded from the Soviet and party authorities that the existing laws should be observed.[1] Pleas for legality, by writers, students and scientists, among others, addressed to the authorities centred around protest against the enactment in 1966 of Articles 190^1, 190^2 and 190^3 of the RSFSR Criminal Code,

---

[1] On the religious movements see two books by M. Bourdeaux, *Religious Ferment in Russia*, London, 1968, and *Patriarch and Prophets* London, 1970.

referred to above: the signatories contended that these new laws violated the Constitution of 1936 – as indeed they do. There were numerous protests and collective demands made in connection with the trial and sentence of Siniavsky and Daniel in 1967, and with the several subsequent trials of other dissenters. The documents prepared by groups of dissenters, addressed to Soviet leaders, to the Procurators, to the Supreme Soviet and the like, circulated relatively freely inside the USSR, and found their way in dozens, if not hundreds, abroad. Several clandestine literary and political periodicals were produced and distributed.[1] Four distinguishing features marked this incipient dissent movement. First, the absence of anonymity: full lists of signatures and addresses figured on nearly all the documents. Secondly, the absence of any specifically anti-Soviet content: the signatories in almost every case called for observance of the Constitution and of existing laws, and not for abolition of the Soviet system. Third, the fact that for the first time for thirty years or more dissenters had shown the courage, in Soviet conditions, to take group action, and to band together to make collective protest. And finally, that the dissent movement was not confined to writers and students, but extended at any rate to some scientists[2] – an important aspect, since while writers are presumably expendable from the point of view of the Soviet leaders, scientists are not.

It is not possible to offer an assessment of this new phenomenon in Soviet life. On the one hand, the party, with the aid of the KGB, has asserted itself with repressive action, and there is no reason to suppose that it lacks the means or the will to step up such action. On the other hand, the movement has to date (1969) persisted for several years in spite of all repressions. Evidently those who adhere to it derive courage from the new-found publicity which earlier régimes were able to deny. Will this new call of conscience and sanity be drowned in a future bloodbath? Or will the persistence and vitality of the human spirit triumph in the end over an ageing and outmoded despotism?

[1] There is a useful collection of these documents available in two special issues of *Problems of Communism*, Washington, July–August and September–October 1968.

[2] See, in particular, A. D. Sakharov, *Progress, Co-existence and Intellectual Freedom*, London 1968. (Academician Sakharov is one of the leading Soviet nuclear physicists.)

Reflections on the Changing Role of the Party in the Totalitarian Polity

The Communist Party of the Soviet Union owed its inspiration to the ideas of Marx, fired and transformed in the crucible of Lenin's dynamic revolutionary doctrines. But there was no place in anything that Marx ever wrote for the notion of the party of the proletariat exercising political rule after a successfully accomplished revolution. Indeed such a conception was inconsistent with his entire philosophy of society and of revolution. Marx saw the revolution as the culminating point in the development of the struggle, and therefore of the consciousness, of the working class: the revolution puts an end to the division which exists between society and the state, and thereby brings about the transcendence (*Aufhebung*) of classes and of the state itself. Conversely, a seizure of power effected by a party in the name of an abstraction called socialism, before the social conditions for it existed, could only result in a change from one form of oppression to another – a charge repeatedly made by Marx against the Paris Jacobins.[1]

But the notion that a 'class' can seize and exercise power is utopian and unrealizable in any practical sense. Lenin provided the practical means – the élitist party acting in the name of the class, the proletariat – but in the process played havoc with Marx's utopia. Yet something of the utopian always survived in Lenin, at any rate at the height of his revolutionary euphoria. In *State and Revolution*, written on the eve of seizure of power, he could still speak of the state beginning to 'wither away' (Engels's phrase, never used by Marx) on the day after the revolution, and of harmonious and easy fellowship and co-operation over the administrative chores taking the place, before very long, of all coercion. As time went on, the realities of power left little room for easy optimism about 'withering away'; and faith in the ever-receding utopia had to be sustained by increasing

---

[1] For the most detailed and lucid examination of the political thought of Marx see Shlomo Avineri, *The Social and Political Thought of Karl Marx*, Cambridge, 1968.

devotion to the myth that 'party' and 'proletariat' were indissolubly one and the same. Since the state had not been 'transcended' and the proletariat had not achieved the social consciousness which in theory should have preceded the revolution, ever new duties had to be thrust upon the party: it hunted out enemies in increasing numbers, harried political opponents, waged war on the bourgeois peasants, stiffened the new Red Army, dominated the Soviets and the trade unions, tried to shore up ruined industry. By 1921 Lenin had created a one-party state, in which a monopolistic party claimed in theory the right to run every aspect of public life, even if in practice it had little chance of doing so.

It can scarcely be doubted that the régime laid down by Lenin at the Tenth Party Congress in 1921 has shaped, and continues to shape, the Soviet Communist Party – and indeed many others. Yet it would be unfair to deduce from this that March 1921 represented the final point of Lenin's political philosophy. For one thing, Lenin's last political writings show that he contemplated a long period, lasting generations, perhaps, in which backward Russia would grow into socialism. This time in the wilderness would require, above all, peace between the peasants and the towns – this was the function of NEP. It would also call for the moral regeneration of party members which Lenin, somewhat naïvely, seems to have believed possible right to the end of his days. Lenin recognized that it was reversing the order of Marx to try to achieve social consciousness after the revolution and not before: he justified this by the claim that the necessity of seizing power in October 1917 had been forced upon the Bolsheviks.

Lenin did not live to carry out what he had prescribed. By 1922 he was already being thrust aside by his impatient successors, and in March 1923 he was silenced by a stroke. If, as some have suggested, the régime established at the Tenth Party Congress was only intended as a temporary, emergency measure – though Lenin did not say so – it was certainly true that the emergency did not abate during Lenin's lifetime; and there was therefore at no time an opportunity open to Lenin for modifying the régime. Some, including the present author, have argued that the foundations for the machine erected by Stalin for his tyranny were already laid by Lenin. There is much force in this argument, and much evidence to support it. But it may also be true that Lenin was struck down at a time when his work was still unfinished.

The party as Lenin left it was, in theory at any rate, monolithic: the Tenth Congress had severely restricted all dissent and put an end to fractionalism. It was also – to use a modern phrase – 'monopolistic', in the sense that it was the only party tolerated, and in the sense that it enjoyed a monopoly of the right to interfere in every aspect of public and private life. It did not, of course, during Lenin's lifetime or for many years after, exercise the right in practice to the full extent. Some writers have seen this type of party as the hallmark of the so-called totalitarian state. Leaving this question aside for the moment, if the term 'totalitarian' is properly applicable to the Germany of Hitler or the Russia of Stalin, or even to the Italy of Mussolini (who probably coined the term), there are a number of reasons why it is not so readily applicable to the Russia of Lenin.

However severe the measures taken in 1921 to subdue the party may have been, the party none the less survived as an institution. The dissenters ('oppositionists'), or the greater part of them at any rate, accepted the need for restricting their own activity – but muted dissent was to survive for many years. Congresses met regularly, the control organs of the party retained a modicum of independence (until 1922), and in many spheres not at the time directly associated with political issues some ideological vigour survived for years. Lenin certainly dominated the party: but he did not (as Stalin would do) completely destroy it as an institution. Again, if ideological control, or the use of ideology as a means of exercising control, is a distinguishing mark of the totalitarian polity, this did not develop until after Stalin had launched his Third Revolution.[1]

But is the monopolistic party as defined above a necessary feature of the totalitarian polity as some authors think?[2] Experience during Stalin's rule, at any rate after the purges of 1936–8, would seem to throw doubt on this view. For Stalin destroyed the party as an institution, and undermined its monopolistic position: he ended up by using both the personnel of the security police and of the state bureaucracy as instruments of his personal rule in rivalry with those of the party. Indeed, it is in the nature of the despot of the type which has become known as totalitarian that he cannot tolerate the existence of any institution, with a corporate life and policy of its own, since it will inevitably rival his own supreme authority. Mussolini, the least successful of such modern despots, conducted

---

[1] This assessment of Lenin represents a slight modification of the views expressed by me in the first edition of this book and in earlier works. Re-reading the last works of Lenin has persuaded me that more allowance ought to be made for the suddenness with which his political aims were cut short by illness.

[2] See e.g. Carl J. Friedrich (editor), *Totalitarianism*, Cambridge, Mass., 1954, p. 47.

unceasing warfare against the Fascist Party.[1] Hitler reputedly won Stalin's admiration by the thoroughness with which he subdued his party once and for all on 30 June 1934. The whole course of Stalin's purges, starting on 1 December 1934 with the murder of Kirov, must, in part, be seen as a similar struggle to subdue and destroy the institutional character of the Communist Party.

It is thus, to repeat, in the nature of the rule of the totalitarian despot that he cannot tolerate any rival institution. It is for this reason that he seeks by one means or another to make a sham of Soviets or other assemblies upon the ruins of which his power emerges. But a party, however monopolistic, with a corporate life, an institutional order and a living ideology of its own can be just as much of a threat to the rule of a despot as a free parliament: he must therefore destroy it before it seeks to destroy him. It is sometimes asserted that totalitarian rule consists in the total absorption of society in the state. The experience of Stalin's rule (and the same case could be argued for Mussolini and for Hitler) suggests that this view may be fallacious, and that both society with its groups and institutions, and the state with its legal structure, are equally the objects of the despot's thirst for total power. His ideal is a formless mass on which he can put his own imprint.

Notwithstanding the great amount which has been written about the nature of totalitarianism in recent years, Max Weber's analysis of the three 'pure types' of legitimate authority (legal, traditional and charismatic)[2] still provides most illumination for the study of the Soviet régime. It will be recalled that Weber was emphatic that the 'pure types' were not to be found in practice complete in every respect as he described them. But he regarded their 'conceptual formulation in the sharpest possible form'[3] as a useful method of analysis. Thus, it is true that both the party and the state bureaucracies in the Soviet Union exhibit some of the features of the first pure type – legal authority with a Bureaucratic Administrative Staff. There is a hierarchy of offices, fairly clearly defined, both in the party and in the government bureaucracy; there are fixed salaries and more or less delimited spheres of competence. However, at this point the outward similarity of the Soviet administrative system, party or government,

---

[1] See on this Alberto Aquarone, *L'organizzazione dello Stato Totalitario*, Torino, 1965, pp. 45–7, 187–8; and Renzo De Felice, *Mussolini il Fascista*, 1, *La conquista del potere 1921–1925*, Torino, 1966, pp. 401–38.
[2] Max Weber, *The Theory of Social and Economic Organisation*, translated by A. M. Henderson and Talcott Parsons, Glencoe, Illinois, 1947, pp. 328–92.
[3] *op. cit.*, p. 329.

to a 'legal authority' in Weber's sense comes to an end. In the first place, the means of compulsion open to the administrative machines and the conditions of their use are neither sharply defined, nor strictly enforced: the employment of force is not subject to a well defined and fully enforceable system of legal rules, administered by courts which are independent of those who stand at the head of the administrative hierarchy. These vital aspects of 'legal authority' are totally absent in the Soviet system. Again, the incumbent of an office in the party bureaucracy (or for that matter in the state bureaucracy) has neither rights which he can enforce within the bureaucracy, nor certainty of tenure which he can protect: no independent method exists by which he can challenge the decisions of his superiors. The most that he can hope for is to challenge the ruling of his immediate superior up to the General Secretary of the Central Committee, and even up to the Politburo. The individual outside the bureaucracy, aggrieved by the act of a party official, has no right under Soviet law to challenge such an act in the courts: his redress is once again limited to complaint, either to those who authorized the act or to their superiors. His chance of redress depends on the will of persons not on the rule of law: it depends on the political relationships between the top party leaders and the officials who authorized the act.

It seems that it is to the other types of rule sketched by Weber that we have to look for a paradigm for the Soviet system – traditional authority, or at times charismatic authority. In one form or another what is decisive in such forms of authority is the personal authority of the chief, whether this be subject to traditional restraints or not. In place of officials with clearly defined and enforceable rights (and duties) within the hierarchy, office is dependent on favour, in place of competence and efficiency the prime qualification for office becomes loyalty. Never, at any stage in Soviet history, have these distinctive features been absent from the party machine.

The object of this excursus has been to emphasize how far removed the party and its apparatus are from the classical concept of a 'bureaucracy' – however often this term may be erroneously applied to it as a term of abuse. Whatever it may have been under Stalin, the party was never in any accurate sense a 'bureaucracy'. It remained essentially a body of retainers. The source of the authority of every party official was not his office: it was the fact that his continuing to occupy the office (when everyone knew he could disappear at any moment) was a public mark of the Leader's favour. The power of an official to act was not circumscribed by the law, but by the extent to which he could mobilize the machinery of repression. No doubt for long periods the party machine, or segments of it, could operate regularly, each man acting as best he could within the ill-defined areas of his competence. But ultimate power or the lack of it depended in the end, at the end of a long chain of superiors and subordinates, perhaps, on the will of the Leader. And not only power to act, but the very power to survive, or at least the power to survive in a life of privilege and comfort.

Of course, Khrushchev restored the institutional framework of the party, its organs and regularities, which Stalin had destroyed. Yet this did not make the party into a bureaucracy, nor did the form of party rule develop into a type of legal authority. For one thing, and perhaps most important of all, the party official never won any kind of independence against the First Secretary, the prime manipulator of the party apparatus. The organs to which he could appeal were dominated by the First Secretary. Thus the last engine of control over party officials devised by Khrushchev in 1962, the Party-State Control Committee, was headed at the centre by a man who had graduated from heading the security police to the party Secretariat. At all lower levels the local party-state control committees were headed by the appropriate first secretary of the party. This policy of Khrushchev was the logical continuation of a tradition, established in 1922, that where a conflict arises between a party official (or party member) and the party hierarchy, the leaders of that hierarchy adjudicate upon the case themselves.

Moreover, while Khrushchev did much to restore the authority and influence of the party, he retained to the full the personal authority which as First Secretary he could exercise over party officials, and indeed over all party members. This authority (while it endured) was much enhanced by the fact that during his period of office Khrushchev was at all times able to retain his own nominees in all the vital posts upon which the control over cadres depends. If seldom, or ever, so drastic in its effects on the individual as such control was under Stalin, it was at times no less wholesale in its extent. One has only to recall the removal of over half of the regional first secretaries between January 1960 and October 1961, or the abolition of the jobs of well over half of the district first secretaries in 1962 and 1963. No party official could have been in any doubt under Khrushchev of the extent to which his career depended on the First Secretary. These officials' support for him (until he had fallen) in the Central Committee, where they formed a major segment, was eloquent proof of this fact. If this form of arbitrary, personal rule, as contrasted with rule through institutions, with properly and legally defined areas of competence, is an essential feature of totalitarianism, then the period of Khrushchev's ascendancy must be described as totalitarian.

Indeed it was in large measure *because* of his insistence on asserting his personal will in the matter of appointments and policy that Khrushchev laid the basis for his quarrel with the men of the party apparatus, which contributed to his downfall. Having revived the party as an institution, he did his best to ensure that it did not function as such. Some signs there certainly were. Occasionally, as happened at the Twenty-Second Congress on the question of Stalin, there was a flash of what seemed like unfettered debate. There were hints of many more such occasions when debate took place behind closed doors, and was not reported in the press. From time to time, at the lowest level of party life, in the primary organizations, the right to elect a candidate of their own choice in place of one foisted upon them by the authorities higher up was successfully asserted by party members. But all this was a long way from party democracy: the traditional rule by the apparatus persisted as it had existed under Stalin. There was, however, a difference. The terror of Stalin's rule had habituated party members to accept his arbitrary and unpredictable trampling on all vested rights of office or privilege: in the laxer era of Khrushchev the men of the apparatus resented what they had perforce had to put up with under Stalin. This was one of the factors which led to Khrushchev's downfall. But, once again, the period of Khrushchev's ascendancy shows that a ruler of the one-party polity who wishes to retain a large measure of arbitrary power cannot permit the single party to become in reality a 'monopolistic' party – an institution with a corporate life of its own; and with privileges of office vested as of right in its respect, though not, of course, in many others, the period when Khrushchev was First Secretary resembled the time of Stalin's ascendancy. But it was in complete contrast with Lenin's period, when the party had not yet ceased to be an institution with life of its own, and was to that extent truly 'monopolistic'.

What, then, are the prospects for the party since the fall of Khrushchev and the advent of 'collective rule'? We are too close to events for any confident assessment of the position, which in any case appears to be one of transition. But transition to what? It is not the function of the historian to predict. He can only point to trends and factors which have become apparent, and indicate the possible directions which development can reasonably be expected to take. Even so he may well overlook some trends, the significance of which at the time is not apparent, and which will only become evident in retrospect to future historians.

The primary significance of 'collective rule' – 'or collective leadership', to use the Soviet term – is for the formulation of policy at the top. The division of the offices of General Secretary of the party and of Chairman of the Council of Ministers between two important leaders has necessarily involved some separation of areas, functions and interests. This in turn necessarily involves agreement on policy in the Politburo between the two leaders concerned, and no doubt between the more influential among the other leaders. Some division of primary responsibility is also discernible: the overriding responsibility of the head of the government for industry or for foreign policy, for example, or of the leader of the party for security, ideology and the international communist movement. Some of the cruder party interventions in the economic life of the country which Khrushchev encouraged have been discontinued, and the strange hybrid party-state organs which he created have all been abolished. In spite of this demarcation of areas, it is too early to see the emergence of either the party or the state machine as separate institutions with some degree of independence. All indications suggest that the old traditions persist in spite of 'collective rule'. The question is of some theoretical importance, since the existence in the Soviet Union of two, rival, and to a large degree independent institutions – the State and the Party – would make it very difficult to speak of that country as 'totalitarian' in any meaningful sense of this overworked term.

There are as yet (1970) no signs that such a situation of independent state and party institutions rivalling each other exists. Everything points to the fact that the strings are still firmly held at the centre – in the Politburo, in the Secretariat and its departments and in the instruments such as the security force, which all these bodies control. Within the institutions at lower levels regularity and legal order only persist so long as the centre does not choose to intervene. Politics in the Soviet Union remains what it has always been: the interplay between powerful leaders through their followers and their bases of operation, in an endeavour to maintain and extend their influence. The fact that there exist at least two equally, or almost equally, powerful top leaders has not altered this characteristic feature. In this situation the party remains what it has been for many years: a powerful network of influence and control, but to a large extent atomized, and always dependent for its influence and authority on the personal links which its individual, leading officials or members can forge to the dominant wielders of influence at the top. And in this respect the situation so far as the state machinery is concerned is little different. In neither case can the individual seek protection against the omnipotent summit by invoking the aid of independent courts, or by enforcing a clear and certain code of laws which the top leaders cannot get round.

The Soviet Union must therefore still be seen as a totalitarian state. This view is strongly reinforced by the persistence in the country of the peculiar device of rule known as ideology – a system whereby the secular rulers determine and lay down the beliefs that are required to be enunciated by the entire population; and moreover prevent by forcible means of coercion the expression by anyone of opinions which are believed to be incompatible with the official creed. The zeal with which uniformity of these beliefs is enforced varies at different periods: it was at its highest under Stalin in the last thirty years of his life, and much higher than it has been since 1964; but it has been much more intensified since the fall of Khrushchev than it was during his period of office. The difference is only one of degree – but this is not to minimize the importance of the difference. A vast deal more of discussion, bordering on dissent from the official doctrines, has been taking place in the Soviet Union since 1953 than in twenty years or more before then. There have even been indications of the existence of unofficial groups of dissent – in the churches, among writers and scientists, and elsewhere. Military, economic, even legal opinion can be discerned from time to time taking shape as an influence on policy. It is difficult to assess the importance of these new trends. All that can be stated at present is the following. First, that dissent, even by individuals, let alone in groups, has far from become recognized, let alone institutionalized. The dissenters put their liberty in jeopardy, and the authorities have not hitherto lacked the means or the will to keep them in check or repress them when they consider this course desirable. The invasion of Czechoslovakia in August 1968 was, in part at any rate, motivated by fear of the effects which the example of a relatively free socialist country might have on another in all respects less free one. And secondly, that the opinions of certain important sections of society, though no doubt listened to and taken account of, have not hitherto been allowed to crystallize into group opinion; nor have the individuals who hold views relating to their interest, be it military, economic or other, been allowed to form 'pressure groups', though there certainly have been occasions when military or industrial influence on policy has been discernible. Only time can tell whether this incipient pluralism is destined to alter the nature of Soviet society, and along with it the role of the communist party.

Perhaps the single most important question in Soviet politics in the next few years will be the survival of collective rule, or the re-emergence of the single supreme leader who has been a characteristic feature throughout Soviet history; and the central feature of all known totalitarian régimes in modern times. There are many reasons which favour return to the traditional form of dictatorship. Decisive policy requires the presence of one man – like the President or the Prime Minister, for example – who has the power while in office to decide. 'It is impossible,' as Max Weber pointed out while the Soviet state was in its infancy, 'for either the internal or the foreign policy of a great state to be strongly and consistently carried out on a collegiate basis.'[1] Growing pressure for yet more drastic action against incipient dissent and pluralism would certainly help the emergence of a new single dictator, since terror cannot be conveniently carried on by a committee. Modern warfare envisages the possibility of decisions of life and death being taken in a matter of minutes: there is still no evidence (1970) that the present General Secretary alone possesses this power of decision. Such arguments could be multiplied.

But there are also several factors to be adduced against the possi-bility. The experience of living under a single leader – the unpredict-able terror of Stalin, and the unpredictable whims of Khrushchev – has been sufficiently traumatic to make all Soviet leaders anxious to avoid a repetition of it. The system of the single dictator is an invita-tion to power struggles and conspiratorial *coups d'état*, which are an obstacle to rational government. He cannot designate a successor (as Khrushchev found to his cost with Kozlov) without thereby encourag-ing either intrigue by the successor or intrigue against him. (He cannot even be sure that securing all vital offices for his protégés will ensure safety in his seat of high office: the men who conspired in 1964 to topple Khrushchev were for the most part his close protégés, who owed all their advancement to the exuberant First Secretary.) His colleagues have no constitutional method of removing him (as became evident in June 1957) without resorting to the kind of conspiracy which took place in 1964. None of this is conducive to rational government. Above all, the concentration of power without responsi-bility (apart from the 'responsibility' to the palace revolution) is the least likely to achieve the kind of economic rationality which appears

[1] *op. cit.*, p. 399.

to be the aim of many sections of Soviet society, including the planners and the scientists. Again, these arguments do not exhaust the case.

Should the single dictator re-emerge, it seems most probable that the party will remain moulded on the Stalin–Khrushchev model – un-institutionalized, atomized and without legal order and without its members enjoying established rights. On the other hand, should the balance of advantages and disadvantages sketched above entail a pro-longed survival of collective rule, the emergence of a more confident, institutionalized party, with a policy of its own and with its own distinctive, corporate existence cannot be excluded. In the end, the solution to the question may lie in the age structure of the party. One half of party members are under forty: but the Politburo and the central and the provincial apparatus are firmly dominated by party members over sixty or over fifty. The party member under forty, unlike his seniors, has little or much less to fear from the burden of guilt – from the dread of vengeance – that weigh on the older men who participated in Stalin's terror. The younger party men may not have received any more liberal an education than their older col-leagues. But they know that they live in a world of nuclear power, some of them have learned something of foreign countries, and they have been through the trauma of the conflict with China. They have seen the unity of communist ideology shattered, and, like Caliban, they have glimpsed the image of their own system in the distorting mirror of China. Their gods are technology and material wealth – gods who demand rationality in return for efficiency. When the turn of these younger men comes to occupy the middle and upper ranks of the party, perhaps even to have some say in the kind of leaders that emerge at the top, will they, like their fathers before them, like all Soviet leaders from Lenin to Brezhnev, still live in the shadow of fear of free speech and free thought?

APPENDIX I

Bibliographical Note

The literature on the history of the party is enormous. Another book, at least the size of the present one, would be required to list all the works which I have consulted, and that would be a fraction of all the available sources. I have adopted the practice in general of going to the primary source, if possible, or failing that, the best secondary source. I have not always indicated the source of my information, since to have done so would have been to burden the text with a vastly greater number of footnotes than are already there. But I have tried to indicate in every case the source of every fact which can be regarded as little known, or controversial, and the sources of all direct quotations. I have in the great majority of cases given the titles of books or articles consulted in full. But in a number of instances, where I have had repeated recourse to certain source works, I have used an abbreviation. A list of all the abbreviations used with a key to the source represented by each will be found at the end of this Note. The aim of the present Note is two-fold. First, to give the reader some idea of the extent to which it is possible to base the story which I have tried to tell on primary sources, and to tell him something about those sources. Secondly, to provide a very short guide to the literature in general, so that those who wish to pursue the subject or some aspect of it will be led to scholarly works in English which will in turn introduce them to further literature on the subject.

PRIMARY SOURCES

The most important source of information on the party is provided by the records of the successive congresses and conferences of the party. More or less complete records exist for all of them, with the exception of the First Congress of 1898, of which none has survived. With a few exceptions (notably the Nineteenth Congress in 1952) the records have been reprinted in volume form, and even in the case of the exceptions fairly full press reports exist. The records of many of the Congresses, namely those of the Second, and of the Fourth to the Eleventh inclusive, have been reprinted in the course of the early 30's with many annotations and addenda by the Marx-Engels-Lenin Institute, which contain valuable information based on otherwise unpublished party archives. Within the last few years new annotated editions have appeared of the majority of the earlier conferences and congresses. In the case of some, if not all, of the congresses and conferences Bulletins were published for the information of delegates in the course of the congress or conference, which in some cases, at any rate, contained information which was not subsequently reprinted in the published volume record. (One notable instance was the Bulletin of the Fourteenth Congress, which printed the text of Lenin's 'Testament', which did not figure in the published volume.) But these Bulletins are very scarce, and I have only been able to consult them in a few instances.

No records are available of the meetings of the Politburo or Praesidium, which are naturally of a highly confidential nature. There are a few extracts from Politburo meetings among Trotsky's papers in the library of Harvard University, but they are very short, and of little interest.

No records are normally published of the deliberations of the Central Committee, though its decisions, and frequently the texts of some of the speeches made at meetings are published. There are, however, some exceptions to this general practice. The records of the Central Committee meetings for the period August 1917 to February 1918 have been published, as well as the records of the scarcely less important Petersburg Committee for the 1917 period. Then, at the end of 1958, the full record of a plenary meeting of the Central Committee held in December was published in a large edition and the practice was continued during the period of Khrushchev's tenure of office. However, this is still a very small proportion of the whole.

For the period before 1917, when the party was leading an underground existence, a great mass of somewhat chaotic documentation exists, in the form of reports of various party meetings, contained in pamphlets or illegal newspapers or in post-revolutionary publications of documents from the archives of the party. For the period after the revolution, when the party became the ruling power, considerable information is contained in official documents which, though strictly of a non-party nature, nevertheless throw a good deal of light on party policy and activity – reports of Soviet Congresses and the like, reports of the Central Executive Committee, decrees, legal codes, etc.

Two further sources are of importance for the pre-1917 period. One is the correspondence of party leaders, such as Plekhanov, Aksel'rod,

Potresov, Martov and Lenin, much of which has been published. The other source is the information on revolutionary activity which was available to the Imperial police, largely on the basis of informers' reports. Extracts from the records of the police dealing with revolutionary activity were published after the revolution, and provide a valuable source of information. (I have also used a collection of unpublished police records available in typescript in the Library of Congress.)

A considerable body of documents has been published relating to the revolutionary years of 1905 and 1917, much of it within the last few years. In spite of the fact that the scholarship in the editing of these documents often shows signs of having been influenced by political considerations, and of careful selection evidently mainly designed to conceal the part played in these revolutions by anyone other than the bolsheviks, a great deal of information can be gleaned from these collections. Some of these materials have been utilized by historians of the two revolutions whose work has appeared in recent years outside the Soviet Union, but much still remains to be done.

Memoirs of participants in events form another indispensable source, and exist in great profusion. In recent years the republication of memoirs of old party workers, which had long been out of print and difficult to obtain, has been taking place. Unfortunately the new texts often contain omissions, not indicated, but discoverable on comparison with the rare earlier editions, which are dictated by changing views of party history.

An important source both of memoirs and documents reprinted from central or local party archives, and of articles based on archives which are not available to scholars outside Russia, is provided by a number of periodicals mainly or partly devoted to party history. The most important of these are the following: *Proletarskaia revoliutsiia, Krasnaia letopis', Krasnyi arkhiv, Byloe, Katorga i ssylka, Istoricheskii arkhiv* and *Voprosy istorii.* Since 1957 a special periodical devoted to party history has been appearing – *Voprosy istorii KPSS* – which, although it has published some material of interest, has not so far shown a very high scholarly standard.

The party has since 1919 published an official periodical, including official documents, decrees and factual analysis issued with the authority of the Central Committee. The nature of this periodical has however undergone considerable change over the years. From 1919 till 1929 it was known as *Izvestiia Tsentral'nogo komiteta rossi-*

iskoi kommunisticheskoi partii (*bol'shevikov*) and was devoted almost entirely to purely factual material. Almost all our information for this period on the structure and working of the party is derived from this periodical. In 1929 a new and rather more popular and propagandist journal replaced it, entitled *Partinnoe stroitel'stvo*. In 1946 this was in turn replaced by a yet more popular propagandist periodical entitled *Partiinaia zhizn'*. These later journals contain nothing like the amount of statistical and factual information published in the first though *Partiinaia zhizn'* has recently (in 1962, 1965 and 1967) resumed publication of statistical information on party membership, covering the period 1956–66. But both are indispensable for the light which they throw on the duties of party members and on the problems and developments of party activity mainly at the lower levels, and I have drawn freely on the information which they reveal. Since they are intended as a guide to party officials at the lower levels they can be regarded as an authoritative view on the working of the party. There have also been at different periods various other official publications of the Central Committee which contain important information not available elsewhere. From 1921 until 1936 there appeared annually, with gaps, a handbook for party workers, *Spravochnik partiinogo rabotnika* in which numerous party decrees and instructions, not available elsewhere, are to be found. The publication of this useful work was resumed in 1957. There are also available, at any rate until 1929, when information on such matters became infrequent, detailed publications of the statistical department of the Central Committee, of which the most important was the publication of the results of the party census (the last to be held so far as is known) held in 1927.

The press is of course another source of the greatest importance. For the pre-revolutionary period the files of the mainly illegal newspapers published by the various factions of the party are always an essential and often the only source of information. For the period after 1917 I have in the main relied on the official organs of the party and the government respectively, *Pravda* and *Izvestiia*. But occasionally information of importance can be gleaned from other papers. In particular, information on the party at lower levels can best be discovered by a study of the reports of the republican party congresses which are published in considerable detail in the Russian language newspapers in the capitals of the Union republics. I have drawn on this material extensively for the period after the war, when information on the party from other sources is particularly scanty.

A certain amount of officially approved information, not available from other sources, can be found in the large Soviet Encyclopedia, especially the first edition.

Apart from the published documentary collections already referred to, three further collections deserve special mention. Two collections recently published, selected from the files of the German Foreign Ministry, throw new light on the relations of the Germans to the bolsheviks during the war. These are: *Germany and the Revolution in Russia 1915–1918*. Documents from the Archives of the German Foreign Ministry, edited by Z. A. B. Zeman. Oxford, 1953; and *Lenins Rueckkehr nach Russland 1917*. Die deutschen Akten, edited by Werner Hahlweg. Leiden, 1957. There is a great mass of hitherto unexplored information which throws indirect light on party history in the files which have not been edited, and only part of which are available for consultation by scholars, but I have only been able to consult this unpublished material to a very limited extent. In addition to these Foreign Office files, some 500 files of the records of the Smolensk party organization were captured by the Germans during the war, and fell into American hands. This invaluable source of information has been digested by Professor Fainsod in his *Smolensk Under Soviet Rule*, Harvard University Press, 1958, and I have drawn freely on this work.

Numerous unpublished collections of documents, which have not yet been fully exploited by scholars in most cases, and many of which I cannot claim to have more than skimmed, add to certain facets of the story. Trotsky's papers, in the Library of Harvard University, deal mainly with his oppositional activities. The papers of Aksel'rod and Alexinsky, in the Institute for Social History, Amsterdam and in Columbia University, respectively, cover virtually the whole active life of each of these important party members. Kautsky's papers covering the period of his relationship with the Russian Social Democrats (1910–14), which are also in Amsterdam, and which I have consulted, are essential for the light they throw on the much disputed question of party funds. The late Mr B. I. Nicolaevsky had a large collection covering many years of his activities in the party and as a historian of the party. In the last few years of his life he digested and edited the main documents of his collection and some documents from other collections, and I was privileged to use his manuscript works covering the period 1906–12. It proved an invaluable source. There are many other collections which await full study. There are also a good many unpublished manuscripts of memoirs, some of them of considerable value, which I have been able to use. Among these may be mentioned the memoirs of P. A. Garvi, and of N. V. Volsky (Valentinov).

Finally, among primary sources must be included the works of such leading figures as Lenin, Trotsky, Stalin, Zinoviev and Plekhanov. There are several editions of Lenin's works, and many volumes of a collection called *Leninskii sbornik* published irregularly in Moscow since 1924, which has reprinted numerous hitherto unpublished materials by or relating to Lenin. The best edition of Lenin's works, published in 30 volumes, is the third, which appeared in 1935–37, and which was published concurrently with the second edition. This edition, published under the auspices of the Marx-Engels Institute, contains invaluable annotations and appendices, to which all historians of the Soviet Union are much indebted. The fourth edition, published in 1942–50, though more complete, contains virtually no annotations of value. A fifth edition began to appear in 1959 and has now (1968) been completed. Although stated to be complete, there is some evidence to suggest that there are still unpublished documents of Lenin in existence. The texts of the fifth edition appear to be accurate, and the great value of this edition is that it provides easy access to many documents which have hitherto been scattered in journals and newspapers. The collection of letters is more complete than anything published hitherto. The annotation, though better than that of the fourth edition, is much inferior in quality and quantity to the annotation contained in the third. The collected works of Trotsky, Zinoviev and Plekhanov were all published in the 20's, and are incomplete. The Soviet edition of the works of Stalin is also incomplete, and stopped publication at the 13th volume, which ends with January 1934. But everything published by Stalin between January 1934 and his death has been collected in three volumes by Robert H. McNeal (in Russian) and published, to form Vols. XIV–XVI of the Soviet edition, by the Hoover Institution, Stanford, in 1967.

SECONDARY SOURCES

None of the several comprehensive histories of the party which has appeared in the Soviet Union can be regarded as satisfactory. The writing of party history in the Soviet Union is subject to the risks of the political fashion of the day, as becomes evident when one recalls the comprehensive histories which have been discarded by the Soviet authorities as unorthodox in the past thirty years – the works of Zinoviev, Bubnov, Popov, Yaroslavsky and Stalin, each in turn. A new officially approved history was published in 1959; the exigencies of changes in the official ideology have already necessitated two further editions, with alterations. An official six-volume history is in course of preparation, and the first three volumes have appeared. None of these works can be regarded as a contribution to scholarship. Since the first edition of this book was published, several comprehensive histories of the party have appeared: in English by John Reshetar and by R. Schlesinger, in German by Borys Lewytzky, and in French by Pierre Broné. John L. Armstrong's *The Politics of Totalitarianism: The Communist Party of the Soviet Union from 1934 to the Present* appeared in 1961, and is indispensable for the period covered by it.

On the pre-revolutionary period the works in Russian of Nevsky, Lyadov, Martov and Dan among others are of considerable value. Mention should also be made of the work of Yu. Z. Polevoi, on the early origins of Marxism in Russia, published in 1959, entitled *Zarozhdenie marksizma v Rossii 1883–94 gg*. The best history of the early period in English is *The Rise of Social Democracy in Russia* by J. H. L. Keep (Oxford, 1963). Also valuable are L. H. Harrison, *The Russian Marxists and the Origins of Bolshevism* (Cambridge Mass., 1955) and Allan K. Wildman, *The Making of a Workers' Revolution: Russian Social Democracy 1891–1903* (Chicago and London, 1967). (In German the work of Dietrich Geyer *Lenin in Der Russischen Sozialdemokratie*, Cologne, 1962, is invaluable for the same period.) All these works only carry the story up to around 1906. The remaining ten years, of the greatest importance in party history, have been little explored in any language, with the shining exception of Mr Bertram D. Wolfe's *Three Who Made a Revolution*, which appeared in 1948, in New York.

The history of the party is, however, often inseparable from the history of the country or from the study of its institutions. The best introduction by far to the Soviet system in its evolution up to the end of 1962, in which considerable space is devoted to the development of the party, is Merle Fainsod, *How Russia is Ruled*, Revised Edition, Cambridge, Mass., 1963, on which I have drawn freely, and to which I am much indebted. This book has the further advantage of containing a detailed bibliography of both Russian and English language works.

There are few comprehensive histories of the Soviet Union. Two one-volume studies may be mentioned: that by Georg von Rauch, *A History of Soviet Russia*, London, 1957; and the more accurate and satisfactory work by Donald W. Treadgold, *Twentieth Century Russia*,

Chicago, 1959. There are however many documentary collections, monographs and studies of special subjects which have appeared in English in the past years which are often of the greatest value. I have tried to acknowledge where I have consciously drawn from the works of others. But there are so many instances where such work has become so much part of one's general mental equipment that detailed acknowledgement becomes impossible, and I can only make amends by listing here a very few of the books (it is not possible even to list a selection of articles) which have helped me in the past to form my picture of Soviet history. The list is necessarily very selective and personal, in the sense that I have only been able to name some of the many excellent books which have influenced me, and I am well aware of the fact that a host of admirable works has been omitted for lack of space. I have also here confined myself to works in the English language. I trust that the curious reader will easily be guided to a much wider selection of titles under the various headings by referring to the bibliographies to be found in many of the works which I have been able to list.

I. SPECIAL PERIODS

(a) *The 1905 Revolution, the Duma Period and the War*

Hugh Seton-Watson, *The Russian Empire, 1801–1917*, Oxford, 1967.

Richard Charques, *The Twilight of Imperial Russia*, London, 1959.

Bernard Pares, *The Fall of the Russian Monarchy*, London, 1939.

Donald W. Treadgold, *Lenin and His Rivals*, The Struggle for Russia's Future 1898–1906, London, 1955.

O. H. Gankin and H. H. Fisher, *The Bolsheviks and the World War*, The Origin of the Third International. Stanford, 1940. (An invaluable collection of texts and documents.)

(b) *The Revolution of 1917*

The best history of the revolutionary year 1917 and of the civil war is W. H. Chamberlin, *The Russian Revolution*, two volumes, New York, 1935. It has of course been rendered out of date in many respects by the publication of much new material, and by researches on special subjects, especially by S. P. Mel'gunov, whose vital works on 1917 and on the Civil War years have not been translated from the Russian. On the events leading up to the February Revolution, Dr G. Katkov's *Russia : 1917. The February*

Revolution, London, 1967, is of major importance. There are two quite indispensable collections of documents and texts: James Bunyan and H. H. Fisher, *The Bolshevik Revolution, 1917–1918. Documents and Materials*. Stanford and Oxford, 1934; and James Bunyan, *Intervention, Civil War and Communism in Russia*, April–December, 1918, Baltimore and Oxford, 1936. On 1917 the three volumes of documents edited by Robert Paul Browder and Alexander F. Kerensky on the Provisional Government (Stanford, 1961) are also of value. On Allied intervention and the civil war two volumes by G. F. Kennan and two volumes by Richard Ullmann, and one by John Bradley have appeared.

(c) *1917–1926*

This period is covered in great detail by the first five volumes of E. H. Carr's *A History of Soviet Russia*. This work contains a great deal of information assembled with consummate skill and clarity. It tends to be overinfluenced by Lenin's outlook in the earlier volumes, and in general deals much more with official policies than with their effects on the population of the country.

2. BIOGRAPHIES

There is no adequate biography of Lenin, but the best in my judgement are those by David Shub and Adam Ulam. The best biography of Stalin is that by B. Souvarine. I. Deutscher's biographies of Trotsky and Stalin are eminently readable. Martov's and Plekhanov's biographies have been written respectively by Israel Getzler (1967) and Samuel H. Baron (1963). Bukharin still awaits his biographer.

3. FORMATION OF THE SOVIET UNION AND THE PROBLEM OF NATIONAL MINORITIES

R. Pipes, *The Formation of the Soviet Union*. Communism and Nationalism, 1917–1923, Cambridge, Mass., 1954.
W. Kolarz, *Russia and Her Colonies*. Third Edition, London, 1953.

4. MARXISM

Books on this subject are legion. The following are illuminating, but simple, introductions:

I. Berlin, *Karl Marx*, Second Edition, London, 1948.

Edmund Wilson, *To the Finland Station*, New York, 1947.

R. N. Carew Hunt, *The Theory and Practice of Communism*, Second Edition, London, 1957.

George Lichtheim, *Marxism: An Historical and Critical Study*, London, 1961.

Shlomo Avineri, *The Social and Political Thought of Karl Marx*, Cambridge, 1968.

5. SPECIAL SUBJECTS

(a) *Economic development*

M. Dobb, *Soviet Economic Development Since 1917*, London, 1948.

Solomon, M. Schwarz, *Labor in the Soviet Union*, New York, 1952.

H. Schwartz, *Russia's Soviet Economy*, Second Edition, New York, 1954.

N. Jasny, *The Socialized Agriculture of the USSR*, Stanford, 1949.

——, *Soviet Industrialization, 1928–1952*, Chicago, 1961.

Alec Nove, *The Soviet Economy: An Introduction*, London, 1961.

Alexander Erlich, *The Soviet Industrialization Debate (1924–1928)*, Cambridge, Mass., 1960.

(The work by S. N. Prokopovich from which I have quoted most is available in French and German but not English translation.)

(b) *Inner party matters*

For the period of the 20's Trotsky's works in exile are of great importance. For the purges see Z. K. Brzezinski, *The Permanent Purge. Politics in Soviet Totalitarianism*, Cambridge, Mass., 1956, and the more recent work, embodying all material which has become available since 1956, by Robert Conquest, *The Great Terror. Stalin's Purge of the Thirties*, London, 1968. On the development of the party in the 30's, apart from Fainsod's *How Russia is Ruled*, T. H. Rigby's doctoral dissertation in the University of London, 1954, 'The Selection of Leading Personnel in the Soviet State and Communist Party', which has not been published, is of immense value. On the structure of the party, the same author's *Communist Party Membership in the USSR, 1917–1967*, Princeton, 1968, is quite indispensable.

(c) *Foreign Policy*

On the early period Louis Fischer, *The Soviets in World Affairs, 1917–1929*, Second Edition, Princeton, 1951, is still the main source. For the subsequent period there are the two volumes of Max Beloff, *The Foreign Policy of Soviet Russia*. Also, J. M. Mackintosh, *The Strategy and Tactics of Soviet Foreign Policy*, London, 1962. There are admirable collections of documents on Soviet foreign policy edited by Jane Degras and published by the Royal Institute of International Affairs. For the period up to 1927 see *Soviet Russia and the East*, and *Soviet Russia and the West*, documentary surveys edited by X. J. Eudin and R. C. North, and X. J. Eudin and H. H. Fisher (Stanford, 1957).

(d) *The Communist International*

F. Borkenau, *World Communism. A History of the Communist International*, New York, 1939, for the story up to 1934. A valuable collection of documents on the Comintern has been edited by Jane Degras for the Royal Institute of International Affairs, in three volumes. There is also a recent two-volume history of the three Internationals by Julius Braunthal.

(e) *Religion*

N. S. Timasheff, *Religion in Soviet Russia, 1917–1942*, London, 1943.
Walter Kolarz, *Religion in the Soviet Union*, London, 1961.
(There are also two recently published invaluable collections of documents edited by Michael Bourdeaux.)

(f) *Philosophy*

Gustav A. Wetter, *Dialectical Materialism*, London, 1959.

(g) *Literature*

G. P. Struve, *Soviet Russian Literature, 1917–1950*, Oklahoma, 1951.
Harold Swayze, *Political Control of Literature in the USSR, 1946–1959*, Cambridge, Mass., 1962.

(h) *Law*

Soviet Legal Philosophy. Translated by Hugh W. Babb. With an Introduction by John N. Hazard. Cambridge, Mass., 1951.
Harold J. Berman, *Justice in Russia*, Cambridge, Mass., 1950.
John N. Hazard, *Law and Social Change in the USSR*, London, 1953.
Ivo Lapenna, *Soviet Penal Policy*, London, 1968.

(i) *The Army*

D. Fedotoff-White, *The Growth of the Red Army*, Princeton, 1944.

Raymond J. Garthoff, *How Russia Makes War*, Soviet Military Doctrine, London, 1954.

J. Erickson, *The Soviet High Command*, London, 1962.

R. Kolkowicz, *Army-Party Relations in the Soviet Union*, Chicago, 1967.

(j) *The War*

Alexander Dallin, *German Rule in Russia, 1941–1945*. A study of Occupation Policies, London, 1957.

George Fischer, *Soviet Opposition to Stalin*, Cambridge, Mass., 1952.

John A. Armstrong, *Ukrainian Nationalism, 1939–1945*, New York, 1955.

On foreign policy as it evolved during the war see:

Herbert Feis, *Churchill–Roosevelt-Stalin*, Princeton, 1957.

(k) *Post-War*

For the period up to Stalin's death the surest guide is Fainsod's *How Russia is Ruled*. Excellent documentary records have been published of the party Congresses, beginning with the Nineteenth, edited by Leo Gruliow, under the title *Current Soviet Policies*. See also Boris Meissner (editor), *The Communist Party of the Soviet Union*, New York, 1956; and volume 303 of the American Academy of Political and Social Science *Annals*, January 1956.

For penetrating analysis of the political scene since 1953 see Wolfgang Leonhard, *The Kremlin Since Stalin*, London, 1962, and R. Conquest, *Power and Policy in the USSR: The Study of Soviet Dynasties*, London, 1961.

Even a sketch of bibliographical information of this nature would not be complete without some reference to the immense volume of information made public by former citizens or residents of the USSR who have left their country and written of their experiences. This material is necessarily of varying value, and some of it is almost certainly faked. Nevertheless, a great deal of it has been corroborated by information which has become available subsequently, and there is no doubt that our knowledge of events in the USSR has been enormously enriched by information from these sources. Among those which have proved the most valuable and, in the light of later information, reliable may be mentioned: Trotsky's writings in exile, both his books and his periodical, *The Bulletin of the Opposition*, published in Russian; and among many others, the memoirs of Krivitsky, Barmine, Kravchenko, Leonhard, V. Petrov, Lermolo, Ciliga, Ekart, Scholmer, Agabekov, Herling; and, in Russian, by Gorbatov and Drabkina.

LIST OF ABBREVIATIONS

I. GENERAL

BSE
Bol'shaia sovetskaia entsiklopediia (The Large Soviet Encyclopedia), an official publication of which 65 volumes appeared at various dates between 1926 and 1939.

Izv. Ts.K.
Izvestiia Tsentral'nogo komiteta rossiiskoi kommunisticheskoi partii (*bol'shevikov*) (Bulletin of the Central Committee of the All-Russian Communist Party (bolsheviks)), an official publication for the information of party members which appeared, usually fortnightly, from May 1919 to October 1929.

Lenin, Vol 1, 2, etc.
The reference is, except in a few instances which are indicated in the text of the footnote, to the Second/Third edition of Lenin's collected works, in 30 volumes.

KPSS v rez.
Kommunisticheskaia partiia sovetskogo soiuza v rezoliutsiiakh i resheniiakh s"ezdov, konferentsii i plenumov Ts.K. Three volumes. Seventh edition. Moscow, 1954 (The Communist Party of the Soviet Union in Resolutions and Decisions of Congresses, Conferences and Central Committee Plenary Meetings) – an official collection of the texts published under the auspices of the Marx-Engels-Lenin-Stalin Institute. A fourth volume, covering the period 1954–1960, appeared in 1960.

PS
Partiinoe stroitel'stvo (Party Structure), an official periodical, published with the authority of the Central Committee, twice a month between 1929 and 1946, with gaps during the war.

SPR
Spravochnik partiinogo rabotnika (The Party Worker's Handbook), an official handbook,

containing party decrees, instructions and directives, which in many cases were published nowhere else. Eight volumes appeared between 1921 and 1934, when publication was suspended. Publication of this invaluable handbook was restarted in 1957, and five volumes have appeared at irregular intervals.

Stalin, Vol. 1, 2, etc. The reference is to the collected works of Stalin, of which 13 volumes appeared after 1946.

2. REFERENCES TO PARTY CONGRESSES AND CONFERENCES

I have in general tried to reduce references to congresses and conferences to a minimum, so as to avoid burdening the text with too many footnotes. Where no reference is given it should, I think, be clear from the context that the material is drawn from the report of the relevant congress or conference under discussion, and the reference can easily be traced by looking up the speech referred to in the text under the index of names of speakers. Some references have however been unavoidable, and in order not to quote the very lengthy titles of official stenographic reports, I have adopted what are, I hope, readily recognizable abbreviations. Thus, references to congress verbatim reports are either in the form *Protokoly*, followed by the Roman numeral indicating the congress concerned (e.g. *Protokoly II*), or the Russian word for congress, *S"ezd*, preceded by the Roman numeral, e.g. *XIV S"ezd*. In the case of references to the verbatim reports of conferences the form adopted is always the symbol *Konf.*, preceded by the relevant Roman numeral, e.g. *X Konf.*

The matter is complicated by the fact that in a number of instances more than one edition exists of the verbatim report, since in many cases the official stenogram which was published soon after the congress or conference concerned was later re-edited, with copious annotations and appendices, often of great value, by the Marx-Engels-Lenin Institute between 1928 and 1936. The following table should enable the reader to trace the source of the few references to these congress and conference reports which appear in the footnotes:

Congress or Conference	Edition used
Second Congress	Marx-Engels-Lenin
Third Congress	Contemporary

Fourth Congress	Marx-Engels-Lenin
Fifth Congress	Marx-Engels-Lenin
Seventh Conference	Marx-Engels-Lenin
Seventh Congress	Contemporary
Ninth Congress	Marx-Engels-Lenin
Tenth Congress	Marx-Engels-Lenin
Tenth Conference	Marx-Engels-Lenin
Eleventh Congress	Marx-Engels-Lenin
Twelfth Congress	Marx-Engels-Lenin
Fourteenth Congress	Contemporary
Sixteenth Congress	Contemporary
Sixteenth Conference	Contemporary
Seventeenth Congress	Contemporary
Eighteenth Congress	Contemporary
Twentieth Congress	Contemporary
Twenty-first Congress	Contemporary
Twenty-second Congress	Contemporary
Twenty-third Congress	Contemporary

In a few other instances, where the situation is further complicated by the existence of three editions, the actual edition quoted from is fully indicated in the footnote.

APPENDIX II

Dates of Party Conferences and Congresses 1898–1966

First Congress of the RSDLP	Minsk, 1–3 (13–15) March 1898.
Second Congress	Brussels–London, 17 (30) July–10 (23) August 1903.
Third Congress	London, 12–27 April (25 April–10 May) 1905.
First Conference	Tammerfors, 12–17 (25–30) December 1905.
Fourth (Unification) Congress	Stockholm, 10–25 April (23 April–8 May) 1906.
Second Conference ('First All-Russian')	Tammerfors, 3–7 (16–20) November 1906.
Fifth (London) Congress	London, 30 April–19 May (13 May–1 June) 1907.
Third Conference ('Second All-Russian')	Kotka (Finland), 21–23 July (3–5 August) 1907.
Fourth Conference ('Third All-Russian')	Helsingfors, 5–12 (18–25) November 1907.
Fifth Conference	Paris, 21–27 December 1908 (3–9 January 1909).
Sixth (Prague) Conference	Prague, 5–17 (18–30) January 1912.
Seventh (April) All-Russian Conference of the RSDLP(B)	Petrograd, 24–29 April (7–12 May) 1917.
Sixth Congress	Petrograd, 26 July–3 August 1917.
Seventh Congress of the RCP(B)	Petrograd, 6–8 March 1918.
Eighth Congress	Moscow, 18–23 March 1919.
Eighth All-Russian Conference	2–4 December 1919.
Ninth Congress	29 March–5 April 1920.
Ninth All-Russian Conference	22–25 September 1920.
Tenth Congress	8–16 March 1921.

Tenth All-Russian Conference	26–28 May 1921.
Eleventh All-Russian Conference	19–22 December 1921.
Eleventh Congress	27 March–2 April 1922.
Twelfth All-Russian Conference	4–7 August 1922.
Twelfth Congress	17–25 April 1923.
Thirteenth Conference	16–18 January 1924.
Thirteenth Congress	23–31 May 1924.
Fourteenth Conference	27–29 April 1925.
Fourteenth Congress of the AUCP(B)	18–31 December 1925.
Fifteenth Conference	26 October–3 November 1926.
Fifteenth Congress	2–19 December 1927.
Sixteenth Conference	23–29 April 1929.
Sixteenth Congress	26 June–13 July 1930.
Seventeenth Conference	30 January–4 February 1932.
Seventeenth Congress	26 January–10 February 1934.
Eighteenth Congress	10–21 March 1939.
Eighteenth Conference	15–20 February 1941.
Nineteenth Congress of the CPSU	5–14 October 1952.
Twentieth Congress of the CPSU	14–25 February 1956.
Twenty-first Congress of the CPSU	27 January–5 February 1959.
Twenty-second Congress of the CPSU	17–31 October 1961.
Twenty-third Congress of the CPSU	29 March–8 April 1966.

NOTES

(1) The place of meeting was Moscow, unless otherwise indicated.

(2) The party title in use at the date concerned is only indicated when it changes, viz.—

All-Russian Social Democratic Labour Party (Bolsheviks)
— RSDLP(B);

1918—All-Russian Communist Party (Bolsheviks)—RCP(B)

1925—All-Union Communist Party (Bolsheviks)—AUCP(B)

1952—Communist Party of the Soviet Union—CPSU.

Members and Candidate Members of the Politburo and Praesidium 1917–1966

1. Bureau for the political guidance of the insurrection. Elected at the C.C. meeting 10(23).10.17:
   V. I. Lenin, G. E. Zinoviev, L. B. Kamenev, L. D. Trotsky, I. V. Stalin, G. Ia. Sokol'nikov, A. S. Bubnov.
2. Elected in March 1919 after the 8th Congress:
   Members: Lenin, Kamenev, Trotsky, Stalin, N. N. Krestinskii;
   Candidates: Zinoviev, N. I. Bukharin, M. I. Kalinin.
3. Elected 22 March 1921 after the 10th Congress:
   Members: Lenin, Trotsky, Zinoviev, Stalin, and Kamenev;
   Candidates: V. M. Molotov, M. I. Kalinin and Bukharin.
4. Elected 3 April 1922 after the 11th Congress:
   Members: Lenin, Kamenev, Trotsky, Stalin, Zinoviev, A. I. Rykov, M. M. Tomskii;
   Candidates: Bukharin, Molotov, Kalinin.
5. Elected 26 April 1923 after the 12th Congress:
   Members: Lenin, Kamenev, Trotsky, Stalin, Zinoviev, Rykov, Tomskii;
   Candidates: Bukharin, Molotov.
6. Elected 2 June 1924 after the 13th Congress:
   Members: Kamenev, Trotsky, Stalin, Zinoviev, Rykov, Tomskii, Bukharin (Lenin died 24 January 1924);
   Candidates: Molotov, Kalinin, F. E. Dzerzhinskii, M. V. Frunze.
7. Elected 1 January 1926 after the 14th Congress:
   Members: Bukharin, K. E. Voroshilov, Zinoviev, Kalinin, Molotov, Rykov, Stalin, Tomskii, Trotsky;
   Candidates: Ia. E. Rudzutak, Dzerzhinskii, G. I. Petrovskii, N. A. Uglanov, Kamenev (Frunze died 31 October 1925).
8. C.C. plenary session 14–23 July 1926 – Zinoviev expelled and replaced by Rudzutak.
   Elected Candidates: Petrovskii, Uglanov, G. K. Ordzhonikidze,

A. A. Andreev, S. M. Kirov, A. I. Mikoyan, L. M. Kaganovich, Kamenev (Dzerzhinskii died 20 July 1926).

9. C.C. plenary session 23 October 1926 – Trotsky and Kamenev expelled.

10. C.C. plenary session 3 November 1926 – Ordzhonikidze replaced by V. Ia. Chubar' (Ordzhonikidze elected chairman of the C.C.C.).

11. Elected 19 December 1927 after the 15th Congress:
   Members: Bukharin, Voroshilov, Kalinin, V. V. Kuibyshev, Molotov, Rykov, Rudzutak, Stalin, Tomskii;
   Candidates: Petrovskii, Uglanov, Andreev, Kirov, Mikoyan, Kaganovich, Chubar', S. V. Kossior.

12. C.C. plenary session 29 April 1929 – Uglanov replaced by K. Ia. Bauman.

13. C.C. plenary session 10–17 November 1929 – Bukharin expelled.

14. Elected 13 July 1930 after the 16th Congress:
   Members: Voroshilov, Kaganovich, Kalinin, Kirov, Kossior, Kuibyshev, Molotov, Rykov, Rudzutak, Stalin;
   Candidates: Mikoyan, Chubar', Petrovskii, Andreev, S. I. Syrtsov.

15. C.C. and C.C.C. decision 1 December 1930 – Syrtsov expelled from the C.C.

16. C.C. and C.C.C. joint plenary session 17–21 December 1930 – Rykov expelled; Andreev relieved; Ordzhonikidze elected member (Andreev elected Chairman of the C.C.C.).

17. C.C. plenary session 4 February 1932 – Rudzutak relieved; Andreev elected member (Rudzutak elected Chairman of the C.C.C.).

18. Elected 10 February 1934 after the 17th Congress:
   Members: Stalin, Molotov, Kaganovich, Voroshilov, Kalinin, Ordzhonikidze, Kuibyshev, Kirov, Andreev, Kossior;
   Candidates: Mikoyan, Chubar', Petrovskii, P. P. Postyshev, Rudzutak.

19. C.C. plenary session 1 February 1935:
   Elected Members: Mikoyan, Chubar';
   Candidates: A. A. Zhdanov, R. I. Eikhe (Kirov assassinated 1 December 1934, Kuibyshev died 25 January 1935).

20. October 1937 – N. I. Ezhov elected candidate. Ordzhonikidze committed suicide 18 February 1937.

21. C.C. plenary session in January 1938 – Postyshev expelled and replaced by N. S. Khrushchev.

22. Purged during 1937 and 1938: Kossior, Chubar', Rudzutak, Eikhe, Ezhov. Petrovskii removed early in 1939.
23. Elected 22 March 1939 after the 18th Congress:
    Members: Zhdanov, Khrushchev;
    Candidates: L. P. Beria, N. M. Shvernik.
24. C.C. plenary session 21 February 1941 after the 18th Conference:
    Elected Candidates: N. A. Voznesenskii, G. M. Malenkov, A. S. Shcherbakov.
25. C.C. plenary session in March 1946:
    Elected Members: Beria, Malenkov;
    Candidates: N. A. Bulganin, A. N. Kosygin (Shcherbakov died 10 May 1945).
26. Voznesenskii became member 28 February 1947 (Kalinin died 3 June 1946).
27. In February 1948:
    Elected Members: Bulganin, Kosygin.
28. Zhdanov died 31 August 1948; Voznesenskii arrested in 1949.
29. Praesidium elected 16 October 1952 after the 19th Congress:
    Members: V. M. Andrianov, A. B. Aristov, Beria, Bulganin, Voroshilov, S. D. Ignat'ev, Kaganovich, D. S. Korotchenko, V. V. Kuznetsov, O. V. Kuusinen, Malenkov, V. A. Malyshev, L. G. Mel'nikov, Mikoyan, N. A. Mikhailov, Molotov, M. G. Pervukhin, P. K. Ponomarenko, M. Z. Saburov, Stalin, M.A. Suslov, Khrushchev, D. I. Chesnokov, Shvernik, M. F. Shkiriatov;
    Candidates: L. I. Brezhnev, A. Ia. Vyshinskii, A. G. Zverev, N. G. Ignatov, I. G. Kabanov, Kosygin, N. S. Patolichev, N. M. Pegov, A. M. Puzanov, I. F. Tevosian, P. F. Iudin.
30. Confirmed 6 March 1953 after Stalin's death:
    Members: Malenkov, Beria, Molotov, Voroshilov, Khrushchev, Bulganin, Kaganovich, Mikoyan, Saburov, Pervukhin;
    Candidates: Shvernik, Ponomarenko, Mel'nikov, M. D. Bagirov.
31. C.C. plenary session in May or June 1953 – Mel'nikov replaced by A. I. Kirichenko.
32. C.C. plenary session in July 1953 – Beria expelled from the party.
33. Bagirov arrested during 1953 or 1954.
34. C.C. plenary session in July 1955:
    Elected Members: Kirichenko, Suslov.
35. Elected 27 February 1956 after the 20th Congress:
    Members: Bulganin, Voroshilov, Kaganovich, Kirichenko,

Malenkov, Mikoyan, Molotov, Pervukhin, Saburov, Suslov, Khrushchev;

Candidates : G. E. Zhukov, Brezhnev, N. A. Mukhitdinov, D. T. Shepilov, E. A. Furtseva, Shvernik.

36. C.C. plenary session 13–14 February 1957:
   Elected Candidate : F. R. Kozlov.

37. C.C. plenary session 22–27 June 1957 – Malenkov, Kaganovich, Molotov and Shepilov expelled from the C.C.
   Elected Members : Aristov, N. I. Beliaev, Brezhnev, Bulganin, Voroshilov, Zhukov, Ignatov, Kirichenko, Kozlov, Kuusinen, Mikoyan, Suslov, Khrushchev, Shvernik, Furtseva;
   Candidates : Mukhitdinov, P. N. Pospelov, Korotchenko, Ia. E. Kalnberzin, A. P. Kirilenko, Kosygin, K. T. Mazurov, V. P. Mzhavanadze, Pervukhin.

38. C.C. plenary session 3 November 1957 – Zhukov expelled from the C.C. (and consequently from the Praesidium). Replaced by Mukhitdinov on the Praesidium on 19 December 1957.

39. C.C. plenary session 17–18 June 1958:
   Elected Candidates : N. V. Podgornyi, D. S. Polianskii.

40. C.C. plenary session early September 1958 – Bulganin expelled from Praesidium.

41. May 1960 – Kirichenko and Beliaev removed from Praesidium and replaced by N. V. Podgornyi, D. S. Polianskii and A. N. Kosygin.

42. C.C. plenary session July 1960 – Voroshilov removed from Praesidium.

43. C.C. plenary session January 1961:
   Elected candidates : G. I. Voronov, and V. V. Grishin.

44. Elected 31 October 1961 after the 22nd Congress:
   Members : Brezhnev, Voronov, Kozlov, Kosygin, Kuusinen, Mikoyan, Podgornyi, Polianskii, Suslov, Khrushchev, Shvernik;
   Candidates : Grishin, Rashidov, Mazurov, Mzhavanadze, V. V. Shcherbitskii.

45. C.C. plenary session April 1962 – Kirilenko promoted to full membership.

46. C.C. plenary session November 1962:
   Elected candidate : L. N. Efremov.

47. C.C. plenary session December 1963 – Shcherbitskii replaced by P. E. Shelest.

48. Kuusinen died in May 1964.

49. C.C. plenary session October 1964 – Khrushchev removed from Praesidium.
50. C.C. plenary session November 1964 – Kozlov replaced by Shelest. (Kozlov died in November 1965.)
    Elected member: A. N. Shelepin.
    Elected candidate: P. N. Demichev.
51. C.C. plenary session March 1965 – Mazurov promoted to full membership.
    Elected candidate: D. F. Ustinov.
52. C.C. plenary session December 1965:
    Elected candidate: Shcherbitskii.
53. Politbureau elected 8 April 1966 after 23rd Congress:
    Members: Brezhnev, Voronov, Kirilenko, Kosygin, Mazurov, A. Ya. Pel'she, Podgornyi, Polianskii, Suslov, Shelepin, Shelest;
    Candidates: Grishin, Demichev, D. A. Kunaev, P. M. Masherov, Mzhavanadze, Rashidov, Ustinov, Shcherbitskii.

APPENDIX IV

Organization of the Party Secretariat

CHART I
Organization of the Central Committee Secretariat, 1924–1930

Secretariat—
- —Organization-Assignment Otdel (Orgraspred)
- —Agitation and Propaganda Otdel[1] (Agitprop)
- —Press Otdel[1]
- —Otdel for Work among Women
- —Otdel for Work in the Villages
- —Accounting Otdel
- —Statistical Otdel
- —Information Otdel
- —Administration of Affairs

[1] The Press Otdel was placed under the Agitation and Propaganda Otdel in 1928.
NOTE: *Otdel* means 'department'.

CHART II
Reorganization of the Central Committee Secretariat, 1930

Secretariat—
- —Organization-Instruction Otdel
- —Agitation and Mass Campaigns Otdel
- —Secret Otdel

- —Culture and Propaganda Otdel
- —Administration of Affairs
- —Assignment Otdel
  - —Heavy Industry
  - —Light Industry
  - —Transport
  - —Agriculture
  - —Foreign Cadres
  - —Finance – Planning – Trade
  - —Soviet Administration
  - —Accounting

CHART III

Reorganization of the Central Committee Secretariat, 1934

Secretariat—
- Agricultural Otdel
- Industrial Otdel
- Transport Otdel
- Planning-Finance-Trade Otdel
- Political Administrative Otdel
- Otdel of Leading Party Organs
- Otdel of Culture and Propaganda of Leninism
- Special Section
- Administration of Affairs

CHART IV

Reorganization of the Central Committee Secretariat, 1939

Secretariat—
- Cadres Directorate
- Propaganda and Agitation Directorate
- Organization-Instruction Otdel
- Agricultural Otdel
- School Otdel
- Special Section
- Administration of Affairs

CHART V

Reorganization of the Central Committee Secretariat, 1948

Secretariat—
- Otdel of Party, Trade-Union and *Komsomol* Organs
- Propaganda and Agitation Otdel
- Heavy Industry Otdel
- Light Industry Otdel
- Agriculture Otdel
- Transport Otdel
- Planning-Finance-Trade Otdel
- Administration Otdel
- Foreign Otdel
- Special Section
- Main Political Directorate of the Armed Forces[1]

[1] Functions as Military Otdel of Central Committee Secretariat.

The above five charts are reprinted by permission of the publishers with slight modifications from Merle Fainsod, *How Russia is Ruled*, Cambridge, Mass., Harvard University Press, Copyright 1953 by the President and Fellows of Harvard College.

CHART VI

The following Departments of the Central Committee at the Secretariat were known to exist in 1968, but the list is not necessarily complete, since other departments, to which press references have been made in the past may still survive:

Secretariat—

—Administration of Affairs[1]
—Agriculture
—Administration Organs[2]
—Construction
—Propaganda
—Chemical Industry
—Light and Food Industries
—Machine Building
—Organizational-Party Work[3]
—Science and Educational Establishments
—Heavy Industry
—Transport and Communications
—Planning and Financial Organs
—Trade and Public Services
—Culture
—Defence Industries
—General[4]
—International
—Relations with Communist Parties of Socialist Countries
—Personnel Abroad
—Chief Political Administration of the Army and Navy[5]

Also the following two commissions:
    Party Control Commission
    Ideological Commission

[1] This department deals with the general administration of the office.
[2] This department is concerned with the security organs, the army, the procurators and the judicial service.
[3] This department is responsible for appointments (technically elections) of officials in the apparatus of the party, the Komsomol and the trade unions; and for the supervision of the work of the apparatus.
[4] This department apparently co-ordinates the work of the Politburo.
[5] This is a joint department of the Central Committee and of the armed forces.

Secretaries of the Central Committee: 1959–1964

Plenum 12 Nov. 58	Plenum 4 May 60	Plenum 16 July 60
Aristov, A. B.	Brezhnev	Brezhnev
Brezhnev, L. I.	Kozlov, F. R.	*ceases to be secretary*
Ignatov, N. G.	Kuusinen	(*He had become*
Kuusinen	Mukhitdinov	*Chairman of the*
Mukhitdinov, N. A.	Suslov	*Praesidium of the*
Pospelov, P. N.	Khrushchev	*Supreme Soviet*)
Suslov, M. A.	*Removed :* Aristov	
Furtseva, E. A.	Ignatov	
Khrushchev, N. S.	Pospelov	
Removed : Beliaiev, N. I.	Furtseva	

22 Congress (31 Oct. 61)	Plenum 23–25 April 62	Plenum 23 Nov. 62
Demichev, P. N.	Spiridonov *removed*	*Added :*
Ilyichev, L. F.		Andropov, Yu. V.
Kozlov, F. R.		Poliakov, V. I.
Kuusinen		Rudakov, A. P.
Ponomarev, B. N.		Titov, V. N.
Spiridonov, I. V.		(*all from the apparat*)
Suslov		
Khrushchev		
Shelepin		

Plenum 21 June 63	Plenum 14 Oct. 64	Plenum 16 Nov. 64	Plenum 26 Mar. 65
Added :	Khrushchev *removed*	Kozlov	Ilyichev *removed*
Brezhnev		Poliakov *removed*	Ustinov, D. F. *added*
Podgornyi, N. V.			
Died :			
Kuusinen		(*Kozlov died*	
16 May 1964		*30 Jan 65*)	

Plenum 29 Sep. 65	*Plenum 6 Dec. 65*	*23 Congress 18 Apr. 66*
Kulakov, F. D. *added* Titov *removed*	Kapitonov, I. V. *added*	Kirilenko, A. P. *added* Podgornyi *released*

Index

Index

Index

Bolsheviks – *contd.*

128; Vienna conference, 129; Bolshevik Central Committee, 130; oppose legal daily paper for workers in Russia, 131; compete with mensheviks in trade unions, 132–3; menshevik attitude to, 134; struggle against mensheviks in Duma 'fraction', 135–6; separate 'fraction', 136, 142; and mensheviks and Socialist International, 139; and mensheviks and German social democrats, 139; International Bureau offers to mediate, 139–40; at Brussels Unification conference, 140; outvoted, 141; and split and conference, 141–2; state of organization in 1914, 142; sign menshevik-drafted anti-war resolution in Duma, 144; arrest of five Duma bolsheviks, 144; on revolution, 147, 149; those abroad not united, 149; intellectuals, 149; well organized in Russia during war, 153; oppose War Industry Committees, 154; and war, 161, 163–4; and Provisional Government, 162–5; and Kornilov, 162; seizure of power, 162; some still join with mensheviks, 163; All-Russian party conference, 164–5; and mensheviks, 164; 'German agents' (Lenin's journey), 165; attitude to Soviets, 164–7; still minority at First All-Russian Congress of Soviets, 167; Lenin on immediate revolution, 169, 171; rise in Petrograd, 169; demonstration called for in Petrograd, 167; banned by Congress of Soviets and called off by Central Committee, 167; and position in capital, 168; steps by Provisional Government against, 168; leaders hiding or arrested, 168; 6th Congress, 169–70; increased support for, after Kornilov affair, 170; and *Mezhraiontsy*, 171; exploit mass allegiance to Soviets, 172; strength at 2nd Soviet Congress, 172; 1917 membership, 172–3; Russians and Jews predominate in élite, 173; composition of Central Committee elected by 6th Congress, 174; party organization, 174; Secretariat and Sverdlov's role, 175; new party Rules, 175; discipline, 175; bodies, 175; Red Guard, 175–6; press developed, 176; propaganda funds, 177; Kühlmann's statement, 178; all-bolshevik composition of Council of People's Commissars, 180; on Central Executive Committee, 180; final victory in Moscow, 180; refusal to share power, 181; control of all press given by Central Executive Committee, 181; negotiations for coalition breakdown, 181–2; and Constituent Assembly elections, 182–3; and results, 183; army support, 183; systematic lawlessness, 184; and peace, 184; and general armistice offer, 185; and peace negotiations, 185; left social revolutionaries leave coalition, 186–7; 'Left Communism', 187; open opposition and land nationalization, 189–90; and food supplies, 190; and peasants, 191; and industry, 192; and other parties, 195–6; exercise of power, 246. *See also* Communist Party

Bonch-Bruevich, V., 4 n., 59, 87 n.
Brest-Litovsk, Treaty of: negotiations and Trotsky's part, 185; signed, 186; effects of, 186, 192; terms of, 188; new factor in world revolution doctrine, 197; Lenin on, 356
Brezhnev, L. I., 525, 573, 577, 579, 581, 582, 617
Briandinskii, 125
British-Soviet Friendship Society, 67
Broido, M. I., 115
Brussels conference (1914), 140–1